RUSSIAN
LAW

RUSSIAN LAW

SECOND EDITION

WILLIAM E BUTLER

Professor of Comparative Law, University of London
Director, The Vinogradoff Institute, University College London
Academician, Russian Academy of Natural Sciences and
the National Academy of Sciences of Ukraine
M M Speranksii Professor of International and Comparative Law,
Moscow Higher School of Social and Economic Sciences

OXFORD
UNIVERSITY PRESS

OXFORD
UNIVERSITY PRESS

Great Clarendon Street, Oxford OX2 6DP

Oxford University Press is a department of the University of Oxford.
It furthers the University's objective of excellence in research, scholarship,
and education by publishing worldwide in

Oxford New York

Auckland Bangkok Buenos Aires Cape Town Chennai
Dar es Salaam Delhi Hong Kong Istanbul Karachi Kolkata
Kuala Lumpur Madrid Melbourne Mexico City Mumbai Nairobi
São Paulo Shanghai Singapore Taipei Tokyo Toronto

Oxford is a registered trade mark of Oxford University Press
in the UK and in certain other countries

Published in the United States
by Oxford University Press Inc., New York

British Library Cataloguing in Publication Data
Data available

Library of Congress Cataloging in Publication Data
Butler, William Elliott, 1939–
Russian Law/William E. Butler.—2nd ed.
p. cm.
Includes indexes
1. Law—Russia (Federation) 2. Justice, Administration of —Russia (Federation)
3. Russia (Federation)—Foreign relations—Law and legislation. I. Title
KLB68 .B88 2002   349.47—dc21   2002033660
ISBN 0–19–925400–1

1 3 5 7 9 10 8 6 4 2

Typeset by Hope Services (Abingdon) Ltd.
Printed in Great Britain
on acid-free paper by
Biddles Ltd., Guildford and King's Lynn

To Maryann
and the memory of A J Sommers, Jr (1924–2002)

CONTENTS—SUMMARY

CONTENTS

II THE LEGAL SYSTEM

4. Sources of Law

Contents

III THE SUBSTANTIVE LAW

8. Constitutional and Administrative Law

IV THE LAW AND FOREIGN RELATIONS

18. The Law relating to Foreigners and Foreign Affairs

19. Foreign Investment and Trade Law

V RESOURCE MATERIALS

PREFACE TO SECOND EDITION

Since the first edition of this book was sent to press nearly four years ago Russia has experienced a serious financial crisis (August 1998) which severely tested the viability of fledgling market reforms, economic recovery, a new President, a parliament more sympathetic to the new President, a reformed judiciary, and, most importantly in consequence, the enactment of nearly all of the major first-generation law reform measures intended to lay the foundations of a modern, market-orientated, democratic, rule-of-law, social State.

This edition benefits from student reaction based on my courses at University College London, including the School of Slavonic and East European Studies which is now part of University College London, the Moscow Higher School of Social and Economic Sciences, and the Moscow State Legal Academy, together with instructive comments from fellow teachers at King's College London, Kingston University, Surrey University, the University of Uppsala, among others.

Those who have acquired the first edition are recommended to retain their copies. This edition has been thoroughly reworked to integrate the new materials. Some of what was can only be retrieved through the first edition. Readers will find helpful two companion volumes published by the Oxford University Press: W E Butler, *Civil Code of the Russian Federation* (2003) and *id, Russian Company and Commercial Legislation* (2003).

I am indebted to Consultant Plus in Russia for making available a personal database which has greatly facilitated the preparation of this revised edition.

status juris: 10 January 2003

W E BUTLER
Janurary 2003

PREFACE TO FIRST EDITION

This book is a sequel to my earlier works on the Soviet legal system, notably the treatise *Soviet Law* (1983; 2nd edn, 1988), the casebook *The Soviet Legal System* (1977 and 1984) in collaboration with John N Hazard (1909–95) and Peter B Maggs, and a number of collections of legislation produced from 1978 onwards: *The Soviet Legal System: Legislation and Documentation* (1978), *Basic Documents on the Soviet Legal System* (1983; 2nd edn, 1991; 3rd edn, 1992); *Basic Legal Documents of the Russian Federation* (1992); *Russian Legal Texts: The Foundations of a Rule-of-Law State and a Market Economy* (1998, with Jane E Henderson); looseleaf collections: *Collected Legislation of the USSR and Constituent Union Republics* (1979–91) in seven volumes plus supplements; and more specialised collections referred to in Chapter 21.

It draws upon courses offered since 1970 at the Faculty of Laws, University College London, in the LLB and LLM degrees, the MA programme at the School of Slavonic and East European Studies in the University of London, and during 1978 at the New York University School of Law, 1985 at Ritsumeikan University, 1987 at the Harvard Law School, and since 1996 at the Faculty of Law, Moscow Higher School of Social and Economic Sciences; it also has been greatly enriched by a variety of law reform assignments for the Russian Federation and other members of the CIS and my experience as Of Counsel to Cole Corette & Abrutyn and to Clifford Chance, as a Partner in White & Case, and as Resident Partner in Price Waterhouse CIS Law Offices BV. For all of its indebtedness to what has gone before, however, it is a new study devoted to a new legal order, reflecting the demise of the former Soviet Union, the early searches for a Russian legal identity, and the transition to market-oriented legal rules and democratic institutions.

As in the case of its predecessors, this study is designed for textbook use in law schools and a resource for legal advisers, executives, investors, and practising lawyers, as well as supplementary reading for area specialists who require an introduction to the legal system. Particular attention is given to aspects of Russian law of concern to foreign investors and those who advise them.

In the interests of narrative, footnotes have been kept to a minimum, and no knowledge of the Russian language is presumed. The transliteration of Russian follows the Library of Congress/British Library system simplified by omitting diacritical marks.

W E BUTLER

June 1998

ABBREVIATIONS

БМД	Бюллетень межународных договоров [Bulletin of International Treaties]
CAdR	Code on Administrative Violations of the RSFSR (or Russian Federation)
CIS	Commonwealth of Independent States
COMECON	Council of Mutual Economic Assistance
CPSU	Communist Party of the Soviet Union
ЕжСЮ	Еженедельник советской юстиции [Weekly of Soviet Justice]
FPCivL	Fundamental Principles of Civil Legislation of the USSR and Union Republics
FPLabL	Fundamental Principles of Labour Legislation of the USSR and Union Republics
Goskomimushchestvo	State Committee of the Russian Federation for the Administration of State Property
MID	Ministry of Foreign Affairs
MShC	Merchant Shipping Code of the USSR
NEP	New Economic Policy
RF	Russian Federation
RLT	W E Butler and J E Henderson (eds), *Russian Legal Texts* (1998)
RSFSR	Russian Soviet Federated Socialist Republic
САПП РФ	Собрание актов Президента и Правительства Российской Федерации [Collection of Acts of the President and the Government of the Russian Federation]
СУ РСФСР	Собрание узаконений и распоряжений РСФСР [Collection of Legislation and Regulations of the RSFSR]
СЗ РФ	Собрание законодательства Российской Федерации [Collection of Legislation of the Russian Federation]
СЗ СССР	Собрание законов и распоряжений СССР [Collection of Laws and Regulations of the USSR]
USSR	Union of Soviet Socialist Republics

Ведомости ФС РФ	Ведомости Федерального собрания Российской Федерации [Gazette of the Federal Assembly of the Russian Federation]
Ведомости СНД и ВС РФ	Ведомости Съезда Народных Депутатов и Верховного Совета Российской Федерации [Gazette of the Congress of People's Deputies and the Supreme Soviet of the Russian Federation]
Ведомости РСФСР	Ведомости Верховного Совета РСФСР [Gazette of the Supreme Soviet of the RSFSR]
Ведомости РФ	Ведомости Верховного Совета РФ [Gazette of the Supreme Soviet of the Russian Federation]
Ведомости СССР	Ведомости Верховного Совета СССР [Gazette of the Supreme Soviet of the USSR]
ZAGS	Registry for Acts of Civil Status

TABLE OF LEGISLATIVE ACTS

Russia, the RSFSR, and the Russian Federation

UNION OF SOVIET SOCIALIST REPUBLICS

TABLE OF INTERNATIONAL TREATIES

I

THE SETTING

1

RUSSIAN LAW IN COMPARATIVE LEGAL STUDIES

Russian law and the Russian legal system have yet to find an established place in the world of comparative legal studies. During the nineteenth and early twentieth centuries—the formative period of modern comparative law—Russia and her legal system were basically unknown and by default would have been grouped together with continental Europe.

The demise of the former Soviet Union (1922–91) and its legal system (1917–91) and the re-emergence of the Russian State continue to offer another dimension to the debate amongst comparative lawyers generated by the 1917 Russian Revolution. Soviet law claimed, on the basis of ideological axioms, to be unique amongst all existing and precedent legal systems. While most accepted that 'law' was a component of the Soviet public order, whatever its ultimate fate was postulated to be, it was this claim to uniqueness which challenged the classical classifications of legal systems or families of legal systems.

Some perceived the Soviet legal system as merely a species of the European Romano-Germanic civil law system embellished with ideological encrustations.[1] Professor Albert Ehrenzweig observed that if the Soviet legal system could validly be segregated as unique in the traditional realm of private law, he would be obliged 'to abandon the philosophical pattern of two and one-half millenia and the comparative concern of a thousand years'. Whatever innovations may have been wrought in public law, he believed that the 'essentially civilian structure' in the law of the family, property, succession, contract, and tort remained unchanged, and

---

[1] See F H Lawson, cited in the preface to J N Hazard, W E Butler, and P B Maggs, *The Soviet Legal System* (3rd edn, 1977) vi.

3

he perceived only minor changes in established European patterns of criminal law and procedure.[2]

Presumably those partial to this perception of Soviet law will see nothing novel in the post-Soviet period, merely a discarding of certain Soviet 'forms' of no substantive consequence. Those who truly do know Soviet law will have found the 1990s and early decade of the twenty-first century immensely challenging, for the effort to 'democratise' and to 'marketise' the Soviet legal legacy has been a formidable task going far beyond the rejection or replacement of 'forms'.

Perceptions of uniqueness in the classification of foreign legal systems depend partly upon developments within our own. Those who in the inter-war or early post-1945 era attributed significance in analysing Soviet law to the differences in economic system between East and West found that by the mid-1980s the enlarged State sector in Western economies and greater decentralisation and recourse to economic accountability in socialist economies had reduced a distinction of principle into one of degree.[3] The transition instituted in 1986 by M S Gorbachev to a socialist market economy in the Soviet Union reduced the elements of distinction all the more.

Much, to be sure, depends in the process of comparison on to what one attaches importance and weight when asserting or dismissing claims for uniqueness. All modern legal systems experience legal change of greater or lesser moment, but few claim to be in 'transition' from one developmental stage to another. Soviet law, however, was claimed to be constantly in transition towards the creation of a socialist and eventually a communist society, and Russian law purports to be in transition while dismantling the legacy of the Soviet era. In this sense Soviet and post-Soviet law have been avowedly 'transitional' since February 1917.

The Soviet law codes of the NEP era (1921–28) were modelled upon those of Germany, France, Switzerland, and the draft Russian codes under preparation in the twilight years of the Empire. These years saw the Soviet authorities pursuing mixed economic and legal policies containing capitalist and socialist elements, both reflected in legislation of the NEP. The more considered Soviet codifications of the 1960–70s put the claims of uniqueness and novelty on a rather more profound level, and several of these codes remained in force in the Russian Federation until 2002, leaving but a couple to be replaced or revised.

---

[2] See Ehrenzweig's review of J N Hazard, *Communists and Their Law* (1969), in California Law Review, LVIII (1970), 1007.

[3] René David was amongst those who changed his view with respect to these criteria for classifying legal systems. Compare his *Traité élémentaire de droit civil comparé* (1950) 224, with his *Major Legal Systems in the World Today* (3rd edn, 1985), as translated and revised by J Brierly. Russian legal scholars in the post-Soviet period have their own characterisation of the Soviet past. S S Alekseev, for example, believed the Soviet legal system qualified as a 'totalitarian' legal system, which constituted a distinct family within the world family of legal systems. See S S Alekseev, Теория права [*Theory of Law*] (1993).

Although at a fledgling stage, the Russian science of comparative law—still greatly attracted by the concept of 'families of legal systems'—is of the view that Russian law (and presumably other CIS legal systems too) remains outside the Romano-Germanic legal family. Rather, Russian law in its perception falls into the category of 'transitional' legal systems whose ultimate destination, for comparative law classification purposes, remains undetermined.[4] General Western studies of comparative law have not decided what to do with Russia. Zweigert and Kötz deleted their chapter on socialist legal systems from recent editions, and Glenn gives them scant attention in passing without seriously taking on the issues which the Russian and other CIS legal systems raise for the concept of legal traditions.[5]

A. Teaching and Research on Russian Law

Russian law appears not to have been taught as a distinct subject in European and American law schools before 1917, and the same was true of Soviet law throughout the inter-war era. The rise of Soviet legal studies as a component of legal education dates from the aftermath of the Second World War, when the international status of the Soviet Union changed abruptly from that of a medium power to a major power. Research on the subject, however, commenced in the late nineteenth century, principally in England (Baron A Heyking), France (E Lehr) and Germany, and developed into Soviet legal studies promptly from 1918. In the inter-war era Soviet law was examined principally as the legal system of a large country whose legislation and institutions were part of the corpus of foreign law. Those partial to the changes occurring in what became the Soviet Union believed the legal reforms contained much of possible interest to like-minded individuals abroad. Governments and commercial firms needed to know the rules applicable to transnational transactions. Language was a formidable barrier, and but for a small cadre of Russian *emigré* lawyers (including in England: S Dobrin, B Elkin, A Halperin and M Wolff;[6] in the United States: A N Sack and T A Taracouzio; in Germany: A N Makarow; in France: Baron B Nolde, A Stoyanovitch, M A Taube), the number of Anglo-American law graduates suitably trained to engage in serious comparative study or legal practice was and remains tiny. For

---

[4] See the Uzbek jurist, A Kh Saidov, Сравнительное правоведение [*Comparative Law*] (Tashkent, 1999); id, Сравнительное правоведение [*Comparative Law*] (2000); Iu A Tikhomirov, Курс сравнительного правоведения [*Cours of Comparative Law*] (1996); M N Marchenko, Сравнительное правоведение [*Comparative Law*] (2001); id, Правовые системы мира [*Legal Systems of the World*] (2001).

[5] H P Glenn, *Legal Traditions of the World* (1999). Russian law students have had access to several editions of David since 1967 in the Russian language, as well as to Zweigert and Kötz. Recently translated into Russian were: H Koch, U Magnus, and P W von Mohrenhels, Частное право и сравнительное правоведение [*International Private Law and Comparative Law*] (2001).

[6] The memoirs of Mark Wolff (1891–1987) are serialised in *Sudebnik* (2000–2).

their part, Russian *emigré* lawyers kept alive the Russian legal tradition by founding Russian law faculties abroad in Czechoslovakia, France, Germany, Latvia, Manchuria, and elsewhere.[7]

The principal Western research centre of consequence was founded as the Institut für Ostrecht in Germany and directed by Heinrich Freund at the University of Heidelberg from 1925. It published an excellent journal, *Zeitschrift für Ostrecht*, which during the first decade of its existence included many contributions from the leading Soviet scholars.

Comparative legal studies in general before 1939 were dominated by the view that a principal task of the discipline was to identify or develop general or common principles of law in at least the major extant legal systems. Harmonisation and unification were cherished objectives, especially in the minds of those who sought to reconstruct the world after a devastating carnage in Europe. To those who regarded the Soviet legal system as a variant of the Romano-Germanic civilian tradition, the Revolutions of 1917 posed no insuperable barriers to unification and harmonisation of law. However, insofar as Soviet claims to represent a qualitatively new and higher socio-economic, political, and legal order were of substance, the base for harmonisation and codification even in the most congenial international political climates had narrowed considerably.

Following the Second World War that base appeared to have vanished as the Cold War unfolded. On one hand, the group of states where communist regimes were in control had enlarged from the Soviet Union, the Mongolian People's Republic,[8] the Chinese Soviet Republic,[9] and a brief episode with the Hungarian Soviet Republic to embrace Central and Eastern Europe, China, Vietnam, and Cuba, and arguably even portions of the Third World which had 'legal systems of a socialist orientation'.[10] There followed an era of intense political hostility and confrontation which, while it had the lamentable result of cutting off meaningful contacts, stimulated area and disciplinary studies of the region. Comparative studies had before them not merely a different legal model, but one which was being received, transplanted, absorbed, assimilated into countries of widely varying legal cultures, languages, revolutionary experience, values, and traditions.

Soviet legal studies in the West during this Cold War period were mostly a part of the 'know thine enemy' syndrome: to comprehend how he lived, to facilitate

---

[7] See G S Starodubtsev, Международно-правовая наука российской эмиграции (1918–1939) [*International Legal Science of the Russian Emigration (1918–1939)*] (2000); W E Butler, 'Russian International Lawyers in Emigration: The First Generation', *Journal of the History of International Law*, III (2001), 235–241.

[8] See W E Butler, *The Mongolian Legal System* (1982).

[9] W E Butler (ed), *The Legal System of the Chinese Soviet Republic, 1931–34* (1983).

[10] J N Hazard, *Communists and Their Law* (1969).

means of understanding and communication so as to avoid miscalculation and minimise misperception, to identify and clarify opposed positions and values. Professor Harold J Berman observed in the introduction to his interpretation of Soviet law: 'a legal system expresses in a most vivid and real way what a society stands for. It represents both what is preached and what is practised'.[11] Meaningful harmonisation and unification of law on a worldwide scale were inconceivable under these conditions, indeed ideologically rejected by the East, and so too was the prospect of identifying or developing general principles of municipal law common to the principal legal systems.

Yet it was a period in which Soviet legal studies as a field found its own place in the cosmos of comparative law, pointing up the need to study foreign and domestic law in the larger context of the basic philosophical, historical, sociological, economic, and political premises, first in order better to comprehend them and second, in order better to comprehend our own. Architects of programmes in Slavonic and East European studies were quick to appreciate that some knowledge of law and legal institutions would be essential to an understanding of Soviet society and the group of states called 'socialist'; most who specialised in Soviet law maintained close links to Slavonic studies as part of the infrastructure of their area of concentration.

The last four decades of Soviet law were followed by Western students closely and with fascination: first the processes of de-Stalinisation; then the rise and decline of structures intended to further a 'socialist community law of economic integration', the postulation and then abandonment of policies aimed at eliminating law in a society building communism, the emergence of a Soviet legal profession able to pursue a long-term role for law in society, the stagnation of the economy and social system and the market-oriented measures designed to rectify the situation, and the ultimate dismantling of Soviet structures (although not necessarily of Soviet law). Access to materials has improved beyond imagination, partly due to more democratic attitudes towards disclosure of normative documents, partly to the heavy demand for a knowledge of local law on the part of the foreign legal profession, and partly to the prodigious labours of Western legal specialists in translating Russian texts. It continues to be the case that the Western law student or lawyer has more available to him in English translation concerning the Russian legal system than for any other continental European jurisdiction.[12]

The demise of the Soviet Union has altered in some measure the reasons commonly adduced for studying Soviet law. An improved knowledge and understanding of Russia remains as important today as it was with respect to the closed

---

[11] H J Berman, *Justice in the U.S.S.R.* (rev edn, 1963) 3.
[12] My own contributions in this respect are recorded in W E Butler, *Russian-English Legal Dictionary and Bibliographic Sources for Russian Law in English* (2001).

Soviet society. The ideological component of political tension and mistrust between East and West, while largely dissipated, is not entirely absent, and law remains a shared interest and a mechanism for resolving disputes between Russia and other states. If anything, law has even a larger role to play than in the past. And as governments enlarge their domains of cooperation and foreign investors operate within Russia (and Russian investors abroad), the need to have a thorough command of legal rules and institutions is self-evident.

Although the configuration of Russian law in the larger domain of comparative law has certainly altered, it remains the case that Russian law offers the same scope of comparative enquiry as other continental European systems yet continues to offer in addition fundamentally different and challenging approaches or views for the student's contemplation. Russian law is a legal system within a single state and simultaneously within a federated system of 'subjects of the Russian Federation', some of which are themselves recognised as sovereign states, and it seeks its identity within a cluster or family of legal systems. Marxism-Leninism has been discredited as an ideology, but powerful forces of varying orientations offer substitutes which would differentiate Russia from the West. The transition from a planned economy to a market economy is one which no state has previously attempted in human history; Russian law is the principal vehicle of this transition. The transition from single-Party authoritarianism to multi-party democracy based on a rule-of-law State, political pluralism, and separation of powers is no less absorbing for the comparative lawyer and practitioner.

Whereas one may examine the impact of Revolution upon a pre-existing legal and social order in several societies, including the English, American, and French, Russia offers the more immediate exemplar in double dosage: a Revolution against capitalism, and a second against the socialist authoritarianism which ensued. The effects of both are best viewed through the legal system.

The tensions between revolutionary change and the need for order, stability, and predictability are manifest in the substance of law and law reform, in the nature and role of the legal profession, in the sources of law and schemes for its codification, systematisation, and dissemination, and in the functions of State and non-State organisations created to 'administer' or reinforce legality. While Russian law eschews the explicit educational role of law associated with Marxism-Leninism and concept of 'Soviet Man', it continues to be accepted that law does influence character formation, and consequently the law-maker needs to consider how legislation will affect social behaviour.

But in modern times Russian law, just as Soviet law, sees itself as having more than merely 'national' significance, of being more than a watering place to be frequented when seeking to develop a comprehensive theory of law. In its Soviet guise Russian law was an historical and contemporary model for other legal systems in the socialist and Third worlds; and its experience of the industrial and post-industrial ages[13] contains positive and negative experience instructive for other advanced Western legal systems. In its post-Soviet guise, the Russian legal system continues to exert enormous influence by example over the other independent states of the former Soviet Union and to shape the foundations of what may become the 'law of the Commonwealth of Independent States'. Voices are being heard in the precincts of Russian legal theory which postulate the existence of a 'Russian Legal System' embracing the Slavic peoples of the former Soviet Union and Central Europe.[14]

The legal aspects of the transition from a planned to a market economy are of practical relevance to Western lawyers and investors throughout the CIS. Concepts of ownership, freedom of contract, intellectual property, State immunity, delict, juridical persons, and the proper distribution of legal regulation amongst civil, family, land, economic, environmental, and other branches of law are but some examples which contain difficult issues of reconciling the Soviet past with the Russian present. In the realm of administrative law one encounters a range of offences and penalties which have no equivalent in Anglo/American law, whereas in the criminal law and procedure the equation of public and individual rights and the system of investigation and adjudication proceed, even in their post-Soviet form, from premises, considerations and values quite different from Anglo/American legal systems.

Comparative issues of this magnitude and nature help us to rethink crucial social, economic, and legal questions which confront our own legal system, the reasons those issues arise, the historical bases of our law, and the appropriate role(s) for law in society. Russian law, just as the study of other legal systems, including the Soviet legal system, offers a convenient backdrop, an analytical screen, for approaching our own problems with a fresh and perhaps unique perspective.

For the legal practitioner these considerations take on a different dimension. We no longer speak of commercial transactions with Russia; we speak of investment transactions under which the foreign investor operates within the Russian legal framework and Russian law is the applicable law. Most of the special Soviet institutions created as part of the State monopoly of foreign trade have been dismantled, but in their place arise modes of operation and thought deeply indebted to the Soviet past. The totality of the Russian legal order, including its immediate past, must be within the range of Western practitioners who offer services in or connected with Russia.

Moreover, the value of Russian legal studies, as in the case of the former Soviet Union, transcends the traditional realm of comparative law. Russian State practice

---

[13] See F J M Feldbrugge, 'The Study of Soviet Law', *Review of Socialist Law*, IV (1978), 201–14.
[14] See V N Siniukov, Русская правовая система [*Russian Legal System*] (1994).

in the form of foreign affairs legislation in the broadest sense contributes to the development or clarification of international law. While the ideological elements of hostility are now removed from the equation and Russia is gradually being absorbed into a vast spectrum of international engagements which previously were off limits, there is nonetheless emerging a sense of Russian statehood which will have its own impact upon the codification, reception, and application of international law. The essential components of Russian law will continue to be of fundamental importance to the education of the public international lawyer as part of his understanding of the principal legal systems of the world.[15]

It remains to be seen how rapidly the international legal vocabulary of Marxism-Leninism will disappear from the diplomatic lexicon of the Russian Federation, for Russia is officially the 'legal continuer' of the former Soviet Union and its international treaties. To the extent that this terminology is indebted to domestic legal institutions, it is likely to survive and affect international negotiations (for example, the foreign investment protection treaties concluded by the former Soviet Union with several Western states fail to take account of the repertoire of terms in the Russian language for various forms of 'taking'). And there are nuances in Russian legal terminology which have nothing to do with the Soviet legacy but nonetheless can create awkward moments in international negotiations of a public or private nature.

The Russian international lawyer is himself a product of his municipal system of legal education, be it Soviet or post-Soviet. His concepts of law, the manner and style in which he reasons and expounds his views, are deeply indebted to his domestic legal milieu. Also formed in his municipal legal context is the international lawyer's perception of what role(s) a lawyer has in giving counsel to his employer or client.

On a larger scale, the implementation of international legal arrangements can depend upon the effectiveness of, or obstacles within, national legal systems. The 1993 Russian Constitution is truly revolutionary in its approach to making customary and treaty rules of international law an integral part of the Russian legal system. But within Russia this situation is complicated by the federated structure of the Federation. Those who draft international arrangements must have regard not merely to the municipal formalities for approving international agreements but likewise to the municipal legal context in which they will operate. These are but a few of the concerns to which comparative legal studies, including Russian or CIS legal studies, can make an indispensable contribution to improving our understanding of the nature and effectiveness of international law.

---

[15] See W E Butler, 'Comparative Approaches to International Law', *Recueil des cours* CXC (1985) 9–89.

B. Comparative Law in Russia

The study of foreign law dates back to the earliest days of formal legal education in Russia, not least because the early professors were of foreign origin and had little, if any, command of the Russian language. The Byzantine and European origins of Russian legislation were explored by Russian historians of the eighteenth century; Roman law was taught at Moscow University from its founding in 1755 and included in the teaching syllabus at the Russian Academy of Sciences from 1725 (there were no students). A comparison of Russian and Roman law by A A Artem'ev (c. 1740–1820), based on the lectures by F G Dilthey at Moscow University, may have rightful claim to being the first printed Russian work on comparative law.[16]

Foreign legislation, especially Swedish, was studied and adapted by Peter the Great. Catherine II read Beccaria, Blackstone, and Montesquieu, among others, and had their works translated into Russian in furtherance of her legal reforms. M M Speranskii and his associates were well-schooled in French and German law when they prepared their draft codes under Emperor Alexander I and sufficiently attracted by the ideas of Jeremy Bentham to translate his major work on codification into Russian.

A major bibliography of Russian law published in 1891 listed more than 200 titles under the section 'Comparative-Historical Method Applied to the Study of the History of Russian Law'.[17] Amongst the Russian scholars who pioneered comparative legal studies were N M Korkunov, V I Sergievich, K Malyshev, N P Zagoskin, M M Kovalevskii, P G Vinogradoff, S Muromtsev, G F Shershenevich, F V Taranovskii, and Ia Ia Iakushkin. Kovalevskii in particular produced works on the usefulness of the comparative method in studying Russian law.[18] One comparatist commented that the comparative method had become so popular, so fashionable, that 'at present in Russia there is no textbook on procedure or any branch of law which does not give its due to the spirit of the time; even a manual of

---

[16] A A Artem'ev, Краткое начертание римских и российских прав с показанием купно обоих равномеро как и чиноположения оных истории [*Brief Outline of Roman and Russian Law Showing the Symmetries of Both and the Rituals of Their Histories*] (1777), published by Moscow University in an octavo of 200 pages.

[17] N P Zagoskin, Наука истории русского права [*Science of the History of Russian Law*] (1891) 13–34.

[18] M M Kovalevskii, Историко-сравнительный метод в юриспруденции и приемы изучения русского права [*Historical-Comparative Method in Jurisprudence and Methods of Studying Russian Law*] (1880); also see id, 'Сравнительно-историческое правоведение и его отношенение к социологии' ['Comparative-Historical Jurisprudence and Its Relationship to Sociology'], in Iu S Gambarov (ed), Сборник по общественно-юридическим наукам (1899) I, 9. Legal anthropology in the tradition of these scholars is enjoying a revival in the study of Russian law with special emphasis upon customary law. See A I Kovler, Антропология права [*Anthropology of Law*] (2002).

practical jurisprudence, making pretensions to comprehensiveness, encumbers the innocent reader with a mass of facts compiled without any conclusion and selected from all foreign legislation possible'.[19]

Sir Paul Vinogradoff (1854–1925), who became the Corpus Professor at Oxford University in 1903 upon leaving his Chair at Moscow University, is regarded as having based virtually all of his works upon the comparative method.[20]

Ideological constraints severely circumscribed comparative legal studies during the Soviet period. Several Soviet jurists produced interesting comparative works during the 1920s, but by the end of the decade comparative legal research was reduced either to ritualistic contrastive self-justification of Soviet law in con-tradistinction to 'bourgeois' law or to purely descriptive, albeit often quite useful, accounts of foreign legal systems.

A more enlightened view emerged in the early 1960s. It came to be recognised that the comparative method was indispensable for studying the Soviet legal system itself, the legislative acts of the 15 union republics. Comparison also was essential to investigations of the family of socialist legal systems, the more so as COME-CON pursued measures requiring the harmonisation or unification of law. Moreover, the expanding international contacts of the former Soviet Union required a sound knowledge of foreign legal systems, including those of a 'social-ist orientation'. While Soviet legal research establishments had impressive numbers of specialists on branches of law in foreign countries, neither the aca-demies of sciences nor the universities formed sectors or chairs expressly devoted to comparative law. Even in the *perestroika* era progress was slow, although the term 'comparative law' gradually appeared in the designations of certain sectors of the Institute of State and Law of the Russian Academy of Sciences and a 'labora-tory' at the Law Faculty of Moscow State University. Notwithstanding these signs of progress, however, it must be reported with regret that the nomenclature of legal specialties of scholarly workers, in force from 1 January 1996 in the Russian Federation, does not include the speciality 'comparative law'.[21]

By the 1980s Soviet jurists had begun to recognise what G F Shershenevich had pronounced nearly a century before: 'Russia, forced to catch up with Western Europe, must be acquainted with everything that is done in the West, including

---

[19] See A Bashmakov, in Юридический Вестник [Legal Herald], XXII (1882), 551–552.

[20] Among others, see P G Vinogradoff, Римское право и средние века [*Roman Law and the Middle Ages*] (1910) and *Outlines of Historical Jurisprudence* (1920). On the jurist himself, see W E Butler and V A Tomsinov, 'Pavel G. Vinogradov', *Sudebnik*, II (1997), 405–425.

[21] There nonetheless are some excellent comparative legal studies being undertaken by Russian scholars. See the typologies of legal systems proposed with respect to labour law in I Ia Kiselev, Зарубежное трудовое право [*Foreign Labour Law*] (1998) 36–43.

in the legal domain'.[22] Bilateral symposia with Soviet legal scholars, especially from the Institute of State and Law of the then USSR Academy of Sciences, were arranged on a long-term basis to address the difficult issues of law and law reform. Direct links beween the Institute of State and Law, the Soviet Association of International Law, and the Soviet Association of Maritime Law and The Vinogradoff Institute at University College London generated collected papers for more than 40 symposia, striking new ground in legal research with Soviet legal specialists. The American legal profession sent thousands of attorneys to the Soviet Union through continuing legal education programmes, law teachers, and political scientists under a variety of schemes, and also held bilateral symposia.

Programmes such as these collectively laid the basis for contacts which flourished during *perestroika* and doubtless contributed in their own way to the emergence of *perestroika* itself. Western lawyers began to be invited to contribute officially and unofficially to law reform drafts and even to assume principal responsibility for originating drafts. The Soros Foundation supported collaborative studies of legal aspects of 'open sectors' and an intensive critique of the 'Shatalin Plan' for economic reform. In collaboration with the Union of Jurists in Moscow, the American Bar Association held a massive Soviet/American legal symposium in 1990, followed by a similar venture in 1991 for European lawyers organised by The Vinogradoff Institute and the Union of Jurists.

Applied comparative law took on a life of its own in the late Soviet Union and modern Russia with the opening of offices of foreign law firms in Moscow. Coudert Brothers was the first to appear; Baker and McKenzie and Chadbourne Park were among the first to receive commercial accreditation; Cole Corette & Abrutyn was the first to receive legal accreditation, and other major firms moved quickly to establish some form of presence. In due course the World Bank, the International Monetary Fund, the European Bank for Reconstruction and Development, the European Union, the OECD, the Know-How Fund of the United Kingdom, the United States Agency for International Development, and a host of other international and national agencies began to fund law reform assistance projects which directly involved foreign lawyers in shaping a market-oriented legal framework for the Russian Federation. By 2002 more than 60 foreign law firms claimed a presence in Russia, a levelling off after the August 1998 crisis which caused a number of foreign law firms to withdraw. Programmes such as these helped lay the base for collaborative law reform advice and research on a scale never attempted in East-West relations.

At the turn of the twenty-first century, measures promising to change the face of comparative law in Russia were underway. Translations of important foreign

---

[22] G F Shershenevich, Наука гражданского права в России [*Science of Civil Law in Russia*] (1893) 1.

works on general aspects of comparative law enjoyed large print runs. The Society of Comparative Law, founded in May 2000, publishes the first-ever Russian year-book on comparative law[23] and has attracted a substantial membership. Early CIS textbooks on the subject, while betraying the effects of Soviet isolationist policies in comparative law, offer a promising beginning for university-standard instruc-tion in this discipline.

Russian law, therefore, began a new millennium with a relatively clean slate to configure its new presence in the community of world legal systems. Once the descriptive and empirical prerequisites have been established and access to data on the implementation and effectiveness of Russian law is available, students of the subject will be well placed to advance the quality of comparative generalisation significantly.

---

[23] Ежегодник сравнительного правоведения 2001 год [*Yearbook of Comparative Law 2001*] (2002).

2

THE PRE-REVOLUTIONARY HERITAGE

The 1917 October Revolution proclaimed in the exhuberance of its triumph a complete break with the Russian past, and in 1918 there followed a formal repeal of Imperial legislation (although Soviet courts were allowed for some years to fill gaps in Soviet legislation by having recourse to pre-revolutionary legislation in certain circumstances). But law is not merely the statute book at any given moment of time; it represents an accumulation of experiences, values, terminology, attitudes constructed in the course of human affairs over many centuries, elements which the Revolution could not dispense with no matter how radical the policies it sought to introduce.

Neither was the study of Russian legal history entirely abandoned, although it experienced periods of comparative neglect and, when revived, suffered from the superimposition of ideological constraints. The demise of the Soviet Union has removed those constraints and invited legal scholars to return to the legacy of the past in order to find lessons and solutions for the future development of Russian law.

Reconstructing the pre-revolutionary legal heritage is no easy task. Records for the early period are exceptionally sparse, and for later centuries, hardly touched by legal historians. Moreover, even within the frontiers of the Imperial Russian Empire and the present Russian Federation there were dozens of legal systems operating simultaneously: the customary law of various tribes and peoples, Islamic law, Baltic law, canon law, Judaic law, and others, side by side with Russian law enacted by the central authorities. The development of Russian law itself was influenced by foreign law: Byzantine, Roman, Tatar, Polish, Swedish, German, French, English, Italian, Dutch, Lithuanian, among others, sometimes by precept, more often perhaps by deliberate adaptation.

15

A. Kievan Rus

The importance of legal materials for an understanding of early Russian history may be simply stated: virtually all of the few surviving documents from the Kievan period are legal texts of one kind or another. The earliest are in fact international legal documents, four peace treaties concluded in or about 907, 911, 944, and 971 between the Kievan Prince and Byzantium. These offer insight into penal practices and judicial procedure, the status of foreigners, the law of shipwreck, and the ratification of treaties and legal status of envoys. The first treaty is known through the chronicles; texts of the others exist. Reference is made in them to pre-existing Russian law as an extant legal system. The conversion of Kievan Rus to Christianity (c. 988) created a channel for the reception of canon law and perhaps the means for readily reducing to written form the enactments of the princes and the customary rules applied.

There is a strong supposition that the Slavic peoples inhabiting the lands of what became Kievan Rus had fashioned definite rules for interpersonal and interclan or intertribal behaviour long before the Kievan princes consolidated their authority.[1] Whether the earliest surviving compilations of Russian laws, the Правда Русская [*Pravda Russkaia*, as it is known in English], represented a creative codification of law or a reduction to writing of customary law continues to be debated. So too does the extent to which the substance of the *Pravda Russkaia*, which contains striking parallels with aspects of Frankish and Anglo-Saxon law, was the result of mutual influence or of the independent development of peoples at a similar stage of societal development. The surviving versions pose internal obstacles to understanding. Their obsolete terminology and grammar have spawned interminable debates about the true meanings of terms.[2] Most texts available for study were copied centuries after the original was allegedly composed; the Пространная Правда Русская [*Expanded Pravda Russkaia*], for example, attributed on the basis of internal evidence to the eleventh or twelfth centuries, survives in only three texts prior to the fifteenth century and 92 texts of the sixteenth to eighteenth centuries.[3] The Краткая Русская Правда [*Short Russkaia Pravda*], believed to antedate the Expanded version, is known to us only in manuscript versions that

---

[1] For background, see P M Barford, *The Early Slavs: Culture and Society in Early Medieval Eastern Europe* (2001). Barford's view that 'the Soviet state derived from the Tsarist Russian Empire, which in turn had its origin in the Duchy of Moscow in the late medieval period. There is only the most tenuous of links between this and the Kievan state of the tenth century' (ix) is that of an archaeologist, not a jurist. On the historiography of Kievan Rus, also see A Wilson, *The Ukrainians: Unexpected Nation* (2000).

[2] See the study and subsequent revision and retraction by V M Zhivov, 'История русского права как лингвосемиотическая проблема' ['History of Russian Law as a Lingua-Semiotic Problem and Postscriptum'], in id, Разыскания в области истории и предыстории русской культуры [*Quests in the Domain of History and Prehistory of Russian Culture*] (2002) 187–305.

were transcribed after the earliest manuscripts of the Expanded version. Although the traditional approach has been to consider there to exist three versions of a single law, it is possible that each version may comprise an autonomous enactment to be studied in tandem with the other collected legal texts with which the *Russkaia Pravda* appears.

The initial *Pravda Russkaia* is believed to have been composed in the reign of Iaroslav the Wise (1015–54).[4] It began with the rules of the blood feud, which the Expanded version tells us was abolished by Iaroslav's sons and replaced by a system of monetary compositions; the latter contained provisions treating various forms of stealing, interest, keeping, suits for money, shipwreck, bee-keeping, succession, oaths, slavery, and ownership. The versions of the *Pravda* suggest that the prince's court played a minor role in prosecution and litigation. The system relied upon party initiative; there were no permanent judges, merely officials who presided over the proceedings, and ultimate judgment was decided by kissing the cross or by ordeal, later augmented by numbers of witnesses. So far as is known, there was no possibility of appeal, no system of courts, no legal profession, no legal commentary on the princely legislation or judicial decisions. Nor can we judge with any certainty the territorial extent to which even within Kievan Rus the provisions of the *Pravda* were applied.

It does seem clear that the *Pravda* did influence local legal texts in regions north and west of Kiev. International legal documents are a key: the treaty negotiated by Novgorod with Gotland (c. 1189–99) and the Smolensk treaty of 1229 in its Gotland and Riga versions. Both texts contain provisions that can be traced to the *Pravda* concerning criminal law and commercial matters.

The sources of legal rules in these early documents must have been several. Customary rules, princely decisions, borrowings from Byzantine, German, Scandinavian, Slavic, or other peoples—all are plausible candidates. But Christianity brought an incontestably imported body of canon law whose texts have survived principally in the form of the Book of the Pilot (Кормчая книга, also known in English as the *Kormchaia Kniga*).[5] The collections, varied in content, generally encompassed church canons, epistles, sermons, selections from Byzantine secular legislation, versions of the *Pravda Russkaia*, and princely statutes. Canon law was important throughout the entire pre-revolutionary era,

---

[3] D H Kaiser, *The Growth of Law in Medieval Russia* (1980) 18. Kaiser gives an excellent account of the manuscript sources and the problems they pose for the legal historian. See generally J Martin, *Medieval Russia 980–1584* (1995).

[4] G Vernadsky (transl.), *Medieval Russian Laws* (1947). The fine study of A A Zimin, Правда Русская [Pravda Russkaia] (1999), completed in late 1979, has been published posthumously, and the classic analysis by S V Iushkov, Русская Правда [Russkaia Pravda] (2002) reissued with an excellent biographical sketch of the author.

[5] On the origins and status of the Book of the Pilot, see P I Zuzek, *Kormčaia kniga* (1964).

for it was therein that provisions regarding marriage, divorce, and the family, for example, were to be found. In dispossessing the church of its powers in 1917, the Soviet Government was not merely eliminating a rival source of influence; it also was asserting for the first time in perhaps ten centuries secular authority over certain facets of interpersonal relations. In the Kievan period ecclesiastical courts came to exercise jurisdiction over certain classes of the populace.

The Book of the Pilot often included portions of Byzantine law, notably the *Ecloga* of the eighth century and the *Procheiros Nomos* of the ninth. A Bulgarian compilation of Byzantine law, the *Zakon sudnyi liudem*, was extensively disseminated in Kievan Rus and later manuscript versions sometimes incorporated the *Pravda Russkaia*. It is the Byzantine heritage in these forms which has led one observer to suggest that Roman law provided Russia and the West with a common legal vocabulary, a common set of legal distinctions, and a concept of legislation.[6]

B. Mongol Subjugation 1240–1480

In the mid-thirteenth century there thundered across the Eurasian steppes the most powerful armed adversary Europe had ever encountered. For nearly two and one-half centuries the Golden Horde exacted tribute from Russian communities and episodically laid waste to pockets of resistance. Kievan Rus, which in its prime had flourished as a centre of civilisation with familial and commercial links ranging from England and Scandinavia in the North, to Spain and France in the West, Byzantium, Persia, and India southward, and China to the East, was devastated by the Mongol advance, never to rise again.[7] The Mongol subjugation of Russia is unanimously, it would seem, regarded as the principal reason for Russia's failure to keep up with the pace and course of legal development in Western Europe. Had Kiev survived, in the course of time universities might have opened, law might have been systematically taught, commentaries compiled, a legal profession formed, and the Russian legal system might have come to resemble others of the Romanist tradition more closely.

The Mongols were not a sedentary people. It was not their practice to conquer and then permanently occupy territory. Rather, they preferred to introduce a tributary structure, often relying upon local Russians who appeared to be loyal, and to exact horrible retribution when the tributary obligations were not fulfilled. So far as the legal system was concerned, the Mongols were content that it should operate quite normally; but they imposed a style of autocracy and public administration which

---

[6] H J Berman, *Justice in the U.S.S.R.* (rev edn, 1963) 189.

[7] See D Ostrowski, *Muscovy and the Mongols: Cross-Cultural Influences on the Steppe Frontier, 1304–1589* (1998).

many observers believe left an indelible imprint on subsequent Russian styles of State leadership. Nor, it should be added, did the Mongols in principle oppose commercial or other intercourse between Russian cities or principalities and Western Europe. Why then could not law in Russia, or at least private law, have continued to develop under European stimulus?

There is no conclusive answer, but it may not be amiss to suggest that something other than the Mongol presence needs to be taken into account. It is incontestable, and paradoxical, that the number of manuscript copies of Russian legislation during the period of Mongol subjugation is much larger than for the earlier period and that several medieval Russian legal texts actually originated in the Mongol era, for example, the Charter of Dvina Land (c. 1397), the Charter of the City of Pskov (1397–1467), and the Charter of the City of Novgorod (1471).

The Pskov Charter (*Pskovskaia Sudnaia gramota*), which survives in two versions, represents a Digest of Pskov duties and extracts from earlier Pskov legislation dating as far back as Alexander Nevskii. It was repeatedly reworked after 1397, of which second and third versions are considered to have appeared in 1409–24 and after 1462. Although designed for a particular region, this document and others like it are believed to have been tantamount to local *Russkaia Pravdas* and are important for the insight they offer into the legal and social problems of urban and rural inhabitants. The Novgorod Charter (*Novgorodskaia Sudnaia gramota*), of which one late version survives, is indebted for some provisions to the *Pravda Russkaia* and contains articles devoted to judicial procedure and land disputes. Both the Pskov and Novgorod documents were drawn upon later when all-Russian legislation began to be prepared. The Dvina Charter (*Dvinskaia ustavnaia gramota*), which originated in the chancellery of a Grand Prince, is devoted to dividing the spheres of competence between central and local authorities and has been described as 'the initial stage of forming the legislation of a unified Russian State'.[8]

During the Mongol period, the Book of the Pilot continued to proliferate in versions which more fully reflected Russian legal rules. This period saw the appearance of another collection of legal texts called the Just Measure (*Merilo Pravednoe*); it too owed its origin to the Russian Orthodox Church and included secular and clerical texts. The stages of amalgamation of these texts into successive manuscript collections remains controversial, but the process of consolidation and codification during this era is incontestably in evidence.[9] Nevertheless, the substance of these enactments had developed only marginally beyond the *Pravda Russkaia*.

---

[8] See I N Danilevskii, in Danilevskii, V V Kabanov, O M Medushevskaia, and M F Rumiantseva (eds), Источниковедение: теория, история, метод. Источники российской истории [*The Study of Sources: Theory, History, Method. Sources of Russian History*] (2000) 231.

[9] Kaiser (n 3 above) 26–27.

C. Muscovite Law 1480–1648

Factional rivalries within the Mongol Empire led in due course to its decline and destruction. In Central and Western Russia the Grand Duke of Muscovy gradually asserted his authority over neighbouring appanage princes and fashioned a centralised state which ultimately threw off the surviving remnants of Tatar bondage and then militarily eliminated serious threats to Muscovite lands from that direction. As the Grand Prince's authority extended over newly acquired provinces, charters were issued to confirm the relationship to Muscovy or to grant special privileges to certain communities. The most important surviving text of this nature is the *Beloozero* [White Lake] Charter of 1488, which defined inter alia the powers of the Grand Prince's judges and laid down judicial procedures and penalties.[10]

The Charter was followed nine years later by what has been called the first national Russian Law Code, the *Sudebnik* of 1497. This and the *Sudebnik* of 1550[11] are the two major legal monuments of the period under consideration. Both *Sudebniki* concerned themselves primarily with the technicalities of judicial procedure and to some extent, criminal law. The very few articles devoted to civil law may reflect the inability of the compilers to consolidate satisfactorily the diversity of local rules on the subject. The extent to which they created new rules of procedure or reflected pre-existing patterns is much debated; the evidence of judgment charters prior to 1497 would seem to indicate the transition to a vertical system of justice with a hierarchy of courts and judges was a gradual process rather than an innovation in 1497. Of the 68 articles in the 1497 version, 25 originate in the *Pravda Russkaia*, nine are linked with the Pskov Charter, and ten with other known charters. Some legal historians believe the *Sudebniki* also reflect customary law and judicial practice, and there are indications that the compilers consulted Byzantine texts anew. The 1550 *Sudebnik* is known only through 40 later copies, of which 13 are of the sixteenth century. The text was adopted with the participation of the Boyar Duma in 1550, and confirmed by the Stoglav Assembly in 1551, convoked at the initiative of the Tsar. Consisting of 99 or 100 articles,

---

[10] Translated in H W Dewey, *Muscovite Judicial Texts 1488–1556* (1966) 3–6; commentary in Dewey, 'The White Lake Charter: A Medieval Russian Administrative Statute', *Speculum* XXXII (1957) 74–83.

[11] The first English translation of the *Sudebnik* survives in manuscript at the Bodleian Library, Oxford, and the McLennan Library, McGill University, Montreal in three related manuscripts prepared c. 1599, possibly by Dr Mark Ridley. See Selden supra 50 and Selden supra 60 at the Bodleian; MS McLennan 477 at McGill; and related Selden superius 112 and Selden superius 113 at the Bodleian. See M S Arel, ' "The Lawes of Russia Written": An English Manuscript on Muscovy at the End of the Sixteenth Century', *Oxford Slavonic Papers*, XXIII (N.S. 1990), 13–38. Russian legal historians did not locate an original text of the 1497 *Sudebnik* until 1817, relying until then on excerpts translated in Sigismund Herberstein's account of his Embassy to Muscovy in 1549.

depending upon which copy is consulted, this document had an official title. Reflecting the enhanced stature of the Tsar and further centralisation of power in Russia, this *Sudebnik* began to lay the foundations of a Russian administrative system at central and local levels.

The Grand Prince had the right to act as judge in first instance or as final appellate instance in all cases, if he chose. The right to the personal justice of the ruler was an esteemed privilege in Muscovy which many subjects had secured to them by charters of grant. Certain categories of the populace—the clergy, servitors, and peasants of priests and monasteries, some categories of peasants, guild merchants, foreigners present in Muscovy as merchants or military personnel, among others—were exempted from the ordinary courts and were dealt with by departments [приказы] more responsive to the central authority. The majority of cases, however, came to be heard by regional vice-regents endowed with judicial powers in certain types of cases. Notwithstanding charters of grant and the usual judicial channels, subjects retained the right of direct petition to the Grand Prince to redress wrongs, which ultimately led to the creation of a department specially charged to handle these. The *Sudebniki* would appear to reflect a realisation that the personal dispensation of justice by the Sovereign had become too complex; accordingly, a hierarchy of agents came to perform these functions. Some of the charters of grant even provided for this possibility. But the judgment charters contain no conclusive evidence of a fixed judicial hierarchy; on the contrary, some court officials appeared to have different degrees of authority and sat on the same case on appeal two or more times.[12]

Litigation in Muscovy seems to have been open to anyone, from princes to slaves, women, children, clergy, and bondsmen. Representation and substitution were allowed at trial, even among witnesses and on appeal. Witness testimony was the form of evidence most frequently used; documentary evidence was less common and of great variety, ranging from charters of grant, to purchase deeds, land-exchange or property division instruments, marriage settlements, promissory notes, or rent receipts. Witnesses unable to appear are known to have sent depositions containing their testimony. Extracts from land registry books were employed, and some parties even submitted default judgments. Forgeries were not unknown, and especially in land cases the court would personally verify or authenticate the documentary evidence. Divine justice also might be invoked. An icon or piece of turf might be carried during the boundary inspections and the appropriate oath taken. Kissing the cross also appears on the judgment charters as a means of confirming evidence or independent means of proof. A judicial duel

---

[12] The roles of judges and sundry authority they exercised are described in A M Kleimola, *Justice in Medieval Russia: Muscovite Judgment Charters (Pravye Gramoty) of the Fifteenth and Sixteenth Centuries* (1975) 10–21.

might be invoked, usually by one of the parties but sometimes by initiative of the judge. Yet another method of divine justice was the casting of lots. Foreign visitors to Muscovy have left two descriptions of judicial duel and one foreigner an account of his own involvement in a trial resolved by casting lots (overdue freight account).[13]

In many cases the Muscovite judge merely prepared a trial record (доклад) of the proceedings and submitted this to a higher instance, which read the record and then questioned both parties to the dispute. The trial record could be challenged for inaccuracies and further evidence submitted. The higher instance would then come to a decision and instruct the inferior judge accordingly. Precisely when and why this procedural device was used is not disclosed by legislation or the judgment charter.

On the whole, the Muscovite lawsuits of this period have impressed scholars as an adversary type proceeding in which the two parties had primary responsibility for initiating the case, presenting the evidence, and adducing the arguments. The courts rarely summoned witnesses; judges seemed to have refereed the proceedings by ensuring that each party had full opportunity to present its case. Occasionally the court would carry out on-the-spot views and seek the submission of additional evidence. On the other hand, litigants did not employ professional counsel. There is no evidence of a nascent legal profession. The judge did ask questions, but the records suggest mainly to ensure all the evidence had been presented. Cross-examination or interrogation evidently was not practised.[14]

Judicial corruption was punishable under both the 1497 and 1550 *Sudebniki*. Contemporary accounts by foreigners reported official corruption to be commonplace. Appeals could be lodged by litigants on the ground of deliberate miscarriage of justice, violation of procedural rules, bribery, and an unjust decision. Appeals on the grounds of corruption appear not to have been unduly frequent, however, and one Western scholar who has examined the *ratio decidendi* of judgment charters of the period has concluded that the judges did base their conclusions on the evidence.[15]

In the realm of public law the impact of the Mongol heritage has remained speculative, but many observers believe the centralist autocracy which came to characterise Muscovite administration was the consequence of Mongol despotism.

---

[13] See Butler, 'Foreign Impressions of Russian Law to 1800: Some Reflections', in id (ed), *Russian Law: Historical and Political Perspectives* (1977) 77–8.

[14] Kleimola (n 12 above); the 1497 and 1550 *Sudebniki* are translated in Dewey (n 10 above). Examples of judgment charters, petitions, bailiff documents, deeds, antenuptial agreements, charters of manumission, donation charters, wills, and surety bonds are translated in Dewey and Kleimola, *Russian Private Law in the XIV–XVII Centuries* (1973).

[15] Kleimola (n 12 above) 90.

Ivan the Terrible destroyed the power of the hereditary nobility and abolished the right to pass in service from one lord to another without loss of patrimonial property. The nobility became bound to the Tsar by service, and in turn the peasants were bound to their landlords, gradually being prohibited from leaving their estates and likewise becoming indirectly the servitors of the Tsar. Toward the end of the sixteenth century other progress was to be noted. Trial by ordeal became uncommon, and trial by combat was formally abolished in 1556. But in criminal proceedings the investigation of allegations was by torture, a practice which endured well into the eighteenth century. Evidence and proofs collected in this manner were then sent to Moscow, where they were reviewed and, if the party was deemed guilty, punishment assigned.[16]

From Byzantium, Muscovy had received Christianity via Kievan Rus, and with the fall of Constantinople in 1453 and the marriage of the Tsar to Sophia, the niece and heiress of the last of the Byzantine Emperors, Muscovy assumed the mantle of the 'Third Rome'. The Mongol tradition of tolerance for religious faiths was supplanted in Russia by intolerance for the non-Orthodox. But the Tsar's dual role as head of State and Church contributed, many believe, to an attenuation of some of the harsher features of the Mongol autocratic tradition being adapted by the Muscovite rulers.

D. The Russian Empire 1649–1917

The period 1648–50 was a watershed in Russian legal history, as consequential as the Peace of Westphalia was for European diplomacy and the law of nations. Within that three-year span in Russia, two major law codes, unprecedented in scope and size, were approved and printed for distribution (the first to be printed in all of Russian history) and a substantial German work on the art and laws of war (1615–17) by J J Wallhausen was translated into Russian and printed in 1647. The last was the first printed work treating the law of nations in the Russian language.[17]

Although we have referred principally to the 1497 and 1550 *Sudebniki* for the Muscovite period, there were hundreds of supplemental enactments issued in the late sixteenth and early seventeenth centuries. By 1649 the morass of legislation

---

[16] On punishments, see Butler (n 13 above) 81–5.

[17] Two copies of this book are to be found in England, both in the British Library. The first came from the collection of Sir Hans Sloane (1660–1753) and the second bears the super-libros of King George III (1738–1820), having previously been owned by the Russian geographer and politician, Ivan K Kirilov (1689–1737). See R Cleminson, C Thomas, D Radoslavova, and A Voznesenskij (comps.), *Cyrillic Books Printed Before 1701 in British and Irish Collections* (2000), item 103. Apparently no copies are recorded in the United States.

required a new compilation, and in just over two months during 1648–49 the Land Assembly (Земский собор, also known in English as the *Zemskii sobor*) prepared the most substantial and important achievement of medieval Russian Law: the *Sobornoe ulozhenie* [Соборное уложение] of 1649. Whatever doubt there may be about earlier Russian enactments constituting 'codes', the *Ulozhenie* indisputably qualified. Consisting of 967 articles divided somewhat haphazardly into 25 chapters, the *Ulozhenie* consolidated provisions drawn from the *Pravda Russkaia*, the *Sudebniki*, the *Litovskii Statut* [Литовский статут] (1588) or Lithuanian Code, and sundry individual decrees, and introduced some new provisions. Widely regarded as the benchmark in the transition of Russia from feudalism to absolutism, the *Ulozhenie* in any event came to represent a distillation of the past and the point of departure for Imperial Russian codification. It was printed at once in the Russian language and promptly found a translator in the person of Baron von Mayerburg, who provided a Latin text in the narrative of his diplomatic mission to Russia, published c. 1680.[18]

Legal historians debate to this day the extent to which the *Ulozhenie* represented a reception of Polish-Lithuanian and even Byzantine law in Russia. The scope of the *Ulozhenie* embraced sacrilege, deference due to the Tsar, the Tsar's household, forgery and counterfeiting, jewellers, goldsmiths, and coiners, legal procedure, trials of various classes of the populace, oaths, land law, succession, land tax, serfdom, robbery, capital crimes, the Cossacks, and liquor licensing. Criminal penalties were especially severe under the *Ulozhenie* and became the object of repeated comment in foreign observations about Russia. The gradual enserfment of the peasantry was confirmed and consolidated by the *Ulozhenie*, which forbade peasants to leave their landlords' estates for any reason whatever.

Ecclesiastical jurisdiction remained virtually intact under the *Ulozhenie*, and the Church immediately set about producing a modern version of the Book of the Pilot. This was approved by an ecclesiastical council and printed in 1650 and, with revisions, again in 1653. For the remainder of the Imperial era, this ecclesiastical 'code' continued in effect with minor modifications introduced in the late eighteenth century. Here were preserved tenets of Byzantine and early Russian Law. In 1656 the Patriarch Nikon, acting through the Novgorod ecclesiastical court, ruled on the extent to which a widow's dowry was liable for her late hus-

---

[18] A translation into Danish was made from the Russian in 1721 by Rasmus Ereboe. On the Danish manuscript and its importance, see L P Paulsen-Hansen, 'Русский закон "Соборное уложение" в переводе Расмуса Эребо', in Дания и Россия—500 лет (1996), 153–174. Three copies (one of the first edition and two of the second edition) are recorded in England, one each at the British Library, University College London (SSEES), and the Bodleian Library, Oxford. See Cleminson et al (n 17 above), item 108. Both editions are to be found in the Harvard Law School Library.

band's debts by applying the relevant provisions of the *Ecloga* preserved in the Book of the Pilot.[19]

The systematisation and codification of law accomplished so expeditiously in 1648–50 in the reign of Tsar Aleksei Mikhailovich, father of Peter the Great, is actually part of the process of 'Westernisation' of Russian society accelerated under Peter. If the 1649 *Ulozhenie* did draw significantly upon the Lithuanian Code of 1588,[20] for example, this represented a reception of European law. Peter's modernisation of the Russian State and elimination of the patriacharite as an alternative repository of power had implications for Russian administrative law, and indeed it was here that Peter's chief claim to law reform lay. He acknowledged the need for the continuous systematisation of Russian legislation and appointed no less than three commissions between 1700–20 to attend to the matter. None progressed very far.

It was Peter's reforms of the State apparatus and of military and naval law that gave him claim to the title of law reformer.[21] Russian government was reorganised with close account being taken of Swedish and German practices. Archival research has disclosed that Peter sought and obtained data on both the law and practice of Swedish institutions even while at sword's point during the Northern War[22] and modelled his collegial reform of 1718 on the Swedish practice. Foreigners were extensively recruited to operate the system until Peter could produce sufficient Russian trained personnel. In 1722 Peter established the Procuracy, perhaps also adapting Swedish institutions, to act as the 'eye of the Tsar' and watch over the conformity to law of the actions of local officials and agencies. Military and naval law were fundamentally reformed by the enactment of a Military Statute (1716) and a Naval Statute (1720), both drawing upon European models, including German, French, Swedish, Dutch, and English, remaining in effect with minor modifications for more than a century, and extending to certain civilian matters.[23]

---

[19] Cited in E L Johnson, *An Introduction to the Soviet Legal System* (1969) 13. English libraries hold one copy of each version, the Cambridge University Library having the earliest and the British Library the second. The English copies shed new light on the printing of the two versions. See Cleminson et al (n 17 above), item 114. The Harvard Law School Library holds a copy of each version.

[20] One copy of the Lithuanian Statute of 1588 is recorded in England, at the Francis Skaryna Belarusian Library in London. See Cleminson et al (n 17 above), item 45.

[21] An attractive collection of Petrine legislation is A A Preobrazhenskii and T E Novitskaia (eds), Законодательство Петра I (1997). Also see L Hughes, *Russia in the Age of Peter the Great* (1998) 92–134.

[22] C Petersen, *Peter the Great's Administrative and Judicial Reforms* (1979).

[23] The origins of the 1720 Naval Statute date to 1669, when Captain D Butler, a Dutchman in Russian service, wrote down from memory and had translated into Russian key articles from the Dutch naval disciplinary regulations of 17 September 1662. His version was retained in the Ambassadorial Department together with Russian translations of the 1688 Dutch regulations and English regulations of 1692. Peter the Great drew upon these virtually verbatim when crafting his regulations of 1706, 1710, and, finally, 1720. See P A Krotov, 'Об использовании голландского

These were natural areas of concentration for a ruler intent on modernisation and at war constantly during his reign. Had he lived longer, one may only speculate what changes might have been wrought in private law. In some senses Peter deserved to be classified as a comparativist: he personally drafted or revised many of his enactments; it was he personally who instructed that foreign laws and legal experience be assembled and it was he who read or had specially translated these materials for his own edification. Whatever reception of foreign law may have occurred at earlier stages of Russian history, Russia herself had never before reached so insistently and assertively for foreign legal experience.

It was in the Petrine era, although some believe there were earlier manifestations of this view, that written law [закон] began to be accorded priority over custom as a source of law. So important was this development that in the eyes of some Russian legal historians the periodisaton of Russian legal developments should turn on this. Vladimirskii-Budanov identified three periods in the history of Russian law: the 'princely period' from the ninth to the thirteenth centuries, when customary rules dominated; the Muscovy period of the fourteenth to sixteenth centuries, when custom and written law enjoyed equal stature; and the Imperial period of the eighteenth and nineteenth centuries, when written law had priority over custom.[24]

Peter's immediate successors did not pursue his pace of reform; however, within less than four decades a foreigner came to the Russian throne whose enlightened attitude toward law and law reform rapidly earned her the title 'the Great'. Catherine II set about immediately to bring Russia up to the standard of eighteenth-century Europe.

военно-морского законодательства при разработке уставных положений российского флота во второй половине XVII—первой четверти XVIII века' ['On the Use of Dutch Naval Legislation When Working Out Charter Provisions of the Russian Navy in the Second Half of the 17th and First Quarter of the 18th Centuries'], in Источниковедение: поиски и находки (Voronezh, 2000) 120–130. On the role of the Military Statute in regard to Russian witchcraft trials, see W F Ryan, 'The Witchcraft Hysteria in Early Modern Europe: Was Russia an Exception?', *Slavonic and East European Review*, LXXVI (1998), 49–84, who observes: 'From the introduction of Peter's military law in 1716 onwards, we . . . have in Russia what would now seem distinctly odd, a *church* court administering *military* law in cases of heresy, blasphemy and witchcraft' (77).

[24] See M F Vladimirskii-Budanov, Обзор истории русского права [*Survey of the History of Russian Law*] (Kiev, 1915). A modern authority writes: 'The more radical changes were in the mode of operation of the new formed institutions compared with the Duma and the chancelleries of earlier times. The earlier institutions of government were . . . based to a large extent on custom rather than written procedure. They followed the Conciliar Law Code of 1649 and the many decrees of Tsar and Duma, but much of their operations were still in the realm of orally recorded custom. Peter insisted on written rules of operation as well as adherence to written law . . . The careful records were not just a matter of bureaucratic thoroughness, they were part of the process of orderly and legal government which Peter had learned from observing Western practice': P Bushkovitch, *Peter the Great: The Struggle for Power 1671–1725* (2001) 443.

Peter I had set in motion the measures required to found the Academy of Sciences in Russia, which opened shortly after his death in 1725. Law was among the sciences to be pursued, and the Academy of Sciences was to serve simultaneously as a research and a teaching institution, an Academy and a university. The first appointee in law, J S Beckenstein from Germany, offered lectures on natural law and politics but attracted no students and left in 1735. C F Gross lectured at the same time on moral philosophy, using the Russian translation (1726) of Samuel Pufendorf's *De officio hominis et civis* made at Peter's behest. Beckenstein's successor appointed in 1738 was F H Strube de Piermont (1704–90), who published at St Petersburg in 1740 a major study on the origins of natural law, in the French language; a revised edition issued at Amsterdam in 1744 was reprinted several times with emendations. Under the 1747 Statute on the Academy a sharp distinction was drawn between the academicians and the professors; the last offered lectures in the physical, mathematical, and humanitarian sciences, law falling within the last, and Strube was appointed to offer them. In 1756 Strube delivered a lecture treating the origins of Russian law that was published in both Russian and Latin.[25]

Three chairs of law were initially established within the Law Faculty of Moscow University founded in 1755; the notable professors were P H Dilthey, K H Langer, I A Tret'iakov, and S E Desnitskii. The last especially merits our attention. Desnitskii was the first Russian law professor. Sent abroad in 1761 to read law at Glasgow University, he and Tret'iakov completed the full course of study at what then was Britain's leading university. Desnitskii, elected Academician in 1785, published several works upon his return to Russia, acquainting his countrymen with the ideas of Adam Smith and John Millar, and at Catherine's instruction translated into Russian volume I of Blackstone's *Commentaries*, published at Moscow in three volumes in 1780–83. He offered courses on the history of Russian law, on Justinian's *Pandects*, on a comparison of Russian and Roman law, and on the English language.[26] Since he and Tret'iakov, also appointed at the University and a Glasgow graduate, could lecture in Russian, the number of law students increased appreciably. Z A Goriushkin introduced the practice of teaching Russian law through mock trials and actual proceedings.

Catherine II's own enduring contribution to Russian law occurred in 1767 when there was published a Nakaz composed by herself with extensive borrowings from leading enlightened thinkers, notably Beccaria, Montesquieu, and Voltaire. Although the Nakaz was never enacted, its translation into the major European

---

[25] See W E Butler, 'F. G. Strube de Piermont and the Origins of Russian Legal History', in R Bartlett and J M Hartley (eds), *Russia in the Age of Enlightenment* (1980) 125–141.

[26] A H Brown, 'The Father of Russian Jurisprudence: The Legal Thought of S. E. Desnitskii', in Butler (n 13 above) 117–121.

tongues and issuance in more than 20 editions made it the single piece of Russian legislative material best known abroad. An English version appeared at London in 1768. The Nakaz and perhaps Catherine's administrative reforms of 1775 and 1780, also widely published in Europe, were her major legal achievements; she too appointed codification commissions, but to no effect. However, the intellectual climate and institutions which she fostered, despite her later apprehension about some of their implications, laid the base for an emergent Russian legal elite in the nineteenth century. Foreign perceptions of Russian law had altered dramatically. No longer the epitome of arbitrariness and cruelty, Russia was praised in print and in public law lectures abroad for having set inspired examples which other nations might profitably emulate in their law reform undertakings.[27]

An indigenous legal literature began to complement translations into Russian of foreign works. Pufendorf and Blackstone have been mentioned: Bielfeld, Justi, Nettelbladt, and Montesquieu, among others, were translated, as were extracts from Diderot's *Encyclopédie* relating to law. Strube de Piermont, Dilthey, and Langer all left significant works. V T Zolotinskii published the first original Russian work on natural law in 1764. N I Novikov, M D Chulkov, and others began through their compilations to introduce the Russian public to original texts of their early legal heritage. By the end of the century collections of and indexes to Russian legislation began to appear, essential raw material for teaching Russian law to students.

Russia embarked upon the nineteenth century with a new Emperor in a liberal frame of mind determined to modernise the State apparatus and bring order to the chaotic state of Russian legislation. In 1801 the tenth codification commission since Peter I was instituted. The Commission looked initially to Europe for ideas. The works of Jeremy Bentham were translated into Russian (1805–10) in three volumes and the Code Napoleon was closely followed in preparing the initial drafts. But imposing intellectual or foreign schemes for systematisation did not find favour with Alexander I in the end; codification work fell into desuetude, to be revived in the 1820s in the spirit of Savigny: Russia would look to her own historical experience and legislation to fashion a new code of law.

Alexander I introduced ministerial reforms to supplant the collegial model of Peter the Great. Based upon the French scheme, the administrative reform was accompanied by an expansion of the education system and a transition to a system of civil service recruitment which relied on examination performance rather than exclusively hereditary links. 'Jurisprudence' was among the subjects examined; it encompassed natural law, Roman law, private law, criminal law, and the State

---

[27] Butler (n 13 above) 88–90. Key legislation from Catherine II's reign is collected in two volumes with extensive annotations and bibliography by O N Chistiakov and T E Novitskaia (eds.), Законодательство Екатерины II [*Legislation of Catherine II*] (2000–1).

economy. New universities were founded and faculties of law formed. Foreign law professors had to be recruited in the early decades, but preference was given to Russian candidates and in the course of time Russian graduates came to fill the majority of posts. Moscow University continued to offer legal training in both general law subjects and in the procedures and arts of advocacy in Russian tribunals.

With the accession of Nicholas I in 1825, codification work resumed at an accelerated pace. Drawing upon the talents of a small group of lawyers at St Petersburg University, M A Balugianskii, of Hungarian origin, and M M Speranskii brought to completion the most ambitious and comprehensive systematisation of legislation attempted in Europe. First to appear was the Complete Collected Laws of the Russian Empire (Полное собрание законов Российской империи), a chronological collection of Russian legislation (more than 30,000 enactments) commencing with the *Sobornoe ulozhenie* of 1649 to 1825. Published in 48 massive tomes (1830), this collection formed the base for the next stage: a Digest of Laws of the Russian Empire (Свод законов Российской империи) published in 15 volumes in 1832. Both collections survived with continuations until the end of the Empire. A second series of the Complete Collected Laws was published annually from 1826–81, and the third series, from 1881–1916. From time to time the Digest of Laws would be supplied with supplementary volumes and reissued at intervals in a complete revised edition.[28] This pattern of systematising legislation was taken over by the Soviet Government and is continuing to be used by the Russian Federation.

Speranskii's account of preparing the collections offers much insight into the administration of law and justice in that time. Few enactments had been printed. No chancellery had a complete register of enactments, and those that existed were badly organised. A full record of the law did not exist, and much of what did exist was inaccessible, not to say unknowable, by official and citizen alike. Systematisation, Speranskii wrote, was an absolute prerequisite for the development of a legal system:

> It is not therefore from the Roman Law, nor yet from the isolated efforts of our lawyers, that we can expect to construct a solid foundation for a systematic study of the laws. It must be based upon a body of laws, and will date its commencement from their publication. Until this is done, it would be useless to devise commentaries and prescriptions calculated to develop the science of national legislation.[29]

Although the model of the Digest may appear to be Justinian, the precepts for its compilation were drawn from the writings of English jurists, Sir Francis Bacon

---

[28] See N D Renaud, 'The Legal Force of the 1832 Svod Zakonov', *Sudebnik*, II (1997), 83–124.

[29] M M Speranskii, *A Summary of Historical Sketches on the Formation of the Body of the Russian Laws* (transl. W Wall, 1841) 89–90.

and Jeremy Bentham, especially the former, as Speranskii makes unequivocally clear.

Administrative reforms, expansion and improvement of legal education, the publication of comprehensive law collections, a trained civil service—the gradual implementation of these measures in the nineteenth century contributed mightily to legal professionalisation in Russia.[30] The precise origins of the legal profession remain obscure. It is probable that litigation in medieval Russia was conducted by the parties themselves, although some contemporary accounts referred cryptically to 'attorneys'. In the eighteenth century it is evident that laymen experienced in the ways of the courts often interposed themselves between party and judge and acted as a kind of advocate on behalf of their client. Lord Macartney described them as 'in general very sharp and expert . . . they will undertake to spin out any cause for a term of years, on payment of a certain sum agreed on'.[31] Judges depended for their livelihood upon a percentage of monetary compensation awarded; contemporary accounts provide conflicting evidence on the extent of judicial bribery and corruption in Russia, but there is ample evidence of public opinion, including Peter I, Catherine II, Alexander I, and Nicholas I, profoundly distrustful of judges and lawyers. By the third quarter of the nineteenth century legal professionalisation and legal values were beginning to leave their imprint within the State administration and without. Many observers believe that these were among the factors which contributed to the great nineteenth century reforms of Russian law: the emancipation of the serfs in 1861 and the judiciary reforms of 1864.

The emancipation of the serfs, quite apart from ending an intolerable social injustice, set in motion reforms of land, family, and inheritance law that required several decades to gestate.[32] Reforms of local government, the introduction of the *zemstvo* system, in 1864 and 1870 gave the peasants greater involvement in self-government. The judiciary reform, which originated within the councils of the Tsar, wholly restructured the court system and officially established an organised legal profession. English influence was to be seen, including the intellectual genius of Bentham. The judiciary was made independent of administrative officials, with rights of appeal, and judges not to be removed except for malfeasance in office. *Volost'* courts were retained for the peasants, but otherwise courts based on class were abolished. The English 'justice of the peace' nominated by local *zemstvos* was introduced to handle minor offences. The complicated system of written plead-

[30] R Wortman, *The Development of a Russian Legal Consciousness* (1976). For the emergence of these values and their impact upon criminal punishment, see A M Schrader, 'Containing the Spectacle of Punishment: The Russian Autocracy and the Abolition of the Knout, 1817–1845', *Slavic Review*, LVI (1997), 613–644.

[31] G Macartney, *An Account of Russia* (1767) 103.

[32] See W B Wagner, *Marriage, Property and Law in Late Imperial Russia* (1994).

ings characteristic of Russian procedure was replaced by oral proceedings and trials were to be open, again on the English model. Jury trial was available for serious criminal offences. French influence was to be seen in the creation of two cassational instances in the Ruling Senate (civil and criminal) to review cases when appeal had been exhausted. But although many features of the common law had been adapted and although medieval Russian trial practice had been akin to an adversary-type proceeding, the continental type of inquisatorial proceeding in criminal cases was received, many aspects of which survive in modern Russian criminal procedure. A professional Bar was instituted, and all parties to civil and criminal proceedings were accorded the right to professional representation.

The last half century of Imperial rule has been called the 'Golden Age' of Russian law.[33] The Russian legal profession flowered, producing distinguished practitioners, judges, and legal scholars, successfully challenging in several celebrated jury trials an absolutist autocracy bent upon eradicating political dissent and pluralism. Even to the revolutionary, the legal profession in Russia had its attraction as a channel for effectuating political and social change. Lenin read law at Kazan and St Petersburg universities and passed the Bar precisely for these reasons. In the course of time the reforms came to be attenuated by subsequent legislation. Judicial independence was circumscribed, the jurisdiction of class courts was somewhat enlarged, trial by jury was precluded in a growing number of instances, opportunities for imposing administrative sanctions were increased, the jurisdiction of justices of the peace was narrowed, the openness of trials was limited, and courts martial were used increasingly to try civilians.

Pressure for social and legal reform intensified early in the twentieth century. The Revolution of 1905 brought a constituent assembly, the State Duma, and a form of constitutional monarchy. Political parties became active; attempts at enacting far-reaching economic and social reforms were made. A serious but belated effort to reshape the Russian socio-economic and political order was commenced. Russian jurists were busy with civil and criminal law reform. A draft criminal code of 1903, based on several years of deliberations, was approved only in part, but as a whole it represented the most advanced statement of criminal jurisprudence in the world. A draft civil code compiled in 1910–13 achieved a similar standard of technical and substantive proficiency.[34] Both were drawn upon in the Soviet period and again in the post-Soviet era by those who crafted the RSFSR and then the Russian civil and criminal codes. The legal profession played an increasingly prominent role in Russian political life; many members of the State Duma were

---

[33] S Kucherov, *Courts, Lawyers and Trials Under the Last Three Tsars* (1953).

[34] See A F Povorinskii, Систематический указатель русской литературы по гражданскому праву 1758–1904 гг. [Systematic Index of Russian Literature on Civil Law: 1758–1904], ed. O Iu Shikokhvost (3rd edn, 2001).

individuals with legal background or education, from all parties. But reform could not keep pace with the demands for societal change. In 1917 the Imperial order collapsed under the pressures of war and revolutions.

Imperial Russia it would seem always contained a multiplicity of legal orders operating simultaneously to govern the affairs of the more than 200 ethnic groups inhabiting its territories. Even within the frontiers of the Russian Federation as presently constituted there are more than 100 ethnic minorities, the majority of whom are organised into administrative-territorial entities called 'subjects of the Russian Federation'. In areas conquered or annexed by Russia it was generally the practice to introduce the Russian administrative system, to eliminate some of the worst local practices (slavery, blood vengeance), and to allow local legislation or customary law to otherwise continue to operate. The full introduction of Russian law would have required a political and military commitment to the russification of non-Russian minorities beyond the strength of the Empire. Tolerance of customary rules, however, was in the mainstream of Russian practice with respect to the Russian populace itself. Land relations and succession amongst the rural Russian populace were based chiefly upon local customary rules enforced by peasant courts. It was commonplace to speak of 'peasant customary law'.[35] Amongst the nomadic tribes of Siberia, Russian legislation came gradually to play a larger role, especially through the Code of Steppe Laws of the Nomadic Peoples of Eastern Siberia, but on the whole local customs remained the basic source of law of these peoples.[36]

E. Continuity, Change, and Continuity

What of the pre-revolutionary heritage endured after the October 1917 Revolution, consciously or unconsciously, has engaged the attention of dozens of observers, Russian and foreign. Bolshevism arrived in the initial expectation that it would spark a world revolution and rapidly found itself obliged to contend with the formidable natural limitations of the Russian Empire itself: its size, its vulnerability, its languages, its multi-ethnicity, its standard of industrialisation, its illiteracy and poverty, its hunger for peace and land reform, its historical, religious, and political experience, and its economic order. A Revolution engendered in Russian experience and expectations, it was unavoidable that many responses to problems would draw upon Russian patterns.

The forms of pre-revolutionary legislation were adopted at once. Decrees were cumulated into chronological collections which later served as the base for sys-

---

[35] R Beermann, 'Pre-Revolutionary Russian Peasant Laws,' in Butler (n 13 above) 190.
[36] V A Riasanovskii, *Customary Law of the Nomadic Tribes of Siberia* (1938) 61–62.

tematic compilations and digests. Whereas Decree No 1 of the young Soviet Government was 'On Peace', Decree No 7 dealt with the publication of laws. Habits of neglecting systematisation and codification, of allowing legislation to fall into an appallingly chaotic state of confusion and inaccessability, likewise persisted throughout the Soviet era, despite attempts to eliminate them in the 1970–80s, and already plague the post-Soviet Russian State, which must amalgamate its post-Soviet legislation with that which went before.

In the period since the demise of the Soviet Union, many Russian legal institutions continue to stress their roots in the Russian past which incorporates the Soviet period. In 1997 the Russian Procuracy celebrated its 275th jubilee by the publication of a lavish volume chronicling nearly three centuries of Russian and Soviet and Russian procurators. The Russian legal publishing house, Iuridicheskaia literatura, marked its 80th anniversary in 1998. The system of arbitrazh courts in 1997 traced its roots to the Trade Statute (Торговый устав) of 1667. These are all institutions which have experienced institutional transformations, changes of name and modifications of function, even reorganisation without formal legal succession. Yet Russian they are through contemporary eyes. The debate of the Soviet era regarding elements of continuity and discontinuity has for the present been resolved in favour of continuity: discontinuity never existed, or was never achieved; or, the Soviet claim to uniqueness, to non-Russianness, was never realised.

Modern Russia has inherited its burdens of the past, both Imperial and Soviet. Many believe the Imperial pattern of autocracy, intolerance, russification, bureaucratism, backwardness, and the absence of a modern legal tradition, however much the Revolutions of 1917 may have been directed at these evils and abuses, contributed in the Soviet era to resistance to political pluralism, religious freedom, disregard of the rule of law, a suspicion of legal rationalism, Stalinist arbitrariness, and a reluctance to subject the political system to legal intervention. The post-Soviet Russian legal order must come to terms with the entire Russian historical legacy, and happily shows signs of a willingness and ability to do so.

Continuity and change in law is not a mechanical exercise in identifying what seem to be analogous institutions, rules, or practices. Context is of the utmost significance, nor should one lose sight of the fact that both eras of Russian experience relate to the larger Western and Eastern legal traditions. Some similarities and differences may owe their explanation or more plausible hypotheses to legal developments or traditions beyond the limits of Russia itself.

3

RUSSIAN LEGAL THEORY

For nearly three-quarters of a century the fundamentals of Marxism-Leninism comprised the starting point in the former Soviet Union for university and secondary-level studies in all disciplines, including law. Courses in political economy, historical materialism, dialectical materialism, history of the Communist Party, and basic principles of Marxism-Leninism were required in the first and second years of higher education to create what the Soviet authorities considered to be the proper ideological and philosophical base for the further acquisition of knowledge.

With the demise of the Soviet Union, those ideological foundations were discredited and removed from the curriculum (although not instantaneously). There is nothing comparable to insert in their place, although most Russian legal educators believe that students require an introduction to the philosophical and jurisprudential foundations of their chosen discipline and most, if not all, law faculties offer introductory surveys of legal and political doctrines, historical and contemporary. Russian legal theory accordingly has been set unexpectedly adrift to seek new moorings in the Russian past, in the Russian present, and in the world of legal theory at large. While there is discomfort associated with being adrift, there also has been an explosion of interest in Russian political and legal thinkers whose works were previously inaccessible and a certain interest in contemporary legal philosophy, whose works even in the post-Soviet era seem so alien to Russian values and Russian objectives. The Russian jurist of whatever generation and specialty in the law finds either his previous training in Marxism-Leninism irrelevant and unacceptable or his present training eclectic and uncertain. In either case, his concepts of law, its origins, role, and purpose, and its future are a new intellectual challenge. We examine below the historical foundations to which the Russian jurist is being introduced and some of the contending jurisprudential concerns of post-Soviet Russia.[1]

A. Russian Jurisprudential Roots

In the Russian perception legal theory is not an arid subject to be divorced from the 'practical' subjects of legal study. One modern legal theorist has called his field 'the methodological laboratory of political theory . . . with a view to forecasting the ways and means of the further development and perfection of contemporary historical knowledge on State and Law'.[2] The linkage between State and law, and between politics and law, is crucial in Russian thinking. The 'legal succession of ideological structures as a whole and of politico-legal knowledge in particular is not merely an immutable condition for their further development, but also for perfecting the process of State-legal construction'.[3] In other words, the past is part of a direct continuum to policy decisions of the present regarding the development of law and legal institutions.

---

[1] I draw in this chapter to a significant extent upon my introductory essay to W E Butler (ed), *Russian Legal Theory* (1996), where substantial selections are reproduced from those few Russian legal philosophers whose works have been translated into English.

[2] See V S Nersesiants, Политические учения и современность [*Political Doctrines and Modern Times*] (1976) 6.

[3] See I A Isaev and N M Zolotukhin, История политических и правовых учений России xi-xx вв. [*History of Political and Legal Doctrines of Russia from the Eleventh to the Twentieth Centuries*] (1995) 3. Analogous views are expressed in the magisterial work of V S Nersesiants (ed), История политических и правовых учений [*History of Political and Legal Doctrines*] (1995). Also see V S Nersesiants (ed), История политических и правовых учений. [*History of Political and Legal Doctrines of the Twentieth Century*] (1995). This chapter draws upon these studies and others of the post-socialist era without further citation; collectively they are the most objective and thorough introductions to Russian legal theory to appear in nearly a century in the Russian language.

To say that the depths of the history of Russian legal doctrine remain unplumbed, is itself part of the legacy of the recent and remote past. Russian legal theory was in its infancy before the revolutions of 1917,[4] and the history of Russian legal theory even more so. Russian theorists looked principally to their contemporary European colleagues for inspiration, and to the classics of European political and legal thought in Russian translation. The highly regarded work by B N Chicherin on political doctrines made no mention of Russian legal theory.[5] The Soviet Union had little use for political and legal doctrines of the Russian past, particularly those rooted in theological postulates, and consequently offered the most superficial of surveys in law school compulsory subjects. The considerable attention given to the so-called 'revolutionary-democratic' Russian thinkers, while deserved, was unbalanced by other ideological constraints which prejudiced objectivity. A separate subject, ignored undeservedly in both East and West, is the contribution of the Russian *émigré* community in the twentieth century to legal and political theory.

B. Legal Doctrines of the XI–XIV Centuries

The emergence of the formal trappings of the Grand Princedom of Kievan Rus[6] were accompanied by a manuscript culture which included translations into Church Slavonic of texts by Aristotle, Plato, Plutarch, Homer, Zenon, Epicurus, Herodotus, Demosthenes, and others, together with legal texts from Byzantium and southern Slavdom. These contributed in turn to the tradition of Russian Chronicles that treated, inter alia, issues of law and politics and accounts of voyages by Russian travellers who described laws of the lands they visited. In the course of time these sources addressed the origin of Kievan Rus and the ruling dynasty, the unity and sovereignty of the Grand Prince and his officialdom, possible forms of limitation on the absolute power of the Grand Prince (consultative councils and advisors), legality, and the settlement of disputes. A legal terminology came into being, and concepts such as law (jus [право] and lex [закон]), truth, and justice were discussed.

---

[4] This will be deemed a harsh view by some Russian legal theorists, past and present. Nonetheless, in my perception, Russian legal theory remains profoundly particularistic, most especially those strands drawing upon Russian values and experience. The view expressed by V D Katkov in 1913 would be widely shared today: 'The jurisprudence of the West is not on the right path and can not serve us as a *general* example'. See V D Katkov, *Jurisprudentiae novum organon* (Odessa, 1913), I, vi, quoted by V A Tomsinov, reviewing the first edition of this book, in *Zertsalo* (2000) V, 123.

[5] See B N Chicherin, Политические учения [*Political Doctrines*] (1869–79) (5 vols).

[6] For an excellent summary of those complicated times, see A Wilson, *The Ukrainians: Unexpected Nation* (2000) 1–39.

Ilarion

Assuming that the texts of the documents and chronicles which have survived from the Kievan era or which are attributed to that era are contemporary and genuine—assumptions which are not beyond reproach—the early works of Russian legal theory are several. Perhaps the earliest is the Sermon on Law and Grace [Слово о Законе и благодати], believed to have been written с. 1037–50 by Ilarion, the Metropolitan of Kievan Rus, the first Russian to be elevated to that office in 1051. Composed principally for theological instructional purposes and comprising a unique source of medieval Russian vocabulary, grammar, and literary style, the Sermon is treated by Russian historians as the 'earliest surviving political treatise of Ancient Rus'.[7]

The Sermon addressed three main issues: the relationship between law and grace, the significance of baptism for Kievan Rus, and the future development of the Kievan Rus state.[8] Ilarion did not distinguish sharply between human and divine laws, nor offer any form of classification of legislation. Law amounted to the performance of an obligatory prescription, whether of divine origin or issued by the sovereign, and was contrasted with Truth, achieved as the result of the realization of man's free will, informed by the moral and aesthetic teachings of the New Testament. The divine origins of law, modern Russian political theorists suggest, do not preclude law also being understood teleologically and juridically as external prescriptions regulating behaviour of the individual in society by way of prohibitions.

In Ilarion's perception law and truth were not juxtaposed to one another. Truth was comprehended by man thanks to law, and not despite law; Jesus Christ was sent to this world not to violate law, but to perform, or execute, law. This, in turn, led to a terminological issue which continues to bedevil contemporary discussions of legal theory. The issue turned on his use of the Russian terms 'justice' [правда]

---

[7] See V S Pokrovskii, История политических учений [*History of Political Doctrines*] (1960) 134. There are indications that in 1048 Ilarion headed a Kievan Rus Embassy to Paris for negotiations concerning the marriage of Anna, daughter of Prince Iaroslav, to Henry I of France. The marriage took place in 1051.

[8] Professor V A Tomsinov shares quite a different understanding of this text and its implications for the development of legal thought. In his view, the work is concerned principally with contrasting Judaism and Christianity in the 'political meaning' of those religions. Judaism at the time, Tomsinov argues, was not a pure abstraction for Kievan Rus, but rather a power centre represented by the Khazars and a potential choice for the official faith of Kievan Rus, together with Roman Catholicism and Byzantine Orthodoxy. Ilarion's principal message, Tomsinov believes, was that 'Judaism is a religion which serves only Jews, whereas Christianity is a religion called upon to serve all peoples'. As for State power, Ilarion's teachings, in Tomsinov's view, were directed towards emphasising succession in dynastic rule and the benefits such would bring to the lands of Rus. See V A Tomsinov, in O E Leist (ed), История политических учений [*History of Political and Legal Doctrines*] (1999) 127–136.

and 'lex, law' [закон]. The term 'правда' is associated primarily with positive law codifications or systematisations: the *Sudebnik*, the *Russkaia Pravda*, the *Pravda Iaroslava*, the *Sborniki ulozhenii*, and others, with the power to judge, to chastise, to pardon. But the word also was used in a broader legal and philosophical sense to embrace 'truth', 'virtue', 'justness', and the like, and in this case these elements inform the content of law. In a larger sense, Ilarion uses 'правда' to describe both the content and the moral motivation of law, as a 'legal formula' which 'means consideration of a case according to Law irrespective of the final result'. The approach is believed to have influenced the Teachings of Vladimir Monomakh and later legislative material.

Ilarion declared all Christian peoples to be equal, disputing in so doing Byzantium's claim to hegemony. As for the nature of political society itself, Ilarion treated the essence of the State as divine since it represented a realisation of Divine Will. The bearer of supreme power is in communion with and a descendant of the heavenly Kingdom. The origin of power is by way of inherited succession, and Ilarion sought to establish the legitimacy of rules contemporary to him by tracing their lineage back to the 'ancient Igor'. While supporting the concept of rule whereby the Grand Prince was the sole and sovereign power within the lands subject to his rule, the Prince was not to be arbitrary and was to rule on the basis of law (which presumably meant law in both its positive and moral sense), mercy, generosity towards his subjects, and concern for orphans, the ill, widows, the church and monasteries.

Justice, he wrote, must be administered according to law and with mercy, setting out moral criteria with which a Christian ruler should comply when dispensing punishment. These ideas were accepted almost entirely by Vladimir Monomakh in his Teachings and later developed by Daniil Zatochnik. Ilarion also posited the notion that a ruler was accountable to his subjects before God, a subject much discussed by later Russian writers.

Works of Vladimir Monomakh

In or about 1113 the grandson of Iaroslav the Wise, Vladimir Monomakh, came to the throne in Kievan Rus. To him are attributed three works: Teachings for Children [Поучение детям], Message to Oleg Chernigovskii [Послание Олегу Черниговскому], and an autobiographical sketch known as Fragment [Отрывок]. These works touch upon the powers of the Grand Prince, the relations between Church and State, and the principles for administering justice. The Teachings give considerable attention to organising and exercising supreme power. He advised future princes to rule with the advice of a council and not to permit unlawfulness and injustice in the lands. To be just means to adjudicate according to law. Judicial functions Monomakh proposed that the ruler should exercise himself, not permitting a violation of the laws and dispensing mercy to his most defenceless subjects. Blood feud and capital punishment were rejected, including in inter-princely relations.

Monomakh elaborated Ilarion's notion of the ruler's accountability to his subjects. The military forces should not cause harm to the peasant villagers, and wherever possible internecine conflict should be avoided. The ruler and his princes should seek means to achieve peace and disputes should be settled peacefully. As for Church and State, Monomakh accorded to the Church an honourable but subordinate place.

Daniil Zatochnik

Manuscripts attributed to Daniil Zatochnik of the late twelfth or early thirteenth century, by which time Kievan Rus had broken up into countless warring princedoms and was on the eve of being subjugated by the Mongols and Tatars from the East, counselled centralisation of power in the interests of defending Rus against invaders. Whether the manuscripts were by one author or two, the Sermon [Слово] or Supplication [Моление] (titles vary from one manuscript to another), they posit an idealised Grand Prince who is physically attractive and merciful. He rules with strength, tempered by wisdom and justness. His State is a strong one, well-organised and orderly. He rules with the assistance of advisors and counsellors and accepts their advice. His task is to select good and wise advisors, but not necessarily only the old and experienced. Wisdom is not only age and experience.

This account suggests that Daniil Zatochnik regarded Vladimir Monomakh as having represented the ideal form of power. The Grand Prince also must have good military forces capable of defending his lands against outside enemies. But peace is to be generally desired, as is the peaceful settlement of disputes. Daniil advises the Grand Prince to recruit foreigners to his service for the benefit of his country. Strong warnings are given against internal threats to the Grand Prince in the form of the arrogation of power by boyars, a commentary on the fractionalisation of Rus into warring princedoms underway at the time. These were themes continued and enlarged upon in the manuscript culture that emerged after the celebrated Battle of Kulikovo in 1380, when the Muscovy Grand Prince Dmitrii Ivanovich defeated the Mongol forces amassed against him.

C. Legal and Political Theory 1500–1613

In the period here considered the forces of decentralisation in Muscovy had been overtaken by those of centralisation. The Mongol hordes, gradually defeated in Russia and called back by internal dissension at home, receded and the Grand Princes Ivan III (1462–1505) and Vasilii III (1505–33) succeeded in uniting the appanage princes and their lands under the rule of the Grand Prince of Muscovy. With the fall of Constantinople in 1453 and the marriage of Ivan III to Sophia-Zoe Paleologue, Princess of Byzantium, Muscovy laid claim to the two-headed eagle of the Eastern Roman Empire and to succession as the Defender of Orthodoxy, the Third Rome.

The principal themes of earlier works continued to be debated: the formation of a single sovereign political community, the type of monarchy which should emerge, the origins of the Russian State and the lineage of its princes, the organisation of State administration, the relations of Church and State, and the administration of justice. The position of the Church itself began to be debated, now a centre of wealth, land, and power.

The Russian clergy came to be conditionally divided into those who favoured a reorganisation of the Church under which the Church would renounce all wealth and lands and refrain from any interference into the affairs of the State, and those who preferred preserving the existing forms of church organisation and its economic status.

Nil Sorskii

(1433–1508). Idealising the early Christian communities, Nil Sorskii organised his own Nilo-Sorskii Hermitage in the Vologda Region. There he and his followers drew attention to those passages in the Gospels where Christ and his disciples renounced all worldly goods and counselled his fellow monks to follow that example. In relations between Church and State Nil Sorskii departed from the Byzantine tradition, where there had been a complex combination of the two, and suggested that each had its own domain of activity and therefore its own measures of dealing with problems confronting it.

These rather general propositions were elaborated by his friend and follower Vassian Patrikeev, who directly put the question of depriving monasteries of their wealth and even eliminating monasteries as such. He favoured a sharp delineation in legislative acts of the spheres of operations of State and Church and the principle of non-interference in one another's affairs.

Maksim Grek

(c. 1475–1556). The ideals of Nil Sorskii were most fully elaborated by a theologian of Serbo-Croatian origin who came to Russia in 1518 by invitation of Grand Prince Vasilii III to translate theological works from the Greek language into Russian or correct translations badly done. Born in Albania or Salonika (the sources differ), Maksim Grek studied in Paris, Florence, and Venice, where he had witnessed the movement and heard the teachings of Savonarola, then returned in 1505 to a monastery on Mount Athos before accepting the invitation of the

Grand Prince. His Russian years were not happy ones. He aroused opposition in senior circles of the Russian Orthodox Church; twice condemned by assemblies of the Church, he spent nearly 25 years in exile, where he continued to write.

Drawing upon his years of learning at the University of Paris, he advocated broadly based education in all disciplines and not merely the theological sciences. He developed Nil Sorskii's teaching on free will, laying the groundwork for natural law conceptions that were to follow. His political and legal views have been extensively investigated by Russian historians of political thought.

Maksim Grek argued that a legitimate ruler could come to the throne either by way of succession-descent or by way of election by a representative assembly, citing the example of Alexander of Macedonia. The principal task of the ruler or the State was to ensure the peaceful and quiet life of its subjects and a stable internal order. The preferred form of power was one in which the ruler relied upon wise and conscientious advisors, councils, and councillors, which in Russian conditions meant not merely the boyars but also other representatives of the nobility— an interpretation of Maksim Grek which remains controversial.[9]

The limitation of the ruler's power was to be achieved not only by advisors, but also by law and accepted moral criteria. He interlinked jus, lex, and legality in his concept of justice. Injustice he equated to a violation of law, a crime against law. Although his understanding of 'justice' is broad, it takes on juridical forms in a number of instances, most notably court proceedings in which punishment must be meted out on the basis of law, without hypocrisy and with mercy. Maksim Grek is regarded as being the first in Russian politico-legal literature to develop a detailed doctrine for limiting the actions of a ruler by positive law, following divine teachings and laws.

The quality of justice in Muscovy was remarked upon by virtually all writers of the period. Maksim Grek subjected the judicial system to scathing criticism, condemning the bribery of judges who 'steal estates and property from widows and orphans'. Such practices, he wrote, not only bring harm to subjects of the princedom, but also undermine the authority of the Tsar and the prestige of the State itself. He opposed the mediaeval practice of casting lots as inherently unjust, preferring witness testimony and oath in its stead.

---

[9] For the view that Maksim Grek favoured boyar-aristocratic rule, see S A Pokrovskii, 'Из истории русской политической мысли XVI в.', ['From the History of Russian Political Thought of the Sixteenth Century'], Труды Всесоюзного юридического заочного института [*Proceedings of the All-Union Juridical Correspondence Institute*] (1971) 5–7. This view is challenged in N A Kazakova, 'Максим Грек в советской историографии', ['Maxim Grek in Soviet Historiography'], Вопросы истории [*Questions of History*] no 5 (1973) 155; id, ' Максим Грек и идея сословно-представителей монархии', ['Maxim Grek and the Idea of an Estates-Representative Monarchy'] in Общество и государство феодальной России [*Society and the State in Feudal Russia*] (1975) 159–170.

Maksim Grek linked the application of the law with the extending of mercy. The unlimited power of the ruler would be limited through law by creating a just court system and eliminating extrajudicial types of arbitrariness on the part of the ruler himself and his officials. He held that the Tsar had no right to appropriate another's private ownership, nor to take the things of his servitors. One limit on his power was the right of private ownership protected by law.

The duties of the ruler to his subjects were elaborated in a late work composed about 1545: Message to Tsar Ivan Vasil'evich. There he enumerated the duties of the Tsar: he must rule with justice and reason, respect his officials, reward the military, listen to the advice of his wise counsellors and the clergy, protect orphans and the indigent, and in all order the life of his subjects on the basis of good laws.

Iosif Volotskii

(1439–1515). The philosophical and jurisprudential protagonists of Nil Sorskii and Maksim Grek were those who identified with Iosif Volotskii. Volotskii's principal works were Messages to Various Persons [Послания к различным лицам] and a number of sermons directed against heretics, later collected under the title The Enlightener [Просветитель]. His political orientation in Muscovy changed several times; initially an opponent of the Grand Prince by reason of his secularisation intentions, he came successfully to defend the monastery system for its good deeds—the building of monasteries and churches, provision for monks, assistance for the needy, and the like.

He differed from Nil Sorskii and Maksim Grek in his doctrine of power, distinguishing between the concept of power as being divine in origin from the actual fact of realising power by an individual person acting as the Head of State. While the ruler attempts to achieve divine purposes, he relies in so doing upon ordinary mortals who inevitably err and cause harm to the realm. Consequently, the ruler and his princes are not guilty before God for all misfortune and misadventure that occurs. This distinction opened the possibility for the first time in Russian politico-legal literature for a discussion and critique of the merits and actions of the actual ruler and condemning those who proved to be bad rulers and against whom one might legitimately resist.

Iosif Volotskii also postulated the supremacy of spiritual power over secular. He adhered to the long-established Byzantine concept of the 'symphony' of powers, an alliance of power under which the secular authority is obliged to assist the Church, to persecute enemies of the Church and heretics, and not to appropriate Church property, whereas the Church in turn is to support the authority and lawfulness of the secular ruler, provided however that the dominant role is accorded to the Church. Much attention was accorded by Iosif Volotskii to the issue of heresy. He undertook to prove that heresy was both a crime against religion and

43

the Church, and also against the State, and as a political offence it should be per-secuted (including investigation and punishment) by the State—a position which led Iosif Volotskii to come close to according primacy of place to the State. He drew parallels between ordinary criminal behaviour and heresy which enabled him to justify the trial and punishment, including the death penalty, of heretics in ordinary State courts.

The 'symphony' of powers led Iosif Volotskii to postulate a classification of laws which undertook to combine within a single system all the rules and norms by which man should be guided. Accordingly, he did not distinguish sharply between divine law and positive, man-made law. Divine will, in his view, was both a source of power for the ruler and a source of all legislation, especially as formu-lated in assemblies and councils of the Russian Orthodox Church. Free will had no place in his approach, and he drew no sharp line between law and morality.

After 1504 Iosif Volotskii and his followers became dominant in Muscovy and their ideas played an influential role in Russian legal and political thought throughout the sixteenth century.[10]

Filofei

'Moscow—the Third Rome' is a doctrine in its developed form traditionally asso-ciated with Filofei, a follower of Iosif Volotskii. His social and educational back-ground is uncertain, but he was undoubtedly of a pro-Muscovy orientation. His politico-legal views were formulated in a series of Messages addressed to the Pskov Namestnik Mikhail Grigor'evich Misiur-Munekhin and to the Grand Princes of Muscovy, although precisely which one remains in dispute amongst scholars.

Filofei set out a doctrine of supreme power which stressed the legality of the ori-gin of the Grand Princes, their succession, and their stature as God's representa-tive on Earth. The Tsar was to be concerned for his subjects, and to be so his kingdom must be in awe of God, symbolised by the sceptre in his hand and crowned with a laurel wreath. The image of the Tsar was dwelt upon at length. He was severe with all who depart from justice, but just with all of his subjects, being especially solicitous of the weak. His subjects in turn were to obey him without reservation.

Following many mediaeval thinkers, Filofei did not distinguish between morality and law [jus]. Accordingly, any immoral act was in his view unlawful whether it had a legal basis or not. His concept of justice also included moral principles.

The unification policies of Muscovy *vis-à-vis* its near neighbours convinced Filofei that the time had come for Russia to fulfil its historic mission, a mission

---

[10] See D M Goldfrank, *The Monastic Rule of Iosif Volotsky* (1983).

that in his eyes was inseparable from the mission of Russian Orthodoxy. Russia was the sole remaining kingdom true to Orthodoxy, and consequently the sole successor to its predecessors: 'two Romes have fallen, a third stands, and a fourth will not be'. This historic role of grandeur for Russia was confirmed by her recent experience—fidelity to Orthodoxy, defeat of the Tatar-Mongols, successful defence of Russian frontiers, and a promising diplomacy. The might and glory of Byzantium and Rome had passed to Muscovy, to the Russian State. Whether the doctrine of the Third Rome is an expansionist, aggressive one continues to be much discussed, including comparisons with the Soviet era and more recently renewed Russian interest in other Slavic peoples.

It followed that the centre of Orthodoxy could only be a powerful sovereign state enjoying universal respect and being possessed of sufficient power to defend the faithful Orthodox wherever situated. This was a powerful impetus to those who supported a centralised Muscovite state, and figured as a central tenet of Russian foreign policies for centuries thereafter, at least in words. 'There are sufficient grounds to assert that the political formula of Filofei was part of documents expressing the official ideology of the State and for a long time was a constituent part thereof'.

Fedor Karpov

The emergence of Muscovy as a centralised grand dukedom gave rise to a manuscript literature treating the changes in the form of rule and State structure. Fedor Karpov, publicist and diplomat, was amongst those who addressed these issues. Close to Maksim Grek and his followers, Karpov set out his views in a Message to the Metropolitan Daniil, ascribed to the 1530s. His political discourses and terminology have been studied extensively and variously construed. It is generally accepted that he favoured a representative form of rule of the Grand Prince and his senior officials and accepted the Aristotelian position that every city and kingdom required a Tsar and his counsellors. As regards the categories of justness and law [jus], which he combined into one, Karpov required that all laws must be just and directed attention to existing schemes for payment for labour. Earnings must be just and fair, and wealth fairly distributed. Subjects unfairly paid, including those in military service, might cease to listen to their Tsar. Compliance with law [lex] is both the moral base of social life and the foundation of the well-being of the State. Illegality is the consequence of a decline of morality.

Karpov offered an original interpretation of 'groza' [гроза], widely translated in English as 'terror' but having in fact a strong connotation of 'awe'. Many Russian political theorists held that the ruler should incorporate 'awe' as a vital component of the exercise of power. Karpov held that 'awe' was not an attribute of power, but rather an attribute of law [lex] itself. Order in a state created the necessary foundations for the element of 'awe' in a law and thereby enabled the sovereign and his officials to rule effectively and protect their subjects against 'evil' people. Laws [lex] and the State were human creations. Laws Karpov divided into three categories: natural, divine (the laws of Moses and the laws of Jesus Christ), and positive (State), the last being enacted on the basis of the former. He rejected justifications of any illegal actions, even if founded on such ethical categories as 'patience' and 'forgiveness'.

As a diplomat and public official, Karpov is credited with according greater attention to the interests of the State and the status of its citizens. His theory of law and politics is regarded as being close to that of Niccolo Machiavelli, although there is no evidence of Karpov being aware of Machiavelli's writings, of being a 'material link' in the process of the formation of an autonomous juridical doctrine in Russia based on natural law and human reason. That process was evidence of Muscovy moving into a new stage of 'cultural-historical development' closer to the thinkers of the Renaissance.[11]

Ivan Semenovich Peresvetov

The programme of State and legal reforms associated with the name of Peresvetov may or may not have originated with him, or with a group of individuals, or even, as some suspect, with Tsar Ivan IV himself. Whatever the case, the ideas associated with his name treated a number of principally legal matters, including the creation of a system of unified legislation applied by a centralised judicial system. Without being enmeshed in the religious disputes of the time, his writings elaborated and extended in substance many of the ideas advanced by Maksim Grek.

Judicial reforms favoured by Peresvetov were directed above all towards eliminating the evils of localism. Judges should be appointed directly from the centre and paid from the State treasury. Court costs and duties accordingly should be recovered to the State treasury and not to the judges, and the judges should rely only upon the law [lex] in administering justice. He would have endowed judges also with certain administrative and supervisory functions on behalf of the central authority. The great attention accorded in Peresvetov's writings to matters military were reflected in his proposal for a separate military court to be organised separately from the civil courts. The military court was to be local, expeditious, just, and without cost to those who appeared before it.

In matters of administering justice Peresvetov favoured severe punishments, including the liberal application of the death penalty at least in principle in order to create the right climate of obedience to law. He too introduced the concept of 'terror' or 'awe' to instil respect for law, having in mind the scheme of strict pun-

---

[11] See A K Leont'ev, 'Государственной строй, право и суд', ['State System, Law, and Court'] in Очерки русской культуры XVI в. [*Essays on Russian Culture of the Sixteenth Century*] (1977) 74.

ishments which might be applied to miscreants. Within the half century which elapsed after the period in which his writings originated, many of the reforms proposed were acted upon. With respect to legislation, the *Sudebnik* of 1550 was introduced.

Ivan the Terrible

Foreign impressions of the less salubrious side of Russian mediaeval and subsequent politico-legal thought are invariably associated with the legacy of Ivan IV, known principally through two works attributed to him which may or may not be contemporary: his so-called 'epistles' and a correspondence with Prince A D Kurbskii (see below).[12] The essence of those ideas reduced to absolute autocracy, terror, and a police State. Following the tradition of Russian political thought in tracing the origins of the Russian crown back to its historical roots, Ivan IV reputedly rejected the view that the legitimacy of the ruler depended in part upon his personal and moral qualities. The bearer of ultimate power was accountable solely to God in the hereafter, not on earth in any way to his subjects. And as for representative rule, the Tsar's sole counsel was God himself and no one else. Similarly, he rejected the combining of spiritual and secular power with the Patrichariate, favouring a sharp delineation between the two and rejecting any limitation on secular power by the spiritual authorities.

In the Tsar's view, the supreme ruler combined also the role of law-giver and judge. The type of punishment and precise penalty should be determined not by the law, but by the Tsar himself. The scale of severe punishments applicable was entirely arbitrary and derived principally from examples of various honourable rulers rather than from legislative material. Punishment might extend not merely to wrongful deeds, but to evil and dangerous thoughts.

Ivan the 'Terrible' or 'Awesome' attached new meaning to the word which has come down in history linked with his name. The term no longer implied a concern about the safety of the realm against external enemies or good order for its own sake. 'Terror' or 'awe' was secured by the *oprichnina*, or special police created by the Tsar. 'Awe' came to be associated with fear and the lawlessness associated with his arbitrariness: 'from the beginning of Russian literature until the end of the sixteenth century not a single political doctrine is to be found which understood the power of the Tsar to be as absolute so as to be decisively unlimited'[13] except for the doctrine of Ivan IV.

---

[12] For a useful recent collection, see Ivan IV, Сочинения[*Works*] (2000).
[13] See V Val'denberg, Древнерусские учения о пределах царской власти [*Mediaeval Russian Doctrines on the Limits of Tsarist Power*] (1916) 359–360.

Andrei Mikhailovich Kurbskii

A major source for the political thinking of Ivan IV is correspondence which reputedly passed between the Tsar and Prince Kurbskii, and which in any event proved to be a vehicle by which juxtaposed politico-legal approaches arising out of disagreements between the Tsar and senior officials in the late 1550s and early 1560s could be expressed. Those disagreements led to the disgrace of the senior officials concerned, mass repressions, and the flight into exile of Kurbskii himself.

In the writings attributed to him Kurbskii criticises the style of rule introduced by Ivan IV as tyrannical, comparing the Tsar with King Herod. Addressing matters of law and administration, he reiterated many of the criticisms levied against the courts by Maksim Grek, Otenskii, and Peresvetov, enlarging their comments to embrace legislation. He analysed both the processes of creating legislation and applying it. Invoking the traditional Russian concepts of justness and law, Kurbskii asked whether a law [lex] adopted by the State should always be complied with if it failed to conform to those criteria which a good law must satisfy? His reply, based to some extent upon the actual application of law, was that law [jus] and justness must coincide for a law [lex] to be considered to be lawful.

As for legislation, Kurbskii believed that a law [lex] must contain prescriptions which can actually be complied with; illegality he described as not only the failure to comply with a law, but also the adoption of cruel laws. The latter type of legislation Kurbskii labelled 'criminal'. In the view of V S Nersesiants, Kurbskii was the 'first in the history of political and legal thought to put the question that justness and justice, and also the natural rights of man (natural laws), are a source of rights and freedom of the individual not subject to the arbitrariness of the legislator'.[14]

Following Peresvetov, Kurbskii criticised the actual application of the law within and without the courts. The courts, he said, dispensed neither justice nor mercy. He singled out trials in absentia for special condemnation; a slandered individual had no opportunity to defend himself against his accusers—a fate experienced by those with whom Kurbskii was politically associated. The terrorist regime introduced by the *oprichnina*, Kurbskii argued, rendered judicial and representative organs useless. Accordingly, Kurbskii elaborated upon the theory posited by Iosif Volotskii concerning the right of a people to resist the ill-intentioned exercise of power.

Kurbskii favoured a limited monarchy, a monarch advised by representatives of strata of the populace who took part in all the major decisions of state. A distinction was drawn between what might be loosely described as legislative powers, to

---

[14] See V S Nersesiants, Право и закон [Jus and Lex] (1983) 196.

48

be exercised by the Tsar together with a representative council, and administrative or executive powers, to be exercised by the Tsar together with councils of advisors chosen for their wisdom and experience.

Ivan Timofeev and the Time of Troubles

The turn of the sixteenth-seventeenth centuries in Muscovy found the realm in disarray as the Rurik dynasty came to be succeeded by the Romanovs. A substantial politico-legal literature emerged addressing the issues of succession to the throne and the political organisation of society, of which perhaps the most noted is a manuscript entitled *Vremennik* [Временник]. Discovered in 1834 and attributed to a senior official, Ivan Timofeev [Semenov], the *Vremennik* is regarded as the most significant and influential example of such literature in its day.

Addressed principally to political rather than legal issues, the manuscript treated the legitimate succession of Tsars traditionally, considering those to be legitimate who succeeded by way of inheritance or by way of lawful election. Illegal Tsars were those who seized or appropriated the throne, offending thereby human and divine will and, it would follow, subject to punishment for their misdeeds. A stern opponent of Boris Godunov, Timofeev regarded the False Dmitrii as being sent by God to punish Russia for allowing Boris Godunov to take the throne.

Timofeev supported a limited monarchy, basically following the reasoning of Maksim Grek, F Karpov, Z Otenskii, Ivan Peresvetov, and A Kurbskii, but substantially elaborating the argumentation in favour of such a scheme. He advocated the formation of a Council of Cities of the Realm, which would recognise and confirm the authority of the Tsar and would take part in helping the Tsar exercise his functions.

The formulations advanced by Timofeev persuaded many later students of his manuscript to believe that Timofeev advocated more than a mere Council to assist the Tsar. Such a Council should express and reflect public opinion, which would lay the basis for resisting laws and acts of the Tsar that were considered to be unlawful or unjust. Given the tenor of the times, he strongly endorsed the thesis that subjects of an evil ruler had not only the right, but the duty to resist his reign.

Timofeev accepted the classifications of legislation advanced by Maksim Grek, Otenskii, and Kurbskii. He used the words 'natural law' [lex] and distinguished it from '*ustavnoi zakon*' [lex], or positive law. Natural laws he sometimes called 'reasonable', and he would appear to have accepted the view of Kurbskii that natural law categories emanate from divine will and express eternally just and reasonable principles. Positive law must conform to natural law. By '*ustavnoi zakon*' Timofeev meant all positive legislation in force from the very earliest days of Kievan Rus. His concept of justice, however, went beyond the classical limits of law to embrace elements of faith and morality. Although an opponent of Boris Godunov, Timofeev praised his devotion to justice and to the eradication of injustice.

D. Legal Theory and Romanov Absolutism 1613–1800

The accession of the Romanovs to the Russian throne in 1613 led in the course of time to a decline in those Russian institutions which had contained elements of representative power—the assemblies (*Zemskii sobor*) giving way to the Boyar Duma and the *Osviashchennyi sobor*, both formed on a non-elective basis. By the mid-seventeenth century the Romanovs were firmly in place and under Tsar Aleksei Mikhailovich a series of major reforms commenced that in turn produced deep divisions in Russian society and new politico-legal theories. As noted in Chapter 2, in 1649 law reform was introduced in the form of the *Sobornoe ulozhenie*, followed in 1650–1 by a similar systematisation of canon law and in 1654 by sweeping church reforms. The last led to schisms within the Russian Orthodox Church, of which the group known as the Old Believers continued to adhere to liturgies and scriptural readings of the pre-reform era and to favour a different relationship between Church and State.

Simeon Polotskii

The consolidation of Romanov power led to politico-legal theories which justified various forms of absolute monarchy. Samuil Petrovskii Sitnianovich (1629–80), born at Polotsk and known by his monastic name of Simeon, is associated with the doctrine of 'enlightened absolute monarch' in Russian politico-legal theory.

Simeon first extolled the person of the Tsar, comparing the Tsar with the sun, introducing the formula into the Russian political language: 'Tsar-Sun'. He rejected comparisons between the Tsar as a human personage and his subjects. God and Tsar were of virtually equal greatness: 'The Tsar—a celestial citizen—is the Father of all'. In Simeon's view, the Tsar and the State were identical, and he accordingly gave much attention to the formation and education of the Tsar. The Tsar must above all be an educated individual who acquires knowledge and wisdom from books and from wise people. Books about history were of special importance, so that the ruler might master the historical experience of other countries and peoples and live by their example. Distinguishing between the Tsar and a tyrant, Simeon observed that to know the difference, one should read Aristotle.

An enlightened monarchy, Simeon taught, is one in which the State is based on laws: 'All punishments must be suffered under the law'. There was no exception, neither for the Tsar himself, nor his son, nor any subjects. The courts must establish the truth and not be a source of retribution nor administer harsh sanctions.

He urged the creation of a court before which all were equal and a unified judicial system without 'red tape'.

Iurii Krizhanich

Born in Croatia (1618–83) and educated at Zagreb and then Vienna, and resident in Rome for nearly two decades, Iurii Krizhanich came to Russian service in 1659. Victim of a libellous denunciation in 1661, he was exiled to Tobolsk for 15 years. After two further years in Moscow, he left Russia in 1678 forever. While in Tobolsk he devoted himself to composing reflections on government, best-known in history as his treatise on Politics [Политика].

Krizhanich's European background and education and his command of Russian history and theology placed him in a special position amongst Russian politico-legal theorists. He criticised those Russian thinkers who endeavoured to trace Russian Tsars back to the Caesars of Rome. Such kinship, he suggested, would be shameful rather than honourable. He also questioned the doctrine of Muscovy being the Third Rome, dismissing this view as merely one means of extolling Ivan the Terrible.

His treatise on politics ranged widely over many affairs of State. He accepted the divine origin of the ruler. All kings, he wrote, are placed by God and are themselves divine. The purpose of the State is to achieve the 'common good' for all members of society. Krizhanich considered the best form of rule to be a perfected absolute monarchy which must be secured against transformation into tyranny by certain guarantees. Amongst the guarantees Krizhanich enumerated the presence on the throne of a philosopher-king, compliance with good laws which were in accord with divine and natural law, and the normative regulation of all estates and officials of society under which they would have defined rights and duties.

As an educated European, Krizhanich had been well-schooled in the Digest of Justinian, and his writings frequently contain propositions derived from that source. Those who draft Russian laws, he counsels, should have a thorough command of all laws and customs of the country and when necessary also study the laws of long-established states (including contemporary France) in order to draw upon their experience. All officials of State should strictly comply with the law in their activity. However, the philosopher-king he placed technically above the law; the King is himself the living law and not subject to other laws except divine law— here his writings repeat virtually verbatim the passages from the Digest of Justinian.

Krizhanich criticised Russian laws of his day as being excessively cruel and harsh: 'By reason of such harsh laws all European nations with one voice call the Orthodox Kingdom tyrannical . . . And moreover they say such tyranny is greatest here'. Krizhanich offered certain proposals to improve the judicial system. He recommended that a Boyars' Court be instituted to settle serious criminal cases by a majority vote and that lesser criminal and the civil cases be referred to one judge for settlement who would be chosen from among the boyars.

A L Ordin-Nashchokin

By the late seventeenth century Russia began to manifest mercantile protectionism in its legislation, usually accompanied by various projects and programmes for economic transformation of Muscovy. One of the most able Russian diplomats, Afanasii Lavrent'evich Ordin-Nashchokin (1605–80), proposed to encourage entrepreneurship partly by means of law reform.

He prepared the draft New Trade Statute [Новый Торговый устав] (1667) which contained rules regulating foreign and domestic trade and gave Russian merchants the same legal status as accorded to foreign merchants and others granted certain immunities. Partly the Statute was based on foreign practice and experience. However, it was to be more than a century before the politico-legal underpinnings of his programme came to the forefront of the Russian agenda for reform.

I T Pososhkov

The trends towards absolute monarchy intensified under Peter the Great as a form of rule. In his legislation Peter proclaimed: 'His Majesty is an Autonomous Monarch Accountable to No One in the World'. The Senate and Synod declared Peter to be the Emperor of All the Russias, thereby transforming the Grand Dukedom of Muscovy into the Russian Empire. The Duma of Boyars was replaced by the Ruling Senate; the administrative departments (приказы, also known in English as prikazy) became colleges operating under special Reglaments; the patriarchiate was abolished and a Synod created to administer the Church.

Among the most noted political theorists of the Petrine era was Ivan Tikhonovich Pososhkov (1652–1726), who flourished in a variety of entrepreneurial/industrial capacities and travelled widely throughout Russia. In 1724 he prepared his 'Book on Poverty and Wealth' addressed to the Emperor and set out his views on a number of matters which he believed should be the subject of urgent attention, amongst which was the system for the administration of justice. The book was not published at the time and may have led to the author's arrest and death in prison. Whether Peter the Great ever saw the manuscript or not is unknown. It eventually was rediscovered in 1842 and published, although not without difficulties even then with Russian censorship.

Pososhkov set himself the task of identifying why poverty and illegality were so widespread in Russia. The manuscript was mostly devoted to issues of organising industry and trade. Merchants, he advised, should be given the right of free trade and internal commercial duties and taxes should be uniform throughout the realm. Pososhkov believed the State should ensure enterprises had a labour force, including if necessary by assigning prisoners for this task. Merchants in turn should trade honourably and in certain cases statutory prices should be introduced for goods. As regards serfdom, he recommended the enactment of a special law which would precisely define the extent of duties of peasants and the limits of tied labour. A progressive land tax was suggested as a source of revenue for the State, which should not permit use of land free of charge.

Considerable attention was given to the eradication of injustice. Pososhkov basically accepted the position of Peresvetov with respect to the relationship between justice and law [lex]. Illegality was injustice. He proposed a draft scheme for 'direct justice', which would be effectuated by judge-bureaucrats of the State paid from the State treasury. The judges should come from the lower classes, as the nobility was too susceptible to bribery. For unjust activity Pososhkov proposed severe penalties, including capital punishment.

Court proceedings should be transcribed in writing according to rules laid down in law, and any State revenues from the trial should be paid into the State treasury directly. He also urged that judges should be informed at once about all detentions of suspects so that no one was unlawfully detained.

Codification he recommended on a large scale, to include all ancient and recent laws, to add whatever provisions were necessary, and to set out the entire body of legislation in precise detail. Both Russian and foreign legislation should be used as models, including Turkish examples. He recommended that a special commission be appointed to undertake codification which would include two to three persons from each province of the Empire and of all social strata, including peasants and soldiers. The entire commission would sign the final draft and submit it to the Tsar for confirmation, ensuring democratic participation in the drafting but leaving the final word for the Emperor.

V N Tatishchev

Known as an historian, diplomat, and distinguished military officer, Vasilii Nikitich Tatishchev (1686–1750) was charged in 1717 by Peter the Great with composing a geographic description of Russia and preparing a history of the country. This task he worked on episodically, eventually completing the work after 1745 when he fell into disgrace under the Empress Elizabeth. His views were based on natural law and a contractual theory of the origin of the State.

The State originated in a social contract amongst peoples who could not otherwise secure their safety and security against others and achieve the common good. Historically, he suggested, all known human communities first concluded contracts between spouses, then between parents and children, and ultimately between lords and servitors. As families became extended, entire societies emerged which required a head, who became the monarch and to whom all were subordinate just as children are subject to their father. The social contract was thus a series of contracts, and he regarded serfdom as one of such contracts which could not be dissolved at the instance of one of the parties without the agreement of the other.

Tatishchev devoted considerable attention to the forms of the State. The various forms of rule, he postulated, reflected the size of territory and degree of security from foreign threat. Peoples small in number who were not subject to attack could establish democratic forms of rule, whereas vulnerable and large states required a strong ruler. The worst of all forms of rule was tyranny, and the best, monarchy. In his view the best monarchy would rely upon a two-chambered elective organ, one a Senate composed of 21 representatives from the nobility and the second a consultative Council composed of 100 persons elected on a representative basis. While the monarch was the supreme legislator, the laws he issued must correspond to natural law, justness, and the general benefit. And one individual could not perform the task of legislation alone; the monarch was a formal legislator who must rely upon his departments and elected institutions to prepare the draft laws. The task of the monarch was to sign the draft laws prepared.

Tatishchev urged the preparation of a new *Ulozhenie* to replace that of 1649. The new legislation should be written in precise accessible language comprehensible by all. Codification consisted of eliminating the contradictions and inconsistencies in the law.

As regards court organisation and procedure, Tatishchev advocated the professional training of judges, a view ultimately introduced in the 1864 judicial reforms.

S E Desnitskii

The first Russian professor of law in Russia, Desnitskii (c. 1740–89) studied at the Theological Seminary at the Troitse-Sergiev Monastery and then the Petersburg Theological Academy before being sent by Catherine II to read law at Glasgow University in Scotland in the company of Ivan Tret'iakov. There he came under the influence of Adam Smith and John Millar; upon returning to Moscow, he translated William Blackstone into Russian at the request of Catherine II. He also published a number of works in which he set out rather radical proposals for the legal transformation of Russia.[15]

---

[15] See A H Brown, 'The Father of Russian Jurisprudence: The Legal Thought of S. E. Desnitskii', in W E Butler (ed), *Russian Law: Historical and Political Perspectives* (1977) 117–142; I S Ross, *The Life of Adam Smith* (1995).

Desnitskii did not accept the contractual theory of the origin of the State. He suggested that mankind had proceeded through historically successive 'states': the first period of hunting; the second, herding; the third, cultivation; and the fourth, commercial. The collective possession of things predominated in the first two stages, whereas full-fledged ownership arose in the third and fourth. The right of private ownership, following John Locke, originated in the expenditure of labour. The State was essential only in the fourth stage of societal development.

The purpose of the State was to achieve good for the greatest number of people. The best form of State was the constitutional monarchy founded on the separation of powers. The three principal powers were: legislative, judicial, and punitive. Legislative power would be exercised by the monarch together with a unicameral parliamentary organ called the Senate and consisting of 600–800 persons. Deputies from all social strata would be elected, including the intelligentsia. Senators would be equal irrespective of social origin.

His ideas relating to the courts included a number of proposals of a constitutional character. He believed the judiciary should be entirely separate from the administration and recommended the jury system, open trials, direct and continuous trials, and allowing the accused to defend himself. At the lower levels of the court system, however, he compromised on these principles and allowed links between the courts and local government.

Punitive power was within the jurisdiction of the Emperor and local officials, who were to be responsible for combatting crime, executing court judgments, prisons, and the collection of land duties. He classified law into State (the person and the State), civil (parents, children, spouses), criminal (crimes against society and the State) and judicial (relations between persons). In the domain of court proceedings he favoured the introduction of democratic principles such as equality of all before the law, equal punishment for those who committed the same crimes, commensurate punishment for the gravity of crimes, and greater emphasis on crimes against the individual and private ownership instead of those against religion, the Church, and the State. The death penalty might be applied only for intentional homicide and treason, and must be humane rather than applied so cruelly as in his day.

A P Radishchev

The efforts of Russian legal and political philosophers in the late eighteenth century to identify the most desirable form of law and government produced, in the case of Aleksandr Radishchev (1749–1802), a genuinely radical response. Born into a family of the nobility with large landholdings, he read law at Leipzig University and pursued a civil service career before turning to literary pursuits. His mission was to help to put an end to serfdom and autocracy, understanding by the latter term the concentration of unlimited power in the hands of a monarch. In his works autocracy was no longer a description of the sovereignty and independence of supreme power; it designated a form of rule, which in time came to be accepted as a characterisation of the form of rule in Russia.

In Radichshev's eyes autocracy was a state of being contrary to human nature. All forms of monarchy, whether 'enlightened' or otherwise, in his eyes were equally pernicious. An 'enlightened' monarch had never been and could not be. He also criticised the bureaucracy which surrounded the throne and in Russia was notable for being divorced from both the monarch and the people.

Radishchev proceeded from the theory of natural human rights and the contractual origin of the State. The natural sociability of people was the reason for creating states. Following J J Rousseau, he attributed the formation of states to the emergence of private ownership and the attendant inequalities among people. The social contract was a tacit one, concluded for the purpose of ensuring a prosperous life to all and defending the weak and oppressed.

Positive legislation enacted by a state must be based on natural law; if legislation is contrary to natural law, it is invalid, a point of departure used by Radishchev to reject serfdom. Contradictions such as this between natural law and positive legislation led Radishchev to the revolutionary proposition that an oppressed people had a right to rise up against the State if their natural rights were flagrantly violated.

His social ideal was a society of free and equal owners of property. Land should be given to those who cultivate it. Social privileges should be abolished and the nobility made equal in rights to all other strata of society. The Russian Table of Ranks should be eliminated, and the bureaucracy reduced and made accountable to a representative body. He favoured a Republic within Russia based on the model of the mediaeval city-States of Pskov and Novgorod.

Radishchev rejected the doctrine of the separation of powers on the principle that only the people are the true ruler. The State should secure to its people their sacred natural rights: freedom of thought, speech, action, self-defence when the law could not protect them, ownership, and to be judged by their equals. The administration of justice he would have placed in the hands of land courts elected by citizens of the Republic. The judicial system should be made up of Church, civil, military, and equity courts, and he urged the introduction of juries.

E. Legal and Political Theory 1800–50

The Decembrists

The reformist spirit of the reign of Tsar Alexander I contributed to the emergence of tiny oppositionist organisations created by like-minded individuals who composed programmes for altering the absolute Russian monarchy and abolishing serfdom. These secret societies ultimately contributed to the so-called Decembrist uprising in December 1825 in St Petersburg, the perpetrators being severely punished by death and exile.

A key figure was Pavel Ivanovich Pestel' (1793–1826), born in Moscow, educated at home and then in Germany, and upon returning to Russia became the first graduate of the Corps of Pages. He spurned a promising military career in favour of joining the secret societies and later became the organiser and head of the Southern Society, for which he composed a *Russkaia Pravda* as a programme for action. He was executed in 1826 for his role in the December uprising.

Pestel' was a materialist and an atheist philosophically. He believed in the natural equality of all individuals and their mutual aspiration to satisfy their requirements on the basis of a social organisation through the division of labour. The State, he said, was to introduce legal order into society and to balance mutual rights and duties of the government and the people. The task of government was to choose the best means of achieving general prosperity for each and everyone. Pestel' divided laws into three types: spiritual, natural, and civil. Spiritual laws are disclosed through the Holy Scripture; they link the spiritual and the natural worlds. Natural laws arise from the requirements of nature and natural needs; they are imprinted in our hearts. State or civil laws are decrees of the State whose aim is to secure general prosperity, and consequently they must be issued in full accordance with spiritual and natural laws. Such conformity, he said, was an absolute condition of the validity of State laws.

Pestel' also believed that State laws must conform to social interests in the sense that the advantage of the whole must always prevail over the advantage of the particular. Consequently, civil laws should be so composed that the interests of an individual do not take precedence over the interests of all society. Any action contrary to the general prosperity should be deemed to be criminal. Every just society must be based on the absolute authority of law and not the personal predilections of the ruler.

Addressing the various differences which existed in the basic laws of various countries and peoples, Pestel' argued that such differences arose principally from the various social and political institutes and institutions which existed in each state or society, rejecting Montesquieu's view that such differences originated in varying climates and geographic positions.

The Russian State, said Pestel', did not pursue the achievement of social prosperity and therefore represented an abuse of power which ultimately would lead to the State itself perishing. The flouting in Russia of natural, spiritual, and positive laws required, he suggested, 'changes of the existing State order and the introduction in its place of that which would be based only on precise and just laws and decrees'. In these propositions lay the right postulated by Pestel' of the people to overthrow a government which violated spiritual, natural, and positive laws.

Pestel's *Russkaia Pravda* contained a scheme for social and political transformations in Russia and the means for achieving these ends which was, in the true sense of the word, radical. It proposed the abolition of serfdom and the division of land amongst the peasants free of charge on the premise that land according to natural law is the weal of all of the people. Each individual holds a participatory share therein since land is the principal source for feeding mankind. However, he recognised that private ownership existed and was so deeply imbedded in the consciousness of people that eliminating ownership was impossible. Accordingly, Pestel's idea was not to eliminate land ownership, but to transform all Russians into land-owners.

Politically, Pestel' described himself as a republican because in that form of rule he saw the greatest possibilities for prosperity in Russia. State power would be divided into legislative and executive; all male citizens of 20 years or more enjoyed the right of suffrage except those in service. The legislative branch would be a single-chamber parliament elected for five years, with the annual election of one-fifth of its membership by rotation. No one might dissolve parliament. Executive power would be lodged in five persons elected for a five-year term to a Derzhavnaia Duma; all ministries and governmental bodies would be subordinate to this executive organ. Supervisory power of the legislative and executive branches would be vested in an assembly, or sobor, consisting of 120 persons called boyars who would be appointed for life and not take part in either legislative or executive life. Candidates would be nominated by the provinces. All laws would be sent to the assembly, which would not consider it in substance, but carefully verify that all necessary formalities had been complied with as a condition of the law entering into legal force.

The other supervisory functions of the assembly would be exercised through the appointment of one of its members to each ministry and to each region of the country. The sobor would appoint the supreme military command and could send for trial any official of any level who abused his power.

Pestel' proposed that the Russian State operate under a Constitution, which he called the 'State Testament'. Under his scheme, Russia would be divided into a federation composed of ten regions and three udels; each region in turn would consist of five provinces or national areas, each province of uezds, and each uezd of volosts. He proposed to transfer the capital of Russia to Nizhnii Novgorod, which he regarded as the geographic centre of Russia and the cradle of Russian freemen.

The best means of achieving these transformations in Russian life, Pestel' counselled, was a military-revolutionary coup with immediate elimination of the monarchy and physical elimination of the members of the Imperial family in order to prevent restoration of the monarchy. The creation of a new order would require a provisional supreme ruler headed by a dictator for a period of ten to 15 years. A constitutional order would come into being only when the existing order had ceased to exist and the memories of that order had been erased from the people's memory.

A second key figure in the Decembrist movement was Nikita Mikhailovich Murav'ev (1796–1843), who became head of the Northern Society. His intellectual development was shaped by the ideas of French Enlightenment doctrines, the Greek and Roman classics, and Russian writers and historians, of whom Karamzin was especially important. After the December uprising, he was sentenced to 20 years forced labour in Siberia.

Murav'ev composed three draft constitutions which contained the essence of his social and political programme. The third draft, written while in prison at the behest of the investigative authorities, was the most radical. He was well-grounded in the United States Constitution and the documents of Revolutionary France. Deeply religious, Murav'ev combined natural law doctrines with those of the New Testament and criticised absolute monarchy from these positions as being contrary to natural law. The Russian people, he wrote, are free and independent and may not belong to any person or family. The people are the source of power and have the exclusive right to make the basic provisions of such power for themselves.

The first step by way of transformation of the State, said Murav'ev, should be the abolition of serfdom and slavery. He considered the constitutional monarchy to be the best for Russia based on the principle of separation of powers. Legislative power would be placed in a two-chamber parliament. All individuals who had attained majority and who owned moveable or immoveable property, except those in private service, would have the right to vote. One chamber of parliament would be elected for six years, one-third of its membership being renewed every two years. Members of this chamber must be at least 30 years old and own property of a specified minimum amount. The other chamber would consist of 450 members and be elected for a term of two years, the chamber presupposing the creation of a federated Russian state. Laws would be adopted by majority vote; any member of parliament or a minister had the right of legislative initiative.

The monarch could not as the head of executive power change or repeal laws nor appropriate the functions of legislative power. But he was endowed with extensive powers in Murav'ev's scheme, including being the commander-in-chief of the armed forces and representing Russia in negotiations with foreign powers. The monarch could convoke both chambers of the parliament and change the time of sessions of the chambers, but not for more than two months. All power of the monarch would be supervised by the parliament, including even visits to other countries. His courtiers would enjoy no special rights or privileges and could not be elected or appointed to State offices. Women could not inherit the throne.

A Constitution would make provision for the competence of the chambers of the parliament and for local government on an elective basis. He proposed a rather complex judicial system which would have reinstated courts of equity originally introduced briefly under Catherine II. Amendments to the Constitution could only be introduced according to a special procedure and the election of a people's assembly whose principal responsibility was to draft and submit major laws and constitutional amendments. The monarch would be required to take an oath to comply with the Constitution.

Murav'ev did not accept Pestel's version of social transformation which postulated a temporary dictatorship, for he apprehended this might lead to the creation of conditions encouraging arbitrariness and illegality.

Slavophiles and Westernisers

In the 1830–40s there emerged two orientations in social and political thought which dominated the next decades of Russian politico-legal discourse. The central theme of the dialogue was the historical fates of Russia, the place and role of Russians amongst other peoples, and the distinctiveness of Russia's political and legal experience against the background of European and Oriental experience.

Law and legal institutions were a passing component of this dialogue, but of interest nonetheless. The Slavophiles urged the need to reassess certain elements of earlier Russian experience, of which those of legal interest included the peasant community, local self-government, and the correlation of law and custom. The communities and customs of early Russia had given way to mercenary judges, vain boyars, and power-worship amongst the clergy. The extent of power wielded by the State had led to the destruction of regional rights and the stifling of local self-rule, and under Peter the Great, to a Westernisation of Russia which was completely alien.

The Westernisers responded that Russia should not be juxtaposed to Europe. Russia and Europe shared Christianity in common and the differences between Russia and Europe lay in the special types of Christianity, in a special orientation towards Enlightenment, and in differences in private and personal life. A leading proponent of the Westernisers and one of the founders of the so-called 'State school' in interpreting Russian history was Konstantin Dmitrievich Kavelin (1818–85). This approach argued that the moving force in history was the struggle between the individual for freedom and the gradual changes of social forms from family to the State. Russia had traversed the same historical path as Europe in this regard, but more slowly and therefore, being behind, had to borrow the achievements of civilisation where appropriate. The reforms of Peter the Great placed Russia on the path of Europeanisation with respect to freedom and administration on the basis of modern acts and laws.

F. The Golden Age 1850–1900

The year 1850 as a benchmark of periodisation is purely arbitrary. The socio-legal reforms of 1861 linked with the emancipation of the serfs and the judicial reforms of 1864 gave new stimulus to legal theory, new varieties of political programmes, and new groupings amongst those writing on the subject, which may be classified roughly into the reformers, the radicals, the liberals, and the conservatives.

The Reformers

The practicalities of land reform engaged the attention of legal theorists from the 1850s. Various drafts circulated in the government, the minimal position being granting peasants the right to acquire in ownership their peasant house and immediately adjacent land plot. Under this scheme peasants would obtain only the right of use over other lands, with attendant duties by proceeding from local circumstances and customs. Later drafts recognised that greater rights over land needed to be given, responding to a considerable public reaction that peasants should acquire land and freedom without obligatory duties to the land-owner or to the State. The so-called 'Narodnik' movement pressed this view, drawing upon the earlier discussions of the role of the *obshchina* [община], or community, in Russian life and maintaining that as the community was liberated from the dual yoke of serfdom and bureaucratism, so would it take on its own natural life.

These views were shared to some extent by Aleksei Mikhailovich Unkovskii (1828–1893/94), a reformer from the ranks of the nobility who initiated the most radical draft regarding the peasant question. His draft, submitted to Tsar Alexander II as early as 1857 in the name of the nobility of Tver Province, recommended that peasants be accorded the right to acquire both their personal plot and field allotment immediately and compulsorily. Neither expectation was fully met by the reforms of 1861.

The Radicals

The 1860s also saw the emergence of new social movements advocating radical programmes and radical social actions. Some Russian historians have called this period the formation of revolutionary utopian socialism in Russia, a combining of Russian utopian peasant socialism and the mass revolutionary movement amongst the Russian intelligentsia. Leading representatives of this movement were Alexander Herzen (1812–70) and N G Cherynshevskii. Herzen placed great hopes in the revival of the Russian *obshchina*, a theme pursued in its legal aspects by Nikolai Gavrilovich Chernyshevskii (1828–89).

Chernyshevskii believed that the existence of a high level of civilisation as achieved in contemporary Europe did not preclude the concept of *obshchina* possession of property as the highest form of relations of man and land. This form of ownership in his view was much to be preferred to private ownership because it better secured the general prosperity by combining the owner, master, and worker into a single person. Contrasting intra-*obshchina* regulation with governmental regulation on the basis of legislation, he concluded that the former was preferable for the absence of the interference of any central and outside administration, which enhanced the freedom of the individual. Intra-*obshchina* regulation was inherently more reasonable than governmental as it was formed by generations on the basis of legal customs and agreement. Although private ownership in Western Europe had its virtues, in his eyes it led to excessive individualism and competition which in the end meant the strong triumphing over the weak and labour being the victim of capital. The way out was to create an alliance and brotherhood among people on the basis of the latter combining into a society sharing a common interest and using the forces of nature and science in common. In the domain of land ownership, this brotherhood was to be expressed in the transfer of land to *obshchina* use, whereas factories would become a company of all those working at the factory and also transferred as *obshchina* weal. When he became convinced that the existing State apparatus could not be reformed, he advocated peasant revolution and the formation of a society and State free from bureaucratism, local representative government and self-rule, an independent and just court, limitation of imperial power, and administration on the basis of laws.

Also amongst the radicals, Mikhail Aleksandrovich Bakunin (1814–76) is associated with the ideas of collectivist anarchism, a species of ultra-revolutionary socialism. He cautioned against the uncritical acceptance of the Russian *obshchina*, criticising the *obshchina* in Russian history for its humiliation of women, absolute denial of women's rights and honour, patriarchal absolutism and despotism, disrespect for the *mir*, and the lack of both legal rights and even elementary justness in decisions of the *mir*. Bakunin's treatment of the rights of the individual or duties of State officials was natural-law based; he rejected State laws and regulation as having been formed under the influence of negativist influences and inherently despotic. So-called political legislation was inevitably hostile to freedom and contrary to the natural laws of nature. The greatest guarantee of freedom in Bakunin's view was control over State power.

Another noted anarchist was Petr Alekseevich Kropotkin (1842–1921), who sought to combine the doctrine of anarchism with his studies of the science of nature and society. He linked the historical development of the State with the emergence of land ownership and the aspiration of one class to concentrate such ownership in its hands. The State, he said, in essence was a mutual insurance society composed of the land-owners, military, judges, and clerics each seeking to maintain their respective power over the people and to exploit the poor. The organisation of State power was accordingly closely linked with law and the system of justice. The court administered legalised revenge called justice.

The Liberals

The liberals favoured reforms of autocratic Russia and greater recognition of the worth of the individual. Respect for law was a central theme of liberal writings about legal subjects. Leading representatives of the liberal orientation included B N Chicherin and S A Muromtsev, N M Korkunov, and M M Kovalevskii.

Boris Nikolaevich Chicherin (1828–1904) wrote widely on the history of political and legal thought and the philosophy of law. In his view the State in history was an alliance of the people who were linked by law in a single legal whole and administered by supreme power for the benefit of all. The aim of the State was not the good of the individual, but rather to ensure the safety of the person and create a moral order, defining and defending civil rights and freedoms (but not natural rights). The domain of natural law, as contrasted with positive law, is truth and justness: the system of general legal norms arising from human reason and obligations which serves as a standard and guide for positive legislation. Justness is the standard by which the domain of the freedom of individual persons is demarcated and the requirements of laws are established. The aim of socio-political development is to avoid the extremes of individualistic anarchism and mechanical statism, to know how to combine individual freedom harmoniously with the general law.

Law does not reduce, he said, to benefit or to interest; it is inextricably linked with freedom as an individualistic and *a priori* metaphysical principle. From this standpoint law is the external freedom of the individual, determined by external lex. Lex determines, defines, freedom and its limits or boundaries and the relations arising from them. In part Chicherin was influenced by the Hegelian proposition that law is a development of the idea of freedom, but was critical of its statist and anti-individualistic implications. Chicherin schematised freedom as: external (law), internal (morality), and social. Freedom as subjective morality becomes objectified and is combined with law as a norm of freedom in social linkages—the family, civil society, Church, State.

The essence of liberalism in Chicherin's perception was the essence of the individual as a free being who became part of society while preserving that status. Even when the individual voluntarily limited his freedom in the interests of the freedom of others and accepted civil duties and the authority of the State, he retained his human dignity and inherent right to develop his powers of reason. Freedom of conscience, freedom of thought—these are the divine source of spiritual power which impart freedom to the individual.

Sergei Andreevich Muromtsev (1850–1910) contributed significantly in Russia to the study of law from a sociological perspective, directing attention to law as the existing legal order and justifying the creation of legal rules by judges. He hoped the last would further the evolution in Russia of a more liberal regime. 'There is no reason to fear arbitrariness on the part of judges', he wrote, for their high level of education and orderly progression in the ranks of the judiciary, and the very 'corporation of jurists' reflected in their methods of selection, openness of proceedings, and stability of tenure in office, their adherence to law, custom, and legal doctrine, their social conscience, justness, and morality were all grounds for allowing them to participate in the law-creation process.

Muromtsev's originality lay in his concept that law is not merely the aggregate of legal norms, but rather the aggregate of legal relations, the legal order. This perception contributed in Russian jurisprudence to a more profound understanding of law as not merely the will of the ruler (Tsar, parliament), but to the entire complex of legal relations in Russian society. A strong proponent of constitutional reforms, he was elected chairman of the I State Duma. When he died his students placed a wreath on his grave inscribed: 'To the first Russian citizen—from future citizens'.

Nikolai Mikhailovich Korkunov (1853–1904) developed the ideas of Muromtsev and of Jhering. Society, said Korkunov, is an objective social order representing conflicting personal and social interests in the political, economic, and religious domains. These conflicts are coped with by imposing certain limitations on each subject of legal relations. Law both demarcates the interests and acts as an instrument for ensuring order in the process of the emergence and settlement of conflicts of interests.

Korkunov was influential in his day for his sociological and philosophical approaches to the study of law, contrasted to the formalistic orientation of dogmatic jurisprudence which dominated in university circles. The translation into English of his general theory of law established Korkunov in Western circles as the best-known Russian jurist of his generation.

Maksim Maksimovich Kovalevskii (1851–1916) was a jurist of many parts: legal theorist, comparative lawyer, publicist, publisher, and member of the State Duma. He spent considerable time in England, where he came to know the work of Sir Henry Maine; he pursued and developed Maine's comparative legal studies, combining the study of law with an analysis of its interlinkages with State institutions. Kovalevskii also achieved, through his studies of customary law, considerable reputation as an ethnographer.

The Conservatives

As a group those legal theorists classified as 'conservatives' were noteworthy for their patriotic cultural-nationalism and a growing distrust of the relevance of European political and legal experience for Russia. This meant a distrust of representative rule, of the idea of equality, and of respect for the rights and freedom of man and citizen.

Nikolai Iakovlevich Danilevskii (1822–85), in a monumental work contrasting the cultural and political relations of Russia and Europe, developed a theory of the cultural-historical types of human civilisation. Not a jurist, his views and approach, sometimes described as a species of comparative Russian culturology, nonetheless influenced many Russian legal theorists. In particular, he believed that the only special guarantees of political and civil rights which were possible were those which the supreme power in a society wished to grant to its people. He ridiculed the notion of a social Russian parliament, although unlike many other neoslavophiles, he did value the freedom of speech as a natural right and not merely a privilege granted by the State.

Konstantin Nikolaevich Leont'ev (1831–91) was a strong proponent of the terror of power personified in the status of the Tsar as supreme ruler. Developing the ideas of Danilevskii, Leont'ev believed that the future of various cultures and historical types of society were capable of being predicted, provided that a sufficient time-frame was taken into consideration—at least a half-century or century. State organisms proceeded through cycles, which Leont'ev calculated occurred every 1,200 years.

Leont'ev rejected the egalitarianism of liberalism, which he equated to a species of anarchism. Russian statehood and law he believed were derived partly from Byzantium and partly from Europe. The cycles of statehood led states to commence as aristocracies, develop into monarchies, and then decline and die as egalitarian and liberal democracies.

Vladimir Sergeevich Solov'ev (1853–1900) does not fit neatly into any of the preceding categories but nonetheless made his own contribution to Russian legal thought. A patriot and very much a Russian philosopher, he cautioned nonetheless against the 'extra-European' and 'anti-European' views in Russian society of his day as an 'empty pretension'. Among those ideas of Western Europe of which he approved was the rule-of-law State, which he saw as a step forward towards a more perfected variant of community. He gave considerable attention to theocracy in his published writings, and in later years to social Christianity. In his understanding of law Solov'ev endeavoured to separate out the moral value of law and of legal institutes and principles. He defined law as the 'lowest limit or certain minimum of morality binding equally upon all'. Natural law for him was the formal idea of law rationally derived from the general principles of philosophy. For Solov'ev natural law and positive law were merely two aspects of the same thing. Natural law embodied the 'rational essence of law' and positive law personified the historical phenomenon of law whose realisation depended upon the state of moral consciousness in a particular society and on other historical conditions. Positive law constantly adds to natural law.

Natural law is an algebraic formula which comes down in essence to two factors: freedom and equality. Freedom is a necessary substratum, and equality the necessary formula thereof. The aim of a normal society and law is the common good, and not merely the collective good (the sum of individual purposes). This common good by its essence internally links everyone and everything through joint and several actions to achieve the common aim. Law endeavours to effectuate justness, but this aspiration is merely a general trend, the 'logos' and idea of law. Positive law embodies and realises, albeit not always fully, this common trend in specific forms.

Solov'ev's ideas about law influenced in some measure the legal views of Novgorodtsev, Trubetskoi, Bulgakov, and Berdyaev, amongst others.

As investigations into the history of legal theory from this period continue, there are other important figures whose contribution was real but remains relatively unknown. Among them is K P Pobedonostsev (1827–1907),[16] whose reputation as a jurist has long been coloured and overshadowed by his reputation as an *éminence grise* behind the Russian throne.

G. The Twilight Years 1900–17

Among the thinkers influential at the turn of the century was G V Plekhanov, sometimes styled the 'father of Russian Marxism'. Departing from the '*narodniki*', Plekhanov believed that Russia had to pass through a full phase of capitalist development, which meant not only the development of production forces but also the respective superstructure, including a constitution and parliamentary rule. The Great Mission of the working class of Russia was to complete the task commenced by Peter the Great: the Westernisation of Russia. In August 1903 he advocated the slogan 'The Good of the Revolution is the Highest Law', a phrase which on its face justified any means to the end, but also advocated the existence, adapting the English expression, of a 'Long Parliament' and its rapid demise when necessary. Constitutional revolutionary law played a purely auxiliary role; the dictatorial power of the State was for him the highest law and not bound by constitutional requirements and prescriptions.

---

[16] See V A Tomsinov, 'K. P. Pobedonostsev: State Official and Jurist', *Sudebnik*, V (2000), 781–810.

The mainstream of Russian legal philosophers was preoccupied in the early years of the twentieth century with constitutionalism. Sergei Aleksandrovich Kotliarevskii (1873–1940) wrote a major treatise on the rule-of-law State (1915) in which he observed:

> the idea of the rule-of-law State came into the practice of modern civilised States, in aggregate those expectations which turn a member of a State union into the leaders thereof. A rule-of-law State became one of the political tasks. The crisis of legal consciousness, the loss of faith in the majesty of law and institutions, has been noted many times . . . the conviction that the State must take on the face of a rule-of-law State remains unshakeable.

Kotliarevskii believed that the principal purpose of a rule-of-law State is to be a State of justness, which presupposes that lex must always be just. The first requirement or first principle of a rule-of-law State, wrote Aleksandr Semenovich Alekseev (1851–1916),[17] is the inadmissability of changing the legal order in a State without the participation of popular representation. And the second requirement is the supremacy of jus (and not of lex): 'It is not lex which gives force to jus, but jus which gives force to lex, and the legislator must not create, but must find jus, worked out in the consciousness of society'.

Gabriel Feliksovich Shershenevich (1863–1912), a noted legal philosopher and specialist in civil law, combined a professional legal dogmatism with philosophical positivism, arguing that the State is the source of law since it represents power. Power is linked with the will and knowledge to oblige others to form their behaviour so as to correspond to the will of the rulers. He supported the sociological concept of the State, which rests on the fact that it is difficult to build the concept of the State as power or as a legal relationship, but it is possible to imagine the State as a combination of power and will. State power in this sense is based on the autonomous will of some (those who rule) who subordinate others to their will (the ruled).

Bogdan Aleksandrovich Kistiakovskii (1868–1920) is credited with taking the initiative in posing the question of how a rule-of-law socialist State would be as part of the process of overcoming the imperfections of a bourgeois rule-of-law State. He criticised the Russian intelligentsia for neglecting law and for having an underdeveloped legal consciousness, especially those who linked their fate with revolutionary ideas and causes. He accused the Slavophiles of legal nihilism. The *narodniki*, he felt, exaggerated the so-called ethical preoccupation of the Russian people, and this inhibited the transition from custom to written legislation in the countryside. He was himself partial to a Kantian definition of law, which in terms contemporary to Kistiakovskii was defined as the 'aggregate of norms establishing and delimiting the freedom of persons'. From the sociological point of view, he

---

[17] See V A Tomsinov, 'A. S. Alekseev (1851–1916)', in *Sudebnik*, I (1996), 83–90.

accorded preference to treating law as the aggregate of norms creating a compromise among various demands.[18]

Evgenii Nikolaevich Trubetskoi (1863–1920) defined law as 'external freedom granted and limited by a norm'. He criticised definitions of law based on concepts such as 'power', 'State', and 'coercion' because they failed to appreciate that any state and any power must be conditioned themselves by 'law' [jus]; they overlooked the fact that varieties of law exist independently of whether they may be recognised or not by a particular state, examples being canon law, international law, and certain legal customs.

Trubetskoi sought to harmonise natural law and positive law; natural law was the moving principle in history. The very idea of natural law gave the individual the possibility to climb above his historical milieu and save him from being enslaved by that which existed.

Pavel Ivanovich Novgorodtsev (1866–1924) distinguished himself early as a legal historian and philosopher. He was a member of the Kadet political party and elected to the State Duma. After the Russian revolutions he emigrated to Prague, where he formed the Russian Law Faculty with the assistance of the Czech Government; recognised to be the leader of a school of reborn natural law, his pupils included I A Il'in, B P Vysheslavtsev, N N Alekseev, and A S Iashchenko.

Author of several noted works, most fundamental perhaps is his *Introduction to the Philosophy of Law* (1907–17) published over a decade in three parts. The first treated the need for a renaissance of natural law, and the second, what he called the 'crisis' in the use of ideals and values of the Enlightenment, including those of the rule-of-law State. In his last volume, on the 'social ideal', he analysed the ideals of socialism and anarchism. His own position was that there should be a break with the traditions of exclusive historicism and sociologism and a transition to a system of moral idealism: 'Natural law structures are an integral property of our spirit and evidence of its high calling. A society which has ceased to create ideal structures would be a dead society; each time these structures show a spirit is alive, that there is movement of moral feeling and consciousness'.

H. Russian Legal Theorists in Emigration

In the aftermath of the Russian Revolutions, Russian legal theorists unsympathetic to Bolshevism found themselves in Kharbin (Manchuria), Prague, Berlin, Paris, London, and various cities in Yugoslavia. A detailed study of early Soviet legal experience by a collective of Russian jurists published at Prague in 1925 con-

---

[18] See S Heuman, *Kistiakovsky: The Struggle for National and Constitutional Rights in the Last Years of Tsarism* (1998).

tained essays by Nikolai Nikolaevich Alekseev (1879–1964)[19] and Nikolai Sergeevich Timasheff (1886–1970). They observed that the constitution was not important in order to establish a dictatorship in Soviet Russia; a direct and multifarious political experiment was underway. The category of lex [закон] was irrelevant because in practice the distinction between lex and subordinate enactments, the existence of a hierarchy of legal norms, was inoperative. Alekseev observed that Soviet power rested on the fact that the seizure of power was effectuated by the oppressed, which he understood to mean that naked power had not created Soviet Russia, but a power equipped with the idea of a struggle for liberation. According to this logic the proletarian State possessed a right of limited coercion, which presupposes the elimination of any coercion—propositions which Alekseev based on his interpretation of natural law.

Other noted Russian legal theorists in emigration included Pitrim Aleksandrovich Sorokin (1889–1968), who commenced his academic career at Petrograd University and then at the University of Minnesota and Harvard University. He had been the personal secretary of M M Kovalevskii and in 1919 offered the first course of lectures on sociology. After the Russian Revolution he became the personal secretary of A F Kerenskii. In 1922 he was exiled from Soviet Russia and took up his posts in Western institutions. Petr Berngardovich Struve (1870–1944) evolved philosophically from legal Marxism to State liberalism in the spirit of Kavelin and Chicherin and found himself after the Russian Revolutions in Belgrade and Berlin.

P G Vinogradoff

Although contemporary Russian treatises on the history of legal thought consign Sir Paul (Pavel Gavrilovich) Vinogradoff (1854–1925) to the category of Russian emigrants,[20] his was not the usual emigration and had nothing to do with the coming of the Bolsheviks to power in 1917. A fellow student at Oxford in the 1880s with Henry Maine and Frederick Pollock, he resigned his Chair at Moscow University in 1901 and accepted in England election to the Corpus Chair at Oxford University in 1903. He was elected Corresponding Member in 1892 and full Academician of the Imperial Russian Academy of Sciences in 1914, FBA, and Academician elsewhere.

Vinogradoff came to historical and jurisprudential studies at a time when social history had become fashionable. He was the first Russian legal scholar to choose English history as a field of research, having also devoted considerable time to

---

[19] See Tomsinov, 'N. N. Alekseev (1879–1964)', *Sudebnik* I (1996) 91–100.

[20] See W E Butler and V A Tomsinov, 'P. G. Vinogradoff (1854–1925)', *Sudebnik* II (1997) 405–426; V G Grafskii, in V S Nersesiants (ed), История политических и правовых учений. XX в. [*History of Political and Legal Doctrines. XX Century*] (1995) 27–30; O Kaznina, Русские в Англии [*Russians in England*] (1997) 87–89.

mediaeval Lombardy, and later expanded into the history of jurisprudence, which he viewed as the history of doctrines and institutions.

Legal history, in his perception, dealt with flows of doctrine and institutional activity which across many centuries and State frontiers pass from one historical formation into another. The archetype examples of such cultural succession were the reception of Roman law in mediaeval and modern Europe, or the linkages between Roman codifications and their Oriental predecessors.

His perception of law as a social phenomenon and a part of social experience caused him to range widely amongst the humanities and social sciences in his research. He gave considerable attention to the law of ownership, maintaining that how society structures its law of ownership determines how that society establishes the status of the family, of women, of labour relationships, of crime and punishment, and of State structure and organisation.

Political theory he believed was a constituent part of jurisprudence, part of the 'literary development of State Law'. 'The various branches of State Law and the sundry norms of civil, criminal, and canon law stand together with State Law, covering it like a shield and dustwrapper'.[21] Although Vinogradoff enjoys a kinship with those legal theorists preoccupied with the 'law in action', his historical orientation, which he himself called a 'synthetic' approach, led him always to examine the origins and evolution of law, and in this he also departed from the positivism of Jeremy Bentham and John Austin. The weakness of the analytical school, he counselled, was that it contained the danger of being preoccupied with abstract concepts and terms and losing sight of social realities. The 'world of concepts' becomes an end in itself.

His late works were strongly interdisciplinary, exploring how the other branches of the social sciences and humanities might profitably use legal phenomena in their disciplines. His studies were always comparative in spirit if not in substance, and he remains one of the greatest Russian progenitors of comparative law. In the early 1920s his attention turned to the history and typologies of legal systems and law, a line of enquiry interrupted by his death. In Russia his collected papers are in the process of publication, but in the minds of most Russians he was an historian, and not a jurist.

I. The Soviet Marxian Legacy

Marx and Engels had comparatively little to say about law in their writings, and what they did say appertained principally to their larger critique of the society

---

[21] See P G Vinogradoff, История правоведения (Курс для историков и юристов) [*History of Jurisprudence (Course for Historians and Jurists)*] (1908) 10.

contemporary to them and their explanation of societal change. Law in effect was explained away. Future society, it was supposed, would administer itself without need of legal rules. Those who came to power in October 1917, who confronted, as Marx and Engels had not, the need to govern nations, peoples, an economy, an army, found no specific blueprint in the writings of Marx and Engels. There commenced the process of developing and adapting theories of revolutionary change to cope with a real revolution, a process which continues to this day, by devising substages through which a society was to pass in the course of the transition to socialism and communism. Those levels of societal development were closely linked to and dependent upon law and legal institutions. Intense and important debates about the role or purpose of law figured in Soviet policy dialogues on those issues; at various periods of the Soviet era legal theory, or more properly, the theory of State and law, contributed to those discussions within the Communist Party and without and, of course, duly reflected the ultimate decisions taken. Law was, inter alia, policy as well as politics, whether one spoke of law writ large (jus) or as a single legislative act (lex); it was the product of political processes, it recorded a policy judgment or decision, and it transmitted that decision to whosoever it was addressed in the form of a normative rule.

In his *Critique of the Gotha Programme* Karl Marx spoke of a transition period between capitalist and communist society when the former would transmute into the latter. Politically the State during this period could be nothing, Marx said, other than the 'revolutionary dictatorship of the proletariat'. Lenin developed the notion in his *State and Revolution* (1917), suggesting that a proletarian State would be essential in order to crush the bourgeoisie but would commence the withering away process at once. Much of Soviet Marxian legal theory thereafter was devoted to the relationship between those contradictory processes and the relative weight to be accorded to each.

Once power passed into their hands, the Soviet leadership fashioned a highly centralised form of government within a federated structure. Initial expectations that an untrained, often illiterate, proletariat and peasantry could simply step into a dismantled State apparatus proved illusory. Normative acts represented 'proletarian commands'; they were to be obeyed because they represented the will of the new ruling class. Philosophically, however, the Soviet leadership saw no long-term virtue in those legal rules and institutions governing the personal interests of citizens. Those were expected to disappear during the transition period. The classics of Marxism were explicit with respect to State and law of the old order: it was to be smashed; the power base of the old order was to be dismantled with all the legal institutions which supported it.

The dismantling and restructuring processes simultaneously at work during this early transition period were variously interpreted against the background of the NEP. Some viewed the legal history of 1917–21 as an era primarily of dismantling the old Imperial order and experimenting ad hoc with the minimum legal measures required for transition.[22] To them NEP represented an unfortunate but essential tactical reversal of this process, a restoration of capitalist elements whose doom otherwise was sealed by early proletarian legislation. Others viewed the NEP as a logical continuation and development of the revolutionary measures. The NEP codifications, according to this view, were a consolidation and systematisation of revolutionary achievements and by no means a retreat or compromise; the NEP was a necessary next step in the class struggle to achieve socialism.

In one sense it is perfectly true to say that in the Soviet period the history of legal thought was a battleground in which various forms of Marxism-Leninism fought against what was perceived to be State and law in their non-communist sense, against a bourgeois world-view. Massive resources were dedicated to replacing systematically a history and ideology of law [jus] with one based on a proletarian, Bolshevist, Marxist-Leninist, communist ideology and a reinterpretation of the historical past into one which was congenial to the nature of Soviet institutions and a postulated withering away of State and law.

In the early years after the Russian Revolutions numerous discussions and dialogues addressed the fate of law under the new socio-political circumstances and alternative theories emerged. Law as an instrument of the dictatorship of the proletariat figured centrally in the writings of Dmitrii Ivanovich Kurskii (1874–1932), an early People's Commissar of Justice. Law under the dictatorship of the proletariat, he said, was an expression of the interests of the proletariat, and there was accordingly no place for recognition and defence of the rights and freedoms of the individual. He extolled the revolutionary people's courts as a new source of law-creation; their principal function being 'criminal repression', he asserted the courts should be absolutely free and should be guided above all by their legal consciousness.

The new 'proletarian communist law' was based on the Soviets, a free family, and the ownership by the proletarian State of all the instruments of production. With the transition to the NEP Kurskii asserted that Soviet law had become a species of 'rule-of-law' State, although the interests of the State always were postulated to prevail over competing personal rights of individual citizens.

Petr Ivanovich Stuchka (1865–1932) viewed law as a procedure for social relations. The basic principles for a new revolutionary-Marxist law Stuchka reduced to three: the class character of any law; the revolutionary-dialectical method (in substitution of formal legal logic); and material social relations as the basis for explaining and understanding the legal superstructure (instead of explaining legal relations by proceeding from a law and legal ideas).

---

[22] See J N Hazard, 'Soviet Law: The Bridge Years, 1917–1920', in W E Butler (ed), *Russian Law: Historical and Political Perspectives* (1977) 235–257.

In his role as a senior legal official Stuchka was positioned to pursue his ideas in the drafting of legislation. Writing about the preparation of the 1919 Guiding Principles of Criminal Law of the RSFSR, he said: 'When before us, in the collegium of the People's Commissariat of Justice, was the necessity to formulate our own, so to speak, "Soviet understanding of law", we rested on the following formula: "Law—is a system (or procedure) of social relations corresponding to the interests of the ruling class and protected by the organised power thereof" '.

Much of what was written attempted to draw upon certain strands of European legal philosophy and criticism of them in the light of Soviet experience of Marxian tenets. In the absence of a cohesive Marxist theory of law for the dictatorship of the proletariat, it was easier to react against the ideas of others. Jellinek, Petrazhitskii, Duguit, Renner, and Kelsen were among those who had Marxist followers, albeit in a revisionist spirit, and whose pre- and post-revolutionary writings were subject to avid scrutiny in Soviet legal media. For all of the searching for a Marxist theory of State and law in the 1920s, however, no one seriously challenged the notion that law was expected to die away rapidly.[23] In the interim, law was an instrument for revolutionary social change. Legalism was decried as a 'bourgeois fetish'.

The Soviet jurist who developed original notions of the role of law in a society building socialism and of the rapid withering away of law and who came to lead intellectually the legal policies associated with the transition from NEP to national economic planning and collectivisation was Evgenii Bronislavovich Pashukanis (1891–1937). His ideas acquired considerable reputation in the West at the time through a German translation of his *General Theory* and enjoyed fresh consideration in the late 1970s. He rejected the concept of 'proletarian law' because in his perception bourgeois law, the historically most developed type of law, was not to be followed by another, post-bourgeois law. He accordingly developed an 'anti-law' position and offered instead the 'commodity exchange theory' of law. Those who purchase and sell goods in the market-place rely on contract or other forms of transactions to define and enforce reciprocally their mutual economic relations. The participants identify themselves as juridical persons bearing particular rights and duties. The law of contract, to Pashukanis, is founded upon the intentional voluntary reciprocal conduct or consent of the parties giving effect, in this instance, to their economic relations, but the same consensual base underlies other branches of law: labour relations, between management and employee; family law, in the form of marriage and parent-child relationships; or even constitutional law, based on a social contract reflecting an alleged consensus

---

[23] See on this period A A Plotnieks, Становление и развитие марксистско-ленинской общей теории права в СССР [*Origin and Development of Marxist-Leninist General Theory of Law in the USSR*] (1978).

to govern. All law consequently had an economic basis, in this case founded on commodity exchange.

Pashukanis believed he had accurately diagnosed the legal process in society, not law as an abstract ideal but as a genuine operational element in human relations. Although law was to be found in every level of societal development after primitive communalism, its inherent individualism and contractual or consensual base led naturally to its apogee of development under capitalism. The dictatorship of the proletariat would avail itself of bourgeois law only insofar as the transition to a socialist economy required. With the introduction of national economic planning (hereinafter 'Plan') and elimination of a commodity-exchange economy, the legal superstructure of bourgeois law would die away.

His Soviet critics accused Pashukanis of applying abstract characterisations of law which existed before and outside of socialism; these were not applicable to proletarian law. In the course of time Pashukanis was obliged to accept that a new post-revolutionary and post-bourgeois 'Soviet law' did in fact exist, albeit with a very special and specific nature.

The psychological conception of class law is associated with Mikhail Andreevich Reisner (1868–1928), who even before the Russian Revolutions began to pursue these lines of enquiry under the influence of L Knapp and L Petrazhitskii. The idea of law as a form of social consciousness was developed by I P Razumovskii. He offered a general definition of law: 'The procedure of social relations, ultimately relations between classes, insofar as it is reflected in the social consciousness, is historically inevitably abstracted, differentiated for this consciousness from its material conditions and, objectified for it, receives further complex ideological development in systems of "norms"'. The withering away of bourgeois law Razumovskii described as the 'death of law as an ideology'.

From the late 1920s to the early 1930s there occurred what in Soviet legal history is known as the 'struggle on the legal front'. Soviet jurists of all orientations, influenced by the transition to a Planned Economy, collectivisation of agriculture, and campaigns against various forms of ideological 'deviations', adjusted their jurisprudential positions. This led to an increased politicisation of legal science and greater direct influence of the Communist Party on the substance of legal doctrine. An address by Lazar Kaganovich on 4 November 1929 to the Institute of Soviet Construction and Law of the Communist Academy was the signal for unleashing a campaign of Bolshevist criticism and self-criticism. Kaganovich accused communist legal theorists of being imprisoned by the 'old bourgeois legal methodology', which led to such doctrines as State agencies being subordinate to the commands of the law: 'We have our laws. Our laws determined the functions and ambit of activity of individual agencies of State power. But our laws are determined by revolutionary expediency at each particular moment'.

The struggle on the legal front contributed to a polarisation of the two principal positions in Soviet jurisprudence of the day: those of Pashukanis and Stuchka. Pashukanis subjected himself to self-criticism and began to recant from his views in favour of considering law and policy (or politics) to be identical, interpreting law as one of the forms of policy or as a component of policy (or politics). Stuchka in turn acknowledged an excessive reliance on the bourgeois sociological school of law in his early writings. In 1931 the I All-Union Congress of Marxist specialists in the State and legal sciences attempted to form a single correct position and line. The Congress was dominated by adherents of Pashukanis, but in the end adopted an eclectic resolution which tried to save face for the various approaches.

In the early stages Pashukanis and his followers secured the upper hand and enjoyed an opportunity rarely open to legal theorists: to practise what they preached. The introduction of national economic planning in 1928 brought a revolutionary offensive against law. The day of withering away was believed to have arrived, and the goals were not modest. Large-scale industrialisation required the planned concentration and allocation of resources and investment. Part of the rural labour force had to be released for the factories, and this could be accomplished it was believed only by mechanising agriculture on a large scale and eliminating the potential economic stranglehold of the middle and wealthy peasants over the nation's food supply. Moreover, the State intended to finance industrialisation partly through the export of grain and raw materials, which also required that the State have full control over agricultural production. Survivals of capitalism were to be abolished. By the end of the Second Five-Year Plan antagonistic classes were to have disappeared.

The pace of change gave rise to vigorous debate about economic policy and the human capacity to effectuate short-term vast social change. Those who believed man was not fully capable of shaping his own destiny carried the day. A dynamic approach was preferred to the stability-mindedness of those who counselled caution. In the realm of law, Plan was expected to supplant the remnants of bourgeois law. The transition to socialism had accelerated; an adaptive socio-economic policy needed a flexible set of institutions and policies that would give effect to Plan not in terms of rights and duties but in terms of elastic revolutionary legality. As a means of social control, law would be superseded by Plan in economic relations. Codification and systematisation of legislation, at an advanced stage in 1929–30, were suspended for fear the forms of law would constrain socio-legal change. In the realm of interpersonal relations, civil law was relegated to a minor place in legal studies. Draft penal codes prepared by followers of Pashukanis consisted of broad principles and no Special Part, for Pashukanis had regarded pre-existing criminal law and its fixed penalties for offences as a kind of contractual relationship between society and the individual.

75

By 1936 it was apparent that the pace of imposed change could not be sustained. On the other hand, it was felt that the necessary threshold had been crossed. The adoption of a new Constitution for the USSR in 1936 to mark the transition of the Soviet Union to a society building socialism required a new concept of law. Pashukanis in 1936 advanced the concept of 'socialist law', abandoning his former characterisation of all law as 'bourgeois': 'The Great Socialist October Revolution dealt a blow to capitalist private ownership and laid the principle of a new socialist system of law. Therein is that which is fundamental and principal for an understanding of Soviet law, its socialist essence as the law of a proletarian State'.

The 1936 USSR Constitution declared the Soviet Union to be a socialist society. Antagonistic classes had been eliminated. Those who counselled restoration of stability of laws came to the forefront, and those responsible for earlier policies of rapid change were purged and in many cases, including Pashukanis, executed. The State under socialism would not wither away rapidly. Socialism existed only in one country (the USSR) and was being built in another (Mongolia), neighbours surrounded by hostile capitalist powers, and for self-defence the State would be maintained and strengthened. For the State ultimately to disappear, Stalin said, it must pass through the dialectically contradictory stage of becoming stronger.

The ideological underpinnings of these postulates culminated in 1938 with the Conference devoted to the science of Soviet law and State convoked by A Ia Vyshinskii (1883–1954). From 16–19 July 1938, 600 legal workers, teachers, and practitioners assembled in Moscow to attend the I Conference on Questions of the Science of the Soviet State and Law. The aim of the Conference was to lay down a single true Marxist-Leninist, Stalinist-Bolshevist general line in legal science and on the basis thereof to reorientate all approaches and conceptions posited by Soviet jurists of the earlier periods, most of which were rejected as 'hostile' or 'anti-Soviet'. In his initial theses submitted to the Conference and in his oral address Vyshinskii defined law [jus] as:

> the aggregate of rules of conduct established by State power as the power of the ruling class in society, and also customs and rules of community life sanctioned by State power, effectuated in a compulsory procedure with the assistance of the State apparatus for the purpose of protecting, consolidating, and developing social relations and procedure advantageous and suitable for the ruling class.

This definition was altered as follows in the final written text of Vyshinskii's address and in the theses approved by the Conference. Law [jus] is:

> the aggregate of rules of conduct expressing the will of the ruling class established in a legislative procedure, and also the customs and rules of community life sanctioned by State power, the application of which is ensured by the coercive power of the State for the purposes of the protection, consolidation, and development of social relations and procedures advantageous and suitable for the ruling class.

Together with this general definition of law the Conference also approved a definition of Soviet law:

> Soviet law is the aggregate of rules of conduct established in a legislative procedure by the power of the working people expressing their will and the application of which is ensured by the entire coercive power of the socialist State for the purpose of the defence, consolidation, and development of relations and procedures advantageous and suitable for the working people, the full and final destruction of capitalism and its survivals in the economy, domestic life, and consciousness of people, and the building of a communist society.

This definition dominated Soviet legal thought throughout the remainder of the Stalin era and beyond. The principal doctrinal writings on law repeated it verbatim. The thaw of the mid–1950s was accompanied in legal circles by some embryonic criticism of the Vyshinskii position, and its monopoly as the official line was sundered forever. Now styled a 'narrow-normative' approach by its critics, it began to be supplanted by doctrines of law as a unity of legal norm and legal relations (S F Kechek'ian, A A Piontkovskii) or as a unity of legal norms, legal relations, and legal consciousness (Ia F Mikolenko). The substance of these positions acknowledged the normativity of law as laid down in 1938 but attenuated such normativity by recognising the importance of law-in-action.

Vyshinskii's 'socialist legality' evolved into a standard by which excesses of the Stalinist era came to be condemned and legal reforms to be effectuated in the post-Stalin era. The initial law reforms of the post-Stalin period amounted to an attenuation of the harsher political terror and the introduction of greater substantive and procedural guarantees. Following the XX Congress of the CPSU, most of the jurists criticised during the Stalinist era were rehabilitated. The relaxation in the post-Stalin era likewise brought an extensive preoccupation with Western political and legal philosophy of all periods and orientations, both critiques and translations. The turning point in Soviet legal thought, however, dates from the XXI and XXII Congresses of the CPSU in 1959 and 1961 respectively. At the XXI Congress, Soviet society was said to have entered a higher phase of socialist development, the period of the 'expanded construction of communism'. A new Programme of the CPSU adopted at the XXII Congress called for completion of the first phase of communist construction by 1980, a timetable that was quietly shelved when the economic prerequisites proved too ambitious.

For a brief period the transition to this new level of socialist development refuelled the debate about the imminent withering away of the State. The 1961 Party Programme declared the Soviet Union to be a 'State of the whole people' or an 'all-people's State'. The dictatorship of the proletariat had ceased to be necessary. The all-people's State would rely less on coercion and more on persuasion and would commence the process of divesting its functions to non-State bodies such as social organisations. The comrades' courts and people's guards were introduced as social agencies to assume law enforcement functions. Criminal law reforms placed greater emphasis upon social measures to reform first offenders who committed minor crimes. A constitutional revision commission appointed in 1962 was to prepare a new constitution reflective of the new level of societal development. It may have been intended to reduce the numbers of lawyers; reports persist of an unpublished Party resolution c. 1963–4 calling for a reduction in the numbers of law students. Soviet jurists gave serious thought for the first time to mechanisms for social control in the first phase of communism as the State withered away. Customary law took on special interest in this connection and no longer was deemed to be inherently retrograde. Vyshinskii's definition of law was deemed unsuitable for the new stage of societal development.

The change of leadership in 1964 brought a new style and slight reorientation to the debate. The new codifications of civil and criminal law had been completed. Attention concentrated on economic reforms and upon making the middle and lower levels of State power and administration more democratic, participatory, and responsive. The all-people's State emphasised less the immediate divestiture of its functions and more the greater involvement of citizens in its affairs. The comrades' courts and people's guards were retained as proven quasi-legal institutions but modified to introduce better procedural safeguards. Legislation on local government was reworked thoroughly for the first time since the 1930s. For reasons not wholly clear, the new Constitution was delayed until 1977. Its enactment signalled the full-fledged legislative acceptance of the all-people's State.

Soviet legal theory during this period was preoccupied with the 'nuts and bolts' of legal development. As legislation became more detailed and comprehensive, the theorists were engaged with the minutiae of legal institutions and rules. Larger questions, to be sure, were of concern. Soviet jurists confronted the issue of distinguishing 'good' laws from 'bad'. State command, it was widely recognised, was not always sufficient to establish the 'legality' or the 'justness' of legislation. Various efforts to measure legislation against the larger goals of a socialist society building communism, or against communist morality, or against laws of societal development or analogous basic standards brought Soviet jurisprudence close to some sort of natural law position in the minds of many Western legal philosophers.

Soviet jurists began publicly to question the identification of *pravo* [jus] and *zakon* [lex] which underlay Vyshinskii's theses. To distinguish between the two reflected in some measure a return to the thinking of Russian jurists of the past and involvement in the ratification of the 1966 covenants on human rights. The dialogue is one which has not been followed in detail by Western scholarship, but will repay study in due course, for in that dialogue lie in part the roots of *perestroika* and the eventual dissolution of the Soviet Union. The search for freedom, equality, and rule-of-law [jus] in the post-Soviet era has its roots in the jurisprudential legacy of Russia.

Perestroika itself in the late Soviet era and the developments in Russian law following the dissolution of the Soviet Union were neither foreseen nor shaped by legal theory. Nor has a theory emerged to assist the legislator in pursuing democratic reforms. The Russian legal system remains a theory-minded system in search of a theory.

J. Post-Soviet Legal Theory

The search for a theory has seen three basic orientations emerge in Russian legal doctrine: the liberal-democratic, the modernised Marxist-Leninist, and the so-called traditional. Others agree on the number of basic orientations but categorise them otherwise: normativist-statist, sociological jurisprudence, and libertarian-legal.[24] Of these, the liberal-democratic or libertarian-liberal seems most likely to have something to offer post-Soviet Russia, taking its point of departure from the 1993 Russian Constitution and the legal structures based on it;[25] the principal defect of this orientation in the view of some of its warmest proponents is its excessive preoccupation with bourgeois values and aspirations.[26] The more appropriate foundations for the liberal-democratic approach are, it is argued, a 'civilitarian system' and a 'civilitarian law'. In place of the bourgeois emphasis upon formal legal equality, civilitarian law (accenting the word 'citizen', *civis* in Latin) stresses equal civil ownership, that is, an identical participatory share for everyone in all of the desocialised socialist ownership:

> This conceptual perspective of the movement from nonlegal socialism to civilitarianism and to a civilitarian law has important theoretical-criterial significance and enables one to adequately evaluate the history of the Soviet theory of law and Marxist doctrine on law as a whole in their correlation with the realities of nonlegal socialism and to determine the coordinates of post-socialist paths to law in the general bed of world-historical progress of freedom, equality, and law.[27]

The 1993 Constitution is based in this view on a legal (anti-legist, anti-statist) type of comprehension of law, which in turn determines the legal orientation and aims of Russian jurisprudence. The Constitution serves a society in transition from totalitarianism, anti-law socialism, to a post-socialist legal structure, the commencement of the formation of a civil society, a rule-of-law State, and a law [lex] which must accord with law in the highest sense [jus]. The core of the 1993

---

[24] A V Poliakov, Общая теория права [*General Theory of Law*] (2001) 124.

[25] Works reflecting this approach include: V A Chetvernin, Понятие права и государства [*Concept of Law and State*] (1997); V N Khropaniuk, Теория государства и права [*Theory of State and Law*] (1995); V V Lazarev (ed), Общая теория права и государства [*General Theory of Law and State*] (1996); G N Manov (ed), Теория государства и права [*Theory of State and Law*] (1996).

[26] See V S Nersesiants, Юриспруденция [Jurisprudence] (1998) 156.

[27] Nersesiants (n 14 above) 156.

Constitution is recognition, concretisation, and defence of the rights and freedoms of man and citizen, which is vital for a country with a totalitarian-socialist past whose jurisprudence reflected class-communist positions. The Constitution combines a 'legal-axiomatic' approach (the rights and freedoms of man are the highest value) with a natural law view (the rights and freedoms of man are innate and not conferred by the State). The task of the civilitarian school is to measure the Constitution, its virtues and shortcomings, against the realities of Russian life and seek to identify and repair those domains where the Constitution falls short.[28]

The modernised Marxist-Leninist school seeks to adapt the precepts of the past to the society of the future, whereas the traditionalist approach is anti-Western, endeavouring to find the future of Russian jurisprudence in prerevolutionary Russian legal theory with a Slavophile disposition.

As during the last five decades of Imperial Russian rule and even to a surprising extent during the Soviet era, Russian jurisprudence today gives evidence of a considerable range of innovative and imaginative legal theory, mostly indebted to the distinctively Russian condition and circumstances.

---

[28] On the role of 'civilism' during the Putin era, see Nersesiants, *The Civilism Manifesto: The National Idea of Russia in the Historical Quest for Equality, Freedom, and Justness* (transl. W E Butler, 2000).

II

THE LEGAL SYSTEM

4

SOURCES OF LAW

During the Soviet era, Marxist-Leninist legal doctrine conventionally distinguished between two meanings of 'sources of law'. In their most 'fundamental' sense the 'sources of law' were said to be the socio-economic order of a particular society; it was that order which gave birth to and shaped the distinctive political, economic, and legal superstructure of the society. A socialist society, in this larger sense, formed and shaped the substance of its socialist law and legal system.

In their technical meaning, which is the aspect treated in this chapter, the 'sources of law' are the rules or norms created, sanctioned, or recognised by the State or its agencies in a duly established manner. Not all acts fall within this definition; only those prescribing general rules of conduct, or *normative* legal acts,[1] as they are

---

[1] The legislator has never actually defined 'normative legal act', although definitions appear in doctrinal writings and documents of agencies of State power. On 25 May 2000 the Plenum of the Supreme Court of the Russian Federation by Decree No 19 explained that a normative legal act is an 'act issued in the established procedure by a duly empowered agency of State power, agency of local self-government, or official establishing legal norms (or rules of behaviour) binding upon an indefinite group of persons intended for repeated application and operating irrespective of whether specific legal relations provided for by the act have arisen or terminated'.

often called. Non-normative acts appertain to individual specific matters and are issued on the basis of legal norms. The distinction between normative and non-normative is more easily drawn in theory than in practice, and is one drawn in many different ways.

It also follows from this definition that not all sources of law originate in the State itself. The discussion of jus [право] in Chapter 3 turns entirely upon the proposition that jus is something above the State. 'Customs of business turnover' are also recognised as a subsidiary source of law emanating from non-State bodies, and many local normative acts are adopted by or within non-State entities.

Unlike the common law, which ascribes no special priority to the sources of law, the Russian legal system attaches significance to a formalistic hierarchy of the sources of law. The 1993 Russian Constitution has introduced an entirely new dimension to that hierarchy, whose implications continue to unfold.

A. Jus [право]

Russian law has incorporated from its earliest recorded days the concept of 'jus', of law which originates somewhere other than with the ruler of the day or the State. Whether its origins be the Will of God, or the natural order of the universe, or the laws of societal development, or the fabric of Russian (or Slavic) socio-cultural values, or otherwise continues to be the subject of lively debate. In the post-Soviet era that debate is likely to be of crucial significance for the future of the rule-of-law in Russia. In some measure the Russian legal system has taken refuge in those elements of '*pravo*' incorporated in general principles of international law or in international treaties of the Russian Federation, most notably in human rights treaties. For the rest, proponents of jus [право] equate it with natural law, or a community-based unwritten law which takes precedence over all others. The Constitutional Court of the Russian Federation has yet to consider a case which juxtaposes a provision of the Constitution to some higher law, and much may depend, if such a case be instituted, upon the willingness of that Court to give formal recognition to the existence of Russian law in its most fundamental meaning. The modern Russian general theory of law recognises that 'law [jus] does not reduce itself to the aggregate of laws [lex]. It is considered that law [jus] stands by virtue of its own laws [lex]'.[2]

---

[2] See A A Rubanov, 'Понятие источника права как проявление метафоричности юридического сознания', ['Concept of Source of Law as a Manifestation of a Metaphor of Legal Consciousness'], in Судебная практика как источник права [*Judicial Practice as a Source of Law*] (1997) 47.

B. Soviet Law

Legislation of the former Soviet Union continues to play a significant part, albeit declining, in Russian legal affairs. Its history in the development and application of Russian law is brief but complex. When the RSFSR declared its State sovereignty on 12 June 1990, the First Congress of People's Deputies of the RSFSR established 'the supremacy of the RSFSR Constitution and laws of the RSFSR throughout the territory of the RSFSR; the operation of acts of the USSR which are contrary to the sovereign rights of the RSFSR shall be suspended by the Republic on its territory'.[3] The date of the Declaration, 12 June 1990, thereafter became a benchmark when assessing the applicability of USSR legislation, and indeed is now celebrated as Independence Day in Russia.

On 24 October 1990 the RSFSR adopted the Law on the Operation of Acts of Agencies of the USSR on the Territory of the RSFSR. This Law recognised the operation of laws and other acts of the highest agencies of State power of the USSR, edicts and other acts of the President of the USSR, acts of the Council of Ministers, and of ministries and departments of the USSR only insofar as they were adopted within the powers transferred by the Russian Federation to the USSR in accordance with the Declaration on State Sovereignty of 12 June 1990 and certain other enactments. If USSR enactments met this test, they were of direct application on the territory of the RSFSR; if they violated the sovereignty of the Russian Federation, they were subject to suspension by the RSFSR Supreme Soviet or the RSFSR Council of Ministers. If USSR enactments did not satisfy the criteria set out above, they entered into force in the Russian Federation only after their ratification by the RSFSR Supreme Soviet, RSFSR Council of Ministers, or empowered State agencies of the RSFSR respectively. Acts of agencies of the USSR issued before 24 October 1990 operated on the territory of the RSFSR insofar as they had not been suspended by the RSFSR Supreme Soviet or the RSFSR Council of Ministers.[4]

On 31 October 1990 the RSFSR required that any acts of agencies of State power and administration of the USSR connected with the seizure of material, financial, currency, monetary valuables, and other property belonging to citizens, labour collectives, social organisations, and other owners were not subject to execution on the territory of the RSFSR unless so provided by legislation of the RSFSR, pursuant to the Law on Ensuring the Economic Foundations of the Sovereignty of the RSFSR.[5] Enterprises and organisations situated on the territory of the RSFSR

---

[3] Ведомости СНД и ВС РСФСР (1990), no 2, item 22; translated in W E Butler, *Basic Legal Documents of the Russian Federation* (1992) 35–37.

[4] Ведомости СНД и ВС РФ (1990), no 21, item 237; translated in Butler (n 3 above) 49–50.

[5] Ведомости РСФСР (1990), no 22, item 260; translated in Butler (n 3 above) 45–47.

or effectuating activity on that territory, even if of Union subordination, were required to be guided by RSFSR legislation and apply USSR enactments in accordance with the Law of 24 October 1990.[6]

On 12 December 1991 the RSFSR ratified the Agreement on the Creation of the Commonwealth of Independent States, providing in point 2 of the Decree on ratification:

> For the purposes of creating conditions necessary for the realisation of Article 11 of the said Agreement, to establish that the norms of the former USSR shall apply on the territory of the RSFSR until the adoption of respective legislative acts of the RSFSR in that part which is not contrary to the Constitution of the RSFSR, legislation of the RSFSR, and the present Agreement.[7]

The Agreement itself contained a most cryptic formulation of Article 11: 'From the moment of signature of the present Agreement, the application of the norms of third States on the territories of the States which have signed it, including the former USSR, shall not be permitted'.[8] On one reading, at least, Article 11 of the Agreement would appear to take away that which earlier Russian legislation had permitted, and if that interpretation were correct, being embodied in an international treaty Article 11 would override inconsistent Russian legislation. In practice the formulation of the Decree on ratification of 12 December 1991 has been applied.

Taking all of the foregoing enactments together, the accepted position is that USSR legislation may apply on the territory of the Russian Federation unless it has been expressly repealed or suspended, unless it is contrary to the Constitution of the Russian Federation and other Russian legislation adopted after 12 June 1990, or unless it has become obsolete. In some instances special provision has been made for the continued operation of USSR legislation even though Russian enactments have been adopted. The 1991 FPCivL, for example, were enacted by the former Soviet Union to enter into force on 1 January 1992. Since the USSR had been dissolved before the date of their entry into force, they did not become legally binding, but were specially introduced into force as from 3 August 1992 by the Russian Federation[9] insofar as they were not contrary to the Constitution of

---

[6] See the Edict on Ensuring the Economic Foundations of the Sovereignty of the RSFSR, 20 August 1991; translated in Butler (n 3 above) 41–43.

[7] BBC РФ (1991), no 51, item 1798; translated in Butler (n 3 above) 51.

[8] Signed at Minsk, 8 December 1991; transl. in Butler (n 3 above) 3–6.

[9] See the Decree of the Supreme Soviet of the Russian Federation on the Regulation of Civil Law Relations in the Period of Conducting Economic Reform, adopted 14 July 1992, as amended. BBC РФ (1992), no 30, item 1800; (1993), no 11, item 393; (1996), no 5, item 411; and the Decree on Certain Questions of the Application of Legislation of the USSR on the Territory of the Russian Federation, adopted 3 March 1993. BBC РФ (1993), no 11, item 393. The last Decree has been amended numerous times to reflect the enactment of various Russian codes and remains in force as amended 26 November 2001. СЗ РФ (2001), no 49, item 4553.

the Russian Federation and legislative acts of the Russian Federation adopted after 12 June 1990. The 1964 RSFSR Civil Code continues in force insofar as not superseded by the 1994–2001 Civil Code, the 1991 FPCivL, and other legislative acts of the Russian Federation adopted after 12 June 1990. This would result, for example, in decrees of the Government of the USSR remaining in force on questions which according to the Civil Code of the Russian Federation may be regulated by federal laws that, to date, have not been enacted.

The Family Code of the Russian Federation recognises legal relations established under pre-revolutionary and Soviet legislation, as well as according to international treaties of the Russian Empire, irrespective of whether those treaties remain in force or not.

C. Legislation

Constitution of Russian Federation

The Russian Federation is founded on the principle of popular sovereignty. Article 3 of the 1993 Constitution of the Russian Federation proclaims that the sole source of power is the multinational people of Russia. They exercise their power directly, by way of referendum, and through agencies of State power and agencies of local self-government. State power, in turn, is effectuated on the basis of separation into legislative, executive, and judicial powers (Article 10, Constitution). These principles are the very antithesis of the late Soviet constitutional system, which emphatically rejected the separation of powers and its delegation of power to non-representative organs. 'All power to the Soviets' had been among the hallmarks of the 1917 October Revolution.

The Constitution of Russia, adopted by an all-people's referendum on 12 December 1993, is by reason of the method of its enactment and of its substance the highest source of man-made law in the Russian Federation. It has 'the highest legal force, direct effect' and is applicable throughout the entire territory of Russia (Article 15, Constitution). All laws and other legal acts must not be contrary to the Constitution, and all agencies of State power, local self-government, officials, citizens, and their associations must comply with it. In order to preserve the special stature of the Constitution *vis-à-vis* other types of legislation, Articles 1–16 (Chapter 1) are characterised as the 'foundations of the constitutional system' and may not be changed except in the procedure established by the Constitution. Chapter 1 thus occupies a special place even within the Constitution, reflected in the formulation of Article 16(2) stipulating that no other provisions of the Constitution may be contrary to that Chapter.

The Constitution being the highest law, all other enactments are subordinate [подзаконный, literally, sub-law] legislation (note that I avoid the expression 'delegated legislation', for subordinate acts may be issued without delegation so long as they are 'on the basis and in execution of' the acts of superior agencies or agencies at the same level as the issuing organ). This novel concept sits uneasily with the terminological legacy of pre-revolutionary Russia and the Soviet Union, for never before in Russian history has a constitution been placed above monarch and State. In the Russian psyche, the Federal Assembly remains the source of lex [закон], the President as Head of State the source of edict [указ], and the government the source of decree [постановление]. The language of the sources of law lags behind the realities of the new hierarchy embodied in the 1993 Constitution.

Although legislation is the paramount source of law in the Russian Federation, hierarchical relationships among subordinate acts containing legal rules (normative) are confused and confusing, a situation aggravated by the inconsistent and extensive use of more than 40 denominations for enactments.

Federal Assembly

Primacy of place is given to the constitution [конституция], of which there exist the Constitution of the Russian Federation and the constitutions of the more than 20 republics within Russia. The right to adopt laws [закон] remains with the legislative branch of the State, including at the Federation level, the Federal Assembly, and the respective legislative bodies of the republics within the Russian Federation, down to and including the legislative branch of the City of Moscow. A law also may be adopted by way of referendum.

The Constitution of Russia draws a distinction between two types of laws: federal constitutional laws and federal laws. A qualified majority is required to adopt the first, and a simple majority, the second. Amongst enactments which must take the form of a federal constitutional law are the laws on the Constitutional Court, the Supreme Court, the Supreme Arbitrazh Court, and the judicial system. In the hierarchy of sources of law, federal constitutional laws are superior to federal laws.

In addition, the chambers of the Federal Assembly may adopt decrees [постановление] relegated specifically to their respective jurisdiction. The Soviet of the Federation adopts decrees to appoint the Procurator General, judges of the Constitutional Court, Supreme Court, and Supreme Arbitrazh Court, and others. The State Duma declares an amnesty or appoints the Chairman of the Central Bank by way of decree (see Articles 102, 103, Constitution). The Reglament (yet another type of normative act) of the State Duma also provides that the decree shall be used for certain internal matters, for example, the disposition of draft laws after a first or second reading.

Finally, the Federal Assembly confirms, by way of federal laws, other normative acts: statute [положение], code [кодекс], and fundamental principles [основы]; from time to time the Federal Assembly may adopt an appeal [обращение], declaration [декларация], statement [заявление], or message [послание] for transmission to other governments, parliaments, or peoples, especially in the domain of foreign policy. The Supreme Soviet of the Russian Federation used the form of the 'Declaration' on 12 June 1990 to declare State sovereignty and again on 25 October 1991 to regulate the languages of the peoples of Russia.

In quantitative terms the law-making activity of the Federal Assembly has changed beyond recognition in comparison with the parliaments of the Soviet era. Working in session from eight to ten months per year, the Federal Assembly has been generating hundreds of laws and thousands of decrees each year.

President of Russian Federation

The President of the Russian Federation issues edicts [указ] and regulations [распоряжение] (Article 88, Constitution), which must not be contrary to either the Constitution or to federal laws. Both are a form of subordinate legislation, and the Constitution does not specify which type of act should be used for what purpose. Edicts in practice are used for the most important Presidential enactments; regulations for, as a rule, non-normative enactments addressed to individual administrative matters.

There exists a certain tension between the stature of federal laws and edicts, partly linked to the inherent rivalry of branches of State power and partly to ambiguities in the precise demarcation of legislative and presidential power.[10] In the period leading up to the adoption of the December 1993 Constitution of Russia and following the attempted displacement of Presidential power in September 1993, edicts were used as a surrogate for laws in the absence of parliamentary authority. In the early days of radical economic reform, the Supreme Soviet of the RSFSR conferred additional powers on the President of the RSFSR by virtue of which the President could issue edicts which were contrary to and therefore could alter the operation of laws of the RSFSR. The additional powers were exercised principally in the areas of banking, stock exchange, currency, foreign economic, investment, and customs activities, the budget, price formation, taxation, ownership, land reform, and employment. The Civil Code of the Russian Federation goes to some lengths in an attempt to prevent presidential edicts from introducing rules departing from the Code. It follows from the separation of powers, however, that within their domain of competence edicts of the President enjoy the same stature as sources of law as do the enactments of the legislative branch of the State—a view

---

[10] Some Russian jurists and judges believe the President has greatly abused the power to issue edicts on subject matter which should be dealt with only by laws. See V O Luchin and A V Mazurov, 'Presidential Edicts in Russia: General Characteristics', *Sudebnik*, V (2000), 55–97.

reinforced by the absence in the Constitution of a formulation requiring that edicts be issued 'on the basis of and in execution of' laws.

The procedure for the preparation of edicts and regulations is regulated by a Regulation of the President issued 3 August 1996. The decision to submit a draft edict or regulation to the President for signature is taken by the Director of the Administration of the President of the Russian Federation. Edicts, regulations, and laws are signed by the President in his own hand; only exceptionally is a facsimile signature used, and then only with the personal authorisation of the President himself (the facsimile is kept by the Head of the Chancellery of the President).[11]

Government of Russian Federation

Executive power in the Russian Federation is the responsibility of the Government, which 'on the basis of and in execution of' the Constitution, federal laws, and normative edicts of the President issues decrees [постановление] and regulations [распоряжение]. As a rule, decrees are normative, and regulations treat routine administrative matters. In practice the Government of Russia follows patterns of the past in enacting new legal rules which are within its jurisdiction and not contrary to law or edict. However, if decrees and regulations fail to conform to the Constitution, federal laws, or edicts, the President of the Russian Federation has the power to repeal them (Article 115, Constitution).

Decrees and regulations of the Government are binding throughout the Russian Federation without further confirmation by the Federal Assembly or President and without further action by subjects of the Russian Federation. Thousands are issued each year. However, their importance within the general fabric of legislation has diminished because of the substantial volume of law-making undertaken by the Federal Assembly and the President.

Acts of the Government are superior to all others adopted by agencies of State administration and, paradoxically perhaps, even many decisions of subjects of the Russian Federation.

Ministries and departments

The names of enactments of ministries, State committees, and other departments, and of ministers and similar officials are no longer a matter of constitutional regulation. In practice the denominations of ministry and ministerial enactments are determined by the statutes on the ministries or State committees and the terminology of the past largely survives. The acts of ministries and State committees are

---

[11] СЗ РФ (1996), no 33, item 3982. See M V Baglai, Конституционное право Российской Федерации [*Constitutional Law of the Russian Federation*] (1997) 413.

sometimes called decrees, instructions, instructive regulations, and others. Ministers issue, as a rule, an order [приказ] or instruction [инструкция].

Russian Federation ministries and officials are empowered to issue, and frequently do, joint instructions and other normative acts. These acquire no greater force in the hierarchy of normative acts by reason of their joint issuance. The difference between an instruction [инструкция] and an instructional directive [указание] is not clear in theory or practice, except that one rarely encounters a joint instructional directive. As for orders and instructions, the first may be normative or non-normative, whereas the last are always normative because they elaborate a particular law, edict, or governmental decree.

Other State agencies or officials occupying equivalent positions within the State system as ministries or ministers promulgate enactments. These are sometimes designated as orders or instructions, but may bear other appellations. The Central Bank of the Russian Federation, for example, issues instructions and letters [письмо]. Ministries and departments sometimes issue rules [правила] or a *nastavlenie* [наставление] which may extend to institutions and personnel or their own particular system or may be binding generally. In the latter case they are normative.

Subjects of the Federation

The constitutions of republics within the Russian Federation and the legislation governing the other subjects of the Federation contain analogous terminology with respect to normative acts and are, for the most part, also analogous in their internal State structures. They are required to comply with normative acts issued by Federal agencies within their jurisdiction.

Local self-government

Agencies of 'local self-government', which bear different names in different municipalities although the term 'soviets' is still widely used, adopt decisions within the limits of the powers granted to them by legislation of the Russian Federation. In the City of Moscow an entirely new terminology has accompanied the creation of new urban structures. The Moscow City Duma adopts laws, the Mayorate, decrees, and the Mayor, decisions.

Other appellations for acts do arise in the practice of local self-government. A decision [решение] frequently confirms a statute [положение], provisional statute [временное положение], or model statute [примерное положение] of regulatory agencies attached to local government. Many local soviets have enacted reglaments to govern their own internal procedures.

Some decisions of local self-government concern matters within their exclusive jurisdiction, in which event the enactment is an act independently operative within the territorial jurisdiction of the local soviet. The decision must conform to enactments of superior subjects of the Federation and to superior agencies of federal power and administration. Other decisions are adopted on the basis of and in execution of acts of superior bodies.

The acts of local self-government executive committees and of their departments, sections, and administrations are in all instances issued on the basis of and in execution of acts of superior agencies. Such acts may contain normative prescriptions, and the same is true of orders and regulations issued by the heads of departments and administrations of local self-government executive committees.

D. Treaties of the Federation

On 31 March 1992 the Russian Federation concluded a series of three treaties, collectively known as the Treaty of the Federation, as a step towards drafting a new Constitution of the Russian Federation. These documents delimit the subjects of jurisdiction and powers between federal agencies of State power and the agencies of power of the various subjects of the Federation and are expressly referred to in Section Two, Concluding and Transitional Provisions, of the 1993 Russian Constitution.[12] Since 1993, the Russian Federation has quietly been concluding a series of bilateral treaties with each of the subjects of the Federation on a vast variety of subjects. Five treaties and agreements with Tatarstan, for example, address banking, currency, oil refining, foreign economic relations, ownership, and related issues.[13] The Republic Sakha has concluded more than 15 treaties and agreements with the Russian Federation. Since nearly all 89 subjects of the Federation followed this practice, there were nearly a thousand such treaties and agreements in place. Beginning in November 2001, large numbers of these treaties were terminated by mutual agreement.

The texts of these treaties were not gazetted at the federal level, although some have appeared as unnumbered annexes in the СЗ РФ. Russian doctrine is unanimous that they are not 'international treaties' of the Russian Federation. Their substance differs one from the other so that in reality the shared jurisdiction between the Federation and an individual subject of the Federation may vary considerably from that of others. Moreover, some subjects of the Federation have concluded agreements between themselves without including the Russian Federation as a party.

Russian doctrine is reserved in placing these internal documents in the hierarchy of sources of law. Depending upon their subject matter, they may be a source of

---

[12] The treaties are translated in *RLT* 51–72.
[13] Translated in *RLT* 73–88.

rules of particular branches of law. There is a compelling argument that such treaties and agreements may override inconsistent provisions of federal laws. Since, however, the Federal Assembly is not as a rule involved in their conclusion, there are conceptual problems with this view.

Although the pace of treaty-making has slowed since June 1998, it does continue. Efforts have been made to bring order to the process of concluding such treaties and agreements by the enactment on 24 June 1999 of the Federal Law on the Principles and Procedure for Delimitation of Subjects of Jurisdiction and Powers Between Agencies of State Power of the Russian Federation and Agencies of State Power of Subjects of the Russian Federation.[14] The Federal Law determines what such treaties may regulate (clarification of subjects of jurisdiction and powers established by the Constitution of the Russian Federation and by federal laws; the conditions and procedure for the effectuation of powers delimited by a treaty; forms of inter-action and cooperation when performing the provisions of a treaty; and other questions connected with the performance of a treaty). An agreement, on the other hand, is reserved for the transfer of the effectuation of part of powers; the conditions and procedure for the transfer of effectuation of part of powers; material-financial foundations for transfer of the effectuation of part of powers; forms of interaction and cooperation when performing the provision of an agreement; and other questions connected with the performance of provisions of an agreement. Greater transparency is provided for by requiring that draft treaties and agreements be referred to the parliament of each subject of the Federation and to the Soviet of the Federation of the Russian Federation.

E. Judicial and Arbitration Practice

The introduction of 'checks and balances' into the Russian constitutional order is leading to a reappraisal of the role of judicial practice as a source of Russian law. During the Soviet era, the objections raised against the doctrine of 'precedent' were several: it would diminish the role of legislation; it would give scope for judicial arbitrariness; it would encourage a mechanical concentration on analogous elements in cases to the detriment of their individual distinguishing features. In fact, judicial practice was not ignored in the Soviet legal system and at various periods of Soviet legal history played a creative and unusual role in the development of law. Many appellate court rulings and judgments were reported in supreme court bulletins and other law journals. Practitioners routinely kept or made special card indexes containing the case headnotes of reported cases so that lawyers could review relevant judicial practice with respect to each article of the

---

[14] СЗ РФ (1999), no 26, item 3176.

laws or codes concerned. Procurators, judges, investigators, advocates, and jurisconsults were counselled to read case reports in order to familiarise themselves with errors which higher courts rectify when reviewing judgments.

An Index to published judicial practice over the period 1938–69 cautioned users against regarding 'rulings and decrees of superior courts as a standard or model for deciding other analogous cases. This would be recognition of the practice of "judicial precedent" '.[15] In practice Soviet courts were required to fill 'gaps' in the law, notably the legal rules governing obligations arising out of the causing of harm (delict, or tort, to the Anglo-American lawyer). The law of necessary defence also owed much to judicial decisions and to guiding explanations of the Plenum of the USSR Supreme Court.[16]

At one level the Russian Federation has inherited entirely the legacy of the debate over judge-made law by the USSR and RSFSR supreme courts for the simple reason that the 'guiding explanations' issued by those courts remain in force except insofar as repealed, suspended, or changed by the Supreme Court of the Russian Federation. Although for the most part these 'explanations' interpret rather than create legal norms, the line is no less difficult to draw in Russian law than in other legal systems; many Russian jurists believe that in some instances the Plenum of the Russian Supreme Court has stepped across the line into law-creation. Normative acts in the form of explanations of the Plenum of the Supreme Court, and of the Supreme Arbitrazh Court, are binding upon all lower courts and therefore upon all who appear before those courts. Such explanations continue to be published cumulatively in book form and are repealed and amended as required.[17] The authority for giving such explanations is Articles 126 and 127 of the 1993 Russian Constitution.

The position taken by Soviet jurists, it should be noted, was a doctrinal position. There was no rule of Soviet law which rejected judicial precedent. At a meeting held in April 1997 by the Institute of State and Law of the Russian Academy of Sciences and attended by senior representatives from the entire Russian legal profession, the doctrinal position regarding judicial practice as a source of law was

---

[15] See S V Borodin (ed), Вопросы уголовного права и процесса в практике верховных судов СССР и РСФСР (1938–1969) [*Questions of Criminal Law and Procedure in the Practice of the Supreme Courts of the USSR and RSFSR (1938–1969)*] (2nd edn, 1971) 5.

[16] See W E Butler, 'Necessary Defense, Judge-made Law, and Soviet Man', in W E Butler, P B Maggs, and J B Quigley, Jr (eds), *Law After Revolution* (1988) 99–130.

[17] See Сборник постановлений Пленумов Верховных Судов СССР и РСФСР (Российская Федерация) по гражданским делам [Collection of Decrees of Plenums of the Supreme Courts of the USSR and RSFSR (Russian Federation) with Regard to Civil Cases] (1997); Сборник постановлений Пленумов Верховных Судов СССР и РСФСР (Российская Федерация) по уголовным делам [Collection of Decrees of Plenums of the Supreme Courts of the USSR and RSFSR (Russian Federation) with Regard to Criminal Cases] (1997). The first document in the volume on civil law dates from 22 February 1932.

re-examined and revised. One rapporteur declared: 'In modern reality the decision in a specific case also may be a source [of law]'.[18] The reasons for the change in Russian legal doctrine were several: one is the new and central role of Russian courts in verifying the legality of normative acts. If such acts are found to be illegal or unconstitutional, those acts are vacated by the courts, which action 'gives rise to new rights and duties of the participants of social relations, so that in essence such a decision is norm-creative . . . A judicial decision to vacate a particular normative act proves to be a source of law [jus]'.[19] Another is the role of individual judicial decisions, when construing provisions of legislation, in changing 'prevailing law'. Judicial decisions also fill in gaps in the law and clarify the substance of legal norms otherwise ambiguous. It is accepted that only published judicial decisions can have precedential value. The role of judicial practice in the criminal law has been singled out. A V Naumov observed that 'one can not do without judicial practice when classifying crimes . . . the criminal law is augmented by real content only through judicial practice in respect of concrete cases. Each new judicial decision enlarges . . . or narrows the law enforcer's concept of the content of a criminal-law norm'.[20]

Whether publication is constitutive in this respect and therefore must be in an official organ of the judicial system, or whether any publication for general information is satisfactory, has not been addressed. The classic position of the Soviet era, moreover, commands support still in doctrinal writings, even with regard to explanations of the courts: 'However, it is considered that for all of their significance neither judicial precedents nor decrees of the Plenums of the Supreme Court and the Supreme Arbitrazh Court of the Russian Federation may be regarded as sources of civil law. Judicial institutions do not possess norm-creative functions; they do not create norms of law, but merely interpret and apply them'.[21]

Evidence is accumulating that the Constitutional Court of the RF expects its previous decisions to be followed as *stare decisis*. It has on several occasions indicated that legal positions taken in previous decisions, decrees, rulings, and the like are to be treated as resolved as a matter of law unless and until the Court is persuaded to change them. In a Ruling of 7 December 2001 concerning the right of a defence counsel and a person under investigation to have an interpreter present without the investigator himself being privy to their conversation, for example, the Constitutional Court said:

---

[18] See R Z Livshits, 'Judicial Practice as a Source of Law in Russia', *Sudebnik* II (1997) 632.

[19] Livshits (n 18 above) 629.

[20] See A V Naumov, Уголовное право. Общая часть [*Criminal Law. General Part*] (1996) 109–110.

[21] V V Dolinskaia, in A G Kalpin and A I Masliaev (eds), Гражданское право [*Civil Law*] (1997) I, 38.

From the legal position set out by the Constitutional Court of the Russian Federation in a Decree of 25 October 2001 with regard to the case concerning the verification of the constitutionality of provisions contained in Articles 47 and 51 of the RSFSR Code of Criminal Procedure and Article 16, paragraph two, point (15) of the Federal Law 'On Confinement Under Guard of Suspects and Persons Accused of the Commission of a Crime' it follows that the fulfilment by an advocate having the order of a legal consultation office to conduct a criminal case of the procedural duties of a defender may not be made dependent upon the discretion of an official under whose proceedings the criminal case is situated based on circumstances not enumerated in criminal procedure law limiting the possibility of effectuating the powers of defence. Construing Article 17(4) and (5) and Article 18 of the Federal Law on Confinement Under Guard of Suspects and Persons Accused of the Commission of a Crime as enabling access of an interpreter to a meeting with the defender of an accused under guard who does not possess the language of the court proceeding to be refused is, in essence, contrary to criminal procedure law.[22]

It has not been suggested that published arbitration awards by Russian arbitral tribunals have precedential value or significance for the Russian legal system generally. To a greater extent perhaps than most other countries, however, Russian arbitral tribunals often do publish their awards in the legal media or, in the case of the Russian Court of International Commercial Arbitration, in the form of commentaries or collections of awards. At a minimum these collections are invaluable guides to the reasoning of the arbitrators when applying the applicable law to disputes before them and may be said to represent a repertoire of arbitral practice in the Russian Federation.

F. Customs of Business Turnover

Soviet attitudes toward customary law were ambivalent. During the Kievan Rus and Muscovy eras of Russian legal history, custom was the principal source of law. Written legislation began to achieve priority with respect to custom only from the late seventeenth century. In Imperial Russia customary rules had been widely applied in property, inheritance, family, and other legal relationships, and amongst non-Russian peoples to other legal domains as well. Native courts and customs were supplanted in the early 1920s by Soviet courts and written legislation. Customs deemed to be primitive and retrograde were made illegal in the Russian Federation. Chapter XI of the 1960 RSFSR Criminal Code, for example, contained articles punishing the payment and acceptance of bride price, compelling or obstructing the marriage of a woman, concluding a marital agreement with a person under marital age, and bigamy or polygamy when such acts are

---

[22] See the Case of L S Islamov. СЗ РФ (2002), no 7, item 743.

committed in republics within the Russian Federation or other localities where the acts constitute survivals of local customs.

As a source of civil law, the Civil Code of the Russian Federation introduced the concept of 'customs of business turnover' (Article 5). These are rules of behaviour formed and extensively applied in any domain of entrepreneurial activity and have not been provided for by legislation, although they may have been fixed in commercial or entrepreneurial documents. They are not applicable if they are contrary to legislation or to a contract binding upon the parties; that is, they may not override legislation or contractual provisions agreed between the parties. They are purely sources of 'civil' law and may exist in any sphere of economic life; they may be regional, local, national, international, or relate to branches of industry or activity or inter-branches.[23] In this sense customs of business turnover relate to the law of obligations, and not to the law of things. Russian jurists construe the term widely to embrace commercial customs, business customs, trade customs, and the like. Such customs not having been provided for by 'legislation' is interpreted broadly to include subordinate normative acts: edicts of the President, decrees of the government, and departmental acts. The customs must be stable and generally recognised in the respective sphere of entrepreneurial activity, and may be oral or written. Examples of customs of business turnover include the conditions of model Russian contracts published in the press (Article 427, Civil Code), Incoterms, published collections of the customs of commercial seaports, and others. Proving their existence is a question of evidence. They are dispositive, and therefore the parties to a contract are at liberty to include contractual provisions which are contrary to customs of business turnover. Customs of 'trade turnover' (Articles 309, 311, 314, and 315, Civil Code) are considered to fall within the ambit of business turnover.

The 1999 Merchant Shipping Code of the Russian Federation allows the use of merchant shipping custom to help determine the law subject to application to relations arising from merchant shipping with the participation of foreign citizens or foreign juridical persons or complicated by a foreign element (Article 414(1)) and authorises recourse to 'other international merchant shipping customs' if the law applicable to general average is 'incomplete' or the parties so agree (Article 285).[24] The 1993 Law on International Commercial Arbitration refers to 'trade customs' (Article 28).[25]

---

[23] See V P Mozolin, in T E Abova, A Iu Kabalkin, and V P Mozolin (eds), Гражданский кодекс Российской Федерации: научно-практический комментарий [*Civil Code of the Russian Federation: Scientific-Practical Commentary*] (1996) 19–20.

[24] СЗ РФ (1999), no 18, item 2207. The formulation preceded but is consistent with Part Three of the Civil Code of the Russian Federation, and indeed is based also on Article 5 of the Civil Code.

[25] Ведомости СНД и ВС РФ (1993), no 32, item 1240.

G. Normative Acts of Non-State Entities

Although the roles of trade unions, collective farms, consumer cooperatives, the Communist Party, and other 'social organisations' have changed drastically in the transition to a market economy in the Russian Federation, Russian legal doctrine continues to regard certain non-State enterprises and organisations as being vested with the right to enact normative legal acts. These are called 'local' [локальный] acts. Classic examples occur within the enterprise: collective labour contracts and other acts adopted by the executive of the organisation with the participation of workers or their representatives, in the case of labour law. The authority for the right to enact local normative acts is the 2001 Labour Code of the Russian Federation: 'An employer shall adopt local normative acts containing norms of labour law within the limits of its competence in accordance with laws and other normative legal acts, collective contracts, and agreements' (Article 8).[26] Such local normative acts extend to all workers of the enterprise or to individual categories of workers; they may be adopted for a determined or an indeterminate period, with or without the participation of the representative organ of workers as provided by the Labour Code or collective contract.

The procedure for adopting such acts depends upon the nature of the act. Collective contracts are negotiated between management and workers and then confirmed by the general meeting or conference of workers. Agreements concerning the protection of labour are concluded between the administration of the enterprise and the elective trade union agency of the enterprise. The rules of internal labour order are confirmed by the general meeting or conference of workers upon the recommendation of the administration. Most others are adopted by management after having agreed them with the trade union. There is no obligatory list of local normative acts nor requirements as to their substance, so long as they are not contrary to Russian legislation.[27]

Russian juridical persons also confirm or are subject to other local normative acts. Many Russian jurists regard the charter of a juridical person as a local normative act,[28] together with individual internal statutes regulating, for example, the management organs of the juridical person: statutes on the general meeting of stockholders, council of directors, management board, internal audit commission, and the like.

---

[26] СЗ РФ (2002), no 1(I), item 3.

[27] For earlier practice see A F Nurtdinova, in Iu P Orlovskii (ed), Словарь по трудовому праву [*Dictionary of Labour Law*] (1998) 172–174. In a sense the 2001 Labour Code has strengthened the rights of employers in this respect.

[28] V V Zalesskii, in G S Shapkina (ed), Комментарий к Федеральному закону об акционерных обществах [*Commentary on the Federal Law on Joint-Stock Societies*] (1996) 39.

H. Acts of the Union State

On 8 December 1999 the Russian Federation and Belarus concluded the Treaty on the Creation of the Union State (see Chapter 20), which is in the process of formation. The Union State has its own organs: the High State Council, the Parliament of the Union State, the Council of Ministers, the Court of the Union State, and the Counting Chamber. The agencies of the Union State adopt within the limits of their competence normative legal acts provided for by the Treaty of 8 December 1999: laws, fundamental principles of legislation, decrets, decrees, directives, and resolutions, recommendations, and opinions.

On matters within the exclusive jurisdiction of the Union State laws, decrets, decrees, and resolutions will be adopted. Decrets and decrees are adopted by agencies of the Union State on the basis of the Treaty of 8 December 1999 and laws of the Union State. With regard to questions within the joint jurisdiction of the Union State and the states-participants, fundamental principles of legislation, directives, and resolutions are enacted. These are then to be realised by means of the adoption of national normative legal acts of the states-participants. Although the terminology is not used, it would appear that enactments of the Union State serve as the foundation for 'subordinate' legislation by Russia and Belarus respectively.

Laws and decrets are intended for general application, are binding in all respects, and after their official publication are subject to direct application on the territory of Russia and Belarus. In the event of a conflict between a law or decret of the Union State and norms of internal law of Russia or Belarus, the norm of the law or decret of the Union State has preferential force, except that this rule does not apply in the event of a conflict with norms contained in the constitutions and constitutional acts of Russia or Belarus. Decrees are binding in all respects upon the states and the natural and juridical persons to whom they are addressed. Directives are binding upon each state to whom they are addressed, but the agencies of the respective state retain freedom of choice as to the forms and methods of action. Resolutions are acts by means of which the current activities of agencies of the Union State are ensured. Decisions of the Court of the Union State are binding and subject to official publication; only Russia, Belarus, and agencies of the Union State may transfer questions for the Court to consider which are connected with the interpretation and application of the Treaty of 8 December 1999 or with normative legal acts of the Union State.

I. Documents of the Commonwealth of Independent States

It is estimated that during the first decade of its existence the Commonwealth of Independent States generated more than 8,000 normative documents. The forms are various: international treaties and agreements, decisions of CIS organs, protocols, and others. Their publication is irregular, although many of the matters which these documents address are of considerable legal importance. Insofar as these documents are international treaties, they are pursuant to Article 15 of the 1993 Russian Constitution an integral part of the Russian legal system. The great majority are doubtless interdepartmental agreements.

J. International Treaties

The status of international treaties, and of international law generally, in the Russian legal system has been dramatically transformed by the 1993 Russian Constitution (see Chapter 18). The 1993 Russian Constitution provides (Article 15(4)) that 'generally-recognised principles and norms of international law and international treaties of the Russian Federation' are an integral part of the legal system of the Russian Federation. This is a formulation without precedent in Imperial Russian and Soviet law and legal practice insofar as it, first, accepts generally-recognised principles and norms of international law as part of Russian law and, second, places such norms and principles side by side with norms of municipal Russian law. This may imply that such norms and principles are incorporated into domestic Russian law and overridden by rules of Russian law later in time or lex specialis. It further follows that applicable law clauses in contracts which choose Russian law automatically incorporate the general rules of international law and the norms of international treaties of the Russian Federation.

The expression 'international treaties' embraces all interstate, intergovernmental, or interdepartmental documents irrespective of their form and appellation (treaty, agreement, convention, pact, protocol, exchange of letters, or notes) or other forms and appellations (see Article 1, 1995 Law on International Treaties of the Russian Federation).

The Constitution gives priority to treaty norms over those of domestic law: 'If other rules have been established by an international treaty of the Russian Federation than provided for by a law, the rules of the international treaty shall apply' (Article 15(4)), Constitution).

K. Doctrine

The teachings and writings of jurists have no formal place among the sources of Russian law. It is not the practice of Russian courts to cite the published works of jurists when issuing a decree or judgment. As trained lawyers, Russian judges are of course aware of doctrinal views and doubtless may be influenced by them.

Russian advocates are at liberty to refer to doctrine and commentary in oral pleadings in court and arbitration tribunals.

L. Publication and Entry into Force of Legislation

The publication and entry into force of legal normative acts usually are two closely interrelated processes. Publication is associated with the 'presumption of knowledge of the law'; if a legal normative act has been brought to the information of the general public in a duly established procedure—ordinarily printing the act in a designated official gazette—no one may plead ignorance of the law as a pretext for failure to comply with its prescriptions. Publication in printed form also may establish the official text of the enactment, provide a precise benchmark in time from which the normative legal act takes effect, and enable the legislator to communicate most efficiently with those to whom his enactments are addressed.

For the first time in Russian history the 1993 Constitution of the Russian Federation provides that laws are subject to official publication, that unpublished laws shall not be applied, and that any normative legal acts affecting the rights, freedoms, and duties of man and citizen may not be applied unless they have been published officially for general information (Article 15(3)). In practice this principle has rested uneasily with long-established Russian administrative traditions with the result that access to Russian normative legal acts, although incommensurably improved in comparison with the Soviet period, nonetheless falls short of full disclosure. The Federal Law on State Secrecy of 21 July 1993, as amended 19 September 1997,[29] does not make specific provision for classifying normative legal acts or part thereof, but in enumerating (Article 5) in a general way the information comprising a State secret, it is evident that some information would inevitably be contained in normative acts issued by the President, by the government, or by other agencies of executive power. On the basis of the Law, a List of Information relegated to a State Secret was confirmed by Edict of the President of the Russian Federation on 30 November 1995, as amended 24 January 1998, 6 June 2001, and 10 September 2001. Included on the List is 'information concerning the preparation, conclusion, ratification, preparation for denunciation, content, or fulfilment of treaties, convention, or agreements with foreign States, the premature dissemination of which may caused damage to the defence capability, security, political, or economic interests of the Russian Federation' (point 26).[30]

---

[29] Российская газета, 21 September 1993; СЗ РФ (1997), no 41, item 4673; no 41 8220–8235.

[30] СЗ РФ (1995), no 49, item 4775; (1998), no 5, item 561; (2001), no 24, item 2418; no 38, item 3724. A useful source is A V Kolomiets (comp.), Тайна. Коммерческая. Служебная. Государственная. Сборник нормативных правовых актов [Secrecy. Commercial. Employment. State. Collection of Normative Legal Acts of the Russian Federation] (2001).

Legislative acts

The Law on the Procedure for the Publication and Entry into Force of Federal Constitutional Laws, Federal Laws, and Acts of Chambers of the Federal Assembly of 14 June 1994, as amended 22 October 1999,[31] provides that only those which have been officially published shall be applied on the territory of the Russian Federation. A certain confusion arises over the dates of adoption, approval, and signature of federal laws and constitutional laws. The 1994 Law provides that the 'date of adoption' of a federal law is considered to be the date on which the State Duma adopted the law in its final version. In practice the 'final version' of a federal law is actually in existence only after an editorial commission of the Federal Assembly incorporates the emendations required as a result of the final reading of the draft law; these may be stylistic, or may record changes which the deputies accepted but left to be reduced to final wording by the editorial team. As for federal constitutional laws, the date of adoption is considered to be the day when it was approved by the chambers of the Federal Assembly in the procedure established by the Russian Constitution. The date, however, by which a federal law or constitutional law is commonly referred to is neither of the two dates mentioned above, but rather the date of signature by the President of the Russian Federation. The official number of the law is assigned when the law appears in the official gazette. This can lead to anomalies when the President succeeds in having adjustments made to the final text of a law and delays formal signature for an extended period.

Official publication must occur in the case of federal constitutional laws or federal laws within seven days after signature by the President and within ten days, in the case of acts of the chambers of the Federal Assembly, after adoption. First official publication is considered to be the publication of the full text in Российская газета, a newspaper published five days each week, the Собрание законодательства Российской Федерации, published weekly but approximately two to three weeks after the cover date, or, from October 1999, Парламентская газета, a newspaper issued by the Federal Assembly. Additional publication in other printed media, television, radio, circulation to State agencies, officials, enterprises, institutions, or organisations, on-line, or in machine-readable form are acceptable. They also may be published as separate pamphlets or brochures, and frequently are. Federal laws are also subject to obligatory publication in a computer database prepared by the Scientific-Technical Centre for Legal Information, 'Система' [System], whose machine-readable text has the stature of an official text.[32]

---

[31] СЗ РФ (1994), no 8, item 801; (1999), no 43, item 5124.

[32] On-line publication is authorised by the Edict of the President of the Russian Federation on the Procedure for the Publication and Entry into Force of Federal Laws, adopted 5 April 1994, as amended 9 August 1994 and 1 December 1995. СЗ РФ (1994), no 15, item 1173; no 16, item 1881; (1995), no 49, item 4777.

Entry into force occurs simultaneously throughout the entire territory of the Russian Federation upon the expiration of ten days after official publication unless a different procedure for entry into force is established by the laws themselves or acts of the chambers. The practice varies widely: some laws or codes enter into force many months after signature. Certain portions of a law may enter into force on one date, and other articles or sections at a later date. Frequently a law enters into force on the date of official publication, in which case the date of first official publication becomes significant.

The Constitutional Court has ruled on the date of official publication of laws in connection with a case arising out of the adoption of the Federal Law of 7 March 1996 on Making Changes in the Law of the Russian Federation on Excises. This Law confirmed a new version of the Law on Excises which by its provisions entered into force from 1 February 1996 and introduced excise taxes on goods imported from CIS countries, whereas previously such goods had been exempt. On 15 March 1996 the State Customs Committee circulated the text of the law by teletype to the heads of regional customs administrations, instructing them to recover excise tax with respect to all affected goods as from 1 February 1996. Observing that this Law was retroactive and disadvantageous to the taxpayers concerned, the Constitutional Court held that it was in clear violation of Article 57 of the 1993 Russian Constitution. Invoking Article 4 of the 1994 Federal Law on the procedure for the publication of laws, the Court observed that it was to be determined whether first publication occurred in the СЗ РФ or in Российская газета. The relevant issue of the СЗ РФ was dated 11 March 1996, whereas Российская газета was dated 13 March 1996; however, the Court noted that the cover date of the СЗ РФ was the date on which the issue was signed to press, and not the actual date of publication (which had to have been later and therefore the taxpayers to whom the law was addressed could not have had knowledge of the law on that date). Therefore the newspaper date was that of first publication, and the Law, not providing otherwise, could only enter into force not earlier than 24 March 1996, when ten days had lapsed from the moment of official publication.[33] Each issue of the gazette will bear scrutiny on this basis; the day on which they are signed to press, that is, officially approved for printing, can be days or weeks after the cover date.

Presidential, governmental, and departmental acts

According to the 1993 Russian Constitution, the President issues edicts and regulations (Article 90(1)), and the government issues decrees and regulations (Article 115). The publication of these is regulated by the Edict of the President of the

---

[33] See T G Morshchakova (ed), Конституционный Суд Российской Федерации: Постановления. Определения. 1992–1996 [Constitutional Court of the Russian Federation: Decrees. Rulings. 1992–1996] (1997) 459–465.

Russian Federation on the Procedure for the Publication and Entry into Force of Acts of the President of the Russian Federation and of the Government of the Russian Federation and Normative Legal Acts of Federal Agencies of Executive Power, adopted 23 May 1996, as amended 16 May 1997 and 13 August 1998,[34] and by the Law on the Government of the Russian Federation. Whereas all federal laws are subject to publication without exception, accessibility to Presidential edicts, governmental decrees, and departmental acts is affected by the Law on State Secrecy. Accordingly, under the 1996 Edict, edicts and regulations of the President and decrees and regulations of the Government are subject to obligatory official publication except for those acts or parts thereof which contain information constituting a State secret or information of a confidential character. Publication takes place, when applicable, within ten days after their signature in the same organs as federal laws, noted above, including the computer database.

Acts of a normative character adopted by the President enter into force simultaneously throughout the territory of the Russian Federation upon the expiry of seven days after their first official publication. Other Presidential acts, including acts containing information constituting a State secret or information of a confidential character, enter into force on the date of their signature. However, all Presidential acts may enter into force on a different date as provided therein, commonly on the date of publication. Acts of the Government affecting the rights, freedoms, and duties of man and citizen or establishing the legal status of federal agencies of executive power or organisations enter into force seven days after their first date of official publication unless the acts provide otherwise. Other acts of the Government enter into force on the date of signature unless provided otherwise therein.

The greatest advances in the interests of a rule-of-law State with regard to publication of legislation have occurred with respect to departmental acts. Subject to exceptions (for example, certain acts of the Central Bank of the Russian Federation; see Chapter 12), departmental normative legal acts require registration with the Ministry of Justice of the Russian Federation as a condition of their validity. A departmental act will not be registered if in the view of Ministry of Justice specialists it is contrary to law. The Ministry routinely rejects numerous drafts on these grounds, information concerning which is recorded weekly in the newspaper Экономика и жизнь [*Economy and Life*] and, since 1998, in the Бюллетень Министерства юстиции Российской Федерации [*Bulletin of the Ministry of Justice of the Russian Federation*]. Those departmental acts or parts thereof containing information constituting a State secret or information of a confidential character which have not undergone State registration, or those registered but not published in the established procedure, have no legal consequences

---

[34] СЗ РФ (1996), no 22, item 2663; (1997), no 20, item 2242; (1998), no 33, item 3967.

on the grounds that they have not entered into legal force. Accordingly they may not serve a ground for regulating legal relations or applying sanctions to citizens, officials, or organisations for the failure to comply with the prescriptions contained therein; nor may they be referred to when settling disputes. Departmental acts enter into force simultaneously throughout Russian territory upon the expiry of ten days after the date of official publication unless a different period is specified therein, whereas those which by reason of State secrecy or the confidential information contained therein are not officially published enter into force from the date of their State registration and the conferment of a registration number on them, unless the acts themselves specify a later date.

The Rules for the Preparation of Normative Legal Acts of Federal Agencies of Executive Power and the State Registration Thereof were confirmed by Decree of the Government of the Russian Federation on 13 August 1997, as amended 11 December 1997, 6 November 1998, 11 February 1999, and 30 September 2000.[35] Normative legal acts are issued by federal agencies of executive power in the form of decrees, orders, regulations, rules, instructions, and statutes; the Rules expressly prohibit normative legal acts being issued in the form of letters and telegrams (this provision does not extend to the Russian Central Bank, which is not a federal agency of executive power). The amendments of 11 December 1997 excluded deputy ministers and other deputy heads of federal agencies of executive power from signing, and therefore, confirming, normative legal acts. In April 1998 the Minister of Justice introduced internal procedures to expedite the process of evaluating departmental enactments.

Under the Rules of 13 August 1997, as amended, the Ministry of Justice registers not only normative legal acts affecting the rights, freedoms, and duties of man and citizen or those having an interdepartmental character, but also acts establishing the legal status of organisations (thereby giving effect to the Edict of the President of the Russian Federation of 23 May 1996, referred to above). Ministries and departments seeking registration of a normative legal act must submit an original and five copies of the draft act because, if registered, the act also must be published in the Бюллетень нормативных актов федеральных органов исполнительной власти [*Bulletin of Normative Acts of Federal Agencies of Executive Power*] and copies supplied to the Scientific-Technical Centre for Legal Information 'System' and the Institute of Legislation and Comparative Law attached to the government of Russia. If the act contains information comprising a State secret or of a confidential character, only one original and one copy are submitted. The Ministry of Justice has up to 15 days, with possible extensions for a further ten days, to complete its expert legal evaluation of the draft normative legal act. If

---

[35] СЗ РФ (1997), no 33, item 3895; no 50, item 5689; (1998), no 47, item 5771; (1999), no 8, item 1026; (2000), no 41, item 4081.

draft normative legal acts contain a violation of the established procedure for submission thereof or provisions contrary to law, they are returned to the issuing agency for rectification and possible resubmission. Non-normative acts, that is, acts not containing a legal norm, may proceed to issuance without State registration, a fact which also is confirmed by the Ministry of Justice and recorded in a separate published list.

Nonetheless, there are numerous acts whose form is not mentioned in the 1997 Rules but which meet the definition of normative legal acts subject to State registration and official publication. Within this group are acts containing ecological, sanitary-epidemiological, hygienic, fire prevention, product safety, and analogous rules. In Russian legal doctrine these have been called 'normative legal acts with technical content': State standards, construction norms and rules, State sanitary-epidemiological rules, and the like. In practice some are registered and others are not. In a case which went to the Supreme Court of the Russian Federation a citizen alleged that certain provisions of an Order of the Ministry for Communications and Informatisation on the procedure for introducing technical means to conduct operational and search operations were illegal because they violated his right to secrecy of telephone conversations. The claimant contended that the Ministry Order contained references to orders of certain ministries and departments that were unregistered and not officially published. The respondents averred that the unpublished orders were of a 'technical' nature, non-normative, and did not require State registration. The Supreme Court accepted this distinction in rejecting the claimant's arguments.[36] The reasoning of the Supreme Court is not persuasive against the definition of a normative legal act set out in its Decree No 19 of 25 May 2000.[37]

Departmental acts which are not subject to registration in the view of the Ministry of Justice may be published in designated departmental gazettes.[38]

The overall result is that Russian normative acts are more accessible than in the past, but nonetheless there remain secret, classified, and technical normative acts, particularly with respect to entrepreneurial matters, that make it impossible for lawyers who advise to eliminate elements of legal risk arising in this connection.

---

[36] Бюллетень Верховного Суда РФ [Bulletin of the Supreme Court of the Russian Federation], (2001), no 4, 10–11.

[37] See Ia. Partsii, 'О лицензировании отдельных видов деятельности' [On Licensing Individual Types of Activity], Хозяйство и право, (2002), no 1, 31–40.

[38] An example is Regulation No СФ–13-р of 19 February 2002 issued by the Ministry of Transport of the RF; Ministry acts are subject to publication in the newspaper Транспорт России. See Российская газета, 16 March 2002.

International treaties

Under Article 15(4) of the 1993 Russian Constitution, international treaties of the Russian Federation are an integral part of the Russian legal system. The Federal Law on the Procedure for the Publication of Federal Laws of 14 June 1994 provides that 'international treaties ratified by the Federal Assembly shall be published simultaneously with the federal laws concerning their ratification' (Article 3). This formulation does not specify that the treaties shall be published in the same gazette as the federal law ratifying the Convention, although the СЗ РФ does publish certain international treaties. In any event in practice the requirement of 'simultaneous' is not complied with. For example, the Federal Law on the Ratification of the Convention on the Protection of Human Rights and Basic Freedoms and the Protocols Thereto, of 30 March 1998, was published on 6 April 1998 with the emendation that the 'Convention and Protocols thereto will be published upon their entry into force for the Russian Federation'.[39]

Those treaties which have entered into legal force, except treaties of an interdepartmental character, are subject to official publication in the Бюллетень международных договоров [*Bulletin of International Treaties*] published monthly by the Administration of the President of the Russian Federation.[40] When necessary, they may also appear in the newspaper Российская газета, and in practice they frequently appear in the 'Ведомственное приложение' ['Departmental Annex'] of the same newspaper, available weekly by special subscription. These requirements apply only to international treaties which were concluded or acceded to after 1 January 1992. Interdepartmental international treaties are to be published in the official organs of the ministries or departments which concluded those treaties.

There is another category of treaty which finds no mention in the legislation regulating the publication and entry into force of normative legal acts: treaties concluded between the Russian Federation and subjects of the Federation. The great majority appear to be unpublished, or if published, commonly in the newspapers of the subjects of the Federation concerned or in the departmental annex to Российская газета.

---

[39] СЗ РФ (1998), no 14, item 1514.

[40] See Edict of the President of the Russian Federation on the Procedure for the Publication of International Treaties of the Russian Federation, adopted 11 January 1993, as amended 1 December 1995. СЗ РФ (1993), no 3, item 182; (1995), no 49, item 4777. Some believe the Edict de facto lost force with the entry into force of the 1995 Federal Law on International Treaties of the Russian Federation, a position difficult to sustain in light of the fact that the Edict was amended after the entry into force of that Law.

Official gazettes

An extensive bibliography of official gazettes is contained in Chapter 21. The Собрание законодательства Российской Федерации [Collection of Legislation of the Russian Federation] appears weekly as the official periodical publication in which are published 'Federal constitutional laws, Federal laws, acts of chambers of the Federal Assembly, edicts and regulations of the President of the Russian Federation, decrees and regulations of the Government of the Russian Federation, decisions of the Constitutional Court of the Russian Federation concerning an interpretation of the Constitution of the Russian Federation and concerning the conformity to the Constitution of the Russian Federation of laws, normative acts of the President of the Russian Federation, Soviet of the Federation, State Duma, Government of the Russian Federation, or individual provisions of the enumerated acts'.[41]

Both the internal structure of the gazette and the forms of citation and layout of normative acts are regulated by the 1994 Federal Law. The gazette is divided into five sections. Section One contains federal constitutional laws and federal laws and in practice also contains the texts of international treaties when they are published in this gazette. Section Two consists of the acts of the chambers of the Federal Assembly. In Section Three the edicts and regulations of the President of the Russian Federation appear. Section Four publishes the decrees and regulations of the Government of the Russian Federation. Section Five reproduces the decisions of the Constitutional Court subject to publication in this gazette.

Section Two is subdivided into two parts. The first contains decrees of the chambers of the Federal Assembly adopted with regard to questions relegated by Articles 102 and 103 of the 1993 Russian Constitution to the jurisdiction of the chambers. Part Two consists of other acts of the chambers of the Federal Assembly. Sections Three and Four also are subdivided into two parts; in each case Part One consists of normative acts, whereas Part Two contains acts of a non-normative character.

Acts placed within the gazette are given a consecutive item number; annexes to acts are placed under the same item number as the act itself. The full name of the federal constitutional law or federal law is given, the date of its adoption by the State Duma and the date of its approval by the Soviet of the Federation, the name of the official who signed it, the place and date of signature, and the registration number, which consists of an abbreviation of the type of law and the number assigned; for example, No 5-ФЗ indicates Federal Law No 5. The numeration

---

[41] Article 7, 1994 Federal Law on the Procedure for the Publication and Entry into Force of Federal Constitutional Laws, Federal Laws, and Acts of Chambers of the Federal Assembly (n 27 above), as amended 22 October 1999.

commences anew each calendar year, so that the number of the law without a date is not helpful. International treaties are given an item number when published in the gazette but do not have a registration number as a federal law. Only the law on ratification of the treaty has a registration number.

When changes and additions are made to a federal constitutional law, federal law, or act of a chamber of the Federal Assembly, the new version may be published in an integrated text containing all the changes and additions, or a law instructing the changes and additions to be inserted may be adopted, as the Federal Assembly may choose. In practice both approaches are widely used.

The Federal Assembly of the Russian Federation publishes two gazettes, one official and the other not. The Парламентская газета since October 1999 has been recognised as an official gazette for federal constitutional laws, federal laws, and decrees of chambers of the Federal Assembly whose publication is required by the parliament. The Ведомости Федерального Собрания Российской Федерации [*Gazette of the Federal Assembly of the Russian Federation*] contains the texts of federal constitutional laws and federal laws and decrees adopted by the chambers of the Federal Assembly. The texts, however, do not have the stature of official texts.

Normative legal acts of federal agencies of executive power were subject to official publication for many years in the newspaper Российские вести [*Russian News*] within ten days after their registration by the Ministry of Justice. That organ has virtually disappeared, leaving as the principal source the Бюллетень нормативных актов федеральных органов исполнительной власти [*Bulletin of Normative Acts of Federal Agencies of Executive Power*], issued since 1996 at various intervals and from 1998, weekly. The on-line version of these acts is also official (for details on other departmental gazettes, see Chapter 21).

M. Techniques of Law Reform

With the transition to a market economy, law reform has come to mean the changes in law and legal institutions required to effect that transition. Nonetheless, the classic preoccupations of 'legal technique'[42] remain relevant: the expansion in the sources of law, the varied denominations for enactments, the continued need to distinguish between normative and non-normative legal acts, and the problems of making enactments physically and linguistically accessible.

The amounts of legislation generated by a legal system in transition to a market economy have proved in Russia to be no less and very possibly considerably greater

---

[42] See D A Kerimov, Законодательная техника [*Legislative Technique*] (1998).

than the staggering figures of the Soviet Planned Economy, the more so if Russian legal doctrine persists with the concept of 'local' normative acts. Russia pioneered in the nineteenth century systematic and chronological collections of legislation (see Chapter 2), and these efforts were renewed by the Soviet Government in the 1920s and again in the 1960–80s.[43] They resulted in a looseleaf Свод законов [Digest of Laws] of the USSR and RSFSR (and all other union republics) and a more comprehensive Собрание действующего законодательства [Collection of Prevailing Legislation] in hardback format for the USSR and RSFSR (and other union republics). The enactments in each case were an official text, although neither collection was remotely exhaustive.

Following the enactment of the 1993 Russian Constitution it was decided to revive the concept of the Свод законов Российской Федерации [Digest of Laws of the Russian Federation] organised according to subject and based on a chronological collection of all normative legal acts of the USSR, RSFSR, and Russian Federation in force on the territory of Russia. The chronological collection, reportedly completed, is maintained by the Chief State Law Administration of the President of the Russian Federation. The subject matter classifications have been developed and formally enacted as the General Legal Classification System of Branches of Legislation on 15 March 2000, with later revisions published more or less annually in the СЗ РФ.[44]

The advisability of introducing a Digest of Laws of the Russian Federation, whether in on-line and/or looseleaf form, is disputed by many Russian jurists, who stress the necessarily transitional and consequently imperfect state of Russian legislation for the foreseeable future.[45]

---

[43] See W E Butler, 'Toward a *Svod Zakonov* for the Union of Soviet Socialist Republics', in D Barry, F J M Feldbrugge, and D Lasok (eds), *Codification in the Communist World* (1975) 89–111.

[44] СЗ РФ (2000), no 12, item 1260.

[45] For the debate and draft outlines of the Digest, see S V Polenina and N P Koldaeva, 'On the Digest of Laws of the Russian Federation', *Sudebnik*, III (1998), 28–81.

5

LEGAL PROFESSION AND
LEGAL EDUCATION

The expression 'jurist' (юрист) in the Russian language can be used in a broad sense to encompass all who have a legal education and all who work in a legal specialty, whether as academician, professor, judge, procurator, arbitrator, notary, investigator, advocate, jurisconsult, ZAGS personnel, or whatever. In this chapter we examine two types of jurist who most closely approximate the narrower Anglo-American concept of the lawyer, solicitor, or barrister, that is, those who principally advise citizens and juridical persons or appear in court on their behalf. These in the Russian legal system are the advocate and the jurisconsult.

Advocates and foreign lawyers who 'effectuate advocate activity on the territory of the Russian Federation' again require, as of 1 July 2002, registration in a special register, the procedure for keeping which is determined by the Government of the Russian Federation. The requirement of licensing, introduced by the President of the Russian Federation in 1991 and implemented by the Government of the Russian Federation from 15 April 1995,[1] was effectively abolished when the long-awaited Federal Law on the Licensing of Individual Types of Activity, of 25 September 1998, as amended, failed to include legal services on the list of activities subject to licensing.[2] This had the effect of restoring the long-established practice of regarding Soviet law graduates as immediately qualified in principle to

---

[1] СЗ РФ (1995), no 17, item 1550; repealed by Decree of the Government No 548, of 20 May 1999. СЗ РФ (1999), no 21, item 2637.

[2] СЗ РФ (1998), no 48, item 5853; (1999), no 52, items 6365, 6366.

practice upon receiving their first degree in law from an institution of higher education. When the 1998 law was replaced on 8 August 2001 by another federal law bearing the same name, legal services were omitted again from the list of those requiring a license.[3] However, the Federal Law on Advocate Activity and the Advokatura in the Russian Federation of 31 May 2002 introduced the special register mentioned above.

It is common for auditors in Russia to have a degree in law, although degrees in economics and certain other disciplines are deemed to be acceptable for this profession. Under the Federal Law on Auditor Activity, of 7 August 2001, as amended 14 December 2001, auditing organisations and individual auditors may in the course of rendering auditing services also offer 'concomitant services'.[4] The last include tax advice and legal advice (including representation in judicial and tax agencies with regard to tax and customs disputes); an auditor's license is sufficient to sanction the rendering of such services without any additional licenses. However, in giving such advice, auditors may not engage in any entrepreneurial activity other than auditing and others connected therewith.

A. The Advocate

(1) History

The survival of a group of professional people in the Soviet Union who could be retained on a fee basis by individual citizens came as a surprise to many in the West who imagined that the employment of one citizen by another was no longer possible. The initial reaction of the Bolsheviks to the Advokatura, or 'Bar' as it is sometimes misleadingly styled, in Russia was antipathetic; the pre-revolutionary Russian Advokatura was dissolved on 24 November 1917 in Decree No 1 'On Courts'. The Petrograd and later the Moscow Bars refused to recognise the legality of the dissolution and continued to function for nearly a year. Lenin himself was an advocate in the 1890s. Expelled from his law studies at Kazan University, he completed them externally at St Petersburg University, was admitted to legal practice, and actually appeared in court in several cases before devoting himself wholly to the revolutionary movement. He took a dim view in some of his writings about aspects of the Russian legal profession, but was never opposed to the legal profession in principle. It was Lenin who personally inserted clauses on defenders in the early draft enactments on criminal procedure.

Decree No 1 'On Courts' allowed every citizen who enjoyed civil rights to act as defence counsel,[5] and under this proviso many advocates of the Tsarist era

---

[3] СЗ РФ (2001), no 33, item 3430.
[4] СЗ РФ (2001), no 33, item 3422; no 51, item 4829.
[5] СУ РСФСР (1917–18), no 4, item 50.

continued to practice their profession. Although this right was retained in Decree No 2 'On Courts', adopted 15 February 1918, Lenin modified the draft to allow 'colleges' of individuals to be formed and attached to local soviets; college members might act for remuneration either as prosecutors or defence counsel.[6] The link between prosecution and defence proved to be incompatible and was abolished in May 1918. There followed a period of constant reorganisations of the provision of legal services for some four years. As a rule, regulation of advocates was left to local soviets. Initially a fee system operated on the basis of a schedule fixed by councils within the colleges of defenders; then the colleges were reorganised and defence council became salaried employees just as judges and procurators. Into this new scheme of colleges passed many members of the Tsarist Bar in November 1918 when they resolved to liquidate their former organisations. In 1920 a dramatic new experiment was tried; local soviets were obliged to confirm twice-yearly lists of individuals who were capable of acting as defenders in court. They were paid *per diem* from State funds. Individuals on the list found themselves pressed into the role of defender whether they wished to act or not. The system proved unworkable, and in the majority of instances defenders were appointed from officials of local justice agencies attached to the respective local soviets.

The introduction of the NEP brought a full-fledged Statute on the Advokatura, adopted 26 May 1922.[7] Under the Statute, colleges of defenders for civil and criminal cases were formed and attached to the *guberniia* justice sections. College members were confirmed by the Presidium of the *guberniia* executive committee, but new members could now be admitted by the college itself with subsequent notification of the Committee. Members were precluded from holding simultaneously posts in State institutions and enterprises except for elective offices and law teaching positions. Defenders were free to negotiate their fees with the client except with workers of State and private enterprises or employees of soviet institutions and enterprises, for whom fees were regulated by the People's Commissariat of Justice. Indigents were exempted from legal fees by court decree. The defenders then paid a stipulated percentage of their remuneration to the College for overhead expenses. Defenders did not enjoy a monopoly position. Close relatives of an accused or a victim and authorised representatives of certain State and social organisations also might appear in court as a defender. Other individuals, however, required the special authorisation of the court.

The influence of lawyers from the *ancien regime* in local advokaturas evidently troubled many local party organisations. As late as early 1923 about 25 per cent of the 2,800 advocates in the RSFSR were from the pre-revolutionary era.

---

[6] СУ РСФСР (1918), no 26, item 240.
[7] СУ РСФСР (1922), no 36, item 425. Although entitled as a separate Statute, the enactment was in fact an amendment to Articles 43–49 of the Statute on People's Courts, adopted 21 October 1920.

Should communists be allowed to join? The Central Committee of the Party on 2 November 1922 counselled affirmatively in a circular to all regional and provincial Party organisations; otherwise, the Committee said, the colleges would be taken over by elements hostile to Soviet power. But limitations were imposed. A communist was required to have the advance approval of a senior Party organisation before joining the college; communist advocates must not accept cases, especially civil cases, involving the defence of 'bourgeois interests' in disputes against workers or State enterprises, nor in criminal cases defend clearly counter-revolutionary or other impure elements.[8] Throughout most of the NEP period advocates worked as private practitioners, the fee arrangements being attenuated by legal consultation centres at factories or public places where workers might obtain legal advice free of charge. During the era of forced collectivisation in 1929–31, advocates in most places found themselves pressured to merge into voluntary 'collectives' of advocates. The arrangements varied from locality to locality; as a rule, clients contracted for services with a collective and fees were paid to the collective. Advocates were then remunerated on the basis of quantity and quality of work performed.[9]

Somewhat greater guidance over the legal profession ensued with the creation of a Legal Defence Section within the RSFSR People's Commissariat of Justice by legislation of 20 July 1930. On 27 February 1932 the RSFSR People's Commissariat of Justice adopted a Statute on Collectives of Members of Colleges of Defenders, confirming that the notion of collectives in this realm was on the whole regarded as a positive development. The collectives worked under the direct guidance of the presidium of colleges of advocates, whereas the colleges received their 'general policy guidance and supervision' from the territorial, regional, and higher courts. The collectives admitted new members, subject to final approval by the colleges. Clients selected their own defenders from those available; fees varied depending on the qualifications, socio-legal work, and workload of the advocate but were levied at rates worked out by the Presidium of the College and confirmed by the court.[10]

The 1932 Statute was enacted at a time when the need for a legal profession at all was being serious questioned by the Pashukanis school. In the event, the importance of defence counsel was staunchly defended. Following the adoption of the 1936 USSR Constitution, the system of court organisation was remodelled and for the first time all-union legislation on the Advokatura was approved, on 16 August 1939, by the USSR Council of People's Commissars.[11] The 1939 Law

---

[8] Reproduced in ЕжСю (1923) no 1, 24; signed by V M Molotov.

[9] There are two excellent accounts of the advocate in the Soviet era: J N Hazard, *Settling Disputes in Soviet Society* (1960) 247–300; E Huskey, *The Russian Legal Profession* (1986).

[10] See M V Kozhevnikov, История советского суда 1917–1956 годы [*History of the Soviet Court: 1917–1956*] (1957) 237.

[11] СП СССР (1939), no 49, item 394.

changed the terminology from 'defenders' to 'advocates' and provided that colleges of advocates were to be created in autonomous republics, territories, and regions as voluntary professional associations. The management organs of the colleges were the general meeting of advocates, the presidium, and the audit commission. General direction over the advokatura was exercised by the USSR and union republic people's commissariats of justice, on whom the advokatura was dependent.

In about 1947 the Government of the USSR created so-called 'closed territories' which included at least ten cities with populations from 50,000 to 100,000 persons, each territory having its own courts, procuracy, police, notariat, and advokatura. The names of the towns often consisted of a combination of names and numbers, eg, Tomsk–7, Cheliabinsk–65. The names of the legal consultation offices also were given classified names, which in 1971 were changed to classified numbers, eg, Legal Consultation Office No 9, 10, 19, 20, 25, 33, and others. During this period responsibility for the work of the special advokatura was placed on various agencies, including the USSR Ministry of Justice, Supreme Court of the USSR, RSFSR Ministry of Justice, and RSFSR Supreme Court. On 12 March 1980 the Inter-Republic College of Advocates was founded; it presently has more than 1,340 advocates with legal consultation offices in 54 subjects of the Russian Federation and four independent states. In 1996 advocates of the collegium gave advice on 208,657 matters, nearly 50 per cent free of charge.

The 1958 FPCOrg returned responsibility for the Advokatura to the union republics, each of whom between 1962 and 1963 enacted their own statutes for their respective advokaturas but retained essentially the same internal organisational scheme within the advokaturas. Some central direction was felt to be necessary, however, and in 1976 work commenced on drafting an all-union enactment. The 1977 USSR Constitution (Article 161) provided for a new pattern of regulation—USSR and union republic legislation—and elevated the colleges of advocates to organisations of constitutional stature for the first time in Soviet history. On 30 November 1979 the USSR Supreme Soviet adopted the Law on the Advokatura in the USSR. On the basis of that Law, the RSFSR Supreme Soviet adopted the Statute on the Advokatura of the RSFSR on 20 November 1980, which remained in force until 30 June 2002. It was finally replaced with effect from 1 July 2002 by the Federal Law on Advocate Activity and the Advokatura in the Russian Federation, of 31 May 2002.

(2) *Current Legislation*

Federal Chamber of Advocates of Russian Federation

Beginning in the late 1980s, a number of regional colleges of advocates combined into various social organisations for the purpose of defending the interests of the advocates as a profession. In 1991 an All-Union Congress of Advocates was held in the Soviet Union. The Congress created a Union of Advocates, elected the executive organs thereof, and adopted a Charter. Upon the dissolution of the Soviet Union, several associations of advocates were created within the Russian Federation: the Union of Advocates of Russia, founded in 1990, became the Federal Union of Advocates based in Moscow at the Founding Congress on 12–13 September 1994; the Regional Association of Russian Advocates, head-quartered in Saratov, was established in 1994 and combined 13 colleges of advocates; the Guild of Advocates of Russia, based in Moscow, was formed on 27 January 1995 and combined more than 40 so-called 'parallel' colleges of advocates formed during the early 1990s; and the Union of Advocates of the USSR, founded in 1989, which became after the demise of the Soviet Union, the International Union (or Commonwealth) of Advocates, in Moscow, brought together advocates and their colleges on the territories of Belarus, Uzbekistan, and other CIS States and a number of Russian regions; it was formed in 1994 and re-registered in 1998. These associations neither rendered legal services nor directed the operations of their member colleges of advocates or individual members.[12]

Although the tasks of each association varied one from the other, the Federal Union of Advocates of Russia was not untypical. Under its Charter, the Federal Union was dedicated to strengthening an independent and strong Advokatura, defending the rights of advocates and their honour and dignity, promoting the training of specialists for advokatura work, publishing, strengthening links with academic lawyers, participation in drafting legislation, representing the interests of the Advokatura in State agencies and social organisations, and developing international links of Russian advocates.

These associations were supported by membership dues, publishing revenues, donations, and other private-sector assistance. Their future is uncertain, however, for the 2002 Federal Law on Advocate Activity and the Advokatura in the Russian Federation succeeded in accomplishing a 'centralisation' of Russian advocates within a national framework that the various legal associations had frustrated for so long. They may exist so long as they do not perform the functions reserved by Russian legislation to the chambers of advocates.

Under the 2002 law, the Federal Chamber of Advocates of the Russian Federation has been formed as an all-Russian, non-State, non-commercial organisation in which membership is compulsory for chambers of advocates formed at the level of subjects of the Russian Federation. The aim of the Federal Chamber of

---

[12] For an informal but informed account of the early days of these rival groupings, see Iu Lubshev, Адвокатура в России [*The Advokatura in Russia*] (2001).

Advocates is to represent and defend the interests of advocates in agencies of State power and local self-government and ensure a high level of legal assistance to clients. The Federal Chamber is a juridical person which is formed by the All-Russian Congress of Advocates. The existence of rival organisations is prohibited if they have analogous functions and powers to the Federal Chamber of Advocates. The Charter of the Federal Chamber is adopted by the All-Russian Congress of Advocates and is subject to registration in the same procedure as applies to other juridical persons. Decisions of the Federal Chamber are binding upon all chambers of advocates and individual advocates.

The All-Russian Congress of Advocates meets at least once every two years and is quorate if not less than two-thirds of the delegates to the Congress take part. The Congress also, in addition to the charter, adopts the professional ethics code for advocates, confirms the uniform norm for representation at the Congress, forms the Council of the Federal Chamber, determines the deductions from chambers of advocates for the common needs of the Federal Chamber and confirms the estimate of expenditures, elects the internal audit commission, confirms the reglaments of the Congress, personnel establishment, and performs other functions stipulated by the charter. In intervals between congresses, the affairs of the Federal Chamber are conducted by its collegial executive organ, the Council, which elects the President of the Federal Chamber for a term of four years and, upon his recommendation, three vice-presidents for a term of two years.

A chamber of advocates exists in each of the 89 subjects of the Russian Federation also as a non-State, non-commercial organisation. Membership of advocates is obligatory. These chambers operate on the basis of general statutes for organisations of this type. They are created to ensure that qualified legal assistance is rendered and accessible throughout the territory of the particular subject of the Federation in which they are formed, that such assistance is free of charge when required or necessary, to represent and defend the interests of advocates in agencies of State power and local self-government and other organisations, supervise the professional training of persons admitted to effectuate advocate activity and compliance with the advocates' code of professional ethics. The chamber is formed by a constitutive meeting or conference of advocates. Each chamber is a juridical person and responsible for its own obligations with its property; advocates are not liable for obligations of their chamber. Each chamber is subject to State registration in the procedure established for the registration of juridical persons. There may be only one chamber in each subject of the Federation. No branches, representations, or subdivisions on the territory of other subjects of the Federation are permitted, and inter-regional or other inter-territory formations are prohibited. A chamber may not engage in advocate activity in its own name, nor engage in entrepreneurial activity.

Advocate formations

As of 1 January 2002 there were nearly 47,000 advocates in the Russian Federation,[13] organised into 145 colleges of advocates consisting of 3,316 legal consultation offices and firms containing 26,309 advocates and 50 so-called 'alternative' colleges consisting of 5,500 advocates. The College of Advocates of the City of Moscow grew from 1,068 advocates in 1987 to 1,650 in 1996. Although the traditional colleges of advocates outnumber the 'alternative' colleges by a substantial margin, the Moscow Legal Centre, which is a law office within the Guild of Advocates of Russia, has more than 100 advocates. Even though the number of advocates significantly increased in the 1990s, the per capita ratio of advocates to the populace is much lower than other developed legal systems. However, because the Russian jurisconsult is part of the equation, the per capita figure is lower than the actual position.

Under Article 72(k) of the 1993 Russian Constitution, the advokatura is the subject of joint jurisdiction of the Russian Federation and its subjects. Accordingly, the Federation may issue federal laws on the Advokatura, and so too may the subjects of the Federation in elaboration of and in compliance with the 2002 Federal Law on Advocate Activity and the Advokatura in the Russian Federation and other federal legislation.

Advocates were, prior to 1 July 2002, organised into 'colleges of advocates', which were independent, self-governing professional associations.[14] Under the 2002 Federal Law on Advocate Activity, so-called 'advocate formations' may take one of four forms: the advocate cabinet, college of advocates, advocate office, and legal consultation office. It is for the individual advocate to decide the form and place of his preference, and to notify the council of the chamber of advocates of that choice in the established procedure.

The advocate who prefers to operate as a sole practitioner forms the advocate cabinet, having informed his chamber of advocates by registered letter the requisite information about himself, address of the cabinet, and telephone, cable, postal, and other addresses. An advocate cabinet is not a juridical person. Agreements with clients are concluded between the advocate and the client and registered in the documentation of the cabinet. If the advocate wishes, he may work from home.

Two or more advocates have the right to form a college of advocates, which is a non-commercial organisation based on membership and operating on the basis of a

[13] V N Burobin (ed), Адвокатская деятельность: Учебно-практическое пособие [*Advocate Activity: Instructional-Practical Manual*] (2001) 13.
[14] The foundation documents of a number of colleges are reproduced in V M Anufriev and S N Gavrilov, Организация и деятельность адвокатуры в России [*Organisation and Activity of the Advokatura in Russia*] (2001).

charter confirmed by its founders and constitutive contract concluded by them. The founders and members of the college must be advocates, information concerning which is contained only in one regional register. In the constitutive contract the founders determine the conditions for transferring their property to the college of advocates, the procedure and conditions for admitting new members, the rights and duties of each, and the procedure and conditions for withdrawal. The charter must contain information established in federal legislation, and the same procedure for notifying the formation of the college of advocates to the chamber of advocates applies as in the case of sole practitioners. The college of advocates is a juridical person and may create branches anywhere in the Russian Federation or abroad, but within Russia must also register in the regional register of the relevant subject of the Federation and, if a foreign branch is created, this must be registered in the regional register where they were founded. Property contributed by the founders of a college of advocates belongs to the last by right of ownership. A college of advocates has limited responsibility: members of a college of advocates are not liable for its obligations, and the college of advocates is not liable for obligations of its members. However, agreements to render legal assistance in a college of advocates are concluded between the advocate and the client and are registered in the documentation of the college of advocates. A college of advocates may not be transformed into a commercial organisation or into any other non-commercial organisation (except into an advocate office, under certain conditions). The rules of the non-commercial partnership apply to a college of advocates insofar as they are not inconsistent with the 2002 Federal Law on Advocate Activity.

Two or more advocates also may choose to form an advocate office, which requires the conclusion of a partnership contract in simple written form. Under the partnership contract the advocate-partners are obliged to combine their efforts to render legal services in the name of all the partners. The contract must make provision for its period of operation, the procedure for the taking of decisions by the partners, the procedure for electing the managing partner and the competence thereof, and any other material conditions. Under this structure, agreements with clients are concluded by any partner in the name of all partners on the basis of powers of attorney issued by them. The power of attorney must set out all limitations on the competence of a partner who is concluding agreements with clients and third persons.

A legal consultation office is formed by the chamber of advocates in a subject of the Federation in which the total number of advocates in all advocate formations on the territory of a judicial district comprises less than two per federal judge. The legal consultation office is a non-commercial organisation created in the form of an institution, and is regulated by the Federal Law on Noncommercial Organisations. The conditions for operating the legal consultation office are determined by legislation of the respective subject of the Federation.

Advocates

An advocate, as defined in the 2002 Federal Law on Advocate Activity, is a person who has received the 'status of an advocate' in the established procedure and the right to effectuate advocate activity. He is an independent advisor on legal questions and does not have the right to engage in other paid activity except for scholarly, teaching, and other creative activities. In rendering legal assistance the advocate, according to legislation, (1) gives advice on and references to legal questions in oral or written form; (2) draws up applications, appeals, petitions, and other documents of a legal character; (3) represents the interests of the client in constitutional court proceedings; (4) participates as a representative or defender of the client in a civil, criminal, or administrative proceeding; (5) participates as a representative of the client in an arbitration court, international commercial arbitration, and other agencies for the settlement of disputes; (6) represents the interest of the client in agencies of State power, agencies of social associations, social associations, and other organisations, courts, agencies of State power, courts and law enforcement agencies of foreign States, and non-State agencies of foreign States; (8) represents the client in execution proceedings and tax relations; and may render other legal assistance not prohibited by a federal law.

The status of an advocate may be acquired by natural persons who have a higher legal education received in an accredited institution of higher professional education or a learned degree in a legal specialisation. The individual must have either two years' work experience in a legal speciality or undergo a traineeship. Persons who lack dispositive legal capacity, or who have a record of a criminal conviction may not be advocates. The decision to confer the status of advocate is taken by the qualifications commission attached to the chamber of advocates of the subject of the Russian Federation concerned after a qualifications examination is completed. In a significant change from previous practice, foreign citizens and stateless persons who have received the status of advocate in the procedure established by the 2002 Federal Law on Advocate Activity may engage in advocate activity throughout the entire territory of the Russian Federation.

The status of advocate is conferred for an indefinite period and is not linked in any way with age. An advocate is required to swear an oath as follows: 'I solemnly swear to perform the duties of advocate honourably and conscientiously and to defend the rights, freedoms, and interests of clients being guided by the Constitution of the Russian Federation, law, and code of professional ethics of an advocate'.

Advocate activity

'Advocate activity' is a defined concept in the 2002 Federal Law on Advocate Activity: 'qualified legal assistance rendered on a professional basis by persons who have received the status of advocate in the procedure established . . . to natural and juridical persons . . . for the purposes of defence of their rights, freedoms, and interests, and also ensuring access to justice' (Article 1). This sweeping definition is attenuated by certain exclusions, namely legal assistance rendered by workers of legal services of juridical persons, and also by workers of agencies of State power and agencies of local self-government, and participants and workers of organisations rendering legal services, as well as by individual entrepreneurs; and by notaries, patent attornies (the last subject to certain exceptions). There is a limitation on certain terms associated with advocates. The expressions 'advokatura', 'advocate activity', 'advocate', 'chamber of advocates', 'advocate formation', and 'legal consultation office' in their Russian-language versions, or word combinations thereof, are reserved exclusively for advocate formations.

There are no political constraints on advocates, and they are free to join any political party. Indeed, the Guild of Russian Advocates registered itself as a political party and nominated candidates for the 1999 parliamentary elections, some of whom were successful.

An advocate has the right to remuneration for his work provided that if all or any part of such remuneration is received in circumvention of the cashier in the legal consultation office, this is regarded as tax evasion, a violation of advokatura rules, and a disciplinary offence. Except for legal aid assignments which are compulsory and duty rosters in the legal consultation office, the advocate is at liberty to determine his own professional workload. Some advocates give the greater portion of their time to teaching, research, law enforcement activities, or legislative advice.

Most advocates spend the greater part of their time giving legal advice and drafting documents. As a rule, it is the advocate himself who gathers evidence or other data for submission to an investigator or to a court in a criminal or civil case or who retains a private detective to do so. An advocate has the right to represent the interests of a client in all State and social organisations: the courts, procuracy, Ministry of Internal Affairs, Federal Security Service, and others. On 27 March 1996 the Constitutional Court of the Russian Federation held that the participation of an advocate in a criminal case could not depend upon whether the advocate had clearance for access to State secrets. Article 21 of the Law on State Secrecy, the Court ruled, did not extend to advocates participating as defenders in a criminal proceeding.[15] Construing Article 47 of the 1960 RSFSR Code of Criminal Procedure to exclude privately-practicing jurists who are not members of a college

---

[15] The Russian Supreme Court has held that substituting during the preliminary investigation a lawyer from a law firm who was not a member of a college of advocates for an advocate who was on holiday in order to avoid a two-day delay in the proceedings was an error which required the case to be returned for further investigation. See Бюллетень Верховного суда Российской Федерации [Bulletin of the Supreme Court of the Russian Federation], no 3 (1998), 15. In this case the person under investigation objected to the substitution.

of advocates from participating in the preliminary investigation was held to be unconstitutional by the Constitutional Court in a Decree issued 28 January 1997.[16]

Legal Fees

Fees are determined by the contract with the client and may be based on an hourly rate or a specific fee for certain documents or transactions; in early 2002 about one-third of such contracts were with natural persons and the balance with juridical persons. The difference between Russian and foreign legal fees has narrowed considerably in the transition to a market economy. Certain categories of legal assistance are rendered free of charge to citizens whose earnings are below the living minimum, for example: for recovery of alimony, compensation of harm caused by injury or other impairment of health or death of a breadwinner connected with work, applications for pensions or benefits, and questions connected with rehabilitation for those who suffered political repression.

Legal advice is given, as a rule, on the basis of a written agreement between the advocate and the client. Such a contract for the compensated rendering of services is regulated by Chapter 39 of the Civil Code of the Russian Federation. However, certain types of representation, for example, in a constitutional, civil, administrative, or criminal proceeding, are made on the basis of the contract of commission. In this event the 2002 Federal Law on Advocate Activity imposes obligatory conditions upon the contract of commission that differ somewhat from those contained in the Civil Code of the Russian Federation.

The request of an investigator, procurator, or court for an appointed advocate was mandatory in the past for the presidium of the college of advocates and the managers of legal consultation offices[17] and remains binding upon advocate formations. They were obliged to make an appointment within a 24-hour period after receiving the request. If the financial status of the accused did not enable him to pay the costs of the advocate appointed, the investigator, procurator, or court has the right to exempt him from the payment of legal fees. *Pro bono* legal services are at State expense, although in practice it has been extremely difficult for legal consultation offices to be reimbursed for such legal advice. Outside Moscow it has been estimated that more than half of all legal assistance is granted to clients free of charge.

---

[16] The Letter of the Ministry of Justice of the RF, No 09–09/19–94 containing the Statute was dated 31 January 1994. For the text, see G L Pipilenko (comp), Адвокатура [*Advokatura*] (1998) 69–71. The Statute has been supplemented by various Letters and other documents clarifying its provisions. By a Decision of the Supreme Court of the Russian Federation of 14 November 2000, the Statute was declared to be illegal and not subject to application.

[17] See Hazard (n 8 above) 281–291.

The transition to a market economy has removed ceilings on the earnings of advocates. Those engaged in commercial work are likely to do better than those who concentrate upon family, housing, or labour relations. The practice of contingency fees, however, has met with legal problems; courts have held that a 'contingency' fee is not related to the services performed and the 'result' obtained. For the most part contracts for legal services based on a contingency arrangement have been unenforceable under Russian law.

Legal ethics

Difficult ethical and moral conundrums can arise for Russian advocates no less than other professionals. In 1925 the Moscow College of Defenders published a volume recounting presidium decisions relating to legal ethics.[18] The practice appears to have been infrequent,[19] and so far as can be determined, no Russian College of Advocates has a comprehensive Statute or regulation on the matter. Over the years, however, several draft codes, statutes, or rules of ethics of Russian advocates have been prepared and engendered lively discussion.[20]

The 2002 Law on Advocate Activity relegates to the Federal Chamber of Advocates the adoption of a code of professional ethics. That Law, however, contains certain requirements of an ethical nature which will be incorporated and elaborated in the ethics code. As a matter of Russian legislation, an advocate does not have the right to render legal assistance to a person if the advice requested is known to have an illegal character, nor to accept a person as a client if the advocate has an autonomous interest with regard to the subject of the agreement with the client which differs from that of the client, or if the advocate participated as a judge, arbitrator, mediator, procurator, investigator, inquiry official, expert,

---

[18] See I I Skliarskii, Дисциплинарная практика Московской городской и областной коллегий адвокатов (Методическое пособие для адвокатов) [*Disciplinary Practice of Moscow City and Regional Colleges of Advocates (Methods Manual for Advocates)*] (1971), published by the Moscow City and Moscow Regional colleges of advocates.

[19] A draft Code of advocate's ethics and draft Rules of professional ethics of Russian advocates are published in M Iu Barshchevskii, Организация и деятельность адвокатуры в России [*Organisation and Activity of the Advokatura in Russia*] (1997) 291–308; the Rules of Professional Advocate Ethics confirmed by the General Meeting of the Astrakhan Inter-Territory Specialised College of Advocates on 15 January 1998 are published in K K Lebedev, Правовое обслуживание бизнеса (корпоративный юрист) [*Legal Servicing of Business (Corporate Jurist)*] (2001) 402–408.

[20] In response to the decision of the Constitutional Court, the Pension Fund of the Russian Federation issued a Letter on 17 March 1998, No EB–09–28/1860 observing that the Constitutional Court, in striking down the new rates of contributions, did not specify what rates should be imposed, leaving that decision to the legislator. Rather therefore than reinstating the previous rate (which would seem to be logical given that the new rate was declared illegal and the decision of the Court had direct effect), the Pension Fund ruled that contributions at 28 per cent must continue until the legislature came to a decision about a new rate. This was far from the end of the story, however; litigation continued over the matter in the Constitutional Court for some time. See V I Sergeev, Комментарий к положению об адвокатуре [*Commentary to the Statute on the Advokatura*] (2001) 43–50.

specialist, interpreter in a case or is a witness or victim, or if he was an official within whose competence it was to take a decision with regard to the interests of the client, or if the advocate is a relative or in family relations with an official who took part or who is taking part in investigating or considering the case with regard to the client, or if his interests are contrary to those of his client. Moreover, an advocate may not take a position contrary to the will of his client except in special situations, nor divulge information communicated to him by the client in connection with legal assistance rendered unless the client so consents, nor resign from a defence undertaken. Advocates are prohibited from rendering nontransparent cooperation to agencies engaged in operational search activity.

The duties of an advocate likewise are reflective of certain ethical principles. An advocate must honourably, reasonably, and in good faith insist upon the rights and legal interests of his client using all means not prohibited by Russian legislation. And he must comply with the code of professional ethics of an advocate and execute decisions of organs of the chamber of advocates and Federal Chamber of Advocates.

It is worthy of note that what in the west is routinely referred to as 'client confidentiality' in the Russian Federation is labelled 'advocate secrecy'. Nonetheless, any information connected with the rendering of legal assistance by an advocate to his client is classified as 'advocate secrecy'. An advocate may not be summoned and interrogated as a witness concerning circumstances which became known to him in connection with the application of a client for legal assistance or the actual rendering of such assistance. An advocate's office or dwelling premises may be searched only on the basis of a court decision.

Foreign lawyers and legal services

In the Soviet period the Moscow City College of Advocates maintained a special legal consultation office to handle, principally, civil cases for foreign citizens and organisations. It was one of two such institutions empowered to give legal advice throughout the entire former Soviet Union. Called 'Iniurkollegiia', it is still in existence, specialising as before in inheritance, property, insurance, intellectual property, and related matters. Its fees have historically been approximate to those charged by leading Anglo-American law firms.

Since 1988, foreign law firms have established various forms of presence in the Russian Federation, ranging from a hotel-room office, to a representation office, to a Russian juridical person. Foreigners may apply to them for legal services or to any Russian legal consultation office, law firm, college, bureau, cabinet, or private practitioner. The hourly rates charged by foreign law firms are similar to those in New York and London; Russian law firms as a rule are less expensive than foreign firms but more expensive than for Russian citizens or juridical persons.

In early 2002 there were about 60 foreign law firms who claimed a presence in Moscow, St Petersburg, Novgorod, Samara, Vladivostok, and other Russian cities. They ranged in size from one to 40 lawyers. Many were without Russian-speaking partners, and most concentrated upon serving foreign clients investing in Russia.

B. The Jurisconsult

Jurisconsults in the Russian Federation are legal advisers to the President of the Russian Federation, the Russian Government, the courts, the Federal Assembly, ministries, departments, and local government units at all levels, juridical persons, and social organisations. Foreign lawyers employed by foreign law firms in Russia are classed as jurisconsults who, unless advocates in their own right, may not engage in advocate activity.

(1) History

A thorough study of the jurisconsult in pre-revolutionary Russia has yet to be made. The term itself dates in the Russian language to the late seventeenth century, when it seems to have meant any jurist or lawyer. The position of jurisconsult existed in Russia in the late nineteenth century, appeared at once in Soviet people's commissariats and other governmental agencies after the October Revolution, and survived in a few of the large enterprises, where despite the early expectations of an administered economy and society, their skills were provisionally required. In the categories of Soviet workers established in 1918 for wage scales, jurisconsults were included in category 1 of Group I, the highest classification.[21] By 1920 the need for legally-trained personnel had become desperate. On 11 May 1920 the Council of People's Commissars ordered all individuals with a higher legal education to register so that 'proper use of "their" specialised knowledge' might be made.[22] One week later the same agency created 'consultation subsections of justice' to be staffed by jurisconsults in the 'people's commissariats and all central institutions of the RSFSR'.[23] The Moscow College of Defenders in 1922 requested the Moscow City Soviet to authorise members of the College to hold jointly the post of jurisconsult and practise in the College, which was approved on 23 July 1922.[24]

---

[21] CУ РСФСР (1918), no 48, item 567.
[22] CУ РСФСР (1920), no 47, item 211.
[23] CУ РСФСР (1920), no 51, item 221.
[24] See Yu Luryi, 'Jurisconsults in the Soviet Economy', in D Barry *et al* (eds), *Soviet Law After Stalin* (1979), II 170–171.

The establishment of the Procuracy in 1922 led to a reorganisation in the regulation of the jurisconsult. Supervision over the jurisconsult vested in the People's
Commissariat of Justice in May 1920 was transferred to the Procuracy, which was
to register them and oversee their activity in justice agencies. Outside this commissariat, regulation of jurisconsults largely became a matter for the organisation
employing them. In industry an all-union conference of jurisconsults was convoked at the initiative of the USSR Supreme Economic Council, which on 14
August 1925 enacted a statute on the jurisconsult subordinate to that Council.
On 30 March 1927 the RSFSR Council of People's Commissars enacted a Decree
'On Jurisconsults of State Institutions and Enterprises and Cooperative
Organisations and the Supervision of Their Activity'.[25] The decree confirmed the
supervisory role of the Procuracy over the jurisconsult, which was broadened by
subsequent legislation. Throughout the late 1920s conferences of jurisconsults
were held on an all-union or lesser scale to exchange work experience, hear
reports, and even adopt resolutions about organising and supervising the profession.

Unlike the advocates, however, jurisconsults have never formed a professional
body that transcended ministerial or departmental lines. The transition from the
NEP to the planned economy posed an initial threat to the jurisconsult because
law was expected rapidly to wither away and be supplanted by Plan. The 1927 legislation on jurisconsults had become obsolete; in most branches of industry the
1927 decree was superseded de facto by commissariat statutes on jurisconsults
from 1932–39. The supervisory role of the Procuracy diminished accordingly.
The 1939 Statute on the Advokatura prohibited advocates from serving simultaneously as jurisconsults, but in 1941 enterprises which did not have the post of
jurisconsult included in their personnel establishment were allowed to retain an
advocate's services by agreement.

In 1957 Khrushchev initiated a major reorganisation and decentralisation of the
administration of the national economy. These reforms were followed by local
legislation on the jurisconsult endowing the post with widely varying duties and
status. In the RSFSR a 'model statute' on the jurisconsult was enacted in 1963 to
aid enterprises and organisations in drafting their own.

The 1965 and 1987 economic reforms in the Soviet Union gave State enterprises
greater responsibility for their contractual relations with other enterprises and
expanded the scope of economic accountability. The enlarged discretion accorded
to enterprise management required disciplining; law and contract were the chosen instruments and State Arbitrazh the principal forum. A massive increase
in legal personnel was required, together with other legal improvements. Several

---

[25] СУ РСФСР (1927), no 36, item 238.

tentative measures were taken, but the key document for the jurisconsult was the Decree of 23 December 1970 'On the Improvement of Legal Work in the National Economy'. The Decree, inter alia, required the enactment of the General Statute on the jurisconsult, the formation or strengthening of legal departments in the central apparatus and at all levels of economic administration, local government, and agriculture; the USSR Ministry of Justice was reinforced in its role of effectuating methods direction over legal work in the national economy and improving the substance and systematisation of Soviet legislation; the admission of students to law faculties was greatly increased and measures were introduced to raise the qualifications of jurisconsults already in post.[26]

(2) Current legislation

On 22 June 1972 the USSR Council of Ministers confirmed the General Statute on the Legal Section (or Office), Chief (or Senior) Jurisconsult, and Jurisconsult of a Ministry, Department, Executive Committee of a Soviet of People's Deputies, Enterprise, Organisation, or Institution, which remains in force as amended 4 December 1980, 1 December 1987, and 21 December 1990. On the basis of this General Statute, ministries and departments drafted and confirmed their own internal statutes for their respective legal offices or legal personnel. Social organisations were recommended to use the General Statute as a model when establishing a procedure for carrying on legal work within their organisations. Collective farms and intercollective farm enterprises and organisations arranged their legal services pursuant to an Instruction confirmed jointly by the ministers of agriculture and justice on 3 January 1973.

In the Russian market economy the jurisconsult remains, unlike the advocate, a salaried employee in the establishment where he works. Jurisconsults are by far the largest component of the Russian legal profession. Ministries, State enterprises, and local government continue to employ jurisconsults on the basis of the 1972 and subsequent Soviet legislation. On 23 September 1994, for example, the State Customs Service issued an Order confirming the General Statute on the Legal Section, Legal Group, and Jurisconsult of the Customs Agency of the Russian Federation, in force as amended 24 December 2001. Each subdivision (legal section, legal group, and jurisconsult) is to operate on the basis of its own Statute confirmed at an appropriate level of the State Customs Committee system. On 2 April 2002 the Government of Russia confirmed a Model Statute on the Legal Service of a Federal Agency of Executive Power.

The private sector is the new professional frontier for the jurisconsult: economic societies and partnerships of all types, foreign companies with accredited representations and branches in Russia, and foreign law firms. Except for the law firms,

---

[26] J E Giddings [Henderson], 'The Jurisconsult in the USSR', *Review of Socialist Law*, I (1975), 171–211.

which by definition offer paid legal services, the legal personnel of juridical persons are essentially unregulated except by reference to the legislation of the Soviet era.

(3) Functions

The duties of the classical jurisconsult employed by a ministry, State enterprise, local soviet, or collective farm do not differ materially in principle from those in the Soviet era. In general the jurisconsult verifies whether draft legal enactments conform to legislation in force; whether his 'visa' on documents is required seems to be more a matter of local practice than formal legal requirement. He supervises the conformity to law of internal regulations and enactments and prepares amendments for these when necessary. He helps to draft labour contracts, the collective labour contract if there is one, drafts and reviews contracts, organises and carries on claims work, advises on the procedure for the acceptance of goods and products, represents his employer in arbitration, helps prepare draft normative acts or opinions thereon and gives advice on matters which arise during the course of operations, and prepares materials relating to theft, shortages, and the like for transfer to investigative or judicial agencies. The jurisconsult commonly is called upon to advise other organisations connected with his employer, such as the local trade union committee, or individual employees. He has responsibility for forming the internal law library and informing others about new legislation.

Unlike their foreign counterparts, it is still uncommon for the management of Russian economic societies and partnerships to use their legal staff in direct negotiations with contracting parties or to require jurisconsults to advise on the legal aspects of general business strategy. Jurisconsults are not, as a rule, transaction or 'deal' lawyers.

The ministerial jurisconsult has less responsibility for direct economic operations and more work involving legislation, administration, and supervision of inferior structural subdivisions or enterprises. In some ministries the jurisconsult may be heavily engaged in questions of foreign law or public and private international law. The ministries of foreign affairs, foreign economic relations, and transport are examples. The jurisconsult of an agency of local self-government or a subject of the Russian Federation deals extensively with the legality of draft normative materials and gives legal advice to the local government and to individual deputies.

(4) Methods assistance

With the demise of the Planned Economy in Russia, the Ministry of Justice plays a minimal role in extending assistance to jurisconsults, largely abandoning its issuance of 'methods instructions and recommendations' to jurisconsults. Whether as the market economy develops the profession of salaried legal advisor or jurisconsult splits into those employed by the State and those employed in the private sector remains to be seen.

C. Legal Education

The education or 'formation' of the legal profession in Russia is of crucial importance to an understanding of the Russian legal system. It is in the law schools that the knowledge, skills, and values of the jurist are initially inculcated, often to be followed by a period of further training or 'apprenticeship' in a law office, enterprise, or legal agency. It is in the Russian law schools that the training of the rising generation and the retraining of the Soviet generations of jurist will be initially accomplished or not.

To understand a lawyer from a foreign legal system, how he conceptualises law and reasons in juristic categories, one must have some familiarity with the way he has been educated to perform legal or other roles in society. The teaching of law in turn is influenced by considerations of the kinds of lawyer which educational institutions seek to produce and the values and skills they undertake to impart.[27] As Russia has integrated into the world market economy, the private sector of legal practice has been re-created after four generations of neglect and suppression, the Russian jurist integrated into international law firms, and Russian domestic and international law firms established. And as Russia integrates into the various European communities, the rule of law must be thoroughly absorbed into the entire Russian legal fabric.[28]

(1) Historical background

Ideas about legal education were in turmoil during the early years following the 1917 October Revolution. Throughout 1918 university law courses continued to be taught essentially as they had been before the Revolution, presumably taking due account of the new government's dismantling of the Tsarist courts, laws, and legal order. The extent to which expectations of a rapid 'dying out' or 'withering away' of law may have affected early attitudes toward legal education is debatable, but there was no doubt in the minds of educational policy-makers that the

---

[27] A literature concerning lawyer skills is emerging. See, eg, L A Voskobitova, L P Mikhailova, and E S Shugrina (eds), Профессиональные навыки: опыт практического обучения [*Professional Skills of the Jurist: Experience of Practical Study*] (2001). The study concentrates on legal clinics, advocacy skills, and interviewing techniques.

[28] See A M Lomonosov and R W Makepeace, 'Legal Education in Russia—Present Challenges and Past Influences', *The Law Teacher*, XXXI (1997) 335–347; G Ajani, 'Legal Education in Russia: Present and Future—An Analysis of the State Educational Standards for Higher Professional Instruction and a Comparison with the European Legal Education Reform Experience', *Review of Central and East European Law*, XXXIII (1997) 267–300.

instructional plans extant at the universities were obsolete and non-Marxian.[29] In August 1918 the Soviet authorities altered admission requirements to make university learning accessible to everyone, irrespective of their social status. For students of proletarian origin the reform was inadequate, since most were ill-prepared to undertake university work. By early 1919 it was decided to train legal personnel elsewhere for employment in Soviet universities. The university law faculties were formally abolished and replaced by faculties of social sciences (FON), which offered, inter alia, courses for judicial and administrative personnel on Soviet law. The early teaching syllabi for the FON were prepared by the politico-legal section of the Socialist Academy of Social Sciences, founded in 1918. The Academy itself offered advanced lectures in law during 1918–19 to some 400 evening students, of whom 50 were regular attendees.[30] In many places 'Workers' Faculties' (рабфак) were formed in 1919–20 to provide secondary-level education on a Marxist basis for students of proletarian background who aspired to higher education. In Autumn 1921 legislation was enacted to give children of proletarian origin preference in admission to educational institutions.

The FON offered courses on the history of State and law, the development of political and legal thought, State law of the Soviet Republic, social law, criminal sociology and policy, labour law and social policy, the history of international law and international relations, and social hygiene and sanitation. The introduction of the NEP in 1921 brought a partial restoration and adaptation of legal institutions previously known in Imperial Russia, such as the Procuracy, further stabilisation of the court system, and an urgent need for codifying and systematising legislation. As the demand for trained legal cadres within the State apparatus intensified, the Workers' Faculties and FON were supplemented by the widespread use of short-term (usually four to six months) courses on the basic principles of new Soviet legislation and codes.[31] The FON were officially abolished in 1924 (though some continued to operate until 1926) and their legal sections were superseded by Faculties of Soviet Law formed at the I Moscow University, Saratov, Irkutsk, eventually Leningrad, and later elsewhere in the country.[32]

The university law faculties offered a four-year course of study, including lectures on the basic principles of the Soviet constitutions, criminal law, economic law,

---

[29] Some were openly hostile to legal education per se. M N Pokrovskii commented, when the law faculties were abolished: 'the science of law was an attractive jacket which concealed the enslavement of hundred of millions by tens of thousands . . . of course, for socialist Russia all such "sciences" are completely useless'. See Народное просвещение, nos 23–25 (1919) 31.

[30] A A Plotnieks, Становление и развитие марксистско-ленинской общей теории права в СССР [*Origin and Development of Marxist-Leninist General Theory of Law in the USSR*] (1978) 114.

[31] See E I Kel'man, О системе юридического образования [*On the System of Legal Education*] (1926).

[32] M M Isaev, 'О высшем юридическим образовании РСФСР' ['On Higher Legal Education of the RSFSR'], Советское право [Soviet Law] no 6 (1927) 116–118.

land law, administrative law, court organisation, criminal procedure, international law, and the cooperative and trade union movement. By 1928 there were some 15,000 Soviet jurists with a higher or secondary legal education.

At the end of the 1920s Soviet legal education was being profoundly affected by contending approaches to the Marxist theory of State and law. Those of the university teaching staff most antipathetic to the revolutionary order had left in 1918–19, and many other progressive but non-Marxian figures were screened out when the law faculties were reopened in 1924–26. There remained nonetheless a diverse, creative, and often original community of Soviet legal scholars excited by the prospect of revolutionary social engineering through law who represented a considerable range of non-Marxian, quasi-Marxian, and Marxian thought.[33] Among those a pre-eminent role on the 'theoretical front' was played by E B Pashukanis (see Chapter 3). By the end of the 1920s Pashukanis and his adherents exercised a predominant influence over legal education by virtue of control over the drafting of teaching syllabi, the placement of teaching personnel, and the implications of his commodity exchange theory for the legal system itself.

The preparation of syllabi for law courses had been concentrated by 1929 in the Institute of Soviet Construction and Law of the Communist Academy, directed by Pashukanis. The new syllabi amounted to a fundamental and far-reaching reworking of earlier eclectic approaches to course syllabi, introducing the terminology and conceptual apparatus of the commodity exchange theory. There was an intense campaign against 'bourgeois' legal scholarship, an appraisal of the principal bourgeois legal institutions, and an examination of the theory of State and law as laid down in the works of Karl Marx, Friedrich Engels, and V I Lenin. The syllabi on the 'Doctrine of the Soviet State', which stressed the political rather than the legal dimension of the Soviet State, and on 'economic and administrative law', which contemplated the abolition of the civil law, especially reflected the notions of the Pashukanis school. The first-year law course on the general theory of law became, in effect, an exposition of the commodity exchange theory, and students studying law externally through correspondence courses, including Party activists, offered by the Institute of Red Professors (of which Pashukanis was Rector), similarly were imbued with this approach.[34]

While law students were absorbing the lessons of the commodity exchange school, the larger implications of Pashukanis' views were becoming noticeable in legal education. The imminent withering away of law boded ill for legal careers.

---

[33] An excellent selection of writings from this period is given in M Jaworskyj, *Soviet Political Thought* (1967).

[34] For a detailed account of these developments, see R Sharlet, 'Pashukanis and the Withering Away of Law in the USSR', in S Fitzpatrick (ed), *Cultural Revolution in Russia, 1928–1931* (1978) 169–188; id, 'Pashukanis and the Rise of Soviet Marxist Jurisprudence, 1924–1930', *Soviet Union* (1974) I, 103–121.

Study of the purely 'legal infrastructure'—the constitution and State system—was being phased out of the curriculum, and law school enrolments dropped dramatically. In 1930–1 Pashukanis and his associates were obliged to modify their position that the State would rapidly wither away, but throughout the early 1930s they continued to emphasise the 'flexible' and 'expedient' dimensions of the law as an instrument of revolutionary policy rather than its stabilising role.

The adoption of the 1936 USSR Constitution heralded a transition to a policy of 'stability of laws', which in the realm of legal education meant a restoration and expansion of university-level law teaching and a substantial increase in numbers of law students. Pashukanis himself disappeared from the scene in January 1937 during the purges, to be succeeded in the leadership of the legal profession by A Ia Vyshinskii. Almost immediately after Pashukanis' execution, civil law was restored to the law curriculum in place of economic law and a massive effort undertaken to revise course syllabi and prepare new textbooks.[35]

In 1936 the system of legal education was reorganised. The USSR People's Commissariat of Justice assumed principal responsibility for providing legal education, appointing the directors of law schools, and preparing the syllabi and textbooks for courses to be taught.[36] Four-year courses of legal studies were offered in juridical institutes and university law faculties. Special short-term courses of from six months to one year were established in outlying areas of the country to raise the proficiency of legal personnel in post. In addition, correspondence schools and three-month courses to train what today might be called paralegal and auxiliary legal personnel were introduced, and an advanced two-year course in law for higher level legal personnel at the All-Union Law Academy.[37]

Except for the early war years, legal education expanded from the late 1930s for nearly two decades. The course of law studies in universities was extended to five years in the mid-1940s, and pursuant to a Decree of the Central Committee of the CPSU adopted on 5 October 1946 and a joint Party-Government Decree of 30 August 1954, a number of steps were taken to improve the quality of legal studies. By the late 1950s, however, perhaps influenced by the transition of Soviet society to the stage of the building of communism and a concomitant emphasis on transferring State functions to non-State bodies, sharp reductions in law school

---

[35] An American lawyer's student perspective on Soviet legal education from 1934–7 is recorded in contemporary correspondence and lecture notes, reproduced in W E Butler (intro), *Law Student Life in Moscow: The Letters and Course Notes of John N. Hazard, 1934–1939* (1978); excerpts from the letters are published in D Barry, W E Butler, and G Ginsburgs (eds), *Contemporary Soviet Law* (1974).

[36] For the period 1938–45, see E A Prianishnikov, Страницы истории института-законодательства и сравнительного правоведения [*Pages of History of the Institute of Legislation and Comparative Law*] (2000) 64–80.

[37] See J N Hazard, 'Legal Education in the Soviet Union', (1938) Wisconsin Law Review 562–579.

enrolments were imposed. Between 1956 and 1963 the number of law graduates in full-time study declined by more than 50 per cent (although night school and correspondence courses kept the total number of law graduates in 1963 at a higher level than in 1956). In the summer of 1964 a decree of the Central Committee of the CPSU (unpublished) reasserted the need for better jurists and an expansion and improvement of legal education, a need more keenly felt after the economic reforms of 1965. The economic reforms, inter alia, gave greater discretion and independence to economic units in concluding economic contracts, foreseeing at the same time that economic units would exercise their discretion within the constraints of the applicable law. It followed, of course, that economic units would require more and better advice in these matters from qualified legal personnel. A similar devolution of responsibility within the lower levels of local government also was accompanied by a substantial increase in the number of jurisconsults employed.

The veritable explosion in the number of Soviet law graduates had a dramatic impact upon the qualifications and quality of the corpus of legal personnel as a whole. In 1936, when the reversal of Pashukanis' theories commenced in earnest, less than 6.7 per cent of Soviet judges had any formal higher legal education and more than 50 per cent had no legal education at all.[38] By 1980 virtually all judges and procurators had a higher legal education. Today it is almost impossible to enter any branch of the legal profession without an educational qualification of this level.

(2) Modern legal education

The demise of the Soviet Union and the transition to democratic institutions and a market-oriented economy has brought with it a certain reform of higher legal education, but not a fundamental transformation. Marxism-Leninism disappeared promptly from the syllabus, as one would expect; new legislation brought new courses (taxation, commercial law, entrepreneurial law, etc) or a thorough reworking of traditional staples in the light of new codes (civil law, criminal law, family law, and others). Dozens of educational institutions added law faculties or departments (sometimes even existing law faculties opened additional law schools) and the private sector founded new law schools or faculties. The Institute of State and Law of the Russian Academy of Sciences established the Academy University of Law for undergraduate and postgraduate training; the Academy of National Economy created the M M Speranskii Law Faculty for undergraduate training and collaborated with the University of Manchester to introduce an LLM degree, and with Essex University to initiate a PhD degree, within the Moscow

---

[38] Data published in Ia Berman, 'О правовом образовании' [On Legal Education], Советское Государство и право ['Soviet State and Law'], no 5 (1936) 115.

Higher School of Social and Economic Sciences attached to the Academy; Moscow State University added a college of law to its own law faculty; analogous schools were founded in St Petersburg and other cities. By 1997 some 79 State higher educational institutions contained law faculties, ten higher educational institutions of law operated independently, 47 operated within the system of the Ministry of Internal Affairs plus an additional seven concerned with continuing legal education, three within the Federal Security Service and military, and at least 50 law faculties existed within non-State institutions of higher education. Tuition costs have become for most Russian families a major financial consideration.

The system of university and postgraduate education, including legal education, in the Russian Federation is regulated by the Law on Education of 10 July 1992 in the version of 13 January 1996 as amended 16 November 1997, 20 July 2000, 7 August 2000, 29 December 2001, and 13 February 2002,[39] and by the Federal Law on Higher and Postgraduate Vocational Education of 22 August 1996, as amended to 25 June 2002. These laws determine the principles of State education policy, among which are the humanistic character of education, the priority of universal human values, the free development of the individual, nurturing respect for human rights and freedoms, love for the environment, the Motherland, and the family, general accessibility to education, the secular character of education in State and municipal institutions, freedom and pluralism in education, and others. The principles are pursued through the establishment of State Educational Standards (hereinafter 'GOST') laying down an obligatory minimum for the content of educational programmes, the maximum instructional load for students, and requirements for the training of graduates. An accredited educational institution which trains graduates of poor quality can be sued by the State in court for compensation of additional expenditures needed to retrain the graduates in other educational institutions.

Although law is offered to some extent at the level of secondary vocational education, jurists are trained at the standard of higher vocational and postgraduate professional education. GOST 021100 (jurisprudence) lays down the requirements for training a jurist. The training may take the form of full-time day, evening, or correspondence education. Citizens of the Russian Federation have the right to receive higher vocational and postgraduate professional education in State or municipal educational institutions within the limits of the GOST on a competitive basis.

The aim of Russian higher legal education as set out in GOST 021100 is to train jurists who are experts, or specialists, in law after five years of undergraduate study.

---

[39] СЗ РФ (1996), no 3, item 150; (1997), no 47, item 5341; (1999), no 28, item 3493; (2000), no 30, item 3120; no 33, item 3348; (2001), no 53(I), item 5025; (2002), no 7, item 631.

Whether graduates choose to continue in an academic career, become a judge, or work as a legal practitioner (jurisconsult or advocate) or procurator, all are expected to undergo the same general training in the foundation subjects of Russian law. The general requirements for a jurist are that he or she possesses civic maturity and is socially active, professional ethics, and 'legal and psychological culture', a profound respect for law and an attitude of care towards the social values of the rule-of-law State, the honour and dignity of citizens, a high moral consciousness, humanity, firm moral convictions, a feeling of duty and of responsibility for the fate of people and the task entrusted to them. The jurist is a person of principle and independence in ensuring and protecting the rights, freedoms, and legal interests of the individual. He has the requisite will and insistence to execute legal decisions made and a feeling of intolerance for any violation of law in his own professional activity. He should be acquainted with the basic teachings in the humanities and socio-economic sciences, capable of analysing scientifically socially significant problems and processes, and know how to use the methods of these sciences in various types of professional and social activities. Ethical and legal norms regulating the relations of individuals and of society and of the environment must be part of his make-up, and he must know how to take them into account when working out ecological and social projects. The jurist should have an integral understanding of the processes and phenomena which originate in nature, living and non-living, and comprehend these at a standard needed to resolve tasks which arise in the course of performing vocational functions.

By training, if not ability, the jurist should be capable of continuing his education at the level of postgraduate studies or the magistratura and be able to carry on vocational activities in a 'foreign language milieu'. He should have scientific knowledge about a healthy way of life and the skills for physical self-improvement, possess the culture of thought and art of logical analysis, know the general laws thereof, and be able to express himself in writing and orally both correctly and logically. The jurist organises his labour on a scientific basis and possesses the full range of computer skills applicable to his vocational activities. In an era when science is developing and social policy is changing, the jurist is capable of re-evaluating accumulated experience, analysing his opportunities, knows how to acquire new knowledge, and uses modern information educational technologies. He appreciates the essence and social significance of his future profession, the basic problems of his discipline, and sees their interconnection with the integral system of knowledge. Capable of professionally building and using models to describe and predict various phenomena, he can undertake the quantitative and qualitative analysis of these. He can formulate the tasks connected with performing his vocational functions and can use the methods of the legal and other sciences to realise them. He collaborates with colleagues, knows how to work with and in groups, can take management decisions under trying conditions, knows the psychology of people and individual social groups, has teaching skills, and can assist with the legal education of laymen.

The foregoing general requirements are linked in the GOST with knowledge and skills arising from the study of philosophy, logic, psychology, pedagogy, culturology, history, philology, mathematics, and physical culture. In the field of language, for example, the jurist should, in addition to the Russian language, have a minimum command of 1,500–2,000 words and word combinations in a foreign language and be able to use them correctly in oral and written discourse, be able to translate texts with a dictionary, work without a dictionary when searching for information, and prepare annotations and abstracts in a foreign language.

The educational values and aims which shape the jurist are expected to be achieved through the so-called 'obligatory minimum' of academic subjects. These form the core curriculum for higher vocational education accredited by the State. The foundation humanities, socio-economic, and mathematical subjects include: philosophy, foreign language, culturology, Russian history, sociology, politology, psychology, economic theory, sport, mathematics and informatics, conceptions of the modern natural sciences, and certain elective subjects which, it is recommended, might include logic, Latin, and rhetoric. The courses in law build upon these foundations. The obligatory minimum includes: theory of State and law, history of political and legal doctrines, history of Russian State and law, history of the State and law of foreign countries, Russian constitutional law, the constitutional law of foreign countries, civil law, civil procedure, administrative law, labour law, criminal law, criminal procedure, criminalistics, international law, ecological law, land law, Roman law, private international law, and financial law, plus elective subjects offered by each individual faculty of law. These are followed by special subjects: Russian municipal law, Russian entrepreneurial law, commercial law, family law, criminology, criminal-executory law, law enforcement agencies, and procuracy supervision, together with other specialist courses which the faculty may offer. Each student also spends 21 weeks in so-called 'practice', usually a form of internship with legal agencies or law firms, and 17 weeks preparing a dissertation. In all the obligatory minimum consists during a five-year period of 167 weeks of instruction (8,930 hours), 21 weeks of practice, 17 weeks to prepare the dissertation, four weeks for compulsory State examinations, and 41 weeks of vacation.

Within the above criteria, each individual law faculty may alter the required number of hours for each discipline within certain parameters provided that the weekly workload for students is not increased and the minimum content of the syllabus for each subject is maintained. The hours of instruction include time allocated to prepare essays and other course work.

Pending final approval of the obligatory minimum, State and private instructional programmes share an uneasy alliance. The experimentation of the early

1990s is giving way to the reintroduction of State-imposed standards and curriculum rigidity. Smaller seminars continue to be typical of the last two years of study, with a substantial dissertation as a diploma work. Attention is given to information and computer skills. At least eight major computer banks of Russian legislation compete for the market. Most Russian law graduates know how to use them. Interpersonal skills receive less attention. Advocacy and other team skills are rarely part of the curriculum. Interdisciplinary training, on the other hand, is part of the curriculum. Both the pre-revolutionary Russian educational tradition and Marxism-Leninism itself in their own ways accentuated the importance of the social, economic, political, and historical sciences for a comprehension of law. Comparative law plays a minor role, the Socratic method rarely utilised, practical workshops normally shunned.

Within the law faculties, headed by a dean, the key structural units are the chairs of law created for particular branches or subjects of law. A chair is usually headed by a professor, around whom are grouped senior and junior university staff of a similar specialisation and the students who have chosen to concentrate on that area of law. Each chair has an office where students may meet the teaching staff, diploma theses may be defended, and the affairs of the chair conducted. The number of chairs varies from one university to another, depending upon the number of students and the quality and importance of the teaching staff; in new law faculties more modest physical facilities are requiring adjustments to the accoutrements of the classic chair.

Admission

An applicant for the study of law in an institution of higher education is required to have completed the full programme of secondary education and successfully undergo oral admissions examinations administered by the institution concerned on, as a rule, the Russian language, Russian literature, and the history of Russia. Interest in studying law continues to be exceptionally high, and the best institutions have many more candidates than places. Ability to pay is a major consideration.

Course of study

The full-time course of study in law requires four or five years, depending upon the institution chosen. Evening programmes or correspondence degrees require five or six years. Students who are willing to undertake self-study and sit the examinations when they consider themselves ready can sometimes shorten the degree course by as much as two years. The programmes at Moscow State University illustrate the full range of possible programmes.

The Law Faculty offers on a full-time day-study basis the speciality jurisprudence (правоведение, sometimes called in other universities юриспруденция) over a five-year term. Students may specialise in State law, civil law, or criminal law from the fourth year. There is an evening division which requires six years to complete. Upon completion of the course of study, graduates are awarded the qualification of 'jurist' and the degree of master of legal sciences. If they wish, graduates also may be awarded a bachelor's degree in addition to the master of legal sciences (on the premise that the bachelor's degree requires four years). Foreign students who have a bachelor of law degree may be admitted to the faculty for a two-year course of study resulting in the master of legal sciences and the qualification of 'jurist'. The courses offered closely approximate those in the obligatory minimum described above.

Within the Law Faculty of Moscow University, founded in 1755, a legal college was founded in 1992 as a higher legal educational institution. It offers a bachelor's degree in law after four years of full-time study or five years in the evening division. For those who already have a university degree in a discipline other than law, the bachelor's degree may be obtained in two years of full-time study or three years in the evening division. Graduates receive the qualification of 'jurist'. A less ambitious dissertation is required in the final year, and all graduates are required in both the bachelor's and master's programmes to pass successfully State attestation examinations in the theory of State and law and their chosen specialisation.

Teaching and assessment

The basic method of instruction is the magisterial lecture. Russian full-time law students attend as many as 26 hours of lectures per week, tapering off in the last two years. These are augmented by small seminars, study groups or circles, and the like, to analyse and discuss matters or problems treated in the lectures. During the fourth and fifth years the special subjects often take the form of seminars since the numbers of students involved are smaller. Many subjects require students to present short essays or oral reports on selected topics. Although the case method is not used following the American model, Russian judicial practice is increasingly important and plays a larger role in the curriculum than previously.

Assessment is based on oral examinations administered by the teaching staff. Questions are drafted by persons designated within each chair and approved by the chair as a whole. The questions are then typed on individual slips of paper. When the student appears at the designated hour for his examination, he draws the questions by lot and then may sit for a quarter-hour or so to think about his answer. He is then summoned to a small table opposite the instructor where he gives a discourse on the question. The instructors may ask further supplementary questions to probe the depths of the student's mastery. Failures are not common and resits readily granted. The diploma paper in the fifth year is submitted in writing and formally defended.

Career placement

In the Soviet era law graduates could expect to accept employment assigned by the State for a period of up to three years and then move on within the planned economy to a more satisfactory position. With the transition to a market economy guaranteed employment has disappeared and the graduate finds himself in the employment market immediately upon graduation. Demand for law graduates is high in fact, with opportunities in private practice and as jurisconsults especially lucrative. Those willing to subsist on civil service salaries find ready employment in State agencies, the procuracy, or the courts. Law is increasingly accepted as excellent training for other professions and is a recognised qualification for becoming an auditor or a tax consultant.

Postgraduate studies

There are three postgraduate programmes in Russian universities and a scheme of continuing legal education. The new degree programme is the magister, which exists in a variety of forms. One, discussed above, is simply completion of the five-year course of study. Another route is the bachelor's degree and then enrolment in a magister degree course tailored to meet the wishes and requirements of each individual student. In this case the student offers an individual study programme for a period of two years; the programme is confirmed by the chair which will supervise the course of study. The successful graduate receives the magister of legal sciences, the same degree as those who complete the five-year course for the first degree in law. To complicate matters further, the English LLM is offered in Moscow by the University of Manchester through the Moscow Higher School of Social and Economic Sciences as a one-year programme after either the four or five-year degree at a Russian institution of higher education.

The postgraduate degrees in law of candidate of legal sciences and doctor of legal sciences remain essentially unchanged after being stripped of their ideological components from the Soviet period. Equivalents with the Anglo-American systems of legal education are not easy to identify, particularly in the United States and Canada where the first degree in law is a postgraduate degree, but taking into account the respective national systems of education *as a whole*, the candidate of legal sciences degree would correspond roughly to the British PhD degree and the American MA obtained by thesis. The Russian doctor of legal sciences would correspond to the highest degrees in Britain and the United States, respectively in law the LLD in Britain and the PhD or SJD in the United States.

Entry to postgraduate study in the Russian Federation is open on a competitive basis to individuals who have completed their first university degree and, as a rule, worked for at least two years. Unlike Britain and the United States, postgraduate studies are supervised not only at universities but also within the academies of sciences and other research establishments or even enterprises which have been duly accredited for this purpose.

Postgraduate studies may be either full-time or part-time. Those pursuing the degree of candidate of legal sciences must take certain examinations, the so-called candidate minimum: Russian language, philosophy, and a third subject depending upon the speciality. Having completed these, the individual then prepares and defends the candidate dissertation. The candidate dissertation is the principal result of study for the candidate degree. Russian normative acts require that the dissertation be a scholarly work which contains the 'resolution of a task' having material significance for the respective branch of knowledge or which sets out scientifically substantiated technical, economic, or technological findings ensuring the resolution of important applied tasks.

The doctoral dissertation must be a scholarly work based on the author's research which elaborates theoretical propositions, the aggregate of which may be classified as a new major achievement in the development of the respective branch of scholarship or which solves a scientific problem having important socio-cultural, national economic, or political significance, or which sets out scientifically substantiated technical, economic, or technological solutions, the introduction of which makes a significant contribution to the acceleration of scientific-technical progress. The work will ordinarily have been published in book or article form before submission. It remains possible in the Russian Federation to submit a classified dissertation 'for official use', in which event special procedures apply to the submission and defence.[40]

The procedures for writing and defending the candidate dissertation and doctoral dissertation and for conferring the respective degree are determined not by the supervisory university or institution, but by the Statute on the Procedure for Awarding with Learned Degrees, confirmed on 30 January 2002 by Decree of the Government of the Russian Federation. It is the State which continues through the Supreme Attestation Commission (VAK) to award the degree or which has the right to verify the awarding of such.[41] On 30 April 1998 the State Attestation Commission was abolished and its functions transferred to the Ministry of Education of the Russian Federation. As part of the reforms in this connection a unified register of learned degrees and learned titles is to be created.

---

[40] The Instruction on the Procedure for the Consideration and Defence of a Dissertation with the Cypher 'For Official Use' was confirmed by Decision of the Presidium of the Higher Attestation Commission of Russia on 4 November 1994, No 48/25, portions of which lost force on 7 June 2000 by Order of the Ministry of Education of the RF, No 1707.

[41] СЗ РФ (2002), no 6, item 580. For the relevant legislation, including the previous Decree of 24 October 1994, conveniently collected, see F A Kuzin, Кандидатская диссертация. Методика написания, правила оформления и порядок защиты [*Candidate Dissertation. Method of Writing and Rules for Formalisation and Procedure for Defence*] (1997).

Within each university or institution authorised to supervise postgraduate studies a 'dissertation council' is formed by VAK. It consists of reputable scholars whose membership is confirmed by VAK. Only these councils may accept candidate and doctoral dissertations for defence within their respective specialties. When the dissertation is ready for submission, the author prepares an abstract which is printed and circulated. In the case of law, the abstract would be sent to several law faculties and leading authorities. Two official opponents are appointed to read the dissertation in full; a law faculty or legal institution may be chosen to submit detailed written comments on the thesis. The defence is a public occasion, often advertised in the press. Members of the specialised council hear the author outline his principal contentions and the views of the official opponents, to which the author may reply. Written comments submitted are read aloud to the dissertation council. When the defence is concluded, the dissertation council decides by secret ballot whether the dissertation conforms to the standard of the degree. The ultimate decision to award the degree rests with VAK, which receives a copy of the dissertation, the opinion and petition of the dissertation commission, and the other relevant documents. Although as a rule a dissertation is submitted in the Russian language, a dissertation council has the right in a reasoned petition to VAK to request that the dissertation be submitted in another language, in which case certain materials associated with the dissertation are translated into Russian. The defence also may occur in a language other than Russian.

Although the usual pattern is to defend a candidate dissertation and later in life a doctoral thesis, it is possible for an individual who does not have a candidate degree to proceed directly to the doctorate provided that the candidate minimum requirements are satisfied.

The role of VAK in verifying dissertations is to ensure compliance with the unified standards for scholarship. Each dissertation is reviewed by an expert council, which has up to four months in the case of a candidate dissertation and eight months in the case of a doctoral dissertation to complete its work. Detailed procedures apply if the expert council and the dissertation council differ in their conclusions.

(3) *Other types of legal education*

A knowledge of law or of particular branches of law is regarded as essential for many non-legal professions and for every Russian pupil. An elementary course on the basic principles of Russian law is a part of many secondary school curriculums. Special training is organised for persons serving as people's assessors or as jurors in Russian courts. In higher education Russian law is a required component of the syllabus for economists, engineers, medical personnel, social workers, journalists, transport personnel, and others.

More advanced specialist law courses or subjects are offered at dozens of institutions, for example, the Moscow State Institute of International Relations (MGIMO), the Diplomatic Academy, the Academy of the National Economy, the Ministry of Internal Affairs, the Academy of the Federal Security Service, the Ministry of Transport, and various of the military services. Auditors, bookkeepers, and tax personnel are routinely trained in law as part of their education; many have a degree in law. Many law faculties or colleges offer 'preparatory courses' for those who have a higher education in a discipline other than law and require foundation courses before proceeding on to a shortened law degree programme. Combined law and business programmes are widespread throughout Russia.

Individuals already holding a law degree from the Soviet era are encouraged to enhance their marketability through various continuing legal education ('raising legal qualifications') schemes. These may take the form of a full-fledged post-graduate degree, but more commonly are a continuing legal education certificate attested and recognised by State agencies.

D. Legal Research

In the Soviet era legal research enjoyed significant State financial support and was closely linked to themes singled out for priority at the congresses and in the programmes of the Communist Party and in the State five-year plans for economic and social development. Those days are gone, and legal research struggles for support from a multitude of sources. The numbers of lawyers engaged in full-time research has diminished drastically, partly because remuneration in the private sector is more attractive and partly because of retrenchment in research establishment posts. Russian university teaching staff also undertake legal research, although economic pressures require many to hold two or more teaching positions in order to make ends meet.

The most important and prestigious scientific research institution in the field of law is the Institute of State and Law of the Russian Academy of Sciences (IGPAN). The roots of the Institute as the first autonomous legal research body in the former Soviet Union date to 1925 with the formation of the Institute of Soviet Construction within the Communist Academy. The Institute was merged in 1929 with the Section for the General Theory of State and Law of the Communist Academy and renamed the Institute of Soviet Construction and Law. Several months later, in March 1930, the Institute absorbed the Russian Association for Scientific Research in the Social Sciences (RANION), which had functioned since 1920 attached to Moscow University. Other changes of name occurred from time to time, the present dating from 1960. The Institute has created the Academy

University of Law as a direct adjunct institution which offers undergraduate and postgraduate degrees, including the Magister of Russian Law (LLM).

Attached to the Government of the Russian Federation is the Institute of Legislation and Comparative Law, formed on the base of the All-Union Scientific Research Institute of Soviet Legislation (VNIISZ), created in 1963 as a consequence of the reorganisation in the All-Union Institute of Legal Sciences. The Institute is principally concerned with law reform and carries out studies of Russian and foreign legal experience to that end.

The All-Russian Scientific Research Institute of State Patent Expert Examination evaluates patent applications. The Institute of Justice of the Russian Legal Academy assists with the training of judges. The Centre of Private Law also is concerned with law reform and offers a postgraduate degree programme concentrating upon civil and entrepreneurial law and is closely linked with the Scientific-Consultative Centre for Private Law of the Commonwealth of Independent States.[42]

The Ministry of Internal Affairs has its own All-Russian Scientific Research Institute and a network of regional branches linked to the Russian Institute for Raising Qualifications. Attached to the General Procuracy of the Russian Federation is the Institute for Raising the Qualifications of Procuracy-Investigative Workers and a second Institute for Raising the Qualifications of Executive Personnel of the General Procuracy, as well as the Scientific Research Institute for Problems of Strengthening Legality and Legal Order.

The Ministry of Justice system includes the Scientific Centre for Legal Information, which concentrates upon legislative computer databases, and the Scientific Research Institute of Law Creation and Problems of Law Enforcement. Forensic expertise is within the responsibility of the Russian Federal Centre of Forensic Expert Examination.

E. Legal Publishing

Although a number of publishing houses issued legal materials in the Soviet era, the principal specialist legal publisher was Юридическая литература [Legal Literature]. It celebrated its 85th anniversary in 2002 and continues to operate, having undergone several cycles of internal reorganisation, as a major source for Presidential and governmental materials. The advent of *perestroika* in the late 1980s brought the possibility of legitimate 'Samizdat', which a number of lawyers took advantage of to publish their own monographs at their own risk, and non-State publishing houses eager to respond to a remarkable demand for legal and business literature: treatises, collections of legislation, individual codes and

---

[42] See A L Makovskii, 'Scientific-Consulative Centre for Private Law of the Commonwealth of Independent States', *Sudebnik*, I (1996), 1044–1048.

laws. The opportunity for publishing joint ventures was explored in the field of law by a hardy few: C H Beck, the distinguished German publisher, had made a spectacular success by becoming the quality publisher of legal textbooks, manuals, commentaries, and looseleaf series. Others, such as Interlist (London), had a brief but inspired role which never ripened into a true joint venture. The Soros Foundation through its sundry subfunds and societies included law to some extent within its programme of translations and contributed importantly at a critical moment to foreign legal classics becoming available to a Russian readership.

Russian legal scholars, lawyers, and law firms founded their own publishing houses. Зерцало [Zertsalo] under the leadership of Professor V A Tomsinov has played an outstanding role in the field of textbooks and commentaries; the Law Firm Контракт [Contract] has produced an excellent looseleaf set of Russian legislation, legal encyclopedias, treatises, and dictionaries. Other law firms issue important guides for the layman on key aspects of law. Russian banks have supported significant publications on financial and banking law. The community of Russian international lawyers in Moscow and St Petersburg is indebted to commercial sponsors and a Russian foundation for the publication of journals, yearbooks, and bibliographies.

Legal literature became such a phenomenon that in the mid–1990s the weekly review of books published regular bestseller lists. During the first quarter of 1997 the number one bestseller was a collection of codes of the Russian Federation, supplanted in the second quarter by Professor A R Kunitsyn's compilation of sample forms of judicial documents. Legal titles in 2001 accounted for nearly 30 per cent of the total business book market.

Perhaps 1996 marked the first year that the market for law books began to become satiated and genuine competition amongst legal publishers commenced in earnest. Eminence of authors, attractiveness of book design and typography, quality of paper, presentation, and price all count in a market where the consumer increasingly has choice and is purchasing with discrimination. C H Beck in its Russian guise (Бек) has set the standard, producing quality books with tasteful, even elegant, lines and typeface. But the Russians are book designers par excellence and some stunning volumes have begun to appear, and to win prizes for book design in national and international competitions; among them are annotated collections of legislation from the eras of Peter the Great and Catherine II.

The market for law books remains traditional: advocates, jurisconsults, judicial and procuracy personnel, arbitrators, investigators, policemen (the majority have law degrees), military lawyers, tax and customs personnel, law students, and legal scholars—with some important and unusual additions: entrepreneurs, accountants, auditors (many of whom have a law degree), foreign law firms and lawyers, and the law libraries of the greatly expanded number of law schools and faculties.

6

THE ADMINISTRATION OF LEGALITY

The expression 'administration of legality' is used in a special sense in this chapter to refer both to State and non-State bodies directly concerned in the Russian Federation with the application and enforcement of the law, excluding the advocates and jurisconsults, who have been discussed previously (see Chapter 5).

A. Ministries of Justice

(1) History

The Russian ministries of justice in their present or past forms have no precise analogue in Britain or North America. The first RSFSR People's Commissariat of

Justice created the day after the 1917 October Revolution included among its functions the investigation of offences, the administration of prisons and camps, the administration of the separation of Church from State, and the codification of legislation, among others. In 1921 these functions were broadened to include supreme judicial control and in 1922 to embrace the Procuracy. The repeated reorganisations of the ministries need not detain us here, except to note that from 1963–70 they were abolished completely and their functions dispersed among other agencies. On 31 August 1970 the USSR Ministry of Justice was formed as a union-republic ministry and the Statute on the Ministry confirmed on 21 March 1972.

The Ministry underwent several reorganisations throughout the Soviet era, in time becoming responsible for the organisational direction of the courts, summarising judicial practice, gathering forensic statistics, preparing the Digest of Laws of the USSR, developing methods guidance for legal work in the national economy, helping to distribute law graduates, supporting its own legal research institutions, and exercising State guidance over the Advokatura, the Notariat, and the ZAGS offices.

Since the USSR Ministry of Justice was a union-republic ministry, the disappearance of the former USSR left the Ministry of Justice of the Russian Federation to assume responsibility for the full range of ministerial functions. Republics within the Federation have their own ministries of justice; other subjects of the Federation have justice sections.

(2) Current legislation

The legal status of the Ministry of Justice is determined principally by the 1993 Russian Constitution, the Law on the Government of the Russian Federation, the Statute on the Ministry of Justice confirmed by Edict of the President of Russia on 2 August 1999, as amended on 8 June 2000 and 10 December 2001,[1] and certain decrees addressed to individual Ministry functions or programmes. Among the last is the Decree of the Government of the Russian Federation on Confirmation of the Conception of Reforming Justice Agencies and Institutions of the Russian Federation, adopted 7 October 1996.[2] The principal tasks of the Ministry are to: realise State policy in the sphere of justice; ensure the rights and legal interests of the individual and the State; ensure the legal defence of intellectual property; ensure the established procedure for the activity of courts, the execution of acts of judicial and other agencies, and the execution of criminal punishments.

---

[1] СЗ РФ (1999), no 32, item 4043; (2000), no 24, item 2546; (2001), no 51, item 4872. The 1999 Statute replaced that of 4 November 1993, as amended, which lost force by Decree of the Government of the Russian Federation of 14 December 1999. СЗ РФ (1999), no 51, item 6354.

[2] СЗ РФ (1996), no 42, item 4806.

Pursuant to these tasks, the Statute on the Ministry enumerates 62 principal functions. Amongst them is the provision of support for what is called 'norm-creation activity' of federal agencies of executive power. This involves offering expert advice to the President and Government on draft legislative and other normative acts submitted by federal agencies of executive power, as well as normative legal acts adopted by subjects of the Russian Federation from the standpoint of their constitutionality,[3] effectuating control over the correctness and timeliness of publication of normative legal acts registered by the Ministry, systematising Russian legislation, maintaining the databank of Russian normative acts on computer, participating in the preparation of the Digest of Laws of the Russian Federation, and making proposals to bring existing legislation into conformity with newly-enacted laws, the Constitution, and international treaties. The President of the Russian Federation has enlarged the powers of the Ministry in this domain by requiring that draft federal laws submitted to the Government of Russia first be evaluated by the Ministry of Justice.[4]

The Ministry operates a system of State registration for normative legal acts of federal agencies of executive power which affect the rights and legal interests of citizens, establish the legal status of organisations, or have an interdepartmental character. Normative legal acts of these categories must undergo expert evaluation by the Ministry and be formally registered as a condition of their validity. The Ministry routinely rejects draft departmental acts and publishes a list of those which have been duly registered. The Central Bank of Russia is deemed for these purposes to fall within the registration requirement for many of its normative documents.

The charters of religious and social organisations and associations, and from May 1995 the social associations themselves, are registered with the Ministry of Justice. By 1996 the Ministry had registered more than 32,000 social associations, of which 90 were political parties and 109 were social movements. A Presidential Edict adopted 2 May 1996 enlarged the Ministry's responsibility for supervising such social associations and gave the right to request information regarding their activities. From 30 January 1998 the Ministry became responsible for registering rights to and transactions concerning immoveable property. The State Registry of Juridical Persons established pursuant to the Federal Law on the State Registration

---

[3] The Provisional Procedure for Conducting Legal Expert Examination of Normative Legal Acts of Subjects of the Russian Federation was confirmed by Order of the Ministry of Justice of the Russian Federation on 18 October 2000, No 296. Бюллетень Министерства юстиции РФ, no 11 (2000).

[4] See the Edict of the President of the Russian Federation 'On Additional Functions of the Ministry of Justice of the Russian Federation', No 550, adopted 3 June 1995, as amended 29 November 2000. СЗ РФ (1995), no 24, item 2281; (2000), no 49, item 4826.

of Juridical Persons of 8 August 2001 (in force from 1 July 2002) is no longer the responsibility of the Ministry.[5]

Since 1996 the Ministry has been responsible for implementing State policies regarding the protection of intellectual property, including performing the functions of the State patent agency established by intellectual property legislation. Functions with respect to the Advokatura are mostly determined by the 2002 Federal Law on the Advokatura (see Chapter 5), but include giving consent to the formation of colleges of advocates and maintaining a register of such colleges. In the case of the Notariat, the Ministry of Justice opens and abolishes State notarial offices or directs justice agencies to do so, maintains a register of State and private notarial offices, establishes the procedure for issuing licences to engage in notarial activity, certifies the genuineness of signatures and seals of notaries when documents are legalised for transmission to natural and juridical persons in foreign States, as well as supervising the performance by notaries of their professional duties.

The Ministry plays a key role in developing the legal information systems within the Russian Federation, developing legislative databanks to be used for exchanging materials with subjects of the Federation and with foreign States.

The reforms of the Ministry of Justice are being implemented pursuant to the 'Conception of Reforming Justice Agencies and Institutions of the Russian Federation', confirmed by Decree of the Government on 7 October 1996, No 1177.[6] On 24 July 1997 the Government of the Russian Federation adopted Decree No 930 entitled 'Questions of the Ministry of Justice of the Russian Federation', parts of which were classified.[7] In furtherance of the Conception, the traditional functions of the Ministry in support of court organisation were transferred, in the interests of separation of powers, to the Judicial Department attached to the Supreme Court of the Russian Federation in accordance with the Federal Law on the said Department of 8 January 1998.[8] Not mentioned in the Conception but in furtherance of obligations arising out of membership in the Council of Europe, on 8 October 1997 the President of the Russian Federation issued an Edict on reforming the system for the execution of criminal punishments; a principal element of the reform consisted of transferring in stages the entire system of penal institutions from the Ministry of Internal Affairs to the Ministry of Justice.[9]

---

[5] СЗ РФ (2001), no 33, item 3431.
[6] СЗ РФ (1996), no 42, item 4806.
[7] As amended 10 August 1998 and 17 and 19 August 2000. СЗ РФ (1997), no 30, item 3663; (1998), no 33, item 4023; (2000), no 34, item 3480; no 35, item 3581.
[8] СЗ РФ (1998), no 2, item 223.
[9] СЗ РФ (1997), no 41, item 4683.

B. Judicial System

(1) History

The Bolsheviks came to power determined to completely reshape the pre-existing judicial order. Revolutionary tribunals sprang up immediately, without legislative sanction, under various names. Cases were judged not on the basis of Imperial law, but according to revolutionary consciousness; judgments were not subject to appeal. The first official legislative act creating courts was Decree No 1 'On Courts' enacted 24 November 1917.[10] In place of the old court system the Decree created 'people's courts' presided over by a judge directly elected and two assessors, the latter being laymen who served on a part-time basis. Their jurisdiction was limited to civil cases of up to 3,000 rubles and criminal cases in which the punishment could not exceed two years' deprivation of freedom. Judgments could not be appealed but were sometimes subject to review by cassation. As a separate system of courts Decree No 1 established revolutionary tribunals consisting of seven persons elected by provincial or city local soviets. These tribunals heard cases involving serious crimes or counter-revolutionary acts; their judgments were not subject to appeal, and they administered what came to be known as the 'Red Terror'.

This relatively simple judicial structure was elaborated by Decree No 2 'On Courts' adopted 15 February 1918. Intermediate-level courts were organised in some provinces and a Supreme Judicial Control organ authorised but never actually instituted. The functions of people's assessors were given in greater detail, and the courts were officially authorised to allow persons to speak their native tongue in court. The powers of cassational instances were enlarged.

Decree No 2 said nothing of the revolutionary tribunals. These continued to be the object of special legislation; their numbers were reduced but their jurisdiction was broadened. The All-Russian Extraordinary Commission for the Struggle Against Counter-Revolution and Sabotage (VChKa) worked closely with the revolutionary tribunals as an investigative agency, possessing for some time the power to punish summarily without trial. New statutes on revolutionary tribunals were enacted on 12 April 1919 and 18 March 1920. The last was viewed as a kind of unification act for the tribunals; measures of repression had to be based on legislation. Outside this system there operated revolutionary military tribunals and

---

[10] The draft of Decret No 1 is usually associated with P I Stuchka, correctly, but he was not at the time the People's Commissar of Justice. The true people's commissar, G I Oppokov (who used the pseudonym Lomov) (1888–1937), jurist, economist, theatre critic, and publicist, was never mentioned in the unclassified Soviet press until 1977. See A Smykalin, 'Создание советской судебной системы' ['Creation of the Soviet Judicial System'], Российская юстиция, no 2 (2002) 41.

revolutionary military railway tribunals on the basis of slightly different principles and their own legislation. In mid-1921 the entire scheme of tribunals was unified; the Supreme Tribunals attached to the VTsIK became the sole cassational and supervisory organ for the entire system and a court of first instance for especially important cases.

The people's courts likewise underwent modifications. They had jurisdiction over all civil and criminal cases except those within the competence of the revolutionary tribunals. Most cases were heard by a judge and two people's assessors; especially grave crimes were heard by a college of the court consisting of the judge and six assessors.

At the outset of 1921 moves were underway to set up a single centre of judicial supervision for people's courts and revolutionary tribunals in the person of a body called Supreme Judicial Control; instead the people's commissariat of justice was given judicial supervisory powers, but only partial ones. The introduction of the NEP brought further changes for the judiciary: the VChKa was reorganised into the GPU; the Procuracy was founded; and criminal, civil, labour, civil and criminal procedure codes were enacted. The 'judicial reform of 1922' in the RSFSR instituted a uniform system of judicial institutions consisting of the people's court (in two guises), the provincial court, and the RSFSR Supreme Court, broadened the rights of people's assessors somewhat further, and clarified the competence of each level in the system. These reforms were hardly in motion before they were overtaken by the formation of the USSR (by Treaty of the Union, 30 December 1922) and the creation in July 1923 of the USSR Supreme Court.

The details of the USSR Supreme Court of this period are beyond the scope of this study except to note a few distinctive features. The Court exercised several types of supervisory power: general supervision, constitutional supervision, and judicial supervision, as well as trying important cases at first instance. It issued guiding explanations to inferior courts on all-union legislation. The Procuracy was linked to the Supreme Court in the person of the 'Procurator of the USSR Supreme Court' until 1933, when the two were separated and the Court lost its responsibilities for general supervision over legality.

Several reorganisations of the judiciary ensued. On 29 October 1924 the USSR enacted Fundamental Principles of Court Organisation, followed on 19 November 1926 by the RSFSR Statute on Court Organisation. Military courts were separately regulated by a Statute of 20 August 1926 on Military Tribunals and the Military Procuracy, but were considered to be part of the judicial system; the USSR Supreme Court exercised general guidance over them. Nevertheless, there persisted an inclination to create specialised tribunals. In 1930 'line courts for railway transport' were formed, followed in 1934 by analogous courts for water transport; both were served by the Supreme Court as a cassational instance.

In 1934 a separate body was formed outside the judicial system, the Special Board (Особое совещание) attached to the USSR People's Commissariat of Internal Affairs. The Special Board was authorised to apply to persons deemed 'socially dangerous': (a) exile for up to five years under public supervision in localities listed by the Commissar; (b) banishment for up to five years under public supervision and a prohibition to reside in capitals, large cities, and industrial centres of the USSR: (c) confinement in correctional-labour camps for a term of up to five years; (d) banishment of socially dangerous foreign subjects beyond the limits of the Soviet Union. The Procurator might protest decisions of the Board, but no judicial review was possible under the Decree.[11] The Board was apparently free to decide who was 'socially dangerous' on any basis it chose without regard to substantive or procedural law. The Board's operations were augmented by special legislation, including a Decree adopted by the Presidium of the TsIK SSSR on 1 December 1934 concerning cases relating to the preparation or commission of terrorist acts. This type of case was to be considered within ten days, the conclusion to indict being handed to the accused 24 hours before the trial, the case was considered without a procurator or an advocate, cassational appeal and pardon were not allowed, and the death penalty if assigned was subject to immediate implementation. An analogous procedure was established on 14 September 1937 for cases concerning wrecking, sabotage, and smuggling. Countless Soviet citizens fell victim to this institution and legislation. The enactments of 1934 and 1937 were repealed by Edict of the Presidium of the USSR Supreme Soviet on 19 April 1956, but presumably ceased to function after Stalin's death in March 1953.[12]

The ordinary court system evidently functioned throughout this period in the normal way. The 1936 USSR Constitution transformed a number of established elements of judicial administration—electivity of judges, participation of people's assessors, national language in court proceedings—to the status of constitutional principles. The 1936 USSR Constitution also 'federalised' a number of areas which had been shared between the central and union republic authorities. On 16 August 1938 the USSR Supreme Court adopted the Law on Court Organisation to replace the 1924 Fundamental Principles. The 1936 USSR Constitution having proclaimed the disappearance of antagonistic classes in the Soviet Union, the 1938 Law made provision for the equality of citizens before the court. The concentration of judicial supervision in the Supreme Court, however, while it

---

[11] СЗ СССР (1935), I, no 11, item 84.

[12] Details are emerging of so-called 'courts of honour' created after the Second World War within Communist Party agencies, including the Central Committee, at the behest of Stalin. These were used on occasion, if not always, for the purposes of political reprisal and punishment. Although they had certain analogies with the comrades' courts, apparently they were quite a separate and unrelated phenomenon. See V D Esakov and E S Levina, Дело КР. Суды чести в идеологии и послевоенного сталинизма [*The KR Case. Courts of Honour in the Ideology and Practice of Postwar Stalinism*] (2001).

contributed to uniformity of judgments and perhaps in some areas (the law of tort) to judicial innovation in the law, did complicate and prolong the judicial process. During the war, military tribunals assumed jurisdiction in areas proclaimed to be in a military situation; in areas under siege, the ordinary courts were simply transformed into military tribunals.

In 1957 the USSR Constitution was amended to return responsibility for court organisation to the union republics to be exercised in accordance with all-union Fundamental Principles of Legislation. The FPL were enacted on 25 December 1958, replacing the 1938 Law, and the union republics approved their own laws on court organisation in 1959–61. Those laws continued in force with slight amendments arising out of the 1977–78 USSR and RSFSR constitutions, the RSFSR Law on Court Organisation in the version of 1981 remaining in force as amended to 2 January 2000.

(2) Current legislation

The Russian judicial system is presently regulated by the 1993 Russian Constitution (especially Chapter 7), the 1996 Federal Constitutional Law on the Judicial System of the Russian Federation of 31 December 1996, which entered into force from 1 January 1997, as amended on 15 December 2001,[13] and the 2002 Federal Law on Organs of the Judicial Community in the Russian Federation.[14] These enactments require, inter alia, that judicial power be effectuated only by courts, that the courts be independent of legislative and executive power, and that extraordinary courts and courts not provided for by the Constitution or by the 1996 Law on the judicial system are not permitted.

Three kinds of federal courts are provided for by the 1993 Russian Constitution: the Constitutional Court of the Russian Federation, the federal courts of general jurisdiction, and the federal arbitrazh courts. Military courts fall within the federal courts of general jurisdiction. All are conceived as being part of a unified judicial system, the unity of which is ensured by the shared origin of Russian courts in the Constitution and 1996 Law on the judical system, the concept of the 'judicial community of judges', compliance by all courts with the rules of procedure established by federal laws, the application by all courts of the Russian Constitution, federal laws, generally-recognised principles and norms of international law and international treaties of the Russian Federation, and the constitutions or charters and other laws of subjects of the Russian Federation, recognition that judicial decrees which have entered into legal force are binding throughout the Russian Federation, the unity of the status of judges, and the financing of federal courts and justices of the peace from the federal budget.

---

[13] СЗ РФ (1997), no 1, item 1; (2001), no 51, item 4825.
[14] СЗ РФ (2002), no 11, item 1022.

In addition there are the courts of the subjects of the Russian Federation. These comprise the constitutional or charter courts of each subject (although as of 2002 not all subjects of the Federation have created or activated such courts) and justices of the peace, who are the judges of general jurisdiction in subjects of the Federation where they have been actually established. In all there are about 15,000 judges in the Russian Federation as of June 1998, with about 7.6 per cent vacancies. However, the caseload is such that by 1999 there should have been 35,700 judges, a figure impossible to meet. Under the 2001 Code of Criminal Procedure a judge with 12 jurors or three professional judges hear cases under stipulated situations (Article 30).

The 'judicial community' comprises judges of federal courts of all types and levels together with judges of courts of subjects of the Russian Federation comprising the judicial system of Russia. A judge becomes a member of the community from the moment he takes his oath of office and remains such until the decision terminating his powers as a judge enters into legal force. The purpose of the judicial community is to express the interests of judges as the bearers of judicial power. The organs of the judicial community consist of: the All-Russian Congress of Judges, the conference of judges of subjects of the Russian Federation, the Council of Judges of the Russian Federation, the councils of judges of subjects of the Russian Federation, general meetings of judges of courts, the Supreme Qualifications College of Judges of the Russian Federation, and the qualifications colleges of judges of subjects of the Russian Federation. The principal tasks of the judicial community of judges are to further improvement of the judicial system and court proceedings, defend the rights and legal interests of judges, participate in the organisational, personnel, and resource provision for judicial activity, and affirm the authority of judicial power.

(3) Constitutional Court of the Russian Federation

History

In the early years after the formation of the USSR by the Treaty of the Union on 30 December 1922 there was a certain interest in constitutional control. The 1924 USSR Constitution placed this responsibility on the USSR Supreme Court (Articles 30, 46, and 46(6)) as a subsidiary one,[15] but left most powers in this connection to the TsIK USSR. By the early 1930s the USSR Supreme Court ceased to play any meaningful role in constitutional control. The 1936 and 1977 USSR Constitutions, and all union and autonomous republic constitutions based thereon, placed constitutional supervision in the hands of the highest agencies of State power (the Supreme Soviets) and in intervals between sessions, in their

---

[15] See V K Diablo, Судебная охрана конституций в буржуазных странах и в СССР [*Judicial Protection of Constitutions in Bourgeois Countries and in the USSR*] (1928) 94.

presidiums. On 1 December 1988 Article 125 of the USSR Constitution was amended and renumbered to Article 124 to make provision for the Committee of Constitutional Supervision of the USSR. The establishment of the Committee encountered considerable resistance; the Law on the Committee was not adopted until 23 December 1989 and the full Committee not elected until 26 April 1990. The Committee's ability to function effectively was further hamstrung by a provision in the legislation creating it requiring that provisions of the Law 'affecting supervision over the conformity to the USSR Constitution and laws of the USSR of the constitutions and laws of the union republics enter into force simultaneously with changes in and additions to the Section of the USSR Constitution on national-State structure'. In fact that section of the USSR Constitution was never amended, and constitutional control over those questions rested with the President of the USSR. The Committee on Constitutional Supervision of the USSR, however, did enjoy some successes during its brief existence, including declaring void unpublished legislation which affected the rights and legal interests of citizens. The Committee, of course, was not a court and its opinions could be overridden by a qualified majority of the USSR Congress of People's Deputies. Its intended RSFSR counterpart, authorised by amendments to the RSFSR Constitution of 27 October 1989 (Article 119), was never actually created.

As the Russian Federation moved in 1989–91 towards a Presidential system and separation of powers with checks and balances, the RSFSR Constitution was amended to create a Constitutional Court which functioned on the basis of the Law on the Constitutional Court adopted 12 July 1991.[16] During its period of operation in 1992–3 the Constitutional Court considered 27 cases, of which 19 related to verifying the constitutionality of legal acts and eight concerned individual appeals by citizens. The Court declared unconstitutional two decrees of the Congress of People's Deputies of the Russian Federation in whole or in part, six laws and decrees of the Supreme Soviet of the RSFSR, two decrees of the Presidium of the RSFSR Supreme Soviet, eight edicts of the President of the Russian Federation, two decrees of the Government of the RSFSR, and four acts of the highest agencies of State power of republics within the Russian Federation. Two opinions also were given on the actions or decisions of the President of Russia. A full seven months was devoted by the Court to the constitutionality of the President's ban of the Communist Party of the Soviet Union and collateral issues of the constitutionality of the Party itself.

Russia in those years experienced sharp confrontation between the President and the legislative branch of State which the Constitutional Court was drawn into,

---

[16] Ведомости СНД и ВС РСФСР (1991), no 19, item 621; no 30, item 1017. The Law was suspended by Edict of the President of the RF by virtue of the adoption of the 1993 Russian Constitution and lost force on 21 July 1994. See САПП РФ (1993), no 52, item 5086; СЗ РФ (1994), no 13, item 1447.

endeavouring to play the role of mediator and in the end aligning itself publicly with particular factions. Its decisions became politicised, or were perceived to be so; some judges of the Court appeared in the mass media in a clearly partisan role. After 20 March 1993 the politicisation of the Court grew markedly, ultimately culminating in the 'suspension' of the Constitutional Court by an Edict of the President of the Russian Federation adopted 7 October 1993 'until the adoption of a new Constitution'.

Current legislation

The present Constitutional Court of the Russian Federation was constituted on the basis of the 1993 Russian Constitution and the Federal Constitutional Law on the Constitutional Court of the Russian Federation of 21 July 1994, as amended 8 February 2001 and 15 December 2001.[17] It consists of 19 judges appointed to office by the Soviet of the Federation upon the recommendation of the President of the Russian Federation for a term of 12 years, the compulsory age of retirement being 70 years of age. Reappointment to the Court is not possible. A judge may not be removed from office, although under certain circumstances his powers may be suspended or terminated. The powers of the Court itself are not limited by a determined period.[18]

The jurisdiction of the Constitutional Court is complex and under amendments of 15 December 2001 may not be changed other than by means of making changes to the Federal Constitutional Law which established the Court. With respect to conformity to the 1993 Russian Constitution the Constitutional Court may examine: (a) federal laws, normative acts of the President of the Russian Federation, the Soviet of the Federation, the State Duma, and the Government of the Russian Federation; (b) the constitutions or charters, laws, and other normative acts of the subjects of the Russian Federation issued with regard to questions relegated to the jurisdiction of agencies of State power of the Russian Federation and to the joint jurisdiction of agencies of State power of the Russian Federation and agencies of State power of subjects of the Russian Federation; (c) treaties between agencies of State power of the Russian Federation and agencies of State power of subjects of the Russian Federation, and treaties between agencies of State power of subjects of the Russian Federation; (d) international treaties of the Russian Federation which have not entered into legal force.

The second domain of jurisdiction of the Constitutional Court appertains to disputes concerning competence: (a) between federal agencies of State power; (b) between agencies of State power of the Russian Federation and agencies of

---

[17] СЗ РФ (1994), no 13, item 1447; (2001), no 7, item 607; no 51, item 4824.

[18] V A Kriazhkov and L V Lazarev, Конституционная юстиция в Российской Федерации [*Constitutional Justice in the Russian Federation*] (1998).

State power of subjects of the Russian Federation; (c) between the highest State agencies of subjects of the Russian Federation.

The Constitutional Court also considers appeals against a violation of the constitutional rights and freedoms of citizens and inquiries from courts to verify the constitutionality of a law being applied or subject to application in a particular case; gives interpretations of the Constitution; in the event of an attempt to impeach the President of the Russian Federation, gives an opinion as to whether the procedure for putting forward an accusation against the President has been complied with; and exercises other powers granted to the Court by the 1993 Russian Constitution, the Treaty of the Federation, federal constitutional laws; and treaties delimiting the powers among subjects of the Russian Federation. The Court has the right of legislative intitiative with regard to questions of its jurisdiction.

The Court acts in plenary session and is divided into two chambers containing respectively ten and nine judges of the Court. Which judge serves in which chamber is determined by lot. The chairman and deputy chairman of the Court may not be within the same chamber, and the individual composition of the chambers must be changed at least every three years. In plenary session the Court exclusively settles cases concerning the constitutionality of the constitutions and charters of the subjects of the Federation, interprets the 1993 Russian Constitution, gives an opinion regarding impeachment proceedings against the President, decides whether to exercise legislative initiative, and adopts messages to be issued by the Court, elects the chairman, deputy chairman, and secretary of the Court, forms the chambers of the Court, adopts and amends the Reglament of the Court, determines the sequence for hearing cases and distributes cases between the chambers, and decides whether to suspend or terminate the powers of a judge of the Court or the term of office of the chairman, deputy chairman, or secretary of the Court. Matters not within the exclusive jurisdiction of the plenary session of the Court may be considered in sessions of the chambers of the Court.

The principles of a constitutional court proceeding are the:

* independence of the judges, which requires that judges of the Court be guided exclusively by the law, not represent any State or social agencies, political parties or movements, State, social, or other enterprises, institutions, or organisations, officials, State and territorial formations, or social groups, and adopt decisions under circumstances precluding outside influence or interference;[19]

---

[19] The original draft Law on the Constitutional Court contained a number of provisions intended to ensure the independence of Constitutional Court judges which were excluded during deliberations on the draft Law in the State Duma. A senior judge on the Court has written that 'therefore now there is not a full guarantee of the autonomy and independence of the Constitutional Court in the Russian Federation'. See N V Vitruk, Конституционное правосудие: судебное конституционное право и процесс [*Constitutional Justice: Judicial Constitutional Law and Procedure*] (1998) 95.

- collegiality, which demands that a decision be adopted only by those judges who participated in the consideration of the case in a judicial session with the requisite quorom of three-quarters of the membership of the chamber or two-thirds of the composition of the plenary session;
- *glasnost*, which means cases are considered openly unless the Law on the Court provides otherwise, and requires that decisions are proclaimed publicly;
- orality, which requires the Court to hear the explanations of the parties, testimony of experts, witnesses, and to read out available documents;
- language, being in this instance the Russian language with the right to use of an interpreter if participants in the case do not have a command of Russian;
- uninterruptedness, which mandates that the Court commence and complete a case except for time allotted for leisure or to enable the participants to prepare for further proceedings;
- adversariality and equality of parties, which gives the parties equal rights to support their position in a session of the Court.

The rules of procedure of the Constitutional Court are contained in the Law on the Court and in the Reglament of the Court. Recourse to the Court takes the form of an inquiry, petition, or appeal. The Court is required to reply to every recourse in writing, giving grounds for acceptance or rejection and, where possible, directing the person having recourse to other competent agencies or officials if the matter is not within the jurisdiction of the Constitutional Court. Between 1992–5 the Constitutional Court received and dealt with 41,633 instances of recourse by citizens, State agencies, and social associations.[20]

The Constitutional Court adopts four types of document, depending upon the nature of the matter under consideration. A decision adopted in a plenary session or the session of a chamber of the Court is called a decision (решение) of the Constitutional Court of the Russian Federation. With regard to most matters within its jurisdiction (Article 3(1)–(4), Law on the Constitutional Court), the final decision of the Court is called a decree (постановление); if the matter deals with impeachment of the President, it is called an opinion (заключение); all other decisions of the Court concerning a Constitutional Court proceeding are called a ruling (определение). A decision is adopted in an open vote, each judge being polled by name and the person presiding voting last. A majority of judges who participate in the voting is sufficient to adopt a decision unless expressly provided otherwise by the Law on the Constitutional Court. A tie vote in a case concerning the constitutionality of a normative act or treaty is considered to be in favour of the constitutionality of the act under consideration. Disputes concerning competence must be decided by a majority vote. A decision concerning an

---

[20] Vitruk (n 19 above) 80.

interpretation of the Constitution requires a majority of two-thirds of the total number of judges. There is no right of abstention.

During the initial period of its existence (January 1992 to ca. October 1993) the Constitutional Court considered 27 cases, 19 of which were petitions to verify the constitutionality of legal acts and eight of which related to individual appeals by citizens. More than half dealt with human rights questions, and a quarter with issues of State organisation and structure. Following the adoption of the 1993 Russian Constitution, as of December 1999 the Constitutional Court had issued a further 105 decrees and for the years 1997–8 alone, 337 rulings (compared with 225 for 1995–6).

The form and style of a decision of the Constitutional Court is regulated by the Law on the Constitutional Court (Article 75). Special opinions are possible and may take the form of what in the United States would be called a concurring or a dissenting opinion. The decision of the Court is proclaimed in full in open court immediately after being signed by all judges who participated in the voting. Within a two-week period after signature decrees and opinions are circulated according to a list set out in the Law on the Constitutional Court and are subject to official publication in the Собрание законодательства Российской Федерации [Collection of Legislation of the Russian Federation], the newspaper Российская газета [*Russian Newspaper*], and the official organ of the Court itself, Вестник Конституционного Суда Российской Федерации [Herald of the Constitutional Court of the Russian Federation]. Court decisions also have been collected in individual volumes edited by judges of the Court, sometimes with commentary.[21] The decision is final, not subject to appeal, and enters into force immediately after proclamation. Although publication of the decision is mandatory, the legal force of the decision is not dependent upon or connected with publication. No confirmation by other agencies or officials is required in respect of a Court decision; it has immediate direct effect and is subject to execution immediately.

The judges of the Constitutional Court are served by a Secretariat which arranges the full organisational and informational support of the Court, receives visitors, considers recourses to the Court in a preliminary way, weeding out those not

---

[21] See Комментарий Федерального конституционного закона 'О Конституционном Суде Российской Федерации' [*Commentary on the Federal Constitutional Law 'On the Constitutional Court of the Russian Federation*] (1996); Конституционный Суд Российской Федерации. Постановления. Определения. 1992–1996 [Constitutional Court of the Russian Federation. Decrees. Rulings. 1992–1996] (1997); T G Morshchakova (ed), Конституционный Суд Российской Федерации. Постановления. Определения. 1997–1998 [Constitutional Court of the Russian Federation. Decrees. Rulings. 1997–1998] (2000). For a commentary on Constitutional Court decrees arranged by subject, see B S Ebzeev (ed), Комментарий к постановлениям конституционного суда Российской Федерации [*Commentary on Decrees of the Constitutional Court of the Russian Federation*] (2001). 2 vols.

within the jurisdiction of the Court, assists the judges in preparing cases, and monitors the activity of State agencies in executing decisions of the Court. The Statute on the Secretariat is confirmed by the Constitutional Court itself. As a rule the Court sits in Moscow, but may conduct sessions in another place when the Court considers this to be necessary.

Judges wear gowns when the Court is in session. Designed by E N Korotkova, the gowns and caps were intended to bear the State Arms of the Russian Federation. The design was approved by the Presidium of the Supreme Soviet of the Russian Federation on 18 May 1992 but never submitted for confirmation of the full Supreme Soviet. In practice, therefore, judges wore the gown without the headgear and without the State symbols. The situation changed following the adoption of the Federal Constitutional Law on the State Arms of the Russian Federation of 25 December 2000, as amended 9 July 2002.[22] The Court has developed its own internal protocol and forms of address during judicial sessions. The Court is addressed as the 'High Court', or 'Respected Court'; the judges as 'Your Honour' or 'Respected Judge'; and participants in the proceeding as the 'Respected Party'; 'Respected Expert', 'Respected Witness', and the like, adding the surname of the individual if necessary.

(4) Courts of ordinary jurisdiction of the Russian Federation

The courts of ordinary jurisdiction are headed by the Supreme Court of the Russian Federation, which is the highest judicial agency for civil, criminal, administrative, and other cases within the jurisdiction of courts of general jurisdiction. It is the directly superior instance to the supreme courts of the Republics within the Federation, territory or regional courts, courts of cities of federal significance, courts of the autonomous region and autonomous national areas, military courts of military districts, fleets, and types and groups of forces. The lowest tier of this system is the district court, which acts as a court of first instance, and with respect to the justices of the peace, as the court of second instance. The 1996 Federal Constitutional Law on the Judicial System of the Russian Federation makes provision for a federal constitutional law to be adopted with respect to the Supreme Court and all inferior courts. Until that happens, these courts continue to be governed by the 1981 RSFSR Law on Court Organisation, as amended.

The 1993 Russian Constitution (Article 126) establishes the place of the Supreme Court in the judicial system and confers on it the right of legislative initiative (Article 104). Under the 1996 Law on the Judicial System, the Supreme Court effectuates judicial supervision in the procedural forms provided for by a federal law over the activity of courts of general jurisdiction, including military and specialised federal courts, within its competence considers cases as a court of second

---

[22] СЗ РФ (2000), no 52(I), item 5021; (2002), no 28, item 2780.

instance, by way of supervision, and under newly discovered circumstances, and may act as a court of first instance under certain circumstances, and gives explanations with regard to questions of judicial practice.

The Supreme Court consists of judges appointed by the Soviet of the Federation upon the recommendation of the President of the Russian Federation, which in turn is based upon a recommendation of the Chairman of the Supreme Court and the opinion of the qualifications collegium of the Court. There is no limitation on the term of judges, but they must retire at age 65 under 2001 amendments to the legislation. People's assessors serve for a term of five years. In cases heard at first instance the case is heard by a bench composed of a single judge, although a court of three professional judges also is permitted. Cases heard by way of cassation in regard to appeal and protests are considered by three professional judges in one of the three judicial divisions of the Court: civil, criminal, or military. The same applies to cases heard by way of supervision or with regard to newly discovered circumstances. When the Presidium of the Supreme Court considers a case, a majority of its members must be present.

All judges of the Supreme Court are members of the Plenum of the Court, which is convoked at least quarterly. The Procurator General and Minister of Justice have the right to attend sessions of the Plenum, as do others by invitation, including judges of inferior courts, legal scholars, and procuracy personnel. The Plenum adopts decisions by simple majority vote and requires two-thirds of the judges to be present for a quorum. It is the Plenum which issues Guiding Explanations (see Chapter 4).

The Presidium of the Court consists of 13 judges and is the highest judicial instance in the Russian Federation with regard to cases within the jurisdiction of the courts of general jurisdiction. The Soviet of the Federation confirms the 13 judges who sit on the Presidium upon the recommendation of the President of the Russian Federation. The functions of the Presidium are substantial and include deciding cases heard by way of supervision and for newly discovered circumstances, hearing reports analysing judicial practice of lower courts and forensic statistics, organising the work of the judicial divisions and apparatus of the Court, coordination with the Ministry of Justice, and others. Sessions of the Presidium are held at least monthly. Individual cases are reported upon by members of the Presidium or other judges; the Procurator General or his deputy participates to either support a procuracy protest or to comment on protests brought by the Chairman of the Supreme Court or his deputies. Decrees are adopted by simple majority open vote.

The greater portion of work in the Supreme Court is performed within its judicial divisions. They consider cases at first instance, by way of cassation, by way of supervision, and on the grounds of newly discovered circumstances. The judicial divisions for civil and criminal cases each are divided into benches composed of six to eight judges, one of which acts as chairman to preside at judicial sessions and ensure the preparation of cases for consideration by way of cassation or supervision. Each bench is allocated lower administrative-territorial subdivisions from whose courts cases flow to it. It is felt that such allocation enables the judges to come to know the lower courts in detail, the kinds of errors they are likely to make, and the professional qualities of individual judges.

The rules governing whether cases are dealt with by way of cassation or supervision are complex. In general judicial supervision is exercised by considering appeals and protests against judgments and other decisions of inferior courts which have not entered into legal force, or those which have entered into legal force provided that they were not considered by way of cassation, special appeal, or special protest. It should be borne in mind, when tracing the progress of a particular case, that the presidium of each court and, at higher levels, also the plenum are places of resort for the parties or their lawyers. A particularly difficult case can pass through dozens of procedural stages and instances.

As a court of first instance the Supreme Court can take jurisdiction over virtually any civil or criminal case, as well as try those relegated specifically to its jurisdiction. In practice the Supreme Court tries criminal cases where important State interests are involved, or in which the crimes committed involve several administrative-territorial divisions, entail grave consequences, or are of unusual complexity. During election periods, the Supreme Court hears appeals against the decisions of the Central Electoral Commission of the Russian Federation not to register candidates for elective office.

The role of the Supreme Court in issuing guiding explanations is discussed in Chapter 4. Decisions, judgments, rulings, and decrees of the Supreme Court and other courts of ordinary jurisdiction are published in the monthly Бюллетень Верховного Суда РФ [Bulletin of the Supreme Court of the Russian Federation].

In the past organisational provision for the courts of ordinary jurisdiction was made by the Ministry of Justice of the Russian Federation, a proximity to and dependence upon the Government that in the eyes of many compromised the independence of the courts. The 1996 Law on the Judicial System made provision for a Judicial Department attached to the Supreme Court of the Russian Federation, regulated by the Federal Law of 8 January 1998. Although attached to the Supreme Court, the Judicial Department is a federal State agency whose responsibility it is to organise the activity of the entire system of courts (except the Supreme Court itself, which has its own apparatus) of ordinary jurisdiction, including specialised courts, and the financing of the justices of the peace. 'Organise' for these purposes means personnel, finance, material-technical, and other measures which enable the courts to function independently and efficiently.[23] The Judicial Department therefore constitutes a system having agencies and institutions at every level of State administration where there are courts. It is headed by a General Director who is appointed to and removed from office by the Chairman of the Supreme Court with the consent of the Council of Judges of the Russian Federation.

In effect an entire professional group of court administrators has been created by the 1998 Law on the Judicial Department. Its powers are immense: organising the activity of all courts below the Supreme Court, assisting with the drafting of federal laws and other normative acts relating to questions within its jurisdiction, working out proposals to finance the courts and justices of the peace, making proposals to improve the organisation of the courts, submitting proposals to create or abolish courts, monitoring personnel requirements of the courts, conducting work relating to the selection and training of candidate judges, interacting with educational institutions, training and raising the qualifications of judges and workers of the court apparatus, developing normative standards for the caseload of judges, helping reassign judges to courts with vacancies, keeping forensic statistics and court archives, organising the construction and repair of court buildings, and others.

The training of future judges and continuing legal education for existing judges also is the responsibility of the Russian Academy of Justice, founded by the Supreme Court and the Supreme Arbitrazh Court of the Russian Federation on the basis of the Edict of the President of the Russian Federation of 11 May 1998. The Academy also undertakes fundamental and applied research on the organisation and activities of the courts.[24]

Attached to the Supreme Court is a scientific advisory council, which operates on the basis of a Statute confirmed by the Plenum of the Supreme Court on 21 December 1993, as amended 25 October 1996. This is a consultative body whose responsibility is to make recommendations on questions of principle which arise with respect to judicial practice in the form of draft explanations of the Plenum, draft submissions relating to legislation and interpretations of laws, draft instructions and other documents prepared by the Supreme Court, and legal issues arising out of individual court cases. Similar councils attached to lower courts may receive assistance from the Council attached to the Supreme Court. Members of the Council are confirmed for a term of five years.

---

[23] The threat to the independence of the courts is a real one. Notwithstanding the creation of the Judicial Department and the provisions of the Law requiring that reductions in court financing be made only with the consent of the All-Russian Congress of Judges or the Council of Judges of the Russian Federation, on 3 April 1998 the Minister of Finances issued Letter No 02–02–14 which announced a 26 per cent cut in the appropriations for courts of ordinary jurisdiction for the second quarter of 1998. Similar reductions in 1995–97 left the judicial system savagely underfunded, unable to pay salaries to judges and support staff and electricity and telephones cut off.

[24] СЗ РФ (1998), no 19, item 2110.

The courts of general jurisdiction below the Supreme Court of the Russian Federation correspond to the administrative-territorial subdivisions of the Federation. All have equal powers and are commonly called for the sake of convenience 'territory (or regional) courts and courts equated thereto)'. All hear cases at first instance, and all act at second instance with respect to courts below them. At second instance, therefore, they exercise judicial powers by way of cassation and supervision. Collectively they comprise the middle link between the Supreme Court and the principal court of the Russian Federation: the district court. Until 1 July 2002 each court consisted of judges and people's assessors; however, from 1993 criminal cases were considered at first instance by juries in the Stavropol Territory Court and the Ivanovo, Moscow, Riazan, and Saratov regional courts, and from January 1994, in the Altai and Krasnodar territory courts and the Rostov and Ul'ianovsk regional courts on an experimental basis. Where the jury is used, the case is heard by one professional judge and 12 jurors, plus two jurors in reserve. At second instance cases are heard by three professional judges. Each court contains a presidium and is divided into judicial divisions for civil and criminal cases, each division chaired by a deputy chairman of the court.

Although part of the middle link, the republic supreme courts also are the highest judicial instance in the republic, exercise judicial supervision over district courts, and have the right of legislative initiative in their republic.

The court which acted exclusively at first instance was the district court, formerly the 'people's courts' but renamed under the 1996 Federal Law on the Judicial System. When justices of the peace were installed, the district court became an appeal court with respect to their decisions. The number of judges varies from one court to another; in remote areas there is but one judge, whereas in large urban concentrations there are several.

(5) Military courts

Previously known as military tribunals until 1992, when they were renamed military courts, these institutions have survived in peacetime apparently on the premise that military life has special features which require adjudication in courts composed of military personnel. Russian military courts fall within the system of courts of general jurisdiction headed by the Supreme Court. Until 29 June 1999, they operated on the basis of a Statute adopted in 1958 as amended 25 June 1980, which applied insofar as not overridden by subsequent general legislation on court organisation and the judicial system, and on the armed forces. On 23 June 1999 the Federal Constitutional Law on Military Courts of the Russian Federation was signed by the President and entered into force from the day of publication.[25]

---

[25] СЗ РФ (1999), no 26, item 3170.

The number of military courts and military judges is determined by the Supreme Court of the Russian Federation. Protests against decisions, judgments, rulings, and decrees of the Military Division of the Supreme Court and military courts which have entered into force are heard by the Presidium of the Supreme Court. Cassational appeals and protests are decided by the Cassational Division of the Supreme Court. The judicial activities of military courts are taken into account just as those of other courts when summaries of judicial practice are prepared.

A military judge must be at least 25 years of age and a Russian citizen, have a higher legal education and work experience of at least five years as a lawyer, have committed no offences, have passed a qualification examination and been recommended by the qualifications division of military court judges, be a military officer, and have concluded a contract to perform military service.[26]

(6) Justice of the peace courts

So-called justice of the peace courts were introduced in Russia by the celebrated Judicial Reforms of 1864, adapted from English law and practice. The courts were actually formed in St Petersburg, Moscow, Kharkov, and ten central Russian provinces, gradually expanding until 1889, when as part of a conservative backlash against liberal institutions they were abolished in 37 internal and six western Russian provinces and replaced by judicial-administrative agencies. In those areas where they were not abolished, they continued to operate until November 1917, when the Soviet authorities put an end to them.

Provision was made for justices of the peace in the Conception of Judicial Reform approved on 24 October 1991 by the Supreme Soviet of the RSFSR. They were accordingly included in the 1996 Federal Constitutional Law on the Judicial System and expressly authorised by the 1998 Federal Law on Justices of the Peace in the Russian Federation. Financial considerations severely delayed their introduction, however, although certain regions did undertake to finance their creation. Nevertheless, as of 1 October 2001 some 3,558 justices of the peace had been appointed and 80 (of 89) subjects of the Federation had adopted their own laws on justices of the peace. During the year 2000, justices of the peace considered 4,878 criminal cases and 91,762 civil cases. Since these cases were previously within the jurisdiction of the district courts, there was a considerable decrease in the workload of the latter.[27]

Justices of the peace are judges of general jurisdiction and part of the unified judicial system of the Russian Federation. They issue decrees when deciding cases, and

---

[26] V M Lebedev and N A Petukhov (eds), Комментарий к Федеральному конституционному закону О военных судах Российской Федерации[*Commentary on Federal Constitutional Law on Military Courts of Russian Federation*] (2000) 58.

[27] See Российская юстиция, no 1 (2002) 23.

these, together with other documents issued by them, are binding throughout Russia upon all to whom they are directed. Justices of the peace enjoy the same protections and guarantees as other judges, and these may be augmented (but not reduced) by laws of subjects of the Federation. Their competence at first instance extends to criminal cases concerning crimes for whose commission the maximum punishment that may be assigned does not exceed two years deprivation of freedom;[28] cases concerning the issuance of a judicial order; cases concerning dissolution of marriage if there is no dispute concerning the children between the spouses; cases concerning the division of jointly acquired property between spouses; other cases arising from family law relations except those with regard to establishment or contesting of paternity or motherhood, deprivation of parental rights, and adoption; cases concerning property disputes when the value of the suit does not exceed five hundred minimum amounts of payment for labour; cases arising from labour relations, except for reinstatement at work; cases concerning determination of the procedure for use of land plots, structures, and other immoveable property; cases concerning administrative violations relegated to the competence of justices by the 2001 CAdV.

Justices of the peace act alone; there are no people's assessors or jurors to assist them. They operate within territorial units called judicial precincts. The total number of justices and number of judicial precincts is determined within a subject of the Russian Federation by a federal law to be introduced through the legislative initiative of the subject of the Federation concerned, agreed with the Russian Supreme Court, or vice versa. Judicial precincts are to contain from 15,000 to 30,000 persons, and if there are less than 15,000 persons in the relevant territorial formation, only one justice of the peace operates.

A justice of the peace must be a Russian citizen aged 25 or more having a higher legal education and work experience as a lawyer for not less than five years, have committed no offences, and have passed the qualifications examination and been recommended by the college of judges in the respective subject of the Russian Federation. Federal court judges with more than five years experience are exempt from the examination. They are appointed or elected to office by the legislative agency of State power of the subject of the Russian Federation or elected directly by the populace in the judicial precinct as established by a law of the subject of the Russian Federation. The term of office may not exceed five years and is determined by local law. Subsequent elections or appointments are possible for up to five year terms. Financing of salaries and expenses is from the federal budget; salaries are fixed at 60 per cent of the salary of the Chairman of the Supreme Court

---

[28] Justices of the Peace hear criminal cases in accordance with the 2001 Code of Criminal Procedure of the Russian Federation, Articles 318–323 inclusive laying down special provisons for criminal proceedings decided by a justice of the peace.

of the Russian Federation, except in cities of federal significance, where the coefficient is 64 per cent.[29]

(7) Arbitrazh courts

History

The conviction that commercial or economic disputes required special expertise to resolve, and perhaps special procedures, surfaced early in Soviet legal history. Even during the NEP State arbitration commissions were established for this purpose, by a Statute of 21 September 1922. They functioned in each province, and in Moscow a Supreme Arbitration Commission was formed to decide appeals filed against awards of provincial commissions and hear certain disputes at first instance. In 1924 the USSR Supreme Arbitration Commission was created to take jurisdiction over disputes involving enterprises of all-union stature or enterprises from different union republics. The introduction of national economic planning rendered NEP-style arbitration obsolete. On 4 March 1931 the arbitration commissions were abolished; pending and future litigation between enterprises was to be transferred to the ordinary courts, which would assign two people's assessors employed in economic agencies to hear the case with a judge. For a brief spell unification was achieved in the Soviet judicial system, but it was short-lived. The ordinary courts at the time proved to be wholly unsuited to handle this type of dispute. On 3 May 1931 a system of State arbitrazh was created as an integral system attached to each administrative-territorial level from region upwards.

Introduced at a time when the Pashukanis school of economic law was influential, State arbitrazh initially represented a kind of hybrid between arbitration and adjudication. Reconciliation of the parties was to be the primary object; the enterprise managers themselves often appeared around the table to arrange a settlement. Failing that, arbitrazh was to resolve the dispute on the basis of prevailing economic plans and regulations, having regard to economic policy and expediency. Civil code provisions were but useful guidelines and not binding; for a time even jurisconsults were barred from the proceedings. On 19 December 1933 arbitrazh jurisdiction was extended to pre-contractual disputes between socialist organisations; by the mid-1930s the restoration of 'stability of laws' had left its imprint; arbitrazh was to apply relevant Soviet legislation to disputes, jurisconsults appeared on behalf of their management, civil procedure codes were used when relevant, and the arbitrator was required to produce a reasoned opinion based on an accurate account of the proceedings. Economic expediency had become a sup-

---

[29] For a useful survey of regional experience, see A F Izvarina, Мировые судьи России начала XXI века [*Justices of the Peace of Russia at the Beginning of the XXI Century*] (Rostov on Don, 2002).

plementary consideration to be invoked when legislation or the contract itself did not dispose of all the relevant issues.

The 1931 decree was replaced on 17 August 1960 by a statute which broadened the scope of arbitrazh activity, enlarged arbitrazh control over the terms of economic contracts, and elaborated the rules of arbitrazh procedure. The 1960 Statute was replaced on 18 January 1974. The 1977 USSR Constitution elevated State arbitrazh to an agency of constitutional stature, a status consolidated in the Law on State Arbitrazh in the USSR adopted 30 November 1979 and amended extensively in 1987 to reflect *perestroika* policies and move the arbitrazh system closer to that of a court.

Current legislation

The decision to abandon the system of State arbitrazh, so deeply linked with the Planned Economy, and introduce arbitrazh courts as part of the judicial system was taken by the Russian Federation in the form of the Law on the Arbitrazh Court adopted 4 July 1991. The Arbitrazh Code of Procedure was adopted 5 March 1992 and entered into force 15 April 1992.[30] The 1993 Russian Constitution (Article 127) confirmed the arbitrazh courts as a branch of the federal judicial system and required the enactment of the Federal Constitutional Law on Arbitrazh Courts in the Russian Federation of 28 April 1995 and in force as from 1 July 1995.[31] On 5 April 1995 the Code of Arbitrazh Procedure was enacted to replace the 1992 version, and on 24 July 2002, with effect from 1 September 2002, the third Code of Arbitrazh Procedure was adopted.[32]

The system of arbitrazh courts comprises the Supreme Arbitrazh Court of the Russian Federation, the federal arbitrazh courts of precincts (of which there are ten), and the arbitrazh courts of the subjects of the Federation, of which 92 were in operation in 2000. The full complement of judges for the system of arbitrazh courts is nearly 3,000 (by the year 2006 it is estimated that 10,000 arbitrazh judges will be required); by February 2002, the number of judges in post was 2,591, of which 65 per cent were women. The average age of judges was 39, and about 80 per cent were under age 50 and only 4 per cent above the age of 60. Of the 38 who resigned during 2001, two were dismissed for offences incompatible with the office of judge. During the past ten years (1992–2001), 23 arbitrazh court judges were dismissed for such reasons.

In autumn 1996 14 arbitrazh courts began to experiment with arbitrazh assessors, individual non-lawyers at least 25 years of age, Russian citizens with

---

[30] СЗ РФ (1992), no 16, item 836; the Law was amended on 7 July 1993.
[31] СЗ РФ (1995), no 18, item 1589.
[32] СЗ РФ (1995), no 19, item 1589; (2002), no 30, item 3012. Changes were made in the 1995 Code by the Decree of the Constitutional Court of the RF of 3 February 1998 and Ruling of the same Court of 14 January 2000. See respectively СЗ РФ (1998), no 6, item 784; (2000), no 10, item 1165.

experience in entrepreneurial or economic activity but who were not judges. Although the results of the experiment were reportedly mixed, the scheme evidently was successful and led to the adoption of the Federal Law on Arbitrazh Assessors of Arbitrazh Courts of Subjects of the Russian Federation, of 30 May 2001 as amended 25 July 2002.[33] The requirements for such assessors have been tightened; they must now in addition have a professional higher education and work experience of at least five years in the sphere of economic, financial, legal, management, or entrepreneurial activity and upon taking office are required to swear an oath. Candidacies for appointment are recommended by chambers of commerce and industry and associations of entrepreneurs or other professional associations, the Lists being subject to confirmation by the Plenum of the Supreme Arbitrazh Court of the Russian Federation and names published in the Вестник of that Court. There are to be not less than two arbitrazh assessors for each arbitrazh judge who considers cases at first instance. Arbitrazh assessors serve for two years and are subject to reappointment. Remuneration is based on a formula that takes into account the number of days worked and local levels of remuneration.

In 2001 the arbitrazh courts received 745,626 petitions to sue, an increase of 17.5 per cent over 2000, of which 9.5 per cent were rejected. The growth in the number of cases during the year 2001 occurred in the domain of administrative (as opposed to civil) disputes; administrative disputes comprised 50 per cent of all cases decided by arbitrazh courts. Within this category, the number of tax cases were up by 36 per cent, and the number of cases to declare acts of State agencies to be invalid increased by 40 per cent. As for civil cases, the great majority (84 per cent) concerned the failure to perform contracts. More than 56,000 cases concerned bankruptcy, eight times greater than in 1997.[34]

About 12.5 per cent of cases were appealed to the appellate instance of the arbitrazh court system (nearly 80,000 cases) and 8.7 per cent to a cassational instance (about 55,000 cases). The Supreme Arbitrazh Court in 2001 reviewed by way of supervision 18,167 cases, and less than 10 per cent were satisfied. The number of cases with the participation of foreign juridical and natural persons constituted about 1,200 in 2001, a decrease compared with 1997. Of these about 800 involved Western companies, and 400 CIS countries. The caseload varied greatly from one jurisdiction to another. On average it was nearly 34 cases per month for each judge, but in some jurisdictions it was as high as 59 (Archangel).

All arbitrazh courts are federal courts, even those organised at the level of subjects of the Russian Federation. Accordingly, all judicial appointments to arbitrazh courts are regulated by federal laws and not by legislation of the subjects of the

---

[33] СЗ РФ (2001), no 23, item 2288; (2002), no 30, item 3033.
[34] See Вестник Высшего арбитражного суда Российской Федерации, no 4 (2002) 5–29.

Federation. The Chairman of the Supreme Arbitrazh Court is appointed to office by the Soviet of the Federation upon the recommendation of the President of the Russian Federation. The same procedure applies to the deputy chairmen and other judges of the Supreme Arbitrazh Court, except that in this instance the Chairman of the Supreme Court makes recommendations for appointment to the President of Russia. The other arbitrazh court judges are appointed in accordance with the 1996 Law on the Judicial System.

An arbitrazh court considers cases within its jurisdiction in which Russian citizens or organisations are parties, and also foreign organisations, organisations with foreign investments, international organisations, foreign citizens or stateless persons who are effectuating entrepreneurial activity, unless provided otherwise by an international treaty of the Russian Federation. Although commonly called 'commercial' or 'economic' courts because a considerable measure of their activity arises out of entrepreneurial relations, the arbitrazh courts have jurisdiction over matters which goes far beyond the ordinary understanding of 'commercial'. The jurisdiction of the courts set out in the 2002 Code of Arbitrazh Procedure (Article 27) speaks of 'economic disputes.' Examples of such are: disagreements relating to a contract which according to a law must be concluded or with regard to which the parties have agreed to submit to an arbitrazh court; the change of the conditions or dissolution of contracts; failure to perform or improper performance of obligations, recognition of the right of ownership, vindication suits, compensation of losses, defence of honour, dignity, and business reputation, deeming 'non-normative' acts of State agencies, local self-government, and other agencies to be invalid if they are contrary to laws and other normative legal acts and violate the rights and legal interests of citizens, deeming a writ of execution or other document to be not subject to execution in an uncontested proceeding; appeals against a refusal of State registration or evasion thereof, or against the recovery of fines, the establishment of legal facts having significance for the arising, change, or termination of the rights of organisations and citizens in the sphere of entrepreneurial and other economic activity, and others. In certain instances the arbitrazh courts may hear cases of formations which are not juridical persons and natural persons who are not entrepreneurs. The Code of Arbitrazh Procedure must be read together with decrees of the Plenum of the Supreme Arbitrazh Court construing its application.

The principles upon which the arbitrazh courts function are legality, independence of judges, equality of organisations and citizens before the law, adversarialiness and equality of the parties, and openness of the examination of cases (Article 6, 1995 Law on Arbitrazh Courts). To these the 2002 Code on Arbitrazh Procedure adds directness (Article 10), glasnost (Article 11), and national language of court proceeding (Article 12).

The principle of collegiality operates differently in the arbitrazh courts. Cases at first instance are heard by a single judge except those involving bankruptcy, or declaring the acts of State agencies or agencies of local self-government to be invalid, or cases returned for new consideration or within the jurisdiction of the Supreme Arbitrazh Court, in which case three judges hear the case. By choice of the parties a judge and two arbitrazh assessors may hear a case. Openness means that persons present in the courtroom may take notes, keep a verbatim transcript, or record the proceedings on tape without the permission of the court. Permission is required for making videos, cinema films, and broadcast of the proceedings by radio or television.

The internal structure of the arbitrazh courts is similar in key respects with that of the courts of ordinary jurisdiction. The Supreme Arbitrazh Court consists of the Plenum, the Presidium, and two judicial divisions, one for disputes arising from civil and other legal relations and the second for disputes arising from administrative legal relations. The Plenum consists of the Chairman, deputy chairmen, and all judges of the Supreme Arbitrazh Court. Deputies from the Federal Assembly, the chairmen of the Constitutional Court and the Supreme Court, the Procurator General, the Minister of Justice, judges of arbitrazh courts, legal scholars, and others may be invited to take part in Plenum sessions. The Plenum is concerned principally with organisational matters, legislative initiative, referral of questions to the Constitutional Court, choosing members of the judicial divisions, confirming the Reglament of arbitrazh courts and the permanent sites of federal arbitrazh courts, and the like.

The Presidium of the Supreme Arbitrazh Court consists of the Chairman, deputy chairman, and chairmen of the judicial divisions, together with individual judges who may be elected by the Plenum. It is the Presidium which considers cases by way of supervision upon protests against judicial acts of arbitrazh courts which have entered into legal force. The judicial divisions consider cases at first instance, study and generalise judicial practice, make proposals to improve legislation, analyse forensic statistics, among other functions. Within each judicial division so-called benches of judges are organised to hear cases. A Council of the Chairmen of Arbitrazh Courts, consisting of the chairmen of all arbitrazh courts in the Russian Federation, acts as a consultative organ to advice on organisational, personnel, and financial matters. There also is a Scientific-Consultative Council composed of leading legal scholars and practitioners attached to the Supreme Arbitrazh Court. In 1997 the Supreme Arbitrazh Court organised a sector of private international law to analyse systematically the consideration of cases with the participation of foreign persons; this sector played a key role in persuading the Russian Federation to ratify the Hague civil procedural conventions.

The ten federal arbitrazh courts of precincts have no plenums but do have a presidium and the same judicial divisions as the Supreme Arbitrazh Court. The term 'precinct' in this instance refers to administrative-territorial combinations formed for the sole purposes of the arbitrazh courts; each 'precinct' incorporates a number of geographic administrative-territorial divisions of the Russian Federation. They act purely as a cassational instance and sit collegially with an uneven number of judges.

The remaining arbitrazh courts are organised along analogous lines, having regard to the number of judges in each. The Reglament adopted by the Supreme Arbitrazh Court governs internal organisational matters of the entire court system and relationships among the courts.

The Supreme Arbitrazh Court issues decrees based on summaries of judicial practice which are binding upon lower arbitrazh courts. In exceptional instances these have been issued jointly with the Supreme Court of the Russian Federation. The monthly Вестник Высшего Арбитражного Суда Российской Федерации [Herald of the Supreme Arbitrazh Court of the Russian Federation] is the best of all court gazettes, containing not merely relevant legislation, court decrees, and judicial decisions, but also comparative materials from other CIS jurisdictions and official announcements of pending bankruptcies throughout Russia.

(8) Other tribunals

Article 29(5) of the 1993 Russian Constitution provides that the freedom of the mass media, or mass information, is guaranteed. In the months prior to the adoption of the Constitution, during the election campaign of 1993, an Arbitral Information Court was formed on an experimental basis to consider disputes arising out of access to or reports published in the mass media. The arbitral court's mandate expired on 31 December 1993. Its role during the campaign was regarded as highly successful. In furtherance of Article 29 of the 1993 Constitution it was decided to create in place of the arbitral tribunal the Judicial Chamber for Information Disputes as an improved and permanent successor. Although called a 'judicial chamber', it was not part of the Russian judicial system but was rather a State agency attached to the President of the Russian Federation. Between 1994–6 the Judicial Chamber issued 103 decisions, nine recommendations, 20 expert opinions, 15 statements, and one ruling.[35]

Under the Statute on the Chamber, confirmed by Edict of the President of the Russian Federation on 31 January 1994,[36] the Chamber assisted the President of the Russian Federation in realising his constitutional powers as guarantor of the rights, freedoms, and legal interests in the sphere of the mass media. It consisted

---

[35] These are collected in A V Vengerov (ed), Судебная палата по информационным спорам при Президенте Российской Федерации: 1994–1996. Нормативные акты. Практика. Комментарии [Judicial Chamber for Information Disputes attached to the President of the Russian Federation: 1994–1996. Normative Acts. Practice. Commentary] (1997).

[36] САПП РФ (1994), no 6, item 434.

of a chairman, deputy, and members appointed to and relieved from office by the President of Russia and settled disputes and other cases in the domain of the mass media unless such cases were according to Russian legislation within the jurisdiction of the Russian courts. The Judicial Chamber also considered cases and disputes arising from the requirements of generally-recognised principles and norms of international law and from international treaties of the Russian Federation, or from the ethics of journalism. Its decisions were final. The legislation establishing the Chamber lost force by Edict of the President of the Russian Federation of 1 September 2000.[37]

C. Procuracy

(1) History

The Procuracy is very much a Russian institution whose precise origins await definitive study. Peter the Great created the office of 'fiskal' on 2 March 1711 with supervisory functions in treasury matters and is known to have studied carefully French and Swedish institutions analogous in nature. It is, however, to the classical Petrine model of procurator established by an Edict of 12 January 1722[38] to which the modern Russian Procuracy traces its direct origins. The Russian Procuracy marked its 275th anniversary in 1997 with the publication of a monumental jubilee volume containing the biographies of the principal procurators from the beginning to 1917.[39]

In Peter the Great's concept, the procurator was an official independent of local influence who acted as the 'eye of the Tsar' in supervising the conformity to law of the actions of all government departments, officials, and courts, including the Ruling Senate itself. Subordinate procurators were authorised to submit 'proposals' to local officials who violated the law and to present 'protests and reports' regarding violations to superior procurators. In the three years or so of operation until the death of Peter the Great in 1725, the institution reportedly enjoyed some success. Peter's successors reduced its importance; Catherine II revived the Procuracy in modified form, transforming it into an administrative office rather

---

[37] СЗ РФ (2000), no 36, item 3636.

[38] To commemorate this date the President of the Russian Federation by an Edict of 7 June 1996 declared 12 January to be 'Procurator's Day' in Russia. СЗ РФ (1996), no 24, item 2876.

[39] See A G Zviagintsev and Iu G Orlov, Призванные отечеством. Российские прокуроры 1722–1917 [*Called by the Fatherland. Russian Procurators 1722–1917*] (1997). The most extensive modern study of the Procuracy is the six-volume series by the same authors: Око государево [*Eye of the Sovereign*] (1994); Тайные советники империи [*Privy Councillors of the Empire*] (1995); Под сенью русского орла [*Under the Protection of the Russian Eagle*] (1996); В эпоху потрясений и реформ [*In the Epoch of Shocks and Reforms*] (1997); Приговоренные временем. Российские и советские прокуроры XX век 1937–1953 [*Judged by Time: Russian and Soviet Procurators of the Twentieth Century: 1937–1953*] (2001).

than a supervisory one. Alexander I in his governmental reorganisation of 1802 combined the Procurator General with the Minister of Justice and removed most supervisory powers over State administration. The 1864 judiciary reforms ultimately eliminated these and required the procurators to confine their activities to the judicial department. Nevertheless, in the last half-century of Imperial government the procurators did participate as members of certain provincial committees, but without the right of supervision or protest. Prosecution of cases had become their principal function.

The pre-revolutionary Procuracy was abolished by Decree No 1 'On Courts' of 24 November 1917. The prosecution function was passed initially to the public-spirited or aggrieved citizen. A college of 'accusers and defenders' was formed by Decree No 2 'On Courts', and revolutionary tribunals relied on their own colleges of accusers, to consist of at least three persons for each tribunal selected by the local soviets directly or upon the recommendation of its tribunal or the People's Commissariat of Justice. But these were makeshift measures and in the end proved to be unworkable. The supervisory functions of the pre-revolutionary Procuracy over justice matters was dispersed to organs of local soviets. One archival source of the period (1918) disclosed that the 'Commissar of justice is the representative of central authority in the provinces, replacing the former procurators'. Supervisory functions also were exercised by ancillary bodies, the People's Commissariat for State Control and later the People's Commissariat of the Workers'-Peasants' Inspectorate. These too were inadequate, and at Lenin's behest on 28 May 1922, following prolonged debate, the RSFSR instituted the State Procuracy.[40] The original model combined elements of the Petrine and Alexandrine versions: Peter's notions that the Procuracy was to be independent of all local authorities and that it would supervise the legality of acts of all State agencies, enterprises, and citizens through its powers of protest, proposal, and prosecution; Alexander's policy of placing the Procuracy within the People's Commissariat of Justice and making the Commissar simultaneously the Procurator of the Republic. The Procurator appointed all inferior procurators from candidates put forward by central and local agencies; a separate system of military procurators also was subordinate to the Procurator.

Under the 1924 USSR Constitution, an all-union Procuracy was created within the USSR Supreme Court with powers of constitutional, general, and judicial supervision; its powers were elaborated in a Statute of 24 July 1929.[41] In 1933 the Procuracy was reorganised; its role in constitutional supervision was abolished

---

[40] СУ РСФСР (1922), no 36, item 424.
[41] СЗ СССР (1929), no 50, item 445. On the debates over the revival and powers of the procuracy, see J N Hazard, *Settling Disputes in Soviet Society* (1960); G Morgan, *Soviet Administrative Legality* (1962); S Kucherov, *The Organs of Soviet Administration of Justice: Their History and Operation* (1970) 404–447.

and it was separated from the USSR Supreme Court, but there remained the dual system of the USSR Procuracy and union republic people's commissars of justice acting simultaneously as procurators. The latter found themselves in a position of dual subordination: to the USSR Procurator and to the council of people's commissars of their respective republic. Ultimate centralisation of the Procuracy came in 1936 with the formation of the USSR People's Commissariat of Justice and separation of union republic procuracies from that commissariat at all levels. Curiously, this centralisation was not followed by new unified legislation. Articles 113–117 of the 1936 USSR Constitution became the principal legislative definition of Procuracy powers and functions together with the 1933 Statute. Specialised procuracies for water transport and the railway underwent episodic restructuring in the 1930s, and on 5 November 1936 the structural subdivisions of the Procuracy were reorganised. On 19 March 1946 the Procurator of the USSR was renamed the Procurator General of the USSR. After Stalin's death and the abolition of the special boards, it was decided to reinforce rather than to abandon the supervisory role of the Procuracy.

On 12 April 1955 an editorial in *Pravda* called upon the Procuracy to eliminate 'serious shortcomings' in its work and criticised the institution for having been 'insufficiently principled', not fully taking advantage of the 'rights granted to it by the USSR Constitution', not uncovering violations of law at the time, and not stopping the 'anti-State activities of individual officials'.

The extent to which the Procuracy was a willing collaborator or pawn in Special Board proceedings (Procuracy participation was compulsory under the decree establishing the Boards) has yet to be studied, but it is doubtful that in the political climate of the time that the Procuracy could have effectively altered the course of events when the Communist Party itself was unable, if not unwilling, to do so.[42] On 24 May 1955 the Procuracy received its first comprehensive legislation in the form of the Statute on Procuracy Supervision in the USSR. The Statute enlarged the scope of general supervision by the Procuracy, empowered procurators to

---

[42] Insofar as the institutional foundations are concerned, the evidence is conflicting. The 1933 Statute on the Procuracy contained not a single word about the duty of the Procuracy to defend the rights and legal interests of citizens. A secret Decree of the Council of People's Commissars and Central Committee of the All-Russian Communist Party (Bolshevik) dated 15 June 1935 'On the Procedure for Agreeing Arrests', approved two days later by the Politburo of the Central Committee, provided that all agencies of the NKVD without exception could perform arrests only with the sanction of a procurator, and when it was necessary to perform an arrest at the site of the crime, immediately to notify the procurator thereof for confirmation of the arrest. Arrests of senior union republics' officials required that the NKVD and the Procuracy obtain the prior authorisation of the chairman of the Central Executive Committee of the USSR or chairmen of the union republic central executive committee respectively. The Decree is published, together with others which cast further light on the Procuracy in this era, in V M Kuritsyn, История государства и права России 1929–1940 [*History of State and Law of Russia 1929–1940*] (1998) 116–26.

demand and obtain data and documents from officials, and elaborated the procurators' powers to make proposals, representations, and protests.

Following the adoption of the 1977 USSR Constitution, legislation on the Procuracy was elevated to the status of a fully-fledged Law on the Procuracy of the USSR, enacted in 1979. The 1979 Law strengthened the qualifications required of those aspiring to be a procurator, enlarged the role of collegial decision-making within Procuracy institutions, and expanded the group of State agencies and institutions who were subject to Procuracy supervision. Amendments to the 1979 Law introduced in 1987 conferred on procurators the right to issue a written instruction and caution in addition to their usual armoury of recommendations, protests, and other means of recourse.

During the late years of *perestroika* in the Soviet Union, the Procuracy experienced further transformations, mostly linked to the transition to a market economy and taking the form of internal reorganisation. For a brief period in 1991–2 the prospect of a CIS Procuracy was entertained, the idea being to transform the Procuracy of the USSR into the Procuracy of the Union of Sovereign States, an inter-republic Procuracy supervision agency which would function on the basis of all-union and republic legislation on the Procuracy. To this end a federal collegium headed by the Procurator General of the CIS was formed; the deputies of the USSR Procurator General and the procurators general of the republics were members of the collegium. Many supervision functions previously handled by specialised procuracies or by the USSR Procuracy were transferred to the republics. These schemes came to naught when the USSR Procuracy ceased to exist with the dissolution of the Soviet Union in late December 1991.[43]

(2) Current legislation

In the Russian Federation the decision to create a unified Russian Procuracy was taken on 15 November 1991 pursuant to the Declaration on State Sovereignty of the RSFSR and Articles 176 and 179 of the 1978 RSFSR Constitution. The Procurator General of the RSFSR accepted jurisdiction over all Procuracy agencies on Russian territory and all institutions formerly associated with the USSR Procuracy, including scientific research institutions. A period of dual subordination commenced in which Procuracy agencies were subordinate to the Procurator General of the republic and to the highest agencies of State power. The Procuracy experienced significant resignations from service, the Procurator General of the RSFSR reporting to be short 1,200 persons on 1 January 1992, and a commensurate decline in prestige and authority.

---

[43] On this episode see V I Baskov, Курс прокурорского надзора [*Course on Procuracy Supervision*] (1998) 34–35.

On 17 January 1992 the RSFSR Supreme Soviet adopted the Law on the Procuracy of the Russian Federation which, as amended on 18 October 1995 to incorporate the provisions of the 1993 Russian Constitution, remains in force with further amendments of 10 February 1999, 19 November 1999, 2 January 2000, 27 December 2000, 29 December 2001, 30 December 2001, 28 June 2002, and 25 July 2002.[44]

(3) Structure

True to its Petrine model, the Procuracy is a unified, centralised system of Procuracy agencies and institutions comprising the General Procuracy of the Russian Federation, the procuracies of the republics, territories, regions, cities of Moscow and St Petersburg, autonomous region, cities, and district, and the military, transport, and other specialised procuracies. Basically there are procuracies at each administrative-territorial level of the Russian Federation, with certain adjustments and terminological variations. The Buriat Republic, for example, has *ulus* procuracies instead of district procuracies, and in Moscow the medium-level link is the procuracies of the administrative precincts. Some subjects of the Federation have created 'inter-district' procuracies whose jurisdiction extends to two districts. Although the 1993 Russian Constitution and the 1995 Law on the Procuracy emphasise the centralised and unified nature of the Procuracy, that principle is attenuated by the fact that procurators are appointed to office 'by agreement with the subjects' of the Russian Federation and are accountable in some measure to them.

The General Procuracy of the Russian Federation is headed by the Procurator General of the Russian Federation who is appointed to office for a five-year term by the Soviet of the Federation upon the recommendation of the President of the Russian Federation. The Procurator General has a first deputy procurator and several deputies, all of whom are members of a Collegium, together with other Procuracy personnel appointed by the Procurator General.

The structure of the central apparatus of the General Procuracy is established by an Order of the Procurator General issued 5 February 1996, No 12-Sh. There are some 27 administrations and sections, including the secretariat, personnel department, eight concerned with various types of supervision, and the military procuracy. There also is a Scientific Advisory Council to assist with questions of the organisation and activity of procuracy agencies; its Statute is confirmed by the Procurator General. The Chief Investigative Administration and the Chief Military Procuracy are headed by deputies of the Procurator General; senior aides head the administrations and sections with the rights of an administration, and aides head the sections within administrations of the General Procuracy.

---

[44] СЗ РФ (1995), no 47, item 4472; (1999), no 7, item 878; no 47, item 5620; (2000), no 32, item 3341; (2001), no 1(I), item 2; no 53(I), item 5018 and item 5030; (2002), no 26, item 2523; no 30, item 3029.

The Procurator General directs the activity of Procuracy agencies and supervises their work. He issues four distinct types of subordinate normative act which are binding throughout the Procuracy system: the order (приказ), through which the strategic line for exercising powers of supervision over the execution of laws or other activities of Procuracy agencies are determined; the instructive directive (указание), which elaborate orders of the Procurator General; the regulation (распоряжение), intended to ensure the fulfilment of particular actions by a procurator or investigator; and the instruction (инструкция), which contains directions for the performance of procedural or operational actions, such as statistical reports or the registration of criminal offences. Within budgetary and personnel establishment limits, he determines the personnel requirements and structure of the General Procuracy and of the procuracies and Procuracy institutions subordinate to him. In particular, he appoints and dismisses all personnel of the General Procuracy and all procurators throughout the entire system (subject to the duty to secure agreement to the appointment of procurators of subjects of the Federation).

The procurators of subjects of the Federation and procurators equated thereto direct the activities of city and district procuracies and other procuracies equated to them and operate on the basis of laws of the Russian Federation and normative acts of the Procurator General. Within their budgets and personnel establishments fixed by the Procurator General, they may make changes in their staffing. The procuracies of subjects of the Federation also have collegiums which consider the activities of Procuracy agencies, fulfil normative acts of the Procurator General relating to powers of supervision, hear reports of the heads of administrations and sections and of inferior procurators, and discuss personnel matters.

The Procuracy has a large number of investigators who carry out the preliminary investigation in cases relegated by law or by the Procuracy to their competence. Attached to the Procuracy are senior investigators and investigators for 'especially important cases'; lower levels of the Procuracy have investigators of the same nature.

Attached to the General Procuracy are several institutions of a research or instructional nature. The Scientific-Research Institute for Problems of Strengthening Legality and Legal Order deals with problems of organising the struggle against crime by exploring the causes of crime and preventative measures. This is the head institution in Russia concerned with criminology and Procuracy supervision and is a corporate member of the International Association of Criminal Law. Procuracy personnel are required to undergo periodic attestation and courses to improve their skills. These are conducted principally by the Institute for the Improvement of Investigative Workers in St Petersburg, which trains Procuracy and internal affairs investigators and certain police personnel, and the Institute for Raising the Qualifications of Executive Cadres of the General Procuracy of the

Russian Federation, located in Moscow, which trains senior Procuracy officials. A Scientific Advisory Council within the Procuracy, which includes well-known legal scholars from without the organisation, considers proposals to improve Procuracy supervision and investigative work.

The Procuracy publishes its own monthly journal, Законность [Legality], formerly called Социалистическая законность [Socialist Legality].

(4) Procurators

Citizens of the Russian Federation who have a higher legal education and the requisite professional and moral qualities and sound health may be procurators. A probation period of six months is required. Aides of procurators and certain investigative personnel in exceptional cases at city and district level may be persons studying law in institutions of higher professional education. Age requirements depend upon the level of appointment in the Procuracy system. The minimum is 25 years of age to be appointed procurator of a city or district and at least three years of experience as a procurator or investigator. Procurators of subjects of the Federation must be at least 30 years old. Ranks—there are 11 in all—are conferred on procurators in accordance with the Statute on Class Ranks of Procuracy Workers, confirmed by the President of the Russian Federation. In an effort to attract new recruits and retain existing personnel, the 1995 Law on the Procuracy incorporates a number of provisions intended to make the career of a procurator more attractive: paid tuition while obtaining a law degree, improved social benefits and housing, special protections against threats to his person or family, and other forms of incentive.

Procuracy workers may not be members of social organisations which pursue political purposes, nor may such organisations be formed within Procuracy agencies and institutions. Nor, recalling the close relationship in the Soviet era between the Communist Party and the Procuracy, may procurators and investigators be bound in their official activities by the decisions of social associations.

(5) Branches of Procuracy supervision

The supervisory functions of the Procuracy are multifarious and collectively comprise that institution's claim to uniqueness among bodies with analogous objectives in other families of legal systems. The 1995 Law on the Procuracy divides the supervision function into four principal orientations. The first and most important is the Procuracy's power of 'general supervision' over the execution of laws by federal ministries and departments, representative (or legislative) and executive agencies of subjects of the Russian Federation, agencies of local self-government, military administration agencies, control agencies, officials thereof, and also over the conformity to laws of legal acts issued by them. Acts adopted or issued by these agencies must correspond to the constitutions and other enactments of superior legislative and State agencies and be precisely and uniformly executed by officials and citizens. This formulation makes it clear that the Procuracy is not the supreme guardian of the law; it has no supervisory authority over acts of the Government of the Russian Federation, nor the Federal Assembly, nor the President of the Russian Federation. However, its supervisory authority does extend to the parliamentary and governmental agencies of the subjects of the Russian Federation. Its concern is to ensure that the Russian bureaucracy and citizenry adhere to law and not that the highest agencies of Federation power and administration do so.

The powers of the Procuracy to give effect to general supervision are several. They may personally visit the premises of the objects of supervision to inspect the state of affairs, they have access to materials and documents, and may require the directors and other officials to submit necessary documents, materials, statistical information, and the like, verify materials and appeals submitted to the Procuracy, and conduct an internal audit of the activity or organisations within the control or jurisdiction of the agencies being investigated. If necessary, officials and citizens may be summoned to the Procuracy to offer explanations regarding the violation of laws.

Once a violation of law is established, a procurator may react by submitting a recommendation to eliminate the violation, bring a protest against a legal act which is contrary to a law, or apply to a court or arbitrazh court to demand that a legal act be deemed to be invalid. If material harm was caused by a violation of law, the procurator may initiate civil proceedings for recovery. A criminal prosecution may be instituted if a crime has been committed, or an administrative proceeding if there was an administrative offence. A person illegally subjected to administrative detention on the basis of a decision of a non-judicial agency may be freed upon the decree of a procurator.

In the domain of general supervision a procurator may bring a protest against a legal act which is contrary to a law. The protest is sent to the agency or official which issued the act and is subject to obligatory consideration within ten days from the moment of receipt; if the protest is against the decision of a representative or legislative agency of a subject of the Federation or agency of local self-government, the protest is to be considered at the next session thereof. Under exceptional circumstances requiring the immediate elimination of the violation of a law, the procurator may fix a shorter period for consideration of the protest. The filing of a protest does not mean the agency which issued the act must necessarily accept the protest. Its obligation is to consider the protest and the reasons for it; if it disagrees with the protest, the protest may be rejected, in which event the procurator may pursue the matter by carrying his protest to the next level of the Procuracy. Whether the protest is accepted or not, the results of the protest must be communicated to the procurator at once in written form. If the protest is considered by a collegial agency, the procurator who brought the protest must be informed about the date of the session and has the right to be present. A protest may be recalled by the person who brought it before it is considered.

Although the Procuracy may not protest decrees of the Government or laws of the Federal Assembly which are contrary to the Russian Constitution, the Procurator General does have the right to bring such inconsistencies to the attention of the President of the Russian Federation. If a violation of law justifies the initiation of a criminal or administrative proceeding, the procurator's decree must be considered by the relevant agency or official within the period established by legislation and the results of the consideration communicated in written form.

New to the Procuracy is the category of supervision over compliance with the rights and freedoms of man and citizen. In exercising this function the procurator considers and verifies applications, appeals, and other communications concerning a violation of such rights, explains to victims the procedure for defending those rights and freedoms, takes measures to prevent or suppress such violations, and initiates proceedings against persons who have violated the law in this connection and seeks compensation for damage caused. If a criminal act has been committed, the Procuracy may institute a criminal proceeding, and if an administrative offence, either institute an administrative proceeding or bring the materials of the verification to the agency or official empowered to consider an administrative proceeding.

If a violation of the rights of man or citizen require defence in a civil proceeding and the victim by reason of health, age, or other reasons cannot personally defend those rights in a court, or if the rights and freedoms of a significant number of citizens have been violated or for other reasons such violation takes on great social importance, the procurator has standing to bring a civil suit in a court of general jurisdiction or an arbitrazh court in the interests of the victims. A protest may be brought by a procurator or his deputy against an act violating the rights of man and citizen to the agency or official which issued it. A recommendation to eliminate violations of rights and freedoms may be submitted by the procurator or his deputy to the agency or official empowered to eliminate the violation. All other procuratorial powers are available, as appropriate, which procurators possess when exercising general supervision.

The third branch of Procuracy supervision relates to execution of the laws by agencies effectuating operational search activities, inquiry, or preliminary investigation. The Procuracy's powers are vast and, to Anglo-American eyes, anomalous in some respects, for the procurator is expected both to discipline and further, by himself if necessary, the investigatory process. The procurators are to ensure that when crimes are investigated, the legal requirements for a 'comprehensive, complete, and objective' investigation of all circumstances of the case are complied with, both those incriminating and vindicating the accused, aggravating and mitigating circumstances, the causes of crime, conditions furthering the crime, and measures taken to eliminate those conditions, and that no one is detained, arrested, or prosecuted other than in the procedure provided for by law.

Inquiry and investigation fall within the field of criminal procedure; the Procuracy has jurisdiction over all investigators with respect to supervision irrespective of their departmental affiliation. Operational-search activities are carried on by subdivisions of the police, investigative isolation cells, institutions which administer deprivation of freedom, the FSB, the federal tax police, customs agencies, and others. The powers of the Procuracy to give effect to supervision over inquiries and investigations are numerous and encompass, among others, the right to verify all materials, give written instructions concerning the course of the investigation, repeal illegal or unsubstantiated decrees, sanction the performance of a search or the removal of an accused from office, extend periods of investigation and inquiry, return a criminal case with written instructions in order to continue a preliminary investigation, and confirm a conclusion to indict.

The Procuracy's powers with regard to operational-search activities are considerably narrower. A procurator may demand to see documents relating to such operations and may give instructions to operational-search agencies about taking measures relating to cases under investigative proceedings. He also may demand the termination of illegal or unsubstantiated operational-search measures or repeal related decrees which he considers not to correspond to legislation. A number of his powers available under general supervision may be used in connection with operational-search measures: protest, recommendations, initiating administrative and criminal proceedings, and others, as defined in the Order of the Procurator General of the Russian Federation, No 48, 'On the Organisation of Supervision Over Execution of the Federal Law "On Operational-Search Activity" ', adopted 9 August 1996.

The fourth branch of Procuracy supervision concerns institutions where individuals may be confined or detained, ranging from preliminary confinement to imprisonment or compulsory medical treatment. The procurator is to ensure that legislation regarding treatment of confined persons is complied with by visiting places of confinement systematically and at any time, familiarise himself with relevant documentation, release immediately persons illegally confined, question detained or confined persons, and verify the conformity to law of orders, regulations, and decrees issued by the administrations of places of confinement. The specific tasks of the Procuracy in this connection are set out in the Order of the Procurator General of the Russian Federation, No 8, 'On Improvement of Procuracy Supervision Over Compliance With Laws When Executing Criminal Punishments and in Investigative Isolation Cells', of 26 February 1997.

The plurality of roles which the Procuracy sometimes faces can raise conflicts of interests, especially when the procurator must act as accuser on behalf of the State yet initiate objections to procedural or substantive violations by the court. To some extent conflicts are avoided or reduced by depersonalising the conflict. Different administrations or sections of the Procuracy are concerned with different types of supervison or other activities. The essence of the Procuracy function is to persuade agencies to correct their own errors; except in certain aspects of inquiries and preliminary investigations, the Procuracy itself has no administrative power to set affairs in order by itself.

In addition to supervision, the Procuracy performs a number of other functions. The best known is that associated with the very name of the institution: acting on behalf of the State to prosecute criminal cases in Russian courts. The Russian Code of Criminal Procedure does not in fact use the expression 'criminal prosection'; rather, it speaks of the initiation of a criminal case with respect to specific persons, the performance of the preliminary investigation by investigators of the Procuracy, and the actions of procurators directed towards ensuring the certainty that individuals who have committed a crime will be brought to criminal responsibility. At the trial stage, the procurator performs the role of State accuser, and in this sense becomes the prosecutor. In civil cases the procurator's role is to defend the rights of citizens and the interests of the State and society, and in doing so may familiarise himself with the materials of the case, take part in investigating evidence, submit evidence, and offer opinions to the court regarding the substance of the case.

If after the court considers a case the procurator comes to the view that judicial error has occurred, he is obliged to take measures to eliminate such error by bringing a cassational or private protest to the next higher court.

Most significantly, a procurator has the right to demand and obtain the file of any case from a court, or any category of cases, and to bring a protest by way of supervision against a decision, judgment, ruling, or decree which has entered into legal force and in the view of the procurator is contrary to law. The decision of a judge in an administrative proceeding also may be protested by the procurator. Exceptionally, the Procuracy has protested judicial decisions relating to the enforcement of arbitration awards.

The Procuracy plays a role in coordinating the work of law enforcement agencies against crime in accordance with the Edict of the President of the Russian Federation No 567, of 18 April 1996.

(6) Specialised procuracies

There exist military, transport, and 'other' specialised procuracies in the Russian Federation which act with the rights of regional or district procuracies.

Supervision over the precise and uniform execution of the laws in the Armed Forces of Russia is effectuated by the military procuracies. The Military Procuracy constitutes a separate integral system, the highest body of which is the Chief

Military Procuracy within the General Procuracy of the Russian Federation. The Chief Military Procurator is a deputy of the Procurator General. The hierarchical structure of the Military Procuracy corresponds to the system of military courts. Therefore there are procuracies for military districts, force groups, fleets, strategic missile forces, the federal border guard, among others. The lowest level is the procuracies of garrisons and formations.

The Military Procuracy is governed by the 1995 Law on the Procuracy and by the 1981 Statute on the Military Procuracy, confirmed by the Presidium of the USSR Supreme Soviet. Its basic functions include taking measures to prevent violations of law, to enhance military discipline, combat readiness, and State security, to ensure that Russian legislation is correctly and uniformly applied, to protect the rights and legal interests of military servicemen and their families, workers and employees of the Armed Forces, and other citizens or military units, institutions, enterprises, and organisations. The supervisory powers of the Military Procuracy extend to ensuring that all military personnel execute the law when performing their duties; that military courts comply with legality when considering civil and criminal cases; and that legality is observed in guardhouses and disciplinary battalions. The ability of military procurators to demand data and information is more limited than their civilian counterparts, but they may obtain orders, instructions, and other acts to verify their conformity to law, conduct on-the-spot verifications, but only in connection with applications, appeals, or other information concerning violations, and demand explanations from officials, military servicemen, and other citizens. In 1995–7 the crime rate in the Russian Armed Forces grew by more than 20 per cent per year, making the task of military procurators all the more burdensome.

The Transport Procuracy first appeared in the former Soviet Union in the 1920s; they were abolished in 1960 and revived in 1977, being subordinate directly to the union republic procurators. In 1980 the system was strengthened and extended to railway, air, and water transport. Severely criticised in 1987 for being sensitive to local interests, they have nonetheless been retained and found their role in the post-Soviet period. The transport procuracies are concerned with supervision over the execution of laws on a particular railway or sector thereof, port, or air terminal. As of 1998 there existed 17 transport procuracies.

Nature protection procuracies are interdistrict institutions within the jurisdiction of the procuracies of the republic, region, or territory where they are situated. They concentrate upon ecological violations: pollution, waste of natural resources, and the like. Their powers of supervision concentrate upon protection of the natural environment, the activities of nature protection agencies, enterprises, institutions, organisations, and officials. The Volga Basin is within the jurisdiction of the Volga Nature Protection Procuracy, which coordinates its activity with the procurators of the republics and regions adjacent to the Volga River.

The reference to 'other' procuracies found in many Russian textbooks includes the so-called procuracies of the 'Second Administration of the General Procuracy'. These date back to the Edict of the Presidium of the Supreme Soviet of the USSR, adopted 1 June 1979, 'On Courts, Procuracy, Advokatura, Notariat, and Internal Affairs Agencies Operating at Special Regime Objects'. The Edict was unpublished at the time, becoming generally known only by reason of the Opinion of the Constitutional Supervision Committee of the USSR 'On Rules Permitting the Application of Unpublished Normative Acts on the Rights and Freedoms of Citizens', issued 29 November 1990. These procuracies were formed in order to protect the State secrecy of and ensure the established regime of secrecy in special regime objects, a list of which was established by the Soviet Government. The legal status of such procuracies was equated to procurators of cities or districts, and are directly subordinate to the Procurator General of the Russian Federation. However, such procuracies enjoy exceptional procedural rights, equivalent to those of the procurators of republics within the Federation. They are also responsible for exercising supervision over local governmental entities within the special regime territories, and act as State accuser in special courts created in such territories.

Procuracies created for supervision over the execution of laws in correctional institutions first appeared in 1983. They act as interdistrict procuracies and may extend their jurisdiction to a territory occupied by several institutions for deprivation of freedom, and such territories may be within more than one subject of the Russian Federation.

It is prohibited to create procuracies which are not within the unified system of the General Procuracy of the Russian Federation.

D. Notariat

(1) History

In mediaeval Russia notarial functions were performed by the senior clerks [подьячие]. The 1649 *Sobornoe Ulozhenie* permitted only minor transactions to be concluded without notarial recording; in particular, transactions transferring immovable property were drawn up and entered in special books by these officials and a State duty recovered for this service. Peter the Great placed this function on special scribes who were attached to the chancelleries of governors and justice colleges. In 1866 the Statute on the Notariat was adopted; it attached notaries to the courts, determined their competence, and laid down the procedures for performing notarial actions. It was the Statute of 1866 which was overtaken by the 1917 October Revolution.

The Decree No 1 'On Courts' of 24 November 1917 omitted to mention the Notariat among the Imperial legal institutions being abolished. The Moscow

Council of People's Commissars repealed on 23 March 1918 the 'presently pre-vailing Statute on the Notarial Office' and municipalised all notarial offices. Local practices varied, but the general pattern was initially for local city soviets to open notarial offices. A Circular of the RSFSR People's Commissariat to eliminate these and distribute their functions among other agencies was not implemented; instead notarial 'tables' operated in some cities attached to the judicial-investigative subsections of provincial justice sections or local people's courts. The exigencies of the NEP required some offices to certify legal transactions and ver-ify their conformity to law. Despite some reluctance within the People's Commissariat of Justice, 'Theses on the Notariat' were published for discussion early in 1922, and on 4 October 1922 the RSFSR Statute on the State Notariat was enacted, superseded on 7 July 1923 by a new version incorporating elements introduced by the 1923 RSFSR Code of Civil Procedure. Divergencies among the legislation of several union republics on the subject contributed to the adoption on 14 May 1926 of an all-union decree 'On the Basic Principles of Organising the State Notariat'. On 4 October 1926 the RSFSR introduced a new Statute on the State Notariat of the RSFSR, succeeded successively by statutes of 20 July 1930, 31 December 1947, 30 September 1965, and 2 August 1974, as amended. The last Statute operated on the basis of the USSR Law on the State Notariat adopted 19 July 1973, which lost force when the Soviet Union was dissolved.

(2) Current legislation

The 1993 Russian Constitution (Article 72) placed the Notariat within the joint jurisdiction of the Federation and the subjects of the Federation. On 11 February 1993 the Russian Federation adopted the Fundamental Principles of Legislation of the Russian Federation on the Notariat, introducing significant reforms reflect-ing the transition to a market economy, as amended 30 December 2001.[45] These are best expressed in the simple removal of the word 'State' from the title of Russian legislation regulating the Notariat. The 1993 reforms introduced two notariats: the private notarial office and the State notarial office. The principal dif-ference between them is that State notaries are salaried by the State and transfer the entire duties and fees for performing notarial actions to the State budget, whereas the private notary recovers the tariff fee for his or her services which remains entirely with the notary, less deductions for taxes, other obligatory pay-ments, and all overhead expenses for operating the private notarial practice. Where notarial action is obligatory, both State and private notaries charge the same tariff fixed by the State; otherwise, the fee is a matter for negotiation with the

---

[45] Ведомости СНД и ВС РФ (1993), no 10, item 357; СЗ РФ (2001), no 53(I), item 5030.

private notary, who often is able to give more efficient and expeditious service than is the State notarial office.[46]

The Fundamental Principles expressly contemplate that subjects of the Federation may enact their own laws on the Notariat, which must be consistent with the Fundamental Principles. In addition to the Fundamental Principles, notaries also are guided by a body of Instructions issued by the Russian Ministry of Justice. Among the most important of these is the Instruction on the Procedure for Performing Notarial Actions by Officials of Agencies of Executive Power, confirmed on 19 March 1996,[47] and the Methods Recommendations With Regard to the Performance of Individual Types of Notarial Actions by Notaries of the Russian Federation, confirmed by Order of the Ministry of Justice of the Russian Federation No 91, on 15 March 2000.

The City of Moscow, in its capacity as a subject of the Federation, abolished in 1999 the State Notariat; all notaries came to be called notaries of the city of Moscow without being divided into those working in State notarial offices and notaries engaging in private practice. As of 1 January 2000 there were about 650 notaries in Moscow, all combined into the Moscow City Chamber. In Russia as a whole there are more than 7,000 notaries, of whom about 5,700 engage in private practice.[48]

Citizens of the Russian Federation who have a higher legal education and who have undergone an apprenticeship period for not less than one year with either a State notarial office or with a notary engaging in private practice (in practice the one-year period may be reduced to six months for individuals who have experience as legal practitioners), and who have passed a qualifications examination and received a licence for the right to engage in notarial activity, may be notaries.

A private notary not only has the right, but has the positive duty to maintain a notarial office. The office must be a premise in a non-housing fund and may be either owned or leased by the notary. It must contain a waiting room, a room for the secretary of the notary, and a notary's office. These minimum requirements are considered essential to ensure the confidentiality of notarial actions. The private

---

[46] This remains controversial in Russian legal doctrine. Some deplore competition amongst notaries in private practice, arguing that all notaries are officials who perform notarial actions in the name of the State. See V N Argunov, in V P Bozh'ev (ed), Правоохранительные органы Российской Федерации. Учебник [*Law Enforcement Agencies of the Russian Federation. Textbook*] (1997) 327. This position is not consistent with the view that notaries act solely in the interests of their clients.

[47] These and other relevant Instructions are collected in E P Mikhailova and I V Taranina, Справочник по нотариату [*Manual for a Notariat*] (Novosibirsk, 1997).

[48] See L A Steshenko and T M Shamba, Нотариат в Российской Федерации [*The Notariat in the Russian Federation*] (2001) 29. The numbers are broken down according to federal districts by O Kamanina in Российская юстиция, no 2 (2002) 67.

notary may not form a juridical person, but also being prohibited from engaging in entrepreneurial activity, is not registered as an entrepreneur. Nonetheless, a private notary has the right to open settlement, deposit, current, hard currency, and other accounts. Accounts with clients may be settled in cash or non-cash remittance. The deposit account is a client account in which the monies are held to be transferred as the client instructs. Private notaries are required to carry insurance to cover professional negligence; policies are arranged through the notarial chamber. If the insured amount is insufficient to cover the damage caused, recourse must be against the notary him or herself in court under the usual procedures.

A private notary also may conclude labour contracts with workers, withholding income tax and making all necessary obligatory payments for pensions, medical insurance, and the like. It is estimated that the introduction of private notaries has created some 30,000 jobs in the Russian Federation.[49]

The procedure for issuing licences to notaries is regulated by the Ministry of Justice of the Russian Federation. Empowered justice agencies of subjects of the Russian Federation issue licences within a month after the candidate takes the qualifications examination on the basis of the decision of the qualifications commission. The decision of a qualifications commission rejecting the issuance of a licence may be appealed to an appeals commission. The appeals commission is formed and attached to the Ministry of Justice jointly with the Federal Notarial Chamber; the decision of the commission may be appealed to a court within a month from its being rendered.

The numbers of notaries are regulated by taking into account a variety of factors. Justice agencies and the notarial chamber jointly determine whether to institute or eliminate the post of notary and the number of notaries in each notarial precinct. Once the decision has been taken with respect to numbers, an open competition is held amongst individuals having a notarial licence to fill the available positions. The notarial precincts correspond more or less to the administrative-territorial structure of the Russian Federation. Although a notary is not required to reside in her notarial precinct, her office must be opened in the precinct designated. A private notary may resign her licence or be deprived of the licence by decision of a court because of being convicted of an intentional crime, or being held to lack or to be limited in dispositive legal capacity, upon the petition of the notarial chamber for repeated disciplinary offences, a violation of legislation, or being unable by reason of health to perform her professional duties. A State notary may be dismissed in accordance with labour legislation of the Russian Federation.

---

[49] V S Repin, Комментарий к Основам законодательства Российской Федерации о нотариате [*Commentary on the Fundamental Principles of Legislation of the Russian Federation on the Notariat*] (1998) 17.

State notarial offices were opened or abolished by the Ministry of Justice of the Russian Federation or on its behalf by the justice ministries or sections of the subjects of the Federation. As a rule, there is a State notarial office in each city, and in large cities, in each district thereof.

Notaries in the Russian Federation perform many functions which in the Anglo-American legal system would be done by lawyers or solicitors and commissioners for oaths. Since notaries are concerned with routine aspects of legal life, Anglo-American lawyers involved in Russian legal matters are certain to encounter them. They are not necessarily concerned exclusively with the private affairs of their clients. Russian legislation requires that a notary refuse to perform a notarial action which is not in accordance with Russian legislation or international treaties, and that in certain instances a notary submit to a tax agency a reference note concerning the value of property passing to the ownership of citizens by way of gift.

A notary is obliged to maintain the confidentiality of information which became known to him or her in connection with professional activity; however, a court may relieve the notary from this duty of confidentiality if a criminal case is instituted against her in connection with the performance of a notarial action. Information about such activities and documents are issued only to those on whose behalf or with regard to whom they were performed. Wills, however, are protected until the testator's death. The duty of confidentiality extends to all personnel of the notarial office who become aware of notarial activities in connection with their official duties, including the typist. Criminal penalties apply to unlawful disclosure under the Russian Criminal Code.

A notary is required to perform the notarial actions provided for by legislation for any person who applies to her unless the place where the notarial action must be performed is stipulated by legislation or by an international treaty, and assuming that a period of limitation has not elapsed.

Notarial activities fall into three basic categories.[50] The first concerns the certification of the authenticity of copies of documents. Although legislation requires the submission of notarially certified copies of documents in a number of cases, in practice virtually all ministries and departments so require. A notary must decline to certify the trueness of copies if their content is contrary to Russian legislation or if they have no legal significance. If the notary is doubtful about the document, she is obliged to submit it for expert examination.

---

[50] The number of notarial actions increased by about three million merely in the city of Moscow between 1998 and 1999, including a tenfold increase in the number of inheritance certificates issued and a 20 per cent increase in transactions with regard to the alienation of property. See Steshenko and Shamba (n 48 above) xi.

The second category encompasses the certification of transactions, such as contracts, wills, powers of attorney, and others. Russian law requires many transactions to be notarially certified before they may become legally valid, and the notary will not do so if the contract or other document is contrary to law. A purchase-sale contract for a dwelling house or dacha, for example, must be notarially certified. The notary acts as the guardian of legality in transactions between private citizens, refusing to allow unlawful transactions to proceed. A certified contract, on the other hand, constitutes prima facie evidence of the facts recited in the document and the identity and legal capacity of the parties. The notarial office also keeps one copy of the contract and can supply replacements if the others are lost or destroyed.

The Notariat also offers another service arising out of contractual relations when one party has not discharged his indebtedness. If there is no dispute between the parties as to responsibility for the debt and no issue requiring judicial settlement, and the contract falls among the list of documents subject to notarial execution, the creditor can secure a notice to pay from the notary which, if not contested or answered, can be followed by a notarial endorsement of documents of execution. These documents will be given to a court bailiff for execution in the same procedure as a civil court judgment. As a simplified procedure for execution, this method is extensively used to recover sums due for rates, utilities, or other local taxes. The debtor has recourse to the courts against any notarial action if he has any defence against the failure to pay.

Inheritance is a third major category of notarial activity. Wills to be valid must be notarially certified, with certain exceptions provided for by law. Standard forms are widely used. The notary must verify the legal capacity of the testator, his identity and residence, and explain to him the relevant provisions of Russian civil legislation. In 2000 Russian notaries attested 535,819 wills.

There is an inheritance tax in the Russian Federation. Administrators or executors of estates may be designated by a testator to manage property or oversee that testamentary dispositions are correctly effectuated. When evidence of the right to inherit is necessary, it is obtained through a certificate concerning the right to an inheritance issued by the notary; such a certificate may be necessary, for example, to claim monies due under an insurance policy, recover debts, establish heirs, divide property amongst heirs, or settle with the tax agencies. Notaries in such instances explain to the heirs their rights and duties and may help to decide disputes between them, although the right to appeal to the court is always available against the notary's determinations. In 2000 notaries issued 1,052,666 certificates concerning the right to an inheritance.

The Fundamental Principles contain a lengthy enumeration of other types of notarial activities. These include taking measures to protect inheritance property, certifying rights of common ownership, certifying translations, certifying that a person is alive or in a particular place, accepting money, securities, or documents for deposit or safekeeping, performing maritime protests, and others.

Notaries give a great deal of legal advice and assistance. They routinely draft transaction documents and are required by law to explain not merely the rights and duties of the parties to a transaction but also to anticipate the consequences of notarial activities so that the lack of legal information or literacy cannot work to the prejudice of those seeking advice.

Foreign natural and juridical persons have the right to apply to notarial offices, other agencies which perform notarial activities, or Russian consular institutions. If it is within their competence, Russian notarial offices will also execute commissions on behalf of foreign justice agencies.

(3) Notarial chamber

Private notaries are members of a professional association called the notarial chamber. A non-commercial organisation in which membership of private notaries is obligatory, the chamber is a juridical person formed in each subject of the Federation. Its activities are carried on in accordance with Russian legislation and its own charter. Although non-commercial, the chambers may engage in entrepreneurial activity insofar as is necessary to fulfil their charter tasks. They are exempt from the tax on property of enterprises. Their principal tasks are to represent and defend the interests of notaries and further the development of private notarial practice; organise the training of persons who wish to become notaries and improve the skills of notaries, ensure compensation for expenditures for expert examinations assigned by a court in regard to cases connected with notarial activity, and arrange professional insurance for private notaries. A notary pays dues to maintain the chamber and submits information and documents to the chamber required by legislation. Self-governing in principle, the highest organ of the chambers is the meeting of notaries of the chamber; daily activities of the chamber are managed by the president and his staff.

All notarial chambers are members of the Federal Notarial Chamber, which has its own charter and is supported by dues of members. In May 1998 the I Congress of Notaries was held at Moscow for the first time in Russian history.

In population centres where there are no State or private notaries, notarial actions are fulfilled by officials of agencies of executive power. In isolated areas this is a convenience to citizens especially, who otherwise would have to travel vast distances in order to obtain notarial services.

Absent from present Russian legislation on the notary is the duty of the notary to inform the Procuracy about violations of legality discovered in the actions of officials or citizens. This omission might be thought to reflect, in a market economy, the transition of the notary from being a Soviet State official, the humble guardian of socialist legality, to being an impartial neutral force serving his or her client. Russian doctrinal writings, however, suggest that the duty to inform the Procuracy continues to exist, being based on the 'general sense of legislation on the notariat' and in particular on the formulation in Article 1 of the Fundamental Principles calling upon the notary to defend the rights and legal interests of citizens and juridical persons. In practice notaries also report violations of legality to their notarial chambers, as a rule, forged documents and the theft of notarial documents.

The Russian notarial profession is considering whether to request a return to the pre-revolutionary system whereby notaries were linked with the courts. Under this scheme the court would supervise the work of the Notariat, minimising the opportunities for extraneous influences to affect notaries in the performance of their duties.

E. Registry for Acts of Civil Status (ZAGS)

(1) History

In pre-revolutionary Russia vital statistics concerning birth, marriage, divorce, death, or adoption were kept principally by the ecclesiastical authorities. By Decree of 18 December 1917 these functions were entrusted to the local administrative authorities, many of whom formed special sections for the registration of acts of civil status (ZAGS). The activities of ZAGS agencies were governed principally by the 1918 RSFSR Family Code and those family codes which supplanted it. In the post-Soviet period the regulation of ZAGS activities has been removed from the Family Code and become the subject of independent regulation in the form of a federal law.

(2) Current legislation

Vital statistics are registered in the Russian Federation at ZAGS offices formed by agencies of State power of subjects of the Russian Federation and, beyond the limits of Russia, by consular institutions of the Russian Federation. The Federal Law on Acts of Civil Status of 15 November 1997, as amended 25 October 2001 and 29 April 2002,[51] provides that State registration of acts of civil status is established for the purpose of protecting the property and personal non-property rights of citizens and only secondarily in the interests of the State. Seven acts of civil status are recognised: birth, marriage, dissolution of marriage, adoption, paternity,

---

[51] СЗ РФ (1997), no 47, item 5340; (2001), no 44, item 4149; (2002), no 18, item 1724.

change of name, and death. The Law acknowledges that in certain respects the criteria for recognising acts of civil status may vary from one subject of the Federation to another, for example, the age of marriage. Acts of civil status performed as part of religious rites are recognised only insofar as agencies for the registry of acts of civil status had not been formed or reinstated on the territory concerned. In this event they are equated to acts of civil status duly registered by the State in conformity with the legislation which was in force at the time the acts were performed and do not require subsequent State registration. This provision would affect acts of civil status on territories incorporated into the former Soviet Union in 1939–44 and places such as Chechnia in the 1990s.

The registry books exist in two examples, known as the first example and the second example. Each is sewn, numbered, sealed, and kept in the agency for the registry of acts of civil status where the acts were registered. The so-called second examples, also sewn, numbered, and sealed, are kept in the agency of executive power of the subject of the Federation concerned together with metric books compiled before the registry was formed or reinstated. After 75 years the first examples are sent to the State archives, and the second examples are subject to being destroyed.

Individual subjects of the Russian Federation have enacted legislation regulating certain aspects of civil status, for example, the age of marriage.[52]

F. Administrative Commissions

Illegal conduct in the Anglo-American legal system is punished in accordance with the criminal law. Under Russian legislation anti-social behaviour may likewise be criminal or it may fall into a category unknown to the Anglo-American legal world: administrative offences. The 1993 Constitution of the Russian Federation relegates administrative and administrative procedure legislation to the joint jurisdiction of the Russian Federation and the subjects of the Russian Federation. For many years the principal Law regulating administrative offences was the Code of the RSFSR on Administrative Violations (CAdV), adopted 20 June 1984 and in force, as amended, from 1 January 1985.[53] It was replaced by the Code of the Russian Federation on Administrative Violations of 28 December 2001 as amended.

---

[52] A number of relevant laws are collected in I M Kuznetsova, Комментарий к законодательству о регистрации актов гражданского состояния [*Commentary on Legislation Concerning the Registration of Acts of Civil Status*] (2002) 167–188.

[53] See I I Veremeenko, N G Salishcheva, and M S Studenikina (eds), Комментарий к кодексу РСФСР об административных правонарушениях [*Commentary to the Code of the RSFSR on Administrative Violations*] (1997).

The number of agencies and officials empowered to levy administrative sanctions is difficult to calculate because most are named generically rather than specifically; ie, 'agencies and institutions of the criminal executory system'. It is estimated that more than 30 million persons are brought to administrative responsibility in the Russian Federation each year.

An administrative offence is an unlawful, guilty action (or failure to act) of a natural or juridical person for which administrative responsibility has been established by the CAdV or by laws of subjects of the Russian Federation on administrative violations (Article 2.1, 2001 CAdV). The subjects of the Russian Federation and local government adopt their own enactments providing administrative responsibility, for example, for environmental, construction, and traffic offences. An administrative violation may be committed intentionally or through negligence, and the minimum legal age for the commission of such offences is age 16. Defences of extreme necessity and imputablity are recognised. Administrative sanctions which may be applied under the 2001 CAdV include a warning, an administrative fine, seizure with compensation or confiscation of articles and implements used to commit administrative violations, deprivation of a special right granted to a natural person (right to hunt, to drive, etc), administrative arrest for a term of up to 30 days, and for foreigners and stateless persons, administrative deportation beyond the limits of the Russian Federation. The 2001 CAdV introduced 'disqualification' as a sanction, which includes depriving a natural person of the right to hold executive offices in an executive management organ of a juridical person, to be a member of a council of directors or supervisory council, to effectuate entrepreneurial activity with regard to management of a juridical person. The agencies which may consider cases of administrative violations are diverse, ranging from judges of courts of ordinary jurisdiction, arbitrazh courts, internal affairs agencies or State inspectorates, and other agencies and officials duly empowered by law. A great number are heard by administrative commissions attached to agencies of local self-government or by commissions for cases of minors.

Judges, agencies, and officials, together with administrative commissions which exist purely to dispose of cases concerning administrative violations, considered administrative cases as designated by the 2001 CAdV. Some local governments have several administrative commissions. Unless the administrative offence is subject to a fine levied on-the-spot (failing to pay public transport fare, for example), a protocol of the violation is drawn up and signed by the alleged offender and the apprehending person. The protocol usually follows a standard form of a page or two containing: the date, place, data on the apprehending person, full name of the offender, year and place of birth, place of residence and telephone, place of work and position, amount of earnings, pension, or stipend, marital status and dependants, previous administrative sanctions, including details as to who imposed the sanction and when, the Article of the CAdV, identity document (passport data), the Article number, subpoint, and name of the normative act providing administrative responsibility for the act committed, details of any witnesses or victim, and an indication that the rights and duties of the natural or juridical person under the 2001 CAdV have been explained to the offender. There is space for the offender to give his explanations and any additional information, any relevant documents of materials being appended, and signatures by the offender, witnesses and victim, and the person drawing up the Protocol. Under the 2001 CAdV there are 81 categories of officials empowered to draw up protocols.

The judge, agency, or official hears the case on the basis of the protocol. The alleged offender has the right to familiarise himself with the materials of the case, give explanations, present evidence, make petitions, be represented by an advocate or defender, and appeal the decree in the case. If necessary, there may be an investigation and experts may be summoned. The case must be considered by the commission in the presence of the alleged offender, or in absentia if he fails to appear after timely notification. The case is considered openly, and the commission is obliged to ascertain when the violation was committed, whether the particular person committed it, whether he is subject to administrative responsibility, whether there are aggravating or mitigating circumstances, whether property damage was caused, and any other relevant considerations, including possible challenges to those who are considering the case. The commission (or other agency considering the case) renders its judgment in the form of a decree, which may be appealed as laid down in legislation; the decree itself should state the period within which the decree may be appealed (ten days); the appeal is lodged with the judge, agency, or official which rendered the decree, who then has three days within which to forward the appeal onwards to the relevant appellate instance. A procurator may protest a decree, which has the effect of suspending execution until the protest is considered. If the offender does not pay the administrative fine imposed, the administrative commission may issue a notice to the local court to levy execution against the earnings or the personal property of the offender. In the case of an employed offender, the notice may be issued to the employer with instructions to withhold the amount of the fine from earnings. The court also may issue a proposal to enterprises and agencies concerning eliminatinon of the causes of the offence (for example, failure to take proper security measures in order to deter petty theft). The period of limitations for execution of a decree is one year from the day of entry into legal force thereof.

Although administrative violations are often very petty transgressions, the sanctions imposed are intended to be more than perfunctory. The 'tasks' of legislation on administrative violations are 'defence of the individual, protection of the rights and freedoms of man and citizen, protection of the health of citizens, sanitary-epidemiological well-being of the population, defence of public morality, protection of the environment and the established procedure for effectuating State power, public order, and public security, ownership, defence of legal economic interests of natural and juridical persons, society, and the State against administrative violations, and also the prevention of administrative violations' (Article 1.2, 2001 CAdV). The principles of equality before the law and presumption of innocence both operate with respect to administrative violations.

More serious categories of administrative violations (for example, petty hooliganism, petty stealing) are considered by judges in the courts of ordinary jurisdiction or, in the case of a traffic violation, by the State Motor Vehicle Inspectorate, or by police agencies or inspectorates. The procedures for considering the violation are the same, but the penalties can be far more severe, including administrative arrest for a term of up to 30 days. An administrative offence is not a crime, and an offender who commits what otherwise would be a criminal act but is subjected to administrative responsibility does not acquire a criminal record. Even the record of an administrative offence is expunged within a year if a second is not committed. Although an offender does not have the full protection of the Code of Criminal Procedure in administrative proceedings, the 2001 CAdV does considerably tighten due process elements of an administrative proceeding to bring them much closer to those of the criminal justice system.

Commissions for Cases of Minors operate in many respects just as the administrative commissions. They are attached to the administration of agencies of local self-government and continue to be governed by the Statute on Commissions for Cases of Minors confirmed by Edict of the Presidium of the Supreme Soviet of the RSFSR on 3 June 1967, as amended to 1993. The commissions are concerned with juvenile delinquency, child neglect or abuse, school-leavers, orphans, foster parents, child labour, adoption, guardianship, protection of children's rights and interests, leisure time, education, and various kinds of reform schools. There is almost no aspect of a child's being that is not within a commission's purview. The commission also may consider administrative violations committed by a minor and impose the sanctions provided for by legislation.

The sanctions which a commission may impose on a minor who has committed an offence range from making a public apology, to a severe reprimand, to the duty to make compensation, to a fine on a minor who has independent earnings, to being bound over to parents, to being placed in a reform school. Parents also may be punished by a public warning, duty to pay compensation, or a fine for various forms of child neglect or abuse. Cases are considered at the initiative of the commission or citizens, the recommendation of schools, the police, or other agencies or officials. The commission chairman has broad latitude in deciding whether the case should be heard or not. When preparing and considering cases the commission must establish the age, occupation, living conditions, and education of the minor, the fact of a violation, whether there were accomplices or instigators, and whether measures of pressure have previously been applied to the minor. Citizens and officials may be summoned to give explanations. The procurator must be notified of commission sessions, but his participation is not obligatory.

The commission must consider the materials collected, hear explanations of the minor, his parents, the victim, witnesses, and come to a balanced decision either to apply sanctions, terminate the case, conduct a supplementary verification, or transfer the case to the Procuracy. The case record is brief and takes the form of a protocol signed by the persons presiding and the secretary. The decree of a commission is adopted by majority vote and must set out the essence of the violation, the evidence on which the decision was made, the relevant articles of legislative acts, the measure of pressure assigned, the reasons for assigning it, and the procedure and periods for appeal.

G. Law Enforcement Agencies

Police functions are vested principally in two agencies: the Federal Security Service of the Russian Federation (FSB) and the Ministry of Internal Affairs (MVD). Both agencies and the various functions they perform have been the subject of special legislation in the 1990s intended to make them more transparent and accountable.

The expression 'special services' is increasingly being used to describe agencies engaging in external policing, investigative, and protection functions, both State and private. In this larger sense one would speak of the Foreign Intelligence Service of the Russian Federation (SVR Russia), the FSB, the Federal Service for the Protection of the Russian Federation, the Federal Border Service of Russia (FPS Russia), the federal agencies for governmental communications and information, the foreign intelligence agency of the Ministry of Defence of the Russian Federation; the Ministry for Extraordinary Situations of the Russian Federation, the Federal Migration Service of Russia, the courier services, the State Fire Prevention Service of the Ministry of Internal Affairs of Russia; the passport-visa service of internal affairs agencies; private security companies; and private detective agencies, amongst others.

(1) Security Council of Russian Federation

The Security Council of the Russian Federation is a constitutional agency charged with determining the vitally important interests of society and the State, working out the principal orientations for the strategy of ensuring the security of the Russian Federation and organising the preparation of federal special-purpose programmes, preparing recommendations for the President of Russia concerning the taking of decisions of issues of internal and foreign policy of Russia in the domain of ensuring the security of the individual, society, and the State, preparing proposals for the President of Russia concerning the introduction of an extraordinary situation, amongst others.

The Council adopts decisions by a simple majority vote of the total membership; these are formalised in the form of Edicts of the President of the Russian Federation or protocols if they involved lesser questions. The present Statute on the Security Council of the Russian Federation was confirmed by Edict of the President of the Russian Federation No 949, on 2 August 1999, as amended 15 November 1999 and 28 December 2000.[54]

(2) Federal Security Service (FSB)

The FSB is a federal agency of executive power under the direction of the President of the Russian Federation and the Government of the Russian Federation; it is the legal successor to the Federal Counter-Intelligence Service of the Russian Federation. Its activities are governed by the Federal Law on Federal Securities Service Agencies in the Russian Federation, adopted 3 April 1995 and in force as from 12 April 1995, as amended.[55] The FSB is a unified centralised system of agencies with administrations or sections at the levels of the subjects of the Federation and in military units and its own system of enterprises, educational institutions, scientific-research, expert and military-medical institutions and subdivisions, military construction subdivisions, special training centres, and special-purpose subdivisions. The 'creation of Federal security service agencies not provided for' by the Federal Law is not permitted, and neither may organisational structures nor political parties operate or mass social movements pursuing political purposes, pre-election campaigns, or political agitation take place (Article 2). Neither the subjects of the Russian Federation nor local self-government agencies may adopt normative acts affecting the FSB or its activities.

The Statute on the FSB was confirmed by Edict of the President of the Russian Federation on 23 June 1995, as replaced on 6 July 1998 and as amended to 11 June 2001.[56] Other enactments directing activities of the FSB include the Edict on

---

[54] СЗ РФ (1999), no 32, item 4041; no 47, item 5684; (2001), no 1(II), item 68. Replacing the Statute of 10 July 1996. СЗ РФ (1996), no 29, item 3479.

[55] СЗ РФ (1995), no 15, item 1269; (2000), no 1(I), item 9; no 46, item 4537; (2001), no 53(I), item 5030; (2002) no 30, item 3033; (2003), no. 2. Many foundation documents of the Soviet security services previously classified are published in V V Korovin, История отечественных органов б езопасности [*History of Fatherland Security Agencies*] (1998) 103–247, including an extract from the Decree which created the acronym made famous by Ian Fleming, 'Smersh', adopted on 19 April 1943 and forming the Chief Administration for Counter Intelligence of the People's Commissariat of the Defence ('Smersh'); an analogous administration was created in the Soviet Navy.

[56] СЗ РФ (1995), no 26, item 2453; as superseded by the texts in СЗ РФ (1998), no 28, item 3320; no 35, item 4384; no 41, item 5004; (1999), no 2, item 267; no 35, item 4305; (2000), no 25, item 2677; (2001), no 24, item 2422.

Measures Relating to Ensuring Coordinated Actions of Agencies of State Power in the Struggle Against Fascism and Other Forms of Political Extremism in the Russian Federation, adopted 23 March 1995;[57] the Rules for Relegating Information Constituting a State Secret to Various Degrees of Secrecy, confirmed by Decree of the Government on 4 September 1995, as amended;[58] the List of Information Relegated to a State Secret, confirmed by Edict of the President on 30 November 1995, as amended 24 January 1998, 11 June 2001, and 10 September 2001;[59] the Law of the Russian Federation on the Struggle Against Terrorism of 25 July 1998,[60] and relevant international treaties of the Russian Federation.

The FSB also is regulated by and gives effect to the Federal Law on State Protection, adopted 27 May 1996, as amended 18 July 1997 and 7 November 2000;[61] the Law on the State Boundary of the Russian Federation, adopted 1 April 1993, as amended; the Law on Federal Governmental Communications and Information Agencies of 19 February 1993, as amended 7 November 2000;[62] and the Law of the Russian Federation on Security of 5 March 1992, as amended 24 December 1993 and 25 July 2002.[63] The Law on State Secrecy of 21 July 1993, as amended 6 October 1997, and the Federal Law on the Procedure for Exit from the Russian Federation and Entry into the Russian Federation of 18 August 1996, as amended,[64] are major concerns of the FSB.

In provisions which are unprecedented in Russian history, the State 'guarantees compliance with the rights and freedoms of man and citizen' by the FSB agencies. A person who believes that FSB agencies or officials have violated his rights and freedoms has the right to appeal against the actions of the agencies or officials to the superior FSB agency, to the Procuracy, or to a court. State agencies, enterprises, organisations, social associations, and natural persons have the right to request explanations and information from FSB agencies if their rights and freedoms are limited and to seek material and moral compensation for damages caused by the FSB agencies and officials.

The FSB combines intelligence and police functions, 'intelligence' encompassing both counter-intelligence and intelligence. The Law on the FSB gives greater

---

[57] СЗ РФ (1995), no 13, item 1127. Also see the Federal Law on Counteracting Extremist Activity of 25 July 2002. СЗ РФ (2002), no 30, item 3031.

[58] СЗ РФ (1995), no 37, item 3619; (1998), no 5, item 561; (2001), no 24, item 2418; no 38, item 3724.

[59] СЗ РФ (1995), no 49, item 4775; (1998), no 5, item 561; (2001), no 24, item 2418; no 38, item 3724.

[60] СЗ РФ (1998), no 31, item 3808; (2000), no 33, item 3348.

[61] СЗ РФ (1996), no 22, item 2594; (1997), no 22, item 2594; (2000), no 46, item 4537.

[62] Ведомости СНД и ВС РФ (1993), no 12, item 423; СЗ РФ (2000), no 46, item 4537.

[63] Ведомости СНД и ВС РФ (1992), no 15, item 769; (1993), no 52, item 5086. СЗ РФ (2002), no 30, item 3033.

[64] СЗ РФ (1996), no 34, item 4029; (1998), no 30, item 3606; (1999), no 26, item 3175; (2003), no. 2 and changes introduced by Decree of the Constitutional Court of the RF, 15 January 1998. СЗ РФ (1998), no 4, item 531.

prominence to the intelligence function: to inform the President, the Chairman of the Government, and on their behalf federal agencies of State power and agencies of State power of subjects of the Federation about threats to the security of the Russian Federation, elicit, prevent, and suppress intelligence and other activity of special services and organisations of foreign States and also of individual persons directed towards inflicting damage on the security of the Russian Federation, and extracting intelligence information in the interests of ensuring the security of Russia and increasing its economic, scientific-technical, and defence potential. The FSB is designated in the Law on Foreign Intelligence of 10 January 1996, as amended 7 November 2000, as an 'agency of foreign intelligence of Russia'.[65]

Police functions are directed towards eliciting, preventing, and supressing crimes, the inquiry and preliminary investigation of which is relegated by primarily criminal procedure legislation to the FSB and to search for individuals suspected of committing them, to combat terrorism, and to collaborate with other State agencies in working out and implementing measures against corruption, illegal circulation of weapons and narcotic means, smuggling, illegal armed formations, criminal groups, and individuals or social associations whose purpose is forcibly to change the constitutional system of the Russian Federation.

The FSB is subject to Procuracy supervision, except, however, that information concerning persons rendering or who have rendered assistance to FSB agencies on a confidential basis and concerning the organisation, tactics, methods, and means of effectuating activity are not subject to Procuracy supervision.

The number of federal laws regulating the Russian special services has become sufficiently complex to justify, in the opinion of some Russian jurists, a Code of the Russian Federation on the Special Services of Russia.[66]

(3) Internal Affairs Agencies

The ordinary day-to-day functions of protecting public order and crime prevention fall upon the Ministry of Internal Affairs (MVD) and its various substructures. The principal tasks of the MVD are set out in the Statute on the Ministry of Internal Affairs of the Russian Federation, confirmed by Edict of the President of the Russian Federation on 18 July 1996, as amended 6 September 1997, 24 April 1998, 27 May 1998, 20 October 1998, 1 December 1999, and 13 January 2001.[67] The Ministry system consists of structural links at the levels of all subjects of the Russian Federation, administrations or sections on railway, air, and water

---

[65] СЗ РФ (1996), no 3, item 143; (2000), no 46, item 4537.
[66] For a draft structural model, see A Iu Shumilov, Спецслужбы России: Законы и комментарий [*Special Services of Russia: Laws and Commentary*] (1997) 319–321.
[67] СЗ РФ (1996), no 30, item 3605; (1997), no 36, item 4133; (1998), no 17, item 1915; no 22, item 2413; no 43, item 5333; (1999), no 50, item 6197; (2001), no 3, item 220.

transport, so-called 'regime objects', and regional administrations for the struggle against organised crime. The Ministry also has an Investigative Committee, Chief Administration of the State Fire Prevention Service, Chief Administration for the Execution of Punishments, material-technical supply and military supply administrations, a vast network of educational and training institutions, scientific-research institutes, and special subdivisions, units, enterprises, institutions, and organisations formed for special tasks. The MVD also has its own internal forces to perform designated tasks. The Ministry organises the search on Russian territory for missing persons, individuals who have escaped from custody or investigation, or stolen property, the identification of unidentified corpses, the administration of the passport-visa and other authorisation systems, and establishes the rules for the entry, exit, sojourn, and transit through the territory of the Russian Federation of foreign citizens and stateless persons. The MVD will contract with owners to protect specified property and issues licenses for engaging in private detective or personal security activity. There are special detachments of the police (OMON) and motorised units. The MVD also drafts and confirms the rules for traffic safety, organises the registration and recording of means of transport, issues driver's licences, and is responsible for the State Road Traffic Safety Inspectorate (legal successor of GAI), whose Statute was confirmed 15 June 1998.[68]

The police (милиция) within the MVD are governed by the Law of the RSFSR on the Police adopted 18 April 1991, as amended to 10 January 2003.[69] This was the first Law to regulate police agencies comprehensively, an event described by Russian jurists as part of the 'processes of democratisation which led, finally, to the broad awareness of the position long recognised by the international community in accordance with which officials who guard the Law must be free in their activity from political partiality, being "politically neutral" under all conditions and serving only the Law and the people'.[70] The tasks of the police are to ensure the safety of the individual, prevent and suppress crimes and administrative violations, uncover crimes, protect public order and ensure public safety, defend private, State, municipal, and other forms of ownership, and render assistance to natural and juridical persons in the defence of their rights and legal interests (Article 2, Law on Police). The Law on the Police divides them into 'criminal police' and 'public security police'. The criminal police are concerned with preventing and detecting crimes for which the conducting of a preliminary investigation is obligatory and searching for persons who have fled agencies of inquiry

---

[68] СЗ РФ (1998), no 25, item 2897.

[69] Ведомости СНД и ВС РФ (1991), no 16, item 503; (1993), no 10, item 360; no 32, item 1231; СЗ РФ (1996), no 25, item 2964; (1999), no 14, item 1666; no 49, item 5905; (2000), no 31, item 3204; no 46, item 4537; (2001), no 1(II), item 15; no 31, item 3172; no 32, item 3316; no 53(I), item 5030; (2002), no 18, item 1721; no 30, item 3029; (2003), no. 2.

[70] See B P Kondrashov, Iu P Solovei, and V V Chernikov, Российский закон о милиции [*Russian Law on the Police*] (1992) 22.

or investigation or the court. The public security, or local, police maintain public order, prevent and suppress crimes and administrative violations, investigate crimes for which a preliminary investigation is not obligatory, and assist citizens and juridical persons. The local police comprise about 60 per cent of the total number of police.

Among the other structural divisions of the MVD is the Investigative Committee, which supervises the investigative subdivisions and exercises procedural and departmental organisational control over the performance of preliminary investigations and organises the investigation of the most complex criminal cases. The head of the Investigative Committee is directly subordinate to the Minister of Internal Affairs and has the status of a deputy minister. The State Fire Prevention Service works out fire safety and prevention rules, educational programmes, promotes voluntary fire prevention associations, and organises the extinguishing of large fires and rescue work. It is governed in its work by the Federal Law on Fire Safety, adopted 21 December 1994 as amended to 10 January 2003.[71]

The traditional functions of the MVD in overseeing the execution of punishments were transferred in the late 1990s to the Ministry of Justice of the Russian Federation.

Under the Federal Law on Internal Forces of the Ministry of Internal Affairs of the Russian Federation of 6 February 1997, as amended 20 June and 7 November 2000,[72] the MVD maintains armed units whose responsibility is to assist in the protection of public order, protect important State objects and special cargoes, escort convicted persons and persons confined under guard, participate in the territorial defence of the Russian Federation, and render assistance to the Federal Border Service in protecting the State boundary. State control over the activity of the internal forces is exercised by the President of the Russian Federation and the Government of the Russian Federation. The Procurator General of the Russian Federation and subordinate procurators effectuate supervision over compliance with the law by the internal forces.

H. Preliminary Investigation Agencies

(1) History

Reference has been made above on several occasions to the preliminary investigative functions to a number of State agencies, including the Procuracy and internal affairs agencies. These functions have become sufficiently differentiated within each

---

[71] СЗ РФ (1994), no 35, item 3649; (2002), no 1(I), item 2; no 30, item 3033; (2003), no. 2.
[72] СЗ РФ (1997), no 6, item 711; (2000), no 26, item 2730; no 46, item 4537.

institution and characteristic of the general approach of Russian law to imposing responsibility for offences to justify independent treatment in this chapter.

Prior to 1860 in Russia investigative functions were performed largely by various components of the Russian police. Quarter overseers commonly acted as investigators, and in large cities the post of investigative bailiff existed for civil and criminal cases. By an Edict of 8 June 1860 the investigative function was removed from the police and placed on the office of judicial investigator, created in 44 provinces of the Empire within the system of the Ministry of Justice. At the same time two nakaz were issued which laid down the procedure for a preliminary investigation and determined the relations between the judicial investigators, on one hand, and the police and the courts, on the other. Judicial investigators carried the rank equivalent to the judge of an uezd court. They were appointed to and dismissed from office by the Minister of Justice upon the recommendation of the governor and with the consent of the procurator of the province. This procedure immediately created difficulties, for although formally appointed by the Minister of Justice, each judicial investigator was in fact dependent upon the local governor. By the Statute on Criminal Procedure of 20 November 1864 it was provided that judicial investigators would perform the preliminary investigation concerning crimes and offences which were within the jurisdiction of okrug courts with the assistance of the police. In the absence of an investigator, the Statute required the police to perform an inquiry and then turn over the materials collected to the investigator.

Over the years the system was expanded. In 1867 the post of temporary investigators for especially important cases was instituted to investigate forged State credit notes. The post of judicial investigator for important cases was established in 1870, and in 1875, attached to okrug courts, the permanent post of investigators for especially important cases was created; these investigators were allowed to sit in individual cases as a judge provided they had not been involved in investigating the particular case and there were no other judges available.

The office of judicial investigator was abolished in November 1917 by Decree No 1 'On the Courts' together with most other institutional survivals of the Imperial legal system and the investigative function placed on the local judges themselves. There followed a period of rapid changes of policy. The judges could not cope with the investigative burden, which was passed mostly to investigative commissions of the Military-Revolutionary Committee. Analogous commissions to investigate counter-revolutionary crimes were formed and attached to local soviets. Then investigative commissions for grave crimes (homicide, rape, banditism, etc) were established and attached to the okrug courts.[73] The Statute on the

---

[73] See Decrees No 1, 2, and 3 'On the Court'. СУ РСФСР (1917), no 4, item 50; (1918), no 26, item 420; no 52, item 589.

People's Court of the RSFSR placed investigative responsibilities on investigative commissions, on the police (in the form of an inquiry), and sometimes on the judges.[74] The VChK, formed 20 December 1917, investigated certain crimes against the State. The Statute on the Court of the RSFSR, confirmed in October 1920, introduced the post of people's investigator; these were to be elected by the provincial executive committees of soviets and attached to councils of people's judges. At the same time the office of investigator for especially important cases was attached to the provincial justice sections and to the People's Commissariat of Justice of the RSFSR.[75] The first Code of Criminal Procedure of the RSFSR, confirmed 25 May 1922, defined the term investigator as encompassing the people's investigators, investigators attached to provincial courts, investigators of military tribunals, and investigators for important cases attached to the People's Commissariat of Justice.[76] Only a very general definition of preliminary investigation agencies was offered by the 1924 Fundamental Principles of Court Proceedings of the USSR and Union Republics.[77] Thus by the mid-1920s Soviet legislation had laid the foundations for the preliminary investigation and designated certain agencies to conduct these.

Thereafter it was legislation on the Procuracy which addressed the preliminary investigation. The Statute on Procuracy Supervision confirmed 28 May 1922 placed on that institution, inter alia, the duty to supervise the investigation of criminal cases, which until 1928 continued to be carried out by investigative units that remained within the administrative jurisdiction of the courts. Amendments made in September 1928 to the Statute on Court Organisation of the RSFSR removed the investigators from the courts to procurators.[78] In 1936 the investigative apparatus was removed from the justice system and placed within an independent Procuracy, formed in 1933. Throughout the 1930s the inquiry functions of police agencies also were greatly enlarged for the great majority of crimes; in 1940 an investigative apparatus was formed within the Chief Police Administration of the USSR People's Commissariat of Internal Affairs (NKVD), and they retained throughout the 1940–50s principal responsibility for investigating most ordinary crimes.

The adoption of the 1958 FPCrimProc and attendant 1960 RSFSR Code of Criminal Procedure resulted in the abolition of the investigative apparatus within

---

[74] СУ РСФСР (1918), no 85, item 889.

[75] СУ РСФСР (1920), no 83, item 407.

[76] Article 23(5). СУ РСФСР (1922), no 20–21, item 230.

[77] СЗ СССР (1924), no 24, item 206.

[78] I I Kolesnikov argues that the change of jurisdiction was purely nominal because investigators continued to be under the control of the People's Commissariat of Justice and local soviets and the Procuracy remained within the structure of the People's Commissariat of Justice. See V P Bozh'ev (ed), Правоохранительные органы Российской Федерации [*Law Enforcement Agencies of the Russian Federation*] (2nd edn, 1997) 272.

the MVD (although specialised agencies of inquiry continued to investigate many crimes) and the transfer of preliminary investigation functions to the Procuracy and to State security agencies (KGB). The system was unsuccessful, as the Procuracy could not cope with the caseload. On 6 April 1963 the internal affairs agencies (then called the Ministry for the Protection of Public Order) were given back the right to perform preliminary investigations and the police retained the right to conduct inquiries in a substantial number of cases.[79] In the 1990s the federal tax police agencies and State Customs Committee agencies were authorised to act as agencies of inquiry and in 1995 an investigative apparatus was created in the Federal Tax Police Service and re-created in the Federal Security Service. At present, therefore, an investigative apparatus for the preliminary investigation exists in four ministries or State committees.

(2) Current legislation

Investigators are officials empowered by the State to establish in accordance with law the event of a crime, to engage in a search for and unmasking of the person(s) guilt of committing the crime (if one is determined to have been committed), to take measures for compensation of the damage caused by the crime, eliminate the causes and conditions which led to the crime being committed, and to prevent the commission of new criminal acts. The 2001 Code of Criminal Procedure of the Russian Federation is the principal source for the rights and duties of investigators. The competence of Procuracy investigators extends to the gravest crimes against life, sexual crimes, official crimes, crimes committed by judges, procurators, investigators, and officials of internal affairs agencies, the tax police, and customs agencies, and cases concerning crimes with respect to the said persons in connection with the performance of their official duties. The investigators of the Military Procuracy investigate crimes committed by military servicemen, persons called up for military exercises, military builders, and persons equated to military servicemen of the Armed Forces, the FSB, and the Foreign Intelligence Service, and others. The investigators of the internal affairs agencies investigate crimes in accordance with Article 151 of the 2001 Russian Code of Criminal Procedure, as do the investigative agencies of the FSB. The investigative activities of the Federal Tax Police agencies are defined to some extent by Article 126 of the RSFSR Code of Civil Procedure, but their principal concern is the crimes defined in Article 198, paragraph 2, and Article 199 of the 1996 Criminal Code of the Russian Federation.

All of the investigators are empowered to consider applications and communications concerning crimes, the Procuracy investigators having somewhat broader powers than the others.

---

[79] Ведомости СССР (1963), no 16, item 181. The investigative apparatus formed under the NKVD Order of 1940 operated until 1958.

The basic link in the Procuracy investigative apparatus is the investigators of the city, district, and interdistrict procuracies, who are appointed, transferred, and removed from office by the procurator of the superior Procuracy. Investigators at these levels work mostly on a zonal principle, whereas those in large cities are likely to specialise in certain types of criminal cases. At the levels of the Russian Federation itself, republics, territories, and regions there are investigative administrations or sections within the Procuracy staffed by investigators for specially important cases, senior investigators, and aides thereof. The same posts exist within the specialised procuracies. The entire system is headed by the Chief Investigative Administration of the General Procuracy of the Russian Federation. The military procuracies have military investigators, senior military investigators, and military investigators for specially important cases, and equivalent ranks exist within the FSB and the Federal Tax Police. As noted above, the Investigative Committee of the MVD heads the investigative apparatus within that Ministry.

The initial work of gathering evidence of a crime and conducting operational search activities to apprehend culprits is performed by agencies of inquiry. These under Article 40 of the 2001 Russian Code of Criminal Procedure are enumerated as the internal affairs agencies and 'other agencies of executive power' endowed in accordance with a federal law with powers to effectuate operational-search activity, the Chief Judicial Bailiff of the Russian Federation and various officials subordinate to or connected with him, the commanders of military units, and heads of military institutions or garrisons. The FSB agencies, the heads of correctional-labour institutions, State fire supervision agencies, operational agencies of the Federal Border Service of the Russian Federation, the masters of sea-going vessels, Federal Tax Police agencies, and customs agencies of the Russian Federation would fall generally within the agencies of executive power so endowed. The specific jurisdiction of each agency is established, with distinctions drawn between cases in which a preliminary investigation is obligatory and those in which such investigation is not obligatory.

When the preliminary investigation is obligatory, the inquiry is directed towards an inspection of the site of the crime, performance of searches, seizures, the detention and interrogation of suspects, interrogation of the victim and witnesses, and similar urgent investigative actions. Under the second form of inquiry, the investigation of the case is performed by the agency of inquiry in full, up to and including a conclusion to indict or to termination of the proceedings in the case.

I. Arbitration

Informal dispute settlement, or to use modern parlance, alternative dispute resolution, has a venerable history in Russia. During the late nineteenth century,

Russian jurists wrote major treatises as contributions to the emerging dialogue about the creation of permanent international institutions to settle interstate disputes. L A Kamarovskii's treatise on an international court was translated into French, and F F Martens is an acknowledged father of the Hague arbitral tribunal and court.[80]

For many years Russian legislation on arbitration was in a chaotic state, no less than three federal laws regulating arbitration: Annex 3 to the 1964 RSFSR Code of Civil Procedure; the 1992 Provisional Statute on the Arbitration Court for the Settlement of Economic Disputes, as amended 16 November 1997 and 9 July 1999,[81] and the 1993 Law on International Commercial Arbitration.[82] They were inconsistent with one another and contained unjustified differences on issues of principle.[83] On 24 July 2002 the first two were replaced by the Federal Law on Arbitration Courts in the Russian Federation.

As a matter of Russian law, however, arbitration is not a part of judicial power and accordingly is not mentioned in the Russian Constitution. The Civil Code (Article 11) does refer to arbitration in connection with the 'judicial defence of civil rights', and the 1964 RSFSR Code of Civil Procedure makes provision for the 'transfer of disputes for settlement to arbitration courts' (Article 27). A contract clause to transfer a particular dispute for settlement to an arbitration court requires the judge in a court of first instance to refuse to accept an application in a civil case (Article 129, RSFSR Code of Civil Procedure) and if the proceeding is underway, constitutes grounds for termination of the proceedings in the case (Article 219, RSFSR Code of Civil Procedure). The position is rather different under the 2002 Code of Arbitrazh Procedure. The parties may transfer a dispute which has arisen or which might arise from civil-law relations and within the jurisdiction of an arbitrazh court to an arbitration court up to the moment that the arbitrazh court adopts a decision in the case (Article 4). Under this formulation, the arbitrazh court may hear a case even though there is an arbitration clause if the parties have chosen to bring suit there. However, the arbitrazh court will refuse to accept a petition to sue or leave a case without consideration if there is a case

---

[80] See V V Pustogarov, *Our Martens: F. F. Martens. International Lawyer and Architect of Peace* (transl W E Butler, 2000) 195–216.

[81] Ведомости СНД и ВС РФ (1992), no 30, item 1790; СЗ РФ (1997), no 47, item 5341; (1999), no 28, item 3493.

[82] Ведомости СНД и ВС РФ (1993), no 32, item 1240.

[83] For an elaboration of these problems and draft legislation prepared to address them, see the Commentary by E A Vinogradova (comp), Третейский суд. Законодательство, практика, комментарий [Arbitration Court. Legislation, Practice, Commentary] (1997) 327–336. The texts of Russian court decisions relating to the enforcement of arbitral awards and other judicial material are given here, and different materials available in K Hober, *The Enforcement of Foreign Arbitral Awards in Russia* (1994). On the formative era of Russian arbitration legislation, see Vinogradova, Третейский суд в России [*The Arbitration Court in Russia*] (1993). For the late Soviet era, see W E Butler, *Soviet Arbitration* (1989). For the Law on Arbitration Courts, see СЗ РФ (2002), no 30, item 3019; transl. in W E Butler, *Russian Commercial and Company Legislation* (2002).

regarding the dispute between the same persons, concerning the same subject, and with regard to the same grounds under proceedings in a court of general jurisdiction, arbitrazh court, or arbitration court, or if there is an agreement of the persons participating in the case concerning the transfer of this dispute for settlement by an arbitration court and the possibility of recourse to the arbitration court has not been lost and if the defendant, objecting to consideration of the case in an arbitrazh court, petitions for transfer of the case for settlement by an arbitration court not later than its first application with regard to the substance of the dispute (Articles 148 and 150). This has implications for the grounds on which the proceedings in a case must be terminated in an arbitrazh court. The Code of Arbitrazh Procedure stipulates: 'if there is an award of an arbitration court which has entered into legal force between the same persons, on the same subject, and with regard to the same grounds, except for instances where the arbitrazh court has refused to issue a writ of execution for the compulsory execution of the award of an arbitration court.' (Article 150).

There are several possible alternatives to arbitration under Russian law: ad hoc arbitration, recourse to various tribunals which have been or may be organised under Russian law, recourse to specialist arbitration tribunals, recourse to two permanent Russian arbitration courts, recourse to international arbitration.[84]

Ad hoc arbitration between citizens seems to be uncommon but could be arranged under the 2002 Law on Arbitration Courts in the Russian Federation.

Chambers of commerce, stock exchanges, unions of jurists, and even networks of enterprises and organisations have formed permanently operating arbitration courts which are now governed by the 2002 Law on Arbitration Courts. The Law on Chambers of Commerce and Industry in the Russian Federation of 7 July 1993, as amended,[85] empowers chambers of commerce to promote the settlement of disputes arising between enterprises and entrepreneurs (Article 3) and grants them the right to form arbitration courts, confirm statutes on them, and the procedure for the consideration of disputes by the arbitration courts (Article 12). Subjects of the Russian Federation (for example, Bashkortostan on 14 October 1994) have adopted analogous legisiation. Each permanently operating arbitration court adopts its own rules (which may be known by various names: statute, charter, reglament, and others) laying down the procedures for the consideration of cases, in each instance any matters not regulated by the said rules being governed by the 2002 Law on Arbitration Courts. That law requires that there be an odd number of arbitrators, that any natural person possessing dispositive legal

---

[84] G K Dmitrieva, Международный коммерческий арбитраж [*International Commercial Arbitration*] (1997).
[85] Ведомости СНД и ВС РФ (1993), no 33, item 1309; СЗ РФ (1995), no 21, item 1930; (1997), no 20, item 2231.

capacity and consenting to act may serve as an arbitrator (a formulation which includes foreign arbitrators) on condition that the chairman or sole arbitrator must have a higher legal education, that the parties may by *compromis* agree the procedure for forming the court, in the absence of which three arbitrators shall be appointed; and that the arbitration court itself shall decide whether an arbitration agreement exists and whether it is valid. If the answer to the last is negative, the dispute is referred to an arbitrazh court for settlement.

The Law on Goods Exchanges and Exchange Trade of 20 February 1992, as amended 24 June 1992, 30 April 1993, 19 June 1995, and 25 October 2001,[86] requires that disputes connected with the conclusion of exchange transactions be considered in an exchange arbitration commission, in a court or in an arbitrazh court. The exchange arbitration commission is created as an organ to reconcile the parties or to fulfil other functions of an arbitration court (Article 30).

The Association of Russian Banks (Statute on Arbitration Court confirmed 30 April 1993), the Union of Jurists (Reglament on Arbitration Court confirmed 17 July 1993), and the Moscow Interbank Currency Exchange (Statute on Arbitration Commission confirmed 7 April 1994) have each formed specialised arbitration courts.

Those who were successful in the competition conducted to receive stocks in federal ownership on pledge were required to accept as an obligatory condition of the credit contract an arbitration clause which referred disputes, if a party was a foreign juridical person or an enterprise with foreign investments, to the International Commercial Arbitration Court attached to the Russian Chamber of Commerce and Industry, and if a party was a juridical person registered in one of the Independent States or was a Russian juridical person without foreign participation, to the Arbitration Court for the Settlement of Economic Disputes attached to the Chamber of Commerce and Industry of the Russian Federation. Analogous clauses were required for the contract of pledge and commission agency arising out of such competitions.[87]

The Federal Law on Production Sharing Agreements of 30 December 1995, as amended,[88] allows disputes between the State and the investor connected with the use, termination, and invalidity of production sharing agreements to be settled in accordance with the conditions of the agreement in a court, arbitrazh court, or arbitration court, including institutes of international arbitration (Article 22).

---

[86] Ведомости СНД и ВС РФ (1992), no 18, item 961; no 34, item 1966; (1993), no 22, item 790; СЗ РФ (1995), no 26, item 2397; (2001), no 44, item 4148.

[87] See the Edict of the President of the Russian Federation, No 889, adopted 31 August 1995, setting out the Rules for Conducting Auctions for the Right to Conclude Contracts of Credit, the Pledge of Stocks in Federal Ownership, and Commission Agency. Model Contracts for each transaction appeared in Российская газета [*Russian Newspaper*], 14 November 1995.

[88] СЗ РФ (1996), no 1, item 18; (1999), no 2, item 246; (2001), no 26, item 2579.

Analogous provisions have been imposed on Russian and Belarus parties who conclude contracts pursuant to the Agreement between the Governments of the Russian Federation and Belarus on Cooperation in the Development of the Oil and Gas Industry of Russia, concluded 2 March 1993 (Article 15).[89]

Ad hoc arbitration to settle collective labour disputes is a mandatory stage before workers have the right to strike against an employer. The Federal Law on the Procedure for the Settlement of Collective Labour Disputes, adopted 23 November 1995, as amended 6 November and 30 December 2001,[90] makes provision for the formation of an ad hoc tribunal consisting of three persons who do not represent the parties to the dispute. The parties may choose the arbitrators by agreement or from those recommended by the Conciliation Service attached to the Ministry of Labour of the Russian Federation. They have five work days to consider the dispute from the moment of their appointment; however, their recommendations are binding only if the parties have so stipulated in advance in writing. These tribunals are called 'labour arbitration tribunals'; even though they may only issue recommendations, the Russian word used is '*arbitrazhnyi*' [арбитражный] rather than, as one would expect, '*treteiskii*' [третейский].

(1) International commercial arbitration

Reference has been made above to the unhappy choice of terminology in the Russian language to characterise the system of State arbitrazh courts. This confusion is perpetuated and exacerbated by the Law on International Commercial Arbitration, adopted 7 July 1993 to establish the framework for international commercial arbitration of all types in the Russian Federation. Here the Russian word '*arbitrazhnyi*' is used to mean '*treteiskii*', which is genuine voluntary third-party arbitration. It is common to see genuine arbitration confused with the State arbitrazh courts in commercial contracts, the parties sometimes never ultimately understanding which type of dispute settlement they had intended to choose. One consequence is certain from the confusion: a State arbitrazh court decision is not enforceable under the 1958 New York Convention on the Recognition and Enforcement of Arbitral Awards.

The Law on International Commercial Arbitration encompasses any arbitration irrespective of whether it is formed ad hoc or effectuated by a permanently operating arbitration institution. Specifically named are two such: the International Commercial Arbitration Court and the Maritime Arbitration Commission, both attached to the Chamber of Commerce and Industry of the Russian Federation. With insignificant changes, the 1993 Law on International Commercial

---

[89] See Бюллетень международных договоров [Bulletin of International Treaties], no 5 (1994) 25–28. Analogous provisions are to be found in Russian treaties with Armenia and Slovenia.

[90] СЗ РФ (1995), no 48, item 4557; (2001), no 46, item 4307; (2002), no 1(I), item 2.

Arbitration introduces into Russian law the 1985 UNCITRAL Model Law on international commercial arbitration and thereby brings the Russian Federation into the forefront of the select number of European capitals who compete for the stature of being centres for alternative dispute resolution.

The International Commercial Arbitration Court is the legal successor to the Foreign Trade Arbitration Commission, founded in 1932 and attached to the USSR Chamber of Commerce and Industry.[91] Its Statute as amended comprises Annex 1 to the 1993 Law. The Reglament of the Court was confirmed 8 December 1994 and entered into force on 1 May 1995. A major reform of the Court was to include foreign jurists on the panel of arbitrators, which previously consisted exclusively of Soviet jurists. Of the 148 jurists elected to the Court in 2000, more than 50 are experienced Western arbitrators proficient in the Russian language.

The Maritime Arbitration Commission attached to the Chamber of Commerce and Industry of the Russian Federation is the legal successor to the Maritime Arbitration Commission founded in 1930; its Statute as amended comprises Annex 2 to the 1993 Law. It continues to operate substantially as before in accordance with the 1993 Law.

(2) Enforcement of arbitration awards and judicial decisions

The autonomy of the arbitration clause is no longer doubted in Russian doctrine and legislation, but the legal nature of the arbitration clause continues to be the subject of debate and can, depending upon its characterization, affect enforcement. Some Russian jurists consider the arbitration clause to be a civil-law transaction; others believe such a clause to be fundamentally a procedural measure; and yet others are of the view that an arbitration clause is a provision *sui generis*. Those who favour the *sui generis* approach point in particular to the combination of contractual and procedural elements inherent in an arbitration clause as making it unique, sometimes called a 'civil law transaction of a special type'.

The 'autonomy of the arbitration clause' carries the further implication that the legal regime of the clause is regulated first by arbitration legislation and only secondarily by the general provisions of civil legislation; that is, the 1993 Law on International Commercial Arbitration takes precedence over the Civil Code of the Russian Federation. It would follow that, in the absence in a contract or arbitration clause of special provisions to the contrary, rules of civil and company

---

[91] The Court has a substantial caseload: 256 (1992), 268 (1993), 260 (1994), 486 (1995), and 393 (1996). In 1998 there were more than 400. See M G Rozenberg (comp), Практика международного коммерческого арбитражного суда: научно-практический комментарий [Practice of the International Commercial Arbitration Court: Scientific-Practical Commentary] (1997), where the principal awards are collected and commented upon and a similar volume for 1998, published in 1999, and for 1999/2000 published in 2002.

legislation providing for special requirements to conclude a valid civil-law transaction (large-scale transaction, interested transaction, for example) are not applicable to arbitration agreements or clauses.

Russian international arbitration practice is consistent with this view. Credit and
pledge agreements, for example, have been found to be invalid for failure to comply with Russian legislation and the requirements of charters of joint-stock societies. Jurisdiction over the dispute was assumed on the basis that even though the
principal and derivative contracts were not valid, the arbitration clause contained
therein survived that invalidity and conferred jurisdiction on the tribunal. It is
presumed by the commentators that the legislative and charter provisions that
rendered the principal civil-law transactions invalid did not affect the arbitration
clause by reason of its special status, not merely its autonomy.

It was long a principle of Soviet law that the awards of foreign arbitration courts
and decisions of foreign courts were subject to recognition and execution in the
USSR if this had been provided for by an international treaty of the USSR. The
position was elaborated last in the Soviet era in an Edict of the Presidium of the
Supreme Soviet of the USSR adopted 21 June 1988.[92] That Edict remains in force
in the Russian Federation (as do the international treaties of the USSR containing
relevant clauses), and the principle has been incorporated in the Federal
Constitutional Law on the Judicial System of the Russian Federation of
31 December 1996, as amended (Article 6). The formalities of an execution proceeding are laid down in the Federal Law on an Execution Proceeding of 4 June
1997, as amended by Decree of the Constitutional Court of the RF of 30 July
2001,[93] and in the 2002 Code on Arbitrazh Procedure.

Although treaties regulating the mutual recognition and execution of judicial
decisions were concluded with all of the Central and East European countries and
with the Independent States of the former Soviet Union, there are but a tiny handful with the rest of the world (among them, Greece, Italy, Spain) and none with
the leading investment countries. As a result, the 1958 New York Convention, to
which the USSR was and the Russian Federation therefore is a party, assumes special significance for most foreign investors and gives arbitration a far more
prominent role than it would otherwise have in a normal investment climate.[94]

---

[92] See Ведомости Верховного Совета СССР (1988), no 29, item 427. Also see the Letter of the
USSR Ministry of Justice of 9 March 1972 and the Instruction of the same Ministry on legal assist-
ance to Foreign States by courts and the notariat of 28 February 1972, as amended 26 June 1985.
Закон [Law], no 8 (1998) 40–45.

[93] СЗ РФ (1997), no 30, item 3591; (2001), no 32, item 3412.

[94] See Hober (n 83 above); Kaj Hober, 'Enforcing Foreign Arbitral Awards Against Russian
Entities', in id, *Transforming East European Law* (1997) 427–463; A I Muranov, Исполнение
иностранных судебных и арбитражных решений. Компетенция российских судов [*Execution
of Foreign Judicial and Arbitral Decisions. Competence of Russian Courts*] (2002).

J. Role of Non-State Entities

Comrades' courts and people's guards are institutions of the Soviet era whose foundation legislation has not been repealed by the Russian Federation.[95] According to press reports, comrades' courts continue to be used in some communities, including parts of Moscow. People's guards, having fallen into desuetude, began to be revived in 1997 under various names to help cope with the incidence of street crime in individual cities.

Both comrades' courts and people's guards represent a community response to law enforcement. A market response has been the emergence of private detective and bodyguard services pursuant to the Law on Private Detective and Protection Activity in the Russian Federation, adopted 11 March 1992, as amended 21 March 2002.[96] Under this Law, specially licensed juridical persons may offer investigative and personal protection services on a contractual basis to natural and juridical persons. The rising crime rate experienced during the 1990s, especially contract killings, kidnappings, and armed robberies, created considerable demand for private sector provision of such protection. Investigative services included background checks on potential business partners, bodyguard services, search for lost or stolen property, data on unfair competition, information on business reputation, and the like. Licences are issued by internal affairs agencies.

A private detective or protector must be a Russian citizen who has reached at least 21 years of age, has a law degree, or has special training of not less than three years in operational or investigative subdivisions of law enforcement agencies, internal affairs agencies, or the FSB. Individuals with a record of mental illness, alcoholism, drug addiction, criminal record for committing an intentional crime, or dismissed from State service under compromising circumstances, are not eligible to receive a licence. The licence to be a detective does not in and of itself make one a detective. There must follow a labour contract with an enterprise or the registration of an 'individual private detective enterprise'. A list of the types of special means which detectives and protectors are authorised to use in their work was confirmed by Decree of the Government of the Russian Federation No 587, adopted 14 August 1992, as amended to 10 January 2003.[97]

---

[95] See W E Butler, *Soviet Law* (2nd edn; 1988) 136–141.
[96] Ведомости СНД и ВС РФ (1992), no 17, item 888; СЗ РФ (2002), no 12, item 1093.
[97] САПП РФ (1992), no 8, item 506; СЗ РФ(2000), no 31, item 3299; (2003), no. 2.

K. Law Enforcement Coordination in the CIS

Within the framework of the CIS a number of law enforcement coordination groups and councils have been created to encourage cooperation in law enforcement, training, and research. In December 1997 for the first time these bodies held a joint session: the Coordination Council of Procurators General,[98] the Council of Ministers of Internal Affairs, the Council of Heads of Security Agencies and Special Services, the Council of Those Commanding Border Forces, and the Council of Heads of Customs Services. The heads of Tax Police and respective services of CIS member states are in the process of completing the foundation of their CIS organs. The priorities for cooperation are joint efforts against organised crime, to revise the 1993 Minsk Convention on mutual legal assistance with regard to civil, family, and criminal cases, and to encourage the preparation of model codes for consideration by CIS member states.

---

[98] The Council publishes its own quarterly journal: Прокурорская и следственная практика [*Procuracy and Investigative Practice*], since 1997.

CIVIL, ARBITRAZH, AND CRIMINAL PROCEDURE

Russian civil, arbitrazh, and criminal procedure represent a model of procedure which contains a number of distinctive elements not found in the Western European continental model to which the Russian system is akin. Russian legal doctrine continues to regard these types of procedure as parts of a larger whole rather than as three entirely distinct legal realms.[1] In the case of civil and criminal procedure the same courts hear each type of proceeding, although at higher levels of the judicial system special divisions are created for civil and for criminal cases. However, a separate system of courts, called arbitrazh courts (see Chapter 6), considers arbitrazh cases.

The 1993 Russian Constitution lays down procedural principles and guarantees that are applicable to all court proceedings: the right to use the national language,

---

[1] Proponents of this approach sometimes refer to such law as 'judicial law'. For early views, see I V Mikhailovskii, 'Судебное право как самостоятельная юридическая наука' ['Judicial Law as an Autonomous Legal Science'], Право [Law], no. 32 (1908) 1737; N N Rozin, Уголовное судопроизводство [Criminal Procedure] (1914) 8–17.

the independence of judges and their subordination only to law, the purposes of justice, the equality of citizens before the law, the effectuation of justice in precise conformity with the law, and the open examination of cases in all courts. Unlike Anglo-American proceedings, moreover, it is common under Russian law for a civil suit to be dealt with simultaneously in a criminal proceeding. The victim of a crime is usually the plaintiff, but a third person also may have sustained injury by the offence and appear as the civil plaintiff. So too may there be a civil defendant, for example, when an employer is civilly liable for an employee's criminal behaviour.

At one time in Soviet doctrine consideration was given to developing a single law of civil procedure which would extend to all jurisdictional activity: State arbitrazh, the Notariat, arbitration and comrades' courts, and other agencies empowered to settle civil cases. The principal proponent, N B Zeider, was supported by a number of jurists, but the great majority opposed 'Zeiderisation', in the phrase of A A Dobrovol'skii, in the belief that it was theoretically unwise and in practice hopeless to unite all forms for the defence of rights under the common roof of the law of civil procedure.[2] Arbitrazh procedure has a special place in this debate insofar as some legal scholars consider arbitrazh procedure not to be a subspecies of civil procedure but rather one of the forms of economic administration or economic direction; under this view arbitrazh procedure is part of economic law.[3] Others saw arbitrazh procedure as part of Soviet administrative law.[4] And yet others saw arbitrazh procedural law as an autonomous branch of the law of procedure.[5]

Notwithstanding these elements of unity, civil, arbitrazh, and criminal proceedings are the object of individual codification and treated independently in textbooks and teaching. Accordingly, we shall treat them individually below.

A. Civil Procedure

(1) Historical background

Both the French Revolution of 1789 and the Russian Revolutions of 1917 harboured deep grievances against the respective pre-existing systems of civil procedure in their countries. The judicial systems were overburdened with cases; litigation was cumbersome, expensive, time-consuming, and favoured the wealthy

---

[2] See D M Chechot, in V A Musin, N A Chechina, and D M Chechot (eds), Гражданский процесс [Civil Procedure] (1998) 13.

[3] See V V Laptev (ed), Хозяйственное право [Economic Law] (1970) 397.

[4] A T Bonner, in M S Shakarian (ed), Арбитраж в СССР [Arbitrazh in the USSR] (1981) 24.

[5] A A Dobrovol'skii (ed), Арбитражный процесс в СССР [Arbitrazh Procedure in the USSR] (1983) 23.

classes; complex and incomprehensible procedures allowed cases to drag on for years, adding to the expense and contributing to nefarious practices within the court system and legal profession; and innocent people were ruined or degraded by unjust civil judgments against them. The celebrated judicial reforms of 1864 in Russia brought some relief, including a simplified Code of Civil Procedure, but patterns of thought and habit were not so readily transformed.[6]

The system of appellate procedure introduced by the Soviet Government on 24 November 1917 conformed in several essential respects to that introduced by the French Revolution in 1790.[7] For a brief period Soviet courts were authorised to apply the 1864 Russian Imperial Code of Civil Procedure (2,175 articles) unless such application was contrary to Soviet decrees, but soon any reference to the pre-1917 legislation was prohibited.[8] Not until 1923 was civil procedure the object of special legislation. Such regulations as existed were scattered amongst a plethora of acts on court organisation. In general the early legislation introduced greatly simplified court structures, a lay element in the disposition of civil cases, a system of cassational review of cases to replace the usual appellate process, and greater judicial initiative in ascertaining the facts in both civil and criminal cases. Civil litigation was not infrequent during those early years of revolutionary upheaval; by mid-1918 the Soviet courts were obliged to enlarge their staff in order to cope with a flow of civil cases which far outstripped the rate of criminal proceedings; most related to contract, tort, divorce, or maintenance.

The decision of the Soviet leadership to restore the national economy, ravaged by the First World War and civil war, through the NEP had implications for civil procedure just as for other branches of legislation. The RSFSR People's Commissariat of Justice published a draft code of civil procedure in instalments between August 1922 and February 1923, inviting comments. Enactment of the code met with delays, however, largely attributed to apprehensions that civil procedure might become a weapon to be used by NEP-men against the working class or by money-lenders, and the like. An interim decree on civil procedure had to be adopted on 4 January 1923 pending a resolution of these apprehensions. The full RSFSR Code of Civil Procedure ultimately was approved on 7 July 1923 and entered into force on 1 September 1923.[9] With amendments and sometimes de facto superseded in part by subsequent legislation, the Code remained in force until 1964.

The 1923 Code was but one-fifth as long as its Imperial predecessor. The 'return to law' epitomised by the NEP was reflected in the Code by omitting any reference

---

[6] See S Kucherov, *Courts, Lawyers and Trials Under the Last Three Tsars* (1953); R Wortman, *The Development of a Russian Legal Consciousness* (1976).

[7] See D W Chenoweth, *Soviet Civil Procedure: History and Analysis* (1977) 3.

[8] Statute on People's Courts of the RSFSR, adopted 30 November 1918. СУ РСФСР (1918), no 85, item 889.

[9] СУ РСФСР (1923), no 46–47, item 478.

to 'revolutionary consciousness' when deciding cases. Well-enshrined, however, was the principle that the State was entitled to take an active role in the settlement of civil disputes both through the initiative of the court and the intervention, when necessary, of the Procuracy in a civil proceeding. The Code impressed nearly all Western observers as being a modification of the model used in European continental jurisdictions, a 'framework similar to that of any European country'.[10]

Although 'revolutionary consciousness' had been dispensed with, class attitudes were not irrelevant in civil procedure. Soviet commentators in the 1930s often looked upon civil procedure as an anachronistic borrowing from the capitalist world destined to disappear as law withered away. They stressed the importance of a class approach to evidence and its evaluation (the Code gave no guidance to courts for weighing evidence). The adoption in 1936 of the Soviet Constitution and transition to a 'restoration of stability of laws' entailed a new attitude toward civil procedure. Antagonistic classes were declared to have disappeared; the private sector of the economy stimulated by NEP policies had largely vanished with the collectivisation of agriculture and introduction of national economic planning. Civil procedure could now in principle be complied with and enforced impartially, although its scope of operation would be reduced. As time passed, civil procedure 'provided an increasingly stable and important element in the system of Soviet socialist legality'.[11] During the darkest days of Stalinist terror, when so many facets of human behaviour seemed to pose a threat in the minds of the regime, civil procedural relations would be singled out as an area of the legal order which functioned in a more or less normal fashion in the daily life of people.[12]

Aside from certain individual all-union enactments, most notably the 1938 USSR Law on Court Organisation, civil procedure had been regulated in the USSR until 1961 by the 1923 RSFSR Code of Civil Procedure. On 11 February 1957 the USSR Supreme Soviet introduced a constitutional amendment which placed, inter alia, civil procedure within the jurisdiction of the union republics while retaining jurisdiction for the all-union authority to enact Fundamental Principles of civil procedure; this amendment reversed the original intention of the draughtsmen of the 1936 USSR Constitution—never realised—to prepare an all-union code of civil procedure. On 10 December 1961 the USSR Supreme Soviet adopted the Fundamental Principles of Civil Procedure of the USSR and Union Republics (FPCivL), which entered into force on 1 May 1962. These were incorporated and elaborated in the 1964 RSFSR Code of Civil Procedure adopted 11 June 1964 and in force as from 1 October 1964; as amended, it remained in

---

[10] V V Gsovski, *Soviet Civil Law* (1949) I 855. Gsovski added: 'The Soviet civil procedure is like a new building erected of old bricks' (at 856).

[11] See J N Hazard, W E Butler, and P B Maggs, *The Soviet Legal System* (3rd edn, 1977) 135.

[12] See the preface and introduction by Harold J Berman, editing B A Konstantinovsky, *Soviet Law in Action: The Recollected Cases of a Soviet Lawyer* (1953).

force in the Russian Federation until 1 February 2003. The Code contained three annexes, each unchanged since 1964: (1) a list of property which may not be levied against; (2) rules for reinstating a lost judicial or execution proceeding; and (3) a statute on arbitration tribunals, repealed on 24 July 2002. Chapters 34–36 of the 1964 Code remain in force.

In this chapter we consider civil procedure as set out in the 2002 Code of Civil Procedure. It should be noted that cases falling within the purview of Russian arbitrazh courts are considered in accordance with the Code of Arbitrazh Procedure (see below). The Code of Civil Procedure may be applicable sometimes in the arbitrazh courts, but only when the Code of Arbitrazh Procedure does not contain provisions on the relevant point.

(2) Sources of civil procedure law

Nearly 30 articles of the 1993 Russian Constitution affect matters of civil procedure, including those provisions stipulating that all are equal before the court (Article 19), that all are guaranteed judicial defence of their rights and freedoms (Article 46), that no one may be deprived of the right to consideration of his case in that court and by that judge to whose jurisdiction it has been relegated by a law (Article 47), and the provisions generally which apply to judicial power (Chapter 7).

The 1964 Code of Civil Procedure had been augmented by new chapters and articles and by additional parts. These included Chapter 24^1 concerned with appeals against the actions of State agencies, social organisations, and officials which violate the rights and freedoms of citizens, Chapter 11^1 on the judicial order [приказ], and Chapter 16^1 on the decision in absentia. Material changes were made in the provisions regulating the explanations of parties and third persons, the procedure for submitting or demanding and obtaining written and material evidence, and the amounts of fines which may be imposed for procedural violations (substantially increased).

Other principal sources of the law of civil procedure include the Law on State Duty, as amended; the Law on the Procuracy of the Russian Federation, as amended; certain provisions of the Civil Code of the Russian Federation (Articles 11, 152, 162, 203, and 204), and the 1995 Family Code of the Russian Federation. Procedural rules also are to be found in the 2001 Labour Code, the 1983 Housing Code, as amended, the 1992 Law on the Defence of the Rights of Consumers, as amended, and others. Legislation from the Soviet period also remains in force. There are a number of international treaties, most notably bilateral legal assistance treaties, which affect civil procedure.

(3) Scope of civil procedure

The legal relationships directly regulated by the Code of Civil Procedure are more limited than in the Anglo-American legal system for principally two reasons. First, economic disputes are considered mostly in the arbitrazh court system, which has its own Code of Arbitrazh Procedure. Second, many categories of cases under Russian law are relegated for consideration to particular administrative agencies. However, the trend of the 1990s was to enlarge the role of the judiciary, and the courts of general jurisdiction find themselves handling many cases of a type rarely seen in the Soviet era, for example, taxation.

Jurisdiction of the courts is a key issue in any civil proceeding. The Code of Civil Procedure assigns to the courts those cases which arise out of civil, family, labour, housing, land, ecological, and other legal relations if one party to the dispute is a citizen, organisation, on State or local agency. Among administrative cases within court jurisdiction are appeals against the imposition of administrative penalties by agencies or officials or against the unlawful actions of officials which impinge upon the rights of citizens and have been relegated to court jurisdiction. Certain categories of special proceedings fall within special provisions of the Code of Civil Procedure. Cases involving housing, family, or intellectual property legislation are among those which require special reference to the appropriate codes in order to determine whether a civil proceeding will lie. The courts also will hear cases in which foreign citizens, stateless persons, or foreign enterprises and organisations take part, although the latter commonly stipulate contractually that their disputes will be referred to international arbitration or to the Russian arbitrazh courts.

(4) Purpose and features of civil procedure

Russian law continues to adhere to the position of Soviet law that civil procedure is not merely a mechanism for the impartial State adjudication of disputes between persons and organisations. Article 2 of the 2002 Code of Civil Procedure sets out as tasks of civil procedure the proper and rapid consideration and settlement of civil disputes and, interpolating modern values, the promotion of legality and legal order. From this concept of purpose flow certain features of Russian civil procedure which differentiate it from the Anglo-American and the Romanist models.

Participation in civil proceedings

Russian law speaks of the 'subjects of civil procedure relations'. This is a broad category embracing all who participate in a civil proceeding: plaintiff, third persons, defendant, agencies of State administration, expert, procurator, witness. All have their own interests and are collectively referred to in civil procedure legislation as 'persons participating in a case'. Although the Code of Civil Procedure does not mention them in this capacity, most Russian jurists also would include advocates, interpreters, and other representatives in this category.

The Code of Civil Procedure operates as a manual for conducting civil proceedings. Each of the persons participating in the case has been endowed with particular procedural rights. These include the right to familiarise themselves with all of the materials in the file of the case, to make copies or copy out extracts from the files, including materials submitted by other persons, the procurator, agencies of State administration, and others. The advocate or other representative of persons in the proceeding enjoys the same right without a special power of attorney, that is, enjoys this procedural right as a representative. The persons participating in the case have the right to challenge the composition of the court, the procurator, expert, interpretor, or the secretary of the judicial session, submit evidence and participate in the investigation of evidence submitted, put questions to other persons participating in the case and to witnesses and experts, and to offer explanations of circumstances known to them which are relevant to the case. Such explanations are subject to verification and evaluation just as other evidence in the case. They may also submit petitions to demand and obtain evidence, appoint expert examination, secure the suit, suspend the proceedings, and others; they may also give oral and written explanations to the court, present their arguments and reflections regarding all questions which arise during the course of the judicial examination and object to those presented by other persons and anyone else who has offered views on the matter. When judgment is rendered by the court, the persons participating in the case may appeal or, in the case of the procurator, protest the decision or ruling in the procedure and within the periods provided for by legislation.

The Code of Civil Procedure requires that these rights be used in good faith by all and that procedural duties be performed as required. An abuse of rights or failure to perform duties established in the Code can reflect unfavourably on the substance of the judicial decision. For example, the Code requires that each party must prove those circumstances to which they refer as the basis of their demands and objections. If either party fails actively to assume its burden of proof, they are likely to lose, or to find themselves subject to sanctions by the court. Citizens or officials guilty of failing to submit written evidence to the court when they have a duty to do so may be subject to fines.

Russian legal doctrine speaks of civil procedural legal capacity. Closely linked with civil legal capacity as defined in the Russian Civil Code (see Chapter 9), it is not the same, for it encompasses not only civil cases, but also cases arising from administrative, labour, family, tax, housing, and other relations. Natural persons, whether citizens, foreigners, or stateless persons, enjoy civil procedural legal capacity from birth until death. Russian and foreign juridical persons, the Russian Federation, subjects of the Federation, and municipal formations have civil procedural legal capacity from the moment they become subjects of material law. Whether procedural legal capacity extends beyond the parties and third persons to the court, Procuracy, and judicial representatives remains controversial.[13]

Dispositive civil procedural legal capacity is the ability autonomously to effectuate the defence of one's rights in a court by personally instituting proceedings, personally participating in the judicial examination and exercising one's rights, retaining a judicial representative, and the like. Full dispositive civil procedural capacity arises from the age of 18, although 16-year-olds who qualify for emancipation under the Russian Civil Code may also personally effectuate their rights and duties in court, and likewise if they are employed under a labour contract or with the consent of their parents or guardian engage in entrepreneurial activity.

The parties to a civil proceeding are the persons in whose names the proceeding is being conducted and whose dispute in substance is being settled by the court. In every suit proceeding there are always two parties; plaintiffs and defendants may be natural persons, citizen-entrepreneurs, State enterprises and institutions, cooperative organisations, social associations, and other subjects enjoying the rights of a juridical person, including foreign firms, and the State. The names of the parties personify the case, which has implications for *res judicata*. Russian law prohibits the bringing and consideration of a suit already settled between the same parties, concerning the same subject, and on the same grounds. It is the parties who are officially in dispute, who have a material legal interest in the outcome of the case, who enjoy the procedural rights and status as parties, and who bear the court costs of the proceeding. Their rights are too numerous to enumerate, but include the right to participate in all judicial sessions relating to the case, to be present when procedural actions are performed, to determine the extent of the rights and interests to be defended, to modify their demands, to withdraw (plaintiff) or acknowledge (defendant) the suit, to change the grounds for or subject of the suit, and to reach an amicable settlement. Counterclaims may be filed.

Procedural duties are divided into general and special. Acting in good faith is a general procedural duty usually performed voluntarily by the parties; however, a party who has brought an unsubstantiated suit in bad faith or who systematically obstructs the proper and rapid consideration of the case may be required by the court to pay remuneration to the other party for actual loss of work time of up to 5 per cent of the portion of the suit which is satisfied. Other procedural actions are expected to be performed promptly and according to the form required by law; if not, the party may lose the right to perform the procedural actions concerned. Special procedural duties arise out of individual procedural actions; for example, a person requiring written evidence from persons not participating in the case must indicate what evidence is required, why, for what reasons he cannot obtain

---

[13] See M S Shakarian (ed), Гражданское процессуальное право России [*Civil Procedure Law of Russia*] (1996) 58.

the evidence himself, and the grounds on which he considers that the evidence is with a particular person or organisation.

The Code of Civil Procedure provides that 'any interested person' has the right to apply in the procedure established by a law to a court for the defence of a violated or disputed right or an interest protected by a law (Article 3). A waiver of the right to apply to a court is invalid, but does not preclude concluding a contract containing an arbitration clause or referral to another jurisdictional agency besides a court when the parties have the right to do so. 'Person' here refers to both natural and juridical persons, and the concept of 'interested' has been held to include the relatives of a deceased person: a daughter filed suit in Leningrad to seek retraction of libels published in the press about her father, a victim of the purges, as he had been rehabilitated posthumously. After the lower court refused to hear the case on the grounds that only the person defamed could bring suit, the superior court reversed, indicating that any interested person might defend the honour and dignity of an individual.[14]

When filing suit, the plaintiff must submit data to the court from which it is evident that he is the proper plaintiff and that the defendant is the proper defendant. In Russian civil procedure this is called 'legitimation' of the plaintiff and defendant, and it applies equally when the Procuracy or persons acting in the interests of another bring suit. Substitution of an improper party is unusually complicated under the Code of Civil Procedure, which has not satisfactorily foreseen all of the eventualities which may occur. For example, to replace an improper defendant requires the consent of the plaintiff. If the plaintiff does not so consent, the court involves who it considers to be the proper defendant as a second defendant.

Procedural legal succession will normally occur as a result of legal succession in material legal relations. A citizen may be succeeded by heirs, or a reorganised juridical person by its legal successors. A party may assign a right of demand or transfer a debt. In all instances procedural legal succession is unlikely when the interests involved are deeply personal (recovery of alimony, reinstatement in work, and the like). But material legal succession does not automatically give rise to procedural legal succession. The last is dispositive and depends upon the will of the successor.

The filing of suit does not depend exclusively upon the individual seeking to defend his right or interest, although that is the most common situation. A procurator may institute civil proceedings on behalf of another and in some instances other State agencies, trade unions, social associations, or citizens may bring suit on behalf of others. Trade unions may represent workers and employees in matters of

---

[14] Бюллетень Верховного Суда РСФСР [Bulletin of the RSFSR Supreme Court], no 4 (1965) 14.

production, labour, and the like. Cases concerning the deprivation of parental rights may be brought by the procurator or by State or social organisations, as well as by a parent or guardian. Under the Law on the Procuracy in its 1995 version a procurator may enter a case at any stage of the proceeding if the defence of the rights and interests of society and the State so require. Procuracy participation in a case may be at its own initiative or at the initiative of a court. Whether to participate in a case is for the Procuracy itself to decide, although such participation is mandatory if the court so decides or a federal law so provides.[15] Procuracy participation is almost always imperative in cases concerning the deprivation, restoration, or limitation of parental rights, declaring a person to be missing or deceased, or to lack dispositive legal capacity, and appeals against inaccuracies in electoral lists. In practice procurators take part in cases concerning compensation of material damage caused by a crime, freeing property from arrest, and other labour and housing cases, and family cases affecting the interests of children.

Having instituted or entered a proceeding, the procurator is not bound by the interests of the person whose rights and freedoms have been violated. If it transpires that the demands he presented were illegal or unsubstantiated, he not only has the right but also the duty to withdraw the suit in full or in unsubstantiated part. His withdrawal, however, does not mean the interested person has to concur with the procurator's view; he may insist that the case be heard on the merits, and the case may be terminated only with his consent. More awkward is when the procurator brings a suit in defence of the rights of an individual who then refuses to act as plaintiff or insists upon termination of the proceedings, although the procurator does not agree with this. In some instances the proceedings must nonetheless continue and the interested person in whose interests the procurator acted be involved as a co-defendant, for example, in a suit to deem a marriage to be invalid or to deem a transaction to be invalid. But where a citizen who by reason of health, age, or other reasons cannot personally defend his rights but does not wish the proceedings to be pursued, freely expresses his will and understands the significance of his decision, and the case is not of public significance or great social interest, the court will terminate the proceedings notwithstanding the Procuracy involvement.

Third persons are those who do not have the procedural status of a party but whose rights and interests may be influenced by the decision in the case. Russian civil procedure distinguishes between third persons who have autonomous demands regarding the subject of the dispute and those who have no such demands. Those who have demands may enter the case at any time before the decision is decreed; they enjoy the same rights and duties as the plaintiff. They must formalise their participation by filing suit and comply with all requirements

---

[15] See A A Ferents-Sorotskii, in Musin *et al* (n 2 above) 92.

of the Code of Civil Procedure in doing so, including the payment of State duty. The court must issue a formal ruling as to whether to admit a third person to the case. However, the rights of the third person are not identical to those of the plaintiff and may give rise to unusual situations, as for example when the third person is in dispute with both the plaintiff and the defendant. As a rule, the third person enters a case at its own initiative, although the court may notify a third person that its interests are affected by a case being considered. If the third person does not enter the proceedings before the decision in the case is rendered, it must bring an independent suit later in its own name.

Third persons who have no autonomous demands may enter the case on the side of the plaintiff or defendant if the decision in the case may affect their rights or duties with respect to one of the parties. They may be involved in the case upon the petition of the parties, the procurator, or the initiative of the court.

The involvement of State agencies and social organisations in a civil proceeding is modelled closely upon the example of the procurator. They have the right in the instances provided for by legislation to bring suit in defence of the interests of other persons and to act in a proceeding already underway in order to give an opinion with regard to a case. Unlike the procurator, these agencies and organisations may institute a case only with regard to determined categories of cases stipulated in legislation. Under the Russian Family Code commissions for cases of minors and trusteeship and guardianship agencies may defend the interests of minor children, including the revocation of an adoption; organisations empowered by authors to protect their rights may bring suit to defend personal non-property rights of the author; any person may bring a suit against inaccuracies in electoral lists; trade unions, social organisations, and trustee and guardianship agencies may bring suit to have a person declared to lack dispositive legal capacity as a consequence of abusing alcoholic beverages or narcotics; enterprises, institutions, and citizens may bring suit in a court or arbitrazh court to have ecologically harmful activity terminated; federal anti-monopoly agencies, agencies of local self-government, and social associations of consumers may bring suit to defend the rights of consumers, including an indeterminate group of consumers; among others. Cases classified by civil procedure legislation as special proceedings often require the obligatory participation of agencies of State administration. Social security sections, for example, are required to take part in cases connected with the assignment of a pension to establish the facts of dependence, de facto marriage relations, and declaration of a citizen to be deceased.

Representation in civil proceedings

Civil matters engage the attention of lawyers and courts to a far greater extent than any other. Nevertheless, it is common for civil cases to be decided without legal counsel present, taking time away from their jobs and perhaps travelling to another city to do so. The Code of Civil Procedure speaks of a 'representative', a person who performs necessary procedural functions for another, including undertaking the full defence of his rights and interests in court. There are in essence three types of representation: voluntary, legal, and statutory.

Citizens may conduct their own cases in court personally or through a representative, and a citizen's personal participation in a case does not deprive him of the right also to have a representative. Citizens who lack dispositive legal capacity must have a representative. Juridical persons conduct cases in court through their management organs or by using a representative. The concept of civil-procedural representation is quite different from the contracts of representation and commission regulated by the Russian Civil Code. Civil-law representation has the aim of changing or terminating civil rights and duties of the person being represented, whereas civil-procedural representation defends in court the interests of the person being represented in order to assist him in effectuating his procedural rights and performing duties.

Although an advocate is frequently designated as a representative, civil procedure legislation also recognises as representatives workers of State enterprises, institutions, organisations, cooperative organisations, enterprises, and institutions, persons empowered by trade unions or by organisations which by law, their charter, or their statute have the right to defend the rights and interests of those organisations or of other persons, a co-participant of a proceeding on behalf of the others, and individuals allowed by the court considering the case to undertake representation in the case. Certain persons are disqualified, including advocates expelled from a college of advocates, minors, judges, investigators, and procurators. When the circumstances of a case so require, the court may require a citizen to take part personally even though he has appointed a representative. 'Legal representatives' appear on behalf of adopted persons, minors, mentally-retarded persons, and the like. 'Statutory representatives' usually are jurisconsults or officials duly authorised by the charters of their organisations to appear in court on their behalf.

A representative has the right to perform all procedural actions in the name of the person represented. However, the right of a representative to sign a petition to sue, submit it to a court, transfer the dispute to an arbitration court, submit a counterclaim, renounce suit demands, reduce the amount of demands, recognise the suit, change the subjection grounds of the suit, conclude an amicable agreement, appeal, and so on must be specially stipulated in the power of attorney issued to the representitive.

Court costs and fines

Court costs and fines under Russian law are the State duty and other expenses incurred for conducting a civil case in court. Their object is not fully to reimburse the State for the costs of civil proceedings but rather to deter people from filing clearly unsubstantiated suits and to encourage the parties to perform their civil law obligations promptly.

A unified State duty was first introduced by the Soviet Union in 1930. The Russian Federation has retained the essential approach to State duty, which is set out in the RSFSR Law on State Duty of 9 December 1991, as frequently amended to 25 July 2002. State duty is recovered for each petition to sue, whether the initial petition or a counterclaim, and for the petition of a third person who files autonomous demands, for applications or appeals in special proceedings, and for appeal proceedings against the decision of the court. A distinction is drawn between a fixed State duty and a proportional (or percentage) State duty. In some instances the Law on State Duty requires the payment of a fixed amount, and in others imposes a percentage of the value of the suit or demand. The 'price' or value of the suit, as that phrase is used in Russian civil procedure, means the monetary expression of the property or financial interest of the plaintiff, and sometimes of the defendant. The Code of Civil Procedure, for example, stipulates that the value of a suit for the recovery of money is the amount of money to be recovered; for the demanding and obtaining of property, the value of the property to be recovered; for the recovery of alimony, the aggregate payments for one year. As a rule the plaintiff indicates the value of the suit; if the value is difficult to determine at the moment of filing the suit, it will be established preliminarily by the judge, with subsequent adjustments being made by the court when the case is settled.

State duty is subject to refund in the event of overpayment, if the application, appeal, or other recourse to the courts is returned or rejected, or if an empowered agency refuses to perform notarial actions, termination of proceedings in the case or leaving the case without consideration if the case is not subject to consideration in a court of general jurisdiction, or when the plaintiff has not complied with the established pre-judicial claims procedure for settlement of the dispute, and certain other instances. The refund is not a speedy process and may take from a month to a year.

A fixed amount of State duty is imposed for suits of a non-property nature. If a suit combines both property and non-property elements, State duty is collected for both elements. Reduced rates of State duty may be applicable to simplified proceedings.

Other court costs include amounts paid to witnesses and experts, expenses for conducting views on the spot or for searching for the defendant, and expenses connected with execution of the court decision. Exemptions from paying court costs are given in certain instances—to plaintiffs suing to recover labour earnings, individuals holding high State honours (Hero of the Russian Federation, and others), veterans, persons who qualified as having suffered from Chernobyl radiation, authors defending their author's rights, suits to recover alimony, certain personal injury suits, and others. The list of exemptions is vast. In addition the court has a residual power to exempt a citizen partly or wholly from court costs in light of his financial need. Experts and interpreters are paid, by court ruling, remuneration for their work and travel, *per diem*, and accommodation expenses at rates fixed by the State. Translation and interpreting costs affect not only foreigners, but those within the Russian Federation whose native language is not Russian.

Court costs are apportioned only between the parties to the case whose material-law interests were the subject of dispute. If there were several plaintiffs or defendants, or a third person with autonomous demands, all of them are in principle to share in the apportionment. The basic approach is as follows: Russian courts award all court costs against the losing party even if the winning party's costs were paid by the State. If the plaintiff succeeds in part of his suit, he will bear that proportionate share of court costs for the part in which he was unsuccessful. If the suit is rejected, expenses are not compensated to the plaintiff and he must pay the costs incurred by the defendant. If a higher court modifies a lower court decision or decrees a new decision, respective adjustments must be made in the distribution of court costs. Reasonable costs for legal assistance are awarded to the winning party from the losing side, taking into account the specific circumstances of the matter. If the advocate was assigned to work without remuneration, the court may award the costs of his services to the legal consultation office to which the advocate is attached.

A plaintiff who withdraws his suit will not be awarded costs against the defendant, but may petition for costs if the defendant voluntarily settles the demand. When the parties come to an amicable settlement, the usual practice is to distribute court costs as part of the settlement. When a civil suit is filed by the procurator or another agency or person on behalf of other interested persons and recovery is not awarded or only partially awarded, the defendant is compensated proportionately from the State budget for court costs. The rulings of courts' fixing and distributing the value of a suit and court costs may be appealed, or be protested by the procurator, without payment of State duty for the appeal.

Court fines may be imposed by a court or a judge for the failure to perform civil-procedural actions in a timely manner. They are recoverable from the personal means of citizens or officials, and a copy of the ruling imposing the fine is sent to the person being fined. Witnesses, experts, and interpreters may be fined for failure to appear in court upon summons. Individuals may be fined for disturbing a court session, or an official for losing a document of execution, and others. The lowest fine is ten minimum amounts of payment for labour, imposed on a translator for failing to appear in court; the largest fine is two hundred times the minimum amount of payment for labour for the failure to execute the decision of a court which obliged the debtor to perform certain actions. Continued failure to execute the decision can result in the fine being imposed repeatedly.

Procedural economy

An enlightened system of civil procedure accepts as axiomatic that justice delayed by congested court calendars or the procedural tactics of the parties is justice frustrated. The Russian legal system, adhering to the Soviet tradition, has attempted to cope with the matter by imposing strict procedural deadlines or time periods within which specified actions must be performed, documents submitted, or cases heard, and by introducing simplified proceedings for designated categories of cases. Procedural periods are divided into two types: periods established by law, and periods established by the court itself. Unless there are justifiable reasons, the penalties for failure to comply can be draconian: the action or suit is terminated to the benefit of the other party.

The Code of Civil Procedure imposes various deadlines for different kinds of cases. With respect to the courts themselves a distinction is drawn between general and special periods for considering a case. The general period for considering civil cases is within one month from the date the case was filed. Special periods apply to cases for the recovery of alimony, compensation for impairment of health caused by injury, death of a breadwinner, and labour cases: ten days if the parties live in the same city, otherwise 20 days. For appeals against inaccuracies in electoral lists the period is three days, and ten days for considering appeals against the actions of administrative agencies. Individual procedural actions by the court are subject to time requirements: drawing up a reasoned opinion, explaining the decision, execution of judicial commissions, and others. The participants in a civil proceeding must file appeals and requests with the deadlines imposed. If the law is silent on the matter, the court may assign the procedural period itself. Detailed formulas for calculating the running, suspension, extension, or restoration of the periods are given in the Code of Civil Procedure.

The consequences of a court failing to comply with procedural periods do not affect the course of the proceeding or the rights of the parties. The judge himself, however, may be subject to disciplinary responsibility for systematically failing to comply with procedural periods. Non-compliance forms part of the routine forensic statistics submitted by each court to superior courts and to the Judicial Department, as well as part of the personal review of judges undertaken for the purposes of promotion and evaluation.

Procedural economy as a goal of civil procedure was addressed in another way by amendments to the Code of Civil Procedure introduced on 30 November 1995.[16] These amendments added Chapter 11¹, containing ten new Articles 125¹⁻¹⁰, under the title 'Judicial Order', and comprise Chapter 11 in the 2002 Code. Such orders are issued by a judge under simplified rules of civil procedure which do not

---

[16] СЗ РФ (1995), no 49, item 4696.

require that the parties be heard or that the case be considered in substance. The order issued has the status of a document of execution and may be enforced in accordance with the rules for an execution proceeding.

The demands with regard to which a judicial order may be issued are enumerated in Article 122: demands based on a notarially certified transaction, on a written transaction, on the protest of a bill of exchange for non-payment, non-acceptance, or undated acceptance performed by a notary, recovery of alimony for minor children not connected with the establishment of paternity, arrears in taxes and State obligatory insurance, and earnings calculated for but not paid to a worker. The demands in each instance involve a creditor proceeding against a debtor for the recovery of money or moveable property. There are no special requirements concerning evidence, so that any evidence accepted by the court under the general rules of evidence will be acceptable. Although it has been suggested that the simplified procedure may be used only when there is 'no clearly expressed dispute concerning a right',[17] the better view is that there is no real dispute over the evidence supporting the demand of the plaintiff.[18] The court proceeds to issue the judicial order if evidence supporting the demand is produced and not contested by the defendant; the defendant has 20 days within which to contest the case from the moment of being notified by the court about the suit. State duty is levied in the amount of 50 per cent of the duty normally applicable to such a suit in a fully-fledged civil proceeding. A suit will be rejected by the court if the subject matter falls outside Chapter 11, if the evidence does not support the demand, or if State duty has not been paid. Several creditors or debtors may be joined in a single proceeding. The precise formalities and requisites for filing suit to receive a judicial order differ slightly from those of an ordinary proceeding.

This simplified proceeding is used extensively by finance companies, banks, and insurance companies, which before its introduction had massively congested the Russian judicial system, especially in Moscow and St Petersburg, with demands against debtors.

The Code of Civil Procedure also makes provision for so-called 'special proceedings' which are considered in an expeditious and simplified manner. The cases which may be heard by way of a special proceeding are those concerning: the establishment of facts having legal significance, deeming of a citizen to be missing or deceased, deeming a person to have limited dispositive legal capacity or to be without such, establishment of an adoption, deeming property to be masterless, establishing the incorrectness of entries in books of acts of civil status, appeals against notarial actions or a refusal to perform such, and restoration of rights under lost bearer documents.

---

[17] See N A Gromoshina, in M S Shakarian (n 13 above) 177.
[18] N A Chechina, in Musin *et al* (n 2 above) 180.

Filing suit

The 1993 Russian Constitution (Article 46) guarantees to each Russian citizen judicial defence of his rights and freedoms. A suit is the legal means by which a court becomes involved in the defence of a violated or contested right or interest protected by law. A civil proceeding is commenced in the Russian Federation through the filing of a written petition to sue by a person having dispositive legal capacity (or his legal representative) in the court of proper jurisdiction. The petition to sue must contain the information specified in the Code of Civil Procedure and be signed by the plaintiff or a duly empowered representative. A properly drafted petition must be accepted by the judge unless it falls within certain specified criteria for rejection (not triable by a court, failure to exhaust preliminary pre-judicial procedures, *res judicata*, same case already pending in court, lack of jurisdiction, lack of dispositive legal capacity on part of plaintiff, and others). An improperly drafted petition may be amended and proceedings stayed until that is done. A counterclaim may be brought by the defendant in the same procedure as an ordinary action at any time before the court renders a decision on the original demands. The counterclaim must be set off against the original demand, must wholly or partially exhaust that demand, and must be linked with the original demand, on condition that the civil dispute would be more expeditiously considered if the demands were heard together. A demand for damages arising out of a criminal act may be heard simultaneously with the criminal proceeding, or separately.

Security for a suit may be required upon application of a party to the case or upon the initiative of the judge or the court.

Preparation for trial

The preparation of a case for trial is a distinct stage of a Russian civil proceeding. The purposes of this procedural stage are to clarify the circumstances having significance for the proper settlement of the case, determine the legal relations of the parties and the law by which they should be guided, settle who precisely shall be the persons participating in the case, and determine the evidence which each party must present in substantiation of its assertions.

After a petition to sue is accepted, a judge acting alone takes a number of measures to guarantee an expeditious and proper decision. First, the judge questions the plaintiff about the demands of his case, elicits possible defences which may support the defendant, requests additional evidence when necessary, and briefs the plaintiff on his procedural rights and duties. When necessary, the defendant will be summoned for the same purpose. The judge decides the issue of joinder of co-plaintiffs, co-defendants, and third persons, or whether an improper party should be replaced. He also explains to the parties their right to have recourse to an arbitration court and the consequences of doing so. Citizens and organisations interested in the outcome of the case but not participating in it are notified about the time and place for the examination of the case by the court. The judge also decides whether to summon witnesses or to appoint expert examination or experts. At the request of the parties written or material evidence may be requested and demanded from citizens or organisations, and when the matter is urgent, the judge conducts an inspection on the spot of written and material evidence, having notified the persons participating in the case. He sends judicial commissions to other courts, if required, and settles the question of whether security should be posted.

The judge sends or hands over to the defendant copies of the petition to sue and appended documents supporting the demands of the plaintiff and requests that evidence be submitted by the defendant in substantiation of his defence within a stipulated period. The failure of the defendant to submit written explanations and evidence or to appear for the judicial session does not prevent consideration of the case on the basis of the evidence available. The ultimate determination of when the case is ready for trial belongs to the judge alone, who issues a ruling to this effect and notifies the parties and other participants of the proceeding about the time and place for consideration of the case.

Trial

At trial the case is heard by a judge or panel of judges. The proceedings are to be direct, oral, and uninterrupted; that is, the court must personally examine the evidence, hear witnesses, experts, and trial participants, and consider the case with only the usual recesses until it is completed and before hearing another or until it has adjourned the case for reasons specified in the Code of Civil Procedure. The bench may not change during the trial; any changes require retrial from the beginning.

The judicial session passes through four stages: preparatory, investigation of the circumstances of the case, pleadings, and the decree and disclosure of the court decision.

In the preparatory stage the person presiding opens the judicial session and announces which case is under consideration. The secretary of the judicial session reports to the court which of the persons summoned to appear have done so and for those who have not appeared, the reasons for failure to appear. The court establishes the identity of those present and verifies the powers of officials and representatives, removes witnesses from the courtroom until questioned, taking care to ensure that questioned witnesses cannot have contact with those witnesses not yet heard. The person presiding then announces the composition of the court and who is participating as procurator, expert, interpreter, and secretary of the judicial session, and explains the right of challenge. If there is no challenge, the court explains to interpreters, experts, and persons participating in the trial their rights and duties, and also their right to settle the dispute in an arbitration court and the consequences of doing so. Petitions and applications are heard by the court from the parties and their representatives regarding the obtaining of new evidence or other matters. The court next turns to determining the consequences of the failure of a participant in the case to appear; depending upon the circumstances, this may result in postponement of the trial or not.

Commencing the investigative stage of the case, the judge then formally opens the case by reporting on the essence of the case, asking whether the plaintiff persists in his demand, whether the defendant admits the demand in whole or in part, and whether the parties wish to conclude an amicable settlement. The court may refuse to accept a withdrawal by the plaintiff, admission of the demand by the defendant, or an amicable settlement of the parties, but must give its reasons. If the defendant admits the demand, the court renders a decision on the substance of the case satisfying the demands and apportions court costs. Otherwise the court proceeds to hear explanations from all persons participating in the case. Written explanations are read out by the person presiding. Once explanations are completed, the court determines in which sequence the witnesses, experts, and other evidence are to be heard; the parties may take part in this determination. Once the sequence is decided, it may be altered at a later stage if necessary by petition of persons participating in the case. In practice witnesses are usually heard first, each questioned separately. Those who have not testified may not be present in the courtroom until they have done so, whereupon they must remain until the trial is concluded or leave only with permission from the court. Before questioning commences, the person presiding establishes the identity of the witness and cautions the witness about the consequences of perjury. The witness must sign a confirmation that he has been explained his rights and duties; the confirmation is appended to the protocol of the judicial session. The witness is asked to explain his relationship to persons participating in the case and then asked to convey to the court everything personally known to him about the case. Then questions may be put to the witness, first by the person who summoned the witness or his representative and then by other persons participating in the case and their representatives. The plaintiff first questions a witness summoned by the court. The judge may put questions at any time to a witness. If the judge considers that a question put is not relevant, he may disallow the question. Witnesses may be re-examined or confronted with other witnesses in order to eliminate contradictions in their testimony. Witness testimony obtained through judicial commissions or heard at other times is disclosed to the judicial session after witnesses personally present have been heard.

Written evidence or protocols concerning inspections on-the-spot are then read aloud to the judicial session and thereafter submitted to the persons participating in the case and, if necessary, to experts and witnesses. Questions may be put to experts, first by the person who appointed the expert and then by the other persons participating in the trial. The judge may question an expert at any time during his testimony. If agencies of State administration are participating in the case, their opinion is requested; the court, persons participating in the case, and representatives may then put questions to the representative of the State agency.

After considering all the evidence, the person presiding invites those taking part to add in any way to the materials of the case if they wish. In the absence of such request, the judicial examination is declared to be completed and the court proceeds to hear the pleadings.

The court pleadings consist of speeches by those taking part in the case, summing up their position, emphasising relevant evidence and arguments to the court, and asking for judgment in their favour. The plaintiff and his representative speak first, followed by the defendant and his representative, then any third party who has an autonomous demand, followed by any other third party, the procurator or empowered representatives of State agencies or social organisations, or others acting to protect the rights and interests of other persons, followed by empowered representatives, if any, of State agencies joined to the case by the court or at their own initiative. The last word is the prerogative of the defendant. If a procurator is present, he gives his opinion on the substance of the case as a whole after the court pleadings.

In the final stage the bench retires to its consultation room to draw up its judgment. After the judgment is signed by all members of the bench, or a dissenting opinion is attached, the bench returns to the courtroom to announce its decision and explain the procedure and terms for appeal. In exceptional instances arising out of complex cases, the drawing up of a reasoned opinion may be deferred for a period of not more than three days, but the resolutive part of the decision the court must announce at the same session in which it completed examination of the case.

Evidence

Russian courts have enormous latitude in admitting and evaluating evidence. The role of the judge in assembling the evidence already has been noted. In civil cases 'evidence' means any factual data on the basis of which the court establishes the presence or absence of circumstances supporting the demands or defences of the parties and other circumstances material to deciding the case correctly. Each party must prove those circumstances on which his demand or defence rests. In some instances there are statutory requirements as to what type of evidence is necessary; otherwise the court is obliged to admit only relevant evidence. A court is required to weigh evidence according to its own inner conviction based on a comprehensive, full, and objective consideration of the case looked at as a whole and being guided by the law and its legal consciousness. No kind of evidence is accorded any *a priori* established weight. The Code of Civil Procedure treats in detail the evidence of witnesses, documentary evidence, real evidence, and expert evidence.

Appeal

The right of appellate (from justices of the peace) or cassational appeal (all other courts) appeal to the next higher court is available for ten days after the decision of the court is rendered in final form. When that period has lapsed, the decision enters into legal force. The cassational instance reviews the entire case and not merely the errors of law or fact alleged by the appellants. Its decision is not subject to appeal and enters into legal force as soon as it is rendered. Thereafter, review of a judicial decision in a civil case is possible only on the basis of a submission of the Procuracy or in a higher judicial instance by way of judicial supervision.

(5) Civil procedural rights of foreign citizens and stateless persons

Foreign citizens and stateless persons, under the Code of Civil Procedure, enjoy the same civil procedural rights as Russian citizens. These rights are accorded on the principle of national regime irrespective of whether other countries grant analogous rights, although the Government of the Russian Federation may establish reciprocal limitations. 'Foreign organisations' have the right to apply to courts of the Russian Federation and to enjoy civil procedural rights in order to defend their interests.[19]

The principle of national regime for these purposes means that all norms of the Code of Civil Procedure extend to aliens, including those regulating legal capacity and dispositive legal capacity (a foreigner 18 years of age, for example, enjoys full civil-procedural legal capacity in Russia even though he may not do so in his country of citizenship). Foreigners may appear as plaintiff, defendant, or third persons with or without autonomous demands. They bear the same rights and duties as persons participating in a case and may conduct their case personally or through their representatives. On the basis of international treaties, consuls of a sending State often are empowerd to defend the interests of their citizens in a Russian court, sometimes without a special power of attorney.

The 1964 Code of Civil Procedure did not contain special rules treating territorial or generic jurisdiction for cases having a foreign element. Consequently, civil

---

[19] The term 'foreign enterprises and organisations' was used instead of 'juridical persons' in recognition of the fact that organisations and enterprises may exist abroad which are not juridical persons; for example, the English partnership. See Article 433, Code of Civil Procedure; see V A Musin, in Musin *et al* (n 2 above) 458. In 2002 the term became 'foreign organisations'. (Article 398).

cases in which foreign citizens, stateless persons, foreign enterprises or organisations were participating, and disputes in which one of the parties resides abroad, were dealt with in matters of court jurisdiction on the same principles used for allocating purely internal cases by way of analogy of law. In addition to those general provisions, those articles of the Code of Civil Procedure which enable the plaintiff to select his jurisdiction in certain types of cases (alimony, tort, and others) would apply equally to foreigners. In the 2002 Code, Chapter 44 was introduced to address all aspects of systemic and particular jurisdiction.

A foreign citizen or foreign enterprise or organisation has the right to be represented by a Russian advocate or other duly licensed representative, or if a foreign lawyer or law firm not having a presence in the Russian Federation is preferred, the question of admitting such a civil-procedural representative would be decided by the Russian court. In all cases the representative would require a power of attorney to act.

(6) Suits against foreign states

Soviet legislation with respect to suits against foreign States was based on the principle of absolute immunity. The Code of Civil Procedure still reflects this doctrine, providing that 'The bringing in a court of the Russian Federation of a suit against a foreign State, enlisting a foreign State to participate in a case as a defendant or third person, imposition of arrest on property belonging to a foreign State and situated on the territory of the Russian Federation, and the taking with regard to this property of other measures with regard to securing the suit, levy of execution against this property by way of execution of decisions of a court shall be permitted only with the consent of competent agencies of the respective State, unless provided otherwise by an international treaty of the Russian Federation and federal laws' (Article 401). However, the Russian Civil Code, reflecting the principles of a market economy, rejected the principle of absolute immunity for the Russian Federation itself, subjects of the Federation, and municipal formations. These entities, when they act in relations regulated by civil legislation, do so 'on equal principles with other participants of these relations—citizens and juridical persons' (Article 124(1)).

The logical consequence of the position taken in the Russian Civil Code is abandonment of absolute immunity in favour of the principle of functional immunity. In an Opinion sent to the State Duma with regard to a draft Federal Law on the Management of State Foreign Financial Assets Inherited by the Russian Federation, the President of the Russian Federation observed that in accordance:

> with the norms of international law ownership of property (including State property) is determined according to the law of the State where this property is situated. Foreign State ownership enjoys functional immunity in this connection. If a State used its ownership for the purpose of ensuring its sovereignty or fulfilling State-political functions, that is as a subject of international law, for example, to maintain

diplomatic and consular representations, this property always enjoys immunity against the jurisdiction of the State where it is located. However if the State through specially empowered agencies takes part in property turnover or in commercial activity, it is considered as a foreign juridical person and its State ownership does not enjoy immunity. The turnover of such property is regulated by the norms of private international law and by legislation of the country of location of the property . . . This approach has been consolidated in the European Convention on the Immunity of States of 16 May 1972, which in accordance with generally-recognised international practice the Russian Federation may regard as a codified digest of customary norms of international law.[20]

B. Arbitrazh Procedure

(1) Historical background

The history of arbitrazh procedure spans merely a decade or so. With the abolition of State and departmental arbitrazh agencies on 1 October 1991,[21] following the adoption of the RSFSR Law on the Arbitrazh Court, the requirement for a code of arbitrazh procedure was evident. The Code of Arbitrazh Procedure was adopted 5 March 1992 and entered into force 15 April 1992, as amended 7 July 1993.[22] Following the 1993 Russian Constitution, the Civil Code of the Russian Federation, and other market-oriented legal developments, the Federal Constitutional Law on Arbitrazh Courts in the Russian Federation of 28 April 1995 was enacted and in force as from 1 July 1995.[23] On 5 April 1995 the Code of Arbitrazh Procedure was enacted to replace the 1992 version and operated until 1 September 2002, when it was replaced.[24]

The prototype of the arbitrazh courts has been described as the pre-revolutionary Russian commercial courts which considered cases concerning trade and bills of exchange, including trade insolvency.[25] The arbitrazh court is a specialised court for the consideration of economic disputes connected with entrepreneurial activity.

---

[20] Российская газета [*Russian Newspaper*], 13 May 1998.

[21] The Decree of the RSFSR Supreme Soviet on the Introduction into Operation of the Law of the RSFSR on the Arbitrazh Court provided in point 2: 'To abolish from 1 October 1991 on the territory of the RSFSR arbitrazh and other analogous agencies in the systems of ministries, State departments, associations, concerns, and other associations, and also at enterprises and organisations'. See Ведомости Верховного Совета РСФСР (1991), no 30, items 1013–1014.

[22] Ведомости СНД и ВС РФ (1992), no 16, item 836; (1993), no 32, item 1236.

[23] СЗ РФ (1995), no 18, item 1589.

[24] СЗ РФ (1995), no 19, item 1589. Changes were made in the Code by the Decree of the Constitutional Court of the RF of 3 February 1998 and Ruling of the same Court of 14 January 2000. See respectively СЗ РФ (1998), no 6, item 784; (2000), no 10, item 1165. For the 2002 Code, see СЗ РФ (2002), no 30, item 3012.

[25] M K Treushnikov, in M K Treushnikov and V M Sherstiuk (eds), Арбитражный процесс [*Arbitrazh Procedure*] (4th edn, 2000) 13.

(2) Sources of arbitrazh procedure law

The 1993 Constitution of the Russian Federation defines the status of the Supreme Arbitrazh Court of the Russian Federation (Article 127) and the basic functions of the arbitrazh court system. The 1996 Federal Constitutional Law on the Judicial System of the Russian Federation and the 1995 Federal Constitutional Law on Arbitrazh Courts in the Russian Federation both characterise the arbitrazh courts as a system and contain norms regulating procedural relations. At the procedural level, primacy of place is accorded to the 2002 Code of Arbitrazh Procedure of the Russian Federation, accompanied by a large number of federal laws which contain procedural rules and/or references to the arbitrazh courts. Among them are the Civil Code of the Russian Federation (Article 11); the Federal Law on the Defence of the Rights of Consumers (Article 40); the Tax Code of the Russian Federation (Article 138), and the Federal Law on the Procuracy of the Russian Federation (Article 1). The distinctive aspects of considering certain types of cases in arbitrazh courts are provided for in, for example, the 1997 Federal Law on Insolvency (or Bankruptcy), the 1999 Federal Law on the Insolvency (or Bankruptcy) of Credit Organisations, and the 1991 Federal Law on State Duty, as amended.

International treaties of the Russian Federation are sources of arbitrazh procedural law pursuant to Article 15(4) of the 1993 Russian Constitution. Among specific relevant treaties are the 1992 Kiev Agreement on the Procedure for the Settlement of Disputes Connected with the Effectuation of Economic Activity; the 1993 Minsk Convention on Legal Assistance and Legal Relations with Regard to Civil, Family, and Criminal Cases; and the 1998 Moscow Agreement on the Procedure for the Mutual Execution of Decisions of Arbitrazh and Economic Courts on the Territory of States-Participants of the CIS. On 11 June 1999 the Plenum of the Supreme Arbitrazh Court of the Russian Federation adopted Decree No 8 'On the Operation of International Treaties of the Russian Federation Relating to Questions of Arbitrazh Procedure'.[26]

Decrees of the Constitutional Court of the Russian Federation struck down as unconstitutional certain rules of the 1995 Code of Arbitrazh Procedure (Article 192(2)). As for decrees of the Plenum of the Supreme Arbitrazh Court itself being a source of law, the same debate revolves around them as with respect to other courts (see Chapter 4). Nevertheless, many decrees of the Plenum touch upon arbitrazh procedure and are of key importance in applying the Code of Arbitrazh Procedure.

---

[26] See Вестник Висшего Арбитражного Суда Российской Федерации [Herald of the Supreme Arbitrazh Court of the Russian Federation], no 8 (1999) 5.

(3) General principles

The 2002 Code of Arbitrazh Procedure contains a number of general principles which underlie the application of the Code in a particular case. They include: the effectuation of justice by the court (Article 1); the right to have recourse to the court (Article 4); the normative legal acts applicable when settling disputes (Article 13); the independence of judges and their subordination only to law (Article 5); the equality of participants in a proceeding before law and court irrespective of the forms of ownership, subordination, and other circumstances (Article 7 and 8); the *glasnost* of the examination of cases (Article 11); the binding character of judicial acts or decrees (Article 16); the contentiousness and equality of rights of the parties (Article 9); the language of the proceeding (Article 12); the directness of the judicial examination (Article 10); and the application of norms of foreign law (Article 14).[27]

Cases are considered in arbitrazh courts, as a rule, by a single judge. However, if the case involves declaring acts of State agencies, agencies of local self-government, or other agencies to be invalid, or insolvency or bankruptcy, or cases within the jurisdiction of the Supreme Arbitrazh Court, or cases referred back for new consideration collegially, the case is heard collegially. All cases at appellate, cassational, and supervisory instances are heard collegially. 'Collegial' for these purposes is three or a larger uneven number of judges.

Under the principle of 'dispositiveness' the parties and other persons participating in a case may freely dispose of their material and procedural rights at all stages of the proceeding. This follows from the general tenet that proceedings arise because the interested parties to a particular dispute applied to the arbitrazh court for defence of the interests violated or contested. Waiver of the right to have recourse to a court is invalid. The Procuracy and other State agencies also have the right to apply to an arbitrazh court, subject to certain qualifications.

An obligatory pre-judicial claims procedure applies in certain instances established by a law or by contract before there may be recourse to an arbitrazh court. If recourse is made for the purpose of defending State or social interests, such procedure is not necessary for a procurator or State agency to file suit. The principle of dispositiveness is the basis for the rule that the parties to an arbitrazh court proceeding may, before the arbitrazh court adopts its decision, transfer the case to an arbitration court.

The principle of 'operativeness' refers to resolving disputes in a proper and timely manner within the briefest possible periods and with a minimum expenditure of

---

[27] See on the 1995 Code, W E Butler and N Iu Erpyleva, 'Comparative Arbitrazh Procedure: Belarus and the Russian Federation', *Sudebnik*, V (2000), 245–297.

means and efforts by the court and those participating in the dispute, without compromising the other principles applicable to an arbitrazh court proceeding. Provision is made for the parties to challenge a judge, expert, or interpreter, the inadmissability of a judge sitting a second time on the same case, the possibility of a judge removing himself from the case, and the consequences of satisfying a challenge. No provision is made, however, for challenging a procurator in an arbitrazh court.

(4) Systemic and particular jurisdiction

With the emergence of arbitrazh courts as a distinct and autonomous system of courts, the delimitation of systemic jurisdiction between them and the courts of ordinary jurisdiction is of the utmost importance. The correct determination of which court system is empowered to consider a specific dispute is essential at the earliest stage for both the party applying to the court and the judge who considers the petition to sue. The Code of Arbitrazh Procedure defines systemic jurisdiction by reference to:

(1) organisations which are juridical persons of the Russian Federation, and also foreign organisations; juridical persons with foreign investments; and international organisations;

(2) citizens of the Russian Federation, foreign citizens, and stateless persons who effectuate entrepreneurial activity without the formation of a juridical person and have acquired in the established procedure the status of an individual entrepreneur;

(3) the Russian Federation, subjects of the Russian Federation, municipal formations, State agencies, agencies of local self-government, other agencies, officials and citizens not having the status of entrepreneurs;

(4) in the instances established by the Code of Arbitrazh Procedure and other federal laws, also organisations which are not juridical persons and citizens who do not have the status of an individual entrepreneur (Article 27).

The character of the relations being contested are less clearly set out in the Code of Arbitrazh Procedure: cases with regard to 'economic disputes' are within the systemic jurisdiction of an arbitrazh court which are connected with the effectuation of entrepreneurial and other economic activity, as well as 'other cases'. The terms 'economic disputes', 'other economic activity', and 'other cases' are construed variously by legal scholars and practitioners. Their ambiguity is compensated to some extent by a list of economic and other disputes within the systemic jurisdiction of arbitrazh courts.

'Particular' jurisdiction within the system of arbitrazh courts concerns precisely which arbitrazh court, at what level and on what territory, should accept a case for proceedings. The basic rule is that all cases within systemic jurisdiction are within the particular jurisdiction of respective courts of the subjects of the Russian

Federation, except for those within the jurisdiction of the Supreme Arbitrazh Court. Economic disputes between the Russian Federation and subjects of the Russian Federation; between subjects of the Russian Federation themselves; cases concerning the deeming of non-normative acts of the President of the Russian Federation, Soviet of the Federation, State Duma of the Federal Assembly of the Russian Federation, and Government of the Russian Federation to be invalid as not corresponding to a law and violating the rights and legal interests of organisations and citizens, and cases contesting the legality of normative legal acts of the President, Government, or federal agencies of executive powers on designated matters are within the particular jurisdiction of the Supreme Arbitrazh Court (Article 34).

'Territorial' particular jurisdiction is, as a rule, subdivided into: general, alternative (at the plaintiff's choice), contractual, exclusive, and particular jurisdiction with regard to the linkage of cases. The rule of general territorial particular jurisdiction is: a suit is brought at the arbitrazh court at the place where the defendant is located. A suit against a juridical person arising from the activity of a solitary subdivision thereof is brought at the place where the solitary subdivision is located (Article 36). The standards for alternative territorial particular jurisdiction deal with multiple defendants who are subjects of the Russian Federation (in which case at the location of one of the defendants); suits in which the location of the defendant is unknown (in which case at the location of its property or last known location in the Russian Federation); suit against a defendant which is an organisation or citizen of Russia but is situated beyond the limts of Russia (the suit may be brought at the location of the plaintiff or location of property of the defendant); a suit arising from a contract in which the place of performance is specified (suit may be filed at the place of performance).

'Contractual' particular jurisdiction provides that the jurisdiction determined under Articles 35 or 36 of the Code of Arbitrazh Procedure, discussed above, may be changed by agreement of the parties. It should be noted that confusion over the distinction between an arbitrazh court and an arbitration court, based on contractual arrangements, can complicate the choice of jurisdiction.

With regard to 'exclusive territorial particular jurisdiction', suits concerning recognition of the right of ownership of immoveable property, the seizure of such property from another's illegal possession, and eliminating violations of the right of an owner or other legal possessor not connected with deprivation of possession, are brought at the location of the property. A suit against a carrier is to be brought at the location of the transport agency. Particular jurisdiction in bankruptcy cases is determined by the place where the debtor is situated.

Particular jurisdiction in cases concerning the establishment of facts having legal significance is fixed as the place where the applicant is located, except for establishing the fact of possession of immoveable property, which follows the principle of exclusive territorial particular jurisdiction.

Particular jurisdiction with regard to the linkage of cases, which refers to counter-claims, is not determined in detail by the Code of Arbitrazh Procedure, except to provide for joint consideration of the primary and counterclaims. The last are to be brought according to the general rules for bringing suit (Article 132).

(5) Features of arbitrazh procedure

Participation in arbitrazh proceedings

Russian doctrinal writings sometimes refer to the entire group of subjects of an arbitrazh court proceeding as the 'participants in the proceeding'.[28] This view includes the judges as participants. Others distinguish between persons participating in the case and persons facilitating the resolution of the dispute.[29] Chapter 4 of the Code of Arbitrazh Procedure does not make such a distinction nor classify judges as participants, although an analysis of Chapter 2 on the composition of an arbitrazh court does confer a special procedural status upon the judge.

The persons participating in an arbitrazh court case are: the parties, third persons, applicants and other interested persons (in cases concerning the establishment of legal facts), a procurator, State agencies, agencies of local self-government who have brought suit to defend State and social interests, and, when necessary, witnesses, experts, interpreters, and representatives. The parties are the plaintiff and defendant. The plaintiff is the person who brought the suit in his own interests or in the interests of whom the suit was brought. The defendant is the person against whom the suit demand is made (Article 44). The persons or agencies who bring suit in the interests of the plaintiff are not themselves the plaintiff, although there is a view that such persons act as procedural plaintiffs. An analysis of the 1995 Code provisions discloses that when suit is brought by a procurator or State and other agencies in the interests of a plaintiff, the figure of the plaintiff has a completely autonomous character;[30] the same is true in the 2002 Code.

The parties and other persons participating in a case have the full complex of rights and duties, together with rights inherent only in the parties: the right of a plaintiff before the arbitrazh court adopts its decision to change the subject or grounds of the suit, to increase or reduce the amount of suit demands, to renounce or withdraw the suit. The defendant has the right to recognise the suit wholly or partially. Both plaintiff and defendant may end the case by an amicable agreement

---

[28] See S A Ivanova, Арбитражный процесс [*Arbitrazh Procedure*] (1995) 72; id, in Treushnikov and Sherstiuk (n 25 above) 87.

[29] R E Gukasian, Арбитражный процесс [*Arbitrazh Procedure*] (1996) 66; V V Iarkov (ed), Арбитражный процесс. Учебник [*Arbitrazh Procedure. Textbook*] (1998) 52.

[30] Butler and Erpyleva (n 27 above) 257.

between them. The exercise of these exclusive rights is under the supervision of the arbitrazh court.

The Code of Arbitrazh Procedure envisages the possibility of several plaintiffs or defendants in a case. But procedural co-participation is not defined, nor are the grounds for co-participation. Each of the plaintiffs and defendants acts in the case autonomously. When it is necessary to involve another defendant the arbitrazh court shall before adopting a decision involve this defendant with the consent of the plaintiff (Article 47).

The Code of Arbitrazh Procedure does not require the consent of an improper defendant to being replaced; however, the consent of the plaintiff is required. If the plaintiff does not consent to substitution of the improper defendant by another person, the court may involve the other person as a second defendant. In this event the initial and the proper defendants are not co-defendants because they have opposed interests.

'Procedural legal succession' is an expression used to refer to the replacement of a party who has withdrawn from a case. There are two types: universal and singular. Universal legal succession refers to the transfer of all rights and duties from the legal predecessor to the legal successor. Such a transfer is possible, for example, in the event of the reorganisation of a juridical person or the death of a citizen-entrepreneur. Singular legal succession has in view procedural legal succession to an individual legal relation; this occurs, for example, in the event of the assignment of a demand or transfer of a debt. Procedural legal succession occurs only in the event of legal succession having taken place with regard to a material or substantive legal relation. The Code of Arbitrazh Procedure makes provision for the right of an arbitrazh court to substitute parties in a case in the event of the reorganisation of a juridical person or organisation as a person participating in the case, assignment of demand, transfer of debt, on death of a citizen (Article 48).

With regard to third persons who declare autonomous demands, the Code of Arbitrazh Procedure stipulates that they act in the proceedings at their own initiative; they participate in order to defend their interests until the decision of the arbitrazh court is adopted, and they enjoy all of the rights and bear the duties of a plaintiff except for the duty to comply with pre-judicial claims procedures. Third persons who do not have autonomous demands have a rather different procedural status. They act in the proceeding on the side of the plaintiff or defendant for the purpose of defending their own rights and legal interests in future since the outcome of the case may affect their rights and duties in respect of the plaintiff or defendant; they act in the proceedings at their own initiative or initiative of other participants in the proceedings; and they enjoy the rights and bear the duties of a party except for the exclusive rights of the parties to change the grounds or subject of the suit, increase or reduce suit demands, renounce the suit, recognise the suit, conclude an amicable agreement, or demand compulsory execution of a judicial act.

Representation in arbitrazh court

Although parties in arbitrazh proceedings commonly retain legal counsel to assist or represent them, the Code of Arbitrazh Procedure does not so require. Organisations may be represented by their duly empowered organs or officials; citizens may conduct their own cases personally or through a representative. A representative may be any citizen duly empowered to act. Legal representatives may act in the interests of citizens who do not have full dispositive legal capacity. A power of attorney is the customary way of demonstrating a power to represent.

Evidence

Evidence is defined in the Code of Arbitrazh Procedure as information concerning facts received in accordance with the procedure provided for by legislation on the basis of which the arbitrazh court establishes the presence or absence of circumstances substantiating the demands and objections of persons participating in the case, as well as other circumstances having significance for the proper resolution of the dispute (Article 64). Such information is established by written or material evidence, opinions of experts, testimony of witnesses, and explanations of persons participating in the case. The use of evidence obtained in violation of a federal law is not permitted.

The Code of Arbitrazh procedure speaks of the 'duty' of proof, rather than the burden of proof. Each person participating in the case must prove those circumstances to which he refers as the grounds of his demands and objections. However, with regard to cases concerning the deeming of acts of State and other agencies to be invalid, the duty to prove circumstances serving as the grounds for the adoption of such acts is placed on the agency which adopted the act. Moreover, the arbitrazh court may propose to persons participating in the case that they submit additional evidence if consideration of the case on the basis of available evidence is considered to be impossible.

The principles of relevance and admissibility of evidence are directly formulated: an arbitrazh court accepts only that evidence which is relevant to the case being considered; and circumstances of a case which according to a law or other normative legal act must be confirmed by determined evidence may not be confirmed by other evidence. The evidence must be evaluated according to the inner conviction of the judge(s) based on a comprehensive, full, and objective investigation of the evidence available in the case. No evidence has *a priori* force for an arbitrazh court.

Acknowledgement by a person participating in the case of facts on which the other person bases his demands and objections is not binding upon the arbitrazh court.

Securing of suit

When an arbitrazh case is being readied for judicial examination, one of the questions to be resolved is whether the suit should be secured or not, and if so, how. The purpose of securing the suit is to guarantee the timely and real performance or execution of the judicial act. Although securing a suit is permitted at any stage of the proceedings, it is actually possible as a rule only from the moment of instituting the proceedings. It is the right, but not the duty, of the court to take measures to secure a suit. Specific measures to secure include: arrest against property or monetary means belonging to the defendant; prohibition against the defendant performing determined actions affecting the subject of the dispute; suspension of levy with regard to a document of execution contested by the plaintiff under which the penalty is recovered in an uncontested proceeding; suspension of the realisation of property in the event suit is brought to release such property from arrest. There must be a demand from a person participating in the case to render a ruling concerning the securing of the suit. The arbitrazh court must consider the demand to secure by not later than the next day following receipt of the application. Appeal against the ruling to secure does not suspend execution of the ruling. Where appropriate, several measures to secure a suit are permitted.

The defendant may petition that provision of security by the plaintiff be required in order to compensate possible losses of the defendant. Failure to comply with measure to secure a suit entails a fine payable to the State budget, and the plaintiff may recover losses occasioned by the failure to comply with measures to secure. The substitution of one type of security by another is permitted. If the defendant wishes, he may place monies sufficient to cover the security on deposit with the arbitrazh court in place of other security measures. The ruling to secure a suit is subject to immediate execution, and if the plaintiff renounces the suit, the defendant has the right to demand compensation for losses caused to him by securing the suit.

(6) Proceedings in cases with participation of foreign persons

About 1,200 cases a year are heard in the arbitrazh court system with the participation of foreign organisations, international organisations, and foreign citizens or stateless persons effectuating entrepreneurial activity. All have the right to apply to arbitrazh courts in the Russian Federation to defend their violated or contested rights and legal interests. The principle of national regime applies: foreign persons enjoy procedural rights and fulfil procedural duties equally with organizations and citizens of the Russian Federation. Although the Code of Arbitrazh Procedure provides (Article 254) that the Government of Russia may establish retaliatory limitations with respect to foreign persons of those States in whose courts special limitations of the procedural rights of Russian organisations and citizens are permitted, no such limitations have been established. The rights of foreign persons include the right to appear in a case as a third person, to declare or not to declare autonomous demands, to appear in cases concerning insolvency or to establish facts having legal significance, and to conduct a case through representatives.

Arbitrazh courts have competence to consider cases with the participation of foreign persons if the defendant is situated and a citizen has a place of residence on the territory of the Russian Federation. Such cases also may be considered if a branch or representative of a foreign person is situated on the territory of Russia; if the defendant has property on the territory of Russia; if the suit arises from a contract under which performance should occur or did occur on the territory of Russia; if with regard to a case concerning compensation of harm caused to property, an action, or other circumstance serving as grounds for bringing a demand to compensate the harm, occurred on the territory of Russia; if the suit arises from unsubstantiated enrichment which occurred on the territory of Russia; if with regard to a case concerning the defence of honour, dignity, and business reputation the plaintiff is situated in the Russian Federation; and if there is an agreement concerning the competence of the arbitrazh court between an organisation or citizen of the Russian Federation and the foreign person. Special rules apply to cases concerning ownership of immoveables and carriage.

Judicial immunity is recognised in arbitrazh courts when suit is brought against a foreign State, or a foreign State is involved in a case as a third person, or arrest is imposed on property belonging to a foreign State and situated on the territory of the Russian Federation, or when other measures are taken to secure a suit or levy execution against such property by way of compulsory execution of a decision of an arbitrazh court. Such actions may be taken only with the consent of competent agencies of the respective States unless provided otherwise by federal laws or international treaties of the Russian Federation. The same is true with respect to international organisations.

The Code of Arbitrazh Procedure treats the procedural consequences of the consideration of a case by a court of a foreign State with regard to a dispute between the same persons, the same subject matter, and on the same grounds. The consequences are that the arbitrazh court should leave such a case without consideration, with the proviso that such consequences do not ensue if the decision of the foreign court is not subject to recognition and execution on the territory of the Russian Federation or the relevant case is within the exclusive competence of an arbitrazh court of the Russian Federation.

(7) Suspension and termination of proceedings

In this context suspension means the termination of procedural actions for an indefinite period in connection with circumstances which preclude resolution of the case at a particular session of the arbitrazh court for reasons beyond the control of the participants. The Code distinguishes between obligatory and optional suspensions. The arbitrazh court is obliged to suspend proceedings if the case cannot be considered until the adoption of a decision with regard to another case or a question being considered in a constitutional, civil, criminal, or administrative proceeding; the plaintiff-citizen or defendant-citizen is on active service in the Armed Forces of the Russian Federation; a citizen dies where the legal relations in dispute permit legal succession; and if a citizen loses dispositive legal capacity. Optional suspension may occur when expert examination is designated by an arbitrazh court, an organisation participating in the case undergoes reorganisation, or a citizen participating in a case is involved in performing a State duty. The last ground is so abstract that virtually any State duty could be involved.

Proceedings in a case may be renewed after elimination of the circumstances which precluded consideration.

Termination of proceedings means ending the judicial examination without rendering a decision on the merits of the dispute for reasons that make it impossible or senseless to continue the proceedings. The grounds for termination are complex, but include: the dispute is not subject to consideration in an arbitrazh court; *res judicata*; a juridical person or other organisation who is a person participating in the case has been liquidated; an amicable agreement has been concluded and approved by an arbitrazh court; and others. A second recourse to an arbitrazh court with regard to a dispute between the same persons, on the same subject matter, and on the same grounds, is not permitted. However, the ruling of the arbitrazh court to terminate the proceedings may be appealed.

A third possibility is leaving a suit without consideration. This may happen if there is a case under proceedings in a court of general jurisdiction, arbitrazh court, or arbitration court between the same person, concerning the same subject matter, and on the same grounds; or if the parties to a case agree to transfer the dispute to an arbitration court under certain conditions; if the petition to sue was not signed or was signed by a person who did not have the right to sign it, or was signed by a person whose office was not indicated; and others. Once the circumstances which caused the case to be left without consideration have been removed or eliminated, the plaintiff may bring suit in an arbitrazh court again by following the general procedures.

(8) Proceedings at first instance

Proceedings are instituted by filing a petition to sue in written form at the arbitrazh court. Certain requirements of form must be complied with, including proper signature of the petition and sufficient copies for the defendant(s) and others participating in the case together with appended documents. Having received the petition to sue, the court will either return it, refuse to accept the petition, or accept the petition and institute proceedings. The petition will be returned for failure to comply with the requirements of form and content, for want of signature or proper signature, for failure to give evidence that copies of the petition were sent to other persons participating in the case, if the case is not within the jurisdiction of the particular arbitrazh court, if documents have not been submitted to confirm payment of State duty in the established procedure and amount, if documents have not been submitted confirming compliance with pre-judicial claims procedures where relevant, unconnected demands have been included in the petition to sue, the plaintiff recalls the petition to sue before proceedings are instituted, or evidence has not been submitted of recourse to a bank or credit institution to recover indebtedness from the defendant when according to a law or contract the monies should have been received in this manner.

The judge renders a ruling to return the petition to sue, which may be appealed and does not prevent a second recourse to the arbitrazh court in the general procedure.

A refusal to accept a petition to sue may follow when the arbitrazh court lacks systemic jurisdiction, *res judicata*, or proceedings have been terminated or an amicable settlement reached with regard to the same persons in a dispute concerning the same subject matter and same grounds. The procedural consequences of a refusal to accept a petition, which may be appealed, are that a second recourse to an arbitrazh court is precluded.

A ruling to accept a petition to sue can be confusing under the Code of Arbitrazh Procedure. The substance of the ruling might be set out in the ruling to prepare the case for examination. There is a certain ambiguity as to which ruling is the primary one, whether they may be combined in a single ruling, or whether the substance of one ruling may be set out in another.

The judicial examination is that stage during which the case is considered and resolved in substance. It might be called an arbitrazh trial, during which the arguments and objections of the parties and third persons are verified against the evidence submitted. Prior to the judicial examination the judge will consider whether to involve another defendant or third person in the case, notify interested persons about the proceedings, suggest to the persons participating in the case or to other organisations or officials the performance of certain actions, including the submission of documents and information of significance for resolving the dispute, verify the relevance and admissability of the evidence, summon witnesses, consider whether expert examination should be designated, send judicial commissions to other arbitrazh courts, summon the persons participating in the same, attempt to reconcile the parties, decide whether to summon executives of organisations participating in the case to give explanations, and take measues to secure the suit. A ruling is then issued specifying actions with regard to preparation of the case, assigning the case for judicial examination, and setting the time and place for conducting the case. The ruling is despatched by registered post under return receipt. Procedural periods and fines have been introduced to discourage delays in complying with pre-trial requirements.

The case must be considered and a decision taken within a period not exceeding one month from the day of rendering the ruling to assign the case for judicial examination. When the case is heard, the judge opens the session and announces which case is being considered, verifies the appearance of persons participating in the case and their powers, whether persons who have not appeared were duly notified and what are the reasons for their failure to appear, announces the composition of the court and indicates who is participating as an expert or interpreter and explains the right to challenge, explains to the persons participating their procedural rights and duties, warns the interpreter about the consequences of a translation known to be false, the expert for giving an opinion known to be false or refusing to give an opinion, and a witness for giving testimony known to be false or a refusal or evasion to give testimony, removes witnesses from the courtroom until it is their turn to testify, determines the procedure for conducting the session and investigating the evidence, directs the session so as to elicit all circumstances having significance for the case, and takes measures to ensure order in the courtroom. Those present have the right to make written notes, a verbatim record, or a recording. Filming, photography, videos, and broadcasting on radio or television are permitted with the authorisation of the court.

All rise when the judge enters the courtroom and when the decision of the arbitrazh court is read out. Those addressing the court, giving testimony etc, also stand, unless the judge has permitted otherwise. The court investigates the evidence by hearing the explanations of persons participating in the case, the testimony of witnesses, the opinions of experts, familiarising itself with written evidence and examining the material evidence. The same judge(s) must hear the case from beginning to end. The court session should, as a rule, be uninterrupted in each case except for recesses designated for rest. In exceptional instances an arbitrazh court may decree an interruption in a session for a period of not more than five days.

The failure to reply to a petition to sue or to submit additional evidence which the judge suggested might be presented is not an obstacle to consideration of the case. Nor is the failure of a duly notified defendant to appear an obstacle. Even the absence of a duly notified plaintiff will not prevent consideration of the case if the plaintiff has consented in his petition to sue to absentee consideration of the case. An amicable settlement between the parties must be formalised by them in writing and a ruling rendered by the arbitrazh court confirming the settlement. The proceedings in the case are then terminated.

If there is no amicable settlement, and after considering all the evidence in the case, the judge asks the persons participating in the case whether they have additional materials with regard to the case. In the absence of such, the court turns to oral pleading. The plaintiff speaks first, followed by third persons in the case, then the defendant or their representatives. Each then has the right of reply, the defendant always speaking last. The judicial session is declared to be completed and the judge(s) retire to adopt their decision.

The arbitrazh court decision must be legal and substantiated, based only on the evidence investigated in the judicial session, adopted in a separate room after finishing the judicial session. If the case is heard collegially, a majority vote of the judges adopts the decision. When adopting their decision, the judge(s) evaluate the evidence, determine which circumstances having significance for the case have been established and which have not, decide which laws and other normative legal acts to which the persons participating in the case referred should not apply, determine which laws and other normative legal acts should be applied, establish what are the rights and duties of the persons participating in the case, and decide whether the suit is subject to satisfaction. The decision is set out in written form and signed by all the judges participating in the session.

The decision is adopted in the name of the Russian Federation and consists of the introductory, descriptive, reasoned, and resolutive parts. The introductory part must contain the name of the arbitrazh court adopting the decision, the composition of the court, the case number, date and place of consideration of the case, names of the persons participating in the case, subject matter of the dispute, surnames of persons present at the session and their powers. The descriptive part contains a brief account of the petition to sue, reply thereto, other explanations, applications, and petitions of persons participating in the case. The reasoned part indicates the circumstances of the case established by the arbitrazh court, evidence on which the conclusions of the arbitrazh court are based concerning these circumstances, and the reasons why the arbitrazh court rejects other evidence or does not apply laws and other normative legal acts cited by the persons participating in the case, and also the laws and other normative legal acts by which the court was guided when adopting the decision.

The resolutive part of the decision contains the conclusions to satisfy or refuse to satisfy each suit demand. When several plaintiffs and defendants participate, the decision must indicate how the dispute is resolved with respect to each of them. If the primary suit and counterclaims are partially or fully satisfied, the set-off between them must be specified. The distribution of court costs between the parties is indicated in the resolutive part.

The decision is announced at the session in which the case was considered. In exceptional instances in especially complex cases the reasoned decision may be postponed for a period of not more than five days, but the resolutive part is announced at the same session in which the examination of the case ended. The presiding judge then explains the procedure for appeal. The decision enters into force upon the expiry of a month after the adoption thereof, except, however, that a decision of the Supreme Arbitrazh Court enters into force from the moment of adoption.

Rulings of arbitrazh courts are an individual act used when postponing the consideration of a case, suspension or termination of proceedings, leaving a suit without consideration, and in other instances provided by the Code of Arbitrazh Procedure. When issued during the consideration of a case in judicial session, the court may render the ruling without formalising it in the form of an individual act. The ruling is announced orally and entered in the protocol of the judicial session.

(9) Review of judicial acts

The review of judicial acts is intended to verify their legality and well-foundedness for the purpose of defending the rights of juridical persons and citizens. The Code of Arbitrazh Procedure provides for three autonomous stages of an arbitrazh proceeding in order to rectify errors committed or permitted by a court when considering and resolving disputes, and a fourth stage when judicial acts may be reviewed other than in connection with judicial error.

These are:

(1) proceedings in appellate instances with regard to appeals against decisions and rulings of an arbitrazh court of first instance which have not entered into legal force; such an appeal must be filed within a month after adoption of the decision by the arbitrazh court;

(2) proceedings in cassational instance with regard to appeals against decisions, rulings, and decrees of arbitrazh courts of the first and appellate instances which have entered into legal force; the same one-month period applies for filing the appeal;

(3) proceedings by way of supervision with regard to protests against decisions, ruling, and decrees of arbitrazh courts of the first, appellate, and cassational instances which have entered into legal force; and

(4) review of decisions, rulings, and decrees of arbitrazh courts which have entered into legal force on the basis of newly discovered circumstances.

The 1995 Code of Arbitrazh Procedure was reviewed by no less an institution than the Supreme Arbitrazh Court itself. Exercising its right of legislative initiative, the Plenum of the Supreme Arbitrazh Court of the Russian Federation submitted to the State Duma a draft federal law on making changes in and additions to the Code of Arbitrazh Procedure of the Russian Federation. Although cast in the form of amendments, the proposal was in effect a new version of the Code which contained 320 articles (as compared with 215 in the 1995 Code).[31] This draft was the basis of the 2002 Code of Arbitrazh Procedure.

C. Criminal Procedure

(1) Historical background

Distinctive elements in the development of Russian criminal procedure already have been discussed (see Chapter 2). In the early years after the October 1917 Revolution, criminal procedure was regulated haphazardly and incidentally by a profusion of individual enactments treating court organisation. For a brief period judges were instructed to apply the 1864 judiciary reform legislation unless expressly repealed, together with the revolutionary consciousness of the working people. In July 1918 the People's Commissar of Justice issued basic guidelines to judges counselling them on how to acquaint themselves with the materials of the case, to evaluate the evidence, summon the parties and witnesses, and on the procedure for conducting the proceedings. The legal press of the day debated whether criminal procedure rules were purely technical guidance or had a legally binding character and whether the element of adversariality was essential to a criminal proceeding or the court might act without prosecutors and defence counsel. Later in the 1920s some suggested there should be two criminal procedure codes: one based on 'socialist democratism' for the working people and another without procedural guarantees for elements of antagonistic classes. With the abolition of the VChKa, the creation of a unified judicial system early in the NEP, and the cessation of civil war, procedural due process was accorded greater priority. Demand intensified for a systematised procedural law that would regulate a proceeding from beginning to end. On 25 May 1922 the RSFSR enacted the first Code of Criminal Procedure, in effect as of 1 August 1922;[32] it was rapidly supplanted, on 15 February 1923, by a new RSFSR Code[33] that survived with amendments until the 1960 Code. On 31 October 1924 the USSR enacted a set of Fundamental Principles of Criminal Procedure of the USSR and Union Republics which laid down certain all-union principles to which the union republics must conform.[34]

---

[31] See the draft with commentary in V M. Sherstiuk, Новые положения проекта третьего арбитражного процессуального кодекса Российской Федерации [*New Provisions of the Draft Third Code of Arbitrazh Procedure of the Russian Federation*] (2001).

[32] СУ РСФСР (1922), no 44, item 539.

[33] СУ РСФСР (1923), no 7, item 106.

[34] СЗ СССР (1924), no 24, item 206.

The 1923 RSFSR Code of Criminal Procedure underwent distressing amendments in the 1930s, for example, the additions on 10 December 1934 and 2 February 1938 allowing cases concerning terrorist organisations, terrorist acts, and counter-revolutionary wrecking and sabotage to be investigated within ten days, to be heard in absentia, to be not subject to appeal, and the death penalty, if assigned, to be carried out as soon as judgment was rendered. Many modifications of the Code of Criminal Procedure, however, seem to have occurred through judicial interpretation or departmental legislation. The RSFSR Supreme Court, for example, issued a special decree in 1927 altering Article 10 of the Code of Criminal Procedure with respect to Procuracy participation in certain categories of cases. From 1929–33 the formalities of criminal procedure were abbreviated through circulars issued by the RSFSR Commissariat of Justice, a trend that was reversed from 1935–36 by the same process.

The 1936 USSR Constitution required the enactment of all-union legislation on court organisation and criminal procedure. The Law on Court Organisation adopted 16 August 1938[35] supplanted the 1924 Fundamental Principles of Criminal Procedure to some extent, but the various commissions appointed to draft an all-union code of criminal procedure never produced an acceptable version. A draft published in 1939 received brief comment in the Soviet legal media, and another of 1948 was limited to internal circulation only. The drafts were prepared by order of the People's Commissariat of Justice within the All-Union Institute of Legal Sciences. In the early 1950s several decrees of the Plenum of the USSR Supreme Court actually amended or repealed provisions of criminal procedure legislation, a display of judicial law-making that contributed in 1957 to giving the USSR Supreme Court an express right of legislative initiative. Discussions of new union republic codes of criminal procedure and a set of all-union Fundamental Principles were well underway when the constitutional amendment abandoning an all-union code was adopted in February 1957. The Fundamental Principles of Criminal Procedure of the USSR and Union Republics were enacted on 25 December 1958,[36] followed by the RSFSR Code of Criminal Procedure on 27 October 1960[37] (entered into force 1 January 1961). The 1960 RSFSR Code of Criminal Procedure remained in force as amended in the Russian Federation[38] until 1 July 2002, when except for certain individual

---

[35] ВВС СССР (1938), no 11, p. 2.

[36] ВВС СССР (1959), no 1, item 12.

[37] ВВС РСФСР (1960), no 40, item 592.

[38] A useful and massive collection of enactments relevant to criminal procedure has been prepared by V N Galuzo (comp), История законодательства СССР и РСФСР по уголовному процессу 1955–1991 гг. [History of Legislation of the USSR and RSFSR on Criminal Procedure (1955–1991)] (1997).

provisions whose repeal is by stages, it was replaced by the 2001 Code of Criminal Procedure of the Russian Federation, as amended 29 May 2002 (twice), 24 July 2002, and 25 July 2002.[39]

The need to reform criminal procedure was acknowledged in the earliest days of *perestroika*. Dozens of changes, additions, and amendments had produced a 'mass of inconsistencies, contradictions, and gaps that have reached a critical level and begun to tell on the effectiveness of the law'.[40] Hundreds of additional amendments introduced in the intervening decade made the situation far worse, not least because the original 1960 Code of Criminal Procedure, for all of its reforms of Stalinist principles and practices, was built on an ideological structure of State power which gave priority to State interests over the individual and favoured the prosecution over the defence.

The introduction of a democratic Constitution in 1993 superimposed principles upon a Code drafted for a different social system, new legislation on the courts and the Procuracy, and a Constitutional Court which took a dim view of a number of provisions of the 1960 Code. The 1960 Code's value as a manual for a criminal proceeding was consequently reduced, for many Code provisions had to be read against other legislative acts, international treaties, or judicial decisions. Nevertheless, it continued to be the central document applicable in a criminal proceeding until the 2001 Code of Criminal Procedure was enacted.[41]

The 2001 Code of Criminal Procedure is slightly shorter than its predecessor (474 articles, as compared with 503 in the 1964 Code), but more intricate in structure. The 2001 Code consists of five Parts incorporating 18 sections, subdivided into 55 chapters, whereas the 1964 Code had no parts and many fewer sections. The official text of the 2001 Code contains 123 appended model procedural documents which, however, virtually double the length of the Code in comparison with its predecessor; these are routinely amended just as provisions of the Code. Among the normative blocks of provisions new to the 2001 Code are the chapters on the Principles of a Criminal Proceeding (Chapter 2), Rehabilitation (Chapter

---

[39] СЗ РФ (2001), no 52(I), item 4921; (2002), no 22, items 2027 and 2028; no 30, items 3015 and 3029.

[40] See A M Larin, in V M Savitskii (ed), Проблемы кодификации уголовно-процессуального права [*Problems of Codification of Criminal Procedure Law*] (1987) 7.

[41] See on the 2001 Code of Criminal Procedure, V T Tomin (ed), Комментарий к уголовно-процессуальному кодексу Российской Федерации (Вводный) [*Commentary on the Code of Criminal Procedure of the Russian Federation (Introductory)*] (2002); V V Moziakov (ed), Комментарий к уголовно-процессуальному кодексу Российской Федерации [*Commentary on the Code of Criminal Procedure of the Russian Federation*] (2002). On criminal procedure under the 1960 Code during the 1990s see V P Bozh'ev (ed), Уголовный процесс. Общая часть [*Criminal Procedure. General Part*] (1997); V M Lebedev (ed), Научно-практический комментарий к Уголовно-процессуальному кодексу РСФСР [*Scientific-Practical Commentary on the Code of Criminal Procedure of the RSFSR*] (2nd edn, 1997); Kh Ts Rustamov, Уголовный процесс. Формы [*Criminal Procedure. Forms*] (1998).

18), Special Procedure for Adopting a Judicial Decision When the Accused Agrees with the Accusation Presented to Him (Chapter 40), the Peculiarities of Proceeding with Respect to Individual Persons (Chapter 52), and International Cooperation in the Sphere of Criminal Procedure (Part 5). Excluded from the 2001 Code is the section found in the 1964 Code on the Protocol Form of Pre-Judicial Preparation of Materials. On 29 May 2002 amendments were adopted which affected 69 articles and three annexes to the Code.

Taken as a whole, the 2001 Code of Criminal Procedure has become more of a mixed version combining elements of the inquisitorial and adversarial models. The pre-trial phases retain their predominantly inquisitorial features, what Russian proceduralists sometimes call their 'investigative-search' form, whereas the judicial proceedings themselves are more adversarial in the sense of strengthening contentiousness, dispositiveness, legal formalism, and protection of the rights and freedoms of man and citizen. While there are numerous innovations in the Code, it does not represent a global or revolutionary change in comparison with the past.

(2) Sources of criminal procedure law

Unlike the substantive criminal law, which is largely concentrated in the Criminal Code of the Russian Federation, the Russian law of criminal procedure is scattered about many sources, including the 2001 Code of Criminal Procedure of the Russian Federation itself. The 1993 Russian Constitution (Article 71(n)) places criminal procedure within the exclusive jurisdiction of the Russian Federation. All Russian legislation determining the organisation, structure, and competence of the courts, the Procuracy, investigative agencies, the police, and advocates is of relevance to criminal procedure, as are all international treaties of the Russian Federation concerning criminal procedure. International obligations of the Russian Federation during the 1990s were a major source of changes in criminal procedure, whether by the legislator or through court decisions applying those norms. Decisions of the Constitutional Court of the Russian Federation on several occasions declared individual provisions of the 1960 Code of Criminal Procedure to be unconstitutional.

(3) General principles

Although not without considerable controversy, the 2001 Code of Criminal Procedure introduces a chapter on the principles of a criminal proceeding (Chapter 2) which commences by defining the 'designation', or purpose, of a criminal proceeding and then sets out 13 principles for such proceedings. The designation of a criminal proceeding as defined in the 2001 Code of Criminal Procedure is to defend the rights and legal interests of persons and organisations who are the victims of crimes, defend the individual against illegal and unsubstantiated accusations, convictions, and limitations of rights and freedoms, and to ensure criminal prosecution and assignment of a just punishment to the guilty, as well as to see that innocent persons are not prosecuted, are relieved from punishment, and rehabilitated (Article 6). Absent from this formulation, when compared to analogous provisions in the 1964 Code of Criminal Procedure, is any reference to 'objective truth' as the aim of the proceeding. No longer does a criminal investigation have to be full, comprehensive, and objective; it must establish 'judicial' truth, not objective truth. The possibility of returning the file of a case for additional investigation has accordingly been removed from the 2001 Code. The criteria for judicial truth are reflected in Articles 90 and 369 of the 2001 Code. The new formulation thus represents the 'intrusion' of adversariality into the foundations of Russian criminal procedure and a fundamental reorientation of the procedural model.

The reorientation is elaborated in the 13 principles. For example, the principle of legality in proceedings with regard to a criminal case stipulated that a violation of procedural norms contained in the Code by a court, procurator, investigator, agency of inquiry, or inquiry official means that evidence obtained by such means is inadmissable. The principle of 'contentiousness of the parties' requires that a court is not an agency of 'criminal prosecution and does not act on the side of the accusation or side of the defence'. The court rather is to create the 'necessary conditions for the performance of their procedural duties and effectuation of the rights granted to them' (Article 15). The other principles are the effectuation of rights only by a court, respect for the honour and dignity of the individual, inviolability of the individual, protection of the rights and freedoms of man and citizen in a criminal proceeding, inviolability of dwelling, presumption of innocence, ensuring the right to defence, freedom of the judge in evaluating evidence, language of the criminal proceeding, and the right to appeal against procedural actions and decisions.

Criticism of the principles relates principally to their being in the Code of Criminal Procedure at all. A code of procedure, according to this view, should consist of rules subject to direct application by those who apply them, not of abstract ideas. Indeed, many procedural rules represent a compromise among the necessarily overlapping and competing principles, this view holds, which makes the abstract formulation of standards the more pernicious.[42]

(4) General provisions

Russian criminal procedure is a variant of the inquisitorial model of continental Europe and very different from the Anglo-American adversarial model, notwithstanding the adjustments made during the 1990s and in the 2001 Code of Criminal Procedure to accommodate democratic values and principles. The investigation of serious offences is entrusted to an official, called an investigator, who is required to conduct an investigation of the evidence and to issue a decree

---

[42] See Tomin (n 41 above) 27, 37.

when there is sufficient evidence giving grounds for accusing a person of the commission of a crime. Depending upon the nature of the decision concerned, the investigator may act autonomously or be subject to judicial or Procuracy control, or even to the control of other State agencies, including internal affairs agencies, Federal Security Service, and tax police. As noted previously, Russian law encourages the joinder of civil suits to criminal cases when these are related. When a jury is not involved, a sharp distinction is not drawn between law and fact. Opportunities for defence counsel to participate at the investigative stage have been massively increased, although advocates report that they encounter resistance to participation in individual cases from the authorities from time to time.

A Russian criminal proceeding is 'event-oriented', that is, the occurrence or alleged occurrence of a crime is investigated, and not a person. A Russian court, procurator, investigator, agency of inquiry, or person conducting an inquiry is required to initiate a criminal case whenever the indicia of a crime are present on the grounds and in accordance with the procedure established by a law (Article 140, 2001 Code of Criminal Procedure). This categorical requirement is ameliorated in the Code of Criminal Procedure by a list of circumstances or situations in which criminal proceedings are precluded or may be terminated, for example, transfer of a case for the imposition of administrative penalties.

(5) Jurisdiction

All levels of the Russian courts of ordinary jurisdiction have original jurisdiction in criminal cases, including justices of the peace. The 2001 Code of Criminal Procedure (Article 31) provides that justices of the peace have jurisdiction over cases concerning crimes for whose commission the maximum punishment does not exceed three years deprivation of freedom, excluding certain designated crimes. The district courts have jurisdiction over all cases except those reserved to justices of the peace or higher courts or to military courts, the latter courts being vested with jurisdiction over cases arising under specified articles of the Russian Criminal Code. Moreover, a higher court always has jurisdiction at first instance over any case within a lower court's jurisdiction. Territorial jurisdiction is based on the place where the crime was committed. If complications arise, the provisions of Articles 32–36 of the 2001 Code of Criminal Procedure apply.

(6) Operation in time and space

The Code of Criminal Procedure is applied as in force at the time of the performance of the respective procedural action or adoption of the procedural decision, unless the Code provides otherwise (Article 4). If the rights of a participant of the proceedings are prejudiced by a change in legislation which repeals or limits directly or indirectly their rights under the Code, these changes have no retroactive force under Article 54(1) of the 1993 Russian Constitution.

Since criminal procedure is within the exclusive jurisdiction of the Russian Federation, the 2001 Code of Criminal Procedure is applicable throughout the entire territory of Russia and elsewhere to the extent that the Russian Criminal Code is applicable (aircraft, sea-going and river vessels beyond the limits of Russian territory but under a Russian flag provided that the vessel or aircraft is registered in a Russian port) unless provided otherwise by an international treaty of the Russian Federation.

(7) Pre-trial proceedings

A Russian criminal proceeding may pass through several stages before trial. The term 'preliminary examination' is used as a general expression to describe the two forms which it may take: preliminary investigation or an inquiry. A preliminary investigation is obligatory with regard to all criminal cases except for those enumerated in Article 150(3) of the 2001 Code of Criminal Procedure, in which event an inquiry is conducted.

Initiation of criminal case

The initiation of a criminal case is the beginning and obligatory stage of a criminal proceeding. In this stage the empowered State agencies and officials, having received information about the commission or the preparation of a crime from other sources, establish the existence or the absence of grounds for a criminal proceeding and adopt a decision to initiate a criminal case if such grounds are present. A case may be initiated on the basis of statements or oral complaints of citizens, or of someone giving himself up, or through direct discovery of the indicia of a crime by a procurator, investigator, or inquiry official.

The potential sources of information are essentially unlimited by the 2001 Code of Criminal Procedure in this connection, such that the Code introduces no limits on the basis for initiating a criminal case. However, if information is received from the mass media, only the procurator may initiate a criminal case; the investigator and agency conducting an inquiry must draw such material to the procurator's attention rather than acting independently themselves (Article 144). New to Russian criminal procedure is the requirement that the person reporting a crime must be issued a document confirming that the report was made, to whom, and the date; previously such requirements were regulated by departmental normative acts.

Anonymous statements may not serve as grounds for initiating a criminal case (although an anonymous statement contained in a report might so serve, in which case the person submitting the report would be responsible for its veracity). Oral statements are recorded in a protocol and signed. A case may be initiated only when there is sufficient data pointing to the indicia of a crime. The decision to initiate a criminal case must be taken within 72 hours of receipt, a period that may be extended up to ten full days by a procurator, head of an investigative section, or head of an agency of inquiry.

Only the investigator or inquiry official with the consent of a procurator, or the procurator himself, may set the procedure for initiation in motion by issuing a formal decree, whereupon measures must be taken simultaneously to prevent or suppress the crime or preserve any traces thereof. The decree to initiate adopted by an investigator or inquiry official is in force only from the moment the procurator gives his sanction and not from the moment of issuance. A refusal to initiate must also be by decree of the same officials with reasons given (and the procurator notified of the decision) and may be appealed to the appropriate procurator or a court. No investigative actions may be undertaken until a criminal case is initiated except when an inspection of the site of the incident, expert examination, taking of witness statements, detention of a suspect, or personal search is required urgently (Article 146). Initiation of a case is, as a procedural stage, subject to Procuracy supervision. Either an improper initiation or refusal to initiate may be vacated by decree of a procurator.

If the decision to initiate a criminal case is taken by the master of a vessel or head of an expedition or the head of a Russian diplomatic or consular institution, the matter must be referred to a procurator as soon as is practicably possible.

A 'private-law accusation' may be made under the 2001 Code of Criminal Procedure upon the application of the victim of the crime and a criminal case initiated through an application to a court (Article 147).

A criminal case may not be initiated, inter alia, in the absence of the event of a crime or of the constituent elements of a crime, expiry of the period of limitations, the minority of the person being brought to responsibility, the failure of the victim of the crime to make a complaint, the death of the person who committed the crime, or the immunity of an individual against having a criminal case initiated without a waiver of immunity by a designated agency.

Once the decree to initiate a criminal case is adopted, the procurator sends the case for preliminary investigation. If the decree is adopted by the investigator, he commences the preliminary investigation, and if the decision is made by an agency of inquiry, the said agency performs the urgent investigative actions and completes the inquiry.

Inquiry

Under the 2001 Code of Criminal Procedure the distinction between those cases in which a preliminary investigation is obligatory and those in which it is not has disappeared, although traces of that distinction can still be found in individual provisions. The trend is in the direction of unifying the two types of pre-judicial proceedings.

In the great majority of instances consideration of a criminal case by a court is impossible without conducting an inquiry or a preliminary investigation. When a decree to initiate a criminal case is issued, the case is either referred by the procurator or judge for inquiry or preliminary investigation or an agency of inquiry sets about its respective task. 'Agencies of inquiry' under Russian law are several. Most commonly they are police agencies, but the commanders of military units, FSB agencies, tax police, heads of correctional labour or similar institutions, bailiff agencies, customs agencies, State fire supervision agencies, border guard agencies, masters of sea-going vessels, or heads of polar stations may act when necessary. An agency of inquiry undertakes the immediate steps to discover whether a crime has been committed and by whom. These include views, searches, seizures, detention and interrogation of suspects and interrogation of witnesses and victims, listening to telephone and other conversations, imposing arrest on property, and, when necessary, designating expert examination. Agencies of inquiry also may take actions to discover and collect evidence which might disappear, spoil, be lost, or be falsified if not gathered promptly. The Code of Criminal Procedure contains an exhaustive list of measures to be taken by an agency of inquiry, and these are not subject to expansive interpretation.

The duty of the agency of inquiry is to take all steps to establish the facts that must be proved in the case. In performing these duties the agency of inquiry follows the rules established for the performance of a preliminary investigation. Certain categories of cases require completion of an inquiry within 15 full days from the day of initiating the criminal case (mostly enumerated in Article 414, Code of Criminal Procedure), subject to extension by a procurator but for not more than ten full days. Moreover, the criminal case must be initiated not simply against the fact of a crime, but with respect to a specific person.

When the inquiry is completed, the inquiry official draws up an act to indict (Article 225), which is confirmed by the head of the agency of inquiry and sent together with the materials of the file of the case to a procurator. An advocate is permitted to participate in the case from the moment the accusation is presented by the agency of inquiry, and if a person suspected of committing the crime is detained, or such person is confined under guard before the accusation is presented, the advocate may participate from the moment the protocol of detention or decree concerning confinement under guard is presented. There are exceptions for minors, blind, deaf, and dumb persons, individuals who do not know the language in which the proceeding is conducted, and others, in which event the participation of the advocate is obligatory from the moment of detention or confinement under guard.

Russian law draws distinctions, not observed in Anglo-American legal systems, between detention and arrest. The Code of Criminal Procedure authorises an agency of inquiry, investigator, or procurator to *detain* a person suspected of committing a crime for which deprivation of freedom may be assigned as a punishment under certain circumstances, for example, a person apprehended committing a crime or immediately thereafter, or when eyewitnesses or the victim directly indicate a particular person, or when obvious traces of the crime are discovered on the suspect, his clothing, or in his dwelling. Otherwise an individual may be detained only if he attempts to escape, or if he has no permanent place of residence or identification, or if a procurator, investigator, or inquiry official petition the court for confinement under guard of the individual concerned. A protocol of detention must be drawn up within three hours of delivering the suspect to the agency of inquiry, investigator, or procurator which indicates that the suspect has been explained his rights under Article 46 of the 1993 Russian Constitution. Written notification indicating details, grounds, reasons, and the explanations of the person detained must be given to the procurator within 12 hours from the moment of detention by the agency of inquiry or investigator. The procurator has 48 hours from receipt of notice within which either to sanction the detention (arrest) or to release the person detained. Consequently, the period of detention may not exceed 60 hours. Within the periods and under the circumstances laid down in Article 49 of the Code of Criminal Procedure, an advocate must be allowed to participate in the case in pursuance of Article 48(2) of the 1993 Russian Constitution.

'Arrest' may arise under other circumstances. The 2001 CAdV provides (Article 3.9) for the imposition of 'administrative arrest' for a term of up to 15 days, or for a violation of the requirements of an extraordinary situation or of the regime in a zone for conducting anti-terrorist operations, up to 30 days by a judge. In this instance 'arrest' is a punishment, and not an investigative safeguard. Arrest also is a punishment under the Russian Criminal Code (Article 54), consisting of confinement of the convicted person under conditions of strict isolation from society for a term of from one up to six months. During the inter-war and early post-war period the Soviet distinction between detention and arrest worked to the disadvantage of foreigners detained in the Soviet Union for criminal investigation because applicable international treaties governing consular access to such individuals provided for access only in the event of arrest. Detention in those times could be several days in duration, but because 'arrest' had not been imposed consuls sometimes found access delayed or denied. Current international practice is to refer to 'arrest or detention in other form' in order to surmount the divergent attitudes toward police custody in Anglo-American and Romano-Germanic legal systems.

Russian legal terminology, it should be observed, changes with respect to individuals at each stage of the pre-trial proceedings. An individual detained on suspicion of committing a crime or to whom a measure of restraint has been applied before an accusation is presented is called a 'suspect' [подозреваемый].

Once the accusation is presented the individual is the 'accused' [обвиняемый], and when the conclusion to indict is accepted by the court and a judicial session assigned, he becomes the 'person on trial' [подсудимый].

During an inquiry a suspect is summoned and interrogated. He must be informed of his right to give explanations, submit petitions, and appeal against the actions of the person conducting the inquiry, and he must be told what crime he is suspected of committing. When under detention, the suspect must be interrogated within 24 hours of being detained, or of the decree being rendered to initiate a criminal case unless his whereabouts was unknown. His advocate has the right to participate in the first interrogation of the suspect and to familiarise himself with the protocol of detention and the decree on the application of a measure of restraint, and to meet alone with the suspect. If the suspect is not held in detention, the law does not prescribe a period within which interrogation must take place. A suspect may refuse to give testimony during interrogation and bears no responsibility for failure to testify.

Preliminary investigation

The preliminary investigation may be conducted by investigators of the Procuracy, of the FSB, internal affairs agencies, or the tax police (Article 151). The 2001 Code of Criminal Procedure stipulates which agencies are to investigate which crimes. In general the FSB investigates serious crimes against the State.

When investigating crimes all decisions concerning the direction of the investigation and the performance of investigative actions are taken autonomously by the investigator, who bears responsibility for the course and the results of the investigation unless the approval of a judge or sanction of a procurator is required. He may appeal to a higher procurator against instructions of a procurator with which he disagrees. The superior procurator either repeals the instructions of the inferior procurator or assigns the case to another investigator. As a rule, one investigator is assigned to a case, but in a large or complex case a brigade or team of investigators may be involved; in the last instance one investigator is assigned the case and directs the actions of the others. He signs all important decrees and other procedural acts, although his colleagues also retain the right of investigator autonomy. The 2001 Code of Criminal Procedure regulates in greater detail the operations of investigative groups.

Direct guidance over an investigation and control over the work of the investigator is the responsibility of the head of the investigative committee, administration, service, section, or group of the agencies within whose jurisdiction the alleged crime falls. The head of the investigative department has the right to verify the file of the case, give instructions to the investigator, transfer the case from one investigator to another, decide whether to assign several investigators to the case, and take other decisions. The instructions of the head of the investigative department are binding upon the investigator, who may appeal them to the procurator. However, the decrees of an investigator may be changed or repealed by the procurator, but not by the head of the investigative department. Supervision over execution of the law by the head of the investigative department is effectuated by the procurator, whose instructions are binding upon the head of the investigative department but may be appealed to the superior procurator.

Under the 2001 Code of Criminal Procedure, certain investigative actions may only be performed on the basis of a court decision, for which the investigator must petition with the sanction of the procurator. Such petitions must be considered within 24 hours of receipt (some of these investigative actions will not come under judicial purview until 1 January 2004; until then, they are within the jurisdiction of the procurator). When performing the investigation, the investigator takes the decision to involve the suspect as a participant in the case or to deem a person to be a victim, civil plaintiff, or civil defendant; such decision also may be taken by a judge, procurator, court, or inquiry official. The law requires that a decree be rendered to deem, for example, a person to be a victim and inform the victim or his representative thereof. If material damage has been suffered by the victim, then these officials are obliged to explain his right to file a civil suit. If a civil suit is brought, a reasoned decree must be issued deeming the person to be a civil plaintiff or rejecting such status. Arrest must be imposed on the property of the accused in order to secure the suit. The sanction of the procurator is required to impose arrest on monetary means and other valuables in accounts, deposits, or other kept by credit organisations. The advocate, suspect, accused, victim, or civil plaintiff or defendant may not be denied the right to interrogate witnesses, conduct an expert examination, or perform other investigative actions to collect evidence if the circumstances they petition to establish may be of significance for the case. A petition must be denied with reasons. For his part, the investigator may engage an interpreter or summon specialists or witnesses to assist him. The preliminary investigation must be completed within two months from the date of initiating the case until the case is referred with an act to indict, transferred to a court in order to consider the possible application of compulsory measures of a medical character, or terminated or suspended. An extension of up to six months is possible, and in cases of great complexity, up to 12 months. A further extension may be made only in exceptional instances by the Procurator General of the Russian Federation or his deputies.

If having collected the evidence the investigator concludes a particular person has committed a crime, the investigator renders a decree involving the said person as an accused. The significance of the decree is that it creates the legal fact giving rise to criminal procedure relations betwen the accused, the investigator, and the procurator. This decree must be presented within 48 hours of being rendered or the date fixed for compulsory appearance. The accused must be informed of his rights to know of what he is accused, to offer explanations, present evidence, submit petitions, familiarise himself with the materials of the case, and, if he has not already retained an advocate, to do so as provided in the Code of Criminal Procedure, among others. Interrogation may begin at once, but not at night except in an urgent situation. Witnesses and victims likewise are interrogated, and searches, views, and expert examination conducted. An accused or suspect may be committed for expert examination to a medical institution.

If the investigator decides there is no basis for prosecution, the accused is released; otherwise, the investigator draws up the act to indict. At that point he must invite the victim, civil plaintiff, or civil defendant, or their representatives to acquaint themselves with the materials of the case. Then the accused is informed that the evidence will support an act to indict and he too has the right to examine the materials of the case. The accused or his counsel may request further investigation, which must be granted or a reasoned refusal given.

By Anglo-American standards the proceedings now move very rapidly. The accused may not have retained defence counsel yet, or his counsel may be occupied with other matters. Defence counsel has the right to meet with the accused alone, to acquaint himself with all materials of the case and copy necessary information, to discuss the filing of petitions with the accused, to file petitions or challenge officials who took part in the investigation, to appeal to the procurator against investigative actions that prejudice or violate the rights of the accused or defence counsel, and to be present during supplementary investigative actions. A formal record is kept of the presentation of the materials of the case. The investigator must explain to the accused his rights to petition for a jury trial, to hold preliminary hearings, and to petition for a trial held as a special proceeding. The explanation of these rights to the accused and his reply thereto are formally recorded, dated, and signed.

When the offence is not serious, the investigator may with the procurator's consent decide not to prosecute, or transfer the case to a commission for minors, or refer the case to a court for the possible application of compulsory measures of a medical character. If the case is to be pursued, the conclusion to indict is issued which sets out the substance of the case, the place and time of committing the crime, the methods, motives, consequences, and other relevant circumstances, the evidence confirming the occurrence of a crime and the guilt of the accused, mitigating or aggravating circumstances, evidence referred to by the defence, data on the victim and the nature and extent of harm caused by the crime. Page references must be given to relevant passages in the file of the case. Information also must be given about the personality of the accused and the specific article(s) of the Criminal Code which make provision for the crime cited. Appended to the conclusion to indict is a list of persons who should be summoned to the judicial session and also a reference concerning the period of the investigation, the measure of restraint and time of confinement under guard, material evidence, civil suit, measures to secure the civil suit, possible confiscation of property, and court costs. The case must be referred immediately to the procurator. If a translation of the conclusion to indict is necessary, the investigator must arrange this.

The procurator has five days to consider the conclusion to indict and either to confirm it and refer the case to a court, to return the case for supplementary investigation, to terminate the proceedings, to request a proper conclusion to indict be drafted if it is defective, or to draw up a new conclusion to indict and return it to the agency of inquiry or investigator, specifying the errors discovered, or to refer the case to a superior procurator for confirmation of the conclusion to indict. The procurator may strike out sections of the conclusion to indict or apply provisions for a less grave crime, but if a more serious crime is called for, the case must be returned for the preparation of a new accusation. If the procurator confirms the conclusion to indict or draws up a new one, he refers the case to the appropriate court. The procurator also may add to or reduce the list of persons subject to being summoned to court except for the witnesses to be called by the defence.

Administrative session

When the conclusion to indict is received by the court, a judge sitting alone must decide whether the case should be assigned for a judicial session. That decision must be taken within 30 days from the moment the file of the case comes to the court, unless the accused is confined under guard, in which event the decision must be taken within 14 days. The judge at this stage examines whether the case is within the jurisdiction of his court, whether copies of the conclusion or act to indict have been handed over, whether the measure of restraint is subject to being vacated or changed, whether petitions and appeals filed should be satisfied or not, whether measures have been taken to secure compensation of harm caused by the crime or possible confiscation of property, and whether there are grounds for holding a preliminary hearing. The judge may rule to refer the case to the proper jurisdiction, or designate a preliminary hearing, or designate a judicial session.

If the judge considers it possible to assign the case for trial, the place and time of the trial must be determined, whether the case should be heard by a single judge or collegially, whether a defender should be appointed if one has not been retained already, who should be summoned to the trial, whether the case should be considered in open or closed session, which measure of restraint should be applied, except for home arrest or confinement under guard. Once the judge decides to bring a person to trial, the judicial consideration of the case must commence within 14 days, unless there is to be a jury trial, in which event the period is 30 days. However, a minimum seven-day period must elapse from the day on which the accused received the conclusion or act to indict before trial may commence.

The 2001 Code of Criminal Procedure has therefore transformed the administrative session into a stage of the proceedings principally concerned with removing any procedural obstacles to trial. No longer is the judge concerned at this stage with the admissability of evidence or whether the accusation is well-founded. In particular, the judge may not refer the case back to earlier procedural stages.

Preliminary hearing

Although preliminary hearings were introduced in the 1960 RSFSR Code of Criminal Procedure by amendment in order to deal with jury trials, the institution has been transformed into one of general applicability under the 2001 Code of Criminal Procedure. Preliminary hearings are conducted at the request of a party to a criminal proceeding by a judge acting alone in closed session. Parties are summoned to such a hearing at least three full days in advance. The person on trial may by petition not be present, and the failure of other participants summoned to appear who fail to do so does not obstruct the hearing being held.

A preliminary hearing may be held to consider applications of a party to exclude evidence, to establish the alibi of the person on trial, to demand and obtain additional evidence or articles, or to interrogate witnesses. A formal record of the preliminary hearing is kept.

It is during the preliminary hearing that a Russian judge may perform certain actions which under the 1960 Code of Criminal Procedure fell under the administrative session. Depending upon the results of the preliminary hearing, under the 2001 Code of Criminal Procedure the judge must come to one of the following decisions (Article 236): to refer the case to the proper court of jurisdiction; to return the case to the procurator; to suspend proceedings, to terminate the case, or to designate the judicial session. If it is decided to exclude evidence and nonetheless designate a judicial session, the decree of the judge must specify precisely which evidence is to be excluded and which materials of the case may not be further investigated nor divulged during the trial. The procurator may decide in the course of the preliminary hearing to change the accusation, in which event the judge notes this in the decree and where appropriate refers the case to the proper jurisdiction.

Either upon the petition of a party or at his own initiative a judge may return a criminal case to the procurator in order to eliminate obstacles to the case being considered if the conclusion or act to indict was drawn up in violation of the requirements of the Code of Criminal Procedure, or a copy thereof was not handed to the accused, or if compulsory measures of a medical character are involved. These are matters of a technical nature and no longer linked with the requirement that a preliminary investigation establish the objective truth on the basis of a full, comprehensive, and objective investigation.

(8) Trial

Judicial examination

The judicial examination of a case at first instance under the 2001 Code of Criminal Procedure reflects the new role of the judge and the parties. The judge(s) now assume a passive role and the parties an active one, especially with respect to evidence.

The judicial examination of a case at first instance usually takes place in open court. A court secretary keeps a record of the judicial session. The procurator supports the State accusation, but is given considerable 'dispositive' latitude during the trial to withdraw the accusation wholly or in part, giving reasons for doing so. The consequence is that the criminal case itself is terminated in respective whole or part.

Although the 2001 Code of Criminal Procedure (Article 244) speaks of equal rights of the accuser and defence during the judicial session to make challenges and submit petitions, submit evidence, participate in the investigation of the evidence, make pleadings, and so on, in line with the move towards a more adversarial proceeding there is no longer a reference to the 'trial participants' nor any suggestion that the civil plaintiff, civil defendant, defence counsel, and others enjoy autonomous procedural status in the proceedings. The trial is now conceptualised as purely a two-sided contest. Both sides offer the court their 'opinions' on issues which arise during the trial and 'appeal' against the actions and decision of the court.

The general conditions of a judicial examination include directness and orality, *glasnost*, unchanged composition of the court, and the role of the court officials, the parties, and others. All evidence in the case is subject to direct investigation, with certain exceptions. The court hears the testimony of the person on trial, the victim, witnesses, and experts, itself views the material evidence, reads out protocols and other documents, and performs other actions necessary to investigate the evidence. The judgment of the court may be based only on the evidence investigated during the judicial session.

Glasnost in this context refers to the openness of the judicial session. A closed session is permitted when the examination may lead to the divulgence of a State or other secret protected by a federal law, the alleged crime was committed by a person under 16 years of age, or the case concerns crimes against sexual inviolability or sexual freedom of the individual or other crimes that may lead to the disclosure of intimate aspects of the life of trial participants or information demeaning their honour and dignity, or a closed trial is required in the interests of protecting participants in the judicial examination or their close relatives. Correspondence, recordings of telephone or other conversations, telegraph, postal, and other communications, and personal films, videos, and the like may be divulged in open court only with the consent of the persons involved; otherwise, they are considered in closed session. Persons present at a trial have the right to keep a written record, and with the permission of the court photography, videos, or cinema filming may be permitted unless the parties object. Persons under the age of 16, unless they are participating in the trial, require the permission of the court to be present. The judgment of the court must in any event be announced in open session, although not in full if the case was heard in closed session.

The same judge or judges must hear the case from beginning to end. If a judge is forced to withdraw for any reason, a new judge is designated and the case commences from the beginning. The person presiding directs the judicial session and takes all necessary measures to ensure equality of the parties and adversariality. He enforces order in the courtroom, explains to the participants their rights and duties and the procedure for effectuating them, and instructs them on the fundamentals of courtroom etiquette.

The secretary of the judicial session keeps a protocol of the session and must fully and accurately set out in the protocol the actions and decisions of the court and the actions of the participants which occurred during the judicial session. The secretary verifies whether the persons who should participate in the judicial session have appeared. Reflecting the adversarial nature of the proceeding, the 2001 Code of Criminal Procedure contains detailed requirements for the protocol of the session, which may be written out in hand, typewritten, or composed on a computer. Stenographic and other technical means may be used. The parties have three full days after familiarising themselves with the protocol to make remarks upon its substance. The person presiding at the trial must consider these remarks at once and may summon the persons who made the remarks in order to clarify their meaning. The person presiding then issues a decree to satisfy or reject the remarks, and both are attached to the file of the case.

An accuser must be present in every case, and the State accuser must take part in criminal cases involving either a public or a private-public accusation. In the event of a purely private accusation, the victim appears as the accuser. There is no requirement of continuity with respect to the State accuser. If necessary, several procurators may appear in the case and if the replacement of a procurator is essential, this may be done without affecting what already has happened in the case. The State accuser presents evidence and participates in the investigation thereof, gives the court his opinion on the essence of the accusation, and offers his view on applying the Criminal Code and assigning punishment. As noted above, the State accuser may withdraw or modify the accusation at any time before the court withdraws to consider its judgment. Any such withdrawal or modification is without prejudice to a civil suit arising out of the same case.

The person on trial must be present unless, in the case of a crime of small or average gravity, the person on trial petitions to have the case heard in his absence. If the person on trial fails to appear, the judicial session must be postponed, and the court may require that he be brought to court under escort or that the measure of restraint be changed to ensure his appearance.

The defender of a person on trial participates in investigating the evidence, submits petitions, offers the court his view on the essence of the accusation and whether it has been proved, circumstances mitigating punishment or exculpating the person on trial, the punishment which the court should assign, and other matters arising during the trial. The judicial session is postponed if the defender fails to appear; if the defender must be replaced, his successor is given time by the court to familiarise himself with the case. However, replacement of a defender does not automatically involve a repetition of what has transpired in the courtroom already.

The judicial examination proceeds with the participation of the victim and/or his representative unless the victim fails to appear but his presence is not essential to continuing with the trial. If the victim fails to appear in support of his private accusation, the criminal case is terminated.

The 1960 RSFSR Code of Criminal Procedure devoted an entire chapter to the joining of a civil suit to a criminal case. In the 2001 Code of Criminal Procedure the subject is reduced to a single article (Article 250). A civil plaintiff, civil defendant, or their representatives may participate in a judicial examination. However, the court may in the absence of the civil plaintiff consider the case if the plaintiff or his representative so petitions, or the procurator supports the civil suit, or the person on trial completely agrees with the presentation of the civil suit. Otherwise, the civil suit is left without consideration, and the plaintiff must bring a separate civil proceeding.

When the judge(s) enter the courtroom, all rise. The person presiding opens the judicial session and announces which criminal case is being examined. The secretary of the judicial session reports to the court on who has appeared and the reasons for failure to appear, if there are such persons. If an interpreter is present, the person presiding explains to him his rights and responsibility; the interpreter affirms by signature that such explanation has been made, and this is appended to the protocol of the judicial session. Witnesses present then withdraw from the courtroom and measures are taken so that witnesses who have not yet given testimony are unable to communicate with those who have or with others in the courtroom.

The person presiding then establishes the identity of the person on trial, where and when he was born, whether he has a command of the language in which the proceedings are conducted, place of residence and work, occupation, education, family status, and other personal information. No longer is he asked whether he is a member of a political party or not. Then the court determines whether and when he was handed a copy of the conclusion or act to indict or a copy of the procurator's decree to change the accusation. The judicial session must be commenced not less than seven full days after such handing over occurred. Next the presiding person announces the composition of the court and who is the accuser, defender, victim, civil plaintiff, civil defendant, or representatives thereof, secretary of the judicial session, expert, specialist, and interpreter. Each is explained their right to challenge the composition of the court or any of the judges. If any challenges are made, these are settled by the court at once.

The person presiding then explains to the person on trial his rights during the judicial examination, after which the rights and responsibility of the victim, civil plaintiff, and civil defendant or their representatives, expert, and specialist are explained to each of them. The parties are asked whether they have petitions to summon new witnesses, experts, and specialists, to demand and obtain material evidence and documents, or to exclude evidence obtained in violation of the Code of Criminal Procedure. The views of the participants of the judicial examination are solicited with respect to each petition, whereupon the court decides whether to satisfy or reject each petition and issue a respective ruling or decree. If a witness or specialist has appeared in court at the initiative of the parties, the court may not reject a petition to interrogate this person during the judicial session. If any of the trial participants have failed to appear, the court hears the views of the parties as to whether the proceeding may continue in their absence and issues a ruling or decree either to postpone or to proceed.

Individuals stand when addressing the court or giving testimony. The court is referred to as 'respected court' and the judges are addressed as 'your honour'.

Judicial investigation

The procurator (State accuser) opens the case for the accusation by setting out succinctly the essence of the accusation and the precise articles of the Criminal Code involved. The person presiding asks the person on trial whether he has understood the accusation, whether he considers himself to be guilty, and whether he wishes himself or his defender to express his attitude towards the accusation presented. No longer does the judge read out the accusation in court.

The sequence for investigating evidence is determined by the party which is presenting the evidence to the court. The prosecution submits evidence first, and after it has been investigated, the defence submits its evidence. The person on trial, if he consents to give testimony, may do so at any time during the judicial investigation with the authorisation of the person presiding. If there are several persons on trial, the sequence of testimony is determined by the court, having taken into account the views of the parties. The person on trial giving testimony is questioned first by his defender and the participants in the proceeding on the side of the defence, and then by the State accuser and participants in the proceeding on the side of the accusation. The person presiding rejects leading and irrelevant questions. Written notes may be used by the person on trial while being examined, but at the request of the court must be submitted to it. When the two sides have completed their questions to the person on trial, the court may put questions. Under certain circumstances the testimony of the person on trial given during the preliminary investigation may be read out in court.

The victim and witnesses are questioned in a similar way, except that the victim likewise may give testimony at any moment during the judicial investigation with the authorisation of the person presiding. Witnesses are questioned separately and in the absence of any previously questioned. The person presiding commences witness proceedings by determining the identity of the witness, his relationship to the person on trial and the victim, and explains to the witness his rights, duties, and responsibility; the witness signs a paper indicating this has been done, which is appended to the protocol of the judicial session. The party which has summoned the witness opens the questioning, and the judge may ask questions when the parties have completed their examination. The victim and witnesses may use notes while testifying and read out documents relating to their testimony. Special measures apply to testimony given by a minor victim or witness.

An expert who gave an opinion during the preliminary investigation may be summoned to be questioned in court when necessary upon the petition of the parties or at the initiative of the court. After his opinion is read out, the parties may put questions, the first question being asked by the side upon whose initiative the expert was appointed. The court may allow the expert time in which to prepare answers to the questions of the court and the parties. Such expert evidence differs from forensic expert examination, which is undertaken also upon petition of the parties or by the court at its own initiative. The questions in this event are submitted in written form to the expert, having been read out in court to all the parties and their views solicited with regard to the questions. The court, having heard those views, may by ruling or decree reject questions it considers to be irrelevant or beyond the competence of the expert, and may also formulate new questions. If there are contradictions between the opinions of experts which cannot be resolved by way of questioning them in court, a further forensic expert examination may be ordered.

Material evidence may be examined or viewed at any time during the judicial investigation upon the petition of the parties. Persons who submit material evidence have the right to direct the attention of the court to circumstances of significance. The court may view material evidence where it is located. Sites and premises may be viewed by the court with the participation of the parties and, when necessary, witnesses, an expert, or a specialist. A court ruling is required to view a premise. The protocols of investigative actions or other documents appended to the file of the case or submitted during the judicial session may be read out in full or in part pursuant to a court ruling or decree.

Upon completing the study of evidence submitted by the parties, the court asks the parties whether they wish to add anything to the judicial investigation. If there is such a petition, the court discusses the matter and takes a decision, together with performing any other necessary judicial actions. The judicial investigation is then declared to be completed.

Oral argument

The court then passes to oral argument, or pleadings. The oral argument consists of speeches to the court by the accuser and defender, or the person brought to trial if there is no defender. The victim or his representative may take part in the oral argument. A civil plaintiff, civil defendant, their representatives, and the person on trial have the right to petition to participate in the oral argument. The sequence of addresses is determined by the court. However, without exception the accuser is heard first, and the person on trial or his defender is heard last. And the civil defendant speaks after the civil plaintiff, or representatives thereof.

Participants in oral argument may refer only to evidence considered in the judicial investigation. The court may not limit the duration of oral argument but may stop persons if they touch upon irrelevant circumstances or upon evidence deemed inadmissable. After all the participants have given their speeches, they each may speak in rebuttal, the right of last rebuttal always belonging to the defence counsel and the person brought to trial.

When oral argument is completed but before the court withdraws to consider its judgment, the parties have the right to submit in written form suggested formulations of the decisions on questions which the court must decide under Article 299 of the Code of Criminal Procedure. These formulations are in no way binding upon the court.

The person brought to trial then is offered the right of the last word; he may be neither questioned nor limited in time, so long as he speaks about circumstances relating to the case. The court then retires for conference to decree judgment, having informed the trial participants when judgment will be announced.

Judgment is declared in the name of the Russian Federation. The judgment must be legal, well-founded and just. 'Legal, well-founded, and just,' means in this context that the judgment was decreed in accordance with the requirements of the Code of Criminal Procedure and was based on a correct application of the criminal law. Judgment must be decreed in complete privacy only by the judges who considered the case and in the conference room. When decreeing judgment, the court must decide the following questions:

(1) whether it has been proved that the act which the person on trial is accused of committing took place;

(2) whether it is proved that the person on trial committed the act;

(3) whether this act is a crime and under what article, paragraph, and point of the Criminal Code of the Russian Federation it is provided for;

(4) whether the person on trial is guilty of committing this crime;

(5) whether the person on trial is subject to punishment for the crime he has committed;

(6) whether there are circumstances mitigating or aggravating the punishment;

(7) what punishment should be assigned to the person on trial;

(8) whether there are grounds for decreeing judgment without assignment of punishment or relieving from punishment;

(9) what type of correctional institution and regime should be determined for the person on trial when punishment in the form of deprivation of freedom is assigned to him;

(10) whether the civil suit is subject to satisfaction, to whose benefit and in what amount;

(11) how to treat property on which arrest has been imposed to secure the civil suit or possible confiscation;

(12) how to treat material evidence;

(13) on whom and in what amount should procedural costs be placed;

(14) whether the court should deprive the person on trial of a special, military, or honorary title, class rank, or State awards;

(15) whether compulsory measures of an educational nature should be applied;

(16) whether compulsory measures of a medical character should be applied;

(17) whether the measure of restraint with respect to the person on trial should be changed or vacated.

When a case is heard collegially, each question is decided seriatim by simple majority vote, without abstention. The person presiding votes last. If a judge who voted for acquittal is in the minority, that judge may abstain from voting on questions concerning the application of the criminal law. If the judges differ on the classification of the crime or the measure of punishment to be assigned, the vote cast for acquittal is joined to the vote cast for a less grave crime or a less severe punishment. The death penalty may be assigned only by unanimous decision of all the judges. Any member of the court who holds a dissenting opinion may set it out in writing. In this event the dissent is not disclosed when judgment is proclaimed but is attached to the file of the case, where it may be considered by a higher court during an appeal or review.

The judgment must be either of guilty or acquittal, with the disposition of any civil demand being jointly considered. After deciding the 17 questions set out above, the court drafts the judgment in the language in which the judicial examination was conducted. The judgment consists of three parts: introductory, descriptive-reasoned, and resolutive. It is either written out by hand or with the use of 'technical means' by one of the judges. After the judgment is signed by all the judges, including a judge who has a dissenting opinion, the bench returns to the courtroom. All stand, including the court, while the judgment is read out. If a translator is required, the interpretation is made simultaneously, aloud, or immediately after it is proclaimed. If the death penalty is assigned, the presiding judge explains to the person on trial his right to petition for a pardon. In certain cases only the introductory and resolutive parts of the judgment are read out in court. Within five days of proclamation, a copy of the judgment must be handed over to the convicted or acquitted person and may be handed over to the civil plaintiff, civil defendant, victim, or their representatives.

Content of court judgment

The introductory part of a judgment contains the following information:

(1) decreeing of the judgment in the name of the Russian Federation;
(2) the date and place of decreeing judgment;
(3) the name of the court decreeing judgment, the composition of the court, data concerning the secretary of the court, accuser, defender, victim, civil plaintiff, civil defendant, and their representatives;
(4) surname, forename, and patronymic of the person on trial, date and place of birth, place of residence, place of work, nature of occupation, education, family status, and other data concerning the personality of the person on trial having significance for the criminal case;
(5) the article, paragraph, and point of the Criminal Code of the Russian Federation providing responsibility for the crime of which the person on trial is accused of committing.

The substance of the descriptive-reasoned and resolutive parts of a judgment vary depending whether the judgment is one of acquittal or conviction. In the event of acquittal, the descriptive-reasoned part sets out:

(1) the essence of the accusation presented;
(2) the circumstances of the criminal case established by the court;
(3) the grounds for acquittal and the evidence confirming such;
(4) the reasons for which the court rejected the evidence submitted by the accusing side;
(5) the reasons for the decision with respect to the civil suit.

It is inadmissable to include any formulations which cast doubt on the innocence of the accused. The resolutive part must contain:

(1) the surname, forename, and patronymic of the accused;
(2) the decision deeming the person on trial to be innocent and the grounds thereof;
(3) the decision to vacate the measure of restraint, if such was selected;
(4) the decision to vacate measures with regard to securing confiscation of property or compenstion of harm, if such measures were taken;
(5) an explanation of the procedure for compensation of harm connected with the criminal prosecution.

The civil suit is either left unsatisfied or left without consideration. In the latter instance the plaintiff may bring a separate civil suit later.

If the court finds the person on trial to be guilty, the descriptive-reasoned part of the decision must contain:

(1) a description of the criminal act deemed by the court to be proved, specifying the place, time, means of commission, form of guilt, motives, purposes, and consequences of the crime;
(2) evidence on which the conclusions of the court are based with respect to the person on trial and the reasons for which the court rejected other evidence;
(3) the circumstances mitigating or aggravating punishment, and if the accusation is deemed in any part to be unfounded or the classification of the crime to be incorrect, the grounds and reasons for changing the accusation;
(4) the reasons for deciding all questions relevant to the assignment of criminal punishment, relieving therefrom, or the serving thereof, and the application of measures of pressure;
(5) substantiation of decisions adopted with regard to other questions in the list of 17.

The resolutive part of the decision consists of:

(1) the surname, forename, and patronymic of the person on trial;
(2) the decision deeming the person on trial to be guilty of the commission of a crime;
(3) the article, paragraph, and point of the Criminal Code of the Russian Federation providing responsibility for the crime which the person on trial was deemed to be guilty of committing;
(4) the type and extent of punishment assigned for each crime which the person on trial committed;
(5) the final measure of punishment subject to being served;
(6) the type of correctional institution in which the punishment is to be served by the person sentenced to deprivation of freedom and the regime of that correctional institution;
(7) the duration of a probation period in the event of a conditional conviction and the duties placed on the convicted person;

275

(8) the decision concerning supplementary types of punishment;

(9) the decision concerning the set-off of time of preliminary confinement under guard if the person on trial was before decreeing of the judgment detained or if measures of restraint were applied to him in the form of confinement under guard, house arrest, or he was placed in a medical or psychiatric in-patient facility;

(10) the decision concerning the measure of restraint with respect to the person on trial until the judgment enters into legal force.

If the accusation engaged several articles of the Criminal Code, the resolutive part of the judgment must indicate precisely under which of them the person on trial was convicted or acquitted.

The resolutive part of the judgment must, in addition, contain the decision with regard to a civil suit brought, the material evidence, and the distribution of procedural costs. If the court must make additional calculations with regard to the civil suit, the suit may be satisfied and the question of the amount of compensation deferred to a separate civil proceeding. The resolutive part must explain the procedure and periods for appeal and the right of a convicted or acquitted person to take part in the consideration of the case by way of cassation.

Simultaneously with decreeing judgment the court determines in a ruling or decree the care of minor children and other dependants or aged parents requiring outside care, or the protection of property owned by the convicted person which requires protection. If the defender was assigned by the court, a ruling or decree is rendered with regard to the amount of remuneration subject to payment for legal services.

Special proceedings

Admission of guilt

Newly introduced in 2002 is a special procedure for adopting a judicial decision when the accused concurs with the accusation against him. If the State or private accuser and the victim so agree, the accused may petition for judgment to be decreed without a judicial examination being held, provided that the punishment provided for by the Criminal Code for such crimes does not exceed five years' deprivation of freedom. The court may decree judgment provided that it is certified that the accused is aware of the character and consequences of his petition and that the petition was made voluntarily and after consultations with his defender. If the court is not satisfied on these issues or if the State accuser, private accuser, and/or victim object, the trial must proceed in the usual way.

The petition must be made by the accused to the court in the presence of his defender and may be made either when the accused is familiarised with the materials of the criminal case or at the preliminary hearing, when such is obligatory.

The court must nonetheless come to the conclusion that the accusation is well-founded and confirmed by the evidence collected with regard to the case. The right to appeal must be explained to the parties, and procedural costs may not be recovered from the person on trial.

Justice of the peace proceedings

The intentional causing of light harm to health (Article 115), beating (Article 116), slander (Article 129), and insult (Article 130, paragraph two) are crimes under the Criminal Code of the Russian Federation whose prosecution proceeds, in accordance with the Code of Criminal Procedure, on the basis of a private accusation instituted by the victim, his legal representative, or representative, or by a procurator in stipulated instances, before a justice of the peace. Other cases within the jurisdiction of a justice of the peace court are set out in Article 30(1) of the Code of Criminal Procedure. The formula is exclusionary; that is, justices of the peace have jurisdiction over crimes for which the maximum punishment does not exceed three years' deprivation of freedom, except for a lengthy list of enumerated individual crimes.

In the case of private accusations the justice of the peace will reject an application which does not meet the procedural requirements, indicating how it must be adjusted and setting a time to do so. Upon petition, the justice of the peace has the right to assist in the collection of evidence which the parties cannot obtain alone. The person complained against may be summoned within seven days from receipt of the application to familiarise himself with the materials of the criminal case, be handed a copy of the application and be explained his rights in a judicial session, and to determine whether witnesses should be summoned. In the event of a failure to appear, these materials are sent by post.

The justice of the peace explains to the parties the possibility of reconciliation, in which case the criminal proceedings are terminated. If reconciliation is not achieved, the criminal case is considered by the court in the usual procedure, subject to certain exceptions, and must commence within not less than three and not more than 14 days from the receipt of the application or criminal case. If there is a counter-application from the accused, it may be joined to the principal application, and the parties in this event are simultaneously applicants and persons on trial. Judgment is rendered by the justice of the peace in the usual way, and appeal lies within ten days from the day of proclamation, except that an appeal or submission of a procurator is filed with the justice of the peace and sent by the last together with the materials of the criminal case to the district court for consideration by way of appeal.

Trial by jury

Jury trial, as noted above (see Chapter 2), was introduced in Russia as part of the judiciary reforms of 1864 and abolished in 1917. Restoration of jury trial was a central provision of the Conception for Judicial Reform in the Russian Federation of 24 October 1991.[43] On 16 July 1993 the Code of Criminal Procedure was amended to incorporate a new Section X devoted to a court of jurors. Section X consisted of five chapters (36–39) and 47 articles (Articles 420–466). Consequential changes were introduced into other relevant Russian legislation. The Supreme Soviet of the Russian Federation adopted a Decree making provision for the introduction of trial by jury on an experimental basis in nine territories and regions of Russia, some from 1 November 1993 and the others from 1 January 1994. The experiment was arranged with exceptional care and attention and monitored thoroughly.[44]

Trial by jury under Article 30(2)(2) of the 2001 Code of Criminal Procedure is an alternative proceeding which an accused person may choose if he is accused of a crime falling under Article 31(3)(1) of the Code. The choice is made at the end of the preliminary investigation, when the investigator must explain the differences between the usual court trial and a trial by jury and then advise the accused to discuss the choice with his advocate. If the accused decides in favour of a trial by jury, he must submit a petition which is set out in a separate protocol and signed by the investigator and the accused. If the person is accused of committing crimes which fall under several articles of the Russian Criminal Code, he has the right to trial by jury even though only one of the crimes falls within the jurisdiction of the relevant court. If there are several defendants and one of them opts for trial by jury, then the entire case must be heard by a jury.

A single professional judge presides in a trial by jury. Before the judge begins to form the jury, he must formally open the judicial session, announce what case is subject to examination, settle any challenges made, elicit who is present, establish the identity of the person on trial, explain to all participants their rights and duties and settle any petitions submitted. Once these formalities have been completed, the judge instructs the secretary to invite into the courtroom those persons summoned to act as jurors.

The jurors are greeted with a brief speech from the judge explaining what case is being heard, the tasks of a juror, and the conditions under which they participate in the case, including under what circumstances their participation may be challenged. They are instructed that questions will be put to them requesting informa-

---

[43] Концепция судебной реформы в РФ [*Conception of Judicial Reform in the Russian Federation*] (1992).
[44] See M V Nemytina, Российский суд присяжных [*Russian Court of Jurors*] (1995); N. V. Radutnaia, Зачем нам нужен суд присяжных [*Why Do We Need a Court of Jurors*] (1995); S. A. Pashin, Судебная реформа и суд присяжных [*Judicial Reform and the Court of Jurors*] (1995); Суд присяжных. Научно-практический сборник [*Court of Jurors. Scientific-Practical Handbook*] (1993); Суд присяжных. Пособие для судей [*Court of Jurors. Manual for Judges*] (1994).

tion about themselves and their relationships with other persons participating in the case. They also are cautioned about their duty to perform the functions of juror in accordance with Russian law. A juror may disqualify himself if there are conflicts of interest, although his reasons for doing so are subject to discussion by the parties. When self-disqualifications have been completed, the parties may question the remaining candidates for juror individually to determine whether there are reasons to submit a reasoned challenge to selection of the juror. Challenges are submitted in writing to the judge and not disclosed to the jurors; the judge decides the petitions to challenge without leaving the courtroom. Possible grounds for disqualification include being a minor, having a record of conviction for a crime, not having dispositive legal capacity, already holding an opinion with regard to the case based on information previously received, being the relative of a person who suffered in an analogous crime, and the like. If after reasoned challenges there remain less that 18 candidates for juror, the judge must take measures to increase the number of candidates up to 18 from a reserve list. If there remain 18 or more candidates, the State accuser and the person on trial or his defender each have the right to make two unsubstantiated challenges by simply crossing names off the list of candidate jurors. That leaves 14 persons, two of whom will be reserve jurors.

The jurors are seated separately from the judge, unlike Russian proceedings of the past where the judge and two lay assessors sat together. The jurors elect their foreman by majority vote. The foreman directs the course of the meeting of jurors, puts requests and questions to the judge on their behalf, reads out questions put by the court, writes down the answers to them, calculates the results of voting within the jury, formalises the verdict, and when asked by the judge, proclaims the verdict at the judicial session. The jury may communicate with the judge only through the foreman and may not communicate with the participants in the trial at all. A sharp distinction is drawn between questions of law and questions of fact. Being ordinary citizens with no special knowledge of the law, jurors may not decide questions of a purely legal character. However, being guided by their experience in life and sound reason, they are to decide whether determined actions were committed, whether the accused committed them, and whether the accused is guilty of what the State accuser or victim accuse him of. The jurors are, therefore, the judges of fact.

After electing the foreman, the jury is required to take an oath administered by the judge, as follows: 'In taking up the performance of the responsible duties of juror, I solemnly swear to perform them honestly and impartially, to take into account all evidence considered in court, both incriminating and exonerating the person on trial, to resolve the criminal case according to my inner conviction and conscience, not exonerating the guilty nor condemning the innocent, as befits a free citizen and just man'.

Among the distinguishing features of a jury trial as compared with a non-jury trial in Russia are the following: the trial begins with the introductory statements of the State accuser, followed by the defender. The State accuser sets out the essence of the accusation and proposes the procedure for investigating the evidence he will present. The defender offers his view with regard to the accusation, which is agreed with the person on trial, and on the procedure for examining the evidence. The jurors may through the judge put questions in written form to the person on trial, the victim, witnesses, and expert after the parties have finished their interrogations. The questions are formulated by the judge and may be rejected if irrelevant. At his own initiative or by petition of the parties the judge excludes evidence that is inadmissible, and if a question of admissability is raised, the judge considers the issue in the absence of the jurors. Information concerning the personality of the accused is investigated with the participation of the jurors only to the extent this is necessary in order to establish the individual indicia of the constituent elements of a crime which he is accused of committing. It is prohibited to investigate facts of a prior record of conviction, whether the accused is a chronic alcoholic or drug addict, and other information capable of prejudicing the jury against the accused.

The oral argument before a jury is confined to the questions which the jurors must decide. Circumstances connected with a civil suit are established in the jury trial only to the extent that this relates to evidence of the commission of a crime by the person on trial. The parties may not mention matters subject to consideration after the verdict has been rendered. After each party completes its pleadings, each has a right of reply. The last reply belongs to the defender. The person on trial has the right of last word in the usual way.

The judge formulates in written form the questions subject to being decided by the jury. He reads them out and passes them to the parties, who have the right to comment on them and propose new questions. The judge may not refuse to allow the person on trial or his defender to put questions as to the existence of factual circumstances excluding criminal responsibility or entailing responsibility for a lesser crime. The jurors are not present during the formulation of questions and discussion thereof. Taking into account the observations and proposals of the parties, the judge then retires to the conference room and formulates the questions in final written form for the jurors. These are entered on a questionnaire and signed by the judge. The questionnaire is read aloud in the presence of the jurors and handed to the foreman.

After the list of questions is handed over to the jury and before the jurors retire to the conference room, the judge offers a 'parting word' to the jury. He reminds them of the substance of the accusation and of the criminal law providing responsibility for the commission of the act of which the person on trial is accused. He recalls the evidence investigated in the courtroom which both incriminates and exonerates the person on trial without expressing his attitude towards such evidence and without drawing any conclusions. Next he sets out the positions of the State accuser and the defence. The jurors are explained the basic rules for evaluating evidence in aggregate, the meaning of the presumption of innocence, the position concerning the construing of ineradicable doubts to the benefit of the person on trial, that their verdict must be based only on that evidence directly investigated during the juridical session, that no evidence has *a priori* force, that their conclusions may not be based on presuppositions nor on evidence deemed to be inadmissable. The judge draws the attention of the jurors to the fact that a refusal of the person on trial to give testimony or silence in court has no legal significance and may not be construed as evidence of the guilt of the person on trial. The procedure by which jurors are to conduct their meeting is explained, including preparing replies to the questions put, voting, and rendering the verdict. The judge concludes by reminding the jurors of the oath which they swore at the outset of the proceedings.

In retiring to consider their verdict, the jurors may seek an explanation from the judge with regard to ambiguities in the questions but without touching upon the essence of possible answers to those questions.

The meeting of jurors is secret. The foreman presides, voting is open, no juror may abstain from voting, and the foreman votes last. The jury is required to reach a unanimous verdict if possible; after three hours, if unanimity is not possible, the decision is taken by voting. If a majority of jurors vote in favour of each of the three questions put to the jury, the person on trial is deemed to be guilty. If not less than six jurors voted in favour of a negative reply to any of the three questions put, the person on trial is acquitted. Even in the event of a guilty verdict, however, the judge may acquit if in his opinion the act of the person on trial did not contain the constituent elements of a crime. If the judge believes a verdict of guilty has been rendered with respect to an innocent person and there are sufficient grounds to decree a verdict of acquittal in view of the fact that the event of a crime was not established, or the participation of the person on trial in committing the crime was not proved, the judge may by decree dissolve the jury and send the case for new consideration from the stage of preliminary hearing with a new bench. This last decree may not be appealed by way of cassation.

The Code of Criminal Procedure provides (Article 334) that jurors decide only whether it has been proved whether the act took place, whether it is proved that the person on trial committed that act, and whether the person on trial is guilty of committing a crime. If the person on trial is deemed to be guilty, the jurors have the right to say whether he deserves leniency, special leniency, or none at all. The judge must take their reply into account when assigning punishment.

Having answered the questions put to them, the foreman signs the questionnaire and the jury returns to the courtroom. All stand while the foreman reads out the verdict and answers to the questions put. The verdict is then passed to the judge in order to be attached to the materials of the file of the case. The judge then thanks the jurors and declares that their participation in the judicial examination has been completed. If they wish, the jurors may remain in the courtroom to view the further proceedings in places reserved for the general public.

The judge then invites the parties to investigate the evidence which is not subject to being submitted to the jury. This evidence would include prior convictions and the character of the person on trial. The victim may submit evidence concerning funeral expenses, costs of medical care, and moral harm. Oral argument then follows in which the parties address the classification of the act which the jurors deemed to be proved, the punishment to be assigned, the civil suit, and any other purely legal matters. The parties may not cast doubt at this stage on the verdict reached by the jury. If the jury acquitted the person on trial, he is released immediately from custody.

All legal questions are decided by the judge alone without the participation of the jurors. This effectively divides the judicial examination into two stages. The first includes the formation of the panel of jurors and ends with the jury verdict as to the guilt or innocence of the person on trial. The second stage is completed with the decree of the court, which incorporates the jury verdict, addressing all of the legal consequences arising from the decision of the jury.

In the case of a jury trial the decree of judgment differs from that in an ordinary proceeding. The introductory part does not mention the names of the jurors. If the person on trial was acquitted, the descriptive-reasoned part sets out the essence of the accusation and refers to the verdict of acquittal or the retraction of the accusation by the State accuser. Evidence need be cited only in that portion not arising from the verdict itself. If there is a guilty verdict, this part also contains a description of the act of which the person on trial was convicted, a classification of the crime, the reasons for the assignment of punishment, and a substantiation of the decision of the court with respect to the civil case. The resolutive part must explain the procedure for appeal by way of cassation.

Enhanced adversariality

Although Soviet and Russian criminal procedure have always contained elements of adversarialness, the introduction of the jury system in Russian criminal procedure has significantly increased adversariality. With the enactment of the 2001 Code of Criminal Procedure, adversariality became a principle of criminal procedure irrespective of whether there is a jury trial or not. The Code provides that 'the functions of accusation, defence, and settlement of a criminal case have been separated from one another and may not be placed on one and the same agency or official. The court is not an agency of criminal prosecution and does not lean to the side of the accusation or to the side of the defence. The court creates the necessary conditions for the parties to perform their procedural duties and effectuate the rights granted to them' (Article 15).

The presence of a State accuser and a defender is obligatory not only during the consideration of the case, but the defender must be present when the preliminary investigation is completed and the materials of the case are presented to the accused and during the preliminary hearing. If there are several accused, the Code of Criminal Procedure requires that each have their own defender irrespective of the articles of the Criminal Code under which they are charged. If an accused refuses to have a defender, his position is no longer binding upon the investigator, procurator, or court, and the failure to provide a defender is a material violation of criminal procedure.

Presumption of innocence

Soviet jurists debated for decades the meaning of the presumption of innocence and the extent to which in substance that presumption existed in Soviet criminal law and procedure.[45] The expression was denounced during parliamentary debates in the USSR Supreme Soviet preceding the adoption of the 1958 Fundamental Principles of Criminal Legislation of the USSR and Union Republics, by B S Sharkov, Secretary of the Central Committee of the Communist Party of Lithuania, as a 'worm-eaten dogma of bourgeois doctrine'. A decade later the eminent proceduralist M S Strogovich was so bold as to recommend in his treatise on Soviet criminal procedure (at 351) that a formulation of the presumption of innocence be incorporated as a separate legal norm in the Code of Criminal Procedure. The entire print-run of the book (13,200 copies) was recalled and the offending page removed, replaced by a new page which omitted that offending suggestion.[46]

That debate continues, but in an entirely different context. The 1993 Russian Constitution undertakes to set out the essence of the presumption of innocence (Article 49): each person accused of committing a crime is considered to be innocent until his guilt is proved in the procedure provided for by a federal law and established by the judgment of a court which has entered into legal force. As regards burden of proof, an accused person is not obliged to prove his innocence. As regards the balance of probabilities, ineradicable doubts of the guilt of a person are to be interpreted to the benefit of the accused person. Second, as noted above, in a jury trial the judge is required to explain the presumption of innocence to the jurors and the fact that no adverse implication is to be drawn from the refusal of a person on trial to testify.

---

[45] See W E Butler, *Soviet Law* (2nd edn, 1988) 360–362.
[46] Related by V M Savitskii, in A M Larin, E B Mel'nikova, and V M Savitskii, Уголовный процесс России [*Criminal Procedure of Russia*] (1997) 16–17.

Having triumphed by securing an acceptable formulation of the presumption of innocence in the Russian Constitution, the Russian legal community directed its attention to the true substance of the principle as reflected in the minute detail of applicable Russian legislation as a whole: court organisation, administrative procedure, separation of powers, checks and balances, status of judges, role of investigators, powers of the Procuracy, and others. In the 2001 Code of Criminal Procedure the essence of the presumption of innocence, as a principle of criminal procedure (Article 14) is set out as follows:

1. The accused shall be considered to be innocent so long as his guilt in the commission of a crime is not proved in the procedure provided for by the present Code and established by the judgment of a court which has entered into legal force.
2. A suspect or accused shall not be obliged to prove his innocence. The burden of proof of the accusation and refutation of the arguments put forward in defence of a suspect or accused lies on the side of the accusation.
3. All doubts of the guilt of an accused which can not be eradicated in the procedure established by the present Code shall be interpreted in favour of the accused.
4. A judgment of conviction may not be based on presuppositions.

(9) Appeal, cassation, and supervision

The 1993 Russian Constitution provides that each person convicted for a crime has the right to a review of the judgment by a superior court in the procedure established by a federal law (Article 50). Russian criminal procedure distinguishes between appeals by way of appellate or cassation procedure against court judgments that have not entered into legal force and review by way of supervision with respect to those that have entered into force.

The terminology has been complicated by the 2001 Code of Criminal Procedure, which speaks of appellate [апелляционный] and cassational [кассационный] appealing [обжалование] by bringing an appeal [жалоба] or representation [представление]. The parties may appeal, and the procurator presents a representation. The first, 'appellate appealing', is applicable only with respect to judgments and decrees rendered by justices of the peace which have not entered into legal force. The appealing party applies to the relevant district court. A convicted or acquitted person, their defenders or legal representatives, the State accuser, and the victim and his representative may all lodge an appeal, whereas a civil plaintiff, civil defendant, and their representatives may appeal the judicial decision only in the part concerning the civil suit. Certain rulings and decrees may not be appealed: those concerning the procedure for investigating the evidence; those rejecting or satisfying petitions of participants in the judicial examination; and measures for ensuring order in the courtroom, excluding monetary sanctions imposed. The appeal or representation must be filed within ten full days from the day of proclamation of judgment, and with respect to a convicted person confined under guard, within ten days from being handed over the judgment of the court.

If the ten-day period lapses for a justifiable reason, the court may be petitioned to reinstate the lapsed period, and a refusal to reinstate also may be appealed to a superior court.

The filing of an appeal or representation has the effect of suspending execution of the judgment (except for release of an acquitted person). The appellate instance is charged by the Code of Criminal Procedure with verifying the 'legality, well-foundedness, and justness' of a judicial decision in that part which is appealed and only with respect to those convicted persons who are affected by the appeal or representation (Article 360). This formulation has the effect of removing the general review or audit jurisdiction which appellate instances enjoyed during the Soviet era.

Appealing against the judgment or decree of a justice of the peace actually involves a retrial at the district court level. The case must be considered within 14 days of receipt of the appeal or representation, which must contain:

(1) the name of the court of appellate instance in which the appeal or submission is filed;
(2) data concerning the person filing the appeal or representation, specifying the procedural status, place of residence or location;
(3) an indication of the judgment or other judicial decision and name of the court which decreed or rendered it;
(4) the arguments of the person filing and the evidence substantiating his demand;
(5) a list of materials appended to the appeal or representation;
(6) the signature of the person filing.

New materials may be submitted and petitions to summon witnesses and experts may be made.

If the filing is correct, the judge in the district court issues a decree to designate a judicial session. This decree determines the place, date, and time of the consideration of the criminal case; the summoning of witnesses, experts, and other persons; the retention, selection, vacating, or change of measures of restraint with respect to the person on trial or convicted person; and, when necessary, whether the judicial session is to be closed or not. There must be present at the judicial session the State accuser or private accuser who filed the appeal, the person on trial or convicted person who filed the appeal or in the defence of whose interests the appeal was filed or representation made, and the defender.

The judicial investigation is opened by the judge, who sets out the substance of the judgment, the essence of the appeal or submission, and the objections thereto. The court then hears the arguments of the filing party and the objections of the other side. Next the court examines the evidence. Witnesses who appeared in the first trial and have been summoned again are interrogated. The parties may petition to have new witnesses summoned, forensic expert examination, the provision of new material evidence and documents which the court refused at first instance. After completion of the judicial investigation, the parties are invited to submit additional petitions if they wish. The court then passes on to pleadings; the person who filed the appeal or representation speaks first. The person on trial is again offered the last word, after which the judge retires to adopt his decision. The judge may adopt one of four decisions:

(1) to leave the judgment of the court of first instance without change and the appellate appeal or representation without satisfaction;

(2) to vacate the judgment of conviction of the court of first instance and acquit the person on trial or terminate the proceedings in the case;

(3) to vacate the judgment of acquittal of the court of first instance and render a judgment of conviction;

(4) to change the judgment of the court of first instance.

Judgments and decrees of a court of appellate instance may be appealed to a superior court by way of cassation.

Appeal by way of cassation applies to all courts of first and appellate instance except justices of the peace. The grounds for appeal and fundamental procedures are similar to those for an appeal by way of appellate instance. The cassational instance is to consider the case within not later than one month from the day of receipt of the case. Additional materials submitted may not be obtained by performing investigative actions; the person submitting such materials is required to explain by what means they were obtained and why the need arose to submit them.

There are four grounds for vacating or changing a judicial decision by way of cassation (and the same apply in an appellate proceeding). The first is the failure of the conclusions of the court set out in the judgment to correspond to the factual circumstances of the case established by the court of first or appellate instance. This is understood to mean the conclusions of the court not being confirmed by evidence considered in judicial session, or the court failing to have regard to circumstances which could have materially influenced the conclusions of the court, or the existence of contradictory evidence having material significance for the conclusions of the court but without an indication as to why the court relied on some evidence and not other, or the conclusions of the court set out in the judgment contain material contradictions which did or could have influenced the decision as to whether the person on trial was guilty or innocent, the proper application of the criminal law, or the determination of the measure of punishment.

The second concerns a violation of a law on criminal procedure, which violation by means of depriving or limiting the rights guaranteed by the Code of Criminal

Procedure to participants in a criminal proceeding or by failure to comply with the procedure for a court proceeding, or otherwise influenced or could have influenced the decreeing of a legal, well-founded, and just judgment. Within this category in any event are the failure to terminate a criminal case under designated circumstances, decreeing of judgment by an improperly constituted court or jury, consideration of a case in absentia, unless expressly authorised, consideration of a criminal case without the participation of a defender when his participation is obligatory or other violations of the right of an accused to use the assistance of a defender, violation of the right of a person on trial to use the language which he commands and the services of an interpreter, the failure to give the person on trial the right to take part in the oral argument or to the last word, breach of the secrecy of the meeting of jurors or judges when decreeing judgment, substantiation of the judgment on the basis of inadmissable evidence, the failure of a judge(s) to sign the respective decision, or the absence of a protocol of the judicial session.

The third ground, incorrect application of a criminal law, means a violation of the requirements of the General Part of the Russian Criminal Code, the application of the wrong article, point, and/or paragraph of the Special Part of the Criminal Code, or the assignment of a punishment more severe than is provided for by the Special Part of the Criminal Code. An unjust judgment, the fourth ground, is one under which a punishment is assigned that does not correspond to the gravity of the crime or the personality of the convicted person, or a punishment which is excessively severe or mild, even though within the range permitted by the Special Part of the Criminal Code.

A judgment enters into legal force when either the time for bringing an appeal by way of appellate or cassational procedure has lapsed or the respective appeal has been decided. Review by way of judicial supervision is still possible, but only upon the petition of the convicted person, acquitted person, their defenders or legal representatives, victim or his representative, or a procurator. The petition of a procurator is called a 'supervisory representation', and that of the other participants, a 'supervisory appeal'. A complicated scheme is outlined in Article 403 of the Code of Criminal Procedure to determine which courts in the judicial hierarchy exercise supervisory jurisdiction over which inferior courts. However, review by way of supervision which would entail a worsened position for a convicted person is not permitted, nor is review of a judgment of acquittal or a ruling or decree to terminate the proceedings in a criminal case.

A court of supervisory instance considers supervisory appeals or representations within 30 days from the day of receipt. The case is assigned to a judge, who prepares a decree either to refuse to satisfy the appeal or representation or to initiate a supervisory proceeding and transfer the case for consideration by a court of supervisory instance. In the event the judge denies the appeal, the chairmen of designated courts have the right to vacate that decision and permit the appeal or representation. A judicial session is held not later than 15 days, and if the Supreme Court of the Russian Federation, within 30 days, from the day the preliminary decision is taken with regard to the appeal or representation. The procurator, and also the convicted or acquitted person, their defenders and legal representatives, and other persons whose interests are directly affected by the appeal or representation, may take part. A judge-rapporteur is designated to report on the case, after which the procurator is invited to support his representation or offer an opinion on a supervisory appeal. Oral explanations may be offered by other participants in the proceeding if they wish. All leave after the judicial session is completed, whereupon the judges decide the supervisory appeal or representation by majority vote and issue an appropriate decree or ruling. In the event of a tied vote, the appeal or representation is considered to be rejected, subject to certain exceptions.

When considering a case by way of supervision, the court is not confined to the arguments of the supervisory appeal or representation. The entire proceeding in the criminal case is subject to verification, including with respect to convicted persons who may not have been involved in the supervisory action.

Criminal proceedings may be 'renewed' under Russian law by reason of new circumstances or newly-discovered circumstances. New circumstances include the deeming by the Constitutional Court of the RF of a law applied by the court in a particular criminal case to be unconstitutional, or the European Court for Human Rights establishing that a provision of the Convention on the Defence of the Rights of Man and Citizen have been violated which is connected with the application of a federal law not corresponding to the said Convention, or other violations of the Convention. There is no period of limitation with respect to a renewal of proceedings on these grounds.

Russian criminal procedure has for many years made special provision for proceedings with regard to minors and with regard to the application of compulsory measures of a medical character. Completely new in the 2001 Code of Criminal Procedure are the provisions concerning special proceedings for individual categories of natural persons: members of the Soviet of the Federation and deputies of the State Duma, and other legislative personnel; judges; chairman, members, and auditors of the Counting Chamber; the plenipotentiary for human rights; the retiring President and presidential candidates; procurators; investigators; and advocates. Persons in these categories may have criminal proceedings instituted against them in a procedure more complicated than the usual procedure, by a relatively narrow group of officials. There are also special requirements or limitations with regard to procedural detention, choice of measures of restraint, and the performance of certain investigative actions.

The 2001 Code of Criminal Procedure reflects the new position of the Russian Federation in the international community by regulating the procedure for the interaction of Russian procedural agencies and international organisations. Extradition procedures are the subject of Chapter 54 of the Code.

Appended to the Code of Criminal Procedure are some 120 pages or so of official forms of procedural documents. These are considered to be normative in character, a stature which follows from the Law introducing the Code of Criminal Procedure into operation: 'When manufacturing forms of procedural documents specified in the Annexes to the Code of Criminal Procedure of the Russian Federation, a change of the column is not permitted except for those changes which have been specially stipulated'.

III

THE SUBSTANTIVE LAW

8

CONSTITUTIONAL AND ADMINISTRATIVE LAW

The enactment for the first time in Russian history of a genuinely democratic Constitution has given a new dimension to the branch of legal science devoted to State structures. Soviet legal doctrine traditionally preferred the term 'State law' [государственное право], partly a legacy of the German *Staatrecht* and partly a legacy of the Statist orientation of the Soviet legal era; in some quarters the term still finds favour in Russia. This branch of law treated State sovereignty, authority, and structure, and the rights and duties of the citizen conferred by the State. The great majority of Russian jurists now prefer the term 'constitutional law' [конституционное право], partly as a break with the past and partly to reflect the new relationship between the individual and the State.

In conformity with its federative structure, the Russian Federation is a country of many constitutions and constitutive documents—one for the Federation itself and one for each subject of the Federation, plus three treaties of the Federation (sometimes collectively referred to as the Treaty of the Federation), and a supplementary network of individual treaties concluded between the Federation and each subject of the Federation. During the late Soviet era, the sundry entities making up the Union of Soviet Socialist Republics spawned nearly one hundred constitutions, of which 36 were in force on Soviet territory when the Soviet Union was dissolved. The Russian Federation has exceeded that target, for the number of constitutions, other constitutive documents and treaties in force within the Federation as of 1998 is several hundred at least.

A. Concept of Federationism

The 'federation' as a form of Russian statehood originated in Leninist doctrines directed towards coping with the nationality problem in Russia. 'Federated in form, but socialist in substance' was the formula often posited by Soviet legal textbooks. Federation also was a structure which the early Bolsheviks believed might be adapted to a world in which socialism had triumphed. The Russian Federation as such was proclaimed in the guise of the Russian Soviet Federated Socialist Republic (RSFSR) at the III All-Russian Congress of Soviets in January 1918. Originally it was intended to encompass all of what became the former Soviet Union and not merely what falls within the boundaries of the contemporary Russian Federation. That vision of the future did not happen as the Grand Duchy of Finland, Russian Poland, the Baltic States, Ukraine, and Tuva each declared its independence and Belorussia, Turkestan, and the Caucasian republics, also declared to be independent, entered into negotiations with the RSFSR about treaty relationships. Various formations came into being with sundry denominations on the territory of the present Russian Federation, complicated by the absence of well-defined pre-existing boundaries or frontiers and the lack of a clear distinction, for example, between an autonomous republic or a region. Other entities which had acquired some sort of administrative-territorial identity under the Russian Empire retained this, often with an elevated status. In 1923 the RSFSR consisted of 11 autonomous republics, 14 autonomous regions, and 63 provinces and regions.

The formation of the Union of Soviet Socialist Republics by the Treaty of the Union on 30 December 1922 superimposed, from the Russian perspective, another type of federation upon the RSFSR, which itself became a member of the new confederated Union. There remained throughout the existence of the Soviet Union a tension between the desirability of preserving nationality identification at various levels and strong pressures in favour of the centralisation of economic management and unitary administration of the State. Throughout all, however, the federative principle was retained, and there is a compelling argument that its persistent existence considerably facilitated the dismantling of the Soviet Union in 1991 without violence.

Throughout the sunset years of the RSFSR the Constitution in force dated from 1978. During the *perestroika* era more than 200 changes and additions were introduced, including the post of President, the Constitutional Court, elimination of the leading role of the Communist Party of the Soviet Union, a revised parliamentary structure, a more democratic chapter on the rights and freedoms of man and citizen, and the restructuring of the Federation in accordance with the 1992 Treaty of the Federation. The resultant amalgam was pure 'scissors and paste', and the rivalries between the parliament and the President contributed to a number of attempts to shackle Presidential authority. In December 1992 the VII Congress of People's Deputies incorporated Article 126[6] into the RSFSR Constitution which provided that in the event of the dissolution or suspension of the activity of any legally elected agencies of State power the powers of the President would be subject to immediate termination. Preparations were openly made to impeach the President by using Article 126[10] of the RSFSR Constitution. Relations worsened between the President and the Supreme Soviet of the RSFSR. On 20 March 1993 the President signed an edict introducing a special procedure for governing until the crisis of power was overcome, whereupon the next day the Supreme Soviet condemned the edict and on the day following the Constitutional Court of Russia (nine judges of 12), having nothing in their hands except a television account of the edict, decreed that the edict was contrary to the Constitution in at least nine respects. On 24 March 1993 the President signed an edict authorising a referendum vote of confidence in the President, fixing the date of 25 April 1993 for the ballot. The referendum was held (although the questions put were altered by the Congress of People's Deputies), and 60.5 per cent of those voting expressed confidence in the President and favoured new elections of the parliament. The existing RSFSR Constitution was entirely unable to cope with these conflicts.

It had been recognised in 1990 as soon as Russia had declared her State sovereignty that a new Constitution would be required. The I Congress of People's Deputies (22 June 1990) formed a Constitutional Commission under the chairman of Boris El'tsin (then a deputy of the Supreme Soviet of the RSFSR) containing 102 members from throughout the Federation. Within four months the Commission had produced a draft for public discussion, which was countered immediately by alternative drafts emanating from various circles or by proposals for amendments. The draft was considered in October 1991 by the V Congress of People's Deputies, reworked and again published for discussion. In April 1992 the VI Congress of People's Deputies approved the general conception of the draft. The Supreme Soviet and the Constitutional Commission were directed to revise the draft for the next session of the Congress.

The VII (December 1992), VIII (March 1993), and IX (April 1993) Congresses of People's Deputies did not consider the draft further, although the VII Congress had voted to submit the basic provisions of the draft to a national referendum, a decision that was repealed by the VIII Congress. When in May 1993 the draft version approved by the Supreme Soviet was published, it was proposed to convoke the Congress of People's Deputies on 17 November 1993 to consider and adopt the Constitution; it was this same Supreme Soviet which planned to impeach the President at the next Congress.

The President in the meantime pursued his own course of action. On 12 May 1993 he issued an Edict on Measures Relating to Completion of the Preparation of a New Constitution of the Russian Federation,[1] pursuant to which a Constitutional Assembly was convened in Moscow on 5 June 1993 widely representative of the entire country. On 24 June 1993 the Supreme Soviet refused cooperation with the Constitutional Assembly on the grounds that some of its coordinators and organisers were corrupt. The President of the Russian Federation submitted his draft Constitution to the Assembly for consideration, but encouraged the Commission to find compromises between his draft and its own. On 23 July 1993 the Constitutional Assembly completed its work[2] and by a majority vote approved the draft which it had produced (the verbatim proceedings of the Constitutional Assembly have been published in 21 volumes: see Chapter 21).

The crisis deepened in autumn 1993. Both the President and the Supreme Soviet had their own versions of the Constitution, and neither wished to compromise. On 21 September 1993 the President issued an Edict on the Step by Step Constitutional Reform of the Russian Federation which terminated the powers of the people's deputies, introduced a transition period for governing based on the draft new Constitution approved by the Constitutional Assembly, fixed elections to the State Duma for 11–12 December 1993, and an all-people's referendum on 12 December 1993 to consider the adoption of the new Constitution.[3] On the same day the Presidium of the Supreme Soviet, citing Article 121[6] of the RSFSR Constitution, terminated the powers of the President of the Russian Federation and transferred the powers of the President to the Vice President of Russia, A V Rutskoi. In the view of the Supreme Soviet, the President had effectuated a *coup d'état*; the Constitutional Court declared the Presidential edict to be unconstitu-

---

[1] САПП РФ (1993), no 20, item 1757.

[2] For a superb annotated text of the 1978 RSFSR Constitution in all of its versions and the draft Constitution produced by the Constitutional Assembly, see S A Avak'ian, Конституция России: природа, эволюция, современность [*The Constitution of Russia: Nature, Evolution, Contemporaneity*] (1997).

[3] САПП РФ (1993), no 39, item 3597. The Edict was amended on 1 October 1993, 11 October 1993, 24 December 1993. See САПП РФ (1993), no 41, item 3907; no 42, item 3993; no 52, item 5086; (1994), no 6, item 437.

tional and called for his impeachment. Appointments were made to the so-called 'power' ministries, and the Criminal Code of the RSFSR was amended to introduce the crime of anti-constitutional activity, a capital offence. The opposition rested on an existing RSFSR Constitution out of step with democratic change, and the President relied upon the electorate and the subjects of the Federation.

The dramatic confrontation at the White House in Moscow led to Presidential rule. On 7 October 1993 the President issued an Edict on Legal Regulation in the Period of Step by Step Constitutional Reform in the Russian Federation.[4] This edict confirmed the operation throughout the territory of Russia of all laws and decrees adopted by the Supreme Soviet and by the Congress of People's Deputies before 21 September 1993. It further provided that legal regulation usually within parliamentary competence would during the transition period be effectuated by edicts of the President. The Constitutional Court was suspended until the new Constitution was adopted. The Chairman of the Constitutional Court resigned, and the Vice President of Russia, although also directly elected by the people, was removed from office by the President of Russia.

The President terminated, by an edict of 9 October 1993,[5] the powers of soviets of people's deputies and by an edict of 27 October 1993 confirmed Basic Provisions on elections to representative agencies of State power in the regions.[6] This last edict effectively eliminated the last remnants of authority originating in the Soviet system. The draft Constitution to be considered at the referendum was published on 10 November 1993. In the referendum held on 12 December 1993, 54.8 per cent of registered voters participated, and of those, 58.4 per cent voted in favour of the new Constitution.

During 1990–1 most autonomous republics and a number of autonomous regions in the RSFSR proclaimed themselves to be sovereign states within the RSFSR. In a few, separatist sentiments were strongly expressed (Chechnia, Tatarstan). The IV Congress of People's Deputies of the RSFSR voted to exclude the word 'autonomous' from the designation of autonomous republics, which became 'republics within the Russian Federation'. These forces led to the conclusion of the Treaty of the Federation on 31 March 1992 and the formal incorporation of that Treaty into the 1978 RSFSR Constitution on 10 April 1992 (and then into the 1993 Russian Constitution). In greater detail than any preceding Russian or Soviet constitutional document, the Treaty of the Federation delimited the areas of jurisdiction between the Russian Federation and the 89 subjects of the Federation. The

---

[4] САПП РФ (1993), no 41. The Edict lost force on 24 December 1993. САПП РФ (1993), no 52, item 5086.
[5] САПП РФ (1993), no 41, item 3924. Lost force by Edict of the President of the RF of 17 June 2000. СЗ РФ (2000), no 25, item 2678.
[6] САПП РФ (1993), no 44, item 4189; no 45, item 4192. Lost force by Edict of the President of the RF, 17 June 2000. СЗ РФ (2000), no 25, item 2678.

resulting state structure is paradoxical in that the Russian nation has no separate administrative-territorial entity as such but rather sees its interests best expressed in a multinational state formation, that the republics within the Russian Federation are far from homogeneous in nationality, and that the name 'Russia', which identifies the predominant nationality within the frontiers of the Russian Federation, is chosen for what the Constitution describes as a multinational state.

The foundation elements of the Federation are the provisions of the Constitution stipulating that the Russian Federation is a state (Article 1) made up of the subjects of the Federation (Article 65). Subjects of the Federation have no right of unilateral secession; withdrawal from the Federation is possible only by mutual consent of the Russian Federaton and the subject of the Federation in accordance with a federal constitutional law. The number of subjects of the Federation may be enlarged, although the numbers of indigenous peoples and tribes inhabiting the Russian Federation are so fractionated that it is unlikely they will be accorded the status of a subject of the Federation. Their rights are guaranteed separately in Article 69 of the 1993 Russian Constitution 'in accordance with generally-recognised principles and norms of international law and international treaties of the Russian Federation'.

The Constitution establishes the territory of the Russian Federation, the Russian language as the State language, a uniform customs, monetary, and tax system, a delimitation of jurisdiction under which the Russian Federation possesses exclusive and joint jurisdiction with respect to the subjects of the Federation, and the subjects retain residual jurisdiction over matters not otherwise relegated. There is a complex structure for arranging executive and legislative power, but a unified judicial system and Procuracy. Under circumstances determined by the 1993 Russian Constitution, the federal authorities have authorisation to interfere in the affairs of the subjects of the Federation.

The State symbols of the Russian Federation have been controversial. Under the Constitution they are the State flag, Arms, and anthem, the design or wording of which is determined by a federal constitutional law devoted respectively to each of them, of 25 December 2000, as amended 9 July 2002.[7] Those constitutional laws replaced temporary subordinate legislation: the Statute on the State Flag and Statute on the State Anthem, confirmed by Edicts of the President of the Russian Federation on 11 December 1993,[8] and the State Arms, by an Edict of 30 November 1993.[9]

---

[7] On the State Flag, State Arms, and the State Anthem respectively, see СЗ РФ (2000), no 52(I), items 5020, 5021, and 5022; (2002) no 28, items 2780–82.

[8] САПП РФ (1993), no 51, items 4928 and 4929.

[9] САПП РФ (1993), no 49, item 4761.

The capital of the Russian Federation is the City of Moscow (Article 70(2), Russian Constitution), which is a subject of the Russian Federation whose status as capital is defined by the Federal Law on the Status of the Capital of the Russian Federation, of 15 April 1993, as amended 18 July 1995.[10]

B. Subjects of the Federation

All 89 subjects of the Federation are enumerated in alphabetical order and category by the Russian Constitution (Article 65). Although one associates the Russian Federation with the nationality principle, the great majority of the subjects of the Federation (57) are based purely on territorial considerations, and the remaining subjects (32) are far from homogeneous nationality entities. The most senior category is the republic within the Federation, followed by the territory, the region, the cities of federal significance (Moscow, St Petersburg), the one autonomous region, and the national areas. Each has its own constitution, charter, law, or other constitutive document. Although their names are embodied in the Russian Constitution, each retains the right to change its name, such changes to date being incorporated without amendment of the Constitution by edict of the President of the Russian Federation.[11]

The republics within the Russian Federation have the stature of independent States, even though they have surrendered their right of unilateral secession. The hierarchy amongst the others, except for the sequence of enumeration in the Constitution, is obscure. The Constitution speaks of subjects of the Federation changing their status (Article 66(5)), but why they should do so if each has equal rights is unclear. In matters of shared jurisdiction, however, they are identical, as too are they equal in representation in the Soviet of the Federation. As noted elsewhere (Chapter 4), the subjects of the Federation have since 1993 quietly been concluding treaties clarifying the sharing of jurisdiction with the Federation. In some cases the powers of the subject of the Federation were enlarged. No longer can it be said that each enjoys necessarily the same powers as other subjects of the Federation.[12] On 12 March 1996 the President confirmed by Edict, as amended

---

[10] Ведомости СНД и ВС РФ (1993), no 19, item 685; СЗ РФ (1995), no 51, item 4970.

[11] See Edicts of the President of the RF of 9 January 1996, 10 February 1996, and 9 June 2001. СЗ РФ (1996), no 3, item 152; no 7, item 676; (2001), no 24, item 2421.

[12] This process reportedly ceased in the late El'tsin years. From June 1998 to March 2002 no new treaties or agreements were concluded between the centre and the subjects of the Federation and no existing treaties renewed or extended, although agreements were concluded in November 2001 between Far Eastern subjects of the Federation and the Russian Ministry of Justice on bringing regional legislation into conformity with federal laws. See J Kahn, *Federalism, Democratization and the Rule of Law in Russia* (2002) 237. Commencing in November 2001 treaties began to be concluded between the federal government and subjects of the Federation which terminated the earlier treaties on the grounds that they had served their purpose. See, for example, СЗ РФ (2002), no 12, 3277–3280.

25 November 1996, the Statute on the Procedure for Work Relating to Delimitation of the Subjects of Jurisdiction and Powers Between Federal Agencies of State Power and Agencies of State Power of the Subjects of the Russian Federation and on the Mutual Transfer of the Effectuation of Part of Their Powers by Federal Agencies of Executive Power and Agencies of Executive Power of the Subject of the Federation.[13] A Commission attached to the President of the Russian Federation works with the draft treaties and agreements. The principles guiding the Commission include: the principles of delimitation of the subjects of jurisdiction and powers are established by federal laws; a treaty may not establish or change the constitutional status of a subject of the Federation; the treaty may not allow an exception or redistribution of subjects of jurisdiction of the Russian Federation or subjects of joint jurisdiction established in accordance with Articles 71 and 72 of the 1993 Russian Constitution, and powers may not be transferred to a subject of the Federation which relate to guaranteeing the foundations of the constitutional system, the equality of rights and freedoms of citizens, or otherwise which would violate the territory integrity of Russia or the supremacy of the Constitution and federal laws throughout the Russian Federation.

Subjects of the Russian Federation have their own legal systems emanating from their own constitutive documents, laws, and subordinate legal acts. While each therefore has its own constitutional law, it must form part of an integral and non-contradictory whole with the legal system of the Russian Federation. The creation of free economic zones (see Chapter 19) on the territory of subjects of the Federation has the effect of enlarging the rights of the subject of the Federation over customs, taxes, the investment regime, and entrepreneurial activity.

In practice many subjects of the Russian Federation abused their rights either by failing to introduce constitutional and other legislation where they should have done so or by adopting legislation which is contrary to the Russian Constitution or otherwise in violation of the delimitation of jurisdiction. A Commission for the Interaction of Federal Agencies of State Power and Agencies of State Power of Subjects of the Russian Federation When Conducting Constitutional Law Reform in Subjects of the Russian Federation attached to the President of the Russian Federation under an Edict of 25 January 1996 was ultimately abolished in August 2001. In a few instances the President of the Russian Federation has exercised his right to suspend the operation of acts of executive power of subjects of the Russian Federation which are contrary to the Constitution, federal laws, or international treaties of the Russian Federation. The Constitutional Court of the Russian Federation has held unconstitutional a number of enactments of subjects of the Russian Federation on the grounds that those enactments exceeded the powers of the subjects to adopt.

---

[13] СЗ РФ (1996), no 12, item 1058; no 49, item 5534.

In the year 2000 the President of Russia introduced measures of Presidential control over the subjects of the Federation. An Edict of 13 May 2000 on the Plenipotentiary Representative of the President in a Federal District [округ] and accompanying statute divided the Russian Federation into seven federal districts whose boundaries coincided with existing military districts.[14] The seven plenipotentiary representatives appointed to head each district replaced the presidential representatives in each of the 89 subjects of the Federation (established by an Edict of 9 July 1997).[15] Part of their mandate is to further the creation of unified legal space in the Russian Federation. The President of Russia also intensified his use of his own edicts to suspend legislation in subjects of the Federation which was contrary to federal legislation. A variety of lesser measures were taken to assert Presidential vertical control directly over the subjects of the Federation and individual agencies thereof.

There remain on the statute books certain legacies pre-dating the 1993 Russian Constitution. Tatarstan, Sakha (Iakutia), Bashkortostan, Tuva, and others had proclaimed themselves to be not only sovereign states, but also subjects of international law. Tatarstan also declared itself to be 'associated with' the Russian Federation rather than a part thereof. A border dispute between Northern Osetia and Ingushetia remains unresolved, although on 16 March 1996 a State Commission was appointed to consider the matter by the Government of the Russian Federation. Some subjects of the Federation have advanced excessive claims to ownership over the land, subsoil, and natural wealth, whereas others assert the priority of their local laws over federal. The republics within the Federation also vary widely in regulating the status of languages. In only six of the 21 republics within the Russian Federation does the nationality named in the title of the republic actually constitute a majority of the populace.

The 1993 Russian Constitution (Article 65(2)) recognises that new subjects of the Federation may be created or existing subjects transformed into a new subject. On 17 December 2001 the Federal Constitutional Law on the Procedure for Admission to the Russian Federation and Formation Within its Composition of a New Subject of the Russian Federation was adopted in accordance with the Constitution to regulate the process.[16] Admission is open to a foreign state or part thereof by way of accession. The formation of a new subject refers to a procedure under which there is a change in the composition of existing subjects of the Russian Federation which is not linked with the admission of a foreign state or part thereof.

Admission must have regard to the State interests of the Russian Federation, the principles of the structure of the Federation, the rights and freedoms of man and citizen,

---

[14] СЗ РФ (2000), no 20, item 2112.
[15] СЗ РФ (1997), no 28, item 3421.
[16] СЗ РФ (2001), no 52(I), item 4916.

and the historical, economic, and cultural links of subjects of the Russian Federation and their socio-economic opportunities. Formation may involve the combining of two or more existing subjects of the Federation which border one another, including the termination of the existence of subjects of the Federation whose territories are being unified. A change of name does not constitute 'formation'.

In the case of admission, the initiator must be the foreign state, whereupon the President of Russia will submit the proposal to the chambers of the Federal Assembly in the procedure provided for by the 1995 Law on International Treaties. The 2001 Law sets out questions which may be addressed in a treaty with the proposing foreign state. When such a treaty is signed, the President of Russia then applies to the Constitutional Court of the Russian Federation with a request that the treaty be verified for its conformity to the Russian Constitution. If the Constitutional Court finds no non-conformities, the draft treaty is submitted to the State Duma for ratification. Following ratification, a federal constitutional law is to be adopted concerning the consequential amendment of Article 65 and the Constitution republished in a new version.

The initiative for forming a new subject of the Federation must originate with the subjects of the Federation whose territories will form the new subject. A formal proposal must be submitted to the President of Russia which substantiates the reasons for the new formation and addresses the legal consequences thereof. A referendum must be held in the subjects of the Federation concerned. Consequential amendments to the Russian Constitution are adopted in accordance with Article 108 of the Constitution.

C. Electoral System

The President of the Russian Federation and the lower chamber of the Federal Assembly—the State Duma—are directly elected; where senior posts are filled by appointment, commonly in Russia the appointment is made by the agencies of State which were elected to office. The same pattern applies at the middle and lowest levels of State agencies of executive power. Russian legal doctrine draws a distinction between the concept of an 'electoral system' and the 'right of suffrage', although it is recognised that in common usage the two terms are for all practical purposes identical. In Russia the two terms encompass five so-called subsystems:

(1) the procedure for election of the President of the Russian Federation;
(2) the procedure for election of deputies of the State Duma;
(3) the procedure for election of the heads of administration of subjects of the Russian Federation;
(4) the procedure for election of deputies of legislative agencies of subjects of the Federation; and
(5) the procedure for election of agencies of local self-government.

The right to vote is laid down in the 1993 Russian Constitution: 'Citizens of the Russian Federation shall have the right to elect and to be elected to agencies of State power and agencies of local self-government, and also to participate in a referendum' (Article 32(2)). Other articles of the Constitution establish the electivity of the President of Russia and the State Duma. The detailed procedures for elections are set out in the Federal Law on the Basic Guarantees of Electoral Rights and the Right to Participate in a Referendum of Citizens of the Russian Federation, of 12 June 2002.[17] The provisions regulating elections in this Federal Law apply throughout Russia, including the subjects of the Federation. Although subjects of the Federation have their own laws on elections, their provisions may not be contrary to the Federal Law; however, they may establish additional guarantees not found at the federal level. Each individual federal election is then addressed in separate legislation: the Federal Law on Elections of the President of the Russian Federation of 31 December 1999; the Federal Law on Elections of Deputies of the State Duma of the Russian Federation, as amended 24 June 1999, 10 July 2001, 15 January 2002, and 21 March 2002;[18] and the Federal Law on Ensuring the Constitutional Rights of Citizens of the Russian Federation to Elect and Be Elected to Agencies of Local Self-Government of 26 November 1996, as amended 22 June 1998.[19] Referendums are governed by the Federal Constitutional Law on Referendum of the Russian Federation of 10 October 1995.[20] There are in addition a number of other federal laws and subordinate normative acts concerned with, for example, single mandate constituencies, the procedure for forming precinct election commissions, and the regulations for campaign financing. The Central Electoral Commission itself is a considerable source of decrees, instructions, and explanations which elaborate the electoral pocess. As one proceeds down the administrative-territorial ladder in Russia, the constitutive documents of all 89 subjects of the Federation and all agencies of local self-government issue normative acts concerning elections.

Basically, Russian citizens acquire the right to vote at the age of 18 years. Depending upon the election concerned, there may also be a requirement of residence in a particular area of the country in order to vote. Russian citizens abroad also have the right to vote. There is no legal requirement to vote in Russia, however. The validity of elections commonly turns upon a stipulated percentage of the electorate turning out to vote. In the case of the President of the Russian Federation, 50 per cent of registered voters must take part; for elections of deputies to the State Duma the minimum turnout is 25 per cent, and the same is

---

[17] СЗ РФ (2002), no 24, item 2253.
[18] СЗ РФ (1999), no 26, item 3178; (2001), no 16, item 1532; no 29, item 2944; (2002), no 12, item 1093. This Law also was changed by Decrees of the Constitutional Court of the RF of 25 April 2000 and 15 January 2002. СЗ РФ (2000), no 19, item 2102; no 6, item 626.
[19] СЗ РФ (1996), no 49, item 5497; (1998), no 26, item 3005.
[20] СЗ РФ (1995), no 42, item 3921.

true in most subjects of the Federation for elections at that level. Instances do occur of sufficient voter apathy for elections to be deemed invalid for want of participation. Russian elections are, in sum, universal, equal, direct, secret, and held periodically.

Russian law rigorously regulates the so-called 'electoral process'. Once that process is underway, interference is not tolerated. In November 1995 the Constitutional Court of the Russian Federation declined to examine the constitutionality of certain provisions in the 1995 version of the Federal Law on Elections of Deputies of the State Duma of the Federal Assembly of the Russian Federation because the request for review had been made two months after the election campaign had commenced, that is, after the nomination and registration of candidates had occurred. The Court held that conducting a judicial examination in the course of an election campaign immediately before voting could unjustifiably complicate the electoral process, tell negatively on the expression of will by the voters, and ultimately influence the results of the elections. Once electoral legal relations had been engaged, the Constitutional Court believed that any decision it might render could impinge upon voting rights and prejudice the basic constitutional principles of the electoral process.

Referendums may be of three types: all-Russian, subject of the Russian Federation, or local. The 1993 Russian Constitution was adopted by an all-Russian referendum. Certain questions may not be put to a referendum, amongst them changing the status of a subject of the Federation, terminating before time or prolonging the terms of office of the President of Russia or deputies of the State Duma, or members of the Soviet of the Federation, amnesties and pardons, or questions of limiting or abolishing generally-recognised rights and freedoms of man and citizen or the constitutional guarantees for realising them.

Subjects of the Russian Federation have introduced quite diverse electoral laws with regard to their own State agencies of power. Some which have their own citizenship, for example, Buratia, limit electoral participation to individuals who have such citizenship; others have introduced minimum periods of residence on the territory of the subject of the Federation. These are accepted by federal legislation, as a rule, but residence requirements may not exceed one year. The Constitutional Court of the Russian Federation has struck down as unconstitutional legislation of subjects of the Federation which introduced formulas that in practice gave some citizens greater or more equal rights to elect than others.

Under the 2001 Federal Law on Political Parties, the duly registered political parties have an exclusive right to participate in federal and regional elections by means of nominating candidates for elective office. A transition period up to 14 July 2003 is in effect under the Law enabling existing political associations to transform themselves into political parties and to register as such; during the

transition period somewhat different rules operated for the participation of political parties in elections.[21]

D. The Presidency

In the Soviet era the Head of State was the chairman of a collegial organ, the
Presidium of the Supreme Soviet, which operated in the intervals between sessions
of the Supreme Soviet. This has been construed by some Russian lawyers to mean
that the post of Head of State did not in fact exist.[22] The post of President of the
Russian Federation was instituted by an all-people's referendum held on 12 April
1991, and elections to this post were held in the same procedure on 12 June 1991,
precisely one year from the date of the Declaration of State Sovereignty of the
Russian Federation, for a five-year term. The 1978 Constitution of the RSFSR
was amended to introduce the Presidency, although the expression 'Head of State'
was not used. Instead the President was referred to as the 'highest official' (Article
121[1], 1978 RSFSR Constitution) and the 'head of executive power'.

Under the 1993 Russian Constitution the President is the Head of State (Article
80), representing the Russian Federation within the country and in international
relations. There is no post of Vice President; introduced in the amendments to the
1978 RSFSR Constitution, it became such a source of political conflict and
rivalry that the architects of the 1993 Constitution deliberately excluded it. The
principal functions of the President, besides acting as Head of State, are to be the
guarantor of the Constitution of the Russian Federation and of the rights and freedoms of man and citizen, to take measures to protect the sovereignty of the
Russian Federation, its independence and State integrity, and ensure the coordinated functioning and interaction of agencies of State power, and to determine the
basic orientations of internal and foreign policy of the Russian Federation in
accordance with the Constitution and federal laws.

The President is elected for a term of four years in accordance with the Federal
Law on Elections of the President of the Russian Federation of 31 December
1999[23] by citizens of the Russian Federation on the basis of universal equal and
direct suffrage by secret ballot. A second successive term is possible, but a third
term or more may be served only if there is an interruption after the second term.
Russian citizens aged 18 on election day or older may vote in the Presidential election.

---

[21] See D B Katkov and E V Korchigo, Избирательное право [*Electoral Law*] (2001).
[22] M V Baglai, Конституционное право Российской Федерации [*Constitutional Law of the
Russian Federation*] (3rd edn, 2002) 411.
[23] СЗ РФ (2000), no 1(II), item 11. This Law replaced that of 17 May 1995. СЗ РФ (1995),
no 21, item 1924.

The constitutional requirements for a Presidential candidate are few: a Russian citizen at least 35 years of age and permanently resident in the Russian Federation for not less than ten years may run for office. No special education or experience is required, nor is there a maximum age limit, as in the case of judges. At least 50 per cent of the voters must take part in the election for there to be a valid result, and the winning candidate must receive a simple majority of the votes. If there are more than two candidates and no one receives a majority of the votes, a second election is held between the two candidates who received the most votes. The winning candidate of the second round must receive a larger number of votes than the other candidate including abstentions. In 1996 about 70 per cent of the electorate voted in the Presidential elections; none of the ten candidates received a majority. The second ballot resulted in the winner receiving 53.7 per cent of the votes, and the loser, 40.4 per cent. The elected individual takes office on the 30th day after the official announcement of the election result, swearing the oath of office set out in the Constitution (Article 82) in the presence of the Soviet of the Federation, State Duma, and judges of the Constitutional Court of the Russian Federation. From the moment of taking the oath, the President is in office.

The President of the Russian Federation stands down from office upon the expiry of his term at the moment when the newly-elected President takes the oath of office. His term may be terminated before time by resignation (which happened in the case of Boris El'tsin in 1999), by becoming unable for health reasons to effectuate his power, or by impeachment. Resignation presupposes a statement or application of the President himself. Neither the Constitution nor Russian legislation offers any guidance as to procedures for determining whether the President's state of health requires that he leave office or is unable to perform his duties, although a 2001 Instruction of the Ministry of Public Health may offer guidance. Impeachment requires the implementation of procedures set out in Article 93 of the Russian Constitution; in practice such accusations have been brought but failed to secure the required majority in the Federal Assembly. When the President is unable to perform his duties, the Chairman of the Government temporarily performs them; the same applies if the President were to die in office[24] or is ill for an extended period. When the President of the Russian Federation had a serious operation, his powers were distributed by Edict of the President to the Chairman of the Government and others on 19 September 1996. An individual serving as acting President may not dissolve the State Duma, designate referendums, or propose amendments to or revision of the Russian Constitution; the

---

[24] The vexed question of when a Head of State is actually deceased in Russia has been addressed in the Instruction With Regard to Stating the Death of a Person on the Basis of Diagnosis of Death of the Brain, confirmed by Order of the Ministry of Public Health of the Russian Federation on 20 December 2001, No 460, and registered by the Ministry of Justice of the Russian Federation on 17 January 2002, No 3170. Although the Instruction was issued in connection with the transplant of organs, it doubtless would serve as guidance more generally.

logic of these limitations is that the acting President, unlike the individual being replaced, has not received the direct mandate of the Russian voters.

Presidential power and the Federal Assembly

There is little overlap between Presidential and parliamentary powers. The President has the right to designate elections of the State Duma in accordance with the 1993 Russian Constitution and the federal law on elections, whereas the Soviet of the Federation has the right to designate elections for the President. The formation of the Soviet of the Federation proceeds without the participation of either the State Duma or the President.

The President has, and actively uses, the right of legislative initiative to submit draft laws to the State Duma, and also possesses the right of veto over laws adopted by the Federal Assembly. The veto may be overridden if the vetoed law is adopted a second time by both chambers of the Federal Assembly in separate sittings by a two-thirds vote in each chamber, in which case the President must sign the law within seven days. A refusal of the President to sign under these circumstances on the ground of irregularities in the voting was held unconstitutional by the Constitutional Court of the Russian Federation in March 1998. Otherwise the President has 14 days in which to consider a law adopted by the Federal Assembly, after which either it is rejected or it enters into force.

The President delivers yearly messages to the Federal Assembly on the state of the Federation, the basic orientations of domestic and foreign policy, and the like. The Federal Assembly is not bound in any way by the ideas expressed in these messages. In accordance with a federal constitutional law, the President designates the holding of a referendum.

The President may dissolve the State Duma in accordance with the Constitution, but not the Soviet of the Federation. Dissolution of the State Duma occurs if the Duma rejects three times his proposed candidacy for the Chairman of the Government, a situation avoided by the State Duma in April 1998 when on the third ballot the President's candidacy for Chairman of the Government was approved (Article 111(4), Constitution); when lack of confidence in the Government has been expressed twice by the State Duma within three months (Article 117(3), Constitution); and when the Government requests the State Duma for an expression of confidence and such is refused (Article 117(4), Constitution). If the Duma is dissolved, the President designates new elections so that the newly-elected Duma may convene not later than four months after being dissolved.

Under certain circumstances the State Duma may not be dissolved by the President: within a year after the Duma is elected; from the moment of putting forward an accusation against the President until the Soviet of the Federation takes a decision; when a military or extraordinary situation has been declared throughout the entire territory of the Russian Federation; and within six months of the end of the term of powers of the President. In all instances the Soviet of the Federation remains in office, so that the country is never entirely without a legislative chamber in operation.

Presidential relations with the Federal Assembly are facilitated by the appointment of plenipotentiaries to represent the President in the chambers with regard to a particularly important or technical piece of legislation; they may also explain to the Federal Assembly the reasons a particular draft law was rejected by the President.

Presidential power and the Government

There is no question of a balance of powers between the President and the Government of the Russian Federation. The President enjoys absolute priority; he appoints the Chairman of the Government with the consent of the State Duma, subject to the right to dissolve the Duma if it ultimately does not accept the candidacy, in which case pending the Duma elections the President will appoint the Chairman of the Government himself. The President also takes himself the decision to dismiss the Government, as was done in March 1998, even if no lack of confidence has been expressed in the Government. The President also appoints, upon the proposal of the Chairman of the Government, the deputy chairmen and federal ministers. He has the right, and in practice often has done so, to preside at sessions of the Government, leaving no doubt as to who is in charge. Moreover, within a week after being appointed and confirmed, the Chairman of the Government must submit to the President for confirmation proposals concerning the structure of federal agencies of State power.

The President also exerts decisive influence on the appointment and dismissal of the chairman of the Central Bank of the Russian Federation, even though the Bank is not an agency of executive power. If the State Duma does not confirm the candidacy proposed, the President may make his candidate the acting chairman of the Bank and again submit this candidacy to the Duma. No other agency has the right of initiative in this matter except the President.

Presidential power and the Subjects of the Federation

The 1993 Constitution has little to say explicitly about Presidential powers with respect to the subjects of the Federation. Mostly these powers relate to the role of the President as the guarantor of the Constitution. In practice a key lever of Presidential power has been Article 83(j) of the Constitution enabling the President to appoint plenipotentiary representatives to an individual subject or group of subjects of the Russian Federation on the basis of a Statute confirmed by an Edict of the President of the Russian Federation of 9 July 1997, which was replaced on 13 May 2000 by another Edict dividing Russia into seven federal districts, each with a designated plenipotentiary.

These plenipotentiaries are not part of the agencies of State power of the subjects of the Federation, but rather are part of the Administration of the President of the Russian Federation and accordingly independent of local and regional authorities. Plenipotentiaries may not be members of political parties or socio-political movements, nor hold office in State agencies, local government, enterprises, institutions, or organisations, nor engage in entrepreneurial activity. Their purpose is to interact with political, social, and religious associations and citizens in their respective regions, assist the President in effectuating his Presidential powers, coordinate the activities of federal services in the region, take part in the work of agencies of executive power and be present at sessions of the representative agencies of power of the relevant subjects of the Federation. Although in practice it can be a thin line to draw, the plenipotentiaries may not interfere in the operational activities of agencies, enterprises, institutions, or organisations at the regional level nor adopt decisions binding on them. The aim is to create effective liaison with the regional levels without violating their legal autonomy. If the plenipotentiary discovers that the regional authorities are violating or failing to comply with federal laws, Presidential edicts, or decisions of courts, he brings this to the attention of the Chief Control Administration of the President of the Russian Federation.

Under Article 85 of the Russian Constitution, the President does have the right to intervene in disputes between agencies of State power of the Russian Federation and agencies of State power of subjects of the Federation, using conciliation procedures to this end; if these are unsuccessful, the President may transfer the dispute for consideration of a court. Moreover, if there are election irregularities in a subject of the Federation, the President of Russia may appoint to or relieve from office the head of the respective regional administration. Under Article 78(4) of the Constitution, many Russian jurists accept that the President and Government also may act against deliberate and organised insubordination on the part of regional authorities.

It is widely said that normative legal acts adopted by subjects of the Federation frequently violate the Russian Constitution or federal laws. In the case of some subjects, the figure has been placed as high as 50 per cent of all enactments. The President of Russia may suspend the operation of acts of agencies of executive power of subjects of the Federation if they are contrary to the Constitution, federal laws, international treaties of Russia, or violate the rights and freedoms of man and citizen. Most often the heads of regional administrations repeal the acts themselves when the violation is brought to their attention, but the President has used the power of suspension and referred the matter to a court.

Presidential power and the courts

Although the President is forbidden to interfere in judicial power, he participates in appointments or elections to the courts by nominating candidacies for the Constitutional Court of the Russian Federation, Supreme Court, and Supreme Arbitrazh Court for consideration by the Soviet of the Federation. The President also appoints judges to the other federal courts under Article 129(2) of the Constitution.

In practice there have been occasions when the Soviet of the Federation has repeatedly rejected candidacies for the Constitutional Court of the Russian Federation.

Presidential powers and the military

The President of Russia is the Supreme Commander-in-Chief of the Armed Forces of the Russian Federation. He confirms the Military Doctrine of the Russian Federation, which takes the form of a specific document approved by the Security Council and confirmed by Edict of the President of the Russian Federation on 21 April 2000.[25] The President appoints and dismisses the high command of the Armed Forces. Military formations in Russia exist purely at the Federation level; subjects of the Federation are not permitted their own military forces. Although the President may declare a military situation, immediately upon doing so informing the State Duma and the Soviet of the Federation, the President does not have the right to declare war.

The specific powers of the President in matters military have been elaborated in the Federal Law on the Procedure for the Granting by the Russian Federation of Military and Civilian Personnel for Participation in Activity Relating to the Maintenance or Restoration of International Peace and Security, of 23 June 1995;[26] the Federal Law on Defence, of 31 May 1996, as amended 30 December 1999;[27] and the Federal Law on Mobilisation Preparation and Mobilisation in the Russian Federation, of 26 February 1997, as amended 16 July 1998, 5 August 2000, 15 December 2001, and 31 December 2001.[28]

Presidential power and foreign relations

In his capacity of the Head of State, the President of the Russian Federation represents Russia in international relations and directs its foreign policy. Under the

---

[25] СЗ РФ (2000), no 17, item 1852. The Military Doctrine confirmed on 21 April 2000 replaced that formulated in an Edict of 2 November 1993. СЗ РФ (1993), no 45, item 4329.

[26] СЗ РФ (1995), no 26, item 2401.

[27] СЗ РФ (1996), no 23, item 2750; (2000), no 1(I), item 6.

[28] СЗ РФ (1997), no 9, item 1014; (1998), no 29, item 3395; (2000), no 32, item 3341; (2001), no 51, item 4830; no 53(I), item 5030.

1993 Constitution, the President conducts negotiations with foreign States and signs international treaties of the Russian Federation, signs instruments of ratification, and accepts credentials and letters of recall of diplomats accredited to the Russian Federation. In consultation with the State Duma and Soviet of the Federation, he appoints and recalls Russian ambassadors and other diplomatic representatives of the Russian Federation to foreign States and international organisations.

Presidential power and military and extraordinary situations

In the event of aggression against the Russian Federation or a direct threat of aggression the President of Russia has the right to introduce a military situation on the territory of the Russian Federation or in individual localities thereof, notifying at once the Soviet of the Federation and the State Duma thereof. The procedure and consequences of declaring a military situation, including general and partial mobilisation, are set out in the Federal Constitutional Law on a Military Situation, of 30 January 2002, together with a detailed definition of what constitute acts of aggression.[29]

Under Article 88 of the 1993 Constitution, the President of the Russian Federation has the exclusive right by edict to introduce an extraordinary situation on the territory of the Russian Federation or in a particular locality. Upon doing so, he must immediately notify the Soviet of the Federation and the State Duma thereof and request confirmation of his edict by the Soviet of the Federation. The Federal Constitutional Law on an Extraordinary Situation of 30 May 2001 determines the circumstances and procedure for introducing an extraordinary situation.[30] The declaring of such a situation is a provisional measure to be introduced solely to ensure the safety of citizens and to defend the constitutional system of the Russian Federation. In practice extraordinary situations have been introduced on numerous occasions in individual localities to cope with local conflicts or natural disasters.

An extraordinary situation introduced a special regime of administration which unavoidably impinges upon the rights and freedoms of citizens. The President must give the reasons for so acting and enumerate the extraordinary measures to be implemented not less than six hours before the situation enters into force.

---

[29] СЗ РФ (2002), no 5, item 375.

[30] СЗ РФ (2001), no 23, item 2277. Prior to the federal constitutional law being enacted, the President acted on the basis of a Law of 17 May 1991. Ведомости СНД и ВС РСФСР (1991), no 22, item 773. It is noteworthy that in addition to repealing the Law of 17 May 1991, the Federal Constitutional Law of 30 May 2001 (Article 42) also deemed as not prevailing and not subject to application on the territory of the Russian Federation the USSR Law of 3 April 1990 on the Legal Regime of an Extraordinary Situation. Ведомости СНД и ВС СССР (1990), no 15, item 250.

An exemplary list of such circumstances is given in Article 3 of the Federal Constitutional Law.

Presidential power and State awards

The President of the Russian Federation confers State awards, titles of honour, and senior military and other ranks of the Russian Federation upon recipients in accordance with Statutes on the particular award confirmed by Edicts of the President issued on 2 March 1994 and 1 June 1995, as amended.

The powers of the President relating to citizenship are discussed in Chapter 18. Amnesties are the prerogative of the State Duma; pardons and political asylum are within the discretion of the President (see Chapter 17).

State Council of Russian Federation

By an Edict of 1 September 2000,[31] the President of Russia formed the State Council of the Russian Federation. Viewed by some at the time as a weakening of central authority, the State Council has in practice been hardly visible. It is a consultative agency intended to assist the President in coordinating the functioning and interaction of agencies of State power. Its principal tasks are to discuss problems of especially important State significance concerning relations between the central government and the subjects of the Federation. Draft legislation, including the draft federal law on the federal budget, are routinely on the agenda. The President of Russia is the Chairman of the State Council; its members are ex officio the highest officials of the 89 subjects of the Federation. A Presidium of the State Council composed of seven members who rotate every six months deals with operational issues of the State Council. Sessions are convened, as a rule, every three months but may be held more often by decision of the President, who also determines the procedure for taking decisions within the Council on the basis of discussion. Voting may occur when the President so wishes, and he is free to pursue consensus decisions. Decisions of the State Council are formalised by a protocol which is signed by the secretary of the State Council, but if necessary they may take the form of presidential edicts, regulations, or commissions. Should formal legislation be required from the Federal Assembly, proposals and drafts are submitted to the State Duma by way of presidential legislative initiative.

Presidential Administration and councils

Around the President is a vast variety of aides, advisors, counsellors, and assistants united in a structure called the Administration of the President, which operates on the basis of a Statute on the Administration of the President of the Russian

---

[31] СЗ РФ (2000), no 36, item 3633. The Edict confirms the Statute on the State Council.

Federation confirmed by an Edict of 2 October 1996, as amended frequently thereafter.[32] The Administration includes the Director of the Administration, his first deputies and deputies, amongst them the Head of the Chancellery of the President, the heads of chief administrations and administrations, and the press secretary, Presidential aides, including the head of protocol, plenipotentiaries, and counsellors. All are directly subordinate to the President and appointed by him. Also attached to the President are consultative and advisory agencies under various names: commissions, councils, and others. Reorganisations of these bodies occur with frequency.

E. The Federal Assembly

The parliament of the Russian Federation is called the Federal Assembly. It consists of two chambers: the Soviet of the Federation and the State Duma. By virtue of being named, together with the President, the Government, and the courts of the Russian Federation, as effectuating State power, not even the Federal Assembly may change its own stature in the Russian constitutional system without undergoing the complex procedures for amending the Constitution laid down in Article 135(1) of the Constitution. The parliament is independent in the sense that the Constitution prescribes no precise limits to the legislation which it may enact. It is financially autonomous, determining its own expenses in the State budget, and also determines its own internal structure and procedures, being guided only by the Constitution itself.

Nonetheless, the powers of the Federal Assembly are not unlimited. Certain laws may be adopted by referendum, bypassing the parliament, and during a military or extraordinary situation laws may be suspended. The Constitutional Court has the right to declare laws unconstitutional, and the President may under certain circumstances dissolve the State Duma. International treaties of the Russian Federation may take precedence over laws adopted by the parliament, and certain laws on finances may be enacted only when the Government of Russia has submitted an opinion regarding them.

Although called the parliament of Russia in Article 94 of the Constitution, the Federal Assembly is further characterised as the 'legislative and representative' agency of the Russian Federation. Gone from the Russian Constitution is the vertical integration of legislative power which sought in the Soviet period to make all local soviets subordinate to superior legislative branches of the State. No longer is the parliament conceived as also being a control and administrative agency of State power. Russian constitutional doctrine takes the view that deputies of the

---

[32] СЗ РФ (1996), no 41, item 4689. For the latest version of the Edict, see СЗ РФ (2000), no 34, item 3438.

Federal Assembly once elected, whether directly by the votes in electoral districts or by subjects of the Federation, become representatives of the people at large and not merely the voters of their narrow constituency. They are not bound by imperative mandates from their electors, nor subject to recall for failure to fulfil them.

Many Russian constitutional lawyers continue to adhere to the view, notwithstanding the doctrines of separation of powers and checks and balances, that parliament adopts the enactments of the highest legal force [lex], which no other branch of the State may do. The emotional power of «закон» [lex] has yet to come to terms with the constitutional reality that in Russia only the Constitution itself is lex and that all other enactments—parliamentary, Presidential, governmental—are subordinate [подзаконный]. If this were not the case, the separation of powers would be meaningless. All branches of the State must act in conformity with the Constitution, and the Constitution must conform to Russian law [jus].

Structure of the Federal Assembly

A bicameral parliament was first introduced in Russia by way of constitutional amendments in 1990; prior to that year the highest representative agencies of the RSFSR had from 1917 been unicameral. The experience from 1990–3 was not regarded as very successful; mostly the chambers of the parliament sat in joint session, dominated by its presidium.

Under the Constitution neither chamber of the Federal Assembly is lower or higher; each has equal rights, albeit different powers. The burden of enacting federal laws falls principally upon the State Duma in practice, for the legislative process commences in that chamber. In the popular mind the Soviet of the Federation is more analogous to a Senate, less politicised, less partisan, more deliberate, and more responsive to regional interests. When the chambers have differed on matters of substance, as frequently happens, the conciliation procedures for resolving them have on the whole operated effectively.

The State Duma consists of 450 deputies, whereas the Soviet of the Federation at full strength consists of two members from each subject of the Russian Federation, that is, 178 members from 89 subjects of the Federation. One person may not be simultaneously a member of both chambers. The State Duma is elected every four years, whereas the Soviet of the Federation has no stipulated term of office. Elections to the State Duma are held on the basis of the Federal Law on Elections of Deputies of the State Duma of the Federal Assembly of the Russian Federation, of 21 June 1995, as amended 24 June 1999, 10 July 2001, and 15 January 2002;[33] the Federal Law on the Procedure for Forming the Soviet

---

[33] СЗ РФ (1995), no 26, item 2398; (1999), no 26, item 3178; (2001), no 29, item 2944; (2002), no 6, item 626. The last change is based on a Decree of the Constitutional Court of the RF of 15 January 2002.

of the Federation of the Federal Assembly of the Russian Federation, of 5 August 2000,[34] regulates the formation of the Soviet of the Federation. In compliance with the Concluding and Transitional Provisions of the 1993 Russian Constitution, both chambers were formed initially for a two-year term of office (1993–5); thereafter, the State Duma was elected to a four-year term and the Soviet of the Federation was formed on the basis of the 1995 Law. The word 'deputies' applies only to those in the State Duma; the Soviet of the Federation from 1995 has 'members'. Under the Law of 5 August 2000, the Soviet of the Federation is no longer based upon representation by the head of the legislative or representative agency of the subject and the head of the executive agency of State power. As from 1 January 2002, the representatives from the subjects of the Federation in the Soviet of the Federation are individuals appointed by the heads of executive power and legislative agency in the respective subject. It does not follow that the choices of representatives will be synchronised by the executive and legislative branches within each subject of the Federation, or that the representatives chosen will not be changed at will by the appointing body.

Internal organisation of the Federal Assembly

The Federal Assembly is a permanently operating professional parliament, in sharp contrast to its Soviet predecessors which assembled two to four times yearly for a few days. The convocation of the Federal Assembly does not depend in any way upon the President, but rather its own initiative. The State Duma meets for its first session on the 30th day after the elections, although the President may convoke it earlier. The session of the Duma is opened by its most senior member in age; only from this moment do the powers of the previous Duma lapse (Article 99, Constitution).

The chambers sit separately. Joint sessions are held only to hear messages from the President of Russia or the Constitutional Court of Russia, or to hear addresses by leaders of foreign states who are visiting the Russian Federation. Accordingly, the chambers do not consider questions together or adopt joint decisions, even if they sit in joint session. The absence of a common presidium or official who would manage the two chambers further ensures that they work autonomously. The two chambers are also physically located in different buildings in Moscow and have their own support personnel. Each chamber operates in accordance with its own Reglament, a change from the past when a single Reglament governed both chambers. The Reglaments share much in common but differ in details. The Soviet of the Federation adopted a new Reglament on 30 January 2002 which prohibits political groups or factions from being created within the upper chamber.

---

[34] СЗ РФ (2000), no 32, item 3336. This Federal Law replaced that of 5 December 1995. СЗ РФ (1995), no 50, item 4869.

315

The constitutional foundations for electing the leadership of each chamber are identical, the specific procedures being laid down in each Reglament. Each chamber elects its own chairman, and neither is beholden to the President for this position. The chairman of the State Duma is elected for a four-year term, although he may be removed from office at any time; the chairman of the Soviet of the Federation is elected without limit of term and likewise may be replaced at the pleasure of his chamber.

The Chairman of the Soviet of the Federation and his deputies may not be from the same subject of the Federation. The Chairman presides at sessions of the Soviet, signs decrees, maintains order, send draft laws to committees and, when adopted, to the President for signature, represents the Soviet in relations with the State Duma, Government, and other agencies of State power and with parliaments of foreign States, supervises the administrative apparatus of the Soviet, and the like. In the Chairman's absence his deputy may perform many of his functions, including signing decrees of the chamber. In the State Duma the Chairman, first deputy, and deputies may not represent the same political party or deputy group.

Just as the Soviet of the Federation, the State Duma also forms a Council consisting of the Chairman, the leaders of the factions and deputy groups, and the deputy chairman of the Duma with the right of a consultative vote. The Council is occupied with preparing in advance the organisational decisions of the State Duma: work programme at the current session, calendar for considering draft laws, sending draft laws to committees, deciding whether to hold parliamentary hearings, confirming the distribution of duties among the deputy chairmen, and others. The deputies are informed about all decisions taken.

The 1993 Russian Constitution requires that both chambers of the Federal Assembly form committees and commissions to prepare and give advance consideration to draft laws and hold hearings. All members of the Soviet of the Federation and all deputies of the State Duma, except the chairmen and their deputies, must serve on at least one committee of their chamber. Each chamber determines the numerical size of committees; in the Soviet of the Federation there must be not less than ten persons, whereas in the State Duma the committees vary from 12 to 35 deputies in size. Each member or deputy of the chambers is allowed to express a preference for committee assignment, the final choice being made by vote of each chamber. The State Duma elected the chairmen and deputy chairmen of the committees; in the Soviet of the Federation this is done at a session of the committee, the chairman of the committee then being confirmed by the full chamber.

Committees and commissions have the right to request documents and materials needed for their activities and to invite State officials and officials of social associations, enterprises, institutions, and organisations to their sessions, all of whom are obliged to submit the documents and materials requested. By all accounts the committees and commissions have an active role in law-making, often producing multiple drafts or rival drafts to major legislation. Their deliberations are governed by the Reglaments of the chambers and their own rules and procedures. Each chamber determines which committees to form or to abolish, and committees may themselves form subcommittees. The competence of each committee is confirmed by the Reglament. For example, the Committee of the Soviet of the Federation for Constitutional Legislation and Judicial-Legal Questions has within its competence:

- preparing opinions regarding draft federal constitutional laws approved by the State Duma, federal laws adopted by the State Duma relating to State structure, court organisation, civil law, civil procedure, arbitrazh procedure, criminal procedure, criminal law, and criminal executory law, administrative violations, the Advokatura, Notariat, and intellectual property;
- considering preliminarily proposals to amend or revise provisions of the Russian Constitution;
- conducting the preliminary discussion of candidacies for appointment to the office of judge of the Constitutional Court, Supreme Court, and Supreme Arbitrazh Court and to the office of Procurator General;
- preparing and preliminarily considering draft laws relating to matters within its own jurisdiction and organising parliamentary hearings on these matters.

In addition the Soviet of the Federation has permanent commissions for its Reglament and for parliamentary procedure and ad hoc commissions from time to time. The credentials commission verifies the documents of each newly-elected member of the Soviet of the Federation and submits an opinion to the full chamber for confirmation. The powers of a member of the Soviet are recognised, terminated, or confirmed from the moment that the full chamber adopts a respective decision. Since the Soviet of the Federation operates without a formal term of office, so too do its committees and commissions. Members come and go from the committees as their terms of office change; a committee is quorate if more than half of the members are present. Sessions are held not less than once a month. The committees and commissions often form working groups together with representatives from State agencies, social associations, and academic institutions. They also may enlist the services of individual scholars and other specialists to assist.

The State Duma forms committees for its four-year term of office giving, insofar as possible, proportional representation on each committee to the deputy groups formed in the chamber. Each committee may form subcommittees. Sessions are held as needed, but not less than twice monthly. A deputy group or one-quarter of the members of a committee may demand an extraordinary session, the decision to sit being decided by a majority of those present at the meeting to resolve the issue. Committees and commissions frequently hold joint sessions with one another. Each committee or commission has the right to submit proposals to the Council of the State Duma regarding the session of the Duma, and the chairman of the committee or commission has the right to speak at sessions of the chamber or of other committees and commissions of the State Duma in respect of matters within the jurisdiction of his committee or commission. Working groups may be formed with membership from several committees or commissions and outside specialists or representatives of State agencies, social organisations, and academic institutions.

Commissions of the State Duma are formed from the members of committees of the chamber. They include the credentials commission, commissions to verify particular events or investigate officials, to count the results of secret ballots, to give opinions, and perform other tasks. The remit of each commission is determined by the decree of the State Duma creating it.

The so-called 'deputy associations' are key units within the State Duma; they do not exist in the Soviet of the Federation. The deputy associations take one of two forms: factions and deputy groups. The definition of a faction is complex, but basically amounts to an association of deputies formed on the basis of an electoral association which entered the State Duma under an all-federal electoral district and single-mandate electoral districts. Such groupings are called factions (essentially, but not exactly, political parties or groupings) and are subject to registration in the Duma. Deputies who are not part of factions have the right to form deputy groups, and providing there are at least 35 members, the deputy group will be registered. Factions and deputy groups duly registered have equal rights. A deputy may be a member of only one faction or deputy group. Each association of deputies organises its own internal affairs. The principal factions in the State Duma are: 'Unity', 'Fatherland—All Russia', 'Communist Party of the Russian Federation', 'Liberal-Democratic Party', 'Union of Rightist Forces', 'Iabloko', and deputy groups 'Agrarian-Industrial', 'Regions of Russia', and 'People's Deputy'. From time to time mergers and alliances amongst them result in new names, images, and candidacies.

Internal work procedures of the Federal Assembly

Although they share certain operational procedures in common, the two chambers of the Federal Assembly do differ in many key respects, reflecting their varying competence, the numbers of deputies and members involved, and their constituencies. For each chamber the Reglament operates as an exceptionally detailed manual of operations setting out every stage of daily work. The Soviet of the Federation meets, in practice, less frequently than the State Duma although both chambers operate on a permanent basis. The division of the State Duma into factions and deputy groups imposes requirements of discipline not needed in the Soviet of the Federation. Sheer numbers make it more difficult for a deputy of the

State Duma to speak in plenary session than is the case for a member of the Soviet of the Federation.

The opening and closing of a session of the Soviet of the Federation is marked by performing the national anthem of the Russian Federation. Sessions are quorate if more than half of the total number of members are present, a fact which is determined by registration of members at each morning and evening session of the Soviet. If there is to be a formal vote, an additional registration is conducted to verify the existence of a quorum. Sessions are held between 1 October and 31 July of each calendar year. Extraordinary sessions may be convoked at the request of the President of the Russian Federation, Chairman of the Soviet of the Federation, of the Government of Russia, of a subject of the Russian Federation, or upon the proposal of one-fifth of the total number of members of the Soviet of the Federation. For a subject of the Federation to exercise its right to request an extraordinary session, the request must be formalised by a decision of the legislative or representative agency of State power of that subject. Formal protocols and verbatim transcripts are kept of each session, signed by the person presiding, and published in due course. Members of the Soviet have access to the transcript before publication and may make emendations.

The structure of the agenda, the precise functions of the person presiding, the procedures for granting the floor to a member of the chamber, for putting questions to a vote, for submitting questions, the time to be allocated to types of reports from commissions and committees, for clarifying remarks or explaining votes, for reducing or extending periods of time allotted, and the like are strictly determined by the Reglament. No one may speak without the permission of the person presiding, and no one who has the floor may yield to another member of the chamber except a representative from the same subject of the Federation. A member may not speak more than twice on the same question, and another member may not yield his right to speak a second time to another member.

The State Duma, as noted above, commences its first session on the 30th day after election unless the President of the Russian Federation convokes the session earlier. After electing its Chairman and deputy chairman, the Duma elects a counting commission, provisional commission for control over the electronic voting system, provisional commission for the Reglament of the State Duma, provisional secretariat, and the credentials commission. The President of the Russian Federation or his plenipotentiary representative to the Federal Assembly, the Chairman and members of the Government of the Russian Federation, members of the Constitutional Court, Supreme Court, and Supreme Arbitrazh Court, the Chairman and deputy chairman of the Counting Chamber, the Plenipotentiary for human rights, the Procurator General of the Russian Federation, and the Chairman of the Central Electoral Commission of the Russian Federation have the right to be present at any open or closed session of the State Duma; others may be present at a closed session only by special invitation.

Deference to the President is expressed by allocating to him a special place in the hall above which are placed the State Flag and Arms of the Russian Federation. Protocols and verbatim transcripts are kept and officially published, except for the transcripts of closed sessions. The State Duma assembles in spring and autumn sessions, from approximately 12 January to 20 July in spring and from September to 25 December in autumn. Plenary sessions are held on Wednesdays and Fridays, and the sundry committees, commissions, working groups, hearings, and the like proceed throughout the entire session of the Duma.

The Council of the State Duma meets on a weekly basis. Committees and commissions schedule sessions for Mondays and Thursdays. Tuesday is devoted to work in committees, commission, factions, deputy groups, and to parliamentary hearings. The last week of every month is earmarked for deputies to work with their respective constituencies. The Reglament further stipulates that every Friday is 'question time' during which not more than two members of the Government appear to answer questions.

The 'question time' is highly structured by the Reglament. Deputies submit suggestions in writing to the Council of the State Duma as to who should be invited and the questions it is proposed to put to them. The decision to invite is sent to the member of the Government at least three days before 'question time' together with the question. The member of Government has 15 minutes to reply to the question, whereupon the deputy who formulated the question may submit orally one supplementary question to clarify the answer received and speak not more than five minutes on the substance of the reply received. If the member of Government cannot be present for 'question time', he may submit a written reply to the written questions, and these are brought to the information of the deputies presiding at the session. Members of the Government also may be invited to a 'question time' in which only oral questions will be put, in which case speeches by deputies with regard to the oral responses are not permitted.

A session of the State Duma commences with the registration of delegates present, which is performed by the person presiding. A quorum is a majority (226) of the total number of deputies of the chamber (450). It is a requirement that deputies be present at a session; if this is impossible for justifiable reasons the deputy must inform the chairman of the State Duma beforehand. More often than not, in practice the notification requirement is not complied with by a large number of deputies. Deputies are notified beforehand about the agenda of the session and supplied with draft laws and decrees and other necessary materials not later than three days before their consideration in a session. The daily agenda follows a general work programme confirmed at the first session of the Duma, a calendar drawn up for each month by the Council of the State Duma, and a calendar for each two-week period confirmed by the Duma as a whole by a majority vote. Changes in the calendar are made by written request of a majority of the factions and deputy groups. Certain matters are considered on an urgent or priority basis: messages of the President of the Russian Federation, urgent draft laws submitted by the President or by the Government, draft federal laws on the federal budget and budget system of the Russian Federation, draft laws on the ratification of international treaties, the draft Reglament and decrees of the State Duma, and questions of confidence in the Government of the Russian Federation. Other matters may be considered in priority only if a majority of the chamber so decides.

The person presiding in the State Duma enjoys substantial rights. He directs the general flow of the session, ensures compliance with the Reglament, gives the floor to deputies, fulfils the organisational decisions taken by the State Duma, puts to a vote each proposal of a deputy in the sequence in which they are received, conducts voting and announces the result, oversees the work of the apparatus of the State Duma, and keeps protocols and verbatim transcripts of the sessions. If a deputy violates the Reglament, the person presiding issues a warning; a second violation means the offender no longer has the floor, although a flagrant first violation will result in the same sanction. If legislation of the Russian Federation or the Reglament of the chamber is violated, the person presiding is obliged to point this out, and also to rectify factual errors made in speeches by deputies. He may order removed from the hall any invited persons who obstruct the work of the State Duma. However, the person presiding may not express his own personal view on matters being discussed, nor comment on the speeches of deputies, nor characterise those who have spoken. When voting is open without the use of electronic equipment, the person presiding votes last. If the person presiding himself violates the Reglament, the chamber may appoint another person to preside before adopting a decision on the question under discussion.

Deputies speak in the State Duma from the lectern or in the hall from a positioned microphone. The Reglament requires that deputies wear business attire consistent with the official character of the activity of the State Duma. As in the Soviet of the Federation, speeches, reports, and other addresses to the Duma are strictly timed. The person presiding gives a warning of time expiring and then withdraws the floor from those who exceed their limit. It is common practice for the person presiding to establish with the assent of a majority of deputies present a total time limit for discussing a particular matter on the agenda, including questions and answers, or to extend a time limit previously set. No one may speak without the permission of the person presiding; deputies who do not have an opportunity to speak because of insufficient time may attach the written texts of their intended remarks to the verbatim transcript of the Duma session.

The Reglaments of both chambers of the Federal Assembly lay down a special work procedure for considering questions relegated to the jurisdiction of the chambers, most especially for the adoption or approval of laws.

Voting in the Federal Assembly

Decisions of the Soviet of the Federation are adopted by open or by secret ballot; in the case of open ballot, it may be by roll call. Several methods are used: electronic equipment, ballots, or poll. When the electronic system is used, three methods are available: quantitative, rating, or alternative. Quantitative voting requires that a member vote 'yes', 'no', or 'abstain'. The votes are counted and the results announced in absolute figures and in percentages of votes cast if the question is substantive, but if the question is procedural, only absolute figures are given. A vote by rating constitutes a series of consecutive quantitative votes in which each member of the Soviet may take part with respect to each question put. The results are announced in absolute and percentage figures only after the entire sequence of votes has been cast. Alternative voting is to vote for only one of several variants of a question, the results being disclosed in absolute and percentage figures for all variants of the question simultaneously.

A decision is considered to be adopted if more than half of the total number of members of the Soviet of the Federation have voted in favour unless the Constitution of the Russian Federation or the Reglament of the Soviet provide otherwise. Procedural questions—whether to have a break in the session, carry over a session, or adjourn, terminate speeches relating to the agenda, and the like—are adopted by a majority of members present at a session. Voting is considered to be constituted if the number of members of the Soviet of the Federation present at a session is not less than the number of members needed to adopt a decision. If a quorum is not present, the person presiding has the right to designate a time for voting on a question, the discussion of which has been completed. Members of the Soviet of the Federation from one subject of the Federation may transfer to other members from the same subject by a duly authorised power of attorney the right to cast a vote with regard to all questions to be considered by the Soviet of the Federation except those questions which are decided by secret ballot.

Open voting may be conducted with or without the use of electronic equipment, as the chamber may determine. Once voting has commenced it may not be interrupted except by a point of order. Secret voting is carried out with the use of the electronic system or by ballot, the ballot being deposited in a special box sealed by the Counting Commission. The results of a secret ballot are formalised by a decree of the Soviet of the Federation. One-fifth of the members of the Soviet of the Federation present at a session may require a roll call vote. The results of a roll call are incorporated in the verbatim transcript of the session and may be published in the mass media.

The State Duma also uses both open and secret ballots. When open voting is conducted with the electronic system, each deputy has the right to receive the results with a full list of those who voted and how they voted. In the case of a secret ballot, the list of individual names is not entered in the electronic memory. Decrees of the State Duma are adopted by a majority (226) of the total number of deputies, except with regard to procedural matters, where a majority of those present is sufficient. A deputy who is absent during the voting may not cast his vote once the period allocated for voting has elapsed. When multiple candidacies or matters are put to the State Duma, the Duma may decide to proceed by rounds of voting. If in the second round none of the variants or candidacies has received the minimum number of votes required, the question is removed from further consideration. It is for the State Duma to decide in each instance whether to use electronic voting or not. When the electronic system is not used, the Counting Commission is responsible for counting the ballots. The person presiding announces the results. As in the case of the Soviet of the Federation, voting once commenced may not be interrupted except by a point of order. Secret ballots are conducted by the Counting Commission, which issues a protocol and a report concerning the results; on the basis of these the person presiding announces the result. Roll call votes are conducted in the same procedure as in the Soviet of the Federation. Both chambers have created special groups of members to oversee the electronic voting system and ensure that it performs as it should.

Parliamentary hearings of the Federal Assembly

In accordance with Article 101(3) of the Russian Constitution, both chambers of the Federal Assembly hold hearings on matters within their jurisdiction. Hearings may be open or closed, and may be conducted by commissions or committees of both chambers jointly. Hearings result not in decisions, but in recommendations. Each committee which organises hearings also decides who shall be invited to take part. Hearings may concern draft laws, international treaties submitted for ratification, the federal budget, or other major issues of domestic or foreign policy. Most hearings are open to the press and the general public. Closed hearings discuss, as a rule, issues of State security or secrecy. The duration of hearings is determined by the committee or commission holding them.

Recommendations emanating from hearings are adopted by a majority of the deputies taking part therein and may be published in the press. The materials of closed hearings are submitted to the deputies, empowered representatives of the President of the Russian Federation to the chambers of the Federal Assembly, and to State agencies whose representatives took part in the hearings.

Competence of the Federal Assembly

The subject matter jurisdiction of the Federal Assembly has not been determined precisely by the Constitution of the Russian Federation. In some measure the matters within the exclusive and joint jurisdiction of the Russian Federation

(Articles 71 and 72, Russian Constitution) affect the competence of the Federal Assembly, but that enumeration is much broader, including the competence of the President and the Government, and other federal agencies of State power. However, those Articles of the Constitution which expressly call for a federal law do determine in part the competence of the Federal Assembly. Nonetheless, the competence of the two chambers is not identical even in this respect. The Soviet of the Federation is required to consider laws adopted by the State Duma only with respect to the budget, taxes, war and peace, and others listed in Article 106 of the Constitution. Whether the Soviet of the Federation bothers to consider other laws passed by the State Duma is purely a matter of its discretion. If the Soviet fails to consider them within a stipulated period, the State Duma may pass them along to the President for signature and promulgation (Article 105(4), Constitution).

Each chamber of the Federal Assembly also has special competence expressly provided for by the Russian Constitution. The division of special competence is in part a reflection of the principle of checks-and-balances within the parliament.

Special competence of Soviet of the Federation

Set out principally in Article 102 of the Constitution, but also in others, the Soviet of the Federation has the following areas of special competence.

(1) *Confirmation of changes of boundaries between subjects of Federation.* The Soviet of the Federation considers this matter by mutual consent of the subjects of the Federation whose boundaries are to be changed. The text of the agreement to change the boundaries confirmed by the legislative agencies of State power of each of the subjects concerned, a reasoned case for the change endorsed by each subject, and a map of the locality are submitted to the Soviet of the Federation. The matter is first referred to a committee of the Soviet, whose opinion is submitted to the plenary session. Representatives of the legislative and executive agencies of State power of the subjects of the Federation whose boundaries are being changed are invited to the plenary session, together with representatives of the Government of the Russian Federation. The decision to confirm the change of boundaries is adopted by a majority of the total number of members of the Soviet of the Federation and is formalised in the form of a decree. The decree is final, and is sent to the relevant agencies of the respective subjects of the Federation and to federal agencies of executive power. It will be noted that neither the State Duma nor the President are involved in this matter, and that no federal law is adopted. The decree is the conclusive document.

(2) *Confirmation of edicts of President of Russian Federation on introducing military and extraordinary situations.* When the President of the Russian Federation issues an edict introducing a military or extraordinary situation in a certain locality or throughout the Russian Federation, the edict, together with the consent of the

subject of the Federation if such a situation is declared in a subject of the Federation, is sent immediately to the Soviet of the Federation, which must consider the matter within 72 hours of receipt. Whether the Soviet of the Federation confirms the edict by a majority of members of the Soviet, or refuses to confirm the edict, the decision is formalised in the form of a decree. If the edict is not confirmed, the Soviet of the Federation may propose to the President that a joint conciliation commission be formed to resolve existing disagreements. If the unwillingness to confirm the edict is final, the operation of the edict terminates from the moment that the Soviet of the Federation adopts such a decree.

(3) *Possible use of Armed Forces of Russian Federation beyond limits of territory thereof.* This matter is dealt with on the basis of the Federal Law on the Procedure for the Granting by the Russian Federation of Military and Civilian Personnel for Participation in Activity Relating to the Maintenance or Restoration of Peace and Security of 23 June 1995. The Soviet of the Federation assembles to consider the request of the President of the Russian Federation within not more than five days after receiving it. The President of Russia, the Chairman of the Government, the Minister of Defence, the Head of the General Staff of the Russian Armed Forces, the Minister of Internal Affairs, the Minister of Foreign Affairs, the Head of the Federal Security Service, and the Head of the Federal Foreign Intelligence Service are all invited to the session. A positive decision requires the votes of more than half of the members of the Soviet of the Federation and is formalised as a Decree which, if adopted, is sent to the President within two days of being adopted. By Decree of 31 January 1997, for example, the Soviet of the Federation approved a military contingent of 1,600 persons for peace-keeping operations in Bosnia and Herzogovina. The State Duma plays no role in this matter, and the decree adopted does not require the signature of the President of the Russian Federation.

(4) *Designation of elections of President of Russian Federation.* The grounds for such a decision would be expiry of the Presidential term or termination of Presidential powers in accordance with Article 92(2) of the Russian Constitution. The decision to hold new elections must be taken by the Soviet of the Federation within a week from the moment of the termination of powers, except in the case of impeachment, when the date of election must be announced on the day that the decision to impeach is adopted.

(5) *Impeachment of President of Russian Federation.* Impeachment of the President may occur only on the basis of an accusation put forward by the State Duma of treason or the commission of another grave crime, the said accusation being confirmed by an opinion of the Supreme Court of the Russian Federation that the acts of the President contain the indicia of a crime and an opinion of the Constitutional Court of the Russian Federation that the established procedure for putting the accusation forward has been complied with. In addition to these documents, the Soviet of the Federation must have the opinion of a special State

Duma commission formed to evaluate the well-foundedness of the accusation against the President and a transcript of the session of the State Duma which considered the accusation against the President. These are then referred to a committee of the Soviet of the Federation for consideration and the Chairman of the Soviet requests the Constitutional Court for the aforementioned opinion regarding procedural compliance.

Once the opinion of the Constitutional Court has been received, the Soviet of the Federation must assemble within 72 hours. The date of the session to consider the accusation must be notified to the President and a lengthy list of other senior State officials and judges. The Chairman of the State Duma opens the session by setting out the substance of the accusation, followed by the Chairman of the Constitutional Court to disclose that Court's view on compliance with procedures. Next the Chairman of the Supreme Court speaks to address the substance of the accusation. The opinion is then heard of the Committee of the Soviet of the Federation Regarding Constitutional Legislation and Judicial-Legal Questions. The President of the Russian Federation or his representative may be granted the floor at their wish.

The draft decree to impeach the President is then put to secret ballot without using the electronic system. Not less than two-thirds of the total number of members of the Soviet must vote in favour. If the requisite majority is not achieved, the case is terminated, which also is formalised by a decree. The decision of the Soviet of the Federation must be adopted not later than three months after the State Duma puts forward the accusation against the President.

(6) *Appointment of judges of Constitutional Court, Supreme Court, and Supreme Arbitrazh Court.* The President of the Russian Federation submits candidacies for these judgeships, which must be considered by the Soviet within 14 days from receiving them. The matter is first referred to the Committee for Constitutional Legislation and Judicial-Legal Questions, which submits an opinion for each candidacy. Voting is by secret ballot, and each candidate must receive a majority of all members of the Soviet; if a candidate fails to obtain the requisite majority, the judgeship is deemed to be vacant and another candidacy is submitted to the Soviet within two weeks. After announcing the results of the voting, the Chairman of the Soviet of the Federation administers the oath of office to those successful candidates in a solemn ceremony in which the judge's gown is presented to the new judge. The taking of the oath is confirmed by the personal signature of the judge on a document which is preserved for posterity by the Soviet of the Federation.

The constitutional powers of the Soviet of the Federation in respect of judges have been augmented by the 1992 Agreement on the Status of the Economic Court of the Commonwealth of Independent States, which confirmed the Statute on the said court. The Statute provides (point 7) that the Russian judge on the court shall be appointed in the procedure established for the appointment of judges to the Supreme Arbitrazh Court of the Russian Federation.

(7) *Appointment to and removal from office of Procurator General.* The President of the Russian Federation proposes a single candidacy to the Soviet of the Federation, which must be considered within 30 days following the day of receipt. The candidacy is first discussed in the Committee for Constitutional Legislation, whose opinion is submitted to the Soviet. The candidate must receive a majority of all members of the Soviet by secret ballot, and the result is formalised by a decree. A new candidacy is submitted if the previous one fails to attract the required majority.

Dismissal from office also requires the recommendation of the President of the Russian Federation and the same majority vote from the Soviet of the Federation by secret ballot. If the Soviet of the Federation refuses to either elect the proposed candidate or to remove the existing Procurator General from office, consultations are held with the President to eliminate the disagreements which have arisen.

(8) *Appointment to and removal from office of Deputy Chairman and Members of Counting Chamber of Russian Federation.* Candidacies for these positions are referred first to the Committee of the Soviet of the Federation for the Budget, Finance, Currency and Credit Regulation, Monetary Emission, Tax Policy, and Customs Regulation. A majority of all members of the Soviet is required for appointment, and the decision is formalised by a decree. The question of removing the inviolability of the deputy chairman and auditors of the Counting Chamber appointed to office by the Soviet is decided by the Soviet upon the recommendation of the Procurator General of the Russian Federation.

(9) *Appointment of Central Electoral Commission.* Under the Federal Law on Basic Guarantees of Electoral Rights of Citizens of the Russian Federation (Article 12), the Soviet of the Federation appoints five members of the Central Electoral Commission of the Russian Federation from candidacies proposed by the legislative and executive agencies of State power of subjects of the Federation. The appointment is by secret ballot and is formalised by a decree of the Soviet.

(10) *Recourse to Constitutional Court of Russian Federation.* The Russian Constitution (Article 125) empowers the Soviet of the Federation to request the Constitutional Court for an opinion about the constitutionality of federal laws, normative acts of the President, the State Duma, the Government, and other legal acts. However, the Soviet of the Federation may not request the Constitutional Court to rule on a matter with respect to which a previous decree of the said Court remains in force.

The Soviet adopts a decree referring the matter or petition to the Constitutional Court and also appoints an official representative(s) to represent the Soviet when the Court considers the matter. It is possible that one-fifth of the members of the Soviet of the Federation may refer a matter to the Constitutional Court, in which case the request is signed by the individual members and does not take the form of a decree.

Special competence of State Duma

Although dispersed in several articles of the Constitution, the special competence of the State Duma is concentrated principally in Article 103 and in certain federal laws. A special procedure for considering each matter of special competence is laid down by the Reglament of the State Duma.

(1) *Consent to appointment of Chairman of Government of Russian Federation.* The election of a new Prime Minister in March-April 1998 was a classic exercise of this competence of the State Duma. The Duma must consider a candidacy proposed by the President of the Russian Federation within a week from submission of the candidacy. The candidate addresses the State Duma, setting out the basic orientations of his Government's future activity and answers questions of deputies. At the end of the question period, the representatives of factions and deputy groups indicate whether they support the candidate or not. The decision to consent to the appointment is taken at the Duma's discretion by secret voting either by using the electronic system or by ballot. A majority of the Duma is required for consent, and a decree is adopted with regard to the results of the vote. If the candidacy is rejected, a new candidacy (which may be the same person) is submitted within a week, and if rejected again, a third candidacy may be proposed within a week (which also may be the same person).

(2) *Lack of confidence in Government.* Under Article 117(3) of the Constitution, the State Duma may express lack of confidence in the Government of the Russian Federation. One-fifth of the deputies of the Duma may submit a proposal to this effect, which must be considered by the plenary session within a week of submission as a priority matter. Open voting is practised unless a roll call vote is requested. Adoption of the decree requires a majority of all deputies of the Duma. If the President of the Russian Federation does not agree with the decision of the Duma, a second vote on the same proposal may be held within three months; the Chairman of the Government himself may request a vote of confidence. In the latter instance the vote of confidence must attract the votes of a majority of the deputies; a failure to do so means the State Duma has expressed no confidence in the Government.

(3) *Appointment to and relieving from office of Plenipotentiary for Human Rights.* Candidacies for this post may be proposed by the President or by the Soviet of the Federation or by deputies or deputy associations of the State Duma. The appointment is for a term of five years, which may be renewed once. The candidate addresses the State Duma setting out briefly his programme of action. Questions

may be put by deputies to the candidate and opinions expressed for and against him. If the candidacy is rejected, the same person or another individual may be proposed. A majority of deputies of the Duma is required for appointment to or removal from office, and a decree formalises the position.

(4) *Appointment to and relieving from office the Chairman of Counting Chamber and half of auditors thereof.* Candidacies for the office of Chairman of the Counting Chamber and auditors thereof are proposed by the Committee of the State Duma for Budget, Taxes, Banks, and Finances. The appointment is made for the entire elected term of the State Duma, and requires a majority of all deputies of the Duma for each position, formalised by a decree.

(5) *Appointment to and relieving from office of Chairman of Central Bank.* The President of the Russian Federation proposes the candidate for chairman of the Central Bank of Russia. The candidacy is first considered by the Committee for the Budget, Taxes, Banks, and Finances, whose opinion is submitted to the Duma. The candidate addresses the Duma, setting out briefly his proposed programme. A majority of all deputies is required to approve the appointment. If the appointment is rejected, a new candidacy (including the same person) is considered immediately after submission by the President. Removal from office follows the same procedure.

(6) *Accusation against President of Russian Federation.* A proposal to impeach the President of the Russian Federation may be made at the initiative of at least one-third of the deputies of the State Duma. It must contain specific indication of the elements of the alleged crime and substantiate his involvement in the crime. The proposal is first referred for the opinion of a special commission formed by the Duma so as to determine whether the procedural rules have been complied with and there is factual substantiation for the accusation, and at the same time to the Supreme Court of the Russian Federation for an opinion as to whether the actions of the President contain the indicia of a crime. The special commission of the Duma is elected and consists of a Chairman, deputy chairman and ten to 12 deputies. The Chairman is chosen by open ballot and must receive a majority of the votes of the total number of deputies in the Duma. The commission members are elected by the chamber upon the recommendation of factions and deputy groups from a common list, the same majority being required. The commission should contain equal representation from the factions and deputy groups. The commission verifies whether the accusation is substantiated, compliance with quorum requirements, whether votes were counted properly, and the like. The commission hears the testimony of individuals concerning the facts underlying the accusation, examines relevant documents, and hears the representative of the President of the Russian Federation. By a majority vote of its members, the commission adopts an opinion as to whether there are factual circumstances underlying the accusation or not and whether procedural requirements have been observed.

The opinion of the commission is considered by the State Duma, in a closed session if the Duma so votes. In addition to the deputies, experts and others whose evaluation of the evidence is significant may take part. The decree to put forward the accusation against the President requires a two-thirds vote of all deputies of the State Duma by secret voting with the use of ballots. If adopted, the decree is sent within five days to the Soviet of the Federation; if the required majority is not obtained, the Duma adopts a decree refusing to accuse the President; this decree is final and subject to official publication. It also must be sent to the Soviet of the Federation and to the President.

(7) *Declaration of amnesty.* The State Duma introduces an amnesty in the form of a decree, which also sets out the procedure for implementing it. The decree is submitted and considered in the same procedure as a draft federal law. The signature or endorsement of the President of the Russian Federation is not required. The decree is subject to official publication within three days after adoption and enters into force immediately. The State Duma exercises its right of amnesty from time to time, for example in February-March 1994 in connection with the adoption of the 1993 Russian Constitution.

(8) *Recourse to Constitutional Court of Russian Federation.* Under the 1993 Constitution the State Duma has the right (Article 129) to petition the Constitutional Court of the Russian Federation to settle cases regarding the constitutionality of normative acts and international treaties as stipulated in the Article. This right has been exercised on numerous occasions by the State Duma, which may also seek a formal interpretation from the Constitutional Court on other matters relegated to the jurisdiction of the State Duma by Article 125 of the 1993 Constitution. However, such an inquiry may not be sent with regard to questions already under proceedings in the Constitutional Court.

Within the State Duma the proposal to apply to the Constitutional Court with an inquiry may originate with a faction, deputy group, or committee of the State Duma. A majority vote of the deputies is sufficient to forward an inquiry; however, more formal procedures must be complied with to petition the Court to rule on the constitutionality of normative acts.

Budgetary powers of Federal Assembly

Of all the legislation before the Federal Assembly, the draft federal law on the annual budget generates the greatest controversy and requires the greatest investment of time by the deputies and members. The jurisdiction of the Federal Assembly over the budget originates in Article 71 of the 1993 Constitution, which refers to the right of the Federal Assembly to adopt laws on the federal budget. The budgetary process itself is regulated in great detail by various federal laws which address how agencies of State power are to draw up, consider, and execute the budget. These are augmented by the annual Law on the budget itself which also sets out budgetary procedures.

Unlike other federal laws, which can undergo as many as three readings in the State Duma, the draft law on the budget routinely goes through four readings. If the law is not adopted in final form before 1 January of the relevant financial year, State agencies operate on the basis pro rata of the last quarter of the preceding financial year or, as may also happen, the State Duma adopts a special federal law to cover the interim period.

The State Duma also adopts other financial laws: taxation, and the budgets of the Pension Fund, Federal Fund for Obligatory Medical Insurance, Employment Fund, Social Insurance Fund.

Defence and security powers

Most important of the powers in this domain is the traditional right to declare war and conclude peace. In fact, the 1993 Constitution is silent as to which branch of State exercises this right. Arguably, on the basis of Article 71(j) and 106(f) of the 1993 Constitution, this right is within the competence of the two chambers of the Federal Assembly. On that reasoning the State Duma would adopt a federal law subject to obligatory consideration by the Soviet of the Federation. Presidential signature also would be required.

However, it is the President who has the right to declare a general or partial mobilisation if aggression or a direct threat thereof were committed against the Russian Federation, declare a military situation on Russian territory or parts thereof, and in his capacity as Supreme Commander-in-Chief issue orders to undertake military actions. Russian law therefore distinguishes between conducting military actions, introducing a military situation, and formally declaring war. This view finds support in Article 87(2) of the 1993 Russian Constitution and in the Federal Law on Defence of 31 May 1996, as amended. The Law on Defence expressly stipulates that military actions on the part of the Russian Federation may commence only in the event of aggression, a direct threat, or armed conflicts directed against Russia. Legally speaking, a declaration of war is confined to a defensive situation.

Concluding peace in the form of negotiations falls within the jurisdiction of the Government, but any agreement reached would acquire full legal force only after ratification of the treaty by the Federal Assembly in the form of a federal law and signature by the President.

The legal regime of a military situation is not fully defined pending the enactment of a constitutional federal law on the matter. Such a situation may be introduced by edict of the President of the Russian Federation. The general powers of the Federal Assembly in the domain of defence and security have been clarified and considerably enlarged in the 1996 Federal Law on Defence, which expressly provided that the Federal Assembly shall consider defence expenditures to be included in the federal budget, all federal laws relating to defence, confirm edicts of the President of the Russian Federation introducing a military situation or involving the Armed Forces of the Russian Federation, other forces, and military formation and agencies to perform tasks not within their usual purpose, and decide the question of using Russian forces beyond the limits of the territory of the Russian Federation.[35] There are no constitutional limitations on the types of laws that the Federal Assembly may adopt in the sphere of defence.

The Federal Assembly also has the right to adopt federal laws regulating the State boundaries (see Chapter 18).

Foreign policy and international relations

The Federal Assembly necessarily plays a lesser role in this domain given the extensive powers accorded to the President of the Russian Federation (Article 86, Russian Constitution). Under its Reglament, the State Duma may consider foreign policy issues at its own initiative or at the request of the President of the Russian Federation. The most important power in this domain is the ratification of international treaties of the Russian Federation (Chapter 18). These are submitted by the President of the Russian Federation to the State Duma together with a draft federal law to ratify, an explanatory memorandum, and other necessary documents and materials. The Chairman of the State Duma must notify deputies about the impending ratification, and the Council of the State Duma, depending upon the subject matter of the treaty, assigns it to a committee to consider the matter. The treaty and accompanying materials are sent routinely to the Committee for International Affairs or to the Committee for CIS Affairs. The Council may designate other committees of the chamber to consider the treaty as well. The committees may request additional information or seek the views of independent experts on the draft treaty, and independently may ask other committees of the State Duma to become involved. Parliamentary hearings may be held.

The plenipotentiary of the President to the State Duma or other empowered individual will be heard at a committee session. When these deliberations are completed, the committee prepares a formal Opinion and makes a recommendation to ratify or not, with or without possible declarations, statements, or reservations. A majority vote of all members of the committee is sufficient for adoption of the Opinion. The Opinion is then forwarded to the State Duma, where the Council of the Duma places the question on the agenda as a priority item. The procedure

---

[35] On the use of armed forces outside Russia, see the Federal Law on the Procedure for the Granting by the Russian Federation of Military and Civilian Personnel to Participate in Activity Relating to the Maintenance or Restoration of International Peace and Security, of 23 June 1995. СЗ РФ (1995), no 26, item 2401.

for considering a draft law to ratify a treaty is the same as for other federal laws. A simple majority of all deputies is sufficient for adoption. If the State Duma decides to postpone ratification, it must be reasoned. If an inquiry has been sent to the Constitutional Court of the Russian Federation concerning the constitutionality of the treaty, the State Duma will not consider the question of ratification until a reply is received from the Court.

Appointments and recalls of diplomatic representatives of the Russian Federation to foreign states and international organisations are made by the President of the Russian Federation after consultations with committees and commissions of the chambers of the Federal Assembly. The detailed provisions regulating these consultations are set out in the Reglament of the Federal Assembly.

Stages of the legislative process

The enactment of a federal law requires the completion of several consecutive stages: it is considered to be adopted and to have entered into legal force once it has been submitted, considered, and adopted by both chambers of the Federal Assembly, and then been signed and promulgated by the President, in accordance with the procedure established by the 1993 Constitution. It is therefore technically incorrect to speak of the 'adoption' of a federal law, for that word is used only to characterise the final result of processes within the State Duma, although the Constitution unfortunately also used the term for the entire legislative process (Article 105(1)). The Constitutional Court of the Russian Federation introduced a certain clarity when it observed that the expression 'adopted Federal law' in Article 107(1) of the Constitution refers to the entire legislative process and should be distinguished from the concept of a 'Federal law adopted by the State Duma' (Articles 105 and 106, Constitution).

The Russian legislative process may be divided into eight stages, although some have substages associated with them:

(1) legislative initiative and preliminary consideration;
(2) consideration of draft laws and adoption of laws by State Duma;
(3) consideration by Soviet of Federation of laws adopted by State Duma;
(4) consideration of laws in conciliation commission when disagreements between the chambers arise;
(5) second consideration by State Duma of laws rejected by Soviet of Federation;
(6) second consideration by State Duma of laws rejected by President of Russian Federation;
(7) second consideration by Soviet of Federation of laws rejected by President of Russian Federation;
(8) signature and promulgation of laws by President of the Russian Federation.

We consider each of these in succession.

Legislative initiative and preliminary consideration

Under Article 104(1) of the Russian Constitution, the President of the Russian Federation, Soviet of the Federation, members of the Soviet of the Federation, deputies of the State Duma, Government of the Russian Federation, legislative or representative agencies of subjects of the Federation, the Constitutional Court, Supreme Court, and Supreme Arbitrazh Court of the Russian Federation all enjoy the right of legislative initiative. All draft laws must originate in the State Duma, including those initiated by the Soviet of the Federation; they may be laws having an integral subject matter, amendments to existing laws, proposals to draft new laws or deem existing laws to have lost force, or laws to change the Constitution of Russia, and others. A draft law must be accompanied by certain materials: the text of the draft, a substantiation of the need to adopt it and prediction of likely consequences if the text is adopted, a list of other laws and normative acts which must be changed, amended, repealed, or added to if the proposed new law is enacted, among others. The draft also enumerates by name those deputies who have initiated the draft Law and the State agencies, social organisations, institutions, and organisations and individual persons who helped to prepare it. The draft must include provisions concerning the periods and procedure for its entry into force, the repeal or change of other laws, and the routine proposal to the President and Government to bring their legal acts into conformity with the newly adopted law.

Draft laws submitted to the State Duma are subject to registration by the Duma, which supervises this process through the Committee for the Organisation of the Work of the State Duma. If the requirements of form are not complied with, the Council of the State Duma may return the draft to the initiators to make necessary adjustments. If the draft falls within the purview of several committees, the Council of the Duma determines which committee shall be the lead committee. Working groups may be created, and a deadline may be assigned for producing a revised draft.

If a draft law falls within the joint jurisdiction of the Russian Federation and subjects of the Federation, the draft is circulated to the subjects of the Federation for comments and proposals. They may also be circulated to the Government of Russia, ministries, departments, or to State and social organisations.

Consideration of drafts and adoption of laws by State Duma

Excluding the law on the budget, laws undergo three readings in the State Duma unless the chamber decides otherwise with respect to a particular draft. During the first reading, the basic provisions of the draft law are discussed, whether it should be enacted or not, and the general assessment of the concept of the draft. The initiator of the draft commences the discussion by presenting a report, followed by a report from the committee which considered the draft. Comments and suggestions are received from factions and deputy groups, the plenipotentiary of the President, representatives of the Government or subjects of the Federation, and others. The Duma will either adopt the law at first reading and establish a time for the second reading, reject the draft, or, rarely, adopt it in final form at first reading. A majority of the total number of deputies is required to adopt a draft at first reading, the decision to do so being formalised in the form of a decree.

Amendments to a draft at first reading are sent to the committee of the State Duma responsible for the draft. Amendments may also be submitted by the President, Soviet of the Federation, members of the Soviet of the Federation, deputies of the State Duma, and others who have the right of legislative initiative, except the courts, who may suggest amendments only in respect of matters within their jurisdiction. The committee responsible will consider all of the proposed amendments; the sources of the amendments have the right to clarify them. The revised draft is then submitted to the State Duma for second reading, accompanied by a table of proposed amendments which the committee recommended be rejected and a second table which the committee believes should be accepted. The tables are also circulated to the President of the Russian Federation and to the initiator of the draft law.

At the second reading, the chairman of the committee responsible reports on its deliberation, on the amendments proposed, and on those recommended. He is followed by the plenipotentiary of the President of the Russian Federation and representatives of those who proposed the draft law. The person presiding then determines whether the factions or deputy groups object to the proposed amendments. If there are objections, debate is opened on these and the rapporteur replies to the objections raised. Voting on the amendments then ensues by deciding first whether the original draft law may be used as the basis for the amendments. If that vote is affirmative, voting proceeds on the amendments, and then whether to adopt the draft law as amended at second reading. There are a variety of technical variations on these procedures which are governed by the Reglament of the State Duma.

The version of the draft law adopted at second reading is then sent to the committee responsible which, together with the Legal Administration of the Apparatus of the State Duma, edits the draft to eliminate internal contradictions and correct style, punctuation, and editorial adjustments. When this task is completed, the draft law is sent within seven days to the Council of the State Duma for inclusion on the agenda.

At third reading the draft law cannot be returned for further amendments or discussion as a whole except in the most unusual circumstances when deputy associations representing a majority of deputies so decide. A majority of votes of the total number of members of the State Duma is required to adopt a federal law, and a two-thirds majority if a federal constitutional law is being adopted. After being adopted at third reading, the draft is sent on the basis of a decree of the State Duma to the Soviet of the Federation for consideration.

The phrase 'a majority of votes of the total number of deputies of the State Duma' has been variously interpreted. If, for example, the number of deputies actually elected to office were less than the established size of the chamber, as has occurred, the majority required to adopt a law would differ from the number required if the majority had to be of deputy places. To clarify the problem, the State Duma requested an interpretation of the 1993 Russian Constitution from the Constitutional Court of the Russian Federation, which on 12 April 1995 ruled that this phrase can only mean a majority of the constitutionally-established number of seats in each chamber. In the State Duma the minimum majority required will be 226 votes.

Consideration by Soviet of Federation of laws adopted by State Duma

Laws adopted by the State Duma and sent within five days to the Soviet of the Federation, as provided by Article 105(3) of the 1993 Russian Constitution, are directed to the relevant committee(s) of the Soviet of the Federation for consideration. If the materials forwarded by the State Duma do not include the Opinion of the Government of the Russian Federation, the Soviet of the Federation may immediately reject the federal law if it concerns the introduction or repeal of taxes, issue of State loans, change of State financial obligations, or otherwise engages expenditures to be covered from the federal budget.

Article 105(4) of the 1993 Russian Constitution established a 14-day period within which the Soviet of the Federation must consider certain federal laws. The period commences from the day following the date on which the law was registered for consideration in the Soviet of the Federation. The Constitution further stipulates (Article 106) that federal laws relating to the federal budget, federal taxes and charges, financial, currency, credit, and customs regulation, monetary emission, ratification and denunciation of international treaties, the status and defence of the State boundary of Russia, and war and peace must be considered by the Soviet of the Federation. In practice the Soviet of the Federation has found it impossible always to comply with the 14-day period, raising therefore the question of whether the federal laws enumerated in Article 106 of the Constitution fell under the 14-day requirement of Article 105(4). The question was put to the Constitutional Court of the Russian Federation, which on 23 March 1995 ruled that the 14-day period referred only to the commencement of consideration by the Soviet of the Federation. It was not mandatory that consideration be completed within that period. Questions carried over, however, are subject to obligatory consideration at the next regular session.

A law not subject to obligatory consideration and not considered within the 14-day period is sent to the President for signature and promulgation. If a law is considered and does not receive the required majority, the rejection is formalised by a decree of the chamber. The decree may contain a list of articles, sections, chapters, or other provisions which the chamber considers should be discussed with the State Duma or by a conciliation commission between the two chambers. The decree recording the rejection of a federal law is sent to the State Duma within five days. If the State Duma adopts the law a second time taking into account all of the proposals of the Soviet of the Federation, it is returned to the respective committee of the Soviet, which confirms acceptance of the proposals and recommends approval of the law without further plenary discussion. If the State Duma accepts only some of the proposals, or introduces new provisions, or removes previous provisions, the law returned by the State Duma is reconsidered as though it were an entirely newly adopted text.

Conciliation commissions

When a law is adopted by the State Duma and rejected by the Soviet of the Federation, a conciliation commission is formed from representatives of each chamber on a parity basis elected by the respective chambers. Either chamber may take the initiative to form the commission. The commission considers only those provisions of the law which were the subject of disagreement and seeks to work out agreed provisions in the form of a unified text. The co-chairmen of the commission conduct separate voting within each delegation, and a decision is adopted if both deputations vote for the agreed text. The matter is then referred back to the State Duma, which may or may not accept the result of the conciliation commission. If the result is rejected, the State Duma may propose that the conciliation commission continue its work, and the Soviet of the Federation may either agree or refuse to participate. If the conciliation commission cannot overcome the differences between the two chambers, the law is sent back to each chamber, in which case the Soviet of the Federation has the right to approve the text in any form which it chooses, or to change its delegation to the conciliation commission, or to refuse to continue to take part in the work of the commission. Whatever decrees are adopted are sent to the State Duma within five days.

Second consideration by State Duma of laws rejected by Soviet of Federation

When the conciliation commission refers the results of its deliberations to the State Duma, the latter chamber places the federal law on the calendar for discussion. Only proposals contained in the protocol of the conciliation commission are discussed; no amendments going beyond those proposals are considered. If even one of the conciliation commission proposals are rejected, the State Duma may suggest that the commission continue its work having regard to the amendments approved and that the commission within ten days submit new proposals, which, when submitted, are considered by the State Duma in the same procedure. Each proposal of the conciliation commission is voted upon individually by the State Duma, and each must obtain the majority of total number of deputies of the chamber. The law adopted in the version of the conciliation commission is then sent to the Soviet of the Federation.

If the Soviet of the Federation rejects the law at second consideration, or the State Duma did not accept the proposals of the conciliation commission and disagreed with the decision of the Soviet of the Federation to reject the law, the law is put to a vote in the State Duma in its original form before the conciliation procedures. If not less than two-thirds of the deputies vote in favour of the law, it is considered to be adopted and sent within five days to the President of the Russian Federation for signature.

Second consideration by State Duma of laws rejected by President of Russia

Under the Constitution, if the President of the Russian Federation within 14 days of receiving a federal law for signature rejects it, the State Duma gives second consideration to the law. The Council of the Duma refers the law to the committee responsible or to a specially-created commission, which considers the law within ten days. The committee or commission may recommend that the State Duma approve the law in the version proposed by the President, or agree with the President that such a law should not be adopted, or approve the law again in its original version.

Reconsideration of the law is a priority item on the agenda. The plenipotentiary of the President addresses the chamber, followed by the opinion of the committee or commission. If the President proposes that such a law is not required, this may be put to a vote, a majority of the total number of deputies being required. If the chamber votes to open discussion, only representatives of the factions and deputy groups may take part. At the end of the discussion, the question first put to a vote is whether to approve the law in the version proposed by the President; this requires a simple majority of the total number of deputies. If that proposal is rejected by the Duma, the next question is whether to approve the law in the version originally adopted by the Duma, that is, whether to override the Presidential veto. This requires a two-thirds majority of the total number of deputies. Whichever decision is adopted, the law is sent on the same day to the Soviet of the Federation.

If neither decision is adopted, the State Duma proceeds to vote again on the Presidential version, in this case voting separately on each section, chapter, article, paragraph, and point, the vote required being a simple majority of the total number of deputies. Further consideration is then deferred to the next session of the chamber, during which interval the committee or commission prepares a new version of the law incorporating those proposals of the President which were adopted. This version is then submitted as a whole to the State Duma and requires a simple majority of the total number of deputies for adoption. If adopted, the normal legislative process resumes.

Second consideration by Soviet of Federation of laws rejected by President of Russian Federation

The Soviet of the Federation receives from the State Duma the text of the law and the decree of the Duma concerning the second consideration, together with the text of the President's letter to the Duma. The procedure for overriding the Presidential veto begins with the committee which previously reported on the law reconsidering the text in light of the President's comments together with the version of the law adopted at second consideration by the State Duma. When considering the text in plenary session, the Soviet of the Federation may vote either to approve the text or to open discussion. If not less than two-thirds of the members vote in favour of the version originally adopted, the law is adopted. Approval of the law vetoed by the President is sent in the form of a decree to the President, who is obliged to sign and promulgate it.

The President and the legislative process

Under Article 107(2) of the 1993 Russian Constitution, the President is required to sign a federal law unless within 14 days from the moment of receiving it he vetoes the law. Moreover, if the Federal Assembly overrides his veto, he must also sign the law within seven days of receiving the decrees of the chambers of the Federal Assembly approving the law in its original version. In 1988 the Constitutional Court held that the law must be signed notwithstanding reservations held by the President about voting irregularities in the chambers. In practice the veto has been used rather frequently by the President, and it is rarely overridden.

The President is actively involved in the legislative process at a number of stages. He frequently exercises his right of legislative initiative, gives opinions on draft laws adopted by the State Duma at first and second readings, and through his plenipotentiary makes his views known to the chambers. These actions have become accepted routines on the basis of the Statute on the Procedure for the Interaction of the President of the Russian Federation with Chambers in the Federal Assembly of the Russian Federation in the Law-Formation Process, confirmed by an Edict of the President of the Russian Federation on 13 April 1996, as amended several times.[36] The Statute sets out specific actions to be taken by plenipotentiaries of the President at all stages of the legislative process, the role of the administration of the President, the veto of laws, the submission of opinions on draft laws, and other matters.

---

[36] СЗ РФ (1996), no 16, item 1842; (1997), no 20, item 2238; no 41, item 4680; no 52, item 5912; (1998), no 10, item 1161.

Legal status of deputies and members of the Federal Assembly

The status of deputies of the State Duma and members of the Soviet of the Federation is regulated principally by the 1993 Russian Constitution and the Federal Law on the Status of a Deputy of the Soviet of the Federation and Status of a Deputy of the State Duma of the Federal Assembly of the Russian Federation of 8 May 1994, in the version of 5 July 1999 as amended.[37] The expression 'deputy of the Soviet of the Federation' (originally used in the 1994 Law and reflecting era when the Soviet of the Federation was directly elected, 1991–4), has been changed to 'member'.

Deputies of the Duma represent the people as a whole, being directly elected, work on a permanent professional basis, may not be a civil servant nor engage in other paid activity except teaching, scientific, or creative. Members of the Soviet of the Federation are not full-time, represent their respective subjects of the Federation, and do hold State office elsewhere.

The Russian Constitution is silent as to whether deputies and members of the Federal Assembly have an 'imperative' or a 'free' mandate from their constituencies. In Russian constitutional doctrine the distinction is crucial, for in the late Soviet era the imperative mandate dominated, that is, the powers of a deputy emanated from his electors and he was obliged to fulfil their directions and be responsible to them for his actions. If a deputy did not perform his pre-electoral promises or generally does not perform his duties satisfactorily, he was subject to recall. Under this approach the deputy is not free to vote in the parliament as he believes is in the best interest of his country, but must serve his narrow constituency. The prevailing view in Russian constitutional doctrine is that the imperative mandate no longer operates. The right of recall has been abolished, and there is no legal requirement that a deputy follow the instructions of his constituents, or political party, or other outside source of discipline, although to be sure a deputy will be likely to be guided by his pre-electoral platform and the rights and interests of his constituents and of his political affiliations.

The State Duma is elected for a term of four years, so that the term of office of a deputy of the State Duma commences from the day of election and terminates from the moment that the next newly-elected Duma commences work, subject to certain exceptions provided for by legislation. The term of members of the Soviet of the Federation is determined by the term of office of the respective member as the head of the legislative or representative agency of State power in his respective

---

[37] СЗ РФ (1994), no 2, item 74; (1999), no 28, item 3466; (2001), no 7, item 614; no 32, item 3317; (2002), no 28, item 2785. The amendments of 4 August 2001 extend to members of the Soviet of the Federation from the day of their election or appointment on the basis of the Federal Law of 5 August 2000 on the Procedure for Forming the Soviet of the Federation of the Federal Assembly of the Russian Federation. СЗ РФ (2000), no 32, item 3336.

subject of the Federation. They commence when the Soviet of the Federation decrees to recognise his powers in accordance with the Reglament of the chamber and end when the same chamber decrees to terminate them, but end automatically if the individual member loses his position in his respective subject of the Federation.

The powers of a State Duma deputy will terminate before time if he loses Russian citizenship, resigns in writing, is elected deputy of another representative agency of State power or of local self-government, joins the civil service, engages in other paid activity except those permitted, the State Duma is dissolved, or if he dies in office. A member of the Soviet of the Federation likewise will lose his post if he is no longer a Russian citizen, or if the judgment of a court finds him guilty of committing a crime which has entered into legal force, or if he is deemed to lack dispositive legal capacity by a court, or declared to be deceased by a court, or dies in office.

Under the Russian Constitution (Article 98), deputies and members of the Federal Assembly enjoy inviolability throughout their entire term of office. More than one candidate for office in the State Duma with a criminal accusation pending has used election to the Duma to postpone reckoning or invoke the period of limitations. They may not be detained, arrested, subjected to search (unless detained at the site of a crime) nor subjected to personal inspection unless provided otherwise by a federal law. The inviolability extends to their dwelling, official premises, correspondence, communications, and documents belonging to them. They may refuse to give witness testimony in civil and criminal cases regarding circumstances which became known to them in connection with the performance of their duties. Whether immunity should be waived or not is decided by the respective chamber of the Federal Assembly upon the recommendation of the Procurator General of the Russian Federation; one instance has occurred where such immunity has been waived in the State Duma, but waiver has been refused several times.

The 1994 Federal Law on the status of deputies significantly expanded the enumeration of instances when parliamentary immunity may be invoked, in comparison with the enumeration in the 1993 Russian Constitution. In a Decree of 20 February 1996 the Constitutional Court of the Russian Federation confirmed the constitutionality of the Law, but rejected an expansive interpretation of the Law and abbreviated the list of activities enjoying immunity not connected with deputy activity.

Deputies receive a salary, free life and health insurance equal to the yearly salary of a federal Minister, exemption from military service, right to reinstatement in their former job or equivalent thereto, a lump-sum benefit for the remainder of the parliamentary term if the State Duma is dissolved, free travel to and from their place of residence if the Duma is dissolved and free carriage of personal belongings up to ten tons in weight, inclusion of service in the Federal Assembly as part of labour experience, with the right to receive a State pension earlier, if desired. All deputies receive an identical salary, except that the Chairman of the State Duma receives the equivalent of the Prime Minister of the Government. An expense allowance exists to cover expenses associated with living away from the permanent place of residence. Annual paid leave of 48 work days per year is granted. Each deputy has the right to a furnished office and communications, including governmental, and all types of postal and telegraph expenses connected with official matters are paid for. On the territory of Russia deputies and members of the Federal Assembly may use air, railway, motor vehicle, and water transport, including urban and subur-ban transport, free of charge, excluding taxis. State and municipal hotels must provide deputies and members with a separate hotel room within an hour; deputies from outside Moscow are also provided with living accommodation, with must be vacated within a month after their term of office ends. Each deputy and member may have up to five aides, with the total number per chamber to be determined by each chamber.

The Criminal Code of the Russian Federation and other legislation provide sanc-tions for obstructing a deputy or member of the Federal Assembly in his duties, failure to provide information requested or for providing false information, unlawfully attempting to influence such persons, insulting a deputy or member, and others.

F. The Government

The word 'Government' [правительство] is a narrow and precise term in Russian constitutional law, as it is in English but not necessarily in the United States. It refers to a particular branch of the State and cannot under any circum-stances refer to the State at large. Confusion between the two is usually caused by mistranslating the term 'State' [государство] as 'Government', for which there is no foundation in Russian (or Soviet) law.

The legal status of the Government is regulated principally by the 1993 Constitution of the Russian Federation (Chapter 6) and the Federal Constitutional Law on the Government of the Russian Federation, signed 17 December 1997 and amended on 31 December 1997.[38] The Government is an agency of State power of the Russian Federation and effectuates executive power; it is a collegial organ under the chairmanship of the Chairman of the Government of the Russian Federation and heads the unified system of executive power in Russia. It consists of its

---

[38] СЗ РФ (1997), no 51, item 5712; (1998), no 1, item 1.

Chairman, deputy chairmen, and federal ministers. The Government of the Russian Federation is not a juridical person and enjoys no autonomous legal capacity.

The Chairman of the Government is appointed by the President of the Russian Federation with the consent of the State Duma. The President submits the name of a candidate within two weeks after being newly elected or after the Government has resigned or within a week from the State Duma rejecting a previous candidacy. In practice the State Duma has rejected many candidacies. The State Duma must consider a candidacy within a week of the President making the proposal. If the State Duma rejects candidacies submitted three times, the President appoints the Chairman of the Government himself, dissolves the State Duma, and designates new elections for the Duma. The Chairman is relieved from office if he resigns or if he can no longer perform his duties; such resignation automatically entails the resignation of the entire Government.

Once in office, the Chairman of the Government proposes the names of candidates to the President of the Russian Federation for the office of deputy chairmen of the Government and individual ministers; the same procedure applies to the removal of these individuals from office.

In the interests of eliminating conflicts of interest and undue influence from outside sources the Chairman and deputy chairmen of the Government and federal ministers are required upon appointment to office and thereafter annually to submit information to tax agencies of the Russian Federation about revenues, securities, and property belonging to them by right of ownership which are objects of taxation. This information is sent to the President of the Russian Federation and to the Federal Assembly by the tax agencies. Such information may be published. There are in addition certain limitations imposed on those who hold any of these offices: among them are prohibitions against being a member of the Soviet of the Federation or deputy of the State Duma or of other legislative or representative agencies of State power of subjects of the Russian Federation or deputies of elective agencies of local self-government or holding other offices in agencies of State power or local self-government or in social associations; or engaging in entrepreneurial activity personally or through entrusted persons, including participation in the management of an economic subject irrespective of its organisational-legal form. Members of the Government are, moreover, required to transfer participatory shares or blocs of stock in the charter capital of commercial organisations in their ownership to trust management under guarantee of the State. Any other paid activity is prohibited except teaching, scholarly, and other creative activity. Nor may they act as attorneys or representatives of third persons in agencies of State power, or receive royalties for publications or speaking as a member of the Government, nor receive loans, gifts, monetary or other remuneration, including services or payment for attractions and leisure from natural or juridical persons not provided for by federal legislation, nor receive honorary and special titles, awards, or other marks of distinction of foreign States, nor make business trips outside Russia at the expense of natural or juridical persons except those effectuated in accordance with Russian Federation legislation, international treaties of the Russian Federation, or on a mutually agreed basis between federal agencies of State power and the State agencies of foreign states or of international and foreign organisations.[39]

Standards for State officials and civil servants of this nature are without precedent in Russia. During the Soviet era, it was commonplace for Party and State officials to combine offices in Party and State institutions or for State officials to hold more than one office, or for individuals to serve in both the legislative and executive branches of the State.

The 1993 Constitution of the Russian Federation says relatively little about precisely what the Government is to do. Article 114 provides, without characterising these as duties or functions, that the Government is to work out and submit to the State Duma the federal budget and ensure its execution and submit a report to the State Duma concerning execution of the budget, ensure that unified financial, credit, monetary, cultural, science, education, public health, social security, and ecology policies are implemented in the Russian Federation, effectuate the administration of federal ownership and measures related to ensuring the defence of Russia and State security, the realisation of Russian foreign policy, measures to ensure legality, the rights and freedoms of citizens, protection of ownership and public order, the struggle against criminality, and, under a general powers formulation, effectuate 'other powers placed on it by the Constitution', federal laws, and edicts of the President of the Russian Federation.

On the basis of this language, the Law on the Government devotes numerous lengthy articles to defining the 'powers' of the Government. Some are classified as 'general powers', some as 'powers', and the remainder as 'other powers'. Compared with most constitutions of the Anglo-American family of legal systems, which have no 'law' on the 'Government', the enumeration of powers is vast, but the terminology used to describe those powers is sweeping in scope. In practice the limitation on governmental powers originates more in the status of the Government *vis-à-vis* other agencies of State power and administration than it does in the special nature of the legal capacity which the Government possesses by virtue of the

---

[39] The State officials who are required to comply with these reporting standards are enumerated in the Edict of the President of the Russian Federation of 15 May 1997, No 484, as amended 4 March 1998, 31 May 1999, 25 July 2000, and 5 December 2001 'On the Submission by Persons Holding State Offices of the Russian Federation and by Persons Holding State Offices of State Service and Offices in Agencies of Local Self-Government of Information Concerning Revenues and Property'. СЗ РФ (1997), no 20, item 2239; (1998), no 10, item 1160; (1999), no 23, item 2818; (2000), no 31, item 3252; (2001), no 50, item 4705.

Constitution. With respect to adopting normative acts, this is expressed in Article 115(3) of the 1993 Russian Constitution, which provides that decrees and regulations of the Government may, if they fail to conform to the Constitution, federal laws, and edicts of the President of the Russian Federation, be repealed by the President of the Russian Federation.

The Federal Law on the Government also addresses the internal procedures for adopting certain types of decisions and the allocations of duties among the Chairman, deputy chairmen, and federal ministers. Sessions of the Government must be held not less than once a month. Certain persons who are not members of the Government have the right to participate in sessions, for example, the chairmen of the chambers of the Federal Assembly, the chairman of the Constitutional Court, Supreme Court, or Supreme Arbitrazh Court, the Procurator General, the Central Bank, and others. Individual matters may be considered at closed sessions. There is a list of questions which may be decided solely at sessions of the Government, for example, the decision to submit the federal budget to the State Duma, or to conclude international treaties of the Russian Federation which are subject to ratification. The Government also has the right of legislative initiative in the Federal Assembly and may submit amendments to draft laws being considered by the State Duma.

The Government has the right to form a Presidium in order to deal with operational issues. The Presidium meets as required and operates by majority vote. Its decisions cannot be contrary to acts adopted at sessions of the Government and are subject to repeal by the Government. The Government adopted its own Reglament to help with deciding internal procedural questions and a Statute on the Apparatus of the Government of the Russian Federation on 18 June 1998.[40]

When a new President of the Russian Federation is elected, the existing Government resigns as of the day when the President takes office. At any other time the Government also may offer to resign, and the President is at liberty to accept or reject such offer. The President may also require the Government to resign, and may do so irrespective of whether such decision reflects a lack of confidence expressed by the State Duma or represents the President's own decision. If the State Duma has expressed a lack of confidence and the President does not concur with the State Duma, the Government remains in office; however, if within three months of the first vote of no confidence the State Duma again expresses its lack of confidence in the Government, the President of Russia must either declare the resignation of the Government or dissolve the State Duma for new elections. If the Chairman of the Government himself places the question of confidence in the Government before the State Duma and the latter refuses confidence, the

---

[40] СЗ РФ (1998), no 27, item 3176.

President must within seven days accept the resignation of the Government or dissolve the State Duma and designate new elections. When the Government does resign or lay down its powers, it nonetheless continues to operate until a new Government is formed. There is consequently no vacuum of Government as a result of the exercise of no-confidence options.

The Government is not subordinate to the President but is decidedly inferior to the President. The President of the Russian Federation ensures that the Government and other agencies of State power function and interact on a coordinated basis. The President at any time may preside at sessions of the Government or of its Presidium. Although federal agencies of executive power are part of the Government of Russia, the activity of certain of them is directed by the President and not by the Chairman of the Government; such activity concerns questions of defence, security, internal affairs, foreign affairs, and the prevention of extraordinary situations and liquidation of their consequences. In these instances it is the President who confirms the Statutes on these agencies upon the recommendation of the Chairman of the Government and who appoints their heads. The Government then coordinates the activities of these federal agencies of executive power in accordance with the Constitution, federal constitutional laws, federal laws, and the edicts and regulations of the President of the Russian Federation.

In matters of joint jurisdiction with subjects of the Russian Federation, the Government of the Russian Federation coordinates the exercise of executive power by agencies of executive power of the subjects of the Federation. The Government therefore acts as the channel by which agencies of executive power of the subjects of the Federation communicate with and make proposals to other agencies of the Russian State. Time limits are laid down (not exceeding one month) for the consideration of proposals emanating from subjects of the Federation and the Government likewise must send its own draft decisions to all relevant subjects of the Federation which appertain to matters of joint jurisdiction. The responses of the subjects of the Federation regarding such draft decisions must be considered by the Government. However, the powers of the Government in this domain go beyond coordination. The Government of Russia is also empowered to effectuate control over the activity of federal agencies of executive power generally. It may settle disputes and disagreements between federal agencies of executive power and those equivalent agencies of subjects of the Federation by forming conciliation commissions for this purpose. The ultimate sanction is that the Government of Russia may propose to the President of the Russian Federation that acts of agencies of executive power of subjects of the Federation be suspended if they are contrary to the Constitution of the Russian Federation, federal constitutional laws or federal laws, international obligations of the Russian Federation, or a violation of the rights and freedoms of man and citizen.

As regards the Russian judiciary, the Government of Russia is obliged to finance the courts only from the federal budget and to ensure that the courts are fully independent to perform their functions; the Government is also to ensure the execution of judicial decisions.

G. Local Self-Government

In the Russian Federation local self-government refers to those administrative-territorial entities which are below the subjects of the Russian Federation in stature. The 1993 Russian Constitution refers to them laconically as a system created by citizens autonomously to resolve questions of local significance and the possession, use, and disposition of municipal ownership (Article 130). Although a separate Chapter 8 is allotted in the Constitution to local self-government (Articles 130–133), other provisions of the Constitution touch upon the subject (Articles 8, 9, 15, 24, 32, 33, 40, 41, 43, 46, and 68).

The basic constitutional position is that local self-government is autonomous within the limits of its powers, is not part of the system of agencies of State power, decides questions of local significance and the possession, use, and disposition of municipal ownership, uses referendums, elections, and other means to determine the expression of will of the local populace, and has boundaries which cannot be changed without taking into account the views of the local populace. Autonomy in this context means the right to manage municipal ownership, form, confirm, and execute the local budget, establish local taxes and charges, protect public order, and the like. Under the Constitution local self-government may have recourse to the courts if its rights are infringed and has the right to compensation for additional expenses which arise for it as a result of decisions taken by agencies of State power.[41]

The law of local self-government, often called 'municipal law' in doctrinal writings, rests, in addition to the Russian Constitution, upon the Federal Law on the General Principles of Local Self-Government in the Russian Federation, of 28 August 1995, as amended 22 April and 26 November 1996, 17 March 1997, and 4 August 2000,[42] and upon the charters adopted by each 'municipal formation'.[43] The last expression is a neutral one embracing a city or rural settlement, or several settlements combining a common territory, or part of a settlement within whose

---

[41] A I Kovalenko, Муниципальное право [*Municipal Law*] (1997).

[42] СЗ РФ (1995), no 35, item 3506; (1996), no 17, item 1917; no 49, item 5500; (1997), no 12, item 1378; (2000), no 32, item 3330.

[43] Many of these are collected in N V Varlamova and L E Lapteva (eds), Местное самоуправление в Российской Федерации [*Local Self-Government in the Russian Federation*] (1998).

limits local self-government is exercised—all of the foregoing having their own charter, municipal ownership, a local budget, and elective agencies of self-government. The municipal charter is subject to State registration in the procedure established by the respective subject of the Russian Federation in which the municipal formation is situated; registration may be refused if the charter is contrary to the Russian Constitution.

Municipal charters vary considerably, but contain as a rule the boundaries and composition of the territory of the municipal formation, its jurisdiction, the structure and procedure for forming local self-government agencies, the term of powers of deputies elected, other elective posts, and the procedure for the adoption and entry into force of normative acts of local self-government. In some subjects of the Federation, although local self-government is autonomous and not part of the system of agencies of State power, local agencies of State power have been created side-by-side with local self-government (eg, Iakutia, Komi, Bashkortostan) which are directly subordinate to the 'centre'. In some areas the local self-government has been determined to be simultaneously an agency of State power. The procedure for choosing the chief executive officer, and his stature, also varies. In Tver Region the head of the administration of a city, district, settlement, or rural national area is the head of the superior administration, whereas in other areas the same scheme is augmented by the requirement that the consent of the respective representative agencies of local self-government be obtained, for example, in Arkhangelsk Region. On two occasions the Constitutional Court of the Russian Federation has struck down attempts of subjects of the Federation to interfere in the formation or transformation of local self-government (1 February 1996 and 24 January 1997).

Issues of local significance are decided rather frequently by local referendums, including boundary issues. The procedures for holding referendums are regulated by the charter of the municipal formation in accordance with legislation of the respective subject of the Russian Federation. The same applies to municipal elections to representative organs, except that agencies of State power of the Russian Federation and of the relevant subject of the Federation are required to ensure that local elections do take place. If the municipal formation does not have its own electoral legislation, as happens, the elections are held on the basis of the Federal Law on Ensuring the Constitutional Rights of Citizens of the Russian Federation to Elect and to Be Elected to Agencies of Local Self-Government, of 26 November 1996, as amended 22 June 1998.[44]

Reversion to the ancient tradition of 'assemblies of citizens' may be authorised in municipal formations, provided that the procedure for convoking and conduct-

---

[44] СЗ РФ (1996), no 49, item 5497; (1998), no 26, item 3005.

ing them, adopting and changing decisions, and their precise competence must be determined in the charter of the municipal formation in accordance with legislation of the relevant subject of the Federation. A form of popular legislative initiative exists, called the 'people's law-creation initiative', whereby in accordance with the municipal charter the general public may put forward draft legal acts on questions of local significance. These must be considered by the local self-government in open session and the results of the consideration officially published. Municipal charters may also provide for 'territorial social self-government', whereunder citizens organise themselves at their place of residence and assume responsibility for certain questions of self-government.

Municipal ownership consists of the means of the local budget, municipal extra-budgetary funds, the property of agencies of local self-government, municipal land and other natural resources, municipal enterprises and organisations, municipal banks and other credit institutions, educational, public health, culture and sport institutions, stockholdings or other equity in juridical persons, and other moveable and immoveable property. In large cities the total asset-base can be very substantial and has been successfully used as security to achieve project financing or back the issue of securities. Under the Russian Civil Code (see Chapter 9) municipal agencies of self-government have legal personality and legal capacity and may transfer, lease out, or alienate their property or conclude other transactions with the property in their ownership. The privatisation of municipal property is resolved at the local level, and revenues from privatisation go to the local budget. It has been common practice when major State enterprises are transformed into joint-stock societies to transfer the so-called social infrastructure (housing, clubs, cinemas, children's nurseries, and the like) to the balance sheet of the municipal formation.

Municipal formations may and often do invest in entrepreneurial enterprises, and have the right to engage in foreign economic activity.

H. Constitutional Amendments

The Russian Constitution is not easily amended or revised. Chapters 1 (Foundations of the Constitutional System), 2 (Rights and Freedoms of Man and Citizen), and 9 Constitutional Amendments and Revision of the Constitution) cannot be amended by the Federal Assembly. If a proposal to amend or revise any of those three chapters is supported by the votes of three-fifths of the total number of members of the Soviet of the Federation and of the State Duma, a Constitutional Assembly must be convoked in accordance with a federal constitutional law (which has not yet been enacted). Amendments to Chapters 3–8 of the Constitution may be adopted by the Federal Assembly in the same procedure as is used to adopt a federal constitutional law, but they enter into force only after approval by the agencies of legislative power of not less than two-thirds of the subjects of the Russian Federation (Article 136, Constitution).

If a Constitutional Assembly is convoked, it either confirms the Constitution in its existing form or prepares the draft of a new Constitution. The new draft must be adopted by two-thirds of the total number of delegates at the Assembly or be submitted to an all-people's referendum. If a referendum is held, at least half of the electors must take part for there to be a valid referendum, and a simple majority of the electors must vote in favour of the new Constitution.

Article 65 of the Constitution is subject to yet another procedure for amendment. If a new subject of the Federation is formed or if there is a change in the constitutional legal status of an existing subject, the consequential changes in the Constitution are set out in the federal constitutional law on the admission of a new subject or changing the status of an existing subject of the Federation. If a subject of the Federation simply changes its name, as already has happened, the new name is subject to inclusion in Article 65 of the Constitution; in practice this occurs on the basis of an edict of the President of the Russian Federation.

The constitutional provisions governing amendments to the Constitution have been elaborated in the Federal Law on the Procedure for the Adoption and Entry into Force of Amendments to the Constitution of the Russian Federation, of 4 March 1998.[45] An 'amendment' with respect to Chapters 3–8 of the Constitution means 'any change of the text of Chapters 3–8 of the Constitutions of the Russian Federation: exclusion, addition, new version or any provision of the said chapters'. Interconnected changes of several articles may be incorporated in a single law introducing the amendments, including consequential changes arising out of the proposed amendment. If a section, chapter, or article is to be eliminated from the Constitution, the resulting official text must specify by which law it was excluded, the date, and the number of the law, the original numbering of the text being preserved. The draft law proposing the amendment must also set out the reasons for the amendment and include a full list of federal constitutional laws and laws which must be repealed, changed, added to, or adopted as a result of the amendment.

The proposal to amend the Constitution is first referred to the State Duma, which considers the draft in committee and then subjects the draft law to three readings. A two-thirds vote in the State Duma of all members is required for adoption. Within five days the adopted law is sent to the Soviet of the Federation for obligatory consideration (in this case the Soviet of the Federation cannot fail to take up

---

[45] СЗ РФ (1998), no 10, item 1146.

the law). A three-quarters majority of all members of the Soviet of the Federation must support the draft law; if the law is defeated, the Soviet of the Federation has the right to propose to the State Duma that a conciliation commission be created to discuss the matter. If the Soviet of the Federation approves the law on the amendment, it must be published within five days for general information and also be sent to the subjects of the Federation for consideration.

The subjects of the Federation have one year from the date of adoption by the Soviet of the Federation to consider the law on the amendment to the Constitution; each subject itself determines the procedure for considering the matter. Once they take a decision on the matter, their decree must be sent within 14 days to the Soviet of the Federation, which keeps a record of how many subjects consider the question and when. At its next regular session after the year's period has elapsed for subjects of the Federation to consider the matter, the Soviet of the Federation determines the results of the consideration in the procedure laid down in its Reglament. Within seven days after the results are determined, the President of the Russian Federation or any subject of the Federation may appeal the decree to the Supreme Court of the Russian Federation, which considers the case in accordance with the Russian Code of Civil Procedure. If no appeal is filed within the seven-day period, the Chairman of the Soviet of the Federation sends the law for signature to the President of the Russian Federation and official publication. Should the Supreme Court of the Russian Federation satisfy the appeal against the decree of the Soviet of the Federation, the Soviet reconsiders the matter at its next regular session.

The President of the Russian Federation has 14 days to sign and officially publish the law on the amendment to the Constitution. Within a month after the law enters into force, the President of the Russian Federation must arrange for the new official publication of the Constitution incorporating the amendment.

If the law on the amendment failed to obtain the necessary approval of two-thirds of the subjects of the Federation within one year, the amendment may not be reproposed to the State Duma until a year has elapsed since the results of the consideration were established by the Soviet of the Federation.

I. Political Parties

One of the major steps taken during the *perestroika* era in transforming Russia into a democratic society was the abolition of the constitutionally enshrined stature of the Communist Party of the Soviet Union as the sole political party (Article 6, 1977 USSR Constitution). The 1993 Russian Constitution provides that 'political diversity and a multi-party system' are recognised in the Russian Federation (Article 13). This provision serves as the pretext for the adoption of the

Federal Law on Political Parties of 11 July 2001, as amended 21 March 2002 and 25 July 2002.[46] Russian citizens also enjoy a constitutional right to association, or not to associate (Article 30), and the freedom of social associations is guaranteed.

The true place of political parties in the Russian political and legal systems remains ambiguous and ambivalent. Literally hundreds of political parties were organised and registered as such in Russia after the Soviet Union disappeared. Many were purely the creation of a handful of individuals and enjoyed neither broad support nor a national base. Most have not commanded deep allegiance from their membership, and have split and merged with bewildering rapidity. In the State Duma affiliation to a political party does influence the internal organisation of work, the distribution of committee assignments, and sometimes voting patterns. Yet the President of the Russian Federation is, as a matter of law, not expected to remain a member of a political party while in office.

Legally speaking, a political party is a 'social association' created for the participation of Russian citizens in the political life of society by means of forming and expressing their political will, participating in social and political actions, elections, and referendums, and to represent their interests in agencies of State power and agencies of local self-government. A political party must satisfy certain requirements: (1) it must have regional divisions in more than half of the subjects of the Russian Federation and may have only one regional division per subject of the Federation; (2) the political party must have not less than 10,000 members in total and at least 100 members in more than half of the regional divisions of the party in subjects of the Federation and not less than 50 members in the remaining subjects of the Federation; and the executive and other organs of the political party, its regional divisions, and other structural subdivisions all must be situated on the territory of the Russian Federation.

Each political party must have a charter and a programme. The newspaper Российская газета is required by the Law on Political Parties (Article 14) to publish notice of the place and date for a political party to hold its constitutive meeting or a congress for a social organisation or social movement to transform itself into a political party at least a month in advance and after the political party is duly founded or transformed, to publish free of charge the basic provisions of each political party programme. The Law on Political Parties introduced a clean-slate

---

[46] СЗ РФ (2001), no 29, item 2950; (2002), no 12, item 1093; no 30, item 3029. Prior to the enactment of this Law, Articles 6 and 9 of the USSR Law on Social Associations were in force with regard to Russian political parties. Ведомости СНД и ВС СССР (1990), no 42, item 839. With regard to the 2001 Law, Article 33 enters into force not later than 1 January 2004, and Article 36(1), two years from the date of entry into force of the Law.

policy, requiring all parties to register anew under the Law in order to continue to have stature as a political party.[47]

The creation of a political party is prohibited whose purposes or actions are directed towards a forcible change of the foundations of the constitutional system and a violation of the integrity of the Russian Federation, subversion of State security, creation of armed or militarised formations, or the incitement of social, racial, nationality, or religious enmity. Political programmes which favour social justness, however, are not to be regarded as inciting social enmity. Nor are political parties permitted which are based on professional, racial, nationality, or religious affiliation, by which is understood an indication in the party charter or programme that the aim is to defend professional, racial, nationality, or religious interests. Nor may a political party consist of persons from a single profession. Moreover, political parties must be organised territorially and may not have structural subdivisions within agencies of State power, agencies of local self-government, the Armed Forces, law enforcement and other State agencies or in State and non-State organisations (excluding representative, or parliamentary, agencies at all levels). Political parties are further prohibited from interfering in the instructional process of educational institutions. Political parties, or structural subdivisions thereof, of foreign States may not be created or operated on the territory of the Russian Federation.

The creation of a political party must meet the legal criteria laid down in the Federal Law on Political Parties. As noted above, there must be either a constitutive congress or an existing social association or movement must decide to transform itself into a political party. No authorisations of agencies of State power are required for such congresses or transformations. The founders of a political party are the delegates who attend the constitutive congress. Preparations for the Congress are made by an organising committee consisting of at least ten persons; the organising committee notifies in written form the federal agency of executive power empowered to register political parties of its intention to create a political party and indicates the proposed name of the party, together with the submission of other information documents. The registering agency issues a formal receipt of the submission, which then serves as the basis for approaching the media about publication of the time and place of the constitutive congress.

Registration may be refused to a political party whose charter is contrary to the Constitution of Russia, federal constitutional laws, the Law on Political Parties, and other federal laws; whose name or symbols do not meet the requirements of

---

[47] Political parties set about securing registration in autumn 2001. For examples of party programmes, see those of the Soiuz Party, My Family Party, and Constitutional Party in Российская газета, 12 January 2002, 15.

the Law on Political Parties; which failed to submit the documents necessary for State registration, or whose submitted documents do not contain the information required by the Law on Political Parties, or which has not submitted the required documents in a timely manner.

Membership of political parties is voluntary and individual, open to citizens who have reached 18 years of age. Foreign citizens and stateless persons, and Russian citizens who have been deemed by a court to lack dispositive legal capacity, may not join political parties, and a Russian citizen may join only one political party, and in that event must be associated with a particular regional subdivision at his place of permanent or preferred residence. It is prohibited to ask whether a citizen is a member of a political party or not (a sharp change of practice from the Soviet era, when, for example, even in a criminal proceeding a defendant was asked whether he was a Party member or not).

Political parties enjoy special legal capacity. They may have in ownership any property needed for its activity as provided by the Law on Political Parties and its own charter. The party as a whole is the owner of the party's property, including the property of its regional divisions and other structural subdivisions. Regional divisions and other registered structural subdivisions have the right of operative management over property consolidated to them by the owner, together with an autonomous balance sheet or estimate. Party members have no rights with respect to the party's property, and the property may be used only to realise the purposes and tasks provided for by the party charter and programme. Regional divisions and other registered structural subdivisions are liable for their obligations with the property at their disposition, and if such property is insufficient to meet obligations, the political party as a whole bears responsibility for them.

Against the background of reported widespread abuses in campaign financing, the Law on Political Parties provides a number of requirements intended to reduce the incidence thereof. Political parties may receive money from entry and membership dues, if the Party charter so provides, means of the federal budget provided in accordance with the Law on Political Parties, donations, proceeds from measures conducted by the political party or divisions and structural subdivisions, revenues from entrepreneurial activity and civil-law transactions, and other proceeds not prohibited by law. A political party may have only one settlement account for the party itself and for its regional divisions and other registered structural subdivisions and such accounts must be in credit organisations registered on the territory of Russia. Any donations from natural and juridical persons must have documentary confirmation and the source of revenues must be specified.

There is an extensive list of prohibited donors to political parties: foreign states, foreign juridical persons, foreign citizens, stateless persons, citizens of Russia under 18 years of age, Russian juridical persons with foreign participation if the foreign equity share exceeds 30 per cent, international organisations and international social movements, agencies of State power and agencies of local self-government, State and municipal organisations, juridical persons having charter capital in which there is State or municipal ownership exceeding 30 per cent, military units, military organisations, law enforcement agencies, philanthropic organisations and religious associations or institutions and organisations thereof, anonymous donors, and juridical persons registered for less than one year before the donation was made. Donations in the prohibited category must be returned to the donor within a month, and if that is impossible, they go to the revenue of the Russian Federation. Limited State financing is available to political parties from the federal budget provided that the party meets certain criteria laid down in the Law on Political Parties.

J. Administrative Law

Administrative law, as law, sat uneasily in the Soviet legal tradition. There was a vast body of administrative legislation which formally regulated the rights, duties, competence, and responsibility of State agencies from top to bottom, the civil service, local self-government, enterprises, institutions, and organisations. These materials constituted, broadly speaking, the lines drawn by the State in its own interest to delimit the jurisdiction of State agencies and officials in managing or administering their respective spheres, the so-called 'vertical' lines of authority within the State system and between the State and non-State entities and natural persons. Administrative law was and remains, accordingly, massive in its presence, even in a market economy, yet amorphous in substance.

Much of what comprises administrative law in Russia has been addressed in other chapters: the role of the State in administering the legal profession and legal institutions, the economy, family relations, the banking system and securities market, labour relations and the civil service, the environment, foreign relations, control and supervision functions, the right of citizens to pursue administrative remedies by applying in an administrative procedure to State agencies and officials, and administrative responsibility for violations dealt with mostly in an extra-judicial manner.

For obvious reasons administrative law is also closely linked with constitutional law addressing the management and administration of constitutional structures, especially the executive branch. This is the role of 'government' in its broadest sense. In a transition to a market economy, much will depend upon the extent to which the scope of administrative law is seen to narrow or even, in some domains, disappear in favour of civil-law relations or purely private behaviour. Administrative justice and concepts of administrative *vires* to which adjudicative measures may be applied are at the nascent stage in Russian legal development and rest uneasily with concepts of jus and lex (see Chapter 3) in the discussion of a rule-of-law State. Although less descriptive than their Soviet predecessors, Russian textbooks on administrative law consist principally of a summary of normative legal acts which define and regulate vertical lines of authority and competence in the Russian administrative system without a general sense of boundaries as to where and when the State should administer, supervise, and control and when it should not.

9

CIVIL LAW

'Civil law' is widely used in several senses. Civil law may refer to Roman law, or to the family of modern legal systems concentrated on the mainland of Europe which has developed on the basis of legal science fashioned after Justinian in the Romano-Germanic universities from the twelfth century, and to the legal systems elsewhere that received the European civilist tradition. In a narrower sense civil law may encompass private law, that is, the branch of law regulating legal relations between natural and juridical persons. In the Soviet legal system civil law was the branch of law regulating 'property and personal nonproperty relations' in a socialist society for the object of creating the material-technical base of communism and in order to satisfy more fully the material and spiritual requirements of citizens. Under a market economy Russian law has dramatically transformed the meaning of civil law to encompass 'the legal status of the participants of civil turnover, the grounds for the origin and the procedure for the effectuation of the right of ownership and other rights to a thing and exclusive rights in the results of intellectual activity', the regulation of contractual and other obligations, and also other property and related non-property relations based on equality, autonomy of will, and the property autonomy of the participants thereof (Article 2(1), Civil Code). Anglo-American law, also rooted in the Roman law, has for historical reasons developed with divisions, concepts, vocabulary, and methods that diverge in many key respects from all of the aforementioned notions of civil law.

A. Historical Background

Reduced to the juridical nub of the matter, one may say that the civil law was the principal battleground after the 1917 October Revolution for achieving or not achieving socialism as conceptualised by the Soviet leadership. The reform of Russian civil law in the late twentieth century and the revival of private law has been directed at reversing much of what was introduced in the Soviet period and modernising the legal system to meet the standards of the twenty-first century.

Early Soviet legislation was largely concerned with eliminating or reshaping pre-existing civil-law relationships. Private ownership of the instruments and means of production gradually was abolished in key sectors of the economy, Church property and large structures were nationalised, inheritance was abolished, obligations under stocks and bonds were annulled, many pre-existing debts were repudiated, authors' rights and patents were monopolised by the State, as were banking, foreign trade, and insurance, and rail, sea, river, and air transport became wholly State-owned. Land, water, forests, and subsoil resources all passed from private hands. For a time, private trade in foodstuffs was forbidden.

Comprehensive as these measures were, they represented neither the total extinction of private rights nor of private property. Actual confiscation of property depended often on the discretion of local authorities, and small enterprises employing as few as five, ten, or 20 employees were allowed to continue. The countryside situation was chaotic; attempts to enforce decrees met with resistance or sabotage, and in many areas traditional patterns of land tenure continued in effect.

Economic collapse in the aftermath of civil strife led the Soviet leadership to introduce the NEP, under which land and the 'commanding heights' of the means of production would remain in State hands, but private commerce would be allowed to operate in small-scale industry and trade and foreign private capital would be encouraged to invest in concessions and joint ventures. In the exchange of goods the State assumed more of a regulatory than a proprietary role, although in some fields it intended to compete with the private sector. The NEP required legal reform and stability. On 22 May 1922 the RSFSR enacted a decree on basic private property rights recognised by the Russian Soviet Republic, ensured by the law and protected by the courts thereof,[1] whose provisions presaged the approach of the impending RSFSR Civil Code. The decree denationalised certain structures and small enterprises, prohibiting further confiscations, and offered some basis for Soviet courts to enforce private rights, even some antedating the 1917 October Revolution. The RSFSR Civil Code followed in a remarkably short time, being confirmed by the VTsIK on 31 October 1922 and entering into force on 1 January 1923.[2] As amended, the 1922 Code remained in force until the 1961 FPCivL and 1963–64 Civil Codes were enacted.

Prepared in the course of four months, the 1922 RSFSR Civil Code drew upon continental European models, including Germany and Switzerland, and a draft Imperial Russian code submitted to the State Duma in 1913. The Soviet civilist A G Goikhbarg had a considerable role in preparing both the 1913 draft and the 1922 Code. The obvious roots of the 1922 Code in Romano-Germanic experience led many Western comparatists to look upon the Soviet legal system as a variant of, but firmly within, the civil law family of legal systems. Lenin was disquieted enough by early drafts of the 1922 Code to remind the draftsmen that they were to apply to 'private law relations, not the *corpus iuris romani*, but our revolutionary concept of law'.

The 1922 Code was divided into four parts. The General Part treated the subjects of rights, transactions, and limitations. This was followed by a Part called the 'law of things' (ownership, buildings, and mortgages or pledge), a Part on the law of obligations, and a brief Part on inheritance. Family law, land tenure, and employer-employee relations were left for separate codification. Among the significant innovations introduced into civil law by the 1922 Code were the general confirmation that pre-revolutionary private rights had been extinguished, and the view that private rights acknowledged by the Code were conditional upon not being exercised contrary to their socio-economic purpose. Notarial control over contracts was extensive, and when State enterprises were involved, many contract provisions became imperative and not subject to negotiation by the parties. A juridical person whose activities were contrary to State interests could be dissolved

---

[1] СУ РСФСР (1922), no 36, item 423.
[2] Transl in V Gsovski, *Soviet Civil Law* (1949) II, 15–235. For the full original Russian text with a major account of its drafting history, see Т Е Novitskaia, Гражданский кодекс РСФСР 1922 года [*Civil Code of the RSFSR of 1922*] (2002).

by the State. Unjust enrichment reverted to the State, especially if obtained in a contract concluded under duress or under extreme necessity. With regard to personal injury, the Code minimised and virtually did away with the element of fault. A variety of other provisions struck a balance between State and individual concerns usually in favour of the State. With the transition to national economic planning and collectivised agriculture, the Civil Code provisions affecting private commerce and rights were overridden by subsequent legislation, often without amending the Code. For a time in the early 1930s civil law seemed destined to be supplanted by economic and administrative law and Plan. State Arbitrazh looked principally to economic policy defined in the Plan when deciding disputes. Courses and textbooks on civil law disappeared and were superseded by courses and texts on economic law.

The 1936 USSR Constitution redressed the balance somewhat in favour of the continued usefulness of civil law. The transition to planning and collectivised agriculture was confirmed, but civil law was seen to have a role to play in regulating the legal relationships of State enterprises and non-State entities. Rights to personal ownership, succession, and intellectual property were affirmed. Economic accountability and legal personality were accepted as durable civil law concepts adaptable to the requirements of a completely socialised economy.[3]

When post-Stalin civil law reforms were debated in the late 1950s, the decision was taken to retain the pre-existing scope of civil legislation and not place the regulation of State enterprises in a separate branch of legal science and regulation.

The early 1960s in Soviet history were postulated to mark the transition of the Soviet Union to a socialist State engaged in the building of communism, and the new generation of civil legislation was duly to reflect this achievement. In 1961 the USSR adopted the FPCivL, followed in 1964 by the RSFSR Civil Code. The preamble to the 1964 Code related the concepts of ownership and obligations in the Code to the planned economy and the task of building communism. Civil legislation was said to have an active role in shaping and developing forms of ownership, strengthening plan and contractual discipline, improving product quality, encouraging individual creativity, and harmonising individual and social interests.

The 1964 Code incorporated and extended the principle of the 1922 Civil Code that civil rights are conditional, that is, they are protected by law except for instances when they are exercised contrary to their purpose in a socialist society building communism. Although chiefly concerned with horizontal relations between citizens and juridical persons, the Code recognised that certain planning or other administrative acts could give rise to civil obligations. Freedom of con-

---

[3] See Gsovski, (n 2 above), II, for details of the principal legislative developments and the chapters on civil law by O S Ioffe for a conceptual account of the period in id (ed), Сорок лет советского права 1917–1957 [*Forty Years of Soviet Law 1917–1957*] (1958).

tract was severely limited. A transaction concluded for a purpose knowingly contrary to the interests of the socialist State and society would be deemed void. State property was largely removed from civil turnover, and personal ownership circumscribed and subordinated to linkages in the realm of social production. Accordingly, personal property could not be used to derive non-labour income. A major portion of the law of obligations addressed contracts between socialist organisations and non-natural persons. The role of interpersonal contracts diminished accordingly. And in the interests of promoting the rules of socialist community life, the 1964 Civil Code incorporated obligations arising as a consequence of saving socialist property; the so-called duty to rescue.

B. Contemporary Civil Law

With the transition to a market economy in the late Soviet era, the Russian Federation enacted a series of laws addressing individual aspects of the civil law: the 1990 Law on Ownership,[4] the 1990 Law on Enterprises and Entrepreneurial Activity, as amended,[5] the 1992 Law on Pledge,[6] the 1992 Law on Insurance,[7] and others. In Spring 1992 the Russian Government took the decision to commence work on the preparation of a new Civil Code. Pending completion of that task, the Russian Federation introduced into force as from 3 August 1992 the 1991 FPCivL,[8] which had failed to enter into force in its own right because of the demise of the Soviet Union before 1 January 1992. Part One of the Russian Civil Code was enacted by the State Duma on 21 October 1994, signed by the President of the Russian Federation on 30 November 1994, and entered into force on 1 January 1995. Part Two of the Code was adopted by the State Duma on 22 December 1995, signed by the President of the Russian Federation on 26 January 1996, and entered into force on 1 March 1996.[9] Part Three of the

---

[4] Ведомости СНД РСФСР (1990), no 30, item 416; transl. in W E Butler, *Basic Legal Documents of the Russian Federation* (1992) 71–88.

[5] Ведомости СНД РСФСР (1990), no 30, item 418; (1992), no 34, item 1966; (1993), no 32, item 1231 and item 1256; САПП РФ (1994), no 52, item 5086; СЗ РФ (2001), no 49, item 4553; translated in Butler (n 4 above) 183–206. The Law was repealed on 21 March 2002. СЗ РФ (2002), no 12, item 1093, with effect from 1 July 2002.

[6] Ведомости СНД и ВС РФ (1992), no 23, item 1239. This Law is still in force insofar as not inconsistent with the Civil Code and 1998 Law on Mortgage.

[7] Ведомости СНД РФ (1993), no 2, item 56; translated in W E Butler and J E Henderson (eds), *Russian Legal Texts* (1998) 501–516. The Law was amended on 31 December 1997 and 17 July 1999 and appears in (1998) III *Sudebnik* 173–187.

[8] Ведомости СНД СССР (1991), no 26, item 733; transl. in W E Butler, *The Fundamental Principles of Civil Legislation of the USSR and Republics* (1994).

[9] There were certain exceptions within Parts One and Two of the Code. Chapter 4 of the Code dealing with juridical persons entered into force on 8 December 1994, the date of official publication of the Code, and Chapter 17 of the Code entered into force in 2001, when a new Land Code of the Russian Federation became effective. The entire Code is translated in W E Butler, *Civil Code of the Russian Federation* (2002).

Code was adopted by the State Duma on 1 November 2001, approved by the Soviet of the Federation on 14 November 2001, signed by the President of the Russian Federation on 26 November 2001, and entered into force on 1 March 2002. The relevant provisions of the 1991 FPCivL and the 1964 RSFSR Civil Code on intellectual property continue to operate, together with any relevant special legislation (individual laws on intellectual property).

The Civil Code is the product of a transition era in Russian law. It drew upon the pre-revolutionary Russian civil law tradition and upon models of continental Europe (chiefly the Netherlands, Italy, and Switzerland) without replicating any of them, and gives occasional evidence of influence of the Anglo-American family of legal systems. Although market-orientated and containing major departures from its Soviet predecessors, the Civil Code also retains many elements of the Soviet era, some for the better and others not. In drafting style the Code is less sophisticated than its European counterparts, yet more direct and accessible to the user. In some respects the available European models are unfortunate for the Russian situation. The classic French and German civil codes are informed by concepts long obsolete, and the Dutch, Italian, and Swiss versions regulate small-scale economies on the far periphery of dynamic legal change in the world of commerce.

The Civil Code is sometimes referred to as the 'grandfather' of all codes, or the 'constitution of the economy', reflecting its absolutely central role as a foundation stone of a market economy. The text of the Code contains several provisions intended to reinforce that status, even though in the hierarchy of sources of Russian law the Civil Code is merely a federal law amongst others and inferior to the 1993 Russian Constitution and to federal constitutional laws. Nevertheless, civil legislation is within the exclusive purview of the Russian Federation (Article 71, Russian Constitution), and the subjects of the Federation do not have the right to legislate in this domain.

The Civil Code does not pretend to be exhaustive. The fundamental nature and generality of its rules confers on the Civil Code its central place in the Russian legal system. The Code expressly provides for the enactment of individual federal laws on certain matters (for example, the Federal Law on Joint-Stock Societies), stipulating that such laws must be in accordance with the Civil Code and that the norms of other civil legislation must be in conformity with the Civil Code. The legislator is not bound by these assertions of supremacy, for the federal law latest in time governs. But these provisions are a marker which it is hoped the legislator will respect in the interests of the symmetry, unity, and cohesiveness of the civil law. It is relevant that when the Civil Code does expressly contemplate additional legislation, it refers in most cases to a law and less often to 'other legal acts'. The reference to future individual federal laws is also an attempt by the draftsmen to foresee the essential components of major civil legislation and reduce the possibility of haphazard spontaneous intrusions by the legislator into the civil law.

The Civil Code is merely a part, however, of 'civil legislation', a new concept encompassing the Code and other federal laws adopted in accordance therewith. Edicts of the President of the Russian Federation, decrees of the Government, and subordinate normative acts of the Central Bank of Russia and of ministries or State committees fall into the category of 'other legal acts'. It is expected that the Russian courts will contribute more actively to the shaping of the civil law. As noted previously (see Chapter 4), published judicial decisions and other forms of judicial practice are coming to be recognised as a source of law. When the courts are not able to rely upon civil legislation, the agreement of the parties, or customs of business turnover, they may have recourse to analogy of lex (the application by a court of legislation regulating similar relations) or to analogy of jus (the general principles and meaning of civil legislation).

It is particularly important for the Anglo-American lawyer to comprehend that the Russian Civil Code is not merely a compilation of particular rules. It rests upon principles and definitions developed in the science or doctrine of Russian civil law and *qua* Code constitutes a system of interrelated norms. The arrangement of the Code can be of decisive importance in understanding how the rules contained in the Code should be applied.

The Russian Civil Code consists of six Sections (Parts One and Two of the Code comprise Sections I–IV; Part Three, Sections V–VI). Section I and III are subdivided into subsections; 12 Chapters are subdivided into §§; and §2 of Chapter 4 is further subdivided into points. Articles of the Code are commonly divided into points with consecutive numbering, and an article which does not contain numbered points may have unnumbered paragraphs. These structural arrangements contain the symmetry and logic of the Code, reflecting the perceived relationship of various legal norms to one another. In this respect Russian civil law is part of the 'Pandectian' heritage, the Code being arranged to work from the general to the particular or, if one chooses to begin somewhere in the middle of the Code, in whichever direction is most instructive. Some find it instructive to imagine that the Code is a ladder on which one descends from the very top rungs of generality to the bottom rungs of the special or the particular. Equally, of course, one may choose to ascend rather than descend, in which case one works from the particular to the general. The key to understanding is that one cannot work with individual articles of the Code in isolation; one must comprehend their relationship to other rungs on the ladder, above and below, and the rationale of the arrangement.

It is sometimes said that Russian law has its own internal logic, dissimilar from continental and Anglo-American legal systems. Foreign users of the Civil Code are likely to find that observation helpful, and are cautioned against drawing analogies with foreign law too quickly before considering the logic of Russian law itself.

C. General Principles

The Civil Code encompasses legal relations which in the Anglo-American legal tradition are disparate and diverse but which in the civilian tradition are part of a larger and single uniformity of relations. These are called 'property relations' (and encompass related personal non-property relations), that is, legal relations related to or connected with ownership and the various forms of its use. The second unifying strand is that property relations are based on the equality of the participants in such relations, equality in the sense of having the same rights to determine by whose will relations may arise, be changed, or be terminated with other participants of civil law relations.

This is not to suggest that participants of civil law relations are necessarily equal in economic power or that all participants of civil law relations have precisely the same amount or extent of rights. Natural persons, for example, may bequeath their property by will, or receive maintenance, or be compensated for harm caused to life or health, whereas juridical persons may not. Contracts may be concluded between powerful corporations and individual citizens.

In a market economy it is imperative that the equal participants of property and non-property relations enjoy freedom of contract and the 'unobstructed effectuation of civil rights' (Article 1(1), Civil Code). This proposition is reinforced by Article 1(2), which provides that natural and juridical persons acquire and effectuate their civil rights 'by their own will and in their own interest'. They are at liberty to establish their rights and duties on the basis of contract and to determine any conditions of a contract which are not contrary to legislation. They also effectuate their civil rights 'at their discretion' (Article 9(1), Civil Code). These provisions and others embody the principle that 'what is not prohibited, is permitted', provided that natural and juridical persons do not violate the limitations lawfully imposed by Russian law.

The Civil Code does not recite exhaustively the principles applicable to civil-law relations. The principle of good faith, for example, is alluded to in several articles of the Civil Code, but also is implicit in Article 1 of the Civil Code, as well as being specified in individual enactments of civil legislation.[10] It is an example of a principle of Russian law [jus] whose full substance is not reduced to legislation.

---

[10] There is a 'presumption of good faith of a juridical person or individual entrepreneur when State control or supervision is conducted' at work as a basic principle for the defence of the rights of juridical persons and individual entrepreneurs. See Article 3, Federal Law on Defence of the Rights of Juridical Persons and Individual Entrepreneurs When Conducting State Control (or Supervision), of 8 August 2001. СЗ РФ (2001), no 33, item 3436. See in general V I Emelianov, Разумность, добросовестность, незлоупотребление гражданскими правами [*Reasonableness, Good Faith, and Nonabuse of Civil Rights*] (2002).

The Civil Code itself contains certain limitations: civil rights must be effectuated so as not to violate the principle of humaneness (Article 137), nor cause harm to the rights and legal interests of other persons (Article 209), nor create a danger of causing harm to other persons (Article 1065), for example. Certain objects may be excluded from civil turnover or alienated only under certain circumstances (Article 129).

Rights may not be abused solely with the intention to cause harm to another person (Article 10(1)), nor as part of unfair competition, nor in general (Article 10(3)) as part of the duty to act in good faith in civil-law relations.

Moreover, the Civil Code contains within it 'imperative' norms which the parties to civil-law relations may not change or avoid by agreement between them. The failure to comply with imperative norms will normally result in unfavourable consequences for the parties, including invalidity of the transaction, penalties, interest, and others. These are to be contrasted with 'dispositive' norms, which become binding upon the parties unless they provide otherwise by agreement. The great majority of norms in the Civil Code are dispositive, affording the participants of civil-law relations a vast panoply of opportunities to distribute duties and risk as they deem desirable (for the formulation of this principle in respect of contracts, see Article 421, Civil Code).

The balance in a Civil Code between imperative and dispositive norms can determine the success or failure of a market economy. In one sense a Civil Code is a 'shell' within which commercial and other entrepreneurial relations subsist. To configure the constraints too tightly is to obstruct human ingenuity and encourage innovators to seek other legal systems for support and protection (the very limited Russian approach to the forms of commercial juridical persons may well have this consequence), whereas to grant excessive latitude may lead to fraud and abuse. In this transition era the Russian Civil Code has on balance probably opted for excessive formality and constraint.

Not regulated by civil legislation are property relations 'based on administrative or other power subordination of one party to another'. Examples are tax, financial, and other administrative relations, unless provided otherwise by legislation (Article 2(3), Civil Code). These are lines more readily drawn in the abstract than in practice. Russia has joined other democratic societies by providing, as a rule, that unlawful actions committed by State agencies and officials, or even by the State itself, in exercising power subordination may be redressed in accordance with the principles and rules of civil legislation.

Reference has been made above to personal non-property rights. These are subdivided by Russian legal doctrine into two categories. The first would be classified by Anglo-American jurisdictions as property rights pure and simple: authors' rights, patents, trademarks, firm name, and others. In the Civil Code they are referred to as 'exclusive rights to the results of intellectual activity'. The second category consists of personal non-property rights not connected by Russian legal doctrine directly with property: the right to life and health, dignity of the person, personal inviolability, honour and good name, business reputation, personal and family secrecy, the right to free movement and choice of place of sojourn and residence, the right to name, the right of authorship, and other 'non-material benefits' which belong to a citizen from birth or are otherwise inalienable (Article 150, Civil Code).

As noted above, the domain and even the very existence of civil law was under threat throughout much of the Soviet era. Proponents of an 'economic code' sought ways to combine the regulation of vertical and horizontal relations within a single legal document. Certain proponents of 'entrepreneurial law' continue to advocate a strong State regulatory role in entrepreneurial relations. Others would segregate the horizontal relations of entrepreneurial activity into a 'commercial' or 'trade' code, which would address only juridical persons and forms of entrepreneurship not requiring the formation of a juridical person (simple partnerships, branches). Although the prospects in Russia for such a code are dim, other independent states are experimenting and are producing official drafts for discussion.

D. Persons

There are two categories of 'persons' under Russian civil law: natural (citizens, foreigners, stateless) and juridical persons. The legal status of natural persons is determined by the provisions of the Russian Civil Code governing legal capacity, that is the general capacity to bear civil rights and duties, which arises at birth and ceases upon death, and dispositive legal capacity, that is the complete acquisition of the right to exercise legal capacity upon attaining legal age (18) or marriage (if earlier), unless limitations have been placed on dispositive legal capacity by reason of mental illness, drug addition, alcoholism, and the like. New and fundamental to the Russian concept of legal capacity is the right of citizens to engage in entrepreneurial activity and any other activity not prohibited by a law and to create juridical persons autonomously or jointly with other citizens and juridical persons, and to select their place of residence. Although the right to one's name has been the object of legislation previously in the late Soviet era, it is treated in detail for the first time in Russian civil legislation (Article 19, Civil Code).

The dispositive legal capacity of minors has been broadened by reducing the age at which a minor may conclude transactions and bear property responsibility autonomously from age 15 to 14. Under certain circumstances minors may be deemed to have reached majority at age 16 by a court or a guardianship and trusteeship agency. A contractual form of trust management for property of persons under wardship has been introduced which should not be confused with the Anglo-American concept of fiduciary trust.

The treatment of juridical persons in the Civil Code bears the strong imprint of the Soviet era. The Civil Code defines a juridical person as an organisation which has 'solitary property' in ownership, economic jurisdiction, or operative management, has an autonomous balance sheet or estimate, and is liable for its obligations with such property and may in its own name acquire and effectuate property and personal non-property rights, bear duties, and be a plaintiff or defendant in court. Neither 'economic jurisdiction' nor 'operative management' are market concepts of ownership, and the existence of an 'autonomous balance sheet or estimate' confuses auditing practices with institutes of ownership.

The Civil Code further distinguishes between commercial and non-commercial organisations, the former pursuing the aim of deriving profit as the principal purpose of their activity. The enumeration of types of juridical person is exhaustive and narrowly based on European models developed for economies whose potential does not begin to match the potential of Russia. Commercial organisations are treated in detail below in Chapter 11.

Each juridical person operates pursuant to its charter and/or other constitutive documents. Legal capacity commences with the State registration of the charter. The juridical person operates under its own name, is liable for its own obligations, and is not liable for the obligations of the State nor of other juridical persons, and vice versa, subject to certain qualifications established by legislation (for example, a parent which causes harm to a subsidiary may be liable for the consequential losses).

The Civil Code refers obliquely to 'a commercial organisation not endowed with the right of ownership to property consolidated to it by the owner' (Article 113). These are so-called unitary enterprises in the ownership of the State or in municipal ownership. Although commercial organisations, they have special legal capacity; their sphere of activity is strictly determined by their charters. A subspecies of the unitary enterprise is the 'treasury enterprise' formed on the basis of property in federal ownership. The treasury enterprise has no real autonomy, reflected in the assumption by the State of subsidiary responsibility for obligations of the enterprise if its property is insufficient (Article 115, Civil Code). Most severely constrained are 'institutions' created by the owner to effectuate management, socio-cultural, or other functions of a non-commercial character and financed by the owner wholly or partially.

General provisions regulating the reorganisation or liquidation of juridical persons, including the grounds for insolvency or bankruptcy, are contained in the Civil Code (Articles 57–65). Reorganisation is a general term embracing several stipulated methods (merger, accession, separation, division, transformation).

Creditors must be notified in the event of a reorganisation, and they have the right to require the termination or performance before time of obligations and compensation for damages rather than to enter into relations of obligation with the legal successors. The detailed procedures for bankruptcy procedures in general and for bankruptcy of credit organisations in particular are regulated by separate federal laws.

In furtherance of the Civil Code individual federal laws have been enacted to regulate individual types of non-commercial organisations: the Law on Social Associations of 19 May 1995, as amended 17 May 1997, 19 July 1998, 12 March 2002, 21 March 2002; and 25 July 2002[11] the Law on Philanthropic Activity and Philanthropic Organisations of 11 August 1995, as amended 21 March 2002 and 25 July 2002[12] the Law on Noncommercial Organisations of 12 January 1996, as amended;[13] and the Law on Trade Unions, Their Rights and Guarantees of Their Activity, adopted 12 January 1996, as amended 25 July 2002.[14]

The place of the State, subjects of the Federation, and municipal formations in civil-law relations is considerably clarified by the Civil Code (Articles 124–127). The general position is that these entities act in relations regulated by civil legislation on equal principles with natural and juridical persons unless it arises otherwise from a law or the peculiarities of the particular subjects. The responsibility of these entities for their obligations is also clarified: they are liable for the property belonging to them by right of ownership unless such property may only be in State ownership or has been consolidated by right of economic jurisdiction or operative management to juridical persons created by them. Execution may be levied against land and other natural resources, however, only to the extent provided for by a law.

E. Objects of Civil Rights

Until the Civil Code was enacted, the types of objects of civil rights could only be determined on the basis of doctrinal writings and judicial practice. Article 128 relegates to the objects of civil rights: things, including money and securities, other property, including property rights; work and services; information, the results of intellectual activity, including exclusive rights thereto; and non-material

---

[11] СЗ РФ (1995), no 21, item 1930; (1997), no 20, item 2231; (1998), no 30, item 3608; (2002), no 11, item 1018; no 12, item 1093; no 30, item 3029.

[12] СЗ РФ (1995), no 33, item 3340; (2002), no 12, item 1093; no 30, item 3029.

[13] СЗ РФ (1996), no 3, item 145; (1998), no 48, item 5849; (1999), no 28, item 3473; (2002), no 12, item 1093.

[14] СЗ РФ (1996), no 3, item 148, as amended by Decree of the Constitutional Court of the RF, 24 January 2002. СЗ РФ (2002), no 7, item 745; no 30, items 3029 and 3033.

benefits. The distinctive aspects of the legal regime are addressed, including the definition of immovable and movable things, the requirement of State registration for an immovable (and things equated to an immovable, such as a vessel or aircraft), and an enterprise.

Russian civil legislation has experienced great difficulties in assimilating advanced market concepts of securities, not least because such concepts have originated in the Anglo-American legal systems. The Civil Code at best attempts to consolidate certain general requirements of securities, including amongst them examples which modern legal systems do not treat as securities (for example, cheques, bills of exchange), and recognises the concept of the 'paperless security' (Article 149).[15]

Although Soviet legislation had recognised and defended certain individual personal non-property rights, the Civil Code elaborates and systematises these, offering a conceptual foundation lacking in earlier enactments. The inalienability of such rights is confirmed. The protection of the honour and dignity of citizens may be effected posthumously. Victims of libel in the mass media may apply directly for judicial relief instead of being required, as previously, to request a retraction before applying to a court.

The lawful actions by which citizens and juridical persons establish, change, or terminate civil rights and duties are called transactions. The Civil Code has not significantly changed the provisions of Soviet law on these matters, but rather clarified certain aspects. Transactions may be unilateral (for example, a will, gift) or bi- or multilateral (for example, a contract). Russian law continues, as did Soviet law, to regulate in detail the form of transactions. In principle transactions may be concluded orally or in writing. If the law imposes no specific form, they may be considered to be concluded if the will to do so is manifest from the conduct of the person. Silence may represent such conduct when the law so provides or by agreement of the parties.

Russian law continues to place great emphasis upon the written form of the transaction, whether in simple written form or with notarial certification. Transactions between juridical persons and between juridical and natural persons must be in writing, as too must be transactions between natural persons for an amount exceeding not less than ten times the minimum amount of payment for labour or those transactions which a law requires must be in writing. Notarial certification is required when a law so provides or when the parties to the transaction so stipulate even though the law does not so require. Failure to comply with the form required by law or stipulated by agreement of the parties will entail the transaction being invalid. A foreign economic transaction which does not comply with the simple written form is also invalid. If a transaction must be in simple written

---

[15] See V A Belov, Бездокументарные ценные бумаги [*Paperless Securities*] (2001).

form, the failure to comply with this form deprives the party in the event of a dispute from referring to witness testimony in confirmation of the transaction and may result in its invalidity.

Certain transactions must be notarially certified, for example, the sale of a dwelling house. In all such cases, failure to comply with this form results in the transaction being void unless a law provides that such a transaction is voidable or provides other consequences for the failure to comply. Additions to, changes in, or amendments to transactions must be in the same form as the principal document, unless they can be characterised as transactions in performance of a contract concluded in written form (Article 159(3)). The failure of a foreign economic transaction to comply with the simple written form makes the transaction invalid (Article 162(3)).

Gone from the 1996 Russian Civil Code are requirements of the Soviet era regarding transactions concluded for a purpose known to be contrary to the interests of the socialist State and society or transactions concluded by a juridical person contrary to the purposes specified in its charter. In their place is a much more limited provision: a transaction concluded for a purpose knowingly contrary to the fundamental principles of legal order or morality is void. Ultra vires transactions are addressed differently in the 1996 Civil Code. If a juridical person concludes a transaction which is contrary to activity specifically limited in its constitutive documents, a court may deem such transaction invalid upon the suit of this juridical person, its founder or participant, or the State agency effectuating control or supervision over the activity of the juridical person if it is proved that the other party to the transaction knew or clearly should have known about the illegality of the transaction. An analogous approach is taken when the powers of a person to conclude a transaction have been limited by a contract or in the case of a juridical person, by its constitutive documents.[16] However, the periods of limitation in such matters are, as a rule, one year.

The periods for the defence of a right upon the suit of a person whose right has been violated (limitations) have been fundamentally reworked. In the Soviet era such limitations were relatively brief (one year) in order to encourage State organisations to defend their rights, and courts were empowered to apply limitations

---

[16] The practice of the International Court of Commercial Arbitration in the Russian Federation includes instances in which the arbitrators have refused to deem a contract invalid which was signed by one member of the Board of Directors instead of two, as was required by the charter of the said joint-stock society. The arbitrators took into account the provisions of the relevant civil legislation, the practice of the joint-stock society itself, and the actions of the parties in performing the contract in coming to that view. The arbitrators observed that if such practices by the joint-stock society caused harm to the society, the officials of the society who caused the violation should bear responsibility to the society for any losses caused. Case No 16, in M G Rozenberg (comp.), Арбитращная Практика За 1996–1997 *gr.* [*Arbitration Practice for 1996–1997*] (1998) 61–62.

irrespective of the request of the parties or against their wish. Consistent with a market economy, the Civil Code has introduced a three-year period of limitation for all participants in civil-law relations and the discretion of a court to apply or reinstate the limitation has been eliminated for juridical persons and restricted with respect to natural persons. Reduced periods of limitations are provided for in the Civil Code for particular claims or demands, and extended periods (ten years) for a suit concerning the application of the consequences of the invalidity of a void transaction.

The debates which have raged for decades among Russian jurists as to the legal consequences of the expiry of periods of limitation have not been put to rest by the Civil Code. There has been no doubt that if a suit is brought and it is discovered that the period of limitation has lapsed, there are grounds for the court refusing to consider the suit any further even though the plaintiff plainly has a right which has been violated by the defendant. The debate arises over whether the expiry of the period of limitation extinguishes the very right which has been violated. One school of thought has argued that with the expiry of the period of limitation the subjective civil right is simultaneously extinguished.[17] Others contend that the subject right is lost only when a court decides to reject the suit on the ground that the period of limitation has lapsed.[18] A third view, and the predominant one, is that the subject right exists and is unaffected by the lapse of the period of limitations; it simply becomes unrealisable in a compulsory judicial or arbitral proceeding.[19] This approach better explains the position taken in Article 206 of the Civil Code, pursuant to which a debtor who performs an obligation in ignorance that the period of limitation has lapsed has no right to demand the return of that which was performed. It further explains how a court may reinstate the period of limitation for justifiable reasons and then examine the subjective civil right concerned; if the right has been extinguished by the lapse of the period of limitation, the court would in effect be both reinstating a period of limitation (which the Civil Code provides may be done) and resuscitating a lost civil right (for which there is no provision in the Civil Code).

---

[17] See, for example, O S Ioffe, Советское гражданское право [*Soviet Civil Law*] (1967) 352–354; V T Smirnov, Iu K Tolstoi, and A K Iurchenko (eds), Советское гражданское право [*Soviet Civil Law*] (1982) I, 207–209.

[18] See V P Gribanov, Пределы осуществления и защиты гражданских прав [Limits of Effectuation and Defence of Civil Rights] (1972) 252–253; S M Korneev, Право государственной собственности [*Right of State Ownership*] (1964) 75.

[19] See I B Novitskii, Сделки. Исковая дагность [*Transactions. Limitations*] (1954) 223; M Ia Kirillova, Исковая давность [*Limitations*] (1966) 24–26; A P Sergeev, in Iu K Tolstoi and A P Sergeev (eds), Гражданское право [*Civil Law*] (4th edn, 1999) I, 305–314.

F. Ownership

The law of ownership has changed fundamentally in the post-Soviet era. The Civil Code has incorporated the reforms of the early 1990s and introduced a number of others. The forms of ownership are laid down in the 1993 Russian Constitution: 'Private, State, municipal, and other forms of ownership shall be equally recognised and defended in the Russian Federation' (Article 8(2)). The term 'private' ownership was thus restored to grace and placed in front as the principal form of ownership. However, the very concept of 'forms of ownership' is a survival of the Soviet past; in a market economy there is no reason why the State or municipal formations should own, possess, use, or dispose of property or property rights on the basis of a form of ownership which differs from other actors in property relations.

The Civil Code introduces so-called 'trust management' (Article 209(4)) as a variation of the long-established Soviet principle of 'operative management' and elaborates the contract of trust management in Articles 1012–1026. Under this concept the owner of property may transfer his property in trust management to a trust manager, who is obliged to manage the property in the interests of the owner or a third person specified by him and who does not while acting as trust manager have the right of ownership over the property. The obligatory requisites of a contract of trust management are several: the contract must specify the composition of the property being transferred on trust management; the name of the juridical or natural person who is the beneficiary; the amount and form of remuneration to be paid to the trust manager, if such is to be paid; and the period of operation of the contract (the maximum term is five years). The relationships are of a contractual character and lack any fiduciary element so central to the Anglo-American concept of trust. Although trust management will have little appeal to the foreign investor, the guarantees of the content of the right of ownership laid down in Article 209(2) would appear to give considerable scope for fashioning trust ownership relations with a fiduciary component along the lines of the Presidential Edict on Trust Ownership of 24 December 1993[20] or taking advantage of long-established trust relations based on foreign law. That scope, though, may be reduced by departmental enactments introduced in contravention of the Civil Code with a view to regulating trust management contracts. An example is the Statute on the Trust Management of Securities and Means of Investing in

---

[20] САПП РФ (1993), no 1, item 6. Although some Russian jurists believe this Edict was superseded by Part One of the Civil Code provisions on trust management, they are two quite different legal concepts and institutions. In my view, it would be incorrect to construe the Civil Code as superseding the Edict of 24 December 1993, which has not been repealed.

Securities, confirmed by the Federal Commission for the Securities Market by Decree No 38 on 17 October 1997.[21]

The restoration of private ownership in Russia is legally speaking most dramatically expressed in the elimination of the terminology of 'personal' ownership and the various limitations associated with it. The magnitude of the change is simply and directly expressed in the Civil Code: 'any property' may be in the ownership of natural and juridical persons, except for individual types of property which in accordance with a law may not belong to natural or juridical persons. Rather than singling out and enumerating those items which may belong to individuals by personal ownership, the equation has been completely reversed; those items which may not be in private ownership must be enumerated. Any foreign investor must bear in mind that property in State or municipal ownership which was transferred to natural or juridical persons in ownership by way of privatisation may be subject to conditions of acquisition or termination laid down in privatisation legislation. In that event privatisation legislation prevails over the Civil Code. The Code also addresses for the first time the initial acquisition of property, including by way of creating, collecting, catching, or otherwise obtaining it.

There are in addition to full ownership, or title, rights to a thing recognised for non-owners. The Civil Code enumerates five and stipulates that the transfer of the right of ownership in property to another person does not terminate the other rights to a thing in such property: the right of inheritable possession for life of a land plot; the right of permanent or perpetual use of a land plot; servitudes; economic jurisdiction; and operative management. These rights may be defended against a violation by any person pursuant to Articles 301–305 of the Civil Code.

Accent on private ownership also is present in the provisions regulating found things, treasure trove, and neglected livestock or other stray domestic animals. In the past if the owner could not be found they passed into State ownership. Now they pass to the persons most closely connected with their discovery or location, and amounts of compensation have been significantly increased. The provisions on inheritance create eight priorities partly in order to reduce the incidence of escheat to the State.

The ownership of land is regulated by the 1993 Russian Constitution, Chapter 17 of the Civil Code, and the 2001 Land Code of the Russian Federation. The basic principle is that persons having a land plot in ownership have the right to sell, give, pledge, lease out, or otherwise alienate or dispose of their land except insofar as such land has been excluded from or limited in turnover. In Russia the land classified as being of agricultural designation is effectively limited in turnover so long

---

[21] See the Russian text in Вестник федеральной комиссии по рынку ценных бумаг [*Herald of the Federal Securities Commission*], no 8(13) (5 November 1997) 13–19.

as any owner of such land must use it for the designated purpose. Under the 2001 Land Code, the redistribution of land in federal or other State or municipal ownership will be the next order of business on the privatisation agenda of the Russian Federation and its subjects.

The transition to a market economy has required elaboration of the grounds upon which the right of ownership may be terminated. Depending upon context, the word for 'seizure' and 'withdrawal' in Russian may be the same; if the State, for example, is taking back a land plot in its ownership but allocated for construction of a dwelling house, one would speak of 'withdrawal'. However, if the State is taking property compulsorily which is entirely in the ownership of another, one would speak of seizure. The Civil Code introduces an exhaustive list of instances under which the right of an owner to property may be terminated. There are at least 13 instances, each cross-referenced to another article of the Civil Code. In most cases the compulsory taking of property must be based on a court decision and with payment of compensation. An exception is requisition, recognised to be an extraordinary situation, but whose constitutionality must be doubtful in light of Article 35 of the 1993 Russian Constitution. Nationalisation is recognised to be one such means, in which event the value of the property and other losses is subject to compensation.

The failure to complete a full transition to a market economy is evidenced by the continued presence in the Civil Code of the right of economic jurisdiction and the right of operative management. However, the Code clarifies the circumstances and conditions under which property held thus may be transferred to others.

G. Obligations

The greater part of the Russian Civil Code is devoted to the law of obligations, what in Anglo-American law is roughly encompassed by the law of contract and tort. Since during the Soviet period the greater portion of the law of contract concerned socialist organisations and not natural persons or private juridical persons, the task of the 1996 Civil Code has been to eliminate the 'statist' inclinations of the previous civil law and strike a proper balance between the equal rights of the participants of civil-law relations.[22]

---

[22] The 'institute of freedom of contract received a new life and intensive development with the transition to a market economy. Under these conditions contract completely supplants other acts of individual regulation, such as the planning task, planned distribution of property valuables, centralized formation of the conditions of a contract; for example, prices for which goods, work, and services are realized. Contract under a transition to a market economy becomes in the sphere of civil turnover the principal legal fact. All goods-money links are effectuated on a contractual basis. Contract becomes the principal regulator of economic relations. It is precisely when concluding a contract that the participants thereof establish the conditions on which they structure their relations with regard to the realization of goods, fulfilment of work, and rendering of services'. V F Iakovlev, Россия: экономика, гращданское право [*Russia: Economy, Civil Law*] (2000) 41.

By virtue of an obligation one person, often called the debtor because he owes the performance of an obligation, is obliged to perform to the benefit of another, often called the creditor because he is owed the performance of the obligation, a determined action. Such an action may be to transfer property, to perform work, to pay money, to refrain from a certain action, and others. The creditor in turn has the right to demand from the debtor the performance of his duty. A contract is but one form of an obligation. The causing of harm may give rise to obligations too (to pay compensation, make amends), and so may other grounds specified in the Civil Code.

It follows that in any particular contract, for example, each party is a debtor with respect to certain matters and a creditor with respect to others. One party may be obliged to perform work, and is a debtor in this respect, whereas once the work is performed he has the right to receive remuneration, and is a creditor in this respect (Article 308(2), Civil Code). The Code provides imperatively that an obligation may not create duties for third persons.

The general rule of Russian law is that obligations must be performed duly in accordance with the conditions of the obligation and the requirements of a law and other legal acts, and if such conditions and requirements are absent, in accordance with the customs of business turnover and other usually presented requirements. Unless a law provides otherwise, the unilateral refusal to perform an obligation is not permitted (Article 310). However, a new exception has been introduced for entrepreneurs, who are permitted to provide for unilateral refusal by contract unless it follows otherwise from a law or from the essence of the obligation.

Securing performance of obligations

The transition to a market economy has caused Russian jurists to re-examine fundamentally the means for securing the performance of obligations. On the whole, Russian law continues to insist upon the specific performance of obligations. The Anglo-American concept of liquidated damages for non-performance of a contractual obligation does not exist in Russian law. Neither is assignment regarded as a means of securing performance, although in Western commercial practice assignment often is used to this end and the Russian Civil Code does not prohibit it. The Civil Code enumerates seven means of securing the performance of obligations and does not regard the list as exhaustive.

Perhaps the most widely used means of securing performance in Russian law is not recognised in most Anglo-American jurisdictions: penalties, fines, and forfeits stipulated in a contract, usually as a percentage of the value of the contract to be recovered for each day, week, or month of delay, and not substituting for specific performance. New to the Civil Code is withholding of property from the debtor under circumstances when the property of the debtor is temporarily in the possession of the creditor (keeping, carriage, commission agency, and others). Suretyship has been long established in Russian law as a means of securing performance, and has been extended in the Civil Code to embrace future obligations as well as existing. The bank guarantee is new and is expressly not a derivative obligation (Russian law provides that the invalidity of the principal obligation shall entail the invalidity of the obligation securing it unless a law provides otherwise). A bank guarantee may therefore be irrevocable if so stipulated.

Most revolutionary, however, is pledge as a means of securing performance.[23] Included in the civil codes of the Soviet era, by all accounts pledge was rarely used during the socialist period. In the transition to a market economy, pledge is an instrument whereby the owners of property may deploy their assets in order to increase their capital; project finance is but one extensively employed mechanism for doing so. Of all the means for securing performance, only pledge is the subject of special legislation at the level of a law in addition to the provisions of Chapter 23 of the Civil Code: the 1992 Law on Pledge, and the 1998 Law on Mortgage (or Pledge of Immoveable), as amended 9 November 2001 and 11 February 2002.[24] Presidential edicts and governmental decrees regulate individual aspects of pledge and mortgage. The basic approach taken in Russian legislation is to distinguish between rules of general applicability to all pledges and special rules applicable to immovable property or things equated thereto (mortgage) or routine transfers of possession (pawn). Distinctions accordingly are drawn between pledge (залог), mortgage (ипотека), and pawn (заклад), the last being the usual situation of a licensed pawnbroker taking possession of the object being pledged. Although the Civil Code brings greater clarity to the relationship between mortgaged buildings and structures and the land plots on which they are sited and to the procedure for levying execution against property, inflexibility relating to the realisation of pledged property by public sale serves as a strong deterrent to project finance, finance lease, and other modern financial structures.

Assignment

In Western market economies, assignment plays major multiple roles in financial structures. The terminology of 'transfer' has been applied in the Civil Code to encompass both assignment of a right of demand belonging to a creditor on the basis of an obligation or the passing of rights of a creditor to other persons in instances provided for by a law (as a result of inheritance, the reorganisation of a juridical person, on the basis of a judicial decision, and others). The parties are at liberty to determine the amount of rights of a creditor, including future rights,

---

[23] A A Rubanov, 'Pledge in the Civil Code of Russia', *Sudebnik* I (1996), 415–448.
[24] СЗ РФ (1998), no 29, item 3400; (2001), no 46, item 4308; (2002), no 7, item 629.

passing to another person, under what conditions, including rights securing the performance of the obligation. The debtor to an obligation is not required to perform the obligation to a new creditor by way of transfer until evidence is provided which confirms the transfer of the rights under the obligation. Transfer of debt (in the sense of the law of obligations) remains as before: it is an imperative rule that the consent of the creditor is required.

Violation of obligations

Although the rules regulating responsibility for violation of obligations are predominantly dispositive, the Civil Code has significantly strengthened the relevant provisions. The basic principle is that a debtor is obliged to compensate a creditor for losses caused by the failure to perform or by the improper performance of an obligation. 'Losses' encompass the expenses which the person whose right has been violated made or must make in order to restore the right violated, the loss or damage of his property (real damage), revenues not received which this person who suffered loss would have received under ordinary conditions of civil turnover if his right had not been violated. The last type of loss is called 'lost advantage', which is rather broader than the concept of 'lost profits', although such profits would be included in lost advantage. If a penalty has been established for failure to perform or improper performance, losses are compensated in the part not covered by the penalty; however, the parties may require that only recovery of a penalty is permitted but not of losses, or that losses may be recovered in full above the penalty, or that at the choice of the creditor either one or the other may be recovered.

The grounds for responsibility for a violation of an obligation continue to be based on fault, whether intentional or negligent, unless provided otherwise by the contract or by a law. The criteria for the absence of fault are for the first time set out in detail but differ for an entrepreneur, who is excused from responsibility only if proper performance was impossible for reasons of insuperable force. As part of the move away from the Planned Economy, the Civil Code permits a debtor to pay compensation for losses and a penalty in lieu of specific performance unless provided otherwise by the contract, thereby reversing the presumption of a State-dominated economy.

Termination of obligations

Obligations terminate on the grounds provided for by the Civil Code, other laws, other legal acts, or contract. Unilateral termination is permitted only when a law or the contract so stipulates. The Civil Code formally introduces several grounds for termination unknown to Soviet law: release-money, novation, forgiveness of debt. The line between assignment and novation can sometimes be difficult to draw and requires close analysis under the Civil Code. These had been impossible in a Planned Economy, for otherwise State enterprises would have been able to evade their planned obligations at their discretion. It is still conceivable that the performance of an obligation may become impossible by virtue of the act of a State agency, in which event the parties who incurred losses have the right to demand compensation for such.

Law of contract

The General Provisions on Contract contained in the Civil Code represent the most dramatic departures from the 1964 RSFSR Civil Code and steps toward a market economy. They also reflect practices commonplace to continental European civil-law systems but unusual in the eyes of Anglo-American lawyers. A contract under Russian law is predicated upon 'agreement' of the parties (not 'promise') concerning the 'establishment, change, or termination' of civil rights and duties and, if the law so requires, reduced to written form and appropriately signed and notarised. As has been noted, Russian law does place considerable stress in comparison with Anglo-American law upon requiring a contract to be in written form and notarially certified, either when the contract value exceeds a certain formula or when a particular object is the subject of the contract.

Freedom of contract

The principle of freedom of contract proclaimed in Article 1 of the Civil Code is elaborated in Article 421. Citizens and juridical persons are free to conclude contracts which are or are not provided for by a law or other legal acts. A contract may contain elements of various contracts provided for by a law or legal acts (mixed contract), and the conditions of all contracts are determined at the discretion of the parties unless the content of the respective condition has been prescribed by a law or other legal acts. When the condition of a contract has not been determined by the parties or by a dispositive norm, recourse is made to the customs of business turnover, if any, applicable to the relations of the parties. The conditions of any contract are subject to the imperative rules of law in force at the time the contract was concluded. If a law is adopted, and here the Civil Code has in view formal statutory law (lex) of the highest order (закон), which contains rules binding upon the parties that differ from those of the past when the contract was concluded, the provisions of the contract remain valid and in force unless the law stipulates expressly that its operation extends to relations which arose from contracts previously concluded. What the Civil Code does not address is a change in law (jus, право), and its potential impact of contracts concluded in the past.

The Civil Code presupposes that a contract is for compensation unless it arises otherwise from a law, other legal acts, or the content or essence of the contract. Therefore, if price is not provided for in the contract, performance is to be compensated at the price which under comparable circumstances is usually recovered for analogous goods, work, or services. The public contract is reserved for commercial organisations who provide goods, perform work, or render services for everyone who has recourse to it (public transport, communications services, electric power supply, and others); such organisations may not refuse to conclude a public contract nor to prefer some persons to others.

Preliminary contract

The Civil Code retains the concept of 'preliminary contract' introduced in the 1991 FPCivL.[25] Under such a contract the parties are obliged to conclude in future a contract concerning the transfer of property, fulfilment of work, or rendering of services on the conditions provided for by the preliminary contract. If a party which has concluded a preliminary contract evades concluding the principal contract, the other party has the right to apply to a court to compel the principal contract to be concluded and compensation of losses. It is accepted in Russian legal doctrine that the conclusion of a preliminary contract is a volitional and explicit act; a memorandum of understanding or a protocol of intent, unless expressly characterised to be a preliminary contract and meeting the full requirements of the Civil Code, would not be construed to be a preliminary contract. The recognition of preliminary contracts means that Russian law retains the category of 'precontractual disputes' (Article 446, Civil Code) under which a court determines what the contractual provisions should be if the parties are unable to do so.

A contract is considered to be concluded when agreement regarding all the material conditions of the contract has been reached in the form required. Material conditions are those concerning the subject of the contract, or those specified in a law or other legal acts as being material or necessary for a contract of the particular type, and all conditions which one of the parties states to be material. The Civil Code recognises counter-party contracts concluded by various modern means of communications which enable it to be reliably established that the document emanates from a party to the contract.

Change or dissolution of contract

The Civil Code has introduced more stringent requirements for the change or dissolution of a contract. Such is possible by agreement of the parties or, under circumstances of a material violation of the contract by the other party, by decision of a court upon the demand of one of the parties. 'Material' violation is one which

---

[25] The 1964 RSFSR Civil Code contained no reference to preliminary contracts, which modern commentators regarded as a 'gap' in the Code; the 1922 RSFSR Civil Code had no general norms on the subject but did include two special rules relating to future purchase-sale contracts and loans. Pre-revolutionary Russian judicial practice expressly rejected the preliminary contract. See M I Braginskii and V V Vitrianskii, Договорное право. Общие положения [*Law of Contract. General Provisions*] (1997) 184–185.

entails such damage that the victim party is deprived in significant degree of that which it had the right to count on when concluding the contract. This is to be distinguished from another ground for change or dissolution of a contract, namely, material change of circumstances. In this context 'material' refers to circumstances which have changed such that if the parties could reasonably have foreseen this, they would not have concluded the contract at all or it would have been concluded on significantly differing conditions. If the court is persuaded that the changed circumstances were material, it will dissolve the contract, bearing in mind, however, whether dissolution of the contract would be contrary to 'social interests' or would entail damages for the parties which significantly exceeded those expenditures required to perform the contract on the conditions changed by the court.

Purchase-sale

A large portion of the Civil Code (Chapters 30–49, 51–55, and 58) is devoted to individual types of contracts.[26] The contract of purchase-sale is retained and subdivided into general provisions on the subject and seven particular types of purchase-sale contract: retail, delivery of goods, delivery of goods for State needs, agricultural procurement, electric power supply, immoveable, and enterprise. The single essential condition of a purchase-sale contract is the subject of the contract. The particular types of purchase-sale contract require additional conditions to be explicitly agreed.

The Civil Code proceeds from the principle that the seller has strict responsibility for the quality of the goods unless the contract imposes special quality requirements. The legal minimum is that the seller guarantees to the purchaser at the moment of transfer of the goods that the goods conform to the quality specified in the contract or determined by the purposes for which such goods are to be used and that the said goods will be fit for such use or purposes 'for a reasonable period'. If it is proved that the defects of the goods arose before they were transferred to the purchaser or for reasons which arose before such transfer, the seller bears strict responsibility for those defects. The seller may not rely upon the latent nature of the defects, nor upon the absence of fault, nor upon the fact such defects were clearly obvious to the purchaser, nor upon the fault of its suppliers, nor upon any other grounds. If the seller offers its own guarantee, the matter becomes more complex, for the goods must retain their proper qualities throughout the entire guarantee period and the seller, in order to be free from responsibility, must show that those defects arose after the goods were transferred to the purchaser either because the rules for use of the goods were violated or they were stored improperly, or that third persons caused the defects, or that circumstances of insuperable force were present.

---

[26] These are analysed in detail by B D Zavidov, Договорное право России [*Contract Law of Russia*] (1998).

Barter

Barter has been extensively used in the post-Soviet era, partly to cope with currency regulations of the Russian Federation. The Civil Code provisions address the procedure for compensation when the prices for the goods to be exchanged differ, the precise moment of the transfer of ownership to such goods, and the obligations of mutual performance. Special governmental regulations exist with respect to foreign economic barter transactions which substantially elaborate the Civil Code requirements.

Gift

Gift is regulated in much greater detail than in the Soviet era. The definition has been broadened from tangibles to incorporate the transfer of property rights without compensation or the forgiveness of a property or financial obligation. Gifts between juridical persons are prohibited in principle, although purely nominal amounts are ignored. A contract for a future gift is recognised provided that it satisfies the conditions of the Civil Code. Gifts may be revoked or cancelled if the donee commits actions against the donor or his relatives, or if valuable gifts are improperly treated, or if bankruptcy or insolvency rules were violated by the gift.

Rent

In the Soviet era provision was made in the RSFSR Civil Code for the possibility of lifetime support in exchange for the sale of a dwelling house. This possibility has been greatly enhanced in the Civil Code, the monetary or material support being called 'rent'. In fact the Civil Code contemplates four different types of rent relationship and no longer links them to indigence or life maintenance. Contracts of this nature are strictly regulated as to form, registration, and obligatory notarisation. When rent is linked with the alienation of immoveable property, the rent acts as an encumberment which passes to the new owner, with the previous owner continuing to have subsidiary responsibility if the new owner refuses or otherwise fails to pay. Moreover, in this instance a pledge is imposed by law in favour of the rent recipient with respect to the immoveable property. Other forms of guarantee must be incorporated in the contract of rent itself. Interest is payable if rent payments are delayed.

Lease

There are four different words used in the Civil Code for variants of leasing: the lease, rental, finance lease, and hire; in substance these terms also encompass the charter as a form of lease. In the late Soviet era leasing came for a time to be viewed as a possible alternative to privatisation of State property. Each lease relationship has its peculiarities, which in each case need to be read against the general provisions on lease, and, especially with respect to finance leasing, other legislative acts.

Finance leasing is the subject of a special Federal Law on Finance Lease (Finance Leasing) of 29 October 1998, as comprehensively amended 29 January 2002,[27] which greatly elaborate the Civil Code provisions.

Uncompensated use

Uncompensated use, in effect a form of loaning property for use, is the object of a separate contract. Commercial organisations, however, may not use this contract to transfer property for use to founders, participants, managers, or members of management organs. The lender is liable for defects of a thing which he intentionally or through gross negligence failed to stipulate when concluding the contract. Risk of accidental loss usually rests with the lender unless the loan recipient used the thing not in accordance with the contract or the designation of the thing or transferred it to a third person without the lender's consent. If harm is caused to a third person as a result of use of the thing, the lender is liable unless it is proved that the harm was caused as a consequence of the intent or gross negligence of the loan recipient or person with whom the thing is situated with the lender's consent.

Independent work

Extensively used in Russian contractual practice is the independent work contract. It differs from the ordinary contract for the performance of services by linking the work performed with a clearly defined physical result to be obtained by the customer. The Civil Code recognises four distinct types of independent work contract: domestic independent work, construction independent work, the fulfilment of design and survey work, and independent work for State needs. Excluded from this category, and treated separately, are contracts for the fulfilment of scientific research, experimental construction design, and technological work. In all cases the overall approach to these contracts contains elements of the former planned economy represented, for example, in the approach to pricing work, the role of the budget, the work practices associated with this type of contract, and the continued role of subordinate legislation, much of it dating from the Soviet era. For foreign investors this civil-law contract often is an attractive alternative to the conclusion of labour contracts with Russian citizens.

Compensated rendering of services

Although the Civil Code contains a number of chapters which regulate services (carriage, transport expediting, keeping, commission, commission agency, agency,

---

[27] СЗ РФ (1998), no 44, item 5394; (2002), no 5, item 376.

and others), services relatively new to the Russian economy by reason of the transition to a market economy are caught up generally under the Contract for the Compensated Rendering of Services. These services expressly include communications, medical, veterinary, auditing, consulting, informational, teaching, and tourist services, but the list is not exhaustive. The basic principle is that the customer is obliged to pay for services rendered to him as provided in the contract; that if performance is impossible through the fault of the customer, the services are subject to payment in full unless provided otherwise by a law or by the contract; that if performance is impossible through circumstances for which neither party is liable, the customer shall compensate those expenses actually incurred by the executor of the services unless provided otherwise by a law or by the contract; that the customer may refuse performance of the contract on condition of payment to the executor of expenses actually incurred by him; and that if the executor unilaterally refuses to perform, full compensation of losses must be paid to the customer. The Civil Code offers no definition of 'expenses actually incurred', which may differ greatly in principle and concept from one profession or service to another. Contracts for auditing and legal services commonly fall under this classification.

Carriage

Following long-standing Russian tradition in the pre-revolutionary and Soviet periods, the Civil Code contains basic provisions on carriage, leaving to individual Codes the detailed regulation of types of particular transport (1999 Merchant Shipping Code of the Russian Federation; 1997 Air Code of Russia; 2001 Code of Internal Water Transport, and others). The major departure from the Soviet period is the requirement that the carriage of goods, passengers, and baggage by whatever form of transport must be based on a contract (and no longer planning orders or other administrative acts).[28] While the Code contains limitations of carrier responsibility for loss or damage to freight or baggage, such limitation may not be imposed for death or injury to a passenger, except that increased responsibility above the rules contained in the Civil Code generally may be provided for by a law or by the contract of carriage. The provisions on the transport expediting contract are principally concerned with the responsibility of the expeditor.

Loan and credit

The contracts of loan, credit, and goods and commercial credit are regulated in a single Chapter of the Civil Code within three sections. The general provisions on credit obligations are set out in the section on the contract of loan, subject to exceptions in the remaining two sections. Any contract of loan for an amount

---

[28] See V Moudrykh, 'Insurance Protection on Russian Transport', *Sudebnik*, VI (2001), 598–685.

exceeding five times the average amount of monthly payment for labour is pre-supposed to be interest-bearing. If the contract fails to stipulate the amount of interest, the Civil Code requires that the bank rate be applied. The same rate applies to overdue loans unless provided otherwise by the contract of a law. Loans which result under stipulated conditions in a bill of exchange being issued for the amounts due are then governed by bill of exchange legislation. Pursuant to Article 75 of the 1993 Russian Constitution and Article 124 of the Civil Code, provision also is made for the Contract of State Loan in which the borrower is the Russian Federation or a subject of the Federation, and the lender is a citizen or juridical person. Such loans are voluntary and the conditions of the loan, once issued, may not be changed.

A credit contract expresses the obligation of a bank or other credit organisation to provide credit to the borrower in the future. The creditor may refuse to provide the credit when there are circumstances obviously testifying to the fact that the amount to be provided cannot be repaid on time, and the borrower may refuse to draw down upon a credit for any reason having given due notice. The Code does not determine precisely the moment when a credit is provided or deemed to be provided, however. If the credit were available for draw-down immediately upon conclusion of the credit contract, the credit contract would amount to what Anglo-American practice understands as a credit facility, payment for which may or may not commence from that moment. Russian law has attached importance to the opening of a credit account in the name of the borrower, to the actual trans-fer of means to the borrower, or to the transfer of means to a creditor of the bor-rower. Russian judicial practice has understood an oral instruction from a borrower to change the destination of borrowed means from his own name to that of a third person not as a change of the credit contract, but as an action taken in performance of the contract which need not comply with the formalities of a change of contract. Given these considerations, whether a credit contract should be subject to challenge for impecuniousness is open to question.

Financing under assignment of monetary demand

Factoring has been introduced into Russian law under the expression 'financing under assignment of monetary demand'. The provisions are consistent with inter-national practice and include a prohibition against the assignment by a creditor of its rights to a finance agent.

Bank deposit

Banking is in the process of far-reaching market transitions in Russia, of which the provisions on bank deposit, bank account, and settlement of accounts are a major stage. The contract of bank account concluded with a natural person is a public contract and must be concluded by the bank on the same terms with all depositors;

the same is not true of juridical persons. If a person accepts a deposit from a natural person and does not have the right to do so, or in violation of the law or banking rules applicable, the depositor has a statutory right to demand return of the deposit with interest as laid down by the Civil Code and compensation of all losses. In the case of a juridical person the contract of deposit is invalid. The contract of bank deposit must be in written form, which is satisfied if the savings deposit book, savings or deposit certificate, or other document has been issued which records the deposit. The Civil Code permits demand and time deposits. Banks are required to secure the return of deposits of natural persons by obligatory insurance and other means; such security with respect to deposits of juridical persons is determined by the contract of bank deposit. Savings or deposit certificates, both bearer and inscribed, are used extensively in Russia.

Bank account

In the Soviet era the content of the contract of bank account was dictated by instructions of the State Bank of the USSR. The intention of the Civil Code is to relax the level of statutory regulation of such accounts, affording to clients and banks the opportunity to negotiate individual arrangements, while maintaining necessary minimum standards in order to protect bank clients. An important clause in the transition to the market economy is that providing that the bank does not have the right to determine and control the orientations of use of the client's money nor establish other limitations on the client's right to dispose of his monetary means at his discretion that are not provided for by a law or by the contract of bank account itself. A bank may not refuse to open an account except in instances expressly provided for by the Civil Code. Unless the contract provides otherwise, the bank must make available to the client the entire range of operations associated with a bank account, and maximum periods are provided for transferring funds to the client's account and performing client instructions. Interest is usually payable on monetary means in the client's account.

Funds may be withdrawn from a bank account on the order of the client or on the basis of a judicial decision or in other instances provided for by the contract of bank account. In the case of juridical persons it has been common for the State tax and other agencies to attach bank accounts, and equally for many financial transactions to pledge bank accounts, accounts receivable, and future revenues. Under the 1964 RSFSR Code of Civil Procedure only monetary means actually received in a bank account are in the ownership of the client which opened the account.

In the short life of the Civil Code no provision has been more controversial than that establishing the priority for the withdrawal of monetary means when there are insufficient funds (Article 855). Three amendments have been introduced into the Article and the Constitutional Court has been obliged to rule on the constitutionality of State Duma enactments with regard to the issue.[29] In first priority are documents of execution concerning compensation for harm caused to life or health and alimony demands; in third priority are settlements regarding the payment of severance benefits and payment for labour to persons under the various forms of labour and author's contracts. Social security and insurance payments fall into the third priority, and taxes into the fourth.

Settlement of accounts

The settlement of accounts remains a major problem in Russia's underdeveloped financial system. Although natural persons who are not entrepreneurs may settle accounts in cash, individual entrepreneurs and juridical persons must have recourse to a non-cash procedure through banks and other credit organisations. Those procedures are inefficient and routinely delay payment for weeks to months. The Civil Code lays down general rules regulating settlement and then details regulation of four forms: payment orders, letters of credit, encashment, and cheque. The system of cheques bears little resemblance to the personal banking services in the West. Payment orders are the most extensively used form of settlement: the bank is required to withdraw means from the client account, send the monies to the account of the recipient, and ensure that the monies are deposited in the recipient's account. The bank is responsible for damages caused by a violation and liable to pay interest at the bank rate for the period of delay in fulfilment of the payment order; the precise scope of damages payable remains the subject of judicial development. The regulation of letters of credit, encashment, and cheque is based principally on international commercial practices.

Keeping

The traditional contract of keeping in the Soviet era was concluded by natural persons who checked luggage or a hat. In the Civil Code this contract has been orientated towards the commercial storage of goods and the financial opportunities presented by warehouse receipts. Three types of warehouse document are recognised: dual warehouse certificate, simple warehouse certificate, and warehouse receipt. The first two are classified as securities, and the dual warehouse receipt actually consists of two separable parts: the warehouse certificate and the pledge certificate or warrant. It is relatively simple to pledge the goods being stored by pledging the dual or simple warehouse certificate. The holder of a warehouse certificate separated from the pledge certificate has the right to dispose of the goods in keeping but may not remove them from the warehouse until the credit issued under the pledge certificate has been paid. Both certificates may be transferred together or separately under endorsement.

---

[29] For the amendments and the text of the decision of the Constitutional Court, see W E Butler (ed and transl), *Russian Civil Legislation* (1999) 577–591.

Insurance

Insurance is regulated by the Civil Code and by the Law of the Russian Federation on Insurance, adopted 27 November 1992, as amended 31 December 1997, 11 December 1999, and 21 March 2002. Under the Civil Code two types of insurance are recognised: personal and property. Insurance of civil responsibility is classified as a species of property insurance, although the Law on Insurance considers it to be an independent form of insurance. As the market economy develops in Russia, new types of insurance are being introduced, including the insurance of entrepreneurial risk. Certain interests may not be insured. These include 'unlawful interests', the insurance of losses from participation in games, lotteries, and betting, or expenses which one may be forced to make in order to liberate hostages. It is possible to insure the risk of contractual liability arising from one's own violation when a law so provides; it is on this basis that a bank may insure itself against claims arising from the failure to return deposits made by natural persons.

Commission

In three separate chapters the Civil Code deals with contracts of commission, commission agency, and agency. Under the contract of commission the principal charges his representative, called in this instance an attorney, using the word in its classical English meaning, to perform in the name of and at the expense of the principal specified legal actions. The principal is engaged directly by the rights and duties arising from the transaction concluded by his attorney. When the attorney is acting as a commercial representative for the principal, he has the right to withhold things in order to secure performance of his demand for remuneration or other demands under the contract of commission. The principal must give lawful, practicable, and specific instructions to his attorney, the last having the right to deviate from such instructions when this is necessary in the interests of the principal and there is no time to consult in advance or a reply to an enquiry has not been received within a reasonable period. The principal may at any time revoke, and the attorney renounce, the contract of commission; this right may not be waived by either party.

Commission agency

Under a contract of commission agency, the committent instructs the commission agent to conclude one or several transactions in the name of the commission agent but at the expense of the committent. The commission agent is obliged and acquires rights in a transaction concluded by him with a third person even though the committent also was named in the transaction or was in direct relations with the third person in regard to performance. The parties have great latitude in the contract to determine the period of the contract, the applicable territory, and whether the contract is exclusive to one commission agent or not. Just as the attorney in the contract of commission, so too may the commission agent withhold things from the committent in order to secure demands arising under the contract of commission agency. When the commission agent is acting as an entrepreneur, he may be given the right to deviate from his instructions without prior enquiry and may be released from the duty to inform the committent about the deviations. There is no prohibition against the commission agent who has acted for a committent then becoming an autonomous party and acquiring all or part of the goods acquired for the committent from the committent.

Agency

The contract of agency is new to Russian law and contains elements of both the contracts of commission and of commission agency. Under certain circumstances there may be substantial overlap between them and the parties could have used one or the other. The principal distinction is that under the agency contract the agent is less concerned with individual instructions of the principal or the committent and more with acting exclusively or otherwise in a domain of activity designated by the principal and in doing so fulfilling a vast variety of actions: collecting orders, marketing, servicing aircraft or ships, selling goods, and the like. The relationship between principal and agent is essentially commercial rather than personal, which is reflected in the types of limitations common to the contract of agency (Article 1007, Civil Code).

Commercial concession

The contract of commercial concession empowers the possessor of rights to grant the use of such rights with or without stipulating the period of use to the other party, called the user, in entrepreneurial activity on an exclusive basis. Such rights may include the right to use the firm name or other commercial designation, protected commercial information, trademarks, service marks, and the like, business reputation, and commercial know-how. The use of these rights, reputation, and experience may be confined to a designated territory and stipulated domain of entrepreneurial activity. In Anglo-American law this is the franchise, which enables commercial companies to enlarge the territorial scope of their operations without forming subsidiaries, to raise capital from the franchise holders, and to maximise profit from 'tied' supply and marketing schemes. The Civil Code requires that such contracts be in written form and be registered by the agency which registered the juridical person or individual entrepreneur acting as the right-possessor, and if that right-possessor was created in a foreign state, by the agency which registered the user in Russia. The right-possessor and the user are required by imperative rules of the Civil Code to control and ensure the quality of the goods produced, work fulfilled, or services rendered to the standards of those of the right-possessor. While the right-possessor may require the user to take advantage of its supply and marketing schemes, the right-possessor may not determine the retail price or establish upper or lower limits for such prices. A user who has duly performed his duties under the contract has a preferential right of renewal on the same conditions for a new period; if the right-possessor refuses to do so, disadvantageous consequences flow from the Civil Code.

Simple partnership

The simple partnership, also known in Soviet law as the contract on joint activity, is a popular structure in the natural resources sector, among others, because it enables two or more parties to create a contractual joint venture without the formation of a juridical person in order to derive profit (see also Chapter 11). Natural persons who are registered as entrepreneurs and juridical persons may create a simple partnership.

In Anglo-American parlance, the simple partnership is a legal entity, but not a juridical person. The parties combine their contributions to achieve a common cause. The contributions may be money, other property, property rights, professional and other knowledge, skills, and ability, business reputation, and business connections. The partners agree the monetary value of their contributions and are presumed to contribute equally unless the contract provides otherwise. The parties are given considerable latitude to organise their affairs. Book-keeping for the partnership may be done collectively or entrusted to one of the juridical persons which is a partner. The partners may act jointly, or designate one partner to act for all (in which case a power of attorney is issued to this end). Although the partners may agree to divide profit as they wish, no partner can be entirely eliminated from participation in the profit or exempted from sharing in the losses or common expenses. When the partnership is created to carry on entrepreneurial activity, the partners are liable jointly and severally for all common obligations irrespective of the grounds from which they arise. For the first time in Russian law provision is made for the 'non-transparent' partnership, or silent partnership, in which the very existence of the partnership may not be divulged to third persons.

Games and betting

In the Soviet era lotteries and similar games of chance were a State monopoly. A lottery ticket was a valuable whose forgery was a serious criminal offence. Russia has transformed State lottery enterprises into joint-stock societies and encouraged foreign investors to operate individual lotteries and games with modern technology. Relations between those who organise lotteries, totalisers or mutual betting and other games based on risk and those who participate are based under the Civil Code on a contract which is formalised by the issuance of a lottery ticket, receipt, or other document. These contracts are enforceable against the organisers in a

Russian court. Those who organise such games and betting must have a licence issued by the Ministry of Finances of the Russian Federation.

Demands of natural and juridical persons connected with the unlicensed organisation of games and betting are not subject to judicial protection unless participation therein was based on deceit, coercion, threat, or ill-intentioned agreement with the organiser.

H. Non-contractual Obligations

Of the small number of obligations which arise not from agreement of the parties but rather from the occurrence of an action or failure to act or are otherwise deemed to exist by operation of law, the most important are the obligations arising as a result of causing harm.

Tort

Early Soviet principles of tort were closely linked to social insurance. Responsibility was founded on causation, not fault, and judicial practice was prepared to go to some lengths in order to find causation as a means of protecting weaker parties. The courts were authorised by the 1922 RSFSR Civil Code to have regard when fixing damages to the respective financial status of the victim and the person who caused injury; the person who caused injury could be obliged to compensate even if he did not cause the injury because he was financially well-off; while this policy had the advantage of favouring the less well-off and personal exposure to losses was minimised by free medical care and expanded social insurance benefits, it did little to encourage an attitude of care on the part of tortfeasors, especially the worker. In an economy in which the State sector had absorbed the private sector, responsibility went hand in glove with morality: Soviet Man was to be aware of his duty to exercise care in all circumstances from which harm might arise. Deterrence of harm was as significant as compensation for injury. The change in policy was carried out almost entirely through judicial practice and guiding explanations. The key was the linking of subrogation and the 'criminal act or omission'. If management had failed to adopt proper safety rules or comply with them, the courts were quick to equate this with criminal behaviour even though a criminal prosecution was not brought. Social insurance came to be fixed at levels somewhat lower than full earnings, encouraging the victim to bring suit against the wrongdoer. The defendant avoided responsibility if he proved that he could not have averted the harm, or that he was empowered to cause it, or that the plaintiff himself was guilty of gross negligence or intended the harm to occur.

The Russian Civil Code retains intact the formulation making fault the general basis of responsibility for causing harm introduced by the 1961 FPCivL: 'Harm caused to the person and property of a citizen, and also harm caused to the property of a juridical person, shall be subject to compensation in full by the person who caused the harm' (Article 1064, Civil Code). The person who caused harm is relieved from the obligation to compensate harm if it is proved that the harm was caused not through his fault, unless a law provides otherwise. Harm caused by lawful actions is subject to compensation only if a law so provides, including necessary defence unless the limits thereof were exceeded, but not extreme necessity unless under particular circumstances the court decides to place the duty of compensating it on a third person in whose interests the causer of the harm acted. Reflective of the market economy, an organisation or a natural person must compensate harm caused by a worker employed by them when performing labour, employment, or official duties; the term 'worker' in this context can extend to natural persons working under either a labour or a civil-law contract. Analogous responsibility extends to economic partnerships and production cooperatives for harm caused by their participants or members if the last effectuate entrepreneurial, production, or other activity of the partnership or cooperative. In the Soviet era such responsibility did not reach natural persons because they could not be employers.

The tort liability of the State developed along different lines and in the market economy has had to be adjusted. The Imperial Russian Government limited the responsibility of a treasury government establishment or official to infringements of personal rights while acting as a representative of the proprietary interests of the treasury. There was no liability when the establishment or official acted as an agency of public authority. Soviet law rapidly developed a functional test. The 1922 RSFSR Civil Code gave State institutions immunity, unless a law expressly provided otherwise, for harm caused by the actions of officials in the course of their duties. Enterprises engaged in economic activity were deemed to be outside this structure. The 1961 FPCivL reversed the formulation and made State institutions responsible for harm caused to citizens by the improper actions of their officials in the domain of administrative management on the general grounds of tort liability unless provided otherwise by a law. The Russian Civil Code has revised the formulation once more and broadened the liabiilty of the State. No reference is made to 'administrative management'. State agencies, agencies of local self-government, and officials of these agencies are subject to compensation if caused to a natural or juridical person as a result of the illegal actions or failure to act of such agencies or officials, including as a result of the issuance of an act which does not correspond to a law or other legal act. The harm is to be compensated at the expense of the treasury respectively of the subject of the Federation or the Federation itself whose agency or official was at fault. Treated separately is harm caused by the illegal actions of agencies of inquiry or preliminary investigation, the Procuracy, and the court. Responsibility is again placed on the treasury, but may arise when so provided for by a law irrespective of fault. The Civil Code offers no definition of an 'official'; it is likely that the definition found in the notes to Article 285 of the 1996 Russian Criminal Code will be taken as guidance.[30]

The appearance of personal liability insurance in Russia is reflected in an innovation in the Civil Code requiring a juridical or natural person who has taken out voluntary or obligatory insurance to the benefit of a third person to pay compensation if the amount of damage actually caused exceeds the amount of insurance compensation available under the insurance policy.

An early and enduring principle of Soviet tort law was that of liability for 'heightened' or 'increased' danger, or extra-hazardous activity. Responsibility was placed on the owners of all sources classified as 'increased danger' in the belief that they should and could best bear the losses arising from their operations or activities. That principle is retained in the Russian Civil Code. Juridical and natural persons whose activity is connected with an increased danger for surrounding persons are obliged to compensate the harm caused unless it is proved that the harm arose as a consequence of insuperable force or the intent of the victim. The Civil Code offers an exemplary list of such sources: means of transport (including automobiles), mechanisms, high tension electric power, atomic power, explosive substances, virulent poisons, construction work and other related activity, amongst others. Gross negligence of the victim and the financial status of the responsible natural person may attenuate responsibility. The duty of compensation is placed on the juridical or natural person who possesses the source of increased danger by right of ownership, economic jurisdiction, operative management, or other legal basis, including lease or a power of attorney. The massive increase in the private ownership of motor vehicles in Russia is transpiring notwithstanding the liability implications. If two sources of increased danger cause harm (for example, a collision of motor vehicles), the possessors are responsible to third persons jointly and severally.

As a general principle, Russian law retains the position of Soviet law that any person who has compensated harm caused by another person may take recourse against the latter to the extent of compensation paid unless provided otherwise by a law. 'Person' includes insurance organisations for these purposes and the State itself when harm has been caused by an official of agencies of inquiry or preliminary investigation, the Procuracy, or a court. Minors and persons who lack dispositive legal capacity are not subject to subrogation suits.

When awarding compensation for harm, a court may require the wrongdoer either to make good for the harm in kind by repairing the damaged thing, or pro-

---

[30] See W E Butler (ed and transl), *Criminal Code of the Russian Federation* (3rd edn, 1999) 161–162.

viding a thing of the same kind and quality, etc, or by paying compensation in full for the losses caused, including expenses incurred, loss of or damage to property, and lost advantage. Gross negligence by the victim that contributed to or aggravated the harm may be set off against or cancel any compensation due. Fault of the victim is not taken into account when compensation is paid for additional expenses, for death of a breadwinner, or for burial expenses. While a court may reduce the amount of compensation for harm by taking into account the financial status of a natural person, this may not be done if the harm was caused by intentional actions. If a juridical person obliged to pay compensation caused to life or health is terminated, the obligations to pay compensation pass to its legal successor, and if the juridical person is liquidated, such obligations must be capitalised.

Compensation may be awarded for physical or moral suffering (moral harm), a principle long rejected in the Soviet era. When awarding compensation for moral harm the court is obliged to have regard to the extent of physical and moral suffering against the background of the individual peculiarities of the person who suffered harm.

The procedures for compensation vary depending on whether the tortfeasor has a duty to pay social insurance contributions for the victim or not, whether the victim qualifies for a pension or social insurance benefit, and whether the victim is covered by social insurance at all. Future earnings are taken into account at the victim's level of skill at the time of the injury, although greater consideration is given to the possibility of increased earnings or revenues if the harm had not been caused. Burial expenses are reimbursed if the victim dies, and any benefit for burial is not set off at the expense of the compensation of harm.

New to Russian legislation is the possibility to bring suit in order to prohibit activity which may cause harm in the future. If the harm is caused or would continue to be caused by an enterprise, installation, or other production activity, the court may oblige the defendant to suspend or terminate such activity in addition to paying compensation for harm. The only grounds on which the court may reject a suit of this nature is to conclude that to suspend or terminate such activity would be contrary to social interests.

With the transition to a market economy, the measure of damages when foreigners are involved is less of a problem than in the Soviet era, when the pricing system was internal and administered. There is a full choice of Western medical care available in the principal Russian cities, repairs of vehicles are routinely performed with foreign parts, and price levels are substantially similar to those in the West.

Actions in another's interest

Known to Russian law in the past but long missing, the Civil Code has reinstated the obligation to pay compensation when actions are taken in another's interest without a commission, other instruction, or consent in advance. Such actions are to be taken in order to prevent harm to the person or his property, perform his obligation, or act in his other, not unlawful, interests. Such actions must be performed by proceeding from the obvious advantage or benefit and actual or probable intentions of the interested person and with the necessary concern and circumspection under the circumstances of the case. Actions in the interest of other persons performed by State and municipal agencies whose purpose is to perform such actions are not included.

The amount of compensation is limited to necessary expenses and other real damage incurred by the person who acted in another's interest, except for expenses caused by actions made after the other person failed to approve the actions in his interest. The right to compensation survives even if the actions in another's interest do not lead to the results presupposed; however, if damage is prevented to the property of another person, the compensation due may not exceed the value of the property. Remuneration may be paid to the person whose actions in another's interest led to a positive result for the interested person if such right is provided for by a law, by agreement with the interested person, or by the customs of business turnover. The duties with regard to a transaction concluded in another's interest pass to the person in whose interest it was concluded provided that he approved this transaction and if the other party does not object to such transfer or when concluding the transaction knew or should have known that the transaction was concluded in another's interest.

In some respects the reinstatement of compensation for actions in another's interest replaces the duty to rescue of the Soviet era. Gone is the constitutional duty in the 1936 and 1977 USSR Constitutions to 'care for and reinforce socialist ownership'; and gone too are the obligations arising as a consequence of saving socialist property and the ideological connotations associated with this obligation. However, the rescue of a person or property could qualify as an action in another's interest.

Public promise of reward

Soviet civil legislation did not expressly regulate public offers of a reward, disputes arising out of such promises being resolved on the basis of general principles of law. The Civil Code requires the person who has identified himself as willing to pay monetary remuneration or other reward to whomever performs the lawful action specified in the announcement within the period indicated, particularly to whomever has found a lost thing or communicated necessary information to the person who announced the reward. The person who has responded to the promise bears the risk of ascertaining that the promise is authentic and that the person specified in the promise actually made it. But the duty to pay arises irrespective of whether the actions were performed in connection with the public promise or not. If several persons perform the action specified in the announcement, he who performed the action first has the right to the reward.

Public competition

The Civil Code regulates the public invitation to take part in a competition in return for monetary or other reward in greater detail than did Soviet-era legislation. A public competition must be directed towards the achivement of some socially useful purpose. It may be open, in which case anyone may take part, or closed, when participation is by invitation to each participant. An open competition may involve a preliminary screening to select final participants.

Although the person who accounced a public competition has the right to change the conditions or cancel it during the first half of the period established for submission of the work, such notice must be made by the same means as the competition was announced and expenses incurred by any person who fulfilled the work provided for in the announcement before he knew or should have known about the change or cancellation of the competition must be compensated. The sanction for violating the conditions for changing the conditions or cancelling the competition is draconian: the reward must be paid to all persons who have done work in accordance with the previously announced conditions which satisfies the conditions specified in the announcement.

Unfounded enrichment

Although the expression 'unjust' enrichment is commonly used in Anglo-American practice, the Russian language employs the more apt 'unfounded' enrichment. It is not the 'justness' of the enrichment which is in question, but whether there is proper foundation or grounds for the enrichment. The Civil Code has reconceptualised unfounded enrichment to enlarge its scope substantially. The basic principle is that a person who without grounds established by a law, other legal acts, or transaction acquired or saved property at the expense of another person is obliged to return the property unless the said property falls within the four exceptions set out in Article 1109 of the Civil Code. However, the Civil Code goes beyond this principle to extend unfounded enrichment to demands concerning the return of that performed under an invalid transaction, the demanding and obtaining of property by the owner from another's illegal possession, by one part in an obligation to another concerning the return of that performed in connection with this obligation, and compensation of harm, including that caused by the behaviour not in good faith of the person enriched. The rules apply irrespective of whether the unfounded enrichment is a result of the behaviour of the acquirer of the property, the victim himself, third persons, or occurred outside their will.

The Civil Code thus employs unfounded enrichment to address issues which are not necessarily resolved by the provisions concerning the invalidity of transactions, vindication suits, tort, or the return of excess amounts received under a contract, including revenues derived from property unlawfully received, saved, or withheld, or expenditures for the maintenance of such property.

I. Intellectual Property

Russian and Soviet legal doctrine, just as in many other countries, has been divided as to whether 'intellectual property' can truly be said to exist. The term in the Russian language is not 'property' at all, but 'ownership'. To speak of 'intellectual property' in the strict sense of the word (which in Russian usually connotes a 'thing') would be legal nonsense. There are two principal approaches in Russian legal doctrine: some welcome the terminology introduced in Russian legislation which speaks of the 'results of intellectual activity, including the exclusive rights thereto'. Others regard this concept as inaccurate and inappropriate, a political expression rather than a legal concept.

In the nineteenth century Russian legislation expressly relegated the rights of authors, inventors, possessors of factory drawings and models to the law of ownership.[31] Soviet legal doctrine avoided the term 'intellectual property' or ownership altogether, it being criticised for not only its inaccuracy but for being bourgeois and exploitative.[32] The term re-emerged in the USSR Law on Ownership in the USSR adopted 6 March 1990 and was replicated in the RSFSR Law on Ownership in the RSFSR of 24 December 1990, together with an exemplary list of objects of intellectual property. The 1991 FPCivL avoided the term in favour of the 'results of intellectual activity', but by 3 August 1992, when the 1991 FPCivL entered into force in Russia, the expression 'intellectual property' already had been incorporated in a number of subordinate departmental acts and in the 1992 Patent Law of the Russian Federation.

The 1993 Russian Constitution resolved the issue in favour of 'intellectual property'. Article 44 provided: 'Intellectual property shall be protected by a law'. The Civil Code defined intellectual property as nothing less than the 'aggregate of

---

[31] See Свод законов Российской империи [*Digest of Laws of the Russian Empire*], X, ch 1, Article 420. The same attempt to make rights to creative achievements part of the right to a thing, perhaps influenced by the Civil Code of California in part, is to be seen in the draft Russian civil codes at the turn of the twentieth century. Russian doctrine, however, shifted in favour of 'exclusive rights', and that expression began to dominate.

[32] See A P Sergeev, Право интеллектуальной собственности в Российской Федерации [*Law of Intellectual Property in the Russian Federation*] (2nd edn, 2001) 15; V O Kaliatin, Интеллектуальная собственность (Исключительные права) [*Intellectual Property (Exclusive Rights)*] (2000) 20–30.

exclusive rights to the results of intellectual activity, and also certain other objects equated thereto and the means of individualisation of the juridical person equated to them or the individualisation of a product or the work fulfilled or services (firm name, trademark, service mark, and others)' (Article 138). The Civil Code does not contain an exhaustive list of what qualifies as intellectual property. It is clear, however, that objects of intellectual property are protected only 'in the instances and in the procedure established by the present Code and by other laws' (Article 138, Civil Code). It follows that no result of intellectual activity is protected unless expressly specified by a law. Accordingly, results of intellectual activity in the form of scholarly ideas, hypotheses, theories, and the like would not be protected in Russia.

The open formulation of the Civil Code makes it possible to extend protection to the results of intellectual activity by enacting new relevant laws without changing the Civil Code itself. Since 1993 Russian legislation has extended by way of individual legislation protection to utility models, computer programmes, place names of origin of goods, databases, neighbouring rights, and commercial secrets but left without protection two foundation stones of Soviet protection policies: discoveries and rationalisation proposals.

With the dissolution of the Soviet Union the Russian Federation was well placed to enact its own legislation on intellectual property to supplant relevant provisions of the 1964 RSFSR Civil Code and the 1991 FPCivL. In 1992–3 the Russian Federation adopted the Patent Law of 23 September 1992, the Law on Trademarks, Service Marks, and Names of Places of Origin of Goods of 23 September 1992, the Law on the Legal Protection of Computer Programmes and Data Bases of 23 September 1992, the Law on Author's Right and Neighbouring Rights of 9 July 1993, and the Law on Selection Achievements of 6 August 1993, followed in each case by a substantial body of subordinate acts issued by the President and the Government of Russia and individual ministries and departments. These enactments were followed by institutional reforms. The Patent Department of the Russian Federation heads a unified State patent service. Patent attornies have come into being to represent parties when filing patents; however, the patent court or chamber envisaged in Russian legislation to settle patent disputes has yet to be formed. The Russian Agency for the Legal Protection of Computer Programs, Data Bases, and Integral Microcircuits has been formed to register computer programmes, databases, and topologies and contracts assigning such. The State Commission of the Russian Federation for the Testing and Protection of Selection Achievements has responsibility for registering such achievements.

Agencies for the protection of authors' rights experienced several cycles of reform. The All-Union Agency for Authors' Rights (VAAP), formed in the Soviet era, was replaced in Russia by the Russian Agency for Intellectual Property (RAIS) in

1991, which in turn was liquidated in 1993 and its assets transferred by agreement with the authors to the Russian Society of Authors (RAO), formed on 12 August 1993. Other voluntary associations have been founded by those who possess authors' and neighbouring rights in order to manage collectively those rights on a contractual basis.

Authors' rights

Throughout most of the eighteenth century in Russia the publication of books and journals was considered to be a State monopoly. The first private publishing house opened in 1771, about the same time that censorship of foreign literature was introduced. Although between 1781–96 a general authorisation to open printing houses throughout the Empire was given, renewed in 1801, the State monopoly predominated until about the 1850s. Russian legislation had virtually nothing to say about the relationship between author and publisher. Privileges to publish were given as a rule to the publisher and not to authors, whose remuner-ation was more in the form of a gift than an entitlement. Some publishers delib-erately deceived the public as to who was the author, and the censor at the time had no interest in determining whether the publisher had a contractual right to publish or not. In 1816 the position changed when the Ministry of Public Enlightenment decreed that a manuscript submitted to the censor for permission to publish must be accompanied by evidence certifying that the publisher had the right to publish from the author.

The first express regulation of authors' rights was the Censorship Statute of 22 April 1828; according to this Statute, which affected only literary works, the compiler or translator of a book had the 'exclusive right to use his publication and sale thereof throughout his entire life at his discretion as property justly acquired'. The author's right lasted for 25 years from the date of death of the author, after which it became the 'ownership of the public'. Failure to comply with the regula-tions on censorship deprived the author of any rights. A new Statute was adopted in 1830 on the rights of compilers, translators, and publishers which extended protection to articles in journals, private letters, anthologies, and the like. The right of ownership was recognised expressly for compilers, as was the possibility to extend protection for up to 35 years after the author's death. In the 1840s protec-tion was extended to musical and artistic works, and in 1875 the period of pro-tection extended to up to 50 years after death. In 1877 the regulation of authors' rights was removed from the censorship legislation to the Civil Code as an annex to Article 420.

A new Statute on Author's Right was adopted on 20 March 1911. Based on the best European models, it nonetheless was criticised for offering in sum a low level of protection to authors. The 1911 Statute lost force after the 1917 October Revolution. The Soviet authorities preoccupied themselves with reserving the right to establish a State monopoly over the authors' rights of certain writers and, from 26 November 1918, over any writers, published or unpublished, and following the abolition of inheritance in general by the Bolsheviks, the inheritance rights of authors and their descendants were not recognised. However, by a Decree of 10 October 1919, the Russian Government declared invalid all contracts of publishing houses with authors which required the author to transfer works to the full ownership of the publishing houses. Publishers could acquire only the right to publish, and even that only for the term specified by the contract.

The NEP briefly brought unlimited scope for private publishing, and by early 1925 a set of all-union fundamental principles on author's right had been enacted; these were supplanted in 1928 by a second set of Fundamental Principles, which in Russia were consolidated and elaborated by the Law on Author's Right of 8 October 1928. Although these acts made it possible for the USSR or a union republic to compulsorily purchase an author's right to any work, this was an exceptional measure rarely used in practice. The exclusive right of all authors to their works was recognised under the 1925 enactment for a period of 25 years from the moment of first publication or first public performance, and from 1928 for the life of the author, for the majority of works. Author's right passed to heirs for a period of 15 years after the author's death. The use of works was possible only on the basis of a contract with the author, subject to a rather wide list of exceptions where use was free. Sergeev characterised the 1920s legislation as follows: 'The juridical-technical qualities of the Fundamental Principles were rather high: it is no accident that many of the rules thereof were carried over virtually without changes to subsequent legislation'.[33]

In the early 1960s a decision was taken to incorporate legislation on authors' rights as an autonomous section within the 1961 FPCivL[34] and union republic civil codes based thereon. The rights of authors were somewhat enlarged and the exceptions relating to free use reduced. In 1973 the USSR acceded to the Geneva Convention on Author's Right, which led to Soviet authors being given the right to the translation of the work, the period of operation of author's right being extended up to 25 years after the author's death, and other changes. The Government of the USSR signalled its willingness to accede to the Berne Convention and the Paris Protocol of the Geneva Convention, which in turn led to the 1991 FPCivL and individual laws adopted by the USSR in 1991 on author's right taking these Conventions into account.

The 1991 FPCivL excluded free use of works in the cinema, radio, and television or the public performance of works without the author's consent. The range of

---

[33] Sergeev (n 32 above) 38–39.
[34] See S L Levitsky, 'Continuity and Change in Soviet Copyright Law: A Legal Analysis', *Review of Socialist Law*, VI (1980), 425–464; id, 'The Beginnings of Soviet Copyright Legislation 1917–1925', *The Legal History Review*, L (1982), 49–61.

works subject to protection was enlarged, the period of author's right extended to up to 50 years after the author's death, and neighbouring rights were recognised for the first time. The 1991 FPCivL were with respect to intellectual property in force for but a brief period in Russia, from 3 August 1992 until the entry into force on 3 August 1993 of the Law on Author's Right and Neighbouring Rights,[35] adopted 9 July 1993 and amended 19 July 1995 (hereinafter Law on Author's Right).

The Law on Author's Right is the highest enactment in the hierarchy of legislation regulating the rights of authors. It addresses two groups of legal relations: first, those relations arising in connection with the creation and use of works of science, literature, and art and constituting the traditional subject of the regulation of authors' rights; and second, those relations arising in connection with the creation and use of phonograms, performances, stagings, air and cable broadcasting—relations which are not in the strict sense 'author's' rights but are so closely linked with the author that they have been characterised in the English language as 'neighbouring' and in Russian, literally, as 'mixed' rights. This Law represents for the first time in Russian legal history an attempt to approximate the same standard of legal protection in Russia which developed countries of the world have long accorded to their authors as set out in the Berne Convention and to integrate the concept of neighbouring rights into Russian law. The Law is market-orientated, treating authors' rights as a type of good or commodity which may be assigned, sold, or otherwise alienated in the interests of the author. Although the principle of contract enables the parties to determine the amount of author's remuneration independently, the Government of the Russian Federation has been granted the right to establish minimum levels of remuneration, which right has been exercised by the Decree of the Government of 21 March 1994, No 218, on 'Minimum Rates for Author's Remuneration for Certain Types of Use of Works of Literature and Art'.[36]

In the past the 'freedom of contract' with respect to authors' rights was further limited by so-called 'standard contracts' which were regarded in Russian legal doctrine as normative and contained minimum standards which could not be contracted out of by the parties (see Article 506, 1964 RSFSR Civil Code). With the adoption of the Law on Author's Right, these standard contracts lost force, being transformed at best into model contracts of a recommendatory nature.

There remains the issue of legal capacity to be a publisher, however, which can affect the right of an organisation to conclude a contract with an author. An author is required to undertake due diligence in order to determine whether the

---

contracting organisation has the right to engage in publishing activity, that is, is duly licensed.

The author's right extends to works, whether published or not, found in any objective form whatever on the territory of the Russian Federation irrespective of the citizenship of the author and his legal successors, or beyond the limits of the Russian Federation and recognised for authors who are citizens of the Russian Federation and their legal successors. The author's right for citizens of other states is recognised under international treaties of the Russian Federation if those works are found in any objective form beyond the limits of the Russian Federation.

The objects of author's right include literary works, computer programmes, dramatic and musical dramatic works, film scripts, choreographic works and pantomimes, musical works with or without text, audiovisual works, paintings, sculptures, graphics, designs, graphic narratives, comics, and other works of decorative art, works of applied decorative and film art, works of architecture, urban construction, and garden-park art, photographic works and works obtained by means analogous to photography, geographic, geological, and other charts, maps, sketches, and plastic works relating to geography, topography, and other sciences. The list in the Law on Author's Right is not exhaustive; 'other works' also may qualify, including derivative works (translations, processing, annotations, abstracts, resumés, surveys, dramatisations, arrangements, and other forms of reworking or reprocessing works of science, literature, and art) and collections (encyclopedias, anthologies, databases, and the like) where the creative work consists of selection or arrangement of materials. The derivative works qualify for protection irrespective of whether the works on which they are based or which they include are objects of author's right. Certain exclusions operate: official laws, judicial decisions, and other texts of a legislative, administrative, and judicial character, including official translations thereof; State symbols and insignia; and communications concerning events and facts of an informational character.

The author's right arises by virtue of the fact of its creation and is not dependent upon any form of State registration. One who possesses the exclusive right of authorship has the right to give notice thereof by using the traditional copyright symbol (the Latin letter 'c' in a circle), indicating the name of the possessor of the right, and the year of first publication of the work, but this is not a prerequisite to obtaining the protections and rights granted to the possessor of an author's right.

The Law on Author's Right distinguishes between personal non-property rights and property rights which belong to an author. Personal non-property rights include the right of authorship (that is, the right to be recognised as the author of the work); the right to name (that is, the right to use or to authorise the use of the work under the true name of the author, pseudonym, or anonymously), the right of publication (that is, the right to publish or to authorise publication of the work in any form), and the right to reputation (that is, the right to defend the work, including its name, against any distortion or other infringement capable of causing harm to the honour and dignity of the author).

The property rights of an author are called 'exclusive rights' under Russian law. The Law on Author's Right sets out in detail what an author may do or authorise when exercising his exclusive rights, including the right to dissemination, reproduction, import, public showing, public performance, transmission on the air, communication by cable, translation, or reworking of the work. The author's right is valid throughout the lifetime of the author and 50 years after his death, subject to certain exceptions, and the right of authorship, right to name, and right to reputation are protected in perpetuity. When author's right expires, the work is automatically transferred to the public weal and may be freely used by any person without payment of author's remuneration provided that the author's rights in perpetuity are complied with. Author's right passes by way of inheritance, but not the perpetual rights to authorship, name, and reputation; these last may be defended by heirs but are not their property rights.

Neighbouring rights extend to performers, producers of phonograms, and broadcasting or cable organisations under the circumstances set out in the Law on Author's Right. Exclusive neighbouring rights operate for 50 years after first performance or staging (for performers), recording or publication (producers of phonograms), and broadcast or transmission (broadcasting or cable organisation).

Other laws contain rules of relevance to authors' rights. Among them are the Law of the RSFSR on the Mass Media of 27 December 1991, as amended, which defines such concepts as the issuance of mass media products, the procedure for their dissemination, and the conditions for the use of authors' letters and works. The Law on Architectural Activity in the Russian Federation of 17 November 1995, as amended 30 December 2001, devotes an entire chapter to author's rights with regard to works of architecture.[37]

Since author's rights are regarded by Russian doctrine as an integral part of civil law, all rules in the Civil Code of a general character are applicable to such rights, including the general provisions regulating transactions, legal capacity, dispositive legal capacity, means for the defence of legal rights, and others. The Russian Criminal Code makes provision for criminal responsibility for a violation of an author's right or neighbouring rights (Article 146) and the 1964 RSFSR Code of Civil Procedure for the levy of execution against author's remuneration (Article 385).

---

[37] СЗ РФ (1995), no 47, item 4473; (2002), no 1 (I), item 2; transl in Butler (n 35 above) 78–80.

Computer programs and databases

The 1992 Law on the Legal Protection of Programs for Electronic Computers and Data Bases 'hereinafter Law on Computer Programs' concerns only relations arising in connection with the creation, legal protection, and use of 'program means'.[38] Computer programs are treated as works of literature, and databases, as collections. The great majority of rules in the Law on Computer Programs are the same as those in the Law on Author's Right, the principal differences relating to the individual property rights of the right-possessor and to the rules for registering programs and databases with the special agency created for this purpose.

Patents

The first Patent Law in Russia, following centuries of the granting of special privileges by the Tsar to individual entrepreneurs, was adopted on 17 June 1812. The Law provided that privileges might be issued for own and imported inventions for periods of three, five, and ten years. The privileges were issued by the Minister of Internal Affairs after the State Council considered the application without actually verifying the essence of the invention. Once issued, privileges might be contested in a Russian court on the grounds that the invention contained no element of novelty. Publication of the invention became possible, and from 1814, obligatory. In 1833 material changes were introduced in legislation with the introduction of a scheme for preliminary investigation of inventions, imposition of the duty of the possessor of the privilege to use the invention, and a prohibition against assigning privileges to joint-stock companies. Although the 1833 legislation did not define an invention, it did provide that privileges should not be issued for 'insignificant discoveries, inventions, and improvements giving evidence solely of an acute or inventive mind' or to inventions which 'could harm society or State revenues', and others.

Not until 1870 was a simplified procedure introduced for obtaining privileges and the policy ended of regarding such privileges as an Imperial favour. The privilege had become a document open to anyone who met the requirements of legislation for technical novelty. In 1896 the Statute on Privileges for Inventions and Improvements was enacted; it offered a more precise definition of a protected invention and excluded from patenting scientific discoveries and theories derived therefrom, chemical and food substances, medicines, and others. The privilege was issued for a period not exceeding 15 years by the Minister of Trade and Industry and could be freely assigned or alienated; the possessor could also license

---

[38] Ведомости СНД РФ (1992), no 42, item 2325; transl in Butler (n 35 above) 135–144.

the invention and pass the privilege to descendants by inheritance. The possessor had five years in which to effectuate his invention or lose his privilege.

Early Soviet legislation dispensed with the patent. The Statute on Inventions was confirmed by a Decree of 30 June 1919, the Patent Statute of 1896 being retained in force until then. However, the 1919 Statute repealed 'all laws and statutes on privileges for inventions published before the publication of the Decree' (point 10). The Russian State was declared to have the right to alienate to its use any invention deemed to be useful by the Committee for Inventions. Inventions declared to be the weal of the RSFSR, excluding secret inventions for defence or of special importance to Russia, were in the common use of all citizens and institutions on conditions to be specially stipulated in each case. The author of such an invention was guaranteed recognition and protection of his right of authorship and remuneration certified by an author's certificate. The remuneration, determined by the commission, was more in the nature of a bonus and was not subject to taxation. In reality the remuneration was derisory and most inventors, rather than risk nationalisation of their invention, preferred not to seek protection at all.

The NEP required restoration of a system for protecting inventions, reflected in the Statute on Patents and Inventions confirmed by the USSR on 12 September 1924. Patents were issued for 'new inventions permitting industrial use' and for new means of manufacture. The patent was issued for 15 years, could be alienated freely and transferred for use to third persons at the discretion of the patent-holder. However, the State retained the right, if agreement with the patent-holder could not be reached, to compulsorily alienate the patent to its own use or establish a compulsory licence for State enterprises, paying remuneration to the patent-holder. The patent could pass by inheritance, but was not included within the estate; this was a special privilege, as the maximum estate in those days was 10,000 rubles. The legislation also annulled all patents issued before October 1917 but made it possible to reinstate them within one year by obtaining a Soviet patent.

With the move towards a Planned Economy, the 1924 legislation was replaced in 1931 by the Statute on Inventions and Technical Improvements, which basically restored the author's certificate introduced by the 1919 Decree, although the patent per se was not entirely eliminated. The substance of the 1931 enactment left no doubt that the author's certificate was the preferred method of protection and the elimination of the private sector made it unlikely the patent would have any practical value. Thereafter Soviet patent legislation went through three further major changes: in 1941, 1959, and 1973. Taken together, they provided for both patents and author's certificates, verification of the applications by expert examination, an authorisation procedure for patenting inventions abroad, and the possibility of compulsory acquisition of a patent by the State. As among themselves, they on each successive occasion clarified the criteria for granting protection to inventions, the rights granted to authors of inventions, and the procedure for examining applications. Patent law reforms anticipated in the mid-1980s were overtaken by *perestroika*, which in turn led to the enactment of a market-oriented Law on Inventions in the USSR on 31 May 1991, which entered into force as from 1 July 1991. Ancillary draft laws on a patent court of the USSR, Statute on patent attorneys, Charter of the State Inventions Fund of the USSR, and others could not be enacted before the disappearance of the Union.

With the demise of the Soviet Union, the protection of industrial property in Russia was in a desperate position. Russia itself had no patent department and the 1991 USSR Law on Inventions was inconsistent with several Russian Federation laws, including those on taxation, enterprises, and investments. Efforts to reach general agreement within the CIS on the protection of industrial property were not successful. In Russia, law reform in this domain took the form of the Patent Law of 23 September 1992, as amended 27 December 2000 and 14 December and 30 December 2001, which regulates inventions, industrial designs, and utility models.[39]

Although inventions, industrial designs, and utility models are distinct forms of intellectual property, Russian legal doctrine has generally accepted their combined regulation in a single law with approbation; 80 per cent of the rules in the Law are common to all three types of intellectual property.

The Patent Law applies to legal relations which arose after 14 October 1992, the date on which the Law entered into force. This approach left open the fate of objects of industrial property previously registered or applications in process. All previously issued USSR protection documents for inventions and industrial designs, including author's certificates, are deemed to operate on the territory of Russia. A voluntary procedure has been established by the Patent Law for exchanging such documents for patents of the Russian Federation. The result inevitably is that the USSR legislation governing those documents will continue to be in force with respect to them. But patents issued previously and patents received in place of author's certificates will be deemed invalid on the basis of procedural rules set out in the 1992 Patent Law, having regard to the new standards of patentability. The Patent Law is administered on the basis of subordinate acts issued by the Committee of the Russian Federation for Patents and Trademarks, whose Statute was confirmed by Edict of the President of the Russian Federation on 12 February 1993.

Patents certify the priority and authorship of the invention, utility model, or industrial design and the exclusive right to the use thereof for a period of 20 years

---

[39] Ведомости СНД РФ (1992), no 42, item 2319; СЗ РФ (2001), no 1(I), no 2; no 51, item 4826; no 53(I), item 5030; transl in Butler (n 35 above) 104–124.

(patent on invention), five years (certificate for utility model), or ten years (patent on industrial design). The extent of legal protection granted by a patent on an invention and a certificate for a utility model depends upon the formula thereof, and for a patent on an industrial design, on the aggregate of its material indicia depicted on the photographs, model, or drawing of the manufacture. The legal protection granted by the Russian Patent Law does not extend to inventions, utility models, or industrial designs deemed by the State to be secret. The right of authorship is an inalienable personal right and is protected in perpetuity.

Only a natural person may be an author. Creative labour which creates the invention, utility model, or industrial design is authorship, and if several natural persons participate in the creation, all are considered to be authors, in which event the use of the authors' rights is determined by an agreement between them. Priority of an invention, utility model, or industrial design is established in each instance by the receipt of an application which meets the respective criteria of legislation at the Patent Department or by taking advantage of certain convention procedures.

Perhaps the single most controversial issue of intellectual property in the transition to a market economy has been the right of an employer to an invention, utility model, or industrial design created in connection with the performance of employment duties or under a specific planning task received from the employer. The Patent Law, after prolonged parliamentary debate, took the position that the right to a patent under these circumstances belongs to the employer unless provided otherwise by a contract between the employer and employee. A contract giving the employer the right to obtain a patent would nonetheless make provision for the author's right to remuneration. If within four months of being notified by the author the employer does not file an application with the Patent Department, nor reassign the right to file an application to another person, nor notify the author of the invention, utility model, or industrial design that it should be kept secret, the author may himself make application for the patent. In this event the employer retains the right to use the object of industrial property in own production and pays contributory compensation to the author on a contractual basis. If the author and employer cannot reach agreement on the amount of, and procedure for, payment of remuneration, the issue may be referred to a court.

Industrial designs

The first material legislation on industrial designs in Russia was the Statute on the Right of Ownership to Factory Drawings and Models enacted on 11 July 1864, which in the Digest of Laws occupied a place in the Charter on Industry. The creator of a design or model intended for reproduction could consolidate to himself the exclusive right to such for a period of from one up to ten years upon petitioning the Ministry of Trade and Industry, which investigated the question as to the novelty and affiliation of the industrial design. A special mark was placed on all manufactures using the design. The right to the design could be transferred to third persons, having notified the Ministry thereof. Compensation of losses and a fine were imposed upon violators.

In the Soviet era legislation was first introduced in the form of the Decree of the USSR Council of People's Commissars 'On Industrial Designs (Drawings and Models)' of 12 October 1924. The industrial model as a type of industrial design was so close to an invention, under this Decree, that the creator was at liberty to choose which he would apply for. And if a patent were refused, the creator might still request exclusive rights for an industrial design. A special certificate was issued to confirm the granting of protection for a period of three years with the possibility of a double extension of three and four years respectively. A violation of an industrial design was a criminal offence, just as was the breach of a patent. The 1924 Decree was repealed in 1936 and not replaced. Drawings were relegated to protection by author's right, and models treated as a technical improvement, the last having been introduced as an object of legal protection in 1931. When the USSR acceded in 1965 to the Paris Convention for the Protection of Industrial Property, separate protection of industrial designs was reintroduced by the Decree of the USSR Council of Ministers of 9 June 1965 'On Industrial Designs' and by the Statute on Industrial Designs confirmed by the Patent Department of the USSR. Two forms of protection for industrial designs were possible: a certificate and a patent. The patent was issued for five years and could be extended for an equal period. On 8 July 1981 the USSR Council of Ministers confirmed a new Statute on Industrial Designs which more closely approximated international standards, in particular requiring novelty at world level rather than, as in the previous Statute, at USSR level. On 10 July 1991 the USSR adopted a Law on Industrial Designs which never entered into force because of the dissolution of the USSR before 1 January 1992. The Russian Federation has incorporated, as noted above, the regulation of utility models and industrial designs into the 1992 Patent Law.

Firm name

Only in the 1990s did Russian law begin to acknowledge that the firm name of a juridical person or individual entrepreneur falls within the concept of intellectual property. The concept of 'goodwill' associated with the firm name, having autonomous value, and subject to inclusion on the balance sheet is still in the very earliest stages of being accepted as part of the transition to a market economy.

In pre-revolutionary Russia and throughout the Soviet era there were incidental references in legislative acts to the 'firm' without a definition but gradually with a recognition that for legal purposes a name of the respective economic society or partnership must be registered and might be transferred by way of inheritance, legal succession, or contract. On 22 June 1927 the Government of the USSR confirmed the Statute on the Firm which for the first time in Russian history established the grounds and procedure for acquiring rights to such. But having been adopted on the eve of the transition to a Planned Economy, the Statute played a marginal role if any in Soviet economic life.[40]

The right to a firm name as a special subjective civil right was first established by the 1991 FPCivL (Article 149) and further elaborated in the Civil Code of the Russian Federation (Articles 54, 69, 82, 87, 95, 96, and others). It is the Civil Code which stipulates that the firm name falls within the category of intellectual property (Article 138) and is an integral part of an enterprise (Article 132). Special legislation on the firm name required by the Civil Code has not been enacted.

It follows from the Civil Code that a juridical person whose firm name has been duly registered has the exclusive right to the use thereof. The possessor of a registered firm name has the right to require another person to terminate the use thereof.

Trademark

Russian legislation on trademarks first appeared in 1830, although marks of producers and manufacturers can be traced back to early Rus. It obliged certain manufacturers to place a mark on their product, rather more in the nature of a hallmark; forgery of another's trademark was a criminally-punishable act. On 26 February 1896 Russia enacted a more comprehensive trademark law which established the right, but not the duty (with certain exceptions), to affix a trademark on the basis of registering it with the Ministry of Trade and Industry. However, if the trademark consisted exclusively of the name of the firm or of the owner of the factory, registration was not required. The protection period was from one to ten years, and the exclusive right to the trademark could be alienated only if the enterprise or firm itself were sold or leased.

The Soviet attitude towards the trademark was various. In the early stages of NEP the RSFSR adopted the Decret on Trademarks of 10 November 1922 under which all trading and industrial enterprises, irrespective of the form of ownership, were granted the right to mark their goods with a special mark which distinguished those goods from products of other enterprises. The Committee for Inventions registered trademarks. A USSR Decree of 18 May 1923 prohibited the use of trademarks which belonged to the former owners of nationalised enterprises. It was a criminal offence illegally to use another's trademark for the purpose

---

[40] Nonetheless, the Statute has not been formally repealed. Admittedly obsolete in some respects, the Statute is regarded by many Russian jurists as being in force and useful in regulating certain issues of the firm name. See Sergeev (n 32 above) 100.

of unfair competition. On 12 February 1926 the USSR adopted a new Decree on Trademarks which did not differ greatly from that of 1922 nor indeed that of 1896. In 1936 the USSR adopted the Decree on Production Marks and Trademarks which laid down obligatory rules for marking industrial products with trademarks and introduced a new species of trademark which enterprises manufacturing goods to special order could use. For a brief period the registration of trademarks was decentralised and then in 1940 concentrated in the USSR People's Commissariat of Trade and from 1959 in the USSR State Committee for Inventions and Discoveries. Trademarks were issued without limit of time and transfer to another user was possible on condition of registering the transfer. On 15 May 1962 the USSR Council of Ministers adopted the Decree on Trademarks and on 23 June 1962 the Statute on Trademarks was confirmed by the USSR Committee for Inventions and Discoveries. Under these acts a Soviet enterprise was required to have and use registered trademarks, although in practice this did not happen. Trademarks were issued for ten years with the possibility to extend. Yet another Statute on Trademarks was enacted in 1974 which modernised the application process but made no changes of principle. The USSR Law on Trademarks and Service Marks, adopted 3 June 1991, never entered into force but served as the basis of the Russian Federation Law on Trademarks, Service Marks, and Names of Places of Origin of Goods of 23 September 1992, as amended 27 December 2000, 14 December 2001, and 30 December 2001, and in force from 17 October 1992.[41]

Legal protection is based on State registration of the trademark in the name of a juridical person or of a natural person effectuating entrepreneurial activity. The trademark certificate issued upon registration certifies the priority of the trademark and the exclusive right of the possessor to that trademark with respect to the goods specified in the certificate. A trademark may be registered in any colour or colour combination, and verbal, pictorial, dimensional, and other designations or combinations thereof may be registered. The registration of a trademark lasts for ten years and may be extended upon application for subsequent ten-year periods.

The priority of a trademark is established by the date of receipt of the application at the registering agency, or pursuant to applications submitted under the Paris Convention for the Protection of Industrial Property. Priority also is recognised for trademarks placed on exhibits of official or officially-recognised international exhibitions organised on the territory of a state party to the Paris Convention. Foreign juridical persons or natural persons permanently resident beyond the limits of the Russian Federation may use Russian patent attorneys to register their trademarks.

---

[41] Ведомости СНД и ВС РФ (1992), no 42, item 2322; (2001), no 1(I), item 2; no 51, item 4826; no 53(I), item 5030; transl. in Butler (n 35 above) 81–101.

Service marks and names of places of origin

Service marks were first recognised in Russian legislation during the Soviet era by the USSR Decree on Trademarks of 15 May 1962. Their existence was consolidated by the 1974 Statute on Trademarks and again in the 1991 USSR Law on Trademarks and Service Marks and in the 1992 Russian Federation Law mentioned above.

Protection of names of places of origin of goods as an autonomous object of intellectual property was first introduced by the Russian Federation Law on Trademarks, Service Marks, and Names of Places of Origin of Goods, of 23 September 1992. Names of place of origin may be registered by one or several juridical natural persons provided that the name of the country, population centre, locality, or other geographic object used to designate a good reflects special properties exclusively or principally determined by natural conditions or human factors characteristic of the particular geographic object or by natural conditions and human factors simultaneously. Registration of the name operates in perpetuity.

Discoveries

Singled out as special objects of legal protection by a Decree of the USSR Council of Ministers adopted 14 March 1947, discoveries were in practice registered by the State from 26 June 1957. The legal concept of a discovery, however, was not elaborated until confirmation of the Statute on Discoveries, Inventions, and Rationalisation Proposals in 1959: the establishment of 'previously unknown objectively existing laws of societal development, properties, and phenomena of the material world' in the natural and technical sciences. Geographic, archaeological, and paleontological discoveries are not included in the scheme, nor are discoveries in the social sciences. Those who discover mineral deposits may qualify for remuneration on another basis. The 1964 RSFSR Civil Code recognised and incorporated the discovery but added nothing to its legal regime. The 1973 Statute on Discoveries, Inventions, and Rationalisation Proposals clarified somewhat the concept of discovery by incorporating the 'making of fundamental changes in the level of cognition' a component of a discovery. Sergeev observes that until the 1990s only some 450 discoveries were registered out of more than 30,000 applications; most rejections were for failure to make fundamental changes in the level of cognition or the inability to prove scientific propositions put forward as a discovery. Of those applications approved, more than half were in the field of physics, followed by chemistry, biology, medicine, and geology.[42] From 1988 the question of whether to retain the discovery as a category of intellectual property was the subject of sharp controversy, and from 1992 the acceptance of applications

---

[42] Sergeev (n 32 above) 61–62.

for consideration ceased not least because the Russian Patent Department did not wish to occupy itself with such work. The future of the discovery, even though the legislation regulating it has not been repealed, remains in doubt.

Commercial secrets

This is a new and rather underdeveloped area of Russian legislation. In the Soviet era it was either wrapped up in the concept of a State secret or was irrelevant. The right of parties to a transaction to protect commercial secrets was first mentioned in the USSR Law on Enterprises in the USSR, adopted 4 June 1990: 'information which is not a State secret and is connected with production, technological information, management, financial, and other activity of enterprises, the divulgence of which may inflict harm on its interests' (Article 2). The 1990 RSFSR Law on Ownership mentioned production secrets, know-how, and trade secrets as objects of intellectual property. The 1990 RSFSR Law on Enterprises and Entrepreneurial Activity confirmed the right of an enterprise to commercial secrets as intellectual property without offering a definition. The 1991 RSFSR Law on Competition and the Limitation of Monopolistic Activity on the Trade Markets provided that the receipt, use, or divulgence of a commercial secret without its owner's consent was a form of unfair competition (Article 10). The 1991 FPCivL also gave recognition to commercial secrets (Article 151), and was superseded by the Civil Code of the Russian Federation (Article 139). On 5 December 1991 the RSFSR adopted a list of information which may not constitute a commercial secret.[43]

Topologies of integral microcircuits

Although the USSR contemplated legislation on protecting this type of intellectual property, it was never actually enacted. The first enactment on the subject was the Russian Law on the Legal Protection of Topologies of Integral Microcircuits, of 23 September 1992, as amended 9 July 2002.[44] Since such topologies are regarded as an autonomous object of intellectual property distinct from objects protected by author's right or a patent, the Law incorporates rules regulating all types of civil and other relations.

The legal protection accorded extends only to an original topology created as the result of creative activity of the author. A presumption operates in favour of originality unless it is proved otherwise. Technical, organisational, or material assistance is not sufficient for authorship. The author has the exclusive right to use the topology at his discretion, including by means of manufacturing and disseminating the integral microcircuit, and prohibiting the use of the topology by other

---

[43] СП РФ (1992), no 1–2, item 7.
[44] Ведомости СНД РФ (1992), no 42, items 2328, 2329; СЗ РФ (2002), no 28, item 2786.

persons without authorisation. The property rights in a topology may be transferred in whole or in part to other natural or juridical persons by a written contract or by way of inheritance.

If a topology is created in the course of employment duties, the property rights in the topology belong to the employer unless provided otherwise by a contract between the author and the employer. An author who creates a topology under contract to a customer who is not his employer is not the owner of the rights to the topology unless provided otherwise by a contract. Topologies may be registered, but this is not a requirement for legal protection. The exclusive right to a topology lasts for ten years running from the date of first use or the date of registration of the topology. Foreign natural and juridical persons enjoy the same rights as Russian natural and juridical persons by virtue of international treaties of the Russian Federation or on the basis of reciprocity.

Selection achievements

Protection of selection achievements commenced in Russia with the 1937 Decree of the Soviet Government 'On Measures Relating to the Further Improvement of Seeds of Grain Crops', which provided for the issuance of protection documents to the authors of new plant varieties. Initially protection was given only to newly introduced or improved varieties of grain. On 5 March 1941 such achievements were relegated to the category of objects of creativity protected by the law on inventions, pursuant to the Statute on Inventions and Technical Improvements. Throughout the 1940–50s similar protection was extended to other plants and to livestock in the form of protection documents issued by the USSR Ministry of Agriculture. The 1959 and 1973 laws on inventions confirmed the position that selection achievements were analogous to inventions, and the Ministry of Agriculture confirmed several Statutes regulating the procedure for obtaining protection documents. Equating selection achievements with inventions, however, remained controversial in Russian legal doctrine, and a sharp disctinction between the two was drawn in the decision to adopt the Russian Federation Law on Selection Achievements on 6 August 1993.

The 1993 Law determines the concept, indicia, and types of selection achievements to be protected by law, the general procedure for evaluating whether they can be protected, the exclusive rights of those who are awarded a patent or an author's certificate to such an achievement, and responsibility for violations.[45]

Rationalisation proposals

Special protection for rationalisation proposals was first introduced by the Soviet Union in 1931 under the Statute on Inventions and Technical Improvements.

---

[45] Ведомости СНД и ВС РФ (1993), no 36, item 1436.

There was no definition of such an improvement, only the stipulation that they need not possess novelty. A protection certificate was awarded to those who developed them by the enterprise which introduced the improvement and remuneration paid pursuant to an Instruction of the Committee for Inventions dated 31 October 1931. The Instruction was noteworthy for addressing not only the technical improvement, but also the 'rationalisation proposal', at the time merely a 'proposal of an organisational character' which lay beyond the resolution of technical tasks. In the years that followed the 'rationalisation proposal' altered in meaning somewhat; in 1973 legislation the definition was narrowed to mean only proposals relating to the technical resolution of production tasks. Remuneration was based on a fixed scale and sometimes represented a percentage of savings effected over a prescribed period.

During the late 1980s the future of protection rationalisation proposals was discussed as part of the general reforms of intellectual property legislation. The results were recorded in the Decree of the RSFSR Council of Ministers adopted 22 June 1991 'On Measures Relating to the Development of Inventorship and Rationaliser Activity in the RSFSR'. It provided that until the enactment of new intellectual property legislation, rationalisation proposals should be a matter for each individual enterprise to decide, remunerate, introduce, and otherwise manage. Thus has Russia abandoned for the moment six decades of State regulation of rationalisation proposals and decentralised implementation to the individual juridical person.

International treaties

As the 'legal continuer' of the former Soviet Union, the Russian Federation is a party to international treaties and a member of international intellectual property organisations to or in which the USSR was a party or member. In addition, the Russian Federation has acceded to other international treaties of relevance. The USSR joined the World Intellectual Property Organisations (WIPO) in 1968, acceded in 1973 to the 1952 Geneva Universal Copyright Convention, and was a party to a number of bilateral conventions with regard to intellectual property. Relations with the former republics of the Soviet Union in respect of intellectual property have been addressed in bilateral treaties and most importantly by the multilateral Agreement on Cooperation in the Domain of Author's Right and Neighbouring Rights, concluded on 24 September 1993. In mid-1993 the Russian Government further declared its intention to accede to all of the principal international conventions relating to author's right. In the end it was decided to accede to three: the Berne Convention on the Protection of Literary and Artistic Works as amended in 1971; the Universal Copyright Convention as amended in 1971, and the 1971 Convention on Protection of the Interests of Producers of Phonograms Against the Illegal Reproduction of Their Phonograms, which was accomplished with certain reservations in December 1994 with effect from 13 March 1995.

With respect to patents, the Soviet Union acceded in 1965 to the 1883 Paris Convention on the Protection of Industrial Property and in 1978 to the Treaty on Patent Cooperation. On 27 December 1991 seven members of the CIS signed at Minsk the Provisional Agreement on the Protection of Industrial Property, but the Agreement has never entered into force. The Eurasian Patent Convention, signed on 9 September 1994, was ratified by Russia and entered into force for it on 28 September 1995. A network of bilateral agreements is being negotiated with other CIS members to simplify reciprocal patenting procedures: Armenia (25 June 1993); Kazakhstan, Kyrgyzstan, Ukraine (30 June 1993); Uzbekistan.

The 1883 Paris Convention also relates to trademarks, and Russia is a party to the 1891 Madrid Agreement on the International Registration of Marks, and the 1957 Nice Agreement on the International Classification of Goods and Services for the Registration of Marks.

J. Inheritance

In the eyes of the early Soviet leadership, inheritance was closely linked with the perpetuation of private wealth in the instruments and means of production. A Decree of 27 April 1918 drastically limited both testamentary and intestate succession. Except for families of a deceased working male which otherwise might be left destitute, all property left by individuals upon death passed to the State. Estates not exceeding 10,000 rubles in value and comprising a dwelling house, furnishing thereof, and an individual worker's means of production would pass to those relatives who resided with and were dependants of the deceased. Peasant households were treated similarly, but without any ceiling value. Local soviets undertook to provide for a surviving spouse, children, and ascending or descending relatives, drawing upon the excess value of the estate. The 1922 RSFSR Civil Code broadened the ambit of heirs but initially retained a ceiling on the value of estates. Property could pass by will only to beneficiaries within the statutory group of heirs, or to State or social organisations. Estates were distributed per capita with no right of representation. This liberalisation was tempered by a progressive inheritance tax up to 50 per cent; when the ceiling on estates was abolished in 1926, the tax rate became up to 90 per cent, although State bonds and later cash deposits held in banks were exempted from the normal rules on inheritance. In 1942 the progressive inheritance tax was replaced by a scheme of notarial fees levied for issuing an inheritance certificate. Further reforms were introduced in 1945 to liberalise succession. The 1961 FPCivL removed the restrictions on individuals to whom property may be left.

The 1993 Russian Constitution guarantees the right to inheritance (Article 35). Inheritance relations are governed by Part III of the Civil Code (Articles 1110–1185) and in some respects by the 1995 Family Code of the Russian Federation and 2001 Land Code of the Russian Federation. Inheritance may be by will or by operation of law; it is the latter when and insofar as it is not changed by a will. The property, including property rights and duties, which may pass by way of succession includes both rights and duties, that is, right to property to the performance of obligations, to royalties, or to accept an inheritance, and likewise to debts of the deceased. Some rights do not pass, for example, the right to receive alimony or a pension, or a duty to fulfil an author's contract.

A will must be drawn up in writing (which includes the use of a typewriter, computer, or other technical means such as a video), specify the place and time it was drawn up, be personally signed by the testator, and be notarially certified. In most cases the testator will simply apply to a notary for assistance in drafting the will according to established forms; the original is retained by the notary and a copy given to the testator. Wills of military servicemen certified by their commanding officer, or of citizens on Russian-registered sea or river vessels certified by the master, or of citizens in hospitals or other treatment institutions certified by the appropriate doctors, or of members of polar, prospecting, or other expeditions are equated to notarially certified wills. When certifying a will, a notary is required by law to explain the provisions of the Civil Code requiring a compulsory participatory share in an estate for certain heirs and to make a formal notation that such explanation was given. A compulsory participatory share is reserved for the testator's minor children and for children, a spouse, or parents and dependants who are not capable of working, in an amount of not less than half of the participatory share which would be due to each if the estate were to pass by operation of law. The value of ordinary household property is taken into account for this purpose.

A 'closed will' is possible, written by the testator, placed in an envelope, sealed and transferred to a notary in the presence of two witnesses. The notary then signs the envelope and in the presence of the witnesses places the envelope inside a second envelope, which is then duly signed and sealed. When the testator dies, the notary has 15 days after presentation of the death certificate to open the envelope in the presence of at least two witnesses and heirs by operation of law. The will is read aloud and a protocol signed by the notary and witnesses certifying that the envelope was opened and did contain the full text of the will. An absolute condition of the closed will is that it be written out and signed in the hand of the testator; mechanical means may not be used.

The heirs by will perform the functions of an executor or administrator of an estate unless a designated individual has been appointed by the testator. In the case of inheritance by operation of law, it is common for the notary to act as executor or administrator. The time of opening an inheritance is the date of death or date specified in a declaration thereof. It is this date which determines the group of heirs, the composition of estate property, and the period for heirs to accept or reject the estate. The estate is opened at the last permanent place of the deceased or, if that is unknown, where the property or the major part thereof is situated. Heirs may be, in the absence of a will, citizens alive at the moment of the decedent's death and the decedent's children born after his death; by will, citizens alive at the decedent's death or conceived during his lifetime and born after his death. In the event of intestacy, the following take in equal participatory shares: (1) first priority: children, the spouse, and parents of the decedent; grandchildren of the decedent and descendants thereof inherit by right of representation; (2) second priority: full or half brothers and sisters of the decedent, grandfather and grandmother thereof both on the side of the father and on the side of the mother; children of full and half brothers and sisters of the decedent (nephews and nieces of the decedent) inherit by right of representation; (3) third priority: full or half brothers and sisters of parents of the decedent (uncles and aunts of the decedent); first cousins of the decedent inherit by right of representation; (4) fourth priority: relatives of the third degree of kinship—great-grandfather and great-grandmother of the decedent; (5) fifth priority: relatives of the fourth degree of kinship—children of full cousins of the decedent (grandchildren once removed) and own brothers and sisters of his grandfather and grandmother (grandfathers and grandmothers once removed); (6) sixth priority: relatives of the fifth degree of kinship—children of grandchildren once removed of the decedent (great-grandchildren once removed), children of his brothers and sisters once removed (nephews and nieces once removed), and children of his grandfathers and grandmothers once removed (uncles and aunts once removed); (7) seventh priority: step-sons, step-daughters, step-father, and step-mother of the decedent; (8) eighth priority: dependants of the decedent not having labour capacity and who not less than a year before the death of the decedent were dependent on him and resided jointly with him. Each priority is called upon to succeed only if there are no heirs of the prior priority able or willing to succeed. The priorities were increased from two to eight in order to reduce the apparently rather considerable, in Soviet times, number of estates passing to the State by escheat.

An heir who lived on the day of opening the inheritance jointly with the decedent has when dividing the inheritance a preferential right to receive at the expense of his inheritance participatory share of the ordinary domestic household articles. The commentators suggest that valuable collections, antiques, original paintings, personal libraries used for professional purposes, and the like would not qualify as household articles.

If he so desires, a testator may appoint an executor in his will, who may or may not be an heir, to perform any actions needed to give effect to the testament. These may include determining and identifying the decedent's property, recovering debts, or satisfying creditors. The executor is not regarded as a representative of either the testator or the heirs; no remuneration is paid for his services unless the will expressly so provides, but he is entitled to reimbursement for actual expenses incurred to protect or manage estate property.

An heir may acquire an estate only when he has formally accepted it unconditionally by actually taking possession of the estate or filed a declaration of acceptance within six months from the date of opening. A duly-empowered representative also may accept an inheritance on behalf of an heir. This policy also favours heirs who lived with or near the decedent, although there are procedures for extending the period for acceptance. An heir who has taken possession or control of an estate before other heirs have appeared may not dispose of the estate until the six-month period has elapsed or a certificate of the right to an inheritance has been issued by the notary. Creditors of a decedent likewise must file demands with regard to any obligations, whether due or not, within the same six-month period or lose the right to their demand. Protection of the decedent's property is the responsibility of the notarial office where the estate was opened until the estate is accepted by all heirs or the six-month period has lapsed. If the estate includes property requiring management, for example, a dwelling house, the notarial office may take measures to protect the property by agreement with the executor, if one has been appointed, or the executor may act alone in the interests of the heirs. A notary may also conclude contracts of trust management when there is property that needs special management; for example, securities, exclusive rights, a business, and so on.

Heirs called to succeed apply to a notary for a certificate of the right to an inheritance. Ordinarily it will not be issued until the six-month period has elapsed, but if the notary is satisfied that there are no heirs other than those applying, the certificate may be issued earlier. State duty is payable for the issuance of a certificate of the right to inherit.

The estate is divided by agreement of the succeeding heirs in proportion to their respective participatory shares. Such agreement must comply with the rules of the Civil Code on the form of transactions and the form of contracts. In the absence of agreement the matter is resolved by a court. In dividing an estate due account must be taken of a spouse's right to property by joint or common ownership. Certain heirs have a preferential right to property which cannot be divided physically or are in common ownership. Provisions are made in this event for contributory compensation to be paid to the other heirs.

Special rules regulate the inheriting of certain types of property, such as rights connected with participation in economic partnerships or a consumer cooperative, an enterprise, a peasant (or farmer) economy, or things whose circulability is limited.

The Civil Code also regulates private international law (see Chapter 18).

10

FAMILY LAW

Prior to the 1917 October Revolution matters of marriage and divorce were left to the canon law of each religious denomination. A religious marriage ceremony was essential, and certain restrictions were imposed on the marriage of Christians with non-Christians or pagans. The State had been content to accept the practices of each religious denomination and give effect to their ecclesiastical judgments.[1] The Bolsheviks, intent upon breaking the authority of the Church, secularised marriage and divorce even before formally legislating upon the separation of Church from State and of school from Church. The family in its bourgeois manifestation, as an economic and legal entity based on the inequality of spouses and the dependence of the wife and children upon the husband, was to be transformed into a free association founded on the free will of its members. How precisely that transformation was to be realised proved to be a lively subject of debate in the early post-revolutionary years. Some urged a rapid transition to collective housekeeping and State-reared children. In the end more responsible heads prevailed. Consensual relationships came to be emphasised rather than the abolition of the family unit, formed in a secular context, with liberal opportunities for divorce and the emancipation of the wife and children. By the mid-1930s the pendulum had swung back. The family became important again as a legal and economic entity, a core unit of present and future society, and continued to be so regarded until the end of the Soviet era.[2]

---

[1] H J Berman, *Justice in the U.S.S.R.* (rev edn, 1966) 330–333.

[2] For an overview of the cultural, anthropological, demographic, social, and other factors of Russian sexual patterns throughout the Soviet and early post-Soviet era, see I S Kon, Сексуальная культура в России [*Sexual Culture in Russia*] (1997).

The 1993 Russian Constitution preserves this position, providing in Article 38 that 'motherhood and childhood and the family shall be under the defence of the State'.

A. Historical Background

The Soviet authorities moved expeditiously to divest religious denominations of their authority over marriage and divorce.[3] Two Decrees were enacted within a day of one another. The first, 'On Civil Marriage, On Children, and On Keeping Books for Acts of Civil Status', adopted 18 December 1917, proclaimed that the Russian Republic recognised only a civil marriage, entrusted the keeping of books for acts of civil status to Soviet agencies, and made equivalent the legal rights of children born within or out of wedlock. The following day the Decree 'On the Dissolution of Marriage' placed divorce within the competence of local courts and marriage registry sections.[4] Neither Decree offered much by way of detail, and on 16 September 1918 they were replaced by the RSFSR Code of Laws on Acts of Civil Status, Marriage, Family, and Guardianship Law.[5]

The Code, comprising 246 articles and some appendices, stipulated that only a marriage registered at a section for the registry of acts of civil status (ZAGS) would give rise to the rights and duties of spouses set out in the Code. Religious marriage had no legal effect unless registered in the established procedure.[6] The formalities of marriage were brief. An oral or written application was filed at the local ZAGS with a certificate of personal identification and signed indication that the marriage was voluntary and there were no legal obstacles to marriage. The presiding official made the appropriate entry in the marriage register, read it to those being married, and declared the marriage to be concluded. A marriage certificate would be issued immediately upon request, but the entry in the marriage register constituted legal completion of the marriage. The requirements for marriage were: age (16 for females; 18 for males); sound mind; not married; no marriage to relatives in the direct ascending or descending line; and mutual consent. People of different religious faiths, monks, priests, or nuns, or persons who had taken a vow of celibacy were all expressly allowed to marry.

---

[3] On the history of late Imperial Russian and Soviet family law, see A M Nechaeva, Семейное право [*Family Law*] (1998) 43–91.

[4] СУ РСФСР (1917), no 11, item 160; no 10, item 152.

[5] СУ РСФСР (1918), no 76–77, item 818.

[6] Church and religious marriages concluded before 20 December 1917, the date of publication of the decree in n 4 above, were deemed to have the effect of registered marriages if performed in compliance with the conditions and forms laid down in Articles 3, 5, 20–23, 31, or 90–94 of the Свод законов Российской империи [*Digest of Laws of the Russian Empire*] (1914 edn). Because Soviet power was established at different times throughout the country, an official circular was issued fixing the date prior to which duly concluded religious marriages would be considered valid. For some regions dates as late as 1925 are specified.

The draftsmen of the 1918 Code clearly wished to encourage registered marriages. Nothing whatever was said of de facto marriage in the Code, probably because that would have undermined the registration requirement. Section III of the Code, entitled 'Family Law', however, seemed to introduce an element of inconsistency by providing that 'Birth itself shall be the basis of the family', birth in the sense of lineage or ancestry. On this premise the Code declared there was to be no distinction between illegitimate and legitimate ancestry, and the provision was retroactive to births prior to 20 December 1917. The Code dwelt separately and at length on the rights and duties of spouses, on one hand, and the personal and property rights of children and parents, on the other. Among the latter was the right of the parents to agree to which religion their children under age 14 might affiliate; the agreement had to be in written form.

Divorce was readily obtained under the Code upon the request of either spouse without any statement of reasons. If both spouses consented, the ZAGS office granted the divorce. If only one spouse filed for divorce, the matter was decided by the local court.

Notwithstanding the Code's silence, people's courts began in certain situations to give effect to de facto marriages. When the courts felt women had been taken advantage of in an unregistered relationship, they were prepared to award them a share of property acquired during the de facto relationship, including sometimes a share of an estate (succession having been abolished).

The 1918 Code was replaced by the RSFSR Family Code adopted on 19 November 1926 and in force as from 1 January 1927.[7] The 1926 Code extended formal acknowledgement to earlier judicial practice regarding de facto marriage. Under the Code, in the absence of registration the existence of a marriage became a matter of evidence and could be registered retrospectively. The Code raised the marriage age to 18 for both males and females, an amendment inserted in the last draft of the Code in the belief that early marriage could be harmful to the health of a mother and child and would deprive women of equal opportunities for education or vocational training. In matters of matrimonial property the 1926 Code departed from its predecessor and established that property acquired during marriage was community property whereas that acquired prior to marriage was separable. Freedom of divorce was maintained and placed entirely within the competence of ZAGS agencies. Despite a more flexible attitude toward registration, the formality was encouraged in order to facilitate the compilation of vital statistics and simplify the administration of inheritance. The courts even in the realm of succession allowed women in de facto relationships to inherit property.

---

[7] The 1926 RSFSR Family Code is translated with comparisons to other union republic family codes in V Gsovski, *Soviet Civil Law* (1948) II 239–290.

During the mid-1930s, the previous emphasis upon secularisation, freedom of divorce, and the liberation of women and children altered. The family began to be regarded as a permanent primary societal unit in a socialist and communist society. Family stability was essential, it was said, to the moral, legal, and spiritual awareness of every Soviet citizen. Individual enactments amended or superseded the Family Code to give effect to this new approach. Motherhood was encouraged through limiting the grounds for abortion and introducing financial and other incentives for mothers of large families. Not insubstantial fees were introduced for the successive registration of divorces. Parents were made legally responsible for the delicts and crimes of their children.

In the late years of the Second World War, when it had become apparent that a substantial imbalance in the male/female ratio would persist for a generation and that casual wartime liaisons would require legal reinforcement if the family were to remain intact, the Presidium of the USSR Supreme Soviet enacted an Edict on 8 July 1944 reinstating the requirement that only a registered marriage would be given legal effect.[8] De facto marriages prior to that date could be registered retrospectively. Divorce policy tightened considerably. Only courts could grant divorces under the Edict, and before doing so they were obliged to attempt to reconcile the parties. If reconciliation were impossible, the case proceeded to the next instance for a new judicial consideration. The Edict specified no grounds for divorce. Courts construed the grounds narrowly, in effect forcing the parties to separate, form a new sustained unregistered relationship, and possibly have children therefrom. The fees payable to the State in connection with divorce proceedings increased significantly. Judicial practice liberalised somewhat in the 1950s in reference to divorce, and in 1965 the Family Code was amended to eliminate the double-tiered court proceedings. The decisions to grant divorce, alimony, custody, and property division were all vested in the people's courts.

On 27 June 1968 the USSR Supreme Soviet confirmed the FPMarL, which were deemed to lose force in the Russian Federation as of 1 March 1996.[9] The 1969 Code on Marriage and the Family of the Russian Federation[10] was replaced as of 1 March 1996 by the Family Code of the Russian Federation of 8 December 1995 and amended 15 November 1997, 27 June 1998, and 2 January 2000,[11] except for Section IV of the 1969 Code, which remained in force until November 1997, when the Federal Law on Acts of Civil Status entered into force.

---

[8] Ведомости Верховного Совета СССР (1944), no 37, 1.

[9] Ведомости Верховного Совета СССР (1968), no 27, item 241.

[10] Ведомости Верховного Совета РСФСР (1969), no 32, item 1086.

[11] СЗ РФ (1996), no 1, item 16 (1997), no 46, item 5243; (1998), no 26, item 3014; (2000), no 2, item 153; translated in W E Butler and J E Henderson (eds), *Russian Legal Texts* (1998) 517–592.

B. Current Family Legislation

The Russian Family Code is not divided into General and Special Parts. It consists of eight sections: general provisions; conclusion and termination of marriage; rights and duties of spouses; rights and duties of parents and children; alimony obligations of members of family; forms of nurturing children left without care by parents; the application of family legislation to family relations with the participation of foreign citizens and stateless persons, and concluding provisions. As noted above, the Section on acts of civil status, included in the 1969 Family Code, is the subject of separate federal legislation and no longer part of the Family Code.

Basic principles

The Russian Family Code, in reaffirming the constitutional provision that the family is under State protection, enlarges the formula to include fatherhood. Gone from the Family Code are ideological references associated with the 'communist' family and social engineering. The purpose of family legislation is to strengthen the family, structure family relations on feelings of mutual love and respect, mutual assistance, and responsibility to the family of all of its members, to ensure the inadmissibility of arbitrary interference of anyone in the affairs of the family, and to ensure the unobstructed effectuation by members of a family of their rights and the possibility of judicial defence of these rights.

The principles guiding family policy are the voluntariness of the marriage union of man and woman, the equality of the rights of spouses in the family, the settlement of intra-family questions by mutual consent, the priority of family nurturing of children, concerns for their well-being and development, ensuring the priority defence of the rights and interests of minors and members of the family lacking the capacity to labour. The rights of citizens in the family may be limited only on the basis of a federal law and only to the extent that this is necessary for the purpose of the defence of morality, health, and the rights and legal interests of other members of the family and other citizens. Although the formulation of family law principles has omitted ideological components, in substance there is unlikely to be drastic change in the equality of spouses. Each continues to have the right to choose his or her surname, occupation, profession, and place of residence, and the requirement of mutual consent to resolve intra-family issues is maintained. There is equal right to property, and a variety of other situations where when deciding family disputes the courts continue to be required to proceed from the principle of equality or to compensate for actual inequalities by making appropriate adjustments in the situation.

A major change in Russian family legislation is the relegation of family law to the joint jurisdiction of the Russian Federation and the subjects of the Federation.

The Russian Family Code therefore does not pretend to be exhaustive in two senses: certain family relations are regulated by other federal legislation, and the subjects of the Federation have the right to adopt their own Family Codes and other family laws which are not inconsistent with the Russian Family Code. Some republics within the Federation have enacted their own Family Codes. The Republic Bashkortostan, for example, first adopted a Code on Marriage and the Family in 1994, replacing it entirely by a version of 11 July 1996 and displacing in so doing the Family Code of the Russian Federation by incorporating the essential provisions of the latter into the Bashkortostan version.

The inevitable overlap in certain instances between civil and family legislation is addressed in the Russian Family Code. Civil legislation shall apply, insofar as this is not contrary to the essence of family relations, to the property and personal non-property relations named in the Family Code between members of a family which are not regulated by family legislation. Where neither family nor civil legislation provides the requisite regulation, and there is no agreement of the parties, norms of family and/or civil law regulating similar relations (analogy of lex) apply to such relations unless this is contrary to the essence thereof. In the absence of such norms, the rights and duties of members of the family are determined by proceeding from general bases and principles of family or civil law (analogy of jus), and also the principles of humaneness, reasonableness, and justness.

If other rules have been established by an international treaty of the Russian Federation than those which have been provided for by family legislation, the rules of the international treaty apply.

Marriage

The Russian Family Code retains the reform first introduced in 1968 that a marriage be not merely *registered* in a ZAGS office but that it be *concluded* there. The ceremony or rites of marriage continue to be the prerogative of the State, although the participants are at liberty to have separate religious ceremonies. ZAGS offices are equipped with premises and amenities to emphasise the solemnity of the relationship being concluded. The presiding State official performs rites designed to be more than a perfunctory ceremony, reminding the intending spouses of their responsibilities toward one another and their future children. The application to marry must be filed at the ZAGS office one month in advance of the wedding. The waiting period may be reduced or extended by up to one month for justifiable reasons. Examples of justifiable reasons include pregnancy, birth of a child, or direct threat to the life of one of the parties. Filing an application to marry in and of itself creates no legal relations between the intending spouses and there are no legal consequences if it is withdrawn.

Russian law recognises religious marriages contracted before the formation or restoration of Soviet power and de facto marriages concluded under the 1926

RSFSR Family Code but before 8 July 1944. Under certain circumstances a de facto unregistered marriage before 8 July 1944 is still subject to being proved in a court; no statute of limitations was ever imposed.

Religious ceremonies are increasingly popular in Russia, but they have no legal effect. Only the civil ceremony at a ZAGS office is legally recognised. The date of marriage is the registration date at the ZAGS office. The refusal of ZAGS to register a marriage may be appealed to a court.

The legal requirements that must be satisfied for marriage are:

(1) mutual consent of the intending spouses;
(2) age 18, which in exceptional circumstances may be reduced to 16 or 14;
(3) neither spouse already is legally married;
(4) the spouses are not relatives in direct line of ascendance or descendance, full or half-brothers or sisters, or adoptive and adopted persons;
(5) neither spouse lacks dispositive legal capacity as a consequence of mental disturbance as determined by a court.

Marriages may be performed only between a man and a woman. Whether an intending spouse already is married Russian law determines by examining the time at which the previous relationship was formed. A religious marriage after 8 July 1944 in Russia, for example, would not be recognised, but if concluded before that date the provisions concerning de facto marriages might apply.

Divorce

The vicissitudes of Soviet divorce policies, from the era of 'postcard' divorces for a nominal sum through ZAGS offices until the mid-1930s to the period of restrictive divorce after the 1944 Edict, have been discussed above. The policy, introduced by the 1968 FPMarL, allowing spouses who have no minor children to dissolve their marriage by mutual consent at a ZAGS office remains in place in the Russian Family Code. A one-month period must elapse before the application is formalised and a divorce certificate issued. The ZAGS office under this procedure has no interest in the reasons for the divorce. Consent and the absence of minor children are conclusive.

Under certain circumstances a marriage will be dissolved by ZAGS agencies upon the application of one spouse, for example, if the other spouse has been declared to be missing or to lack dispositive legal capacity, or has been sentenced to deprivation of freedom for three or more years for the commission of a crime.

Otherwise divorce proceedings are within the jurisdiction of the courts. This includes situations when one of the spouses, despite the absence of objections on his part, evades dissolution of the marriage in a ZAGS office (refuses to file application, does not appear for State registration of dissolution of the marriage, and others). The court has the right, but is not required, to endeavour to reconcile the parties and may postpone consideration of the case for a period of up to three months for this purpose. The marriage must be dissolved if measures relating to reconciliation of the spouses proved to be without results and the spouses (or one of them) insist upon dissolution of the marriage. No grounds need be stipulated. The Family Code merely provides that a marriage shall be dissolved in a judicial proceeding if it is established by a court that the further joint life of the spouses and preservation of the family is impossible. Common grounds for divorce have included the abuse of alcoholic beverages by one spouse, non-cohabitation for a protracted period, or the inability of one spouse to conceive a child.

The divorcing spouses are at liberty to decide with which of them any minor children shall reside and may submit for the consideration of the court an agreement so specifying, as well as the procedure for payment of means for maintenance of the children, and/or the lack of labour capacity of a needy spouse, the amounts of such means, or the division of common property of the spouses. If there is no agreement between the spouses with regard to these questions, and also if it is established that the particular agreement violates the interests of the children or one of the spouses, the court is obliged to determine with which of the parents minor children will reside after the divorce, determine from which of the parents and in what amounts alimony is to be recovered for their children, at the demand of the spouses (or one of them) divide the property in their joint ownership, and at the demand of the spouse having the right to receive maintenance from the other spouse, determine the amount of this maintenance. If the division of property affects the interests of third persons, the court has the right to separate out the demand concerning the division of property into an individual proceeding.

A marriage dissolved in ZAGS offices terminates from the day of State registration of dissolution of the marriage in the book for the registration of acts of civil status. If the marriage is dissolved in a court, termination is from the day of entry of the decision of the court into legal force. Dissolution of a marriage in a court is subject to State registration in the procedure established for the State registration of acts of civil status. The court is obliged within three days from the day of entry into legal force of its decision concerning the dissolution of the marriage to send an extract of this decision to the ZAGS office at the place where State registration of the marriage was made. Spouses do not have the right to enter into a new marriage until they receive the certificate concerning dissolution of the marriage at the ZAGS office at the place of residence of one of them.

Invalidity of marriage

A marriage is deemed to be invalid if the conditions for concluding it were violated, or there were obstacles to the conclusion thereof, or if the marriage is fictitious. By fictitious marriage is meant the registration of a marriage without an intention to create a family, but rather, for example, to obtain rights to a pension, dwelling house, or other reason. A court may deem a marriage to be valid if at the moment of consideration of the case concerning the deeming of a marriage to be invalid the circumstances have disappeared which by virtue of a law obstructed the marriage being concluded.

A judicial proceeding is required to declare a marriage invalid. The spouses, any persons whose rights were violated by the marriage, parents of a minor spouse, guardianship and trusteeship agencies, or the Procuracy may bring suit to this end. A marriage deemed to be invalid is regarded as such from the moment it was concluded and no rights and duties arise from the marriage unless fraud was present. A court may not deem a marriage to be fictitious if the persons who registered such marriage have created a family de facto before consideration of the case by a court.

A court is obliged within three days from the day of entry into legal force of its decision deeming the marriage to be invalid to send an extract of this decision to the ZAGS office at the place where the marriage was registered.

The rights of children born of a fictitious marriage or within 300 days of the marriage being deemed to be invalid are not affected by the invalidity. Property relations between the parties to a fictitious marriage are governed by the Civil Code of the Russian Federation, and a marriage contract concluded by them is invalid. When rendering a decision deeming a marriage to be invalid, a court has the right to recognise for the spouse whose rights have been violated by the conclusion of such marriage (spouse in good faith) the right to receive maintenance from the other spouse, and with respect to the division of property acquired jointly before the moment of deeming the marriage to be invalid, has the right to give effect to other property rights and to deem the marriage contract to be valid in whole or in part. A spouse in good faith has the right to demand compensation for material and moral harm caused to him or her pursuant to the Civil Code. A spouse in good faith has the right when the marriage is deemed invalid to retain the surname chosen when the State registration of the marriage was effectuated.

Property of spouses

The Russian Family Code divides the property of spouses into two categories. Property acquired by spouses during a duly registered marriage is in their joint ownership, also called the 'common property of spouses'. If the marriage is not duly registered or if the property was acquired before the marriage or during marriage by gift or inheritance, the property is in their respective individual ownership. The rights of spouses to possess, use, and dispose of property which is the joint ownership of members of a peasant (or farmer's) economy is determined by Articles 257 and 258 of the Civil Code of the Russian Federation.

The Russian Family Code contains an extensive list of property which is considered to be the common property of spouses: the revenues of each of the spouses from labour activity, entrepreneurial activity and the results of intellectual activity, pensions and benefits received by them, and also other monetary payments not having a special-purpose designation (amounts of material assistance, amounts paid in compensation of damage in connection with the loss of labour capacity as a consequence of mutilation or other impairment of health, and others). Moveable and immoveable things, securities, shares, contributions, participatory shares in capital deposited in credit institutions, or in other commercial organisations also acquired at the expense of common revenues of the spouses, and any other property acquired by spouses in the period of the marriage, irrespective of in the name of which spouse it is acquired or in the name of which of the spouses monetary means have been deposited, also are the common property of spouses. The spouse who is a home-maker is an equal participant in common property provided that he or she conducted the household, cared for children, or for other justifiable reasons had no autonomous revenue. Articles of individual use (clothing, footwear, and others), except for jewellery and other articles of adornment, although acquired in the period of the marriage at the expense of common assets of the spouses, are deemed to be the ownership of that spouse who used them. The property of each spouse may be deemed to be their joint ownership if it is established that during the marriage investments were made at the expense of common property of the spouses or the property of each of the spouses or the labour of one of the spouses which significantly increased the value of this property (capital repair, reconstruction, re-equipping, and others).

Should it become necessary to divide property in joint ownership, the shares of the spouses are deemed to be equal. However, the Russian Family Code has introduced the Marriage Contract to allow spouses to make an independent settlement of their property affairs. An agreement of the persons entering into a marriage, or the agreement of spouses determining the property rights and duties of spouses in the marriage and/or in the event of its dissolution, is deemed to be a marriage contract. If the contract is concluded before marriage, it enters into force from the moment of State registration of the marriage. The contract must be in written form and notarially certified. The spouses have the right to change by a marriage contract the regime of joint ownership established by law and to establish a regime of joint, participatory share, or separate ownership to all the property of the spouses, to individual parts thereof, or to the property of each of the spouses. A marriage contract may be concluded either with respect to existing or with respect to the future property of the spouses. The spouses have the right to determine their rights and duties in a marriage contract with regard to mutual maintenance, means of participation in the revenues of one another, the procedure for each of them to bear family expenses, to determine the property which will be transferred to each of the spouses in the event of dissolution of marriage, and also to include in the marriage contract any other provisions affecting the property relations of the spouses. The rights and duties provided for by the marriage contract may be limited to determined periods or made dependent upon the ensuing or non-ensuing of determined conditions. The marriage contract, however, may not limit the legal capacity or dispositive legal capacity of spouses, their right to have recourse to a court in order to defend their rights; regulate personal non-property relations between the spouses, and the rights and duties of the spouses with respect to children; contain provisions limiting the right of a needy spouse lacking labour capacity to receive maintenance; or contain other provisions which place one of the spouses in an extremely unfavourable position or contrary to the basic principles of family legislation.

The marriage contract may be changed or dissolved at any time by agreement of the spouses. An agreement concerning the change of or dissolution of the marriage contract must be concluded in the same form as the marriage contract itself. Unilateral repudiation of the performance of a marriage contract is not permitted. At the demand of one of the spouses, the marriage contract may be changed or dissolved by decision of a court on the grounds and in the procedure established by the Civil Code of the Russian Federation for the change of and dissolution of a contract (see Chapter 9). The operation of a marriage contract terminates from the moment of termination of the marriage, except for those circumstances which have been provided for by the marriage contract for the period after termination of the marriage. A marriage contract may be deemed by a court to be invalid in whole or in part on the grounds provided for by the Civil Code of the Russian Federation for the invalidity of transactions. A court may also deem a marriage contract to be invalid in whole or in part at the demand of one of the spouses if the conditions of the contract place this spouse in an extremely unfavourable position or if certain provisions of the Family Code are violated. A spouse is obliged to inform his creditor(s) about the conclusion, change, or dissolution of the marriage contract. A spouse who fails to do so is liable for his obligations irrespective of the content of the marriage contract. The creditor(s) of a debtor-spouse have the right to demand a change of the conditions or the dissolution of a contract concluded between them in connection with materially changed circumstances in the procedure established by Articles 451–453 of the Civil Code of Russian Federation (see Chapter 9).

Despite the provision for equal rights to the common property of spouses, the Russian Family Code gives the court broad discretion to depart from the rule by taking into account the interests of minor children or one spouse. Instances when the other spouse did not receive revenues for unjustifiable reasons or expended the common property of the spouses to the prejudice of the interests of the family are examples. Factors the courts weigh include the disability of one spouse, the spouse with whom minor children will continue to live, or drunkenness on the part of one spouse. The common debts of spouses when dividing common property of the spouses are distributed between the spouses in proportion to the shares awarded to each.

As a general rule the actions of one spouse with regard to managing and disposing of joint ownership are regarded simultaneously as the actions of the other. A transaction concluded by one of the spouses with regard to the disposition of common property of the spouses may be deemed by a court to be invalid for reasons of the absence of consent of the other spouse only upon the demand thereof and only in instances when it is proved that the spouse in the transaction knew or knowingly should have known about the lack of consent of the other spouse to conclude the particular transaction. For one spouse to conclude a transaction with regard to the disposition of an immoveable or a transaction requiring notarial certification and/or registration in the procedure established by a law, it is necessary to receive the notarially certified consent of the other spouse. A spouse whose notarially certified consent to the conclusion of the said transaction was not received has the right to demand the transaction be deemed to be invalid in a judicial proceeding within a year from the day when he knew or should have known about the conclusion of the particular transaction.

Execution may be levied with regard to obligations of one spouse only against the property of this spouse. If this property is insufficient, the creditor has the right to demand the partition of the share of the debtor-spouse which would be due to the debtor-spouse if the common property of the spouses were divided in order to levy execution against it. Execution is levied against the common property of spouses with regard to common obligations of the spouses, and also with regard to obligations of one of the spouses, if it is established by a court that everything received with regard to the obligations by one of the spouses was used for the needs of the family. If this property is insufficient, the spouses bear joint and several responsibility with regard to those obligations with the property of each of them. If it is established by judgment of a court that the common property of spouses was acquired or increased at the expense of means received by one of the spouses by criminal means, execution may be levied respectively against the common property of the spouses or against part thereof. The responsibility of the spouses for harm caused by their minor children is determined by civil legislation.

Support

Spouses have a duty to support one another from the moment their marriage is registered. Cohabitation without registration gives no right to support, whereas a separation of spouses without divorce in no way alters the duty to support, irrespective of the length of the separation. Assuming there is no agreement between the spouses concerning alimony and that support is refused, certain spouses have the right to demand alimony in a judicial proceeding from the other spouse who possesses the means to pay: a needy spouse lacking labour capacity, a wife while pregnant and within three years from the day of birth of a common child, a needy spouse who has cared for a common disabled child until the child reaches 18 years of age or for a common disabled child of the first disability group from childhood. The criteria vary slightly for a former spouse after divorce, but include a needy spouse who has attained pension age not later than five years from the moment of dissolution of the marriage, if the spouses were married for an extended time.

The duty to support a spouse may be removed or altered by a court decision. The court will have regard to a situation when the lack of labour capacity of the spouse who needs assistance ensued as a result of abuse of alcoholic beverages, narcotic means, or as a result of the commission by him of an intentional crime, the spouses were married for a short period, or in the event of unworthy behaviour in the family of the spouse demanding the payment of alimony. Unworthy conduct must be proved by the other spouse on the basis of judicial decisions or other evidence; it may have occurred before or after the marriage.

The amount of alimony payable to support a spouse is determined by the court as a monthly lump sum (not a share or percentage of earnings), taking into account the material and family status of spouses (or former spouses) and other interests of the parties deserving attention. In practice 'other interests' will include the ability of family members to earn independently, and the like. Either spouse may petition a court to alter the amount of alimony as circumstances change.

The Family

Russian legislation continues to adhere to the principle laid down in the earliest decrees on family law, that blood relationship, the birth of children, is the sole basis for the rights and duties of parents and children. Both parents have an equal duty to nurture and support their child irrespective of what their own personal relationship may be, reversing the situation under the Edict of 8 July 1944 whereby if the parents were not in a registered marriage the father had no responsibility for the child. Rights and duties between parent and child arise from the moment of birth, but the relationship must be duly registered. If the parents are married, there is a legal presupposition that the father is the husband of the mother; accordingly, either parent may apply to register the birth. If the parents are unmarried, they file a joint application for registration of the birth at a ZAGS office.

Under the 1944 Edict paternity proceedings were abolished. Restored by the 1968 FPMarL, they are retained in the Russian Family Code by the provision that if a child is born of unmarried parents and the latter do not make joint application to register the birth, the origin of the child from a specific person (fatherhood) is established in a judicial proceeding upon the statement of one of the parents, trustee (or guardian) of the child, or upon the statement of the person of which the child is a dependent, and also upon the statement of the child himself upon attaining majority. In so doing the court takes into account any evidence confirming with reliability the origin of the child from a specific person. The suit is brought against the putative father or, if the mother prevented the registration, also against her. If the putative father is deceased, the matter takes the form of a special proceeding to establish a legal fact. When establishing paternity, a court takes into account the cohabitation and keeping of a common household by the child's mother and the defendant before the birth of the child, or the joint upbringing or support for the child, or any evidence reliably confirming the acknowledgement of paternity by the defendant. The latter evidence may include witness testimony concerning statements by the defendant, blood tests, and the like.

In the event paternity is not established or the mother refuses to name the father, the child is entered in the birth register under the mother's surname and whatever forenames she may choose. This obviates the embarrassing blank spaces that appeared in such cases under the pre-1968 legislation and disclosed the illegitimacy of the child. The mother does not qualify for paternity support, of course, but she is eligible for State benefits for unmarried mothers.

Persons who are married and who have given their consent in written form to artificial insemination or to the implantation of an embryo, in the event of the birth of a child to them as a result of the application of these methods, are entered as its parents in the book of birth registrations. Persons who are married to one another and who have given their consent in written form to the implantation of an embryo in another woman for the purpose of bearing may be entered as the parents of the child only with the consent of the woman who gave birth to the child (surrogate mother).

Children born out of wedlock have the same rights and duties with regard to parents and their relatives as have children born of persons who were married to one another.

The rights of a child generally are regulated, in addition to the Family Code, by the Federal Law on Basic Guarantees of the Rights of a Child in the Russian Federation, of 24 July 1998, as amended 20 July 2000,[12] and international treaties of the Russian Federation.

---

[12] СЗ РФ (1998), no 31, item 3802; (2000), no 30, item 3121.

11

ENTREPRENEURIAL LAW

The principal civil law jurisdictions in continental Europe have a Civil Code and a Trade or Commercial Code (France, Germany), creating what some have called a 'dualism' of private law. The Digest of Laws of the Russian Empire also contained separate volumes devoted to civil and commercial legal regulation. In 1917–18 Soviet policy-makers had little opportunity to reflect on the role of civil and commercial law in a rapidly socialising economy. Some entertained naive assumptions about the rapid withering away of law and the legal system; however, the survival of the regime in the midst of civil strife and a hostile international community quickly took precedence over any grandiose transition to a new economic order. In the period of War Communism (1917–20) private entrepreneurship was discouraged, only during the NEP (1921–8) to be positively encouraged. It was during the 1920s that economic analytical techniques, such as input-output analysis, were developed as tools for comprehending inter-sectoral relationships in the economy, so essential for economic planning.

The transition to NEP was consolidated in the 1922 RSFSR Civil Code and a substantial body of economic legislation regulating the legal status of juridical persons and obligations. Although rightly characterised as an era of private entrepreneurship, NEP was in fact a mixed economy in which the State sector coexisted with the private, and civil law with State-oriented economic legislation. P I Stuchka was among the Soviet jurists of the period who supported the theory of 'two-sector law' under which property relations would be regulated by both civil and economic law; civil law was regarded as capitalist law and economic law was regarded as the law of a socialist economy.

When the initial transition to planning was made during the late 1920s in the midst of prolonged debates about industrialisation strategy among Soviet economists, the group of Soviet Marxist jurists in the ascendancy, led by E B Pashukanis, counselled the rapid elimination of Romanist legal concepts such as legal personality, contract, mutual rights and duties, and ownership associated with the NEP in the belief that vertical technical regulations based on Plan would suffice to manage the operation of production entities and the distribution of goods and services. In legal theory these views were elaborated by L Ia Gintsburg and Pashukanis, who saw economic law as a special form of policy of the proletarian State in organising the administration of the economy. Those views were rejected in the mid-1930s by the Soviet leadership and played no evident role thereafter.

Nevertheless, the legal and administrative structure that did emerge in the 1930s had produced, largely by separate economic legislation outside the 1922 RSFSR Civil Code, a body of planning, administrative, financial, property, contract, and enterprise law which many Soviet jurists believed in the late 1950s should be dealt with as a special branch of law outside the civil law. An intense debate broke out in connection with the drafting of the FPCivL. Those who favoured 'economic law' preferred a truncated civil law dealing only with the relations of citizens inter se and with socialist organisations. The civilists accepted the sui generis character of the planning and administrative aspects of relations of socialist organisations, but argued that these could be analytically distinguished from the civil law dimension of those relations and that there was real merit in preserving the civil law unity of horizontal relationships, whether between enterprises or citizens. So evenly drawn were the protagonists in the discussions that reportedly a formal debate was held before the late A N Kosygin by representatives of both views. The decision favoured the civilists, and the 1961 FPCivL seemed to have put an end to the issue by incorporating the horizontal regulation of the planned economy into the general body of legal rules governing interpersonal relations.

In fact, the debate had only begun. No sooner were the union republic civil codes enacted in 1963–4 than the issue re-emerged. Economic law concepts were actively used in the post-Khrushchev economic reforms of 1965 to expand the rights of State enterprises and enhance the role of economic contracts: 'This approach enabled the narrow framework of the 1961 FPCivL to be overcome, which had proceeded from the absolute priority of an administrative act over a contract'.[1] By 1967 economic law was acknowledged to be a branch of legal science; textbooks were produced, economic law was officially approved as a specialisation in law faculties, and an economic law sector was formed within the Institute of State and Law of the USSR Academy of Sciences. The economic reforms of the post-Khrushchev era seemed to have injected a renewed vitality into the proponents of economic law. On 4 April 1969 the Social Sciences Section of the Presidium of the USSR Academy of Sciences authorised the preparation of a draft USSR Economic Code 'as a generalised law consolidating the new forms and methods of the economy and leading to a uniform system of normative acts for economic legislation'.[2] The draft, published for discussion in 1970, foreshadowed a number of economic measures enacted during the subsequent five years. Debate over the Code intensified; 'however, the Party-State apparatus of that time with the active support of civilist science rejected this draft—it thus did not become a law'.[3]

In the minds of its progenitors the economic law of the Soviet past has become the 'entrepreneurial law' of the market economy. 'Entrepreneurial' is preferred to 'commercial',[4] 'trade', or 'economic' law, the term 'trade law' being particularly unsuited in the Russian language since to many it implies purely purchase-sale relations. The aim of entrepreneurial law is to combine and integrate the public and private law aspects of economic life expressed in entrepreneurship, a philosophy and an aim which in the minds of most proponents presupposes a large, perhaps massive, dosage of State regulation of the economy.

Although it is a truism to say that there is significant State regulation of entrepreneurial activity in all advanced industrial societies, in the Russian context certain areas and approaches to State regulation suggest a compromise with the market economy rather than a transition to one. The State continues to be the owner of key sectors by outright State ownership of enterprises, the owner of most land in Russia, and the major stockholder in many of the largest joint-stock societies. On 20 July 1995 the Russian Federation introduced a system of State forecasting of and programming for socio-economic development for periods of three to five

---

[1] V V Laptev, Предпринимательское право: понятие и субъекты [*Entrepreneurial Law: Concept and Subjects*] (1997) 5. Also see I V Doinikov, Предпринимательское (хозяйственное) право [*Entrepreneurial (Economic) Law*] (1998); Iu M Osipov and E E Smirnova (eds), Основы предпринимательского дела: учебник [*Foundations of Entrepreneurial Business: Textbook*] (2nd edn, 1996); S E Zhilinskii, Правовая основа предпринимательской деятельности (предпринимательское право) [*Legal Basis of Entrepreneurial Activity (Entrepreneurial Law)*] (1998); I V Ershova, Предпринимательское право: учебник [*Entrepreneurial Law: Textbook*] (2002).

[2] See W E Butler (ed and transl), 'Economic Code of the USSR (Draft of Basic Provisions)', *Soviet Statutes and Decisions*, XII (1976), 433–483.

[3] Laptev (n 1 above) 5–6.

[4] Commercial law nonetheless has its proponents. See V F Popondopulo and V F Iakovleva (eds), Коммерческое право. Учебник [*Commercial Law. Textbook*] (1997); B I Puginskii, Коммерческое право [*Commercial Law*] (2000).

years with annual adjustments.[5] So-called 'special-purpose programmes' based on State financing or subsidies have been enacted in dozens of areas, many of which in other market systems are not the subject of State attention. Some special-purpose programmes require the deliveries of designated products or goods for State needs, the procedure for the delivery of which is regulated by a Law of 13 December 1994, as amended on 17 March 1997, 21 July 1997, 6 May 1999, and 9 July 1999.[6] The Government of the Russian Federation determines who are the State customers which are to conclude State contracts with supplier enterprises. Only monopolist enterprises are required to conclude State contracts; other enterprises are given various incentives to do so.[7]

The forms of State regulation of enterpreneurial activity are various: registration of juridical persons and entrepreneurs, licensing of individual types of activity, anti-monopoly regulation, taxation, price regulation for products of monopolist enterprises, currency and customs regulation, a law on the regulation of foreign economic activity, the Federal Law on the State Regulation of the Development of Aviation, of 10 December 1997,[8] and others.

A. Subjects of Entrepreneurial Activity

Registration

The principal actors in entrepreneurial activity in the Russian Federation are commercial organisations, non-commercial organisations which have the right to engage in limited entrepreneurial activity for certain purposes, individual entrepreneurs, legal entities which are not juridical persons, unitary enterprises, small enterprises, and State and municipal formations.

State registration of enterprises, introduced during the NEP, has always been linked in Soviet and Russian law with the formal legal existence of the enterprise. The classic formulation is that a juridical person exists 'from the moment of State registration'; registration in Russia is therefore constitutive. State registration also formed the basis for other registrations: tax, statistics, social insurance and security, and others. Although the process seemed superfluous during the socialist era, when ministries were responsible for the enterprises within their jurisdiction, and there is some evidence that during the 1950s registration of State enterprises was

---

[5] СЗ РФ (1995), no 30, item 2871.

[6] СЗ РФ (1994), no 34, item 3540; (1997), no 12, item 1381; no 30, item 3595; (1999), no 19, item 2302; no 28, item 3493.

[7] All of these developments also influenced venues for and approaches to dispute settlement in economic disputes. See A M Grebentsov, Развитие хозяйственной юрисдикции в России [*The Development of Economic Jurisdiction in Russia*] (2002).

[8] СЗ РФ (1998), no 2, item 226.

abolished as being superfluous, the transition to a market economy has been accompanied by new registration formalities.

The Civil Code of the Russian Federation requires (Article 51) the adoption of a Law on the Procedure for the Registration of Juridical Persons, which was completed on 8 August 2001, with effect from 1 July 2002. That Law regulated relations arising in connection with the State registration of juridical persons in the event of their creation, reorganisation, and liquidation, making changes in their constitutive documents, and the keeping of a unified State register of juridical persons. State duty is payable for State registrations, which are performed by tax agencies, although the Federal Law itself mentions merely the 'federal agency of executive power empowered in the procedure established by the Constitution of the Russian Federation and the Federal Constitutional Law on the Government of the Russian Federation' (Article 2). The State register is designated as a federal information resource kept on paper and electronic carriers, in the event of an inconsistency the paper records being given priority. The register contains the following information and documents: full and abbreviated name, including the firm name, of commercial organisations in the Russian language and other relevant languages; the organisational-legal form of the juridical person; the address or location of the permanently operating executive organ of the juridical person or the organ or person having the right to act in the name of the juridical person without a power of attorney; whether the juridical person is formed by way of creation or reorganisation; information on the founders of the juridical person; copies of the constitutive documents of the juridical person; information concerning legal succession for juridical persons created by way of reorganisation; the date of registration of changes or notifications concerning the constitutive documents; means of termination of the activity of a juridical person (reorganisation or liquidation); the amount of charter capital, contributed capital, charter fund, share contributions, and so on; full name and office of a person having the right without a power of attorney to act in the name of the juridical person, as well as passport data or other identity documents and his taxpayer number if such there be; and information concerning licences received by the juridical person. Old information is retained in the register unless expunged in accordance with a procedure determined by the Government. All information registered is open and accessible to the general public except the passport and taxpayer data of any natural persons in the registration entry; however, the personal information may be obtained by agencies of State power in accordance with their competence.

Information requested from the register is provided in the form of extracts, copies of documents in the registration file, or a formal reference that the information requested is absent. Data submitted for registration must be duly registered within five days of receipt by the registration agency. The moment of State registration is the making of the respective entry in the State register by the registering agency.

The Federal Law on the Registration of Juridical Persons does not extend to other subjects of entrepreneurial activity (natural persons), which continue to be regulated by the Statute on the Procedure for the State Registration of Subjects of Entrepreneurial Activity, confirmed by an Edict of the President of the Russian Federation adopted on 8 July 1994, as amended 29 August 2001.[9] Commercial organisations with foreign investments register in accordance with the 1999 Federal Law on Foreign Investments in the Russian Federation, of 9 July 1999.[10] The foreign investor must submit a bank reference and evidence of registration or incorporation in his home country.

Legal capacity

The Planned Economy of the Soviet Union extensively used the concept of 'competence' even for State enterprises in order to regulate what in a market economy would be described as 'special legal capacity'. The transition to a market economy in Russia with respect to entrepreneurial activity amounts to a considerable extent to a transition from 'special' to 'general' legal capacity.

Throughout the Soviet era and to this day in the State sector of the Russian economy, State enterprise charters have embodied the principle of special legal capacity, that is, enumerated only those activities which the enterprise could carry on. An enterprise could do only that which was expressly permitted. In the late Soviet era under *perestroika* the principle was modified: all was permitted that was not prohibited by a law, provided, however, that this maxim was applied within the framework of special legal capacity, that is, the activity had to correspond to the subject of activity of the enterprise (Article 21, 1990 RSFSR Law on Enterprises and Entrepreneurial Activity). Although subordinate legislative acts sought to alter the position in favour of general legal capacity, this change was only irreproachably achieved by the Civil Code, which provided that commercial organisations may effectuate any types of activity not prohibited by a law (Article 49) and the subject and purposes of the activity need not necessarily be specified in the constitutive documents (Article 52).

B. General Provisions

Juridical persons may be created only in the organisational-legal forms which are expressly provided for by the Civil Code, of which there are two groups: corporative and unitary.[11] Enterprises whose capital is divided into participatory shares

---

[9] СЗ РФ (1994), no 11, item 1194; (2001), no 36, item 3543. The 2001 Federal Law is translated in W E Butler, *Russian Company and Commercial Legislation* (2003).

[10] See Article 20(2). СЗ РФ (1999), no 28, item 3493; transl. in *Sudebnik*, IV (1999), 229–248.

[11] T V Kashanina, Хозяйственные товарищества и общества: правовое регулирование внутрифирменной деятельности [*Economic Partnerships and Societies: Legal Regulation of*

are corporative; economic societies take the form of joint-stock societies (closed or open) or societies with limited or additional responsibility. Economic partnerships are created as full or limited partnerships or *kommandit* partnerships. Unitary enterprises include State, municipal and treasury enterprises. There are in addition other vehicles for entrepreneurship, such as the small enterprise, subsidiary, simple partnership, joint enterprise, commercial organisation with foreign investments, branch, and representation office, which will be discussed separately.

'Corporative' should not be confused with 'corporation'. In Russian law and doctrine the expression 'corporative' is used to describe all types of Russian economic society and partnership, whereas the 'corporation' in the Anglo-American meaning does not exist in Russian law.[12]

Property of juridical persons

Corporative economic societies and partnerships are the owners of their property. State, municipal, and treasury enterprises are the possessors of their property on the basis of 'economic jurisdiction' or 'operative management'. Exceptionally one may still encounter a lease enterprise which possesses its property on the basis of a lease contract with the State. Irrespective of the nature of ownership, every juridical person must have an 'autonomous balance sheet' (see Article 48, Civil Code). The autonomous balance sheet is the highest expression of the 'property solitariness' of a juridical person, and is to be distinguished from the balance sheet of the subdivision of a juridical person, which has a 'separate' balance sheet. The assets and liabilities recorded on a separate balance sheet are also incorporated in the autonomous balance sheet of the enterprise as a whole. Representative offices and branches have separate balance sheets, although they may not be taxpayers in their own name.

There also exists the 'composite' balance sheet, which is used in associations of commercial organisations or enterprises having subsidiaries. A composite balance sheet includes the autonomous balance sheets of enterprises within the relationship, but does not integrate them, merely accumulates them. The principal enactment governing the procedure for recording the property of an organisation is the Federal Law on Bookkeeping Records of 21 November 1996, as amended 23 July 1998 and 28 March 2002.[13] The property of an enterprise is divided into various types of funds, of which the most central is the charter capital or charter fund

---

Intra-Firm Activity] (1995). For the basic legislation on Russian juridical persons, see W E Butler, *Russian Company Law: Basic Legislation* (3rd edn, 2000).

[12] See W E Butler, 'The Russian Open Joint-Stock Society and the American Corporation: The Principal Attributes Compared', *Sudebnik*, II (1997), 565–594.

[13] СЗ РФ (1996), no 48, item 5369; (1998), no 30, item 3619; (2002), no 13, item 1179.

formed from the contributions of the founders and stipulated in the constitutive documents. When an enterprise is created on the basis of a constitutive contract, and not a charter, the fund is called contributed capital. A distinction is drawn between basic and circulating means. Basic means include all immoveables, equipment, and other durable means of labour, whereas circulating means encompass raw material, materials, fuel, and money ear-marked for the operational activities of the enterprise. Any property of low value or rapidly depreciating property is also treated as circulating means irrespective of its function in the production process.

Wear and tear of basic means are deductible as amortisation in certain instances on an accelerated basis, especially for small enterprises. High levels of inflation have required that basic means be revalued from time to time in accordance with Government decrees. Reserve funds are usually created at the discretion of the enterprise itself. However, joint-stock societies are required to form a reserve fund equal to not less than 5 per cent of charter capital.

The chief book-keeper continues to play a key role in enterprise operations. The signature of the chief book-keeper is required as a matter of law on all monetary and settlement documents and financial and credit obligations. If the chief executive of the enterprise and the chief book-keeper disagree about certain economic operations, the documents regarding those operations may be accepted for execution over the written regulation of the executive, who thereby assumes complete responsibility for the consequences of those operations. The taking of an inventory is obligatory when property is leased out, purchased, or sold, before preparing the yearly report of the enterprise, when replacing materially responsible persons, and certain other instances.

An enterprise is liable for its obligations with the property belonging to it. The participants of economic societies and the owners of State and municipal enterprises are not, as a rule, liable for obligations of the enterprises except in individual instances provided for by law or when liability is inherent in the type of economic partnership.

Management models

The emergence of the private sector in Russia has required drastic changes in approaches to enterprise management. The role of the State, excluding unitary enterprises, has had to be confined to an external regulatory role rather than a directive one, as in the past. In effect economic methods of management have had to replace administrative methods: incentive programmes, economic forecasting, licensing, State orders, anti-monopoly requirements.

With the repeal of the 1990 RSFSR Law on Enterprises and Entrepreneurial Activity and the enactment of the 1994 Civil Code, Russian legislation no longer contains general provisions relating to enterprise management. Such requirements as exist are contained in individual legislative acts relating to particular types of juridical persons. The role of the constitutive documents of each type of juridical person has grown with respect to management as a result, defining as a rule the rights and duties of the principal executive organs and officers. In economic partnerships it is the participants themselves who take the principal management decisions, not least because in the absence of special legislation on each type of partnership, the founders have great latitude to determine internal management structures as they wish. The situation is more complex in joint-stock societies, where sophisticated legislation is in place which imposes certain formalities and hierarchies. The limited or additional responsibility societies offer considerable flexibility to the participants.

The unitary enterprise is headed by a director appointed by the owner of the property or by an empowered agency. Pursuant to the Edict of the Presidium of the Russian Federation on certain measures relating to ensuring State administration of the economy, dated 10 June 1994, the director of a unitary enterprise works on the basis of a contract concluded for a term of not less than three years.[14] The director of a unitary enterprise operates on the principle of 'one-man management', pursuant to the Standard Charter for treasury enterprises confirmed by Decree of the Government of the Russian Federation on 12 August 1994, as amended,[15] but without the constraints of labour collectives, whose powers lapsed with the repeal of the 1990 RSFSR Law on Enterprises except in certain privatised enterprises.

Creation, reorganisation, and liquidation

Corporative economic societies and partnerships are created by decision of their founder-owners and reorganised or liquidated by decision of empowered organs (economic societies) or by the full partners (economic partnerships). With respect to unitary enterprises, the decision lies with the owner or duly empowered agency. In all instances the creation, reorganisation, or liquidation is to be completed by the relevant State registration. The single most important general legislative act governing all three operations is the Civil Code of the Russian Federation.

Russian law speaks of the 'creation' of a juridical person in all possible manifestations, rather than merely 'founding'. Creation is understood to encompass not merely the coming into being of a new enterprise, but also the enterprises that emerge as a result of the reorganisation of existing enterprises. In all cases the

---

[14] СЗ РФ (1994), no 7, item 700.

[15] СЗ РФ (1994), no 17, item 1982; (1998), no 32, item 3893; no 48, item 5946; (1999), no 36, item 4400; (2000), no 49, item 4819; (2001), no 25, item 2575. Also see the Decision of the Supreme Court of the RF of 30 March 2001, excerpted in the Бюллетень Верховного Суда РФ, no 1 (2002).

juridical person has its own constitutive documents, which depending upon the organisational-legal form may comprise a constitutive contract, a charter, or both. The constitutive documents determine the firm name, location, and basic management structure of the juridical person and are subject to State registration. Changes in constitutive documents or the adoption of a new version must be notified to the registering agency and enter into force either upon registration or from the moment of notification.

Reorganisation is a blanket term in Russian law to denote one of five ways in which the organisational-legal form of a juridical person may be altered: merger, accession, division, separation, and transformation. Merger and accession are forms of amalgamating enterprises and were extensively used during the Soviet era with respect to State enterprises. Merger describes the process by which a single new larger enterprise is created from two or more small enterprises and all the enterprises which existed previously no longer exist. Under accession one or more enterprises accede to another enterprise, which continues to exist and operates on a larger scale. The enterprises which acceded to the latter lose their existence. Division and separation are ways of creating several juridical persons in place of one, and were widely used in the early 1990s as part of the curtailment of the State sector. Division refers to the dividing of a larger enterprise into two or more smaller juridical persons and the previously existing large enterprise is liquidated, whereas separation involves hiving off subdivisions of the larger enterprise into new independent enterprises while the larger enterprise continues to exist on a smaller scale. Transformation is the creation on the basis of an existing enterprise of another enterprise having a different organisational-legal form. This was the principal form of reorganisation employed during privatisation: State enterprises were transformed into joint-stock societies. Reorganisation in all instances is a non-taxable event, which for many investors can be a compelling reason for choosing Russia as the situs of corporate readjustments.

Legal succession under each of the five methods of reorganisation needs to be addressed. With respect to merger, accession, and transformation, all the property, rights, obligations, and duties pass to the enterprises newly created or, in the case of accession, remain with the existing enterprise. The Civil Code requires in each case that an act of transfer be drawn up to specify precisely which property is being transferred. As regards division and separation, the matter is more complicated and usually resolved in a special balance sheet drawn up to establish the precise legal succession to rights, obligations, duties, and property. The act of transfer and special balance sheet are confirmed by the person or organ which took the decision concerning the reorganisation and submitted together with the constitutive documents to the State registration agency. The failure of the documents to address issues of legal succession or the absence of the special balance sheet entail rejection of the reorganisation; if for any reason it is not possible to determine legal successors on the basis of the special balance sheet, all the newly-formed enterprises bear joint and several responsibility for the obligations of the enterprises which existed before the division or separation. Every creditor must be informed in advance of the reorganisation and has the right to terminate outstanding contracts, require fulfilment of obligations to it before time, and demand compensation of losses.

Liquidation of a juridical person means the termination of its activity without the transfer of rights and duties by way of legal succession to anyone else. The decision to liquidate may be taken by the founders or participants or by empowered management organs or by decision of a court to deem the registration of a juridical person to be invalid. A court decision may be rendered if there occurred violations of legislation regulating the creation of the juridical person which cannot otherwise be eliminated, or if the juridical person engages in activity without a licence which is subject to licensing or engages in activity prohibited by legislation, or commits repeated or flagrant violations of a law or other legal acts. Insolvency is also grounds for a court to order the liquidation of a juridical person.

The official, organ, or agency which takes the decision to liquidate must immediately notify the State agency which registered the juridical person in writing and appoint a liquidation commission or liquidator to manage the juridical person during the liquidation. An entry is made in the State register that liquidation is underway. The fact of liquidation being underway is published and a period of not less than two months established for creditors to submit demands. When the period for demands has lapsed, an interim liquidation balance sheet is drawn up which must be confirmed by the official, organ, or agency which took the decision to liquidate. Demands of creditors are then satisfied in the priority established by Article 64 of the Civil Code, as amended in 1996. Each category of priority must be satisfied in full before proceeding to the next priority; if assets available are insufficient to satisfy all of a priority, each creditor therein is satisfied in proportion to the amount of its demand against the total demands of that priority. Once the interim balance sheet is confirmed only creditors of the first four priorities are satisfied; the fifth priority must wait for a month after confirmation. The refusal of the liquidation commission to satisfy a demand may be appealed to a court. Demands of creditors submitted after the expiration of the deadline for submitting them are satisfied after all creditors who met the deadline have been satisfied. To the extent that property is insufficient to meet the demands of creditors, the demands are considered to be extinguished. A final liquidation balance sheet is then drawn up and submitted for confirmation by the official, organ, or agency which took the decision to liquidate.

Bankruptcy

The *Russkaia Pravda* in the eleventh century drew distinctions between those debtors who did not meet their obligations by reason of 'misfortune', that is, for reasons beyond the control of the debtor, and insolvency by reason of the debtor's fault, as evidenced in his attempt to flee or to conceal his property. Punishments were severe in the latter instance, including selling the debtor into slavery together with his property at a public sale. Dividing bankrupts into categories depending upon the degree to which they contributed to their own predicament, and shaping remedies and sanctions accordingly, has been characteristic of Russian legislation on bankruptcy throughout much of Russian history, a circumstance which has led to Russian law seeking to determine not merely the fact of bankruptcy, but also the reasons for it. These distinctions were found in the *Sobornoe ulozhenie* of 1649 and carried over to the Bankruptcy Charter of 1740, the Charter on Bankrupts of 1800, and the 1864 Charter on Commercial Court Proceedings. The priority of creditors throughout much of Russian history favoured foreigners, who were placed immediately after the prince or the treasury.

In the Soviet era the 1922 Civil Code of the RSFSR contained rules concerning the insolvency of civil and commercial partnerships and natural persons, but presumably had little application because the 1923 RSFSR Code of Civil Procedure contained no provisions to regulate the declaration of insolvency. However, in 1927 Chapter 37 was added on the insolvency of private persons, natural and juridical, and in 1929 two further chapters on the insolvency of State enterprises and mixed joint-stock societies and of cooperative organisations. With the disappearance of the private sector after the NEP, these provisions were moribund, although they remained in place.

Under present Russian legislation, insolvency or bankruptcy is a separate ground for liquidation, but also entails reorganisational and extra-judicial procedures. There were few State enterprises in the early years after the dissolution of the Soviet Union which were not technically insolvent, a fact which caused the Russian authorities to temporise with the enactment of bankruptcy legislation. A Presidential Edict on the subject, adopted on 14 June 1992,[16] applied only to State enterprises and was not in practice used to any extent. It provided an administrative procedure for bankruptcy, the decision to be taken by Goskomimushchestvo (then the State Committee for the Administration of State Property). On 19 November 1992, with effect from 1 March 1993, the Russian Federation adopted the Law on Insolvency (or Bankruptcy) of Enterprises,[17] which was replaced by the Law on Insolvency (or Bankruptcy) adopted on 10 December 1997 with effect from 1 March 1998, as amended 21 March 2002 and in turn replaced on 26 October 2002, with effect from 1 January 2003 by a law having exactly the same name (hereinafter 2002 Law on Bankruptcy).[18] This Law applies to all juridical

---

[16] Ведомости СНД и ВС РФ (1992), no 25, item 1419.

[17] Ведомости СНД и ВС РФ (1993), no 1, item 6.

[18] СЗ РФ (1998), no 2, item 222; (2002), no 12, item 1093; no 43, item 4190; transl in Butler (n 9 above). On 22 May 1998 the Government of Russia adopted a Decree on Measures Relating to Increasing the Effectiveness of the Application of Bankruptcy Procedures which introduced

persons (except treasury enterprises, institutions, political parties, and religious organisations), and to natural persons, including individual entrepreneurs. The 2002 Law on Bankruptcy extends to relations with the participation of foreign persons as creditors unless provided otherwise by an international treaty.

The 1992, 1997, and 2002 laws on bankruptcy substituted in place of the administrative bankruptcy procedure a judicial procedure. Bankruptcy or insolvency is defined in the 2002 Law as the inability to satisfy the demands of creditors with regard to obligations relating to monetary obligations and/or to perform duties with regard to the payment of obligatory payments. The composition and amount of monetary obligations and obligatory payments are determined as of the moment of the filing of an application in an arbitrazh court to deem the debtor to be bankrupt unless provided otherwise by a federal law. When determining whether bankruptcy exists, the amount of monetary obligations are taken into account, including indebtedness for goods transferred, work fulfilled, and services rendered, loans (with interest) subject to payment (excluding obligations to citizens for tortious actions, royalties to authors, and obligations to founders or participants of a juridical person). Penalties, fines, and forfeits which may be due under obligations are not taken into account, including with respect to obligatory payments to State agencies.

Bankruptcy proceedings are considered in the system of arbitrazh courts (see Chapter 6). An application to deem a debtor to be bankrupt by reason of the failure to perform monetary obligations may be filed in an arbitrazh court by the debtor, creditor, or procurator, and also by other persons when the 2002 Law on Bankruptcy so provides; in the case of a failure to perform duties to make obligatory payments, the application may be filed by the debtor, procurator, tax agencies, and other agencies empowered by a federal law. The case may be initiated by an arbitrazh court only if the creditor's demand exceeds not less than 100,000 rubles, although judicial practice permits several smaller creditors to combine their claims in a single suit; in the case of natural persons, the minimum limit is one hundred times the minimum payment for labour. With respect to banks a proceeding may be commenced only after the bank has been deprived of its licence to carry on banking activities.

Reorganisational procedures may be undertaken in an effort to avoid bankruptcy. The 2002 Law on Bankruptcy is more liberal to debtors than its predecessor of 1992. Deeming a juridical person to be insolvent is regarded as an extreme measure, to be used as a rule only after less drastic methods have failed. And only the arbitrazh court may deem a juridical person to be bankrupt.

---

simplified proceduresfor managing bankruptcy proceedings with regard to debtors of the State. СЗ РФ (1998), no 21, item 2249.

If a bankruptcy application is accepted for consideration by an arbitrazh court, the court will place the juridical person concerned under 'observation', a new procedure introduced in the 1997 Law on Bankruptcy. The aim of this procedural stage is to avoid the bankrupt's property from being cleaned out or plundered and to prepare measures directed either towards the recuperation of the enterprise or towards its liquidation. If during this period the enterprise is able to pay its creditors or the indicia of bankruptcy do not exist, the case is terminated. During the observation period arrest may be imposed on the debtor's property only within the framework of an insolvency proceeding, and demands of creditors may not be satisfied individually. In and of itself the observation period is not grounds for removing the management personnel of the enterprise from office; they continue to perform their functions, but with certain limitations. If the enterprise director does not take corresponding steps to protect the property of the enterprise or obstructs the temporary administrator appointed by the courts in the performance of his observation duties, the arbitrazh court may transfer all of the duties of the enterprise director to the temporary administrator.

Once it is decided to institute a bankruptcy case, the creditors or a meeting of creditors determine the future of the enterprise. All judicial decisions previously adopted with regard to property sanctions against the enterprise are suspended, except for payments of indebtedness related to alimony and analogous demands.

After completion of the observation procedure, the arbitrazh court may have recourse to one of two procedures. External administration is one such measure, pursuant to which the arbitrazh court appoints an arbitrazh (or external, temporary, or bankruptcy) administrator who acts as the director of the enterprise. To him immediately upon appointment are transferred the account and other documentation of the enterprise and the seal. A moratorium is introduced on the satisfaction of demands of creditors, including obligatory tax payments, penalties, fines, and forfeits, and amounts of losses caused. The moratorium may last up to 18 months. Not later than a month after his appointment, the administrator must work out a plan for the financial recuperation of the enterprise and submit it to the meeting of creditors for confirmation.

The administrator must be registered as an individual entrepreneur, have a higher education, and hold a licence; as a rule he is an economist, jurist, or individual experienced in business affairs for at least two years, with no record of a criminal conviction. A licensed arbitrazh administrator registers with a self-regulatory organisation, and upon appointment by the court is obliged to perform the duties as administrator. The arbitrazh administrator has broad powers to replace executives of the enterprise or to reduce their functions and to devise measures to restore solvency. These measures must be set out in a plan submitted to a meeting of creditors, which the administrator has the right to convoke. The meeting of creditors may create a committee of creditors to act *ad interim*. If the plan is confirmed by the committee, it forms the basis of the administrator's actions; if rejected, the arbitrazh court may appoint a new administrator or conclude that reorganisation in the form of external administration is impossible, in which case compulsory liquidation is instituted.

If the results of the external administrator are unsatisfactory, the meeting of creditors has the right to petition the arbitrazh court to deem the enterprise to be bankrupt and to open a bankruptcy proceeding.

The second form of reorganisation is pre-judicial sanation, which has in view the recuperation of the enterprise through the provision of financial resources by interested persons. Usually interested persons are the owners, founders, or participants of a juridical person, including agencies of executive power. The financial assistance is to be sufficient to repay monetary obligations and obligatory payments and to restore the solvency of the debtor and may be accompanied by the assumption of obligations by the debtor or other persons to the benefit of those who provided the financial assistance. The conditions under which agencies of executive power may provide financial assistance at the expense of the federal budget or State extra-budgetary funds is determined by the federal budgetary legislation for the particular year; the same applies to subjects of the Federation.

Although the creditors may petition for a bankruptcy proceeding when external administration proves to be unsuccessful, that measure may be instituted at once if it becomes clear that the solvency of the debtor cannot be restored. Compulsory liquidation is conducted so as to ensure commensurate satisfaction for the demands of creditors within the limits of assets available. It must be opened by decision of an arbitrazh court, after which it is prohibited to transfer any property of the debtor-enterprise to other persons or organisations without the authorisation of the meeting of creditors. Property is inventoried and valued, and a new administrator appointed for this purpose commences to realise the property at open public sales unless the meeting of creditors decides otherwise. The property is realised only at market value. Certain special provisions apply to insurance and securities organisations, agricultural and farming entities, and to enterprises employing more than 5,000 persons.

All obligations are considered to have been performed, whch places creditors in an equal position. The arbitrazh court removes the executives of the enterprise from office and appoints a bankruptcy administrator in their place. The bankruptcy administrator manages the enterprise, forms the liquidation commission, convokes the meeting of creditors, and takes responsibility for organising all work connected with the liquidation. The meeting of creditors makes all decisions relating to alienation of the property of the enterprise, nominates the bankruptcy administrator, and determines his remuneration.

The bankruptcy administrator determines what comprises the property against which demands of creditors may be satisfied. The Law on Bankruptcy specifies certain property which is not subject to bankrupcy demands: property leased by the debtor; property in its custody; personal property of enterprise employees; property in trust management. So-called infrastructure assets, such as the housing fund, pre-school institutions, and the like, must be transferred to the balance sheet of local agencies, which reduces the property against which creditors may receive proceeds. As in the case of liquidation, demands of creditors are satisfied in the priorities established by Article 64 of the Civil Code. Demands not satisfied are considered to be cancelled.

If the bankruptcy was caused by the founders or participants of the juridical person or others who have the right to give binding instructions to the juridical person, they bear subsidiary responsibility to the creditors for the obligations of the juridical person (Articles 56 and 105, Civil Code). Analogous rules are contained in individual laws on economic societies and partnerships.

At any stage of the bankruptcy proceeding an amicable settlement may be reached between the debtor and the creditors. Such an agreement must be in writing and confirmed by the arbitrazh court. The decision to conclude such an agreement in the name of the bankruptcy creditors is taken by the meeting of creditors by a majority vote of the total number of such creditors, provided that all creditors with regard to obligations secured by a pledge of the debtor's property have voted in favour of the decision. The amicable agreement may contain provisions concerning the deferral of payments or payment by instalments, assigning of the rights of demand of the debtor, performance of the debtor's obligations by third persons, a discount on the debt, exchanging demands for stocks, or satisfaction of the creditors' demands by other means which are not contrary to federal laws or other legal acts of the Russian Federation.

The 2002 Law on Bankruptcy contains simplified bankruptcy procedures for situations when the debtor is in the process of liquidation but its property is insufficient to meet obligations, or when the debtor cannot be located and it is impossible to establish its whereabouts.

C. Joint-Stock Societies

By far the most popular Russian organisational-legal form amongst Russian and foreign investors is the closed joint-stock society, widely known by its acronym ZAO. As of 1 July 2001, there were about 60,000 open and more than 370,000 closed joint-stock societies registered in the Russian Federation. Such companies were known in Russia from the eighteenth century.[19] The concept was adapted in

---

[19] In 1698 a proposal was made to form in Russia a company in which any person might join by means of the 'purchase of a "portion" or "stocks" '. See V V Dolinskaia, Акционерное право [*Joint-Stock Society Law*] (1997) 49.

Soviet legislation of the NEP era (there were provisions in the 1922 RSFSR Civil Code and in 1927 a special Statute on Joint-Stock Societies was confirmed). Although most of those formed in that period were later dissolved, a few connected with a foreign element survived until the end of the Soviet Union: Intourist, Vneshtorgbank, Ingosstrakh, for example. From November 1990 the formation of joint-stock societies began to be encouraged in the USSR (the Statute on Joint-Stock Societies and Limited Responsibility Societies was confirmed by Decree of the Soviet Council of Ministers on 19 June 1990)[20] and the Russian Federation as part of market transition policies.

The principal Russian Federation enactments inaugurating joint-stock societies were the 1990 RSFSR Law on Enterprises and Entrepreneurial Activity, as amended,[21] and the Statute on Joint-Stock Societies confirmed by Decree of the RSFSR Council of Ministers, No 601, on 25 December 1990.[22] These were superseded in all relevant respects by the Russian Civil Code and by the Federal Law on Joint-Stock Societies of the Russian Federation of 26 December 1995 and in force from 1 January 1996, as amended 13 June 1996, 24 May 1999, 7 August 2001, 21 March 2002, and 31 October 2002 (hereinafter Law on Joint-Stock Societies).[23] The open joint-stock society was the vehicle of choice in the course of the privatisation of State enterprises. The procedures for the organisation and activities of joint-stock societies created in this way were laid down by privatisation legislation, principally Presidential edicts and most notably the Standard Charter of a Joint-Stock Society confirmed by the Edict of 1 July 1992.[24]

A joint-stock society is distinguished from other economic societies by being a commercial organisation having charter capital divided into common stocks as specified in its charter. The stockholders do not bear responsibility for obligations of the society unless they fail to pay up their debt to the society for the purchase price of the stocks, in which case creditors of the society may proceed against the defaulting stockholder to the extent of the debt owed to the society.[25]

---

[20] Transl in W E Butler, *Basic Documents on the Soviet Legal System* (2nd edn, 1991) 323–343.

[21] Ведомости СНД и ВС РСФСР (1990), no 30, item 418; transl in W E Butler, *Basic Legal Documents of the Russian Federation* (1992) 183–206.

[22] СП РСФСР (1991), no 6, item 92; transl in W E Butler (n 22 above) 209–225.

[23] СЗ РФ (1996), no 1, item 1; no 25, item 2956; (1999), no 22, item 2672; (2001), no 33(I), item 3423; (2002), no 12, item 1093, no 45, item 4436. The amendments of 7 August 2001 affected 66 of the 94 articles in the Law. Transl in Butler (n 9 above). See generally O M Krapivin and V I Vlasov, Практический комментарий к федеральному закону об акционерных об ществах [*Practical Commentary to the Federal Law on Joint-Stock Societies*] (2000); B S Black, R Kraakman, and A S Tarassova, *Guide to the Russian Law on Joint-Stock Companies* (1998).

[24] Ведомости СНД и ВС РФ (1992), no 1, item 3; САПП РФ, no 21, item 1731; СЗ РФ (1993), no 2, item 102; (1998), no 16, item 1832.

[25] It was for a long time a fine procedural point as to whether under these circumstances a creditor must first proceed against the society, which impleads the debtor-stockholder, or whether the creditor may proceed against both together, or whether the creditor may proceed against either. Much turns upon the legal nature of the 'stock' under Russian law. Article 2(1) of the Law on

A joint-stock society may be created by one or several founders. If there is more than one founder, a founder's meeting is held in order to complete certain formalities: adopt unanimously the decision to create the society, confirm the charter, value any contributions in kind to the charter capital, and elect the management organs. The charter of the society is the sole constitutive document; any stockholder agreements concluded do not have the status of a constitutive document and therefore cannot regulate relations between the society and other persons. It is, however, imperative for the founders to conclude a written contract among themselves which determines the procedure for them to effectuate joint activity relating to founding the society, the amount of charter capital of the society, the amount and types of stocks subject to placement among the founders, the procedure for paying up the stocks, and the rights and duties of the founders with regard to creating the society. This contract likewise is not a constitutive document.

Joint-stock societies are either closed or open. The open joint-stock society is based on the open subscription to stocks; the stockholders are at liberty to dispose of their stocks as and when they wish; and open joint-stock societies are held to higher standards of public accountability, including the publication of yearly book-keeping balance sheets and financial reports. There is no ceiling on the number of stockholders.

In a closed joint-stock society all stocks must be distributed among the founders. Stockholders have the right to dispose of their stocks but must first offer them to fellow stockholders for preferential acquisition. Public accountability is not obligatory for a ZAO. Under the Law on Joint-Stock Societies the number of stockholders in a closed society may not exceed 50; the requirement was not retroactive and did not affect closed societies registered before 1 January 1996.

The charter capital is regarded by Russian legal doctrine as a protection of creditors,[26] although that view has long been overtaken in the West by more sophisticated structures. The minimum charter capital for an open society is 1,000 times the minimum amount of payment for labour, and for a ZAO, 100 times. The amount of minimum payment for labour, which is fixed by the State and changed from time to time, is determined as of the date of registration of the society. At least half of the stocks distributed must be paid up within three months of the moment of registration and the balance within a year of registration (this is a change, which means that the stockholder under this formula has paid in full for

---

Joint-Stock Societies now provides that stockholders have joint and several responsibility for obligations of the society to the extent of the unpaid portion of the value of the stocks belonging to them.

[26] That view is recorded in Article 25(1) of the Law on Joint-Stock Societies: 'The charter capital of a society shall determine the minimum amount of the property of a society guaranteeing the interests of its creditors'.

50 per cent of the stocks distributed to him and has paid nothing towards the other 50 per cent; it eliminates the anomaly under the earlier formulation where none of the stocks were paid in full, but only 50 per cent). Unless the charter provides otherwise, a founder may not vote his stocks until they are paid up in full. If the balance is not paid up in good time, the stocks not paid for pass to the ownership of the society; the charter capital is to be reduced within one year (unless the society realises the stocks) and creditors notified accordingly in writing with all of the attendant consequences. Russian law distinguishes between charter capital and net assets; the latter must not be less than charter capital, and if that occurs, the charter capital must be reduced to the level of net assets. The society is subject to liquidation for failure to comply with this rule.

The reserve fund must be formed in the amount of not less than 5 per cent of charter capital, and contributions of not less than 5 per cent of net profit must be made annually to the reserve fund until the requisite minimum level is met. Funds may be created in order to acquire stocks for sale to workers. Inscribed or bearer bonds may be issued by a society after charter capital is fully paid up for an amount not exceeding 100 per cent of the charter capital (par value of the bonds) or the amount of security provided to the society by third persons for the purpose of issuance of the bonds.

Stocks are treated in greater detail elsewhere (see Chapter 12). According to the Law on Joint-Stock Societies, a society may issue only inscribed stocks; however, the Law on the Securities Market, of 22 April 1996, as amended 8 July 1999, 31 December 1999, and 7 August 2001,[27] permits bearer stocks to be issued in proportion to the amount of charter capital established by normative standards adopted by the Federal Securities Commission. Stocks may be common or preferred; the quantity of preferred stocks may not exceed 25 per cent of charter capital. Preferred stocks are not voting stocks except under certain circumstances, for example, when questions of reorganisation or liquidation are considered or the issuance of new preferred stocks on conditions superior to the existing preferred stocks. Cumulative preferred stocks may be issued.

A distinction is made in Russian law between placed and declared stocks. Stocks are placed when they have been acquired by founders and other stockholders at the initial emission. The total par value of such stocks equals the charter capital of the society, and the charter must specify both the par value and the total number to be placed. Under the Law on Joint-Stock Societies as amended 7 August 2001, an increase in the charter capital of a joint-stock society at the expense of property of a society may not exceed the difference between the value of net assets and the amount of charter capital and the reserve fund of the society. If charter capital is

---

[27] СЗ РФ (1996), no 17, item 1918; (1998), no 48, item 5857; (1999), no 28, item 3472; (2000), no 1(I), item 10; (2001), no 33(I), item 3424; transl in Butler (n 11 above) 481–538.

increased by placing additional stocks, such stocks are to be distributed among all stockholders of the same type or category in proportion to the number of stocks which each owns. Split stocks may be created through a placement of additional stocks, but not when this is at the expense of property of the society.

Declared stocks are those which may be issued in the future, are considered to be supplemental to the placed stocks, and may or may not be specified in the charter.[28] But the charter must be amended if it is decided to place additional stocks. Those joint-stock societies created in the process of privatisation may have Type A (preferred) and Type B (preferred) stocks; the last were issued to the State, placed at the disposition of Goskomimushchestvo (now the Ministry of State Property), and converted into common stocks for sale to the general public. Provision is also made for the 'golden stock' issued by decision of the Government in enterprises of special importance; this stock gives the Government the right of veto over certain measures, for example, reorganisation or liquidation, and may be convertible to a common stock when transferred to private persons.

The status of stockholder is acquired from the moment of registration in the stockholder register. The register is kept by the society itself or may be entrusted to a specialist organisation; if there are more than 50 stockholders, the register must be held by a registrar. Dividends are declared once a year unless established otherwise by the Law on Joint-Stock Societies. They may not be paid if the charter capital is not fully paid up, or until all stocks have been purchased by right of redemption, or if there are indicia of insolvency, or if the value of net assets is less than the charter capital and reserve fund; and in certain other instances. Stockholders have the right under Russian legislation of redemption when the society is to be reorganised, changes or additions are to be made in the charter which limits their rights if they voted against the said decision or abstained, or if a large-scale transaction is to be concluded as defined by Articles 78 or 79 of the Law on Joint-Stock Societies.

Common stockholders have the right to vote at stockholder meetings (and preferred stockholders, as noted above); in a ZAO the stockholders have a preferential right to acquire the stocks of other stockholders. In a ZAO a stockholder or group of stockholders owning not less than 2 per cent of the voting stocks may place questions on the agenda of the stockholder meeting and nominate candidates to the council of directors, collegial executive organ, internal audit committee, and counting commission, as well as candidates for the office of the one-man

---

[28] In 1988 a Decree of the USSR Government authorised the issuance of 'quasi-stocks' of enterprises and of labour collectives. The stocks of enterprises were sold to other enterprises in order to raise additional capital, whereas labour collective stocks were placed amongst workers of the enterprise. The issuers were not joint-stock societies, and the stocks were not real stocks. Their issuance is no longer permitted.

management organ. The refusal to include a proposed question on the agenda or to place nominations on the list of candidacies may be appealed to a court.

A major distinguishing feature between the Anglo-American corporation and the Russian joint-stock society is the status of the stockholder meeting in Russia as the highest management organ of a joint-stock society. This means that the Russian stockholder meeting decides a large number of questions enumerated in the Law on Joint-Stock Societies, 19 of which are within its competence and may not be transferred for decision to the executive organ of the society nor, except as the Law provides otherwise, to the council of directors or supervisory council. Most questions are decided by majority vote, but certain questions require a three-quarters majority; the last include changes or additions to the charter, reorganisation or liquidation of the society, determination of the quantity, par value, categories or types of declared stocks and the rights granted by those stocks, and the acquisition by the society of placed stocks. The amendments of 7 August 2001 were directed principally at redistributing these powers among management organs or clarifying the procedures by which the management organs conduct their affairs.[29]

A stockholder meeting is 'empowered' to conduct business when stockholders having more than 50 per cent of the placed voting stocks are present. If that quorum is not present, the meeting may be convoked a second time on another date, in which case the quorum must be not less than 30 per cent of placed voting stocks. Russian law distinguishes between the yearly stockholder meeting and all other meetings, which are called extraordinary meetings. The yearly meeting must be convoked not earlier than two months nor later than six months after the end of the calendar year; it elects the council of directors, internal audit commission, confirms the external auditor, and confirms the yearly reports, yearly bookkeeping records, including profits and losses reports or accounts, the distribution of profit, including the payment of dividends, and losses of the society. Extraordinary meetings may be convoked as necessary by decision of the council of directors at its own initiative, request of the internal audit commission or auditor, external auditor, or a stockholder or group of stockholders who possess on the date of submitting the request for such meeting not less than 10 per cent of the voting stocks of the society. The agenda of stockholder meetings may not include items such as 'any other business' or 'miscellaneous'; these terms have been ruled illegal in arbitrazh judicial practice for being insufficiently precise.

---

[29] For a detailed commentary on the changes introduced by the amendments of 7 August 2001, see G S Shapkina, Новое в российском акционерном законодательстве. Изменения и дополнения федеральново закона 'об акционерных обществахе' [*New in Russian Joint-Stock Society Legislation. Changes and Additions to the Federal Law 'On Joint-Stock Societies*] (2002). As part of the policy of strengthening stockholder rights, on 31 May 2002 the Federal Commission for the Securities Market confirmed the Statute on Additional Requirements from the Procedure of Preparing, Convoking and Conducting the General Meeting of Stockholders. See Российская газета, 18 July 2002, p 7.

The council of directors, which may in a charter also be named the supervisory council, exercises general direction over the activity of the society and may decide all questions not relegated to the competence of the general meeting of stockholders. A society with less than 50 stockholders may choose not to have a council of directors or supervisory council and leave all decisions to the stockholders. The council of directors is elected by the stockholder meeting for a term of up to the next yearly general meeting of stockholders; members may serve an unlimited number of terms. Only natural persons may be elected to the council of directors and they may not be stockholders of the society. Members of a collegial executive organ of the society may not comprise more than one-quarter of the members of the council of directors, and if there is a one-man executive organ, that individual may not simultaneously be the chairman of the council of directors. The size of the council is to be determined by the stockholder meeting or charter of the society; however, there must be not less than seven members if there are more than 1,000 stockholders and not less than nine if there are more than 10,000 stockholders.

In Anglo-American practice the competence of the council of directors is rather narrow because the competence of the stockholder meeting is so vast. Certain issues may be decided by the stockholder meeting only upon the recommendation of the council of directors: reorganisation of the society, confirmation of the yearly report and balance sheet or profits and losses report; retention of outside commercial management organisation or outside manager. The stockholder meeting may not authorise payment of a dividend higher than recommended by the council of directors. If the charter of the society so provides, the council of directors appoints the executive organ of the society; otherwise the stockholder meeting does so.

The executive organ directs the day-to-day activity of the society and may be either a one-man executive organ (director, director-general) or a one-man executive organ together with a collegial organ (board, directorate). If the second model is chosen, the one-man manager may not simultaneously serve as chairman of the collegial organ. The stockholder meeting may decide to entrust the functions of the executive organ to an outside management organisation or individual manager. The one-man management organ operates just as the director of a Soviet State enterprise did in the past: acts in the name of the society without a power of attorney, represents its interests, concludes transactions in its name, confirms the personnel establishment, issues orders and instructions binding on all workers of the society. The members of the executive organ, just as members of the council of directors, bear responsibility for damage caused to the society by their 'guilty' actions or failure to act unless the grounds for and extent of such responsibility have been established by federal laws, and if such damage was caused by a decision of the board, they bear joint and several responsibility unless they voted against the decision or abstained.

Russian law continues to perpetuate a highly 'administrative law' approach to enterprise management. There are expectations that each joint-stock society will, in addition to its charter, confirm internal 'statutes' or 'reglaments' on the stock-holder meeting, the council of directors, the board, internal audit commission or auditor, and others in the form of local normative acts. The functions of audit have not been adequately comprehended in Russian legislation. The internal audit commission consists of amateur workers untrained, as a rule, in accounting or financial analysis, and its reports have no independent standing in the financial community. The external auditor is referred to in passing, although the external auditor's reports are decisive with respect to the solvency of the society and are prepared in the interests of the stockholders and the creditors.

Certain control mechanisms exist with respect to joint-stock societies to minimise corporate abuses. The concepts of a 'large-scale' and an 'interested' transaction' have been elaborated in the 2001 amendments to the Law on Joint-Stock Societies (Articles 78, 81). The first turns on the relative scale of the transaction in the society's operations, and the second on the personal relationship between management personnel and those behind or benefitting from the transaction. Members of the council of directors, persons performing the functions of one-man executive organ of the society, management organisation, or manager, member of the collegial executive organ, or stockholder of the society having jointly with his affiliated persons 20 per cent or more of voting stocks of the society, and persons having the right to give instructions binding upon the society fall into the category, together with their near relatives as defined in the Law on Joint-Stock Societies, of persons who may be 'interested' in a transaction. If such interest exists, the decision to conclude the transaction must be taken by the council of directors or general meeting of stockholders. As a rule the interested persons may not participate in the decision to conclude or approve the transaction.

The organisational-legal form of a joint-stock society is required for banks and investment funds, among others.

On 19 July 1998 a new type of joint-stock society was introduced, called the 'people's enterprise'. Governed by the Law on the Peculiarities of the Legal Status of Joint-Stock Societies of Workers,[30] such an enterprise is created by means of transforming any commercial organisation, except State or municipal unitary enterprises or open joint-stock societies in which the workers own less than 40 per cent of the stocks. Such an enterprise must have a minimum of 51 workers and at least 90 per cent of these must be stockholders. The law entered into force on 1 October 1998. So far as can be determined, this model of joint-stock society has not proved to be a popular one.

---

[30] СЗ РФ (1998), no 30, item 3611; transl in Butler (n 11 above) 377–398. Also see N Iu Kruglova, Комментарий к Федеральному закону 'Об особенностях правового положения акционерных обществ работников (народных предприятий)' [*Commentary to the Federal Law on Peculiarities of the Legal Status of Joint-Stock Societies of Workers (People's Enterprises)*] (1999).

D. Limited Responsibility Society

Second in popularity as a corporate vehicle to the joint-stock society among foreign investors is the limited responsibility society, known by its acronym OOO. In concept the OOO is very close to the joint enterprise introduced by the former Soviet Union on 13 January 1987. The legal status of such societies is determined by Articles 87–94 of the Civil Code and by the Federal Law on Limited Responsibility Societies of 8 February 1998, which entered into force on 1 March 1998, as amended 11 July 1998, 31 December 1998, and 21 March 2002.[31] It would be misleading to refer to the OOO as a 'limited liability society', for although it does indeed have limited liability, so too do all Russian economic societies and partnerships. The Russian legislator has unfortunately chosen a characteristic feature of juridical persons generally to be the name of one in particular.

The charter capital of an OOO is divided into participatory shares (доля), which are not securities. Participants in an OOO bear responsibility for its obligations only to the extent of their contributions to charter capital unless their contribution is not paid up in full, in which event they are liable jointly and severally to creditors of the OOO to the extent of their unpaid contribution.

The principal differences between the joint-stock society and the OOO lie in the distinction between stocks and participatory shares and in the fact that the OOO offers a simpler and less formal internal management structure. The maximum number of participants in an OOO is 50; if that number if exceeded, the OOO must within a year either reduce the number of its participants or be transformed into an open joint-stock society or a production cooperative. If the transformation is not undertaken or the number of participants reduced, the OOO is subject to liquidation in a judicial proceeding upon the demand of the agency effectuating the State registration of juridical persons or other agencies given the right by law to present such a demand.

One or several natural or juridical persons may found an OOO, whose constitutive documents are the contract and charter, but the juridical person may not be a sole participant if it in turn also consists of one person. The minimum charter capital is 100 minimum monthly payments for labour. As in the case of joint-

---

[31] СЗ РФ (1998), no 7, item 785; no 28, item 3261; (1999), no 1, item 2; (2002), no 12, item 1093. See S D Mogilevskii, Общества с ограниченной ответственностью. Комментарий. Практика. Нормативные акты [*Limited Responsibility Society: Commentary, Practice, Normative Acts*] (1999); M Iu Tikhomirov (ed), Комментарий к федеральному закону об обществах с ограниченной ответственностью [*Commentary to the Federal Law on Limited Responsibility Societies*] (1998); V V Zaesskii (ed), Комментарий к федеральному закону об обществах с ограниченной ответственностью (постатейный) [*Commentary to the Federal Law on Limited Responsibility Societies (by Articles)*] (1998).

stock societies, at least 50 per cent of the charter capital must be paid up upon registration and the balance within one year. If the charter capital is not paid up within the period, either it must be reduced or the OOO liquidated. It is prohibited to exempt participants from making contributions to charter capital or to allow such contributions in the form of set-offs to satisfy the demands of participants against the society. These limitations originate in the view that charter capital exists partly to protect the interests of creditors, a position expressly articulated in the Law on the OOO (Article 14). The OOO is required to maintain the correlation of net assets to charter capital which a joint-stock society must comply with. A reduction of capital may occur only after all creditors have been informed; creditors have the right to insist upon performance of their obligations before time and compensation of losses.

Contributions may be transferred by participants of an OOO to other participants or to third persons. As in the case of a ZAO, existing participants have a preferential right over third persons to acquire a participatory share that is to be alienated. The charter of an OOO may prohibit the transfer to third persons of a participatory share, in which case if the other participants refuse to acquire the contribution being alienated, it must be purchased by the OOO, which is then at liberty in future to sell the contribution to the other participants or third persons or to reduce the charter capital. A participant also has the right at any time to withdraw from the OOO, in which case he must be paid the value of the portion of the OOO's property which corresponds to his participatory share in the charter capital.

The management structure of an OOO is relatively simple. The highest management organ is the general meeting of participants which decides exclusively questions provided for by the Civil Code and the Law on the OOO: the principal orientations of the activity of the OOO; change of or addition to the charter; change of charter capital; formation of executive organs and termination of their powers before time; confirmation of yearly reports and book-keeping balance sheets, distribution of net profit; placement of bonds and other emission securities by the OOO; reorganisation and liquidation; election of the internal audit commission; confirmation of the auditor and determination of payment for services; and other questions determined by the Law on the OOO. If the participants so wish, provision may be made in the charter for the formation of a council of directors or supervisory council. The executive organ may be collegial or one-man and is accountable to the general meeting; the members of a collegial executive organ may not comprise more than one-quarter of the council of directors or supervisory council.

The OOO preserves the internal audit commission from Soviet times and is allowed to appoint an external professional auditor. However, there is no public accountability of an OOO.

The OOO is a corporate vehicle which requires a high degree of trust among the investors. The participant in an OOO has the right at any time to withdraw from the OOO irrespective of the consent of the other participants or of the OOO itself. From the moment of filing application to withdraw, the participant's participatory share passes to the OOO, which is obliged to pay the participant the actual value of the participatory share determined on the basis of the data of the book-keeping report of the society for the year during which the application was filed concerning withdrawal from the society. With the withdrawing participant's consent, the value of the participatory share may be paid by the issuance of property in kind. The actual value is paid from the difference between the value of net assets of the society and the amount of charter capital; if such difference is insufficient to pay off the withdrawing participant, the OOO must reduce its charter capital by the insufficient amount.

E. Additional Responsibility Society

This variant of the OOO, known by the acronym ODO, is rarely encountered in practice. It did not exist in Russian law prior to the 1991 FPCivL and Civil Code of the Russian Federation.

The ODO is subject to the same provisions of the Civil Code as the OOO with the addition of Article 95. The material difference between the two is that in an ODO the participants agree to bear additional responsibility for obligations of the society in a multiple of their contribution. If one of the participants of the ODO becomes bankrupt, his responsibility is distributed amongst the remaining participants in proportion to their contributions unless provided otherwise by the constitutive documents.

F. Full Partnership

This species of partnership has little in common with the Anglo-American partnership. It is a juridical person in which each participant is liable for the partnership's obligations with all of the property belonging to the participant. Only natural persons registered as entrepreneurs and commercial organisations may be members of a full partnership, and a natural person may only be a participant in one full partnership. The firm name must contain the name of one, several, or all participants.

The full partnership is regulated only by Articles 69–81 of the Civil Code pending the enactment of a special federal law on the subject. The partnership operates on the basis of the common consent of its participants, each having one vote irrespective of the amount of his contribution, unless the constitutive contract of the partnership provides otherwise.

Each participant of the partnership has the right to act in its name unless the constitutive contract designates one or several participants to do so, in which case the others must have a power of attorney when they do act in the name of the partnership. These limitations do not affect the rights of third persons, as the members of a full partnership may not cite the constitutive contract limiting their powers unless the partnership proves that the third person knew or should have known at the moment of concluding the transaction that the partner concerned was not empowered to act in the name of the partnership.

Each participant must pay up half of his contributed capital at the moment of registration and the balance as stipulated by the constitutive contract; delay in payment engages annual interest of 10 per cent and compensation of losses to the partnership. Profit is distributed amongst the full partners in proportion to their capital contributions, but may not be distributed if the value of net assets is less than the contributed capital.

The responsibility of the partners for liabilities of the partnership is subsidiary, that is, it ensues only if the property of the partnership is not sufficient to cover debts. It is also joint and several, so that a demand for payment of a debt of the partnership may be brought in full against any member of the partnership, who then has recourse against the other partners. The responsibility of a partner continues for two years after withdrawal from the partnership but relates only to obligations which arose while the participant was a partner. Withdrawal from the partnership requires six months' notice. Expulsion from a partnership is possible only by decision of a court rendered at the request of the other partners. A withdrawing partner is paid the value of his share of the property of the partnership which corresponds to his contributed capital.

If a partner dies, his heir may become a member of the partnership only with the consent of the other participants; if such consent is not forthcoming, the heir receives the commensurate property of the partnership which corresponds to the contributed capital of the deceased partner. A partner may transfer his participatory share to a third person only with the consent of the other participants.

Execution may be levied against the partnership for debts of a partner only to the extent of the partner's contributed capital and only if the partner's other property is insufficient to meet the obligation. The partnership continues to exist after the withdrawal of partners unless the constitutive documents provide otherwise; however, if only one partner remains, the partnership must either be liquidated or transformed into an economic society (ZAO or OOO).

G. Limited (*Kommandit*) Partnership

The limited partnership, also known as the *kommandit* partnership, contains two groups of participants. The first consists of full partners who carry on entrepreneurial activity in the name of the partnership and who are liable for its obligations if the property of the partnership is insufficient. The second group consists of contributors who take no active role in the affairs of the partnership but bear the risk of losses connected with the activity of the partnership within the limits of their contributions. Only natural persons who are registered as entrepreneurs and commercial organisations may be participants of the limited partnership and they may be members of only one limited partnership. One may not be a participant of a full partnership and simultaneously a full member of a limited partnership.

The differing roles and legal status of the partners sometimes leads to the limited partnership being characterised as a mixed partnership, and indeed were named such before the Civil Code was adopted. The name of at least one full partner must be included in the firm name, but contributors need not be included and if they are, they become a full partner with all of the respective responsibility.

The limited partnership is created by a constitutive contract signed only by the full partners, whose contribution is individually specified. The contribution of the contributors is specified only in aggregate. Only the full partners take part in the management of the partnership; contributors have no role there, although on the basis of a power of attorney they may act in the name of the partnership. The sole duty of the contributor is to pay up his contribution, which is certified by a certificate of participation issued by the partnership. The contributor has the right to: receive part of the partnership profit; familiarise himself with the yearly reports and balance sheets; withdraw from the partnership at the end of the year and receive his contribution back; transfer his participatory share in the contributed capital or part thereof to another contributor or to a third person; however in the last instance the other contributors have a preferential right against third persons to purchase the participatory share or part thereof.

It is a requirement of the limited partnership that there be both full partners and contributors; accordingly, if all the contributors withdraw, the partnership must be liquidated or be transformed into a full partnership. One full partner and one contributor is sufficient to retain the limited partnership.

When a limited partnership is liquidated, including by way of bankruptcy, the contributors have a preferential right against full partners to receive back their contributed capital once the demands of creditors have been satisfied.

H. Simple Partnership

The simple partnership, sometimes called a contract on joint activity, was known to Soviet law but rarely used (see Chapter 9). The provisions on the subject have been strengthened in the Civil Code and are finding favour with foreign investors. Under the contract of simple partnership, two or several persons (partners) are obliged to combine their contributions and jointly operate without the formation of a juridical person in order to derive profit or achieve another purpose which is not contrary to law. Only individual entrepreneurs and/or commercial organisations may be the parties to a contract of simple partnership concluded in order to effectuate entrepreneurial activity. Because a juridical person is not formed, many Russian legal scholars who write about entrepreneurial law omit the simple partnership, and indeed the Civil Code allocates a Chapter to the subject towards the end of Part Two (Chapter 55), unlike, for example, the Kazakhstan Civil Code which placed the simple partnership close to the provisions on economic societies and partnerships.

In Western eyes the simple partnership is the classic contractual joint venture (not to be confused with the joint enterprise, under Soviet law). Everything that a partner has contributed to the general cause, including money, other property, professional and other knowledge, skills and ability, and also business reputation and business connections, is deemed to be its contribution. The contributions of partners are presupposed to be equal in value unless it follows otherwise from the contract of simple partnership or factual circumstances. The monetary valuation of the contribution of partners is made by agreement between them. The property contributed by partners which they possessed by right of ownership, and also the product produced as a result of joint activity and the fruits and revenues received from such activity, is deemed to be their common participatory share ownership insofar as not established otherwise by a law or by the contract of simple partnership or not arising from the essence of the obligation. The use of common property by the partners is effectuated by their common consent, and in the event of the failure to achieve consent, in the procedure established by a court.

When conducting common affairs, each partner has the right to act in the name of all the partners unless it is established by the contract of simple partnership that the conducting of affairs is to be effectuated by individual participants or jointly by all the participants of the contract of simple partnership. When conducting affairs jointly the consent of all the partners is required for the conclusion of each transaction. In relations with third persons the power of a partner to conclude a transaction in the name of all the partners is certified by a power of attorney issued to him by the remaining partners or by the contract of simple partnership concluded in written form. Decisions affecting the common affairs of partners are adopted by the partners by their common consent unless provided otherwise by the contract of simple partnership. The procedure for covering expenses and losses connected with the joint activity of the partners is determined by their agreement. In the absence of such agreement, each partner bears expenses and losses in proportion to the value of his contribution to the common cause. An agreement wholly exempting any of the partners from participation in covering the common expenses or losses is null. When the contract of simple partnership is linked with the effectuation of entrepreneurial activity by its participants, the partners are liable jointly and severally for all common obligations irrespective of the grounds for the arising thereof.

The profit received by the partners as a result of their joint activity is distributed in proportion to the value of the contributions of the partners to the common cause unless provided otherwise by the contract of simple partnership or other agreement of the partners. An agreement to eliminate any of the partners from particpation in the profit is null. The creditor of a participant in the contract of simple partnership has the right to present a demand concerning the partition of his participatory share in the common property in accordance with Article 255 of the Civil Code.

A contract of simple partnership is terminated as a consequence of any of the following circumstances:

- the declaration of any of the partners to lack dispositive legal capacity, to have limited dispositive legal capacity, or to be missing unless the contract of simple partnership or subsequent agreement provides for the preservation of the contract in relations between the remaining parties;
- the declaration of any of the partners to be insolvent (or bankrupt);
- the death of a partner or the liquidation or reorganisation of a juridical person participating in the contract of simple partnership unless the contract or a subsequent agreement provides for the preservation of the contract in relations between the remaining partners or replacement of the deceased partner (or liquidated or reorganised juridical person) by his heirs (or legal successors);
- the refusal by any of the partners to participate further in a contract of simple partnership without term;
- the dissolution of the contract of simple partnership concluded with a specification of the period, at the demand of one of the partners in relations between them and the remaining partners;
- the expiry of the period of the contract of simple partnership;
- the partition of the participatory share of the partner at the demand of his creditor, unless in all cases the remaining partners agree otherwise.

In the event of the termination of a contract of simple partnership, the things transferred to the common possession and/or use of the partners are to be returned to the partner who granted them without remuneration insofar as is not provided otherwise by the agreement of the parties. From the moment of termination of a contract of simple partnership the participants thereof shall bear joint and several responsibility for the failure to perform common obligations with respect to third persons.

A statement of repudiation by a partner of a contract of simple partnership without period must be made by him not later than three months before the proposed withdrawal from the contract. An agreement to limit the right to repudiate a contract of simple partnership without period is null. If a contract of simple partnership was not terminated by the statement of one participant repudiating further participation therein or dissolution of the contract at the demand of one of the partners, the person whose participation in the contract has terminated is liable to third persons for common obligations which arose in the period of his participation in the contract as though he had remained a participant of the contract of simple partnership.

Provision is made for the possibility of a silent simple partnership (non-transparent partnership). In relations with third persons each participant of a non-transparent partnership is liable with all of his property for transactions which he concluded in his name in the common interests of the partners.

Foreign investors may find themselves in a simple partnership more commonly than they expect. Parallel decrees of the Plenums of the Supreme Court of the Russian Federation (No 4) and Supreme Arbitrazh Court of the Russian Federation (No 8) issued on 2 April 1997 stipulated that the contract concluded by the founders of a joint-stock society concerning the creation of the society is a 'contract of joint activity' by its legal nature under which the founders oblige themselves jointly to act for the purpose of founding a joint-stock society by means of combining their efforts and their contributions and when necessary make provision to cover expenses incurred when founding the society; the registration of the society is the grounds for termination of the contract.[32]

I. Joint Enterprise

Although Western firms operated 'concession agreements' on Soviet territory during the 1920–30s, joint equity ventures on a substantial scale were introduced in 1971 within COMECON in pursuance of the 1971 Comprehensive Programme for socialist economic integration.[33] On 13 January 1987 direct Western foreign

---

[32] See V Iu Bakshinskas, Правовые проблемы учреждения акционерного общества [*Legal Problems of Founding a Joint-Stock Society*], Юрист, no 10 (1997) 21.

[33] For the text, see W E Butler, *A Source Book on Socialist International Organizations* (1978) 33–128.

equity investment became possible on Soviet territory in the form of the 'joint enterprise'.[34] At the time, the joint enterprise was regarded as a special structural type of enterprise. When the RSFSR adopted its Law on Enterprises and Entrepreneurial Activity on 25 December 1990, the joint enterprise was not singled out as an autonomous organisational-legal form. Other terminology began to be introduced: 'enterprise with foreign investments', 'foreign enterprise' (although registered in Russia!). It became, and still remains, unclear whether foreign investment incentives and privileges extended to enterprises of a particular organisational-legal form or merely to any which contain a foreign element (although the 1999 Federal Law on Foreign Investments in the Russian Federation makes clear that subsidiaries and branches of foreign juridical persons do not enjoy foreign investment guarantees).

Few, if any, joint enterprises still exist as such in Russia. They were encouraged after 1992 to become a limited responsibility partnership (TOO) or other organisational-legal form of their choice (for other means of establishing a presence in the Russian Federation, see also Chapter 19).

J. Production Cooperatives

Cooperatives have long been a central feature of Soviet economic life, most notably in the form of the collective farm, or *kolkhoz*. The Law of the USSR on Cooperative Societies adopted in 1988 was intended to help lay the foundations for the transition to a market economy, and it remains partly in force to this day. Cooperatives, however, were not mentioned in the RSFSR Law on Enterprises and Entrepreneurial Activity of 25 December 1990, an omission which led many cooperatives to seek transformation into an economic society or partnership. From 1992 legislation began to appear on individual types of cooperative: the Law on the Consumers' Cooperative, of 19 June 1992, as amended 11 July 1997 and 28 April 2000,[35] the Law on the Agricultural Cooperative Society of 8 December 1995, as amended 7 March 1997 and 18 February 1999,[36] the Law on Production Cooperatives, of 8 May 1996, as amended 15 May 2001 and 21 March 2002,[37] and the Law on Credit Consumer Cooperatives of Citizens of 7 August 2001.[38] The production cooperative was singled out as a special type of commercial organisation in the Civil Code (Articles 107–112).

---

[34] See W E Butler, *Soviet Law* (2nd edn, 1988) 388–392.
[35] Ведомости СНД и ВС РФ (1992), no 30, item 1788; СЗ РФ (1997), no 28, item 3306; (2000), no 18, item 1910.
[36] СЗ РФ (1995), no 50, item 4870; (1997), no 10, item 1120; (1999), no 8, item 973.
[37] СЗ РФ (1996), no 20, item 2321; (2001), no 20, item 2321; (2002), no 12, item 1093.
[38] СЗ РФ (2001), no 33(I), item 3420.

The production cooperative, also known as an artel, is a voluntary association of citizens on the basis of membership for joint production or other economic activity. It is a requirement that all or most members of the cooperative contribute their personal labour. Each member of the cooperative has a common undivided share in the cooperative. It is possible for organisations possessing the rights of a juridical person to participate in a production cooperative, but the legislation on the whole is orientated towards natural persons being the usual members. Citizens aged 16 or older and obliged to take part with their personal labour in the cooperative may be members. There are two principal distinguishing features of the production cooperative: natural persons being the members as a rule, and each contributing with their personal labour to the cause of the cooperative. Persons who do not contribute personal labour may be members of a cooperative provided that such persons do not exceed 20 per cent of the membership, the minimum number of members being five. In the Credit Consumer Cooperatives of Citizens members are expected to take part personally in managing the cooperative.

Members bear subsidiary responsibility for the obligations of the cooperative within the limits provided by legislation and the charter of the cooperative. The Law on Production Cooperatives does not make provison for the extent of responsibility; the Law on Agricultural Cooperative Societies provides that the charter determines the extent of subsidiary responsibility, but the minimum amount is 0.5 per cent of the contribution of the member.

The property of a cooperative belongs to it by right of ownership and is divided into the shares of its members. The property created by share contributions of members is called the share fund. The charter may provide that a certain portion of the property constitutes an indivisible fund. At the moment of registration of the cooperative its members must pay up not less than 10 per cent of the share contribution and the balance within a year from the moment of registration. The amount of the share fund must not be less than the net assets of the cooperative. Shares may be freely transferred among members of the cooperative, but transfer to a non-member requires the consent of the cooperative; other members of the cooperative have a preferential right to purchase the share being offered to a non-member.

Profit is distributed among the members in accordance with their personal labour and/or other participation and the amount of their share contribution; for members who do not contribute personal labour, profits are distributed according to the amount of their share contribution. The portion of profit to be distributed among members of the cooperative in proportion to their share contributions must not exceed 50 per cent of the profit of the cooperative subject to distribution among members.

The highest management organ of a cooperative is the general meeting of members. The general meeting has exclusive competence with respect to the confirmation and change of the charter, determination of the basic orientations of the activity of the cooperative, the formation and termination of the powers of the executive organs, the admission and expulsion of members of the cooperative, the confirmation of yearly reports, book-keeping balance sheets, and distribution of profit and losses, reorganisation and liquidation of the society, and certain other questions. Each cooperative member has one vote at the general meeting. Cooperatives with more than 50 members may create a supervisory council which effectuates control over the activity of executive organs of the cooperative] (and in doing so differs significantly from the equivalent organ in a joint-stock society). The general meeting of members forms and terminates the powers of the supervisory council, if there is one, and all other executive organs, although the charter may transfer the right to create and terminate the executive organs to the supervisory council.

The executive organs are the board and the chairman. They direct the day-to-day activity of the cooperative and are accountable to the supervisory council and general meeting of members. A chairman is chosen in all cooperatives, and a board elected only where the number of members of the cooperative exceeds ten. The chairman acts ex officio in the name of the cooperative without a power of attorney. As in the case of enterprises, a cooperative also elects an internal audit commission.

Since a cooperative is a voluntary association of members, any member may withdraw at any time in his discretion. The cooperative must pay to the withdrawing member the value of his share or issue other property of equivalent value at the end of the financial year after confirmation of the yearly report of the cooperative. A member also may be expelled from a cooperative for failure to perform or for improper performance of his duties placed on him by the charter of the cooperative, in which event such member has the same right to be paid his share as does a withdrawing member.

K. Unitary Enterprises

A major change accompanying the introduction of a market system has been the transformation of the legal status of State and municipal 'formations' which participate in entrepreneurial relations.[39] The essence of the transformation is encapsulated in Article 124 of the Civil Code, which provides that the Russian Federation itself, subjects of the Federation, and municipal formations act in rela-

---

[39] An excellent study is N I Kosiakova, Государственное предприятие в рыночной экономике [*The State Enterprise in a Market Economy*] (2001). Also see Iu P Orlovskii and N A Ushakova (eds), Комментарий к законодательству о федеральных государственных унитарных предприятиях [*Commentary on Legislation Concerning Federal State Unitary Enterprises*] (2001).

tions regulated by civil legislation on equal principles with other participants of such relations, namely natural and juridical persons. State and municipal formations accordingly, in their capacity as the owners of property, have the right to create unitary enterprises by allocating their property to such enterprises on the basis of economic jurisdiction or operative management. The Civil Code requires that, in their capacity as owners, State and municipal formations may not interfere in the economic activity of unitary enterprises, but merely control them, may determine the subject and purposes of their activity, appoint the director, receive part of the profit, and reorganise or liquidate them.

The unitary enterprise is created by decision of the owner or duly empowered agency and operates on the basis of a charter.[40] Such enterprises enjoy special, rather than general, legal capacity. The Charter provisions determining the subject and purpose of activity lay down the 'vires' of the enterprise. Certain transactions require that special procedures be complied with (for example, signature), or that authorisations for the alienation of pledging of property be obtained. Nor is the enterprise the owner of its property; title rests with the State or municipal formation. Property, as noted above, is 'consolidated' to the enterprise by right of economic jurisdiction or operative management.[41] The last category, operative management, is reserved for so-called 'treasury' enterprises. The management structure of the unitary enterprise is simple: the director appointed by the owner controls the enterprise.

The unitary enterprise is liable for its obligations with all of the property belonging to it. The owner of a State or municipal enterprise operating by right of economic jurisdiction is not, as a rule, liable for obligations of the enterprise; and the owner of a treasury enterprise bears subsidiary responsibility for obligations of the enterprise if the latter's property is insufficient. These formulations leave the creditor of a unitary enterprise limited in respect of property which can be levied against and, where such property can be seized, with tainted title; if the unitary enterprise only has the right of economic jurisdiction or operative management, on what basis can a creditor or contracting party acquire more than the enterprise has by way of title or possession?

---

[40] See, eg the Charter of the Federal State Unitary Enterprise 'Russian Television and Radio Broadcasting Network', confirmed by Regulation of the Government of the Russian Federation, No 1516-p, of 17 November 2001, in execution of the Edict of the President of the Russian Federation of 13 August 2001, No 1031. СЗ РФ (2001), no 34, item 3486; no 48, item 4538.

[41] The property regime can be severely limited. The property of the Russian Television and Radio Broadcasting Network, for example, is in 'federal ownership, is indivisible, and may not be distributed according to contributions (or participatory shares, shares), including among workers of the enterprise, belongs to the enterprise by right of economic jurisdiction, and is reflected on its autonomous balance sheet'. And the 'fruits, products, and revenues from the use of property in economic jurisdiction of the enterprise, as well as property acquired by it at the expense of profit received, is federal ownership and ensues to the economic jurisdiction of the enterprise' (points 14, 15, Charter). СЗ РФ (2001), no 48, item 4538.

Until 1994 State federal enterprises were created by decision of Goskomimushchestvo, which in 1997 became a Ministry.[42] The 1993 Russian Constitution relegated the administration of federal ownership to the competence of the Government of Russia (Article 114), pursuant to which on 10 February 1994 the Government adopted a Decree delegating the powers with respect to the administration and disposition of objects of federal ownership. Under this Decree, as amended 3 February 2000, 16 March 2000, 16 February 2001, and 19 July 2001, decisions to create or liquidate State federal enterprises are adopted by the Government, whereas the reorganisation of such enterprises not involving a change of ownership was to be decided by the Ministry of State Property.[43] The rationalisation of unitary enterprises was accelerated by the Decree on Federal State Unitary Enterprises Based on the Right of Economic Jurisdiction, No 1348, of 6 December 1999,[44] and many unitary enterprises transferred to subjects of the Federation at the expense of federal budgetary appropriations, pursuant to the Decree on the Transfer of Federal State Unitary Enterprises to the Ownership of Subjects of the Russian Federation, No 1366, of 9 December 1999.[45] These enactments have been overtaken by the Federal Law on State and Municipal Unitary Enterprises of 14 November 2002.

The charters of State or municipal enterprises are confirmed by the empowered State agency or agency of local self-government. Standard charters and contracts with directors have been confirmed by the Ministry of State Property, which also has the right to confirm specified charters and contracts when this right has been delegated to it by the Government. Since there are no investors in unitary enterprises, there is no charter capital. Instead legislation speaks of the charter fund, the minimum level of which is 1,000 minimum monthly payments for labour; it must be paid up in full before State registration.

Treasury enterprises may be created only at the federal level by decision of the Government of the Russian Federation, which also may reorganise or liquidate them. Unlike the State federal enterprise, therefore, the Ministry of State Property has no voice in the reorganisation of a treasury enterprise. They first came into being pursuant to the Edict of the President of the Russian Federation of 23 May

---

[42] This procedure was based on point 15 of the Decree of the Supreme Soviet of the RSFSR adopted 27 December 1991, which provided that Goskomimushchestvo exclusively had the right to dispose of State property by agreement with ministries and departments or, in subjects of the Federation, by agreement with committees for the administration of property. Ведомости СНД и ВС РФ (1992), no 3, item 89. Although merely a 'decree' and not a law, and therefore never signed by the Head of State, and moreover adopted two or so days after the demise of the Soviet Union, this enactment has in practice been treated as a valid and binding normative act.

[43] САПП РФ (1994), no 8, item 593; СЗ РФ (2000), no 6, item 777; no 13, item 1373; (2001), no 9, item 861; no 31, item 3281.

[44] СЗ РФ (1999), no 50, item 6230; transl in Butler (n 11 above) 429–431.

[45] СЗ РФ (1999), no 50, item 6237; transl in Butler (n 11 above) 433–435.

1994 on the reform of State enterprises[46] and have found their place in the Civil Code. These are enterprises which the State deems essential; they need not be profitable, for any losses are covered from the federal budget. Their charters are confirmed by the Government on the basis of a Standard Charter confirmed by Decree of the Government on 12 August 1994.[47]

The autonomy of the treasury enterprise is extremely limited. The State as owner of its property may withdraw such property from operative management at any time. In principle the treasury enterprise may dispose of its property only with the consent of the owner in written form, the sole exception being finished products, for which the enterprise may autonomously conclude contracts of delivery. Economic planning continues to operate within treasury enterprises in accordance with a procedure confirmed by Decree of the Government on 6 October 1994.[48] The enterprise is financed from its revenues, and any shortfall from the federal budget. Unused budget appropriations are subject to being returned to the State at the end of the fiscal year. In principle the treasury enterprise is liable for its obligations with all of the property consolidated to it (whereas State budgetary institutions are liable only with their monetary means), the State bearing subsidiary responsibility if the treasury enterprise is unable to meet its obligations.

L. Holding Companies

In the late decades of the Soviet Planned Economy amalgamations of State enterprises, research institutes, and other entities were positively encouraged. The names applicable to them were various: production associations, concerns, trusts, syndicates, and others. In the early 1990s the emphasis was upon competition and the breaking up of monopolistic enterprises. It was soon determined, however, that the preservation of large-scale production-economic complexes was desirable in certain branches. The turning point came in an Edict of the President of the Russian Federation adopted on 16 November 1992 which made provision for the integration of production-technological complexes when privatising large State enterprises and associations. Such complexes were to be created in the domain of communications, electric power, oil and gas, precious metals, radioactive and rare-earth elements, armaments, railway, water, and air transport.

The Edict of 16 November 1992, as amended on 16 April 1998, confirmed the Provisional Statute on Holding Companies,[49] to be created when transforming

---

[46] СЗ РФ (1994), no 5, item 393. The creation of treasury enterprises was deemed inadvisable by an Edict of 7 August 1995. See СЗ РФ (1995), no 32, item 3293.

[47] СЗ РФ (1994), no 17, item 1982; (1998), no 32, item 3893; no 48, item 5946; (1999), no 36, item 4400; (2000), no 49, item 4819; (2001), no 25, item 2575. Also see the Decision of the Supreme Court of the RF of 30 March 2001, excerpted in the Бюллетень Верховного Суда РФ, no 1 (2002) 9–10.

[48] СЗ РФ (1994), no 28, item 2989.

[49] САПП РФ (1992), no 21, item 1731; СЗ РФ (1998), no 16, item 1832.

State enterprises into joint-stock societies. A holding company was defined in the Provisional Statute as an enterprise, irrespective of its organisational-legal form, whose assets included the controlling block of stocks of other enterprises. Those enterprises whose stocks are held by the holding company are subsidiary enterprises thereof.

A holding company is created by decision of the Ministry for the Administration of State Property, and the subsidiary enterprise, by decison of the committee for the administration of property or by the holding company itself. The federal anti-monopoly agency must consent to its formation. The Provisional Statute prohibited the formation of holding companies whose market share together with its subsidiaries would exceed 35 per cent and forbade holding companies irrespective of market share in the domains of trade, agricultural production, domestic servicing, and certain areas of transport. A holding company could also not be the legal successor to previously existing associations or agencies of State administration. It may, however, contain private enterprises or non-privatised State enterprises, and therefore natural and juridical persons who have the right to be the purchasers of property being privatised may be the founders of a holding company.

Financial holding companies fall into a special category as more than 50 per cent of their capital consists of securities and other financial assets. These may engage exclusively in investment activity and may carry on securities transactions only on the organised market.

A holding company together with its subsidiaries does not have separate and autonomous legal personality. The unity of the holding company is secured by the right of the holding company to determine the decisions of its subsidiaries by using its controlling block of stocks or by independent contractual arrangements which achieve the same result. The definition of a subsidiary contained in Article 105 of the Russian Civil Code is broader than was true when the Provisional Statute was confirmed. And the concept of a 'group of persons' contained in Russian anti-monopoly legislation is broader than the definition of holding company.

M. Financial-Industrial Groups

Financial-industrial groups began to be founded on the basis of the Edict of the President of the Russian Federation of 5 December 1993[50] and are presently regu-

---

[50] САПП РФ (1993), no 49, item 4766. The Edict confirmed a Statute on Financial-Industrial Groups and the Procedure for their Creation, which was repealed by the 1995 Law, transl in Butler (n 9 above). Under the 1993 Edict, a financial-industrial group was a juridical person; the 1995 Law changed the position but also required re-registration of all existing groups. The Edict lost force pursuant to the Edict of 1 April 1996, as amended 24 August 1998. СЗ РФ (1996), no 15, item 1573; (1998), no 35, item 4381.

lated by the Federal Law on Financial-Industrial Groups of 30 November 1995.[51]
A financial-industrial group is the:

> aggregate of juridical persons operating as the principal and subsidiary societies or
> which have fully or partially combined their material and non-material assets (sys-
> tem of participation) on the basis of a contract concerning the creation of a financial-
> industrial group for the purpose of technological or economic integration in order to
> realise investment and other projects and programmes directed towards increasing
> competitiveness and expanding markets for the sale of goods and services, increasing
> the efficiency of production, and the creation of new jobs (Article 2, 1995 Federal
> Law on Financial-Industrial Groups).

It is a requirement that organisations which produce goods and services and banks
and other credit organisations be participants, but other commercial and non-
commercial organisations may take part, as may State and municipal enterprises,
provided that the owners of the property so consent.

There are two ways of forming a financial-industrial group. The first consists of
enterprises and organisations and a central company created by them. The second
consists of a principal society and subsidiary societies. Foreign organisations may
be part of such a group, and transnational financial-industrial groups may be
formed by Russian enterprises and by enterprises from other CIS countries. In
either case the relations within the group are based on a contract which may be
supplemented by others regulating specific aspects of the group's activities. The
group comes into being from the moment of State registration by the Ministry of
Economy.[52] Unlike economic societies and partnerships, whose State registration
is more or less routine, the registration of a financial-industrial group must both
comply with legislation and be advisable in the eyes of the Ministry of Economy
from the standpoint of industrial policy. To register the group the participants
must submit the contract on its creation, the constitutive documents of each participant of the group, the opinion of the federal anti-monopoly agency, and an
organisational design which must make the case for the advisability of creating the
group. A refusal by the Ministry of Economy to register the group may be
appealed to a court. The contract concerning the creation of the group must
determine the basic conditions and purpose for forming the group, the procedure
and conditions for combining assets of the participants and the amount of such
assets, and the procedure for managing the group.[53]

---

[51] СЗ РФ (1995), no 49, item 4697.

[52] The procedure for keeping the register was established by the Statute confirmed by Decree of
the Government of the Russian Federation on 22 May 1996, as amended: СЗ РФ (1996), no 22,
item 2699; (1998), no 6, item 738. The Ministry of Economy became responsible for performing
the functions of the empowered federal State agency for the State regulation of the creation, activity, and liquidation of financial-industrial groups on the basis of the Decree of the Government of
the Russian Federation, 2 February 1998.

[53] One observer has commented: 'The status of the financial-industrial group now has no institutional significance, but is derivative from organisational-legal forms established by the Civil Code

The management scheme will depend upon which of the two approaches to forming the group has been accepted. The 1995 Law on financial-industrial groups concentrates upon managing the group via a specially-formed central company. The highest management organ of the group is the council of managers. Its competence is determined by the contract forming the group; representatives of all group participants serve in the council. The central company may take the form of an economic society or of an association or a union. It is registered by the State in the same procedure established for the registration of juridical persons, which means that there must be two registrations: the financial-industrial group as such with the Ministry of Industry (or its designated successor), and the central company thereof as a juridical person. The central company has its own charter that reflects the foundation contract, and therefore has special legal capacity enabling the company to perform only those legal actions which correspond to the subject of activity of the company. The financial-industrial group through the contract forming it therefore determines the activity of the company but is not itself a subject of law. The central company acts in the interests of the participants of the group, keeps composite records and balance sheets, prepares a report on the activity of the group, and performs banking operations. The participants of the group bear joint and several responsibility for the obligations of the central company.

State support may be available to financial-industrial groups in the form of setting off obligations of participants of the group to the budget, allowing the group to fix its own amortisation periods for equipment, placing stocks of participants of the group owned by the State in the trust management of the central company, or offering State guarantees for investments. Banks which take part in such groups may receive special privileges, including lower reserve requirements or adjustment of other normative standards. Control over the activities of the groups is exercised by the Ministry of Industry, which has the right to demand that violations be eliminated or request that the Government withdraw State support from the group or even liquidate the group (which in fact would mean liquidation of the central company since the group itself is not a subject of law).

N. Individual Entrepreneurs and Small Business

Individual entrepreneurs are natural persons who are registered in the established procedure to carry on entrepreneurial activity in their own names. The USSR enacted on 2 April 1991 the Law on General Principles of Entrepreneurship of Citizens in the USSR, which was largely superseded by the 1990 RSFSR Law on

---

of the Russian Federation'. See V D Rudashevskii, 'Правовое положение финансово-промышленных групп: возможности и ограничения' ['Legal Status of Financial-Industrial Groups: Possibilities and Limitations'], Государство и право [State and Law], no 2 (1998) 36.

Enterprises and Entrepreneurial Activity (no longer in force from 1 July 2002). The Civil Code of the Russian Federation contains some provisions on entrepreneurship, most notably Article 18 which in defining the legal capacity of natural persons indicates that citizens may engage in entrepreneurial and any other activity not prohibited by a law. Natural persons, therefore, enjoy general entrepreneurial legal capacity and may carry on any types of entrepreneurial activity. Those types of entrepreneurial activity requiring a licence or special authorisation have been laid down in normative acts of the Government.

The Russian Federation offers special incentives and support to what is called 'small entrepreneurship'. The subjects of small entrepreneurship are natural persons who engage in entrepreneurial activity without the formation of a juridical person and commercial organisations which meet certain criteria: not more than 25 per cent of their charter capital may be held by the Russian Federation, subjects of the Russian Federation, social and religious organisations or associations, and philanthropic or other foundations; nor may more than 25 per cent of such capital belong to one or several juridical persons which are not subjects of small entrepreneurship. The actual size of the small entrepreneurship is measured by the average number of workers and varies from one industry to another: in industry, construction, and transport, 100 persons; in agriculture and in the scientific-technical sphere, 60 persons; in wholesale, retail trade, and domestic servicing, and other types of activity, 50 persons. These are called 'small enterprises', and do not embrace individual entrepreneurs, who are treated separately. State support takes the form of tax reductions, simplified accounting, reporting and registration requirements, personnel training programmes, and information and other services in the sphere of foreign trade links. Financial assistance is offered through State Programmes and the creation of foundations for the support of small entrepreneurship, organised as non-commercial juridical persons and headed by the Federal Fund for the Support of Small Entrepreneurship, created by the Government of the Russian Federation.[54] State policy in this domain is administered principally by the State Committee of the Russian Federation for the Support and Development of Small Entrepreneurship.[55] As of 1 July 1997, 837,900 small enterprises operated on Russian territory, of which 92 per cent were entirely privately owned and 43.5 per cent were in the trade and public

---

[54] See the Federal Law on State Support of Small Entrepreneurship in the Russian Federation, of 12 May 1995. СЗ РФ (1995), no 25, item 2343. On the Federal Fund, see the Decree of the Government of the Russian Federation on the Federal Fund of Support of Small Entrepreneurship, adopted 4 December 1995, as amended 27 November 2000. СЗ РФ (1995), no 50, item 4924; (2000), no 49, item 4823.

[55] Established by Edict of the President of the Russian Federation, 6 June 1995, as amended 9 July 1997. СЗ РФ (1995), no 24, item 2262; (1997), no 28, item 3422. The Statute on the State Committee was confirmed by Decree of the Government of the Russian Federation on 28 October 1995. СЗ РФ (1995), no 45, item 4320.

dining sector. Enterprises with foreign investment which met the standards of small entrepreneurship were not included in these statistics.[56]

O. Non-commercial Organisations

The Civil Code of the Russian Federation (Article 50) draws a distinction between commercial and non-commercial organisations. Non-commercial organisations are juridical person which do not have as their purpose the deriving of profit and, if profit is received, they do not distribute the profit among the participants. The Civil Code contains a non-exhaustive enumeration of non-commercial organisations: consumer cooperatives, social or religious organisations or associations financed by the owner of institutions, philanthropic and other foundations, and other forms provided for by law. Non-commercial organisations may effectuate entrepreneurial activity only insofar as this serves the attainment of the purposes for which they were created and corresponds to such purposes.

The legal status of non-commercial organisations is regulated in detail by the Federal Law on Noncommercial Organisations of 12 January 1996, as amended.[57] The Law does not extend to consumer cooperatives, which are regulated by separate legislative acts (see above). Non-commercial organisations may be created to achieve social, philanthropic, cultural, educational, scientific, and management purposes, health protection, physical culture and sport, the satisfaction of spiritual and material needs of citizens or to defend their rights and legal interests, settle disputes and conflicts, render legal assistance, and other purposes directed towards the public good. In form a non-commercial organisation may be a social or religious organisation (however, the special features of these are regulated by separate federal laws), a non-commercial partnership [партнерство], institution, autonomous non-commercial organisation, social or philanthropic foundation,[58] association, or union, or any other forms provided for by federal laws. They are created as a juridical person from the moment of State registration and have solitary property in ownership or in operative management, are liable (except for institutions) for their obligations with that property, bear duties, and may be a plaintiff or defendant in court. Unless their constitutive documents specify otherwise, they exist in perpetuity. They have the right to open bank accounts in Russia and abroad.[59]

---

[56] Закон [Law], no 3 (1998) 5–6.

[57] СЗ РФ (1996), no 3, item 145; (1998), no 48, item 5849; (1999), no 28, item 3473; (2001), no 12, item 1093; transl in Butler (n 9 above).

[58] See the Federal Law on Philanthropic Activity and Philanthropic Associations, of 11 August 1995. СЗ РФ (1995), no 33, item 3340; transl in Butler (n 9 above).

[59] See O G Drokin *et al*, Некоммерческие фонды и организации. Правовые аспекты [*Non-commmercial Foundations and Organisations: Legal Aspects*] (1997); M L Makal'skaia and N A Pirozhkova, Некоммерческие организации в России: создание, права, налоги, учет, отчетности [*Non-commercial Organisations in Russia: Creation, Rights, Taxes, Records, Reports*] (1998).

Under 1999 amendments to the Law on Noncommercial Organisations, a State corporation may be founded by the Russian Federation on the basis of a property contribution for the purpose of effectuating social, administrative, or other socially-useful functions and not having membersip. Each must be created on the basis of a federal law; property transferred to a State corporation of the Russian Federation is the ownership of the corporation, which also enjoys limited liability. The corporation may engage in entrepreneurial activity only insofar as this is necessary to achieve the purposes for which it was created and corresponding to those purposes. Constitutive documents required by Article 52 of the Civil Code are not necessary in order to create a State corporation.

Activities bringing profit include the production of goods and services which correspond to the purposes of creating the non-commercial organisation, and also the acquisition and realisation of securities, property and non-property rights, and participation in economic societies or limited partnerships as a contributor. A non-commercial organisation may be the owner of, or possess by right of operative management, buildings, installations, a housing fund, equipment, inventory, monetary means in rubles and foreign currency, securities, and other property, as well as have land plots in ownership or perpetual use. The non-commercial organisation is liable for its obligations with that of its property against which execution may be levied under Russian legislation. There are detailed conflicts of interest provisions governing transactions concluded by non-commercial organisations and their officers or executives.

In accordance with Russian legislation non-commercial organisations may open branches and representations in the Russian Federation. A branch is a solitary subdivision situated outside the location of the non-commercial organisation and effectuating all or part of the functions thereof, including the function of representation, whereas the representation performs only representation functions. Neither is a juridical person; both operate on the basis of a Statute confirmed by the non-commercial organisation. The property of the branch and representation is kept on a separate balance sheet and also on the balance sheet of the organisation which created them. The executives of the branch and representation act on the basis of a power of attorney issued by the non-commercial orgaisation.

This being a chapter on entrepreneurial law, we concentrate upon the non-commercial organisation in the form of a non-commercial partnership. Such a partnership is a juridical person, being described in the Law on Noncommercial Organisations as a non-commercial organisation based on membership founded by citizens and/or juridical persons in order to assist its members in the effectuation of activity directed towards achievement of the purposes mentioned above (Article 8). The property transferred to the non-commercial partnership by its members is the ownership of the partnership. Members of the partnership are not liable for its obligations, and the partnership is not liable for obligations of its members. The partnership has the right to effectuate entrepreneurial activity corresponding to the purposes for which it was created.

The members of a non-commercial partnership have the right to take part in managing the affairs of the partnership, receive information about the activity of the partnership in the procedure established by the constitutive documents, and at their discretion withdraw from the partnership. Unless provided otherwise by a federal law or by the constitutive documents of the partnership, a member has the right to receive, when withdrawing from membership, part of its property or the value of such property within the limits of the value of the property transferred by members to its ownership, except for membership dues. The constitutive documents must set out the procedure for the dispositon of such property to a withdrawing member. If the partnership is liquidated, the members have the right to receive the residual property after settlement of accounts with creditors or the value of such property within the limits of the property transferred by members to the ownership of the partnership unless provided otherwise by a federal law or the constitutive documents of the partnership.

A member of a non-commercial partnership may be expelled by decision of the remaining members in the procedure provided for by the constitutive documents. The expelled member has the right to receive part of the property of the partnership or value thereof as stipulated in the previous paragraph. The constitutive documents may give members other rights so long as they are not contrary to legislation.

A non-commercial organisation may be created either by founding or by way of reorganisation of an existing non-commercial organisation. The constitutive documents are the charter confirmed by the founders, constitutive contract and charter, or decision of the owner to create the organisation and the charter confirmed by the founder. Which of the three patterns is used depends upon the type of non-commercial organisation. There are detailed provisions governing reorganisation, the types of which follow the provisions of the Civil Code. A non-commercial partnership, for example, may be transformed into a social or religious organisation, foundation, or autonomous non-commercial organisation. In this event they would be governed by the Law on Social Associations, of 19 May 1995, as amended 17 May 1997, 19 July 1998, 12 March 2002, 21 March 2002 and 25 July 2002.[60]

Non-commercial organisations are of more than passing interest because stock markets and most forms of advocate activity are required to be created in the form of a non-commercial organisation.

---

[60] СЗ РФ (1995), no 21, item 1930; (1997), no 20, item 2231; (1998), no 30, item 3608; (2002), no 11, item 1018; no 12, item 1093; no 30, item 3029.

12

SECURITIES REGULATION

Russian law, following the Soviet law tradition, continues to be distinctive for a broad definition of what falls into the category of 'securities'.[1] The Russian Civil Code defines a security as a 'document certifying, in compliance with the established form and obligatory requisites, property rights whose effectuation or transfer' is possible only when presenting it (Article 142). Specifically singled out as 'types' of securities in the Civil Code are: State bond, bill of exchange, cheque, deposit and savings certificates, bank bearer savings book, bill of lading, stock, and privatisation securities (Article 143). Laws on securities may designate other documents as securities or create a procedure for making such a determination. Notwithstanding the reference to a security as a 'document', the Russian Civil Code also recognised 'paperless securities' (Article 149). Of the types of security

---

[1] See generally V K Andreev, Рынок ценных бумаг: правовое регулирование [*The Securities Market: Legal Regulation*] (1998); V A Belov, Ценные бумаги в российском гражданском праве [*Securities in Russian Civil Law*] (1996); A G Karatuev, Ценные бумаги: виды и разновидности [*Securities: Types and Varieties*] (1997); V G Keshchian, Правовое регулирование рынка ценных бумаг [*Legal Regulation of the Securities Market*] (1997); A A Kiliachkov and L A Chaldaeva, Практикум по российскому рынку ценных бумаг [*Practical Manual Regarding the Russian Securities Market*] (1997); E V Semenkova, Операций с ценными бумагами: российская практика [*Securities Operations: Russian Practice*] (1997); V A Belov, Бездокументарные ценные бумаги : научно-практический очерк [*Paperless Securities: Scientific-Practical Essay*] (2001).

mentioned, stocks and bonds are the subject of the most extensive regulation, and
we shall dwell on them in this chapter.

A. Historical Background

The term for stock [акция] came into the Russian language in the Petrine period,
as early as 1705.[2] Joint-stock companies were registered in Russia in the eighteenth century[3] and stocks actively traded, sometimes as part of scandalous
schemes, from the 1840s. At the end of 1912 the turnover on Russian stock
exchanges was the fifth highest in the world.[4] During the Soviet era legislation on
securities played a small role, being chiefly concerned with State bonds. However,
on 15 October 1988 a Decree of the USSR Council of Ministers, No 1195,[5] 'On
the Issuance of Securities by Enterprises and Organisations' sought to encourage
working people to invest personal resources in State enterprises on economic
accountability or in cooperatives by acquiring securities issued by such enterprises
or cooperatives. With the introduction of joint-stock societies on the basis of all-
union legislation in June 1990, savings certificates, stocks, and bonds, including
bearer, were introduced into commercial circulation.[6] These were followed in the
Russian Federation by the Statute on the Issuance and Circulation of Securities
and on Stock Exchanges in the RSFSR, confirmed by Decree No 78 of the
Government of the RSFSR on 28 December 1991,[7] and followed by Instruction
No 2 of the Ministry of Finances of Russia on the Rules for the Issuance and
Registration of Securities on the Territory of the Russian Federation, of 3 March
1992; Instruction No 53 on the Rules for Concluding and Registration of
Securities Transactions, of 6 July 1992 (lost force 25 February 1997); and the
Statute on Licensing the Activity on the Securities Market of Investment
Institutes, of 21 September 1991.

Privatisation legislation created a separate regime for securities issued in the course
of privatisation, particularly the emission of stocks by State and municipal enterprises being transformed into joint-stock societies. The alienation of stocks issued

---

[2] See Словарь русского языка XVIII века [*Dictionary of the Russian Language of the Eighteenth
Century*] (1984–) 42. On the history of Russian joint-stock societies, see L E Shepelev,
Акционерные компании в России [*Joint-Stock Companies in Russia*] (1973); T C Owen, *The
Corporation Under Russian Law 1890–1917: A Study in Tsarist Economic Policy* (1991).

[3] See W E Butler and M E Gashi-Butler, 'On the Development of Russian Company Law', in
Butler (ed and transl), *Russian Company Law: Basic Documents* (3rd edn, 2000) vii–xvi.

[4] N T Kleshchev (ed), Рынок ценных бумаг: шаг России в информационное общество [*The
Securities Market: A Step of Russia Towards an Information Society*] (1997) 167.

[5] СП СССР (1988), no 35, item 100.

[6] See the Statute on Securities, confirmed by Decree of the USSR Council of Ministers on
19 June 1990. СП СССР (1990), I, no 15, item 82; transl in W E Butler, *Basic Documents on the
Soviet Legal System* (2nd edn, 1991) 345–353.

[7] Repealed by Decree No 1402 of 17 December 1999. СЗ РФ (1999), no 52, item 6399.

as part of privatisation was limited, and the 1991 RSFSR Statute on securities did not extend to privatisation issues. The privatisation plan of the enterprise operated as the decision to issue the emission prospectus.

Privatisation cheques were so-called special-purpose bearer State securities bearing a par value of 10,000 rubles and distributed free of charge to every Russian citizen alive at 00:00 hours on 2 September 1992. These securities were the principal form of distributing the wealth of the whole people to the entire population of the Russian Federation. The privatisation cheques were negotiable and enjoyed certain preferences in acquiring stocks of State enterprises being privatised or in participation in State property auctions.[8] One method of realising privatisation cheques was to exchange them for stocks in specialist investment funds, which in turn invested on a large scale in the stocks of enterprises being privatised.[9] The procedure for conducting specialised privatisation cheque auctions, in which only privatisation cheques could be used to bid for the stocks of enterprises privatised, was laid down by the Statute on Specialised Cheque Auctions, confirmed by Regulation of Goskomimushchestvo Russia issued 4 November 1992.[10]

B. Current Legislation

Under the 1993 Russian Constitution the unity of economic space, free movement of goods, services, and financial means, and freedom of economic activity are guaranteed (Article 8).

State loans

The Constitution further provides that State loans are to be issued in the procedure determined by a federal law and to be placed on a voluntary basis (recalling the Soviet era, when State loans were acquired by the general public under intense official social pressure). The Federal Law on the Peculiarities of the Emission and

---

[8] See the Statute on Privatisation Cheques, confirmed by Edict of the President of the Russian Federation on 14 August 1992. СП СССР (1992), no 8, item 501; no 16, item 1235; (1993), no 3, item 167. The total number of stocks of each enterprise subject to being sold for privatisation cheques was established by the Edict of 14 October 1992 'On the Development of the System of Privatisation Cheques in the Russian Federation'. Ведомости СНД и ВС РФ (1992), no 42, item 2381.

[9] These operated on the basis of the Edict of the President of the Russian Federation of 7 October 1992, as amended 23 February 1998, 'On Measures Relating to the Organisation of the Securities Market in the Process of the Privatisation of State and Municipal Enterprises', which confirmed the Statute on Investment Funds, the Statute on Specialised Privatisation Investment Funds Accumulating Privatisation Cheques of Citizens, the Model Investment Fund Charter, the Basic Provisions of a Depositary Contract, the Model Contract with the Manager Concerning the Management of an Investment Fund, and the Standard Emission Prospectus of an Investment Fund. See САПП РФ (1992), no 15, item 1155; СЗ РФ (1998), no 9, item 1097.

[10] The Regulation was amended several times and lost force on 28 June 1999.

Circulation of State and Municipal Securities of 29 July 1998[11] addresses these matters, together with subordinate normative legal acts: the Decree on the General Conditions for the Issuance and Circulation of Debt Obligations of the Russian Federation in the Form of Bonds of Federal Loans, set out by Decree of the Government of the Russian Federation of 15 May 1995, No 458, as amended 30 June 1998, 27 February 1999, and 16 May 2001, provides that the Russian Ministry of Finances issues these bonds of federal loans in the name of the Russian Federation.[12] The total issuance in a year of such bonds must comply with a ceiling established in the yearly federal budget for the financial year. The General Conditions for the Emission and Circulation of State Federal Bonds were confirmed by Decree of the Government of the Russian Federation on 15 May 1998.[13] The acquirers of such bonds, under more liberal legislation, may be juridical and natural persons who are, as defined by Russian legislation, residents or non-residents. The types of internal State debts of the Russian Federation and of subjects of the Federation are classified in Annex No 7 to the Federal Law on the Budgetary Classification of the Russian Federation of 15 August 1996, as amended 5 August 2000 and 8 August 2001.[14]

Civil Code

As noted above, the Civil Code of the Russian Federation contains Chapter 7 devoted exclusively to securities. The 1996 Federal Law on the Securities Market does not purport to regulate all securities, only those which are capable of being freely purchased and sold on the market. Purchase-sale therefore presumes the use of the contract of purchase-sale, and not other transactions (for example, barter) relating to the alienation of securities. Article 454(2) of the Civil Code expressly refers to special rules governing the purchase-sale of securities. The Civil Code also regulates securities as objects of civil rights (Articles 66(6), 128, 130(2), 224(3), 302(3), and 338(3)); the conclusion of contracts of loan by means of issuing a bill of exchange, bonds, State bonds, or other State securities (Articles 815–817); the right of a bank to encourage deposits by selling stocks and other securities or by issuing a bill of exchange (Article 835); and limitations on the issue of stocks and bonds by joint-stock societies (Article 102).

Because, uncharacteristically for many countries, Russian banks have the right to issue documents which are securities (bearer savings bank books, savings or deposit certificates, and cheques), they perform securities operations (issue, purchase, sale, recording, keeping, and others) with documents that serve as means of

---

[11] СЗ РФ (1998), no 31, item 3814.
[12] СЗ РФ (1995), no 21, item 1967; (1998), no 27, item 3193; (1999), no 11, item 1296; (2001), no 21, item 2089.
[13] СЗ РФ (1998), no 20, item 2155.
[14] СЗ РФ (1996), no 34, item 4030; (2000), no 32, item 3338; (2001), no 33(II), item 3437.

payment and do not require a special licence but rather are authorised by the Federal Law on Banks and Banking Activity (Article 6).

Joint-stock society legislation

Controversy arose in Russian legal doctrine over an inconsistency between the 1995 Law on Joint-Stock Societies and the 1996 Law on the Securities Market. The Law on Joint-Stock Societies permits only the issue of inscribed stocks, whereas the Law on the Securities Market also authorised the issue of bearer stocks. One view held that the Law on Joint-Stock Societies is specifically called for by the Russian Civil Code, and therefore the Law on the Securities Market, which is not mentioned in the Civil Code, must conform to the Law on Joint-Stock Societies in furtherance of Article 96(3) of the Civil Code. On 28 December 2002 the Law on the Securities Market was amended to eliminate the discrepancy.

The alternative interpretation was that the Civil Code makes provision (Article 145) for bearer securities and stipulates that the types of rights certified by securities are determined by a law or in the procedure established by a law. The Law on the Securities Market is the Law in question, and therefore bearer stocks are regulated not by the provisions of the Civil Code concerning juridical persons, but rather by the Chapter on the contract of purchase-sale. One may as well ask, this view suggested, whether the Law on Joint-Stock Societies is not in violation of Chapter 7 of the Civil Code on securities.

Russian joint-stock society legislation regulates the issuance and circulation of stocks in considerable detail and must be read in tandem with the Civil Code (Articles 96–104). The 1995 Law on Joint-Stock Societies, as lex specialis specifically called for by the Civil Code and as amended in 2001, clarifies and elaborates provisions of the Civil Code, yet also contains gaps, for example, in regulating stockholder rights and duties. However, in defining the difference between an open and a closed joint-stock society, the Law on Joint-Stock Societies determines the distinction between an open and closed subscription for stocks and the procedure for exercising a preferential right to acquire stocks being offered by other stockholders. The charter of a joint-stock society must contain information concerning the quantity, par value, and categories of stocks (common or preferred), and if preferred stocks are to be issued, the types thereof. Limitations may be imposed on the size of the stockholding by a particular stockholder(s) or on the maximum number of votes that a single stockholder may cast. If various categories of stock are introduced, the rights attendant on each category must be specified. The charter may distinguish between stocks placed and stocks declared. The procedure for paying up stocks and other securities is regulated by the Law on Joint-Stock Societies (Article 35). The reserve fund of a joint-stock society may under stipulated conditions be used to redeem stocks of the society. Under certain circumstances stocks may be placed by a joint-stock society at a price below market value.

The stockholder register must be maintained by a joint-stock society in accordance with Articles 44–46 of the Law on Joint-Stock Societies and subordinate normative legal acts. The duties of the holder of the stockholder register have been elaborated in the Edict of the President of the Russian Federation of 27 October 1993 'On Measures Relating to Ensuring the Rights of Stockholders', as amended by an Edict of 31 July 1995 'On Additional Measures Relating to Ensuring the Rights of Stockholders'.[15] The rights of stockholders (and of depositors in credit organisations) are protected too by the Federal Social-State Fund for Defence of the Rights of Depositors and Stockholders, created on the basis of the Edict of the President of the Russian Federation of 18 November 1995, as amended 2 April 1997, 'On Certain Measures of Defence of the Rights of Depositors and Stockholders'.[16] The founders of the Fund consist of federal agencies of executive power and social associations, including committees formed spontaneously to defend the rights of defrauded depositors and stockholders. The Fund pays compensation to persons who were victimised on the stock market, maintains a database of such stockholders, and a list of juridical persons and individuals who perpetrated fraudulent actions. Stockholder protections arising out of the 1995 Law on Joint-Stock Societies were elaborated in the Edict of the President of the Russian Federation of 18 August 1996 'On Measures Relating to the Defence of the Rights of Stockholders and Ensuring the Interests of the State as Owner and Stockholder', as amended.[17] These were enhanced by the establishment of a National Depositary System incorporating a Central Fund for Keeping and Processing Stock Market Information (Central Depositary). The system also included licensed professional securities market participants who are required to work to the standards laid down by the National Depositary System. The Central Depositary upon the requests of courts, federal agencies of State power or agencies of State power of subjects of the Federation, agencies of local self-government, or the owners of securities would issue documents confirming the rights to securities placed for keeping in the National Depositary System or rights recorded in that System. Documents issued by the Central Depositary in the procedure established by the Government of the Russian Federation would not require notarial certification or State registration in order to confirm the rights to the security concerned.[18]

Decisions concerning the number of declared stocks, an increase or reduction of par value or other decision concerning an increase or reduction of charter capital,

---

[15] САПП РФ (1993), no 44, item 4192; СЗ РФ (1995), no 31, item 3101.
[16] СЗ РФ (1995), no 47, item 4501; (1997), no 14, item 1607.
[17] СЗ РФ (1996), no 35, item 4142; (1999), no 32, item 4051.
[18] СЗ РФ (1997), no 38, item 4356.

the redemption of stocks issued, the splitting or consolidation of stocks, or the cancellation of stocks not fully paid-up are within the competence of the general meeting of stockholders of a joint-stock society unless the Law on Joint-Stock Societies permits such decisions to be passed to the council of directors of the society. In any event the council of directors is empowered to decide questions of increasing the charter capital by increasing the par value of stocks or by placing stocks within the limits of the quantities and categories or types of stocks declared if the charter so authorises. Depending upon the charter, the general meeting of stockholders or the council of directors may make a decision with regard to concluding a transaction or several linked transactions connected with the placement of common stocks or preferred stocks convertible into common stocks which constitute more than 25 per cent of common stocks previously placed by the society.

The procedure for the placement of bonds and other securities of a joint-stock society is determined by decision of the council of directors unless the charter provides otherwise. Bonds may be bearer or inscribed, and may be repaid in a lump sum or over periods fixed in the bonds themselves.

Federally-owned stocks

A series of Presidential edicts have guided the Russian Federation in its struggle to cope with the massive portfolio of stocks amassed as a result of the transformation of State enterprises into joint-stock societies and release these by way of privatisation into the general stock market. Partly these have addressed the rights of federal agencies to dispose of these stocks and partly the rights of stockholders who acquire them. On 30 September 1995, as amended 8 July 1997, the Edict of the President of the Russian Federation on the Procedure for the Adoption of Decisions Concerning the Management and Disposition of Stocks in Federal Ownership provided that decisions of federal agencies of executive power, organisations, and institutions concerning the management and disposition of federally-owned stocks, including decisions to transfer these stocks to trust management by juridical and natural persons, or to contribute stocks to the charter capital of organisations, or to pledge stocks or otherwise encumber them were to be taken only on the basis of edicts of the President which determined the periods and forms for the management and disposition of specific stocks.[19] The Government of the Russian Federation was given the right to sell stocks in federal ownership in order to obtain the proceeds from privatisation and meet outstanding indebtedness by an Edict of 8 July 1997.[20] The Russian Federation experienced difficulties in obtaining reports on the economic performance of the joint-stock societies in which it was a stockholder and to remedy this situation authorised a scheme to monitor the joint-stock

---

[19] СЗ РФ (1995), no 41, item 3874; (1997), no 28, item 3417.
[20] СЗ РФ (1997), no 28, item 3417. This Edict addressed indebtedness to civil servants and military servicemen.

societies more closely in Decree No 336 of the Government of the Russian Federation 'On Measures Relating to the Development of the Securities Market in the Russian Federation' of 15 April 1995.[21] In a not entirely successful initiative auctions were instituted to dispose of securities in federal ownership under the Decree of the Government of the Russian Federation of 28 April 1995 'On the Procedure for Conducting Inter-Regional and All-Russian Specialised Auctions for the Sale of Stocks of Joint-Stock Societies of the Open-Type Created by Means of Transformation of State (or Municipal) Enterprises'.[22] 'Interregional' for these purposes meant an auction in which participation was sought from not less than 15 subjects of the Federation, and an all-Russian auction, from at least 25 subjects of the Federation.

Subjects of the Federation were encouraged to settle accounts with the federal budget pursuant to an Edict of the President of the Russian Federation of 27 February 1996 'On the Transfer to Subjects of the Russian Federation of Stocks in Federal Ownership of Joint-Stock Societies Formed in the Process of Privatisation'.[23] Provided that subjects of the Federation submitted a plan for the sale, preferably to citizens, at regional and interregional auctions of these stocks in conformity with privatisation plans previously confirmed, the Government would effect the transfer and arrange an appropriate set-off of obligations to the federal budget. Improved portfolio management by way of trust management was authorised by an Edict of the President of the Russian Federation of 9 December 1996 'On the Transfer to Trust Management of Stocks Consolidated in Federal Ownership of Joint-Stock Societies Created in the Process of Privatisation', as amended 7 August 1998.[24] Pursuant to this Edict, on 7 August 1997 the Government of the Russian Federation confirmed the Rules for Conducting Competitions for the Right to Conclude Contracts of Trust Management for the Stocks Consolidated in Federal Ownership of Joint-Stock Societies Created in the Process of Privatisation, as amended 17 April 1998.[25] The competitions were open to juridical persons who had net assets or own assets equal to not less than 20 per cent of the price of the stocks being transferred on trust management, provided that they also had a licence to manage securities. The intending trust manager must submit a programme of its proposed activity and the amount of remuneration expected. Security must be posed in the form of an irrevocable bank guarantee or a pledge of immoveable property, securities, or monetary means having a

---

[21] СЗ РФ (1995), no 17, item 1543; repealed on 17 December 1999. СЗ РФ (1999), no 52, item 6399.

[22] СЗ РФ (1995), no 20, item 1798; repealed by Decree No 669 of 28 April 1998. СЗ РФ (1998), no 27, item 3189.

[23] СЗ РФ (1996), no 10, item 879.

[24] СЗ РФ (1996), no 51, item 5764; (1998), no 32, item 3847.

[25] СЗ РФ (1997), no 45, item 5193; (1998), no 17, item 1946.

high degree of liquidity and in the full ownership of the trust manager. The value of the security must be at least equal to that of the stocks to be managed.

Federal securities market legislation

On 4 November 1994 the President of the Russian Federation issued an Edict on Measures Relating to State Regulation of the Securities Market in the Russian Federation. The Edict authorised the public placement of State securities, inscribed stocks of joint-stock societies and banks, options and warrants for securities, bonds, including bonds issued by agencies of State power of the Russian Federation and agencies of local self-government, and housing certificates.[26] The intentions of the Russian Federation with regard to the future of the securities market are set out in the 'Conception of the Development of the Securities Market in the Russian Federation' confirmed by Edict of the President of the Russian Federation on 1 July 1996, as amended 16 October 2000.[27] The Conception contains a model structure for the future market and enumerates draft legislation which must be prepared to achieve the desired result.

The 1996 Federal Law on the Securities Market[28] addresses only three types of security under Russian law: so-called 'emission securities', that is, stocks, bonds, and options. The Federal Securities Commission, renamed on 28 December 2002 in the Law on the Securities Market the 'Federal agency of executive power for the securities market' [hereafter the Federal Securities Commission], is empowered to work out methods recommendations concerning the application of securities legislation and has the right to classify securities and determine their types. It has addressed derivative securities (options and warrants) in individual enactments.[29]

C. Regulation of Securities Market in Russia

The early stages of the Russian securities market (1991–5) prior to the creation of the Federal Securities Commission were regulated principally by Goskomimushchestvo, the Ministry of Finances of the Russian Federation, and

---

[26] СЗ РФ (1994), no 28, item 2972; (1996), no 13, item 1312; (2000), no 31, item 3252. Articles 8 and 10 of the Edict were deemed to have lost force by Edict No 60 of 18 January 2002. СЗ РФ (2002), no 3, item 193.

[27] СЗ РФ (1996), no 28, item 3356; (2000), no 43, item 4233.

[28] СЗ РФ (1996), no 17, item 1918; (1998), no 48, item 5857; (1999), no 28, item 3472; (2000), no 1(I), item 10; (2001), no 33(I), item 3424; (2002), no. 52; transl in Butler (n 9 above). The Statute on the Federal Securities Commission was confirmed by Edict of the President of the Russian Federation on 1 July 1996. СЗ РФ (1996), no 28, item 3357; (1999), no 16, item 1967; (2000), no 15, item 1574; (2002), no 8, item 809.

[29] See the Decree of the Federal Commission of 9 January 1997, No 1, 'On the Option Certificate, the Application Thereof, and Confirmation of Standards of Emission for Option Certificates and Their Emission Prospectuses', as amended 31 December 1997.

the Central Bank. Since its creation the Federal Securities Commission has become the agency of executive power responsible for conducting State policy in the domain of the securities market and supervising the activity of professional securities market participants. The powers of the Commission do not extend to the procedure for the emission of debt obligations of the Government of the Russian Federation nor to securities of subjects of the Russian Federation.

The principal functions and powers of the Federal Securities Commission are regulated by the Federal Law on the Securities Market, as amended, and the relevant provisions of the Edict of the President of the Russian Federation of 14 August 1996 'On the System of Federal Agencies of Executive Power', as amended.[30] The Presidential edict provided that federal agencies are created only with the name and status established in the edict; no other status might be conferred on them, and the Federal Securities Commission was stated to be a State committee even though the Federal Law on the Securities Market declared that the head of the Federal Securities Commission enjoyed the status of a federal minister. On 6 September 1996 a further Edict on Questions of Federal Agencies of Executive Power restored the name of Federal Commission but equated the legal status of the Federal Securities Commission to that of a State committee.[31] Reading the Federal Law on the Securities Market and the two Presidential edicts together, the head of the Federal Securities Commission retains his stature equivalent to a federal minister and is a member of the Government, but the Commission itself administers the securities market and coordinates the activity of federal ministries and other federal agencies of executive power with respect to regulation of the securities market. In principle other federal agencies of executive power must, when adopting normative acts within their competence relating to securities regulation, agree these with the Federal Securities Commission; the last in turn within its competence issues decrees which are binding upon all federal ministries and other federal agencies of executive power.

The Director of the Federal Securities Commission is ex officio a federal minister, but the Commission is directly subordinate to the President of the Russian Federation in respect of areas of Presidential competence under the 1993 Russian Constitution.[32] The Federal Securities Commission has a Collegium consisting of 15 members, including the Chairman of the Commission, first deputy chairman, deputy chairmen, and secretary. Five members represent federal agencies of State power whose competence extends to questions connected with the securities mar-

---

[30] СЗ РФ (1996), no 34, item 4081; no 35, item 4152; no 37, item 4264; (1997), no 28, item 3422; (1999), no 16, item 1967.

[31] СЗ РФ (1996), no 37, item 4264 (1997), no 28, item 3422; (1999), no 16, item 1967.

[32] See M E Gashi-Butler, 'The Concept of a Security and Protection of Investor Rights', in W E Butler and M E Gashi-Butler, *The Corporation and Securities Under Russian and American Law* (1997) 123.

ket, and representatives of the Ministry of Finances and of the Central Bank of Russia are obligatory members of the Collegium. There must also be two persons representing the chambers of the Federal Assembly of the Russian Federation, and the Chairman of the Expert Council attached to the Federal Securities Commission is a Collegium member ex officio.

The functions of the Federal Securities Commission fill more than two full pages of text in the 1996 Law on the Securities Market. They include: working out the basic orientations for the development of the securities market, confirming standards and registration procedure for the emission of securities and prospectuses, confirming unified requirements for rules regulating professional securities activity; establishing obligatory requirements for securities operations, public placement, circulation, quotation, and listing, settlement and depositary activity, and keeping the stockholder register; licensing various types of professional securities market activity; issuing, suspending, and revoking general and other licences for securities operations and activities; ensuring disclosure of information about registered issues of securities; determining the procedure for admitting securities registered in Russia to primary placement and circulation beyond the limits of the Russian Federation; fixing the correlation between the amounts of bearer stock and paid up charter capital; and others.

The Federal Securities Commission adopts decisions in the form of decrees. Natural and juridical persons have the right to appeal to a court against published decrees of the Federal Securities Commission on the grounds that they exceed the powers of the Federal Securities Commission or are otherwise contrary to the Constitution or to federal laws. The issuance of an illegal decree by the Federal Securities Commission could result in claims for compensation of losses sustained as a result of the illegal decree.

Regulation of emission of securities

The role of the Federal Securities Commission is set out principally in Section III and Articles 42 and 44[1] of the Federal Law on the Securities Market. As noted above, the Federal Securities Commission is not concerned with the procedure for the emission of debt obligations of the Government of the Russian Federation nor with securities of subjects of the Federation; State and municipal securities are regulated by other federal legislation. The conclusion of a contract of State loan under which the lender acquires State bonds and other State securities is regulated in general by the Civil Code of the Russian Federation (Article 817). However, the powers of the Federal Securities Commission do extend to bonds issued by joint-stock societies and other non-State juridical persons, so-called corporative issues.

The President of the Russian Federation has in a series of edicts directed the Federal Securities Commission to collaborate with the Ministry of Finances of the

Russian Federation in determining the requirements for issuing bonds and other debt obligations as part of restructuring indebtedness of enterprises to the federal budget for obligatory payments. In general these bonds must meet the requirements laid down in the Standards for Emission of Stocks when founding joint-stock societies. They are offered on the market by juridical persons empowered by the Ministry of Finances of the Russian Federation to sell bonds in the ownership of the Russian Federation. Under Article 42 of the Federal Law on the Securities Market, the Federal Commission confirms the Standards for the emission of securities, prospectuses of emitents, the procedure for registering them, and supervises compliance with legislation by emitents.

The Federal Law on the Securities Market gives the Federal Securities Commission the right to establish the correlation between the amounts of bearer stocks and paid-up capital and other requirements which the emitent must comply with, the quantity of unplaced securities which will result in an emission being declared to be unconstituted and the procedure for refunds to investors, the size of blocs of emission securities which may be acquired by owners to be specified in the report on the results of the issue, and the agencies which may register the issue of emission securities. The registering agency must notify the Federal Securities Commission within seven days whether irregularities have been discovered in an emission.

The technicalities of a securities emission are regulated by the Federal Law on Joint-Stock Societies, the Federal Law on the Securities Market, and other normative legal acts. The formalities are increasingly complex and demanding as the market struggles to balance genuine investment opportunities against inadequate financial reporting standards and practices. Violations of the requirements will result in an unlawful placement, which in turn may engage civil, administrative, or criminal responsibility on the part of those who are guilty of the irregularities.

In and of itself an emission of securities is a unilateral transaction which must meet the requirements of Articles 153–181 of the Civil Code of the Russian Federation. It creates duties for the emitent *vis-à-vis* those who acquire the securities and attendant property and non-property rights. To a degree perhaps unmatched in any other type of transaction, a securities emission must comply with draconian legal requirements, including so-called Standards confirmed by the Federal Securities Commission. Moreover, an issue of stocks or bonds must comply with the procedures supervised by the registering agencies and the Federal Securities Commission. The definition of an 'emission not in good faith' is set out in the Federal Law on the Securities Market (Article 26); such an emission is an invalid unilateral transaction. The Federal Securities Commission may bring suit in a court to deem an emission not in good faith to be invalid if the emission deceived investors or the purposes of the emission were contrary to the foundations of the legal order and morality.

When commercial organisations undertake a reorganisation as defined by the Civil Code of the Russian Federation, the ensuing emission of stocks and bonds is regulated by a Decree adopted 12 February 1997 of the Federal Securities Commission 'On Confirmation of the Standards of the Emission of Stocks and Bonds and Their Emission Prospectuses in the Event of the Reorganisation of Commercial Organisations and Making Changes in the Standards of Emission of Stocks When Founding Joint-Stock Societies, Additional Stocks and Bonds and Their Emission Prospectuses Confirmed by Decree of the Federal Securities Commission of 17 September 1996', as amended 11 November 1998.[33]

Russian securities issues intended for placement abroad are regulated by the Decree of the Federal Commission for the Securities Market of 23 November 2001, No 29, which confirmed the Statute on the Procedure for Admittance of Emission Securities Issued by Emitents Registered in the Russian Federation, the Circulation of Which is Proposed Through Foreign Organizers of Trade on the Securities Market for Primary Placement Beyond the Limits of the Russian Federation and for Circulation Through Foreign Organizers of Trade on the Securities Market.[34]

D. Types of Securities

The legal status of securities under Russian law is in some disarray. The Civil Code of the Russian Federation contains a list of securities, many of which are not deemed to be securities in advanced market systems. The conceptual foundations of securities set out in the Civil Code have been, in the case of stocks and bonds, significantly modified and enlarged by other Russian legislation, most notably the 1996 Law on the Securities Market. In no other domain of Russian law have the sheer dynamics of the market so severely shaken the doctrinal and regulatory frameworks devised to fit securities into the mainstream of Russian legal and economic behaviour.

State securities

Governed by a variety of individual normative acts, the basic concept of a debt obligation of the Government of the Russian Federation, acting as the civil-law representative of the Russian Federation itself, was set out in the Law on the State Internal Debt of the Russian Federation, adopted 13 November 1992,[35] succeeded by the 1998 Budgetary Code of the Russian Federation.[36] Such obligations

---

[33] Вестник Федеральной комиссии по рынку ценных бумаг [*Herald of the Federal Securities Commission*], no 2 (1997) 12–34; no 2 (1998) 15–23; no 11 (1998).

[34] Registered by the Ministry of Justice of the Russian Federation, 16 January 2002, No 3164.

[35] СЗ РФ (1993), no 1, item 4.

[36] СЗ РФ (1999), no 28, item 3492. See M V Romanovskii and O V Vrublevskaia (eds.), Комментарий к Бюджетному кодексу Российской Федерации (вводный) [*Commentary on the Budgetary Code of the Russian Federation (Introductory)*] (2nd edn, 2001).

take the form of credits, State loans which usually take the form of a security, and other forms of debt obligation. The State debt of the Russian Federation is secured by property comprising the treasury. State treasury bonds and the like are, therefore, but one form of debt obligation of the Russian Federation.

Stocks

The definition of a stock set out in the Russian Civil Code (Article 142) and replicated in the 1995 Law on Joint-Stock Societies is regarded as having been significantly broadened by the concept of an 'emission security' as defined in the 1996 Law on the Securities Market. In its capacity as an emission security, a stock certifies not only the property rights, but also the non-property rights, of the stockholder—non-property rights which are more than personal. One jurist has justly observed that a stock represents a combination of 'obligation and right to a thing demands', that is, combines elements of the law of obligations and the law of ownership.[37]

Bonds

The definition of an emission security in the 1996 Law on the Securities Market enables a second type of security, the bond, to be classified as an emission security, although in the Civil Code of the Russian Federation it is treated as quite a distinct type of security. It is of interest that the Civil Code, which usually contains a reference to other federal laws on securities, does not do so in this instance.

Options and warrants

Enjoying a significant place in the Anglo-American securities markets, these derivative securities have experienced considerable teething problems in the Russian legal system. The legal basis for issuing them is the Edict of the President of the Russian Federation of 4 November 1994, as amended 18 January 2002, 'On Measures Relating to State Regulation of the Securities Market in the Russian Federation' and the Federal Law on Securities as amended 28 December 2002. In some instances option contracts have not been enforced in Russian courts because judges have doubted the substance of the contract: a right to acquire a right.

On 9 January 1997 the Federal Securities Commission issued a Decree on the Option Certificate, the Application Thereof, and Confirmation of Standards for the Emission of Option Certificates and the Emission Prospectuses Thereof, as amended 31 December 1997. These give formal recognition to the option certificate as a non-bearer derivative emission security.[38]

---

[37] See Andreev (n 1 above) 41.
[38] Вестник Федеральной комиссии по рынку ценных бумаг, no 1 (1997) 1–25; no 1 (1998).

Cheques

Banks have considerable powers to be involved in securities operations in the Russian Federation not least because many means of payment which are not classified as securities in Anglo-American practice are so classified by the Russian Civil Code. The requisites for a valid cheque are set out in the Civil Code (Article 878). It should be borne in mind that Russians do not yet have cheque accounts as exist in the West. Usually a cheque will take the form of a cashier's cheque, as known in the United States, and is issued by the bank against full payment in advance by the payor.

Bills of exchange

Bills of exchange first appeared in Russia during the late seventeenth century. Edicts of the Tsar issued on 31 August 1697 and 29 August 1698 forbade their use to pay customs duties. The first Statute on the Bill of Exchange of 16 May 1729 was based on German models, and indeed the Statute was published in parallel Russian and German language texts. It was replaced a century later by a Statute of 25 June 1832, this one based on French experience, eventually changed on 27 December 1862 to record German practices more familiar to Russian merchants.[39] The transition to NEP required the RSFSR to adopt the Statute on the Promissory Note and Bill of Exchange in 1922; however, by 1930 bills of exchange were prohibited for use on the territory of the USSR by a joint Decree of the TsIK and SNK USSR.

In 1936 the USSR acceded to the 1930 Geneva Convention on the bill of exchange and on 7 August 1937 confirmed a Statute on the Bill of Exchange and Promissory Note which reproduced verbatim (with departures in Articles 31, 38, and 48) the text of the Geneva Convention.[40] Used by the Soviet Union only in foreign trade transactions, the bill of exchange enjoyed a renaissance in the Russian domestic economy when it began to be used to finance inter-enterprise indebtedness on the basis of a Decree of the Presidium of the RSFSR Supreme Soviet of 24 June 1991.[41] The bill of exchange had many virtues for domestic use (no VAT on the purchase or sale of such a security, ease of drawing up the document, ability to use bills of exchange in lieu of currency, and others). On 11 March 1997 the Russian Federation reintroduced USSR legislation of 1937 regulating the bill of exchange on the basis of the 1930 Geneva Convention on the bill of exchange and promissory note, repealing the Decree of 24 June 1991.[42] This is a rare instance of Soviet legislation not merely being applied in Russia, but actually

---

[39] See G F Shershenevich, Вексельное право [*Bill of Exchange Law*] (1909).
[40] СЗ СССР (1937), no 52, item 221.
[41] Ведомости СНД и ВС РСФСР (1991), no 31, item 1024.
[42] СЗ РФ (1997), no 11, item 1238.

re-enacted after having been repealed. The Federal Securities Commission does not treat the bill of exchange as an emission security nor regulate their issuance. The Russian Federation, subjects of the Russian Federation, city and rural settlements, and other municipal formations may become obligated under bills of exchange or promissory notes only in instances specially provided for by a federal law.

Savings books

Russian citizens may open savings accounts in Russian banks and receive as certification of the amounts deposited a bearer savings book, which has the status of a security under the Russian Civil Code. If the book is lost, there are procedures available under the Russian Code of Civil Procedure to reinstate the depositor's rights even though the book is a bearer document.

Savings certificates

Sometimes called a deposit certificate, these may be inscribed or bearer securities that certify the right of the depositor or holder of the certificate to receive the face amount plus interest when the certificate matures.

Bills of lading and warehouse certificates

Classified as 'goods disposition securities' under Russian law, both act as a surrogate for the transfer of the goods specified thereon held by a transport organisation or in a warehouse. The so-called dual warehouse certificate is the most interesting, as it consists of two parts, one constituting a storage certificate and the other a certificate of pledge.[43] A valid certificate must satisfy all of the requisites set out in the Civil Code (Article 913). Although the certificates are 'issued' and transferable, they are not deemed to be emission securities and do not require any State registration, nor do they engage any tax associated with securities operations.

E. Principal Actors in Securities Transactions

Sometimes called 'participants in the securities market', they are numerous from the standpoint of legal regulation. The term 'investor' refers to any natural or juridical person, or international organisation, who acquires securities in its own name and for its own account. The definition in this context is considerably narrower than the term as used in Russian legislation on investment activity and on foreign investments. The term 'investment institutes' also survives from the 1991

---

[43] These are discussed with model forms in A V Makeev and V N Savenkov, Вексель [*The Bill of Exchange*] (2nd edn, 1997) 36–41.

RSFSR Statute on the issuance and circulation of securities. These are commercial juridical persons which may operate as intermediaries, investment consultants, investment companies, or investment funds. These activities would extend to professional participants of the securities market, having regard to the Civil Code of the Russian Federation (Chapter 4), the 1996 Law on the Securities Market, and decrees of the Federal Securities Commission.

Prior to 1997 trade in corporative securities within the Russian Federation was exclusively over the counter. Under the Statute on the Procedure for Licensing Various Types of Professional Activity on the Securities Market, confirmed by Decree of the Federal Securities Commission on 19 September 1997, as amended to 23 November 1998, only a commercial organisation created in the form of a joint-stock society or a limited responsibility society may be issued a licence to effectuate broker and dealer activities. Brokers as participants in civil-law relations operate principally on the basis of the contract of commission (Articles 972, 973, 977, and 978 of the Russian Civil Code) and commission agency (Article 995, Russian Civil Code) and the relevant provisions, as lex specialis, of the 1996 Law on the Securities Market. Brokers must operate in good faith and execute commissions in the sequence received unless the client stipulates otherwise. Any conflict of interest between broker and client must be reported immediately; if the client suffers prejudice as a result of the failure to communicate a conflict of interest, the broker must compensate losses at his own expense in the procedure established by civil legislation. The contract with the broker may provide that monies received from transactions be reinvested in securities or otherwise retained by the broker pending instructions. Brokers are prohibited from giving guarantees or promises to a client regarding revenues from the investment of monies retained by them. Clauses in the broker contract imposing confidentiality must be respected, including name of the investor and payment requisites.

Whereas the broker acts as a commission agent on behalf of his client, the dealer operates in his own name and on his own account to purchase or sell securities at prices previously announced. If the dealer fails to conclude a contract at the announced prices, suit may be brought against him either for specific performance at those prices or for compensation of losses to the client. A dealer contract may stipulate minimum and maximum quantities or securities to be bought or sold and the period for which the prices stipulated are valid. The 1996 Law on the Securities Market (Article 4(3)) lays down other material provisions which a dealer contract should contain; if they are missing, the client may propose material conditions which the dealer is required to accept.

Broker and dealer activity is carried out on the basis of a licence issued either by the Federal Securities Commission or by a federal agency of executive power or by the Russian Central Bank; the last has been granted a general licence by the Federal Securities Commission to effectuate broker and dealer activity on the securities market. Licences distinguish among the following types of activity: (a) broker activity relating to securities operations, excluding operations with the means of natural persons and broker activity relating to State securities operations and operations with securities of subjects of the Federation and municipal formations; (b) dealer activity relating to securities operations, except for operations with State securities and securities of subjects of the Federation and municipal formations; (c) broker activity with the means of natural persons, excluding such activity with regard to State securities, securities of subjects of the Federation, and municipal formations; (d) broker activity relating to State securities and securities of subjects of the Federation and municipal formations; and (e) dealer activity relating to State securities and securities of subjects of the Federation and municipal formations. Individual licences may contain combinations or all of the above, and may also be combined with depositary, custodial, and management activities. Brokers and dealers must satisfy certain personal requirements laid down by the Federal Securities Commission: financial, professional, and organisational.

Notwithstanding the reservations held by foreign investors with regard to trust management contracts under the Russian Civil Code (see Chapter 9), trust managers are increasingly appearing as actors in the securities market. The Russian Federation itself is perhaps the most frequent founder of such trusts. Title to the securities remains with the founder; the trustee may perform any legal and factual actions in the interest of the beneficiary in accordance with the contract of trust management (Chapter 53, Russian Civil Code). The trustee concluded transactions with the property in trust management in his own name, indicating that he is acting as trustee manager. The 1996 Law on the Securities Market also regulates trust management contracts.

It is commonplace for the Russian Federation as owner of securities to establish its own contractual conditions for trust management. The Edict of the President of the Russian Federation on the Transfer to Trust Management of Stocks of Joint-Stock Societies Created in the Process of Privatisation Consolidated in Federal Ownership, of 9 December 1996, as amended 7 August 1998, required that competitions be held for the right to conclude the contracts of trust management.[44] On 17 October 1997 the Federal Securities Commission confirmed the Statute on the Trust Management of Securities and Means of Investing in Securities.[45] The Statute does not extend to share investment funds or general bank management funds, but it does lay down additional requirements for a valid trust management contract in the domain of securities.

---

[44] СЗ РФ (1996), no 51, item 5764; (1998), no 32, item 3847.

[45] Вестник Федеральной комиссии по рынку ценных бумаг [*Herald of the Federal Securities Commission*], no 8 (1997) 13–19.

Services relating to the keeping of stocks and/or the registration and transfer of stock certificates and bonds fall into the category of depositary activity under Russian law. Only a juridical person may act as a depositary. The contract for a deposit account must be in written form and does not transfer to the depositary any rights of ownership to the stocks and bonds being held on deposit. The depositary may not engage in any transactions or actions other than on behalf of the depositor and in the instances provided for by the contract. The depositary is prohibited from requiring in the contract that the depositor pass certain rights consolidated by the securities to it. The function of the depositary is to hold the securities, receive revenues deriving from the securities, and credit the revenues to the account of the depositor.

The requirements imposed on the parties to a contract for a deposit account by the 1996 Federal Securities Law (Article 7) are tantamount to making the contract one of adhesion. The Provisional Statute on Depositary Activity on the Securities Market of the Russian Federation and the Procedure for the Licensing Thereof, confirmed by Decree of the Federal Securities Commission on 2 October 1996, succeeded by the Statute on Depositary Activity in the Russian Federation of 16 October 1997, distinguished between 'depositary-guardianship' and 'depositary-custodial' activities. A depositary-guardian may be a professional participant of the securities market which also engages in broker and/or dealer activity or a specialist guardian which engages exclusively in such depositary activity. There also exist specialist State institutes which undertake depositary-guardian activity of State securities as part of realising the State privatisation programme; they operate on the basis of a licence issued by the Federal Securities Commission. A depositary-custodian also requires a license from the Federal Securities Commission and, if depositary activity is combined with other securities operations, also an authorisation to so combine. Depositaries must in order to be licensed submit a set of Standards to the Federal Securities Commission which they will meet in carrying on their depositary activities. On 16 October 1997 the Federal Securities Commission confirmed the Statute on Depositary Activity in the Russian Federation which regulates all depositary activity, including both emission and non-emission securities issued in any form, documentary or paperless; it took effect from 1 June 1998.[46]

Registrars under Russian law keep the registers of stockholders and bondholders for juridical persons or the nominee holders thereof. Joint-stock societies having more than the minimum number of stockholders established by legislation must contract with an outside registrar and may not keep their own registers. Registrars

---

[46] Вестник Федеральной комиссии по рынку ценных бумаг [*Herald of the Federal Securities Commission*], no 8 (1997) 1–12.

may not engage in transactions with securities of juridical persons whose securities they register. Since, except for bearer stocks, it is the actual entry in the stockholder register rather than the stock certificate which is the stock, celebrated stockholder battles have occurred in Russia over access to and the keeping of the stockholder register. Various measures have been undertaken to reduce the incidence of 'pocket' registrars who are dependent upon and therefore excessively responsive to the managements of individual enterprises. These measures include the mandatory disclosure of stockholder information to auditors and to stockholders seeking to convoke an extraordinary stockholder meeting; failure to comply may result in suspension or revocation of a registrar's licence. On 17 September 1996 the Federal Securities Commission confirmed in a new version its Decree on Licensing Activity Relating to Keeping the Register of Possessors of Inscribed Securities and the Provisional Statute thereon,[47] which was replaced on 2 October 1997 by the Statute on Keeping the Register of Possessors of Inscribed Securities.[48] The Statute enumerates the documents which must be submitted in order to transfer securities from one owner to another: the instruction of transfer, personal identity documents, original or notarially certified copy of document confirming the rights of an empowered representative to act, and, if the securities take documentary form, the securities certificate which belonged to the previous owner.

The organisation of trade on the securities market is the responsibility of the stock exchanges and, with respect to over-the-counter transactions, so-called organisers of trade. The Federal Securities Commission confirmed the Statute on the Requirements for Organisers of Trade on the Securities Market on 16 November 1998.[49] Both stock exchanges and organisers of trade may not combine their activities in this connection with any other types of professional activity. The stock exchange must be organised exclusively in the form of a non-commercial partnership, whereas the organiser of trade may choose any form of juridical person available under Russian law, either commercial or non-commercial. In either event there must be at least 20 members of the stock exchange or the juridical person created by the organiser of trade. There are minimum capital requirements fixed by the Federal Securities Commission and entry fees to be paid by members, mostly brokers and dealers. The fees may not be discriminatory. Each stock exchange and organiser of trade must adopt a charter or rules which address

---

[47] Вестник Федеральной комиссии по рынку ценных бумаг [*Herald of the Federal Securities Commission*], no 3 (1996) 23–31.

[48] Вестник Федеральной комиссии по рынку ценных бумаг [*Herald of the Federal Securities Commission*], no 7 (1997) 1–25. This Statute replaced its predecessor of 12 July 1995 as amended 17 September 1996, and has itself been amended on 31 December 1997, 12 January 1998, and 20 April 1998.

[49] Вестник Федеральной комиссии по рынку ценных бумаг [*Herald of the Federal Securities Commission*], no 11 (1998).

matters stipulated by the Federal Securities Commission. At least once a year an organiser of trade must undergo an external audit by an independent auditor, whose opinion is submitted to the Federal Securities Commission. The requirements for listing and delisting also must meet the requirements of the Federal Securities Commission. Organisers of trade require a licence issued by the Federal Securities Commission for a term not exceeding two years; stipulated executives of the organiser of trade must undergo attestation at regular intervals in order to receive and retain their individual licences.

The Attestation Commission of the Federal Securities Commission, together with representatives from the Ministry of Finances and the Central Bank of the Russian Federation, regularly administer examinations and issue licences in accordance with the Statute on the System of Qualifications Requirements for Executives and Specialists of Organisations Effectuating Professional Activity on the Securities Market, and also Individual Entrepreneurs-Professional Participants of the Securities Market, confirmed by Decree of the Federal Securities Commission on 2 October 1997, as amended to 2 April 1999.[50]

A stock exchange as an organiser of trade is subject to special regulation. Its principal role is that of intermediary, of offering a forum where buyer and seller can conclude their transactions with ease and reliability. As noted above, a stock exchange is created in the form of a non-commercial partnership in accordance with the 1996 Federal Law on Noncommercial Organisations.[51] A non-commercial partnership [партнерство] is defined as an 'organisation based on membership and founded by citizens and/or juridical persons in order to assist its members in the effectuation of activity directed towards the achievement of purposes relating to the organisation of trade on the securities market'. The property transferred to the stock exchange by its members becomes the ownership of the stock exchange. Members of the stock exchange are not liable for its obligations, and the stock exchange is not liable for the obligations of its members. The highest organ of the stock exchange is the general meeting of members. The general meeting has competence over changing the charter of the stock exchange, determining the priority orientations of activity of the stock exchange and the principles for the formation and use of its property, the formation of executive organs of the stock exchange and termination of their powers before time, confirmation of the yearly report and yearly accounting balance sheet, confirmation of the financial plan of the stock exchange and making changes therein, creation of branches and opening of representations of the stock exchange, participation of the exchange in other organisations, and reorganisation and liquidation of the

---

[50] Вестник Федеральной комиссии по рынку ценных бумаг [*Herald of the Federal Securities Commission*], no 2 (1997) 3–11; no 4 (1998); no 5 (1998); the 1999 amendments are unpublished.
[51] СЗ РФ (1996), no 3, item 145.

stock exchange. If the founders so wish, they may create a collegial management organ to manage the stock exchange and decide certain questions within the competence of the general meeting of members.

The provisions of the Federal Law on Noncommercial Organisations relating to partnerships need to be read against the 1996 Law on the Securities Market, which introduced certain adjustments. A broker, dealer, securities manager, clearing organisation, depositary, and holder of a stockholder register, or organiser of trade on the securities market may be members of a stock exchange. However, the founders and participants of professional participants of the securities market which are juridical persons may not be employees of a stock exchange. Members of a stock exchange may not lease out or pledge their seats on the exchange, nor engage in other actions which would create an unequal status for certain members.

The sale of stocks of joint-stock societies created in the process of privatisation is regulated by special legislation in accordance with the Federal Law on the Privatisation of State and Municipal Property of 21 December 2001,[52] which replaced the Federal Law on the Privatisation of State Property and on the Fundamental Principles of the Privatisation of Municipal Property in the Russian Federation, adopted 21 July 1997 and in force from 2 August 1997, as amended 23 June 1999 and 5 August 2000.[53] All prior normative acts regulating this matter are subject to application only insofar as they are consistent with the 1997 Law and from 26 January 2002, the 2001 Law.

---

[52] СЗ РФ (2002), no 4, item 251.
[53] СЗ РФ (1997), no 30, item 3595; (1999), no 26, item 3173; (2000), no 32, item 3332.

13

BANKING LAW

The growth of private banks in the late Soviet era and in the Russian Federation has astonished observers who believed that such bastions of capitalism would be slow to emerge in the transition to the market economy. In fact it was easier for Soviet investors to create a bank than it was to create a joint enterprise with foreign investors. On 1 March 1994 there were 2,075 banks registered in the Russian Federation, of which 65 per cent were share banks in the form of a limited or additional responsibility society and 35 per cent were created in the form of a joint-stock society; in 1995–6 the Central Bank of Russia encouraged share banks to transform themselves into joint-stock banks, and the great majority are now such. As of 1 January 2000 there were 2,342 registered banks, of which 1,315 were operating and had a licence to conduct banking operations; 1,027 were dormant.[1] The Central Bank of the Russian Federation has gradually raised the capital reserve requirements for Russian banks, each round of increases resulting in mergers and a certain number of bank failures. The professed intention is to reduce the number of banks to about 500 through consolidations and more stringent reserve and other requirements. Most banks are universal in profile. The number of specialist banks—project finance, mortgage, land, and so on—remain few.

---

[1] See V I Bukato, Iu V Golovin, and Iu I L'vov, Банки и банковские операции в России [*Banks and Banking Operations in Russia*] (2001) 72. The same source shows the improved banking climate after the August 1998 crisis. On 1 January 1999, 25.7 per cent of banking assets were held by banks in a critical condition, and 19.8 per cent by banks experiencing serious difficulties. As of 1 July 2000, the figures respectively were 8.3 per cent and 7.8 per cent. Also see N D Eriashvili, Банковское право [*Banking Law*] (2nd edn, 2001).

Insurance companies were no less fashionable and relatively easy to establish. In this domain as well the regulatory agencies have gradually increased capital and reserve requirements to encourage mergers and eliminate the small undercapitalised insurers from the market.

A. Banking Legislation

Banking legislation is relegated by the 1993 Russian Constitution to the exclusive jurisdiction of the Federation (Article 7). The Constitution also contains references to the Central Bank of the Russian Federation (Articles 75, 103) and rules which enable natural persons to carry on banking activities with confidence in the banking system; for example, prohibitions against the seizure of property, including bank accounts (Article 35). The constitutional norms which extend to banking activity the legal regime of entrepreneurship and establish the freedom of the movement of capital and financial services are crucial to an effective banking system. The Decree of the Constitutional Court of the Russian Federation of 17 December 1996 which ruled that the constitutional rights of man and citizen extend to juridical persons to the extent that such rights may be applicable to them is applicable to banks and to the clients of banks irrespective of whether the last are natural or juridical persons. The constitutional foundations of the single market, financial, credit, and currency regulation, and monetary emission—all within the jurisdiction of the Federation—also promote the stability of banking activity.

B. Sources of Banking Law

In addition to the Constitution of the Russian Federation, banking relations are regulated by the Civil Code of the Russian Federation, especially Chapters 42–46, the Law on Banks and Banking Activity, the 2002 Law on the Central Bank of the Russian Federation, and by so-called banking practice or banking customs. Particular note, however, must be taken of normative acts issued by the Central Bank of the Russian Federation and its predecessor, the State Bank of the Soviet Union.

The Law on the Central Bank (Article 7) gives the Bank the right to issue normative acts within the limits of its competence which are binding throughout the territory of the Russian Federation upon federal agencies of State power and similar agencies of the subjects of the Federation and local self-government and all juridical and natural persons. While such normative acts may not be contrary to the Constitution or federal laws of any type, the general view is that Central Bank enactments take precedence over the laws enacted by subjects of the Federation but must, of course, not be contrary to federal laws. All normative acts of the

Central Bank must be published in the Вестник Банка России [*Herald of the Bank of Russia*] and be registered at the Ministry of Justice of the Russian Federation, subject to certain narrow exceptions. Entry into force occurs ten days from the day of publication, except for instances established by the Council of Directors of the Bank. Normative acts of the Bank may not be retroactive.

The *Herald* of the Central Bank is published under circumstances which make it not readily accessible and under restrictions concerning the dissemination of information published therein.

On 15 September 1997 the Central Bank issued Order No 02–395 which, as amended by an Instructive Regulation of 24 June 1998, confirmed the Statute on the Procedure for the Preparation and Entry into Force of Normative Acts of the Bank of Russia.[2] A 'normative act of the Bank of Russia' is defined as that 'directed toward the establishment, change, or repeal of norms of law as permanent or temporary instructions binding upon the group of persons determined by the Federal Law on the Central Bank of the Russian Federation (Bank of Russia) and the present Statute and intended for repeated application on the territory of the Russian Federation' (point 1.2). Excluded from the category of normative acts are administrative acts, acts of interpretation of normative acts of the Bank of Russia and/or other normative legal acts of the Russian Federation,[3] acts containing exclusively technical formats and other technical requirements, and other acts which do not meet the indicia of the definition quoted above.

Normative acts of the Central Bank are issued in three forms: instructive regulation [указание], statute [положение], and instruction [инструкция]. The first is used if the content of the document is to establish individual rules with regard to questions within the competence of the Central Bank, or to repeal a prevailing normative act of the Central Bank as a whole. The statute is intended for documents whose basic content is to establish systemically-linked rules on questions within the competence of the Central Bank. Instructions are reserved for documents which determine the procedure for the application of provisions of federal laws or other normative acts, including those of the Bank of Russia. The right of signature lies with the Chairman of the Bank but may be delegated in accordance with instructive regulations. Normative legal acts of the Central Bank signed by the Chairman must be registered on the same day in the Chancellery of the Bank,

---

[2] Экономика и жизнь, no 42 (1997); the amendments of 24 June 1998 were not published but are available on the database Consultantplus.

[3] The Bank of Russia routinely gives upon request explanations of its rules and regulations to those who so request. These do not have normative effect, although one may rely upon them. Quite separately, though, the Bank issues official explanations in order to, inter alia, 'fill a gap in legal regulation'. These are governed by the Statute on the Procedure for the Preparation and Entry into Force of Official Explanations of the Bank of Russia, adopted 18 July 2000. Вестник Банка России, no 41 (26 July 2000).

which is considered to be the day of adoption. The registration and circulation of normative acts of the Bank of Russia containing information comprising a State secret or of limited dissemination is performed by the Chief Security and Defence of Information Administration of the Bank of Russia. If normative acts are subject to registration by the Ministry of Justice, the Chancellery must transfer such acts to the Ministry on the day following registration by the Chancellery. The Legal Department of the Central Bank determines whether a normative act of the Bank is subject to registration by the Ministry of Justice.

In practice the Central Bank has issued instructions (there are more than 70), letters (about 50–60 per year), telegrams (from 300 to 600 per year), orders, statutes, extracts from protocols of a session of the Council of Directors, decisions of the Council of Directors, instructional directives, communications, joint decrees with the Government, explanations, and others. These create nightmares for lawyers, for they are commonly normative and enjoy limited circulation. Telegrams, for example, in addition to being inaccessible, omit punctuation and other elements of style which make them difficult to construe.[4]

The fact that the Central Bank is not an agency of State power or administration or an agency of local self-government has lead some Russian jurists to doubt whether illegal normative acts of the Central Bank are subject to being appealed to a court. The formulas used in Russian legislation which create such right of appeal omitted the Central Bank[5] or were laconic in the extreme. The 2002 Law on the Central Bank now provides: 'Normative acts of the Bank of Russia may be appealed to a court in the procedure established for contesting normative legal acts of federal agencies of State power' (Article 7).

Normative acts of the State Bank of the USSR continue in some instances to be in force. In September 1991 within a 14-day period the Central Bank of Russia issued two telegrams, the first of which deemed all acts of the State Bank of the USSR to be invalid on the territory of Russia. The second telegram, still in force, provided that all acts of the State Bank of the USSR, unless they are expressly contrary to new Russian legislation, are regarded as being in force until expressly and specially repealed by the Central Bank of Russia. The Central Bank regularly publishes a list of acts of the USSR State Bank which are deemed to be no longer in force on the territory of Russia.

It has been argued by some Russian jurists that certain USSR State Bank instructions should be 'deemed to have lost force' even though the Central Bank of Russia has not expressly so determined. The better view is that the Central Bank must

---

[4] L G Efimova, Банковское право [*Banking Law*] (1994) 16.
[5] Ia A Geivandov, Центральный банк Российской Федерации [*Central Bank of the Russian Federation*] (1997) 123.

make that explicit determination as called for in its Second Telegram of September 1991. An example of what difference the distinction can make is the controversy concerning loan accounts. Normative acts of the President of the Russian Federation and other agencies of State power provided that a credit must be granted by crediting the money to settlement accounts and the bank must notify the tax service about the loan accounts opened. Acts of the USSR State Bank, however, suggest that loan accounts are not the accounts of a taxpayer, but rather contractual accounts which represent a form of performance of a contract and do not engage tax revenue implications.[6]

The concept of 'local acts' as a source of banking law is widely accepted in Russian doctrine, emulating the position in labour law and agrarian law. In the domain of banking, local acts are those normative acts worked out and adopted by commercial banks themselves and regulating on the basis of Russian legislation the relations between the banks and their branches, between internal services of the bank, and between bank officials. It is argued, for example, that the charter of a bank, adopted by the bank itself and subject to State registration, determines the legal status of the specific bank and the operations it may conduct. The Law on Banking Activity requires a bank charter to contain certain information about the banking operations which may be performed, and these in turn depend in some measure on the licences obtained by the bank. Licences are treated as 'local acts' insofar as they determine the competence of the bank, and therefore bind both the bank and its clients. The second type of local acts are rules drafted by the bank itself to regulate, for example, granting credits or loans to clients, or the rules governing bank accounts. The third group consists of internal bank regulations, for example, the Statute on the Legal Service, the Statute on the Credit Committee, post instructions for workers, and the like. These are matters which in Western banks would be treated as internal policies rather than the subject of formal internal documents. Yet the Association of Russian Banks, for example, has drafted and published a Model Statute on the Legal Service for the use of its members.

Banking rules and customs, including international practices and customs, are rapidly being recognised as a source of Russian banking law.[7]

C. Central Bank of the Russian Federation

The status, tasks, functions, powers, and principles for the organisation and activity of the Central Bank of the Russian Federation, also known officially as the Bank of Russia, were determined principally by the Federal Law on the Central

---

[6] See O M Oleinik, Основы банковского права [*Foundations of Banking Law*] (1997) 60.
[7] N Iu Erpyleva, Международное банковское право [*International Banking Law*] (1998) 7–8.

Bank of the Russian Federation of 2 December 1990, as amended 27 December 1995, 20 June 1996, 27 February and 28 April 1997, 4 March 1998, 31 July 1998, 8 July 1999, 19 June 2001, 6 August 2001, 30 December 2001, and 21 March 2002, until replaced by the Federal Law on the Central Bank of the Russian Federation (Bank of Russia) of 10 July 2002.[8]

Legal status

The Central Bank is a legal curiosity, as so many central banks are in the world. It combines the functions of a State agency which regulates banking and carries out banking supervision in the name of the Russian Federation. It services juridical and natural persons, performs budgetary and State debt servicing operations and operations with the gold and hard currency reserves. It also participates in civil-law relations and has management functions with respect to subordinate enterprises, institutions, and organisations. The statutory formulations regarding its legal status are cryptic. The Central Bank may be a State institution, at least in part, but the Bank is not an agency of State power or administration, that is, the Bank is not part of the executive, legislative, or other branches of State and is not part of the Government.

The Law on the Central Bank provides that the Bank is a 'juridical person' (Article 1), but does not stipulate what organisational-legal form of juridical person it may be. A careful analysis of its sundry functions suggests that the Bank does not precisely fit into any of the organisational-legal forms provided for juridical persons in the Russian Civil Code. The failure to indicate organisational-legal form is a violation of Articles 52 and 54 of the Russian Civil Code. Article 3 of the Law on the Central Bank declares that deriving a profit is not a purpose of the Bank, which leads some jurists to suggest that the Central Bank qualifies as a non-commercial organisation under the Civil Code.[9] Others have cautioned against trying to pigeon-hole the Bank into a particular private-law category. Pointing to the public-law features of the Bank, Oleinik observes that 'at the present time there is no institute in Russian Law which might express the specific features of the legal status of the Bank of Russia, and the new version of the Law on it did not work out such a construction, having offered nothing in principle that was new'.[10] She suggests the Bank should be regarded as a 'juridical person of public law', although it is acknowledged that such a concept is as yet unrecognised by Russian Law.

---

[8] Ведомости СНД и ВС РСФСР (1990), no 27, item 356; СЗ РФ (1995), no 18, item 1593; no 31, item 2991; (1996), no 2, item 55; (1997), no 9, item 1028; (1998), no 10, item 1147; no 31, item 3829; (1999), no 28, item 3472; (2001), no 26, item 2585; no 33(I), item 3413; no 53(I), item 5030; (2002), no 12, item 1093; no 28, item 2790.

[9] Geivandov (n 5 above) 20–21.

[10] Oleinik (n 6 above) 131. The same is true of the 2002 law.

The functions of the Central Bank also configure its unique legal status. The Law on the Central Bank (Article 4) prescribes these as interacting with the Government of the Russian Federation in working out and implementing a unified State monetary-credit policy, exercising the exclusive monopoly of issuing and circulating money, acting as the creditor of last instance for credit organisations and organising the refinancing system, establishing the rules for the settlement of accounts in Russia, for conducting banking operations, and managing the gold and hard currency reserves, registering credit organisations, issuing and revoking licences for credit organisations and for the organisations which audit them, registering the emission of securities by credit organisations, performing all types of banking operations and other transactions needed to fulfil the principal tasks of the Central Bank, regulating currency, including the purchase and sale of foreign currency and determining the procedure for the settlement of accounts with foreign States, establishing and publishing official exchange rates, organising and effectuating currency control directly and through empowered banks, forecasting and drawing up the balance of payments of the Russian Federation, as well as studying and analysing the Russian economy with special attention to credit, currency, financial, and price matters, among others.

Competence of Central Bank

The Bank of Russia is the very centre of the Russian banking system. It is capable of formulating its own policies for the banking system, must be responsive to the Federal Assembly, the President, and the Government of the Russian Federation, the public interest, and the private interests of commercial banks and their clients. The Law on the Central Bank made provision for this balancing role amongst conflicting interests by authorising the formation of a National Banking Council composed of 12 persons attached to the Central Bank consisting of representatives from both chambers of the Federal Assembly, the President of Russia, the Government of Russia, and the Bank itself.

The rules for conducting banking operations, keeping bank records and accounting documents, and submitting statistical data are established by the Central Bank for all credit organisations. The Central Bank has the right to request and receive information from individual credit organisations about their activities and to demand explanations about the information disclosed; such information is confidential and may not be disclosed without consent unless Russian legislation provided otherwise. Reference has been made above to the problems experienced by banks and their clients with the forms of normative legal acts issued by the Central Bank. For the most part, the Central Bank operates arbitrarily in this domain, issuing telegrams and letters as before.

The Central Bank has limited functions in comparison with ordinary commercial banks; rather it is the bank for banks and also serves a special client, the State. To the extent that the Central Bank does perform banking operations, these are principally for representative and executive agencies of State power of the Russian Federation and subjects of the Federation, agencies of local self-government, institutions and organisations thereof, State extra-budgetary funds, military units, military servicemen, and employees of the Central Bank itself. The Bank also may serve clients in areas where there are no other credit organisations. Some find it indefensible that the Central Bank offers banking services to its own personnel and to juridical persons.

The operations of the Central Bank with Russian and foreign credit organisations and with the Government of the Russian Federation are set out in the Law on the Central Bank (Article 46). These are central to the banking and financial system, and include: granting credits for a term of not more than one year by taking securities and other assets as security for performance, purchasing and selling foreign currency and payment documents and obligations denominated in foreign currency issued by Russian and foreign credit organisations, buying and selling State securities on the open market, and bonds, deposit certificates, and other securities redeemable within not more than one year, purchasing and selling foreign currency and payment documents and obligations in foreign currency, buying, keeping, and selling precious metals and other types of currency valuables, conducting settlement, cashier, and deposit operations, including the acceptance of securities and other valuables for keeping and management, issuing bank guarantees and suretyships, performing operations with financial instruments used to manage financial risks, opening accounts in Russian and foreign credit organisations in the Russian Federation and beyond its limits, issuing cheques and bills of exchange in any currency, and performing other banking operations and transactions in its own name in accordance with customs of business turnover accepted in international banking practice. The Central Bank grants credits to the Ministry of Finances of the Russian Federation to cover the shortfall between yearly current budget revenues and expenses in those instances when the Law on the Federal Budget so stipulates[11] and performs other functions related to servicing the State debt and operations with the gold and currency reserves of the Russian Federation.

The Law on the Central Bank imposes certain prohibitions on the Central Bank. It may not, for example, perform banking operations with juridical persons unlicensed to conduct banking operations nor with natural persons in general unless expressly provided otherwise by legislation, nor acquire stocks or participatory shares in credit and other organisations, nor become involved in operations with

---

[11] The Statute on the Ministry of Finances of the Russian Federation, confirmed by the Government on 19 August 1994, as amended, empowers the Ministry to conclude agreements in the name of the Government for credits to cover the deficit of the federal budget and for other purposes.

immoveable property, nor engage in trade or production activity, nor prolong credits granted—in all cases subject to legislation providing otherwise.

Certain of the Central Bank's operations generate revenues and profit. Rather than tax the Central Bank on these, the 2002 Law on the Central Bank provides that 50 per cent of the actual profit after payment of taxes and charges under the Tax Code and confirmation of the yearly report of the Central Bank by the Council of Directors should be credited to the Federal budget.[12] The remainder of the profit is directed by the Central Bank to reserves and special-purpose funds, when such remainder is permitted.

The Central Bank is the principal agency of State control and supervision over the legality of commercial banking activities with a view to maintaining the stability and integrity of the banking system and defending the interests of depositors and creditors. These functions are performed by the Committee of Banking Supervision within the Central Bank. Verifications are conducted on commercial bank premises and binding instructions may be issued to commercial banks to comply with normative legal acts or eliminate violations. Several sanctions are available to be applied to recalcitrant banks: fines of up to 1 per cent of the paid up charter capital, but not exceeding 1 per cent of the minimum charter capital; implementing measures to restore the financial health of a credit organisation, including a restructuring of assets, replacement of executives of the credit organisation; or reorganisation of the credit organisation, alteration for up to six months of the normative standards which a bank must comply with (for example, reserves); prohibition of certain banking operations for up to one year; appointment of a temporary administrator to manage the bank for up to 18 months, or revoking the licence to perform banking operations. A number of licences are revoked in practice each year. The Central Bank actually has considerable discretion as to how to react to violations, for the Law on the Central Bank, in enumerating the measures which may be taken (Article 74), does not specify which measure that could be applied should be applied for each violation.

In its management capacity the Central Bank is responsible for the credit and monetary policy of the Russian Federation, regulated by fixing interest rates for Central Bank operations, reserve requirements, open market operations, refinancing of banks, currency regulation, growth of the money supply, and direct limitations. These operations are analogous to those of many European central banks. In the open market the Central Bank will buy and sell treasury bills of exchange, State bonds, and other State securities. Foreign currencies may be bought and sold to stabilise the ruble. Each year the Central Bank submits to the State Duma the basic orientations for a unified State monetary-credit policy for

---

[12] This notwithstanding Article 298 of the Russian Civil Code, which allows institutions earning revenues to retain them.

the forthcoming year after discussions of the draft with the President and Government of the Russian Federation. Money supply and circulation is influenced by Central Bank requirements for, inter alia, the operations of non-cash settlements between clients.

The Central Bank acts in the name of the Russian Federation in the capital funds and activities of international financial and other organisations in accordance with international treaties and inter-bank agreements. Within the Russian Federation the Central Bank is the contracting party of the State as a whole in the person of its agencies. It receives credits and deposits to the State budget and services the State debt. On behalf of the Government of Russia it performs the functions of agent and depositary. However, the Central Bank may not grant credits to the Government of Russia in order to finance a budget deficit or to acquire State securities at first placement unless the Federal Law on the Federal Budget expressly so provides, nor may such credits be granted to subjects of the Russian Federation, local budgets, or the budgets of State extra-budgetary funds.

Accountability of Central Bank

The Law on the Central Bank provides that the Bank is accountable to the State Duma of the Federal Assembly of the Russian Federation. Accountability takes several forms. The State Duma appoints the Chairman of the Central Bank to office and relieves him from office upon the recommendation of the President of the Russian Federation. In practice this has sometimes proved to be a controversial appointment, and the President's preferred recommendation has not always been accepted by the Duma. The State Duma itself appoints to and relieves from office the members of the Council of Directors of the Central Bank upon the recommendation of the Chairman of the Bank agreed with the President of the Russian Federation.

As and when it wishes, the Federal Assembly may conduct parliamentary hearings concerning the activity of the Central Bank. Twice yearly the Chairman of the Central Bank reports to the State Duma, once to present the yearly report and again to submit the principal orientations for the unified State monetary-credit policy for the forthcoming year. The yearly report must be submitted not later than 15 May of the following year. It consists of an account of the Bank's activities and analysis of the economy from a primarily financial point of view, the yearly balance sheet, profit and loss account, and distribution of profit, use of the reserves and funds of the Central Bank, and the outside auditor's opinion. Each year the National Bank Council determines who the outside auditors of the Central Bank will be. The internal audit of the Central Bank is conducted by the Chief Auditor, who is directly subordinate to the Chairman of the Central Bank. The State Duma considers the yearly report before 1 July and adopts a decision with regard to the report. Publication of the yearly report must follow by 15 July, although the Central Bank publishes its balance sheet each month, together with data on monetary circulation and the money supply.

The Central Bank plays a key role in the management of Sberbank Russia, in which the Russian Federation is the principal stockholder through the Bank of Russia. Certain issues of Sberbank to be voted upon by the stockholders can only be the subject of voting if a special federal law has been adopted on the question, eg, alienation of or reduction of the number of stocks of Sberbank in federal ownership.

Ownership of Central Bank

Under the 2002 Law, the Central Bank is a juridical person whose charter capital and other property are federal ownership. It would follow that the Bank itself has the right of economic jurisdiction with respect to property consolidated to it by the State. The 2002 Law on the Central Bank does nothing to clarify the position as to whether the Bank holds property by right of economic jurisdiction or by right of operative management, that is, whether the Bank would be dependent upon authorisation from another federal agency, Goskomimushchestvo, to dispose of its property. The Law on the Central Bank merely confirms that the Central Bank is in federal ownership and that it has the right to possess, use, and dispose of its property—rights which in any event it would enjoy under either the principles of economic jurisdiction or operative management, albeit with limitations.

One Russian jurist has dismissed the Central Bank's status with respect to federal ownership as a 'fiction'.[13] It is assuredly anomalous, and rather surprising that the yearly report is not heavily annotated by the auditors.

Structure of Central Bank

The system of the Central Bank consists of a central apparatus, territorial branches, settlement-cashier centres, computer centres, field branches, educational institutions, the Russian Encashment Association, and others, including security. The national banks of the republics within the Russian Federation are territorial branches of the Central Bank.

The system is hierarchical. Territorial branches are not juridical persons and do not have the right to adopt decisions of a normative character, nor to issue guarantees, suretyships, bills of exchange, and other obligations without the authorisation of the Council of Directors of the Central Bank. Each operates on the basis of the Statute on Territorial Branches of the Bank of Russia, confirmed by the Council of

---

[13] Oleinik (n 6 above) 150.

Directors. In some instances territorial branches have been created for economic areas which combine the territories of several subjects of the Federation.

The field branches actually engage in banking operations. They are military institutions which operate on the basis of military statutes and the Statute on Field Branches of the Bank of Russia confirmed by joint decision of the Bank of Russia and the Ministry of Defence of the Russian Federation. They serve military units, institutions, and organisations and those of other State agencies which perform defence functions, as well as juridical persons ensuring the security of the Russian Federation and natural persons who reside on the territories of objects serviced by field branches.

The highest organ of the Central Bank is the Council of Directors, consisting of the Chairman of the Bank of Russia and 12 members, all of whom work on a permanent basis at the Bank. The members of the Council of Directors are appointed for a term of four years by the State Duma upon the recommendation of the Chairman of the Bank of Russia agreed with the President of the Russian Federation. The Chairman of the Bank presides at sessions of the Council, where decisions are taken by a majority of those present provided that a quorum constitutes seven persons and the Chairman of the Bank or the person replacing the Chairman. The Council meets at least once a month, sessions being designated by the Chairman or person replacing him or by one-third of the members of the Council.

The powers of the Council of Directors are substantial. It works out and ensures the fulfilment of the basic orientations for a unified State monetary-credit policy, confirms the yearly report of the Bank and submits it to the State Duma, confirms the estimate of expenses of the Bank for the forthcoming year, determines the structure of the Bank, adopts decisions to create or liquidate branches and organisations of the Bank, to establish obligatory normative standards for credit organisations, increase reserve requirements, change interest rates, determine the ceilings for open market operations, participate in international organisations, purchase and sell immoveable property, issue and remove from circulation banknotes and coins, and lay down the procedure for the formation of the reserves of credit organisations. The Council also appoints the Chief Auditor of the Bank, makes proposals to the State Duma to change the charter capital of the Bank, and decides under what conditions foreign capital may be admitted to the banking system of Russia. Members of the Council may not join political parties nor hold office in socio-political and religious organisations.

The Chairman of the Bank is appointed to office for a four-year term by a majority vote of the total number of deputies of the State Duma. A candidacy for the post must be submitted by the President of the Russian Federation to the State Duma not later than three months after the predecessor Chairman left office, unless the Chairman resigned before his term had expired, in which event the nomination for a replacement must be submitted within two weeks. If the candidacy is rejected by the State Duma, another must be proposed within two weeks; no candidate may be proposed more than twice. No Chairman may serve for more than three terms in succession.

The Chairman acts in the name of the Central Bank and represents its interests without a power of attorney in relations with agencies of State power, credit organisations, organisations of foreign States and international organisations, and other institutions and organisations. He signs normative acts of the Central Bank, decisions of the Council of Directors, protocols of sessions of the Council of Directors, and agreements concluded by the Bank. If there is a tie vote in the Council, his vote is decisive.

D. Russian Banking System

The Russian banking system is regulated first and foremost by the Federal Law on Banks and Banking Activity of 2 December 1990 in the version of 3 February 1996, as amended 31 July 1998, 5 July 1999, 8 July 1999, 19 June 2001, and 7 August 2001.[14] By banking system in this chapter we have in view the Central Bank of Russia and the banks and other credit organisations and the branches and representations of foreign banks which operate in the Russian Federation to serve juridical and natural persons. In the larger sense the banking system includes various unions and associations created by credit organisations to represent their interests and develop various links, holding companies which include a credit organisation, informal associations of bankers where decisions may be taken quietly, and the National Bank Council of the Central Bank, referred to above.

Certain non-banking credit organisations are part of the Russian banking system. Among them is the Settlement Centre of the Organised Securities Market, which is responsible for opening and operating bank accounts for participants of the Settlement Centre. The centres function in accordance with the Statute on the Procedure for the Effectuation of Settlements of Accounts with Regard to Operations with Financial Instruments on the Organised Securities Market, confirmed by Order of the Central Bank of the Russian Federation on 18 July 1996, as amended 8 June 1998. Settlement centres created in the form of joint-stock societies issue stocks, the operations respecting which are also dealt with by the settlement centre. Clearing institutions likewise fall within the category of non-banking credit institutions, their activities being governed by the Provisional

---

[14] Ведомости СНД и ВС РСФСР (1990), no 27, item 357; СЗ РФ (1996), no 6, item 492; (1998), no 31, item 3829; (1999), no 28, item 3459 and item 3469; (2001), no 26, item 2586; no 33(I), item 3424; transl in W E Butler, *Russian Company and Commercial Legislation* (2003).

Statute on the Clearing Institution confirmed on 10 February 1993 and require a licence from the Central Bank. Several regions have created their own clearing centres with narrower functions than those performed by a clearing institution; in Moscow, for example, a city clearing centre was created by the Mayor on 12 April 1996 in order to facilitate settlements between enterprises and the City budget. Broker and dealer firms, investment and pension funds, credit unions, pawn-shops, finance leasing, insurance, and finance companies are frequently licensed by the Central Bank as non-banking credit organisations.[15]

Foreign banks and their branches and representations are part of the Russian banking system. Under the Law on the Central Bank (Article 52), the Central Bank of the Russian Federation is empowered to issue authorisations for the creation of banks with the participation of foreign capital and the Council of Directors adopts the decision with regard to their opening on the territory of Russia. The status of foreign banks and their ability to acquire participatory shares or stocks in the charter capital of Russian credit organisations is regulated in detail by Russian legislation. On 23 April 1997 the Council of Directors of the Central Bank confirmed the Statute on the Peculiarities of the Registration of Credit Organisations with Foreign Investments and on the Procedure for Receiving Preliminary Authorisation of the Bank of Russia to Increase the Charter Capital of a Registered Credit Organisation at the Expense of Means of Nonresidents.[16] For the purposes of the Statute, a credit organisation is a resident credit organisation whose charter capital has been formed with the participation of means of non-residents irrespective of the amount of the participatory share.

The Law on Banks distinguishes between credit organisations and banks. A credit organisation is a juridical person in the form of an economic society which has the right to effectuate banking operations provided for by the Law on Banks on the basis of a special authorisation or licence issued by the Central Bank. A bank is a type of credit organisation which has the exclusive right to effectuate in aggregate banking operations with regard to attracting deposits of monetary means of natural and juridical persons, placing the said means in its own name and on its own account on the conditions laid down in the Law on Banks, and opening and conducting bank accounts for natural and juridical persons (Article 1, Law on Banks). A non-banking credit organisation may effectuate individual banking operations provided for by the Law on Banks but in a combination determined by the Central Bank.

---

[15] G A Tosunian, Государственное управление в области финансов и кредита в России [*State Administration in the Sphere of Finances and Credit in Russia*] (1997) 123.

[16] Entered into force 15 May 1997, as amended 22 June 1999 and 24 June 1999. Вестник Банка России [*Herald of the Bank of Russia*], no 25 (30 April 1997); no 38 (1999).

Banking operations, in addition to those enumerated in the previous paragraph, include effectuating the settlement of accounts on behalf of natural and juridical persons, including correspondent banks, the encashment of monetary means, bills of exchange, payment and settlement documents and the cashier servicing of natural and juridical persons, the purchase and sale of foreign currency in cash and non-cash forms, attracting the deposit and placement of previous metals, and issuing bank guarantees. In addition to these a credit organisation may effectuate the specified transactions: issue suretyships for third persons which provide for the performance of obligations in monetary form, acquire rights of demand from third persons for the performance of obligations in monetary form, trust management of monetary means and other property under a contract with natural and juridical persons, effectuate operations with precious metals and precious stones, lease out special premises or safes to natural and juridical persons for the keeping of documents and valuables, finance leasing operations, and the rendering of consultation and informational services. A credit organisation may not engage in production, trade, or insurance activity.

From the above provisions, it is evident that banks and other credit organisations enjoy merely special legal capacity under Russian law. That position also must be reflected in the constitutive documents of a credit organisation, where the enumerated activities of the organisation must be in accordance with legislation and exhaustive. In the 1996 amendments to the Law on Banks, the language referring to trust operations was altered and may have dispossessed Russian banks of the legal capacity to become involved in trust activities under foreign legal systems which have trusts in the Anglo-American understanding of the word.[17]

Russian banks are required to create reserves in accordance with requirements established by the Central Bank, to classify assets so as to identify doubtful and hopeless debts, and to create funds to cover potential losses.

Banking secrecy and money laundering

The Law on Banks requires a credit organisation, the Bank of Russia, and all employees of these organisations to observe the secrecy of operations, accounts, and deposits of their clients and correspondents. Information concerning the accounts and operations of juridical persons and individual entrepreneurs may be issued to courts, arbitrazh courts, and judges, State tax service agencies, the tax

---

[17] It is argued that the trust management of money undertaken by Russian banks in accordance with the Law on Banks (Article 5) has nothing in common with the Civil Code concept of trust management. They are rather two different institutes bearing the same name. On this view Article 5 of the Law on Banks contemplates a contract of commission or of agency. See R V Amir'iants and I A Dubov, in K D Lubenchenko (ed), Федеральный закон 'О банках и банковской деятельности'. Введение. Текст. Комментарии [*Federal Law 'On Banks and Banking Activity'. Introduction. Text. Commentary*] (1998) 74–79.

police, customs agencies, and, with the procurator's consent, to agencies of preliminary investigation. Natural persons who are not entrepreneurs have a more protected position; information concerning their accounts and deposits may be issued only to courts and, with the procurator's consent, to agencies of preliminary investigation. If the account-holder dies, the credit organisation may issue information according to a testamentary disposition given to the organisation or to notarial offices handling the estate. In the case of foreign citizens, such information may be released to foreign consular institutions.

The precise information subject to the protection of banking secrecy is set out in the Civil Code of the Russian Federation (Article 857). It includes information on the bank accounts and deposits of clients, on the banking operations of clients, and on the clients themselves which the bank possesses by virtue of having performed contractual obligations to the client. A credit institution may add to this list by virtue of its own regulations or contracts so long as federal legislation is not violated. The commentators believe that secrecy extends not only to banking operations proper but also to transactions which banks and other credit organisations have the right to conclude. Open information about clients (charters, accounting reports) is not protected, although in practice it is said that Russian State agencies often use banks to obtain such materials rather than apply to the client directly.[18]

The illegal collecting or divulgence of information constituting a banking secret is a serious criminal offence under the 1996 Russian Criminal Code (Article 183).

With effect from 1 February 2002 the Federal Law on Counteracting the Legalisation (or Laundering) of Revenues Received by Criminal Means of 7 August 2001, as amended 25 July 2002 and 30 October 2002,[19] superimposed over the banking secrecy protections a scheme intended to 'prevent, elicit, and suppress' so-called 'money laundering'. The Law on money laundering extends to foreigners as well as to Russians and under certain circumstances may operate extra-territorially. For the purposes of the law, 'revenues received by criminal means' are monetary means or other property received as a result of the commission of a crime. Legalising or laundering revenues is 'imparting a lawful appearance to the possession, use or disposition of monetary means or other property received as a result of the commission of crimes, excluding crimes provided for by Articles 193, 194, 198, and 199 of the Russian Criminal Code. The principal agencies whose financial operations fall under the law are credit organisations, professional participants of the securities market, insurance and finance leasing companies, postal, telegraph, and other non-

---

[18] See A A Kozlachkov, in Lubenchenko (n 17 above) 217.
[19] СЗ РФ (2001), no 33(I), item 3418; (2002), no 30, item 3033; no 44, item 4296; transl in Butler (n 14 above).

credit organisations which transfer or remit monetary means, and pawnshops.

The principal measures by which money laundering is counteracted are three: so-called obligatory internal control procedures, which consist of activities within organisations effectuating operations with monetary means and other property to elicit operations that are subject to 'obligatory control' and other operations connected with money laundering; (2) obligatory control, which comprises the aggregate of measures taken with regard to control over operations with monetary means and other property on the basis of information submitted to it by the organisations which effectuate such operations; and (3) a prohibition against informing clients and other persons about measures being taken to counteract money laundering. Operations subject to obligatory control include those which exceed 600,000 rubles and which involved a withdrawal or transfer to the account of a juridical person of cash when the character of the juridical person's economic activity does not so involve such transfers; the purchase or sale of cash foreign currency; the acquisition of securities by a natural person with settlement in cash; the receipt by a natural person of monetary means by a bearer cheque issued by a non-resident; an exchange of banknotes of one denomination for banknotes of another; and the contribution by a natural person of cash money to the charter capital of an organisation. The Government of Russia is to publish a list of states or territories where there is considered to be the illegal production of narcotic means and to which the transfer of money or provision of a credit or loan, or securities is made, and the like; routinely such transactions will attract the attention of obligatory control. Transactions with regard to bank accounts, moveable property, and the like also fall under the Law.

The Central Bank of Russia plays an important role in aspects of enforcing the Law, together with other agencies empowered by the Russian Government to do so. The Law expressly stipulates that supplying information and documents for the purposes and in the procedure laid down by the Law on money laundering is not a violation of employment, banking, tax, and commercial secrecy. Treaty arrangements are required by the Law to extend legal assistance in the collecting of information, preliminary investigation, judicial examination, and execution of judicial decisions, the provision of information to foreign law enforcement agencies, and similar measures. Foreign court judgments relating to money laundering are subject to enforcement in Russia on the basis of treaties, including with respect to the confiscation of revenues received by criminal means and situated in the Russian Federation. Extradition and transit carriage of persons to a foreign State may occur either pursuant to a treaty or on the basis of reciprocity, subject, however, to the constitutional prohibition against the extradition of Russian citizens.

14

TAXATION

In the transition to a market economy taxation has come to assume a more central role in ordering Russian economic life, including Russian citizens and foreigners. There continues to be difficulty in applying Western concepts of taxation to the Russian system, for there continues to be a mixed economy containing treasury enterprises in which the State is the owner of the instruments and means of production, open joint-stock societies in which the State is the sole or principal stockholder, and purely private enterprises in which there is no State involvement.[1] The concepts of 'obligatory payments' to the national budget by State enterprises and of 'taxes' levied against private juridical and natural persons sit uneasily together in the body of normative legal acts comprising what may be broadly called the 'law of taxation'. Moreover, the Russian legal terminology of taxation is in a number of instances plainly inconsistent with Russian civil law and traditional Russian modes of expression.

The first decade of experience with a quasi-market tax system produced on the whole negative results. The vast multiplicity of taxes led to chronic under-reporting and evasion. The State actually indulged in double taxation in certain instances and imposed excessive tax rates. There has been an imbalance between the levels of responsibility imposed on juridical and natural persons who violate tax legislation

---

[1] The leading work in English on the late Soviet period is M Newcity, *Taxation in the Soviet Union* (1986).

and the tax agencies and officials who do the same. While tax legislation changes in all countries, the pace of change has been particularly frequent in the Russian Federation; taxpayers find it difficult to master the system and the changes therein, and there are insufficient professional advisors to assist.

A. Historical Background

Although there were signs as early as 1987 that the former Soviet Union might begin to use taxation in relations between the State treasury and State enterprises, the true transition to taxation commenced with the adoption on 14 June 1990 of the Law of the USSR on Taxes from Enterprises, Associations, and Organisations. This Law imposed the duty on the said taxpayers to pay all-union taxes on profit, turnover, export and import, the fund for the payment of labour of collective farmers, increment of means directed towards consumption, and revenues.[2] An indirect sales tax was introduced in 1991 on juridical persons,[3] who already were paying, from 1988, the tax on possessors of means of transport previously recovered only from natural persons.[4] Natural persons were subject to income tax under the Law of the USSR on Income Tax from Citizens of the USSR, Foreign Citizens, and Stateless Persons, adopted 23 April 1990.

It was contemplated by the Soviet authorities that a second phase of tax reform would commence in 1993 under which all personal revenues of citizens would be taxed on a unified basis with appropriate deductions for certain expenses. To that end in 1990 the USSR adopted a law providing for the staged repeal of the tax on bachelors, single citizens, and citizens with small families.[5] A series of enactments addressed relations between the USSR and the union republics. The Union retained the right to establish and direct partly or entirely to the Union budget the entire complex of all-union taxes, fees, and obligatory payments, the rates of which were exclusively within USSR jurisdiction, leaving to the union and autonomous republics the right to introduce their own taxes, fees, and payments in accordance with Union legislation.[6] Local taxes were relegated to the competence of agencies of local-self-government.[7]

---

[2] Ведомости Верховного Совета СССР (1990), no 27, item 522. The tax on export and import was replaced on 26 March 1991 by customs duties pursuant to the USSR Law on the Customs Tariff.

[3] Ведомости Верховного Совета СССР (1991), no 1, item 55.

[4] Ведомости Верховного Совета СССР (1988), no 12, item 186.

[5] Ведомости Верховного Совета СССР (1990), no 19, item 322.

[6] The key enactments were the Law on the Foundations of Economic Relations of the USSR and the Union and Autonomous Republics, adopted 10 April 1990, and the Law on the Delimitation of Powers between the USSR and Subjects of the Federation, adopted 26 April 1990. See respectively BBC CCCP (1990), no 16, item 270; no 19, item 329.

[7] See the USSR Law on General Principles of Local Self-Government and Local Economy in the USSR, adopted 9 April 1990. BBC CCCP (1990), no 16, item 267.

Consequently, the embryo of a tri-level system of taxation was in place but never to develop. Before the demise of the Soviet Union, taxation became part of the 'war of laws' between the Union and the union republics. On 1 December 1990 the RSFSR adopted a Law on the Procedure for the Application of the Law of the USSR of 14 June 1990 and the following day a similar Law concerning the application of the USSR Law on income tax from natural persons. Relying on its Declaration of State Sovereignty, the RSFSR reserved the right to create exceptions from and additions to USSR legislation on taxation on Russian territory. The result was to create a more favourable tax regime for enterprises of Republic subordination in comparison with those of Union subordination to offer more privileges to individuals and juridical persons, and to reallocate receipts between the Union and the Republic budgets. The war of laws persisted throughout most of 1991 in a variety of legislative acts on taxation and finance and contributed materially to the desperate economic situation in which the Union and the union republics found themselves.

B. Contemporary Legislation

As the Union commenced to dissolve, the Russian Federation on 11 and 18 October 1991 respectively introduced a land tax and road fund tax, followed on 6–7 December 1991 by individual laws on VAT, excises, income tax payable by natural persons. However, the system of taxation was formulated in a law which still remains the point of departure for Russian taxation: the Law on the Fundamental Principles of the Tax System in the Russian Federation, adopted 27 December 1991, with effect from 1 January 1992 as amended.[8] Superseded as of 1999 by the Tax Code of the Russian Federation,[9] Articles 18(2), 19, 20, and 21 of the 1991 Law on the tax system remained in force until Part Two of the Tax Code was enacted and to some extent thereafter. Part Two of the Tax Code (Chapters 21–24) was adopted on 5 August 2000 and entered into force on 1 January 2001.[10] Chapter 25 of Part Two (Tax on the Profit of Organisations) was added on 6 August 2001 with effect from 1 January 2002; Chapter 26 (Tax on the Extraction of Minerals), added on 8 August 2001; Section IX (Sales Tax) was added as Chapter 27 by a Law of 27 November 2001; Article 228 of Part II was amended on 29 November 2001; Articles 149 and 164 of Part II on 28 December

---

[8] Ведомости СНД и ВС РФ (1992), no 11, item 527; СЗ РФ (1997), no 30, item 3593.

[9] СЗ РФ (1998), no 31, item 3824; transl. in W E Butler, *Tax Code of the Russian Federation* (1999).

[10] СЗ РФ (2000), no 32, item 3340; (2001), no 1(I), item 18; no 23, item 2289; no 33(I), items 3413, 3421, and 3429; no 49, items 4554 and 4564; no 53(I), items 5015, 5016, and 5023. Both Parts One and Two of the Tax Code have been amended frequently. In August 2001 alone about 30 articles were changed in Part II to clarify or rectify provisions, and on 29 May 2002, 137 articles.

2001; Article 80 of Part I on 28 December 1991; Section VIII[1] (Special Tax Regimes), incorporating Chapter 26[1] on the single agricultural tax, was added on 29 December 2001; further amendments were introduced on 30 December 2001 in connection with the 2001 CAdV. More than two hundred changes were introduced on 29 May 2002; and more on 24 July and 25 July 2002.

This packet of legislative acts marked the true transition, as yet uncompleted, of the Russian Federation towards using taxation not merely to raise revenues, but also to regulate social policy generally, regional policies, and local self-government. Greater emphasis was placed on taxes in place of obligatory payments so characteristic of the Soviet system. Extensive use was made of foreign models, including indirect taxation, property tax, and tax incentives. The Russian State became reliant upon taxation for the principal portion of its revenues notwithstanding difficulties with collection. More than 80 per cent of State budget revenues come from payments made into the tax system, whereas in the Soviet era the greater share of State revenue came from non-tax payments by State enterprises to the budget.

Natural persons were subjected to taxation on an unprecedented scale: various forms of property tax, gift tax, inheritance tax, road tax, and others. The income tax, which had existed in the Soviet period, was massively expanded to reach the great majority of citizens. No longer were income taxes differentiated on the organisational-legal forms of taxpayer (worker, employee, collective farmer, individual entrepreneur), or the form of ownership of the source of his revenues or object of taxation, as had existed previously.

The taxes on enterprises were unified and no longer depended upon the form of ownership of the enterprise. Taxes payable to special funds were introduced (education, road, ecological) and certain taxes became payable by natural and juridical persons alike (land tax, means of transport, etc). Russian law began to experiment with tax credits and special-purpose tax privileges.

Although the Soviet Union had operated a multi-tiered system of taxation, this was vastly expanded in the 1990s to incorporate local taxes of great variety. A major element of future tax reform in Russia must be to harmonise the federal, regional, and local tax systems. A new body of legislation emerged regulating financial, legal, and other responsibility for tax violations and a system of tax agencies to enforce those rules.[11]

---

[11] On the development of the Russian tax system, see D G Chernik (ed), Налоги. Учебное пособие [*Taxes: Instructional Manual*] (3rd edn; 1997); V I Gureev, Российское налоговое право [*Russian Tax Law*] (1997); N I Khimicheva, Налоговое право [*Tax Law*] (1997); I I Kucherov, Налоговое право России [*Tax Law of Russia*] (2001); S G Pepeliaev (ed), Основы налогового права [*Fundamental Principles of Tax Law*] (1995); Pepeliaev, Законы о налогах: элементы структуры [*Laws on Taxes: Elements of Structure*] (1995); G V Petrova, Налоговое право [*Tax Law*] (2nd edn, 2001); O V Staroverova, Налоговое право [*Tax Law*] (2001).

On 23 May 2000 the President of the Russian Federation sent a special tax message to the State Duma outlining the principal orientations and stages of tax reform. The general aim is to reduce the tax burden by repealing inefficient taxes and revising the taxable base for computing enterprise profit, equalising the conditions of taxation by eliminating or reducing unjustified tax privileges and exemptions, and simplifying the tax system and reducing the number of taxes. During the first phase the income tax was lowered to a flat rate of 13 per cent for natural persons, and the taxes on securities operations, roads, and housing fund maintenance were repealed. In the second phase, from 2002–3, the profit tax on the profit of organisations was reduced to a maximum of 24 per cent, a more flexible regime introduced for deductible expenses, and from 1 March 2002 the tax on exchanging foreign currency was abolished. From 1 January 2002 enterprises are required to keep in parallel two entirely separate sets of accounts: bookkeeping and tax. During this phase it is intended to abolish the sales tax, deductions for regeneration of the mineral-raw material base, and to replace the property and land taxes with a tax on immoveables.

C. Duty to Pay Taxes

The duty of Russian citizens to pay taxes arises directly from the 1993 Russian Constitution (Article 57), which provides: 'Each shall be obliged to pay legally established taxes and charges. Laws establishing new taxes or worsening the position of taxpayers shall not have retroactive force'. Article 71(h) of the Constitution relegates the establishment of federal taxes to the jurisdiction of the Russian Federation. The 1998 Tax Code provides that the system of taxes and charges in Russia are established by the Code (Article 1(2)). Local taxes and taxes and charges by subjects of the Federation are established by laws and other normative legal acts of those entities adopted in accordance with the Tax Code. The last phrase has reference to the administrative-territorial and other subdivisions of the Russian Federation; they may introduce and repeal taxes in accordance with Russian legislation or grant greater tax privileges within the amounts of taxes to be credited to their budgets.

D. Concept of Tax

The Russian legal system experienced difficulties with the concept of a 'tax'. The 1991 Law on the Tax System obscured the distinction between tax and non-tax payments (obligatory contributions by a State enterprise of revenues to the budget of its owner, charges imposed for services rendered by the State) by wrapping them all up in a single definition: 'the aggregate of taxes, charges, duties, and other payments' are classed as taxes and more generally defined as the 'obligatory contribution to the budget of the respective level or to an extrabudgetary fund' (Article 2). The Tax Code distinguishes conceptually between the 'tax' and the 'charge'. The tax is an 'obligatory, individually uncompensated payment recovered from an organisation or natural persons in the form of an alienation of monetary means belonging to them by right of ownership, economic jurisdiction, or operative management for the purposes of the financial provision of the activity of the State and/or municipal formations' (Article 8(1)). The language of 'contribution' is omitted and the concept of 'contribution' eradicated by substitution of the terminology of 'alienation'. A 'charge' is defined as an 'obligatory contribution recovered from organisations and natural persons, the payment of which is one of the conditions for the performance in the interests of the payers of charges by State agencies, agencies of local self-government, and other empowered agencies and officials of legally significant actions, including the granting of determined rights or issuance of authorisations (or licences)' (Article 8(2)). The expression 'contribution' is linked here to the provision of legally significant actions by State agencies or officials.

E. Taxpayers

The payers of taxes and charges under the Tax Code are the same: 'Organisations and natural persons on whom in accordance with the present Code the duty has been placed to pay respectively taxes and/or charges' (Article 19). The Tax Code resolves the territorial question of to whom branches and other solitary subdivisions of organisations must pay taxes by stipulating that the branches and other solitary subdivisions of Russian organisations 'shall perform duties of these organisations with regard to the payment of taxes and charges at the location of these branches and other solitary subdivisions effectuate the functions of the organisation in the procedure provided for by the present Code' (Article 19).

While the issue of a 'natural person' is uncontroversial, the category of an 'organisation' is defined broadly as 'juridical persons formed in accordance with legislation of the Russian Federation (hereinafter: Russian organisations), and also foreign juridical persons, companies, and other corporative formations possessing civil legal capacity created in accordance with the legislation of foreign States, international organisations, their branches and representations created on the territory of the Russian Federation (hereinafter: foreign organisations)' (Article 11). The phrase of interest is 'companies, and other corporative formations'. In Anglo-American legal systems a 'company' need not be a juridical person, and 'other corporative formations' (*not* 'corporate') would encompass partnerships and unincorporated associations insofar as they possess 'civil legal capacity' (see Chapter 9). So far as Russian entities are concerned, the definition includes both commercial and non-commercial organisations.

These formulations do not rest on the concept of a 'permanent establishment', for the definition requires neither the quality of 'permanent' and leaves open whether 'representation' is confined to a formally accredited representation or may also reach those who act as the civil-law representatives of foreign juridical or natural persons and other formations. The reference to representations being 'created' on the territory of the Russian Federation suggests formal accreditation.

Taxpayers are required under the Tax Code to pay legally established taxes, register with agencies of the State Tax Service of the Russian Federation if the Tax Code so requires, keep records of their revenues and expenses and of objects of taxation, submit to the tax agency where they are registered the tax declarations with regard to those taxes which they are obliged to pay, submit the documents necessary in order to calculate and pay taxes, fulfil the legal requirements of a tax agency to eliminate violations of tax legislation and not obstruct tax agencies in the performance of their employment duties, provide necessary information and documents in accordance with the Tax Code, and keep accounting records and other documents necessary for the calculation and payment of taxes for a period of four years, and bear other duties provided for by legislation (Article 23). In addition to these general duties, taxpayer organisations are required to give notice to their local tax agency about opening or closing accounts, within ten days; of participation in Russian and foreign organisations, within one month; of all solitary subdivisions created on the territory of Russia, within one month from the date of creation, reorganisation, or liquidation of termination of activity, declaration of insolvency or bankruptcy, liquidation, or reorganisation, within three days of taking such decision; and of changing location, within ten days.

The duty to pay a tax or charge terminates from the moment the tax is paid, when circumstances arise which legislation on taxes and/or charges connects with the termination of the duty to pay the tax, or with the death of the taxpayer or his being deemed to be deceased in the procedure established by civil legislation of the Russian Federation (Article 44). In the case of a juridical person the duty to pay a tax terminates with the liquidation of the organisation after the liquidation commission has settled all accounts with the budget and extra-budgetary funds, or when the tax is paid. Inability to pay tax by a juridical person is grounds to deem the juridical person to be bankrupt, in which case the duty to pay tax arrears falls upon the liquidation commission of the juridical person. A violation of these duties will result in financial sanctions, administrative penalties, and possibly criminal responsibility.

Reversing the position in comparison with the 1991 Law on the Tax System, the Tax Code contains an extensive enumeration of the rights of a taxpayer. These include the right to receive from tax agencies at the place of tax registration free information concerning taxes and charges, legislation regulating these matters, and the rights and duties of taxpayers, tax agencies, and their officials; obtain written explanations concerning the application of tax legislation to them; take advantage of tax privileges and exemptions; be given a deferral, the right to pay by instalment, or a tax credit in accordance with legislation, to set off or receive a refund of taxes paid in excess; represent their own interests in tax agencies either in person or through a representative; be present during tax verifications and submit explanations regarding the calculation and payment of tax; receive copies of tax verifications, decisions of tax agencies, and demands for the payment of tax; require that tax agencies and officials comply with tax legislation; not comply with unlawful acts and demands of tax agencies and officials, require compliance with tax secrecy; and demand compensation for losses caused in full by the illegal decisions of tax agencies or by the illegal actions or failure to act of tax officials.

The Tax Code also requires that 'All ineradicable doubts, contradictions, and ambiguities of acts of legislation on taxes and charges shall be interpreted in favour of the taxpayer (or payer of charges)' (Article 3(7)).

F. Objects of Taxation

The Tax Code as a whole draws the Russian tax system closer to established concepts of Russian civil law and other branches of law. This is evident in the approach to the objects of taxation. Following the precedent of the 1991 Law on the Tax System, the Tax Code does not attempt to give an exhaustive enumeration of objects of taxation. Rather an abstract exemplary enumeration is offered: 'Property, profit, revenue, the value of realised goods (or work fulfilled, services rendered) or other object having value, quantitative or physical characteristics with the presence of which with the taxpayer legislation on taxes and charges connects the arising of a duty with regard to the payment of a tax' (Article 38(1)). It is a further requirement that each tax have an 'autonomous object' of taxation; these are to be determined in Part Two of the Code.

The Tax Code defines 'property' as an object of taxation as the 'types of objects of civil rights (except for property rights) relegated to property in accordance with the Civil Code of the Russian Federation' (Article 38(2)). 'Goods' for the purposes of taxation are 'any property realised or intended for realisation', although it is recognised the definition may vary for the purpose of customs duties, in which case reference is made to the Customs Code of the Russian Federation. 'Work' is activity whose results 'have material expression and may be realised in order to satisfy the requirements of an organisation and/or natural persons', whereas 'services' are an activity whose results 'do not have material expression and are realised and consumed in the process of the effectuation of this activity' (Article 38(4)–(5)).

For the first time the Tax Code contains a detailed characterisation of the 'realisation of goods, work, or services', the principles for determining their prices for the purposes of taxation, the principles for determining revenues and whether they emanate from within the Russian Federation or beyond its limits, and dividends and interest. Tax agencies are given the right to control the correctness of prices only in three instances: when transactions are concluded between mutually-dependent persons, and in the case of barter transactions; or when there are price variations of more than 30 per cent with regard to the prices of identical or homogeneous goods with a brief period.

The rates of taxation and the tax base with regard to federal taxes are determined by the Federal Assembly of the Russian Federation in the Tax Code or, pending the enactment of the relevant Part, by individual laws on separate taxes, unless the Tax Code provides that such base and rates may be established by the Government of the Russian Federation in the procedure and within the limits determined by the Tax Code. The tax base with regard to regional and local taxes is established also by the Tax Code, but the tax rates are determined by laws of subjects of the Federation or normative legal acts of agencies of local self-government within the limits established by the Tax Code. Rates of customs duties are determined in the procedure established by the Law of the Russian Federation on the Customs Tariff of 21 May 1993, 27 December 1995, 5 February 1997, 10 February 1999, 4 May 1999, 27 May 2000, 8 August 2001, 29 December 2001, 30 December 2001, and 29 May 2002.[12]

Tax privileges have been widely granted in Russian practice, partly to alleviate the phenomenal mass of taxes and high rates. The Tax Code recognises the need for such privileges but refers to them rather obliquely: 'When necessary, tax privileges and grounds for their use by the taxpayer also may be provided for in the act of legislation on taxes and charges when establishing a tax' (Article 17(2)). This formulation does not require that all tax privileges be provided in the act of legislation establishing the tax. Reference also is made to 'special tax regimes', defined as 'a special procedure for the calculation and payment of taxes and charges during a determined period of time applied in the instances and in the procedure established by the present Code and by federal laws adopted in accordance with it' (Article 18). Examples of a special tax regime given in the Tax Code are the simplified system of taxation for subjects of small entrepreneurship, the system of taxation in special economic zones, the system of taxation in closed administrative-territorial formations, and the system of taxation under concession contracts and production sharing agreements. The Tax Code prohibits in principle the granting of tax privileges of an 'individual character' (Article 56), but in exceptional instances does permit an individual privilege to be established. The taxpayer is accorded the right to decline to use or to suspend the use of tax

---

[12] Ведомости СНД и ВС РФ (1993), no 23, item 821; СЗ РФ (1996), no 1, item 411; (1997), no 6, item 709; (1999), no 7, item 879, no 18, item 2221; (2000), no 22, item 2263 (2001), no 33(I), item 3429; no 53(I), items 5026 and 5030; (2002), no 22, item 2026.

privileges for one or several tax periods unless provided otherwise by the Tax Code. In practice the Russian Federation has granted tax privileges in the form of a non-taxable minimum, exemption from certain elements of an object of taxation, reduction of tax rates, deductions from taxable salaries, special-purpose tax credits, and others.

The experience of foreign investors with tax privileges during the 1990s has been on the whole unfavourable. Joint enterprises created during the Soviet period under individual tax regimes found themselves wholly deprived of these privileges in the Russian Federation. Taxes which did not exist when joint enterprises were created (and therefore were not incorporated into business plans for long-term projects) were later imposed notwithstanding guarantees of a tax-privilege status (for example, VAT when it was introduced). The Russian Ministry of Finances throttled the attempts of the Russian Government to introduce free economic zones by declining to recognise the tax regimes therein. Episodic periods of tax reform swept away privileges previously granted (for example, the introduction of the new Customs Code). And concessions granted by individual Presidential edict or governmental decree have later proved to be abolished by laws of the Federal Assembly on taxation. The hierarchy of sources of Russian law and the disposition of the Russian parliament to enact tax legislation without taking full account of the pre-existing tax commitments have made tax privileges a hazardous and unpredictable terrain for the long-term foreign investor.

G. Responsibility of Taxpayers

During the 1990s, the approach of the Russian legal system to dealing with violations of tax legislation has changed dramatically from an emphasis almost exclusively on so-called administrative measures to a system based in practice principally upon judicial measures. The failure of a taxpayer to pay amounts of tax due in full within the established periods entitles the tax agencies to seek recovery of the arrears in a compulsory proceeding. If the tax is due from natural persons, only a judicial proceeding is possible; if due from a juridical person, the amounts may be recovered in an uncontested proceeding, which normally means directly by the State Tax Service or the Federal Tax Police Service sending a unilateral decision to the credit organisation or bank in which the taxpayer has an account which requires the bank to withdraw the amounts due from the accounts of the juridical person and to credit those amounts to the designated State budgets. If the taxpayer has sufficient funds to pay all obligations presented for payment, the calendar sequence in which such demands are presented will be followed. However, if there are insufficient funds, as there are in most instances, the priorities laid down in Article 855 of the Russian Civil Code are applicable. The interpretation of Article 855 has been contested by the State Duma and the executive agencies of government, resulting in amendments of the Civil Code and litigation in the Constitutional Court.[13]

As noted above, Article 57 of the 1993 Constitution and the Tax Code require taxpayers to pay only legally established tax payments, and a compulsory proceeding can relate only to such payments. Article 242 of the RSFSR Code of Civil Procedure requires courts when considering cases concerning tax arrears to verify whether the type of payment has been provided for by law. The period of limitations for claims to be presented to natural persons is three years, whereas for juridical persons the period is six years from the moment the arrears accrued. In the case of either taxpayer execution may be levied against the revenues of the taxpayer or against the property of such persons.

The Tax Code introduces a series of five means by which performance of the duty to pay taxes and charges may be secured: pledge of property, suretyship, forfeits, suspension of bank account operations, and imposition of arrest on property of the taxpayer. Pledge requires the conclusion of a contract of pledge between the tax agency and the pledgor, who may be the taxpayer himself, another obliged person, or a third person. If the obligation secured by the pledge is not performed, the pledged property is levied against in the procedure established by Russian civil legislation. Virtually any property may be accepted on pledge, provided that it is not already pledged under another contract. Suretyship and forfeit are analogous means of securing performance also known to the Civil Code of the Russian Federation. Suspension of bank accounts means that no withdrawals are made from the account concerned, although deposits will be accepted. The maximum period of suspension is three months. Arrest of property requires the sanction of a procurator and may be resorted to only when there are sufficient grounds to suppose that the taxpayer would take measures to flee or to conceal his property. All property of a taxpayer is subject to arrest except that which under Russian law cannot be levied against, but only property sufficient to cover the tax liability.

Cases against natural persons are heard in the courts of ordinary jurisdiction at the place of residence of the taxpayer or location of his property. Before bringing suit, the tax agency imposes arrest on the taxpayer's property, making an inventory of the property and prohibiting any disposition of that property. The inventory must be compiled in the presence of the taxpayer, a member of his family who has reached majority, or of eye-witnesses. The taxpayer is handed a formal warning that the case will be transferred to court unless the arrears are paid within ten days from the date of arrest of the property. While under arrest the property remains in the custody of the taxpayer in arrears.

---

[13] The relevant documents are translated in W E Butler, *Russian Civil Legisation* (1999).

The application of the tax agency to the court must contain, in addition to the name and address of the taxpayer, the law on the basis of which the arrears are being recovered, the amount of payment due, and the period for payment. Appended must be a copy of the payment notice, the act concerning the arrest and inventory of the property, and other documents. When considering the case the court will verify whether the law provided for the type of payment being demanded by the tax agency, whether the tax agencies have complied with the established procedure for obtaining the payment, whether any relevant privileges have been taken into account, and whether the inventory of property made corresponds to legislation. If the court determines that the amount of payment due has been calculated incorrectly, proceedings in the case are suspended and the materials are sent to the tax agency for verification. If the tax agency disagrees with the ruling of the court, proceedings in the case are recommenced provided that the application to recover the amounts are confirmed by the head of the tax agency superior to that which filed the case.

If the demand of the tax agency is deemed by the court to be well-founded, the court will render a decision to recover the arrears by leving execution first against revenues of the taxpayer and, if there are not such, against his property, including possible amounts owed by debtors to the taxpayer. If the court concludes that the demand of the tax agency is illegal, it will refuse to satisfy the demand of the tax agency.

On 30 November 1995 the RSFSR Code of Civil Procedure was amended to add Chapter 11[1] containing provisions for a simplified procedure to recover, inter alia, arrears of taxes from taxpayers who are natural persons. It is applicable only if there is no dispute between the taxpayer and the tax agency, in which event the case is heard by a judge sitting alone upon the application of the tax agency. The judge issues a 'judicial order' without holding a formal judicial examination, without summoning the taxpayer or representatives of the tax agency, and without hearing their explanations. The judicial order enjoys the status of a writ of execution and may be proceeded under upon the expiration of ten days after being issued. When a court accepts an application from the tax agency to issue a judicial order, the taxpayer in arrears must be notified within three days; he then has a period of up to 20 days in which to reply. If no reply is received, or if the taxpayer does not disagree with the demand submitted, the court will issue the judicial order. The judge may refuse to issue the order if the taxpayer disagrees with the application or if there is a dispute which cannot be decided without the submission of documents. The refusal to issue a judicial order does not deprive the tax agency of the right to bring suit in the usual procedure against the taxpayer, and the same holds true if the Russian court refuses to accept the application for a judicial order from the tax agency.

Once the judicial order is issued, the taxpayer has a further period of 20 days to apply to the issuing court to vacate the order if the taxpayer for justifiable reasons could not object in good time to the tax agency's demand. In this case the judge will vacate the order, and the tax agency must proceed in the usual way with a formal lawsuit.

Even in their simplified form, the judicial proceedings available to protect the personal rights and freedoms of the individual are a more democratic method of addressing the issues. While juridical persons pay the great majority of taxes to the State budget in Russia, in a market economy the justification for treating them in the same way that State enterprises used to be treated is unconvincing. Constitutional issues have arisen out of compulsory tax proceedings. Article 35 of the 1993 Russian Constitution provides that 'no one may be deprived of his property other than by decision of a court'. The founders of two limited responsibility partnerships challenged the right of the tax police to recover tax arrears and related penalties from juridical persons in an uncontested proceeding. The Constitutional Court upheld the relevant Russian legislation on 17 December 1996, observing that juridical persons had the right to appeal the decisions of tax police agencies to a court just as did natural persons.

The Tax Code introduces the concept of tax violations and responsibility for their commission. A tax violation is an unlawful act or failure to act committed with guilt by a taxpayer, tax agent, or their representatives for which the Tax Code establishes responsibility (Article 106). Both natural persons and organisations may be subject to such responsibility, natural persons from the age of 16 years. Certain safeguards are introduced by the Tax Code: no one may be brought to responsibility for the commission of a tax violation other than on the grounds and in the procedure provided for by the Tax Code. The Code introduces a new concept in Russian law: that of 'tax responsibility', which must be added to the categories of civil, administrative, labour, criminal, and disciplinary responsibility. The Code stipulates that no one may be brought to tax responsibility more than once for the same tax violation. Tax responsibility ensues only if the act committed does not constitute a crime under the Russian Criminal Code. If an organisation is brought to responsibility for committing a tax violation, this does not relieve the officials of the organisation from any administrative, criminal, or other responsibility provided for by laws of the Russian Federation, nor does bringing a taxpayer or a tax agent to responsibility for a tax violation relieve them from the duty to pay the amount of tax due.

The presumption of innocence applies to tax violations, and the formulation of the principle is identical to that of the criminal law. A taxpayer or tax agent is not obliged to prove his innocence of committing a tax violation. The burden of proof lies with the tax agencies, who must prove both the fact of the violation and the guilt of the taxpayer in committing such violation. Any ineradicable doubts of the guilt of the taxpayer must be resolved in his favour.

A person may not be brought to responsibility for committing a tax violation if any one of the following circumstances is present: the lack of the event of a tax violation; the absence of guilt of the person in committing the tax violation; the minority of the offender (less than 16 years of age); the expiry of the period of limitation for bringing a person to responsibility for committing a tax violation. Guilt is measured as in the Criminal Code: the tax violation must be an unlawful act committed intentionally or through negligence. The violation is committed intentionally if the person who committed it was aware of the unlawful character of his actions or failure to act and wished or consciously permitted the ensuing of the harmful consequences of such actions or failure to act. Negligence occurs when the person who has committed it was not aware of the unlawful character of the consequences which arose as a consequence of these actions or failure to act although he should and could have been so aware. The guilt of an organisation in committing a tax violation is determined by the guilt of its officials or representatives whose actions or failure to act conditioned the commission of the tax violation.

The Tax Code further sets out circumstances which preclude the guilt of a person who has committed a tax violation. These include the violation being committed as a consequence of a natural disaster or other extraordinary and insuperable circumstances or, in the case of a natural person, his being in a state where he could not account for his actions or direct them by reason of illness, or the taxpayer or tax agent complying with written instructions and explanations given by the tax agency or other empowered State agency or officials thereof within the limits of their competence. The Tax Code also recognises aggravating and mitigating circumstances in connection with the commission of a tax violation. Mitigating circumstances include: the violation being committed as a result of the confluence of grave personal or family circumstances; or being committed under threat or coercion or by virtue of material, employment, or other dependence, or other circumstances which the tax agency or court may deem to be mitigating. A person previously brought to responsibility for an analogous violation is considered to have acted under aggravating circumstances.

A three-year period of limitation applies to the commission of a tax violation, and is calculated from the day following the end of the respective tax period in which the violation was committed.

Persons or organisations who commit a tax violation are subject to a 'tax sanction'. The Tax Code provides for fines in this event, applied individually for each violation and not cumulated or integrated. Tax agencies have three months in which to bring suit in court in order to recover tax sanctions. The types of tax violations and the penalties applicable are set out in Chapter 16 of the Tax Code. Among the tax violations are: violation of the period to register with the tax agency; evasion of such registration; violation of the period for submitting information about the opening or closure of a bank account; violation of the period for submitting the tax declaration and other documents; flagrant violation of the rules for recording revenues and expenses of objects of taxation; violation of rules for drawing up the tax declaration; failure to pay or underpayment of a tax; failure of tax agent to fulfil duties to withhold or credit tax; illegal obstruction of access of tax agency official to territory or premise; failure to comply with the procedure for the possession, use, and/or disposition of property on which arrest has been imposed; the failure to submit information concerning the taxpayer to a tax agency; a refusal to submit documents or articles at the request of the tax agency; and the failure of a witness or an expert, interpreter, or specialist to perform their duties properly .

Many of these violations are treated as from 1 July 2002 under the Code of the Russian Federation on Administrative Violations (see especially Chapter 6). Tax agencies and federal tax police agencies are empowered under the 2001 CAdV to consider designated cases concerning administrative violations related to taxation (see Articles 23.5 and 23.6).

Criminal responsibility for tax violations is established in Chapter 22 of the 1996 Criminal Code of the Russian Federation. The relevant articles include not only those directly affecting taxation, but also those relating to crimes concerning entrepreneurship which involve duties to pay taxes. For example, the crime of pseudo-entrepreneurship—the creation of a commercial organisation without the intention to carry on entrepreneurial or banking activity—would also include the intent not to pay taxes. The penalties include up to four years' deprivation of freedom. The first criminal conviction for tax evasion against a Russian citizen occurred in Moscow in late 1997.

H. Defence of Rights and Interests of Taxpayers

Although taxpayers may defend their rights and interests in both an administrative (extra-judicial) and judicial proceeding, the practice of the 1990s has shifted strongly in favour of the courts. The point of departure is the 1999 Tax Code (Article 137) which allows taxpayers, both natural and juridical persons, to 'appeal' against the acts, actions, or failure to act of tax agencies and officials. There is an analogous provision in the Law on Federal Tax Police Agencies (Article 20) enabling the actions of tax police personnel to be appealed to superior tax police agencies, the Procuracy, or a court.

The Law on the State Tax Service (Article 14) allows enterprises, irrespective of form of ownership, to appeal the actions of officials of State tax inspectorates directly to those State tax inspectorates to which they are directly subordinate. Appeals must be considered and decisions adopted within one month from the date of receipt of the appeal. Those decisions may in turn be appealed within one month to the superior State tax inspectorates, and when the peak of the tax system is reached and still does not produce an acceptable decision, appeal lies to the

Supreme Arbitrazh Court of the Russian Federation. Although there is some disagreement in Russian doctrine, in fact and in practice the same opportunities for
administrative appeal are available to natural persons, who also have the right to
appeal to a court. In bringing an administrative appeal, natural persons may also
rely upon their constitutional right to have recourse to State agencies (Article 33,
1993 Russian Constitution).

Citizens may apply to the Russian courts on the basis of the Federal Law on
Appeal to a Court of Actions and Decisions Violating the Rights and Freedoms of
Citizens, of 27 April 1993, as amended 14 December 1995,[14] a general law whose
provisions also extend to issues of taxation. Suit may be brought at the court near
his place of residence or where the tax agency is situated. Both the actions or decision and the failure to act of a tax official or tax agency, including the tax police,
may be appealed. Appeals under this law must be within three months from the
date when the citizen knew about the violation of his right, or one month from the
date the individual receives written notice that the superior tax agency or official
has refused to satisfy his appeal, or upon the expiry of a month from filing the
appeal if no reply in writing has been received. If these periods lapse for justifiable
reasons, the court may reinstate them.

A citizen also may have recourse to the Procuracy with respect to tax police actions
as under the Law on Federal Tax Police Agencies of 24 June 1993, as amended
17 December 1995, 7 November 2000, 30 December 2001 and 28 June 2002,[15] the
Procuracy has specific responsibility for effectuating supervision over the legality of
tax police actions.

Juridical persons which wish to pursue judicial recourse against tax agencies or
officials would bring suit in an arbitrazh court on the basis of the Code of Arbitrazh
Procedure and the Tax Code. The tasks of arbitrazh courts include defending rights
and legal interests violated or being contested of enterprises, institutions, organisations, and citizens in the sphere of economic activity. Arbitrazh courts have jurisdiction over economic disputes which also touch the domain of taxation (Article
22, Code of Arbitrazh Procedure). Petitions to sue are subject to State duty, and the
defendant will be the tax agency or tax police agency concerned. Natural persons
registered to engage in entrepreneurial activity without the formation of a juridical
person may also have recourse to the arbitrazh courts for this purpose.

The Constitutional Court of the Russian Federation may defend the rights and
legal interests of all taxpayers and has issued a number of decisions concerning taxation and compulsory payments. Both juridical and natural persons have the right
to bring suit in the Constitutional Court; State duty is payable.

---

[14] Ведомости СНД и ВС РФ (1993), no 19, item 685; СЗ РФ (1995), no 51, item 4970.
[15] Ведомости СНД и ВС РФ (1993), no 29, item 1114; СЗ РФ (1995), no 51, item 4973;
(2000), no 46, item 4537; (2001), no 53(I), item 5030; (2002), no 1(I), item 2; no 26, item 2523.

I. Role of Tax Agencies, Tax Officials, and Banks

Three systems of agencies play a major role in Russia in administering the system of taxation.

Ministry for Taxes and Charges

The Ministry of the Russian Federation for Taxes and Charges, created by Edict of the President of the Russian Federation on 23 December 1998,[16] is the federal agency of executive power which effectuates State control over compliance with legislation on taxes and charges and the proper calculation and complete and timely payment of taxes and other obligatory payments.[17] The Ministry is the legal successor of the State Tax Service of Russia, whose legal status was determined by the Law of the RSFSR on the State Tax Service in the RSFSR of 21 March 1991, as amended,[18] the Statute on the State Tax Service of the Russian Federation,[19] and the 1991 Law on the Tax System. The Ministry heads the unified centralised system of tax agencies, amongst them the All-Russian State Tax Academy and the Scientific-Research Institute for the Development of the Tax System. Headed by a Minister, the Ministry has 13 deputy ministers and a collegium of 25 persons. The Ministry contains 15 departments and 12 administrations, together with other subdivisions. The territorial agencies of the Ministry include administrations for the 89 subjects of the Russian Federation, interregional inspectorates, together with inspectorates for districts, districts in cities, cities not divided into districts, and interdistrict inspectorates—mirroring the administrative-territorial subdivisions of the Russian Federation.[20]

Tax service personnel must be citizens of the Russian Federation. A system of ranks exists based on post occupied, years of experience, and skills. There is a service uniform.

The Ministry of the Russian Federation for Taxes and Charges is principally concerned with organising the functions carried out by the State tax agencies. These are laid down in the Tax Code itself (Article 31). It receives reports from and

---

[16] СЗ РФ (1998), no 52, item 6393.

[17] The duties of the Ministry were elaborated in a Decree of the Government of the Russian Federation of 27 February 1999, No 254. See СЗ РФ (1999), no 11, item 1299.

[18] Ведомости СНД и ВС РСФСР (1991), no 15, item 492; (1992), no 34, item 1966; no 33, item 1912; (1993), no 12, item 429; СЗ РФ (1996), no 25, item 2958; (1999), no 28, item 3483 and item 3493; (2001), no 44, item 4148.

[19] Confirmed by Edict of the President of the Russian Federation, 31 December 1991. BBC РСФСР (1992), no 11, item 527; САПП РФ (1994), no 15, item 1174; СЗ РФ (1994), no 34, item 3586; (1998), no 30, item 3757; (2001), no 30, item 3157.

[20] The internal structure of the Ministry for Taxes and Charges is determined by Order No ГБ–3–20/150 'On the System of Agencies of the Ministry of the Russian Federation on Taxes and Charges and Organisations Within its Jurisdiction', issued on 21 May 1999.

analyses the work of the tax agencies, verifies their activities, works out proposals to improve such work, and assists the Government in developing tax policies and drafting tax legislation together with the Ministry of Finances and other State agencies. Quarterly reports are submitted to the President and to the Government about the enforcement of tax legislation and the flow of tax payments to the State budget. Analogous functions are performed by the tax agencies at the middle levels of the system.

The lowest level tax agencies are concerned principally with the registration of taxpayers. Registration is a duty of every taxpayer, without which banks will not open accounts. Compliance with tax legislation is ensured by tax agency verifications on site at enterprises, institutions, and organisations as necessary, at least once every two years. In performing the verifications, tax agencies have the right to search any premises used to derive revenues. Banking and other documents may be verified and other information obtained from officials and citizens, provided that such does not constitute a commercial secret. If documents are discovered which testify to the concealment or under-reporting of revenue or profit or the concealment of other objects of taxation, the tax agency has the right to seize them on the basis of a reasoned decree in writing issued by a tax agency official. A protocol of the seizure must be drawn up relating to the results of the compulsory seizure and when necessary a special inventory of the documents to be seized. If enterprises or individuals refuse to submit accounting reports, balance sheets, accounts, declarations, and other documents, the State tax agency may issue a decision to suspend the operation of the bank accounts of such juridical or natural persons.

The sanctions which may be applied by tax agencies have been discussed above in the form of fines and forfeits. The formal basis for applying tax sanctions is the act of a tax agency drawn up on the basis of a verification. The decision to apply the sanction is taken by the head of the respective tax agency. Other sanctions include the tax agency initiating a petition to prohibit someone from continuing to engage in entrepreneurial activity in a court of general jurisdiction or an arbitrazh court, or to liquidate an enterprise, or to deem certain transactions to be invalid. If evidence is discovered that a tax crime has been committed or is under preparation, the tax agency sends the materials of the case to the federal tax police agencies.

The interregional tax inspectorates are still in the formative stage. They are intended to work in complex domains of tax administration. Three had been set up by Spring 2002: the Inter-Regional State Tax Inspectorate for Operational Control Over Problem Taxpayers, the Inter-Regional State Tax Inspectorate for Control Over the Taxation of Small Business and Services Sphere, and the Inter-Regional State Tax Inspectorate for Control Over Alcoholic and Tobacco Products. Each has its own Statute confirmed by the Ministry for Taxes and Charges. Within their competence each may vacate or suspend decisions of inferior tax agencies.

Tax posts are mentioned in the Tax Code (Article 31(15)). They actually exist on the basis of individual legislative acts, such as the Decree of the Government of the Russian Federation on the Creation of Permanently Operating Tax Posts in Organisations Producing Ethyl Spirit from All Types of Raw Material, of 9 August 1996.[21] Such posts operated round the clock in order to monitor actual production volumes, shipments, the identity of customers, and so on.

Federal Tax Police Agencies

The tax police were introduced in the Russian Federation by the Law on Federal Tax Police Agencies, adopted 20 May 1993.[22] The police were the successors of tax investigation subdivisions formed in 1992 and attached to the State tax inspectorates. These subdivisions were originally intended to prevent violations of tax legislation and ensure the security of tax inspectorate officials; their powers were very limited, consisting principally of collecting primary materials relating to tax violations and passing them to internal affairs agencies for action. In July 1992 their powers were enlarged to encompass operational-search activities and inquiries in cases of tax crimes.

The tax police formed in 1993 retained the powers introduced in July 1992, and these on 17 December 1995 were enlarged again to enable tax police agencies to conduct the preliminary investigations with regard to cases concerning tax crimes.[23] The tax police therefore became law enforcement agencies in the full sense of the word. Their tasks include: eliciting, preventing, and suppressing tax crimes and violations; ensuring the safe activity of State tax inspectorates and protecting their personnel against unlawful infringements when they perform their official duties; and preventing, eliciting, and suppressing corruption in tax agencies. Legislation requires that they carry out their activities on the basis of the principles of legality, respect for the rights and freedoms of man and citizen, and remain under the control of and accountable to the highest agencies of legislative and executive power of the Russian Federation. As in the case of other law enforcement agencies, the tax police may not contain political parties nor engage in political activities. Contacts are maintained between the Russian tax police and equivalent tax services of foreign countries.

The tax police system is headed by the Federal Tax Police Service of the Russian Federation, which has agencies at the level of all subjects of the Russian Federation and a third local level.[24] The Tax Police Service operates with the rights of a State

---

[21] СЗ РФ (1996), no 41, item 5715.

[22] Ведомости СНД и ВС РФ (1993), no 29, item 1114.

[23] СЗ РФ (1995), no 51, item 4973; (2001), no 53, item 5030; (2002), no 30, item 3033. Also see V N Grigor'ev and I I Kucherov, Налоговая полиция: правовое регулирование деятельности [*Tax Police: Legal Regulation of Activity*] (1998).

[24] The Statute on the Federal Tax Police Service of the Russian Federation was confirmed by Edict of the President of the Russian Federation, No 1272, on 25 September 1999. See СЗ РФ (1999), no 39, item 4590.

Committee and is headed by a Director who has the status of the chairman of a State Committee and is appointed to and relieved from office by the President of the Russian Federation upon the recommendation of the Chairman of the Government of the Russian Federation. Members of the tax police are routinely armed.

Citizens of the Russian Federation aged 20 or above, in good health, and possessing the necessary personal qualities may become tax policemen.

The tax police conduct their own verifications of compliance with tax legislation, sometimes jointly with the tax inspectorates. Their verifications may be directed towards the taxpayer or take the form of confirming what the tax inspectorates have done. If documents are not presented, the tax police may suspend the bank account operations of taxpayers. When violations of tax legislation are discovered, the tax police may require proof of identity, impose administrative detention, impose administrative arrest on the property of juridical or natural persons, and apply other measures provided for by legislation on administrative violations. Under the Law on Operational-Search Activity adopted 12 August 1995, as amended,[25] the tax police may question individuals, remove samples of documents, perform control purchases, keep persons and premises under observation, and perform other investigative activities permitted by legislation. Since December 1995 fully-fledged investigative subdivisions have been formed within the tax police agencies to investigate tax crimes under the 1996 Criminal Code of the Russian Federation.

Banks and credit institutions

The third line of tax control is the banks and credit institutions in Russia in their capacity as the organisations which open and administer bank accounts for natural and juridical persons in accordance with the rules established by the Central Bank of the Russian Federation. The 1991 Law on the Tax System was the first legislative act in Russian history to regulate the responsibilities of banks in the domain of taxation. They are required to submit to tax agencies data concerning the financial and economic operations of taxpayers for the preceding financial year in accordance with the procedure laid down by the Russian Ministry of Finances. If the bank fails to do so, the executives of the bank are subject to an administrative fine in the amount of from three up to five minimum amounts of payment for labour for each week of delay (see Article 15.6.1, 2001 CAdV).

The second function of the bank is to deposit tax payments to the account of the treasury in a timely manner. Accordingly, banks are prohibited from delaying payment orders issued by taxpayers in favour of the budget or non-budgetary funds or to use deposits for this purpose as credit resources. Any revenues received by a

---

[25] СЗ РФ (1995), no 25, item 1129; (1997), no 29, item 3502; (1998), no 30, item 3613; (1999), no 2, item 233; (2000), no 1(I), item 8; (2001), no 13, item 1140.

bank as a result of such violations is recovered to the State budget and an administrative fine imposed on the bank executives. In addition a bank pays a forfeit of 0.2 per cent per day of delay in remitting amounts due to the budget which occur through the fault of the bank; the forfeit does not relieve the bank from other forms of responsibility for a violation. The Central Bank of Russia may apply its own sanctions to banks which fail to comply with legislation.

J. Basic Types of Taxes

Russian legislation distinguishes among three types of taxes: federal taxes, taxes of subjects of the Federation, and local taxes. Federal taxes are paid to the federal budget and recovered from throughout the entire territory of the Russian Federation, some of the revenues then being redistributed to the budgets of subjects of the Federation and local budgets. Federal taxes are: VAT, excises on individual goods or groups of goods, tax on profit of organisations, tax on revenues from capital, tax on revenues of natural persons, uniform social tax, State duty, customs duty and customs charges, tax on use of the subsoil, tax on regeneration of the mineral-raw material base, tax on additional revenue from the extraction of hydrocarbons, charge for the right to use objects of fauna and aquatic biological resources, forest tax, water tax, ecological tax, and federal licence charges. Regional taxes and charges include: tax on the property of organisations, tax on immoveables, road tax, transport tax, sales tax, tax on the gambling business, and regional licence charges. If a region introduces the tax on immoveables, the tax on the property of organisations and natural persons and the land tax are to be abolished. Local taxes and charges are: land tax, tax on the property of natural persons, tax on advertising, tax on inheritance or gift, and local licence charges.

Tax reforms during the 1990s have been marked by a gradual transition from direct to indirect taxes.

K. International Treaties

With the demise of the Soviet Union as an independent state, the RSFSR, later renamed the Russian Federation, considered itself to be the 'legal continuer' or the 'state continuer' of Russia, which had existed for more than ten centuries. A diplomatic Note to this effect was circulated to the Heads of Diplomatic Representations in Moscow on 13 January 1992, although the terms 'legal continuer' or 'state continuer' were not actually used.[26] The Russian Federation accordingly assumed

---

[26] See W E Butler, *The Law of Treaties in Russia and Other Member Countries of the Commonwealth of Independent States* (2002) 11.

obligations under all tax treaties in force with the former Soviet Union and is in the process of agreeing with individual countries one by one the extent to which treaties concluded with the USSR may remain in force and renegotiating such treaties when the parties wish to do so.

Most of the new tax treaties reflect the models developed by the Organisation for Economic Cooperation and Development (OECD) and the United Nations Model Convention for developing countries. The 1991 Law on the Tax System requires that the Government of the Russian Federation coordinate tax policy with other states who are members of the CIS and conclude international tax treaties to eliminate double taxation with other states. Such treaties are therefore intergovernmental in nature but always subject to ratification by the Federal Assembly of the Russian Federation because the 1991 Law on the Tax System so stipulated (Article 23). The 1998 Tax Code does not so require.

In accordance with Article 15 of the 1993 Russian Constitution and Article 5 of the Federal Law on International Treaties of the Russian Federation, international tax treaties are an integral part of the Russian legal system and take precedence in the event that norms of Russian law are inconsistent with the treaties.

The tax treaties generally define what is meant by a 'permanent establishment', offer certain allowances to residents of contracting parties which engage in construction work or assembly, and exclude foreign natural persons who are present in the Russian Federation for less than 183 days and receive remuneration from a source which is not a resident of the Russian Federation. The elimination of double taxation usually takes the form of a credit for taxes paid to other states.

15

NATURAL RESOURCES AND THE ENVIRONMENT

Russian law, following the Soviet legal tradition, does not recognise natural resource law as a distinct branch of law or legal science. Land, water, forestry, the subsoil, the atmosphere, flora, and fauna are the subject of individual federal laws, and so-called 'ecological law' has achieved recognition as a branch of legal science and a distinct subject of legal and general education. With the transition to a market economy, environmental legislation has received less attention than during the past two decades. Nonetheless, private interests must contend with environmental standards, whether surviving from the Soviet era or newly-introduced. Privatisation transactions typically contain an environmental component, a major concern being whether the private owner succeeds to environmental liabilities incurred, and perhaps undiscovered, from the past. Foreign participation in oil and gas exploitation in remote and ecologically-sensitive areas of the Russian Federation has given rise to environmental litigation in Russian courts. The dismantling of the Russian nuclear missiles and naval vessels has raised novel and difficult ecological issues. The legal techniques and institutions created by the Russian legal system continue to be of interest as a model whose effectiveness and failures are instructive to others.

A. Historical Background

Soon after coming to power, the RSFSR nationalised or socialised all land, subsoil, forests, water, and other natural resources in decrees modelled upon the RSFSR Basic Law on the Socialisation of Land.[1] There followed an assortment of individual normative legal acts regulating certain aspects of resource exploitation: fisheries, hunting, minerals, forests, waters, and land. Most of the legislation was of an ad hoc character; in light of the seemingly unlimited abundance of resources, an integrated approach to their exploitation seemed superfluous. During the NEP era, considerable efforts were devoted to codification. Land, forestry, and water codes were enacted in the RSFSR. Some attention was given at the all-union level to statutes or sets of basic principles for particular resources, notably land and the subsoil. All of these enactments were overtaken by the collectivisation of agriculture and the accelerated, planned industrialisation of the Soviet Union, and although they remained formally on the statute books, they were in practice superseded by subsequent legislation.

Between 1957–63 each union republic, including the RSFSR, enacted nature conservation laws that laid down a rudimentary framework of conservation policies and principles, most of which required further implementing legislation. During the 1960–70s, the Soviet Union enacted Fundamental Principles of Land (1968), Water (1970), Subsoil (1975), and Forestry (1977) Legislation, followed in each case by the adoption of individual codes by the RSFSR and other union republics. In June 1980 the USSR enacted a Law on the Protection of the Atmosphere and a Law on the Protection and Use of Fauna. These basic acts were augmented by myriad edicts, decrees, statutes, and other subordinate legislation regulating narrower issues in greater detail.

The conceptual foundation for much of post-Soviet environmental legislation in Russia was the joint Decree of the Central Committee of the Communist Party of the Soviet Union and the USSR Council of Ministers 'On the Fundamental Restructuring of Nature Protection in the Country', adopted 7 January 1988.[2] The Decree informed what for a decade became the single most substantial piece of legislation in Russian history on the environment, the Law of the RSFSR on Protection of the Natural Environment, adopted 19 December 1991.[3] Besides that law, the disappearance of the former Soviet Union left the Russian Federation with its own codes on land, water, forests, and the subsoil. Together with USSR subordinate normative acts and relevant subsequent Russian legislation, these formed

---

[1] For a definitive text of a controversial and complex document, see Декреты советской власти [Decrets of Soviet Power] (1975), I, 406–420.

[2] СП СССР (1988), no 6, item 14.

[3] Ведомости СНД РФ (1992), no 10, item 457.

the background for Russian Federation codes and other environmental legislation. The 1991 Law was replaced by the Federal Law on the Protection of the Environment of 10 January 2002, with effect from the day of official publication.[4]

B. Russian 'Ecological Law'

The discipline of ecological law is now firmly established as an instructional discipline. Its concern is global, and not merely Russian, for the simple reason that the environment is a global and closely interrelated phenomenon: 'everything is connected with everything', as one Russian jurist observed. The use of ecology is the use by man of the natural environment in order to satisfy economic, ecological, and cultural-recreational requirements.[5] The failure to take a global view of the environment and its legal regulation leads to many ecological factors and objects of nature outside the domain of ecological regulation and consequently an under-appreciation of their value, even though there may not be a 'resource' value. The aim of ecological law is to encourage the development of rules which are not contrary to the laws of nature itself, do not contribute to the depletion of nature or to a disturbance of the ecosystem, but rather facilitate the restoration and development of that system.

While Russian legislation continues to be 'resource-oriented', and the branches of legislation are 'resource-based', environmental factors are incorporated in resource legislation. The transition to a market economy, moreover, has raised another serious issue for 'resource-based' legislation: why should it continue to exist autonomously rather than be incorporated into the civil law. The continued desirability of a Land Code has been doubted in this connection, but the enactment on 25 October 2001 of the Land Code expressly foreseen in the Civil Code put an end to the debate over that issue.

C. Environmental and Natural Resource Regulation

The 1993 Constitution of the Russian Federation guarantees (Article 42) to each a 'favourable environment', reliable information concerning the state of the environment, and compensation for damage caused to his health or property by an ecological violation. Each has the duty to 'preserve nature and the environment' and to care for that which is relegated to the category of natural wealth (Article 58).

---

[4] СЗ РФ (2002), no 2, item 133.
[5] See B V Erofeev, Экологическое право России [*Ecological Law of Russia*] (2nd edn, 1996); V D Ermakov and A Ia Sukharev (eds), Экологическое право России [*Ecological Law of Russia*] (1997); V V Petrov, Экологическое право России [*Ecological Law of Russia*] (1995).

Jurisdiction over environmental matters is divided between the Russian Federation and subjects of the Federation. The Russian Federation has exclusive jurisdiction over the establishment of the fundamental principles of federal policy and federal programmes in the domain of ecological development of the Russian Federation, the federal electric power system, nuclear power, fissionable materials, the production of poisonous substances, and other matters which have environmental dimensions. Joint jurisdiction is shared between the Russian Federation and subjects of the Federation over questions of the possession, use, and disposition of land, subsoil, water, and other natural resources, nature use, protection of the environment and ensuring ecological security, specially-protected nature territories, protection of monuments of history and culture, coordination of questions of public health, effectuation of measures relating to the struggle against catastrophes, natural disasters, epidemics, and elimination of their consequences, land, water and forest legislation, legislation on the subsoil, and legislation on environmental protection, and defence of the natural habitat and traditional way of life of small ethnic communities (Article 72).

The 1993 Constitution broadened considerably the scope for ecological legislation in comparison with the 1991 Law on Protection of the Natural Environment. The principal laws of an ecological character include, in addition to those mentioned above, the Land Code of the Russian Federation, of 25 October 2001,[6] the Law of the Russian Federation on Security of 5 March 1992, as amended 24 December 1993 and 25 July 2002,[7] the Federal Law on Sanitary-Epidemiological Well-Being of the Population of 30 March 1999, as amended 30 December 2001,[8] the Fundamental Principles of Legislation of the Russian Federation on Protection of the Health of Citizens, of 22 July 1993, as amended 2 March 1998, 20 December 1999, and 2 December 2000,[9] the Law of the Russian Federation on the Subsoil of 21 February 1992, as amended 3 March 1995, 10 February 1999, 2 January 2000, 14 May 2001, and 8 August 2001,[10] the Federal Law on Natural Resources, Therapeutic-Recreational Localities, and Resorts of 23 February 1995,[11] the Federal Law on Specially Protected Nature Territories, of 14 March

[6] СЗ РФ (2001), no 44, item 4147. See S A Bogoliubov (ed), Комментарий к Земельному кодексу Российской Федерации [*Commentary on the Land Code of the Russian Federation*] (2002); S A Bogoliubov and E L Minina (eds), Комментарий к Земельному кодексу Российской Федерации *(*постатейный*)* [*Commentary on the Land Code of the Russian Federation (Article-by-Article)*] (2002). This Code replaced that of 25 April 1991, published in Ведомости СНД и ВС РСФСР (1991), no 22, item 768; (1993), no 21, item 748; САПП РФ (1993), no 51, item 4935; (1994), no 52, item 5085.

[7] Ведомости СНД РФ (1992), no 15, item 769; (1993), no 52, item 5086; СЗ РФ (2002), no 30, item 3033.

[8] СЗ РФ (1999), no 14, item 1650; (2002), no 1(I), item 2.

[9] Ведомости СНД РФ (1993), no 33, item 1318; СЗ РФ (1998), no 10, item 1143; (1999), no 51, item 6289; (2000), no 49, item 4740.

[10] САПП РФ (1992), no 16, item 834; СЗ РФ (1995), no 10, item 823: (1999), no 7, item 879; (2000), no 2, item 141; (2001), no 21, item 2061, no 33(I), item 3429.

[11] СЗ РФ (1995), no 9, item 713.

1995, as amended 30 December 2001,[12] the Federal Law on the Continental Shelf of 25 October 1995, as amended,[13] the Water Code of the Russian Federation of 16 November 1995, as amended 30 December 2001,[14] the Forest Code of the Russian Federation of 29 January 1997, as amended 30 December 2001 and 25 July 2002,[15] the Federal Law on the Exclusive Economic Zone, and others. Certain Presidential edicts are central to ecological concerns. Amongst the most salient are the Edict on Federal Natural Resources, of 16 December 1993[16] and the Edict on the State Strategy of the Russian Federation for Environmental Protection and Ensuring Stable Development, of 4 February 1994.[17]

The Russian Federation is also party to a substantial and growing number of international treaties on the environment.[18]

D. Ownership of Natural Resources

The 1993 Russian Constitution establishes unequivocally the right of private ownership to natural resources: private, State, municipal, and other forms of ownership are equally recognised and defended in the Russian Federation (Article 8), land and other natural resources may be in private, State, municipal, and other forms of ownership (Article 9), citizens and associations thereof have the right to have land in private ownership (Article 36(1)). The possession, use, and disposition of land and other natural resources is to be effectuated by their owners freely unless this brings damage to the environment and unless this violates the rights and legal interests of other persons (Article 36(2)).

Notwithstanding the constitutional provisions, however, no issue has been politically and ideologically more intractable than that of ownership of natural resources in practice, especially land. The issue goes far beyond the simple juxtaposition of State versus private ownership. The ownership of natural resources exists at the federal, subjects of the Federation, and municipal levels. The Presidential Edict of 16 December 1993, cited above, on Federal Natural Resources delimited federal State ownership to these resources by proceeding from the principles of their general-State significance and the previously determined ownership of subjects of the Federation.

---

[12] СЗ РФ (1995), no 12, item 1024; (2002), no 1(I), item 2.
[13] СЗ РФ (1995), no 49, item 4694; (1999), no 7, item 879; (2001), no 33(I), items 3413 and 3429; (2002), no 1(I), item 4.
[14] СЗ РФ (1995), no 47, item 4471; (2001), no 53(I), item 5030.
[15] СЗ РФ (1997), no 5, item 610; (2001), no 53(I), item 5030; (2002), no 30, item 3033.
[16] САПП РФ (1993), no 51, item 4932.
[17] САПП РФ (1994), no 6, item 436.
[18] These are traced in E A Vystorobets, Атлас международного природоохранного сотрудничества [*Atlas of International Environmental Cooperation*] (2001).

The Edict provided that federal natural resources could include: land plots and other natural objects granted to ensure the defence and security requirements of Russia, protection of the State boundaries, and the performance of other functions relegated to the jurisdiction of federal agencies of State power; land plots occupied by federal electric power, transport, and outer space systems, objects of nuclear power, communications, meteorological service, historico-cultural and nature legacy, and other objects in federal ownership; land plots, waters, and other nature objects of federal State nature reserves, national nature parks, State nature preserves, resort and therapeutic-recreational zones, and other specially-protected nature territories of federal significance; species of flora and fauna entered in the Red Book of the Russian Federation, species of fauna economically valuable and specially-protected which migrate through the territories of two or more subjects of the Federation and those regulated by international treaties of the Russian Federation; mineral deposits or fields having general-State significance, water objects situated on the territory of two or more subjects of the federal, and also border and transborder water objects, and other natural resources as agreed between federal agencies of State power and those of subjects of the Federation.

Land legislation is within the joint jurisdiction of the Russian Federation and subjects of the Federation. Private ownership of land and other natural resources proceeded episodically and slowly in the absence of a modern Land Code. Although the principle of private ownership is firmly embedded in Russian legislation, the State at all levels of the Russian Federation has been slow to dispose of land plots. Some have passed as part of the privatisation of plants and factories; others as part of the disposal of small dacha, garden, and similar holdings; under the 2001 Land Code, the State may be expected to accelerate the disposition of land. Some subjects of the Federation have encouraged private ownership of land, whereas others resisted and even opposed it. Where land is in private ownership, the owner has the right to sell, bequeath, give, lease out, pledge, or exchange the land plot, or to transfer the land plot or part thereof as a contribution to the charter capital of economic societies or partnerships or to cooperative societies, including those with foreign investments.

Although the 2001 Land Code does not expressly so state, the overriding importance of land in comparison with other natural resources makes the Land Code primary amongst equals in comparison with other natural resource codes or legislation. This is illustrated in Article 7 of the Land Code, which provides that lands are subdivided into categories according to their special purpose designation. The seven categories are: (1) lands of agricultural designation; (2) lands of settlements; (3) lands of industry, electric power, transport, communications, radiobroadcasting, television, information, space activity, defence, security, and other special designation; (4) lands of specially protected territories and objects; (5) lands of the forestry fund; (6) lands of the water fund; (7) reserve lands. In effect the Forestry

Code and the Water Code regulate special types of land, and the Subsoil Code the land area beneath the surface layer.

Ownership to land is recognised, first, in the Land Code for citizens and juridical persons who have acquired such on the grounds provided for by legislation of the Russian Federation. State ownership in land is defined as that residual part of the land territory which is not in private ownership or in the ownership of municipal formations, or in the ownership of subjects of the Russian Federation. Land also may be held in permanent use, inheritable possession for life, or lease, and land servitudes are recognised.

With respect to water, forests, and the subsoil, the legislator has considered in unprecedently greater detail the physical characteristics of these objects of ownership and their implications for concepts of ownership. The 1995 Water Code of the Russian Federation defers to the Civil Code of the Russian Federation for the content of the right of ownership to water objects but adds (Article 31) that the concept of possession is not applicable in full to water objects because the waters concentrated in a particular object are in a state of perpetual motion and exchange. Therefore, Russian law speaks of ownership of a water object as a whole (Article 32) and permits non-State ownership, that is, municipal or private ownership, only of solitary water objects (Article 34). All water objects, including solitary or enclosed water objects, which are not in municipal ownership or in the private ownership of natural or juridical persons, are in State ownership (Article 35). The change of course of a river or other change in the location of a water object does not entail a change in the form or type of ownership to the water object unless it follows otherwise from the Water Code. The Code contains a lengthy enumeration of water objects in federal ownership, leaving to the ownership of subjects of the Federation those water objects, aquatories, and basins which are situated entirely within the limits of the particular subject of the Federation and not relegated to federal ownership. Natural and juridical persons are limited in the nature and size of water objects which they may own, the maximum dimensions being determined by land legislation of the Russian Federation.

For those who are not owners of water objects there are three other possibilities: the right of long-term use, the right of short-term use, and the right of limited use (water servitude). These are not rights to a thing, but nonetheless may be defended in the procedure provided for by the Russian Civil Code for the defence of rights of ownership.[19] Long-term use is from three to 25 years; short-term use for up to three years. Water objects may be leased in accordance with civil legislation.

---

[19] See S A Bogoliubov (ed), Комментарий к Водному кодексу Российской Федерации [*Commentary to the Water Code of the Russian Federation*] (1997) 70.

Ownership of the forestry fund is regulated by the 1997 Forest Code of the Russian Federation and by civil and land legislation. The burdens of ownership are specifically set out in the Forest Code, whereas they are not mentioned in the Water Code. The owner bears the costs for the protection, defence, regeneration, and organisation of the rational use of 'objects of forest relations' belonging to it and has the right to receive revenues from the use of the forest fund and forests which are not within the forest fund. The possession, use, and disposition of a forest fund and of forests not within the fund must be effectuated by having regard to the 'ecological significance of forests, their regeneration, duration of growth, and other natural properties of the forest' (Article 18). Although the Forest Code speaks of State ownership of the forest fund and allows private ownership by natural and juridical persons of trees and bushes on land plots in their ownership, a proper delimitation of ownership of the forest fund between the Russian Federation and subjects of the Federation has yet to occur. This has contributed to disputes between subjects of the Federation. On 9 November 1993 the Supreme Arbitrazh Court of the Russian Federation awarded a large sum to the Krasnoiarsk Territory Forest Administration for damage caused by the Norilsk Mining-Metallurgical Kombinat to forests on the territory of the Taimyr (Dolgano-Nenets) Autonomous National Area. Since the forests were situated in the Taimyr Autonomous National Area within the Krasnoiarsk Territory, many believed the Autonomous National Area should have received the compensation, and not the Krasnoiarsk Territory. Although the case pre-dated the Forest Code, the commentators believe that the Forest Code could not have resolved the issue any more than did prevailing legislation at the time.[20] Russian citizens enjoy a public forest servitude enabling them to sojourn in forests; private owners of forests may be subject to a private forest servitude established by contract, acts of State agencies, acts of local self-government, and judicial decisions. The analogy is to water servitudes, set out above, and not to the classical Roman law concept of a servitude.[21]

The rights to use forest fund plots and forest plots not within the forest fund, or lands not covered by forests but within the forest fund, may be limited or suspended to the extent necessary in order to ensure the rational use, protection, defence, and regeneration of forests.

The 1992 Law of the Russian Federation on the Subsoil, as amended, provides that the subsoil within the boundaries of the territory of the Russian Federation, including underground space and minerals contained in the subsoil, is in State

[20] See O I Krassov, in S A Bogoliubov (ed), Комментарий к Лесному кодексу Российской Федерации [*Commentary on the Forest Code of the Russian Federation*] (1997) 60.

[21] O I Krassov, in Bogoliubov (n 18 above) 62.

ownership.[22] Unlike waters or forests, subsoil plots may not be the subject of purchase, sale, gift, inheritance, contribution, pledge, or alienation in any form. Although subsoil plots are immobile, the possession, use, and disposition of the subsoil is relegated to the joint jurisdiction of the Russian Federation and subjects of the Federation. The rights of use may be alienated or otherwise transferred to the extent such turnover is permitted by federal laws. Minerals and other resources extracted from the subsoil on conditions of licence or production sharing may be in private or municipal ownership, or in the ownership of the State or subjects of the Federation (Article 1[2], Law on the Subsoil).

The RSFSR Law on the Protection of the Atmosphere of 14 July 1982, as amended 18 January 1985,[23] was repealed on 4 May 1999 by the Federal Law on the Protection of the Atmosphere.[24] Although the airspace superjacent to the land territory of the Russian Federation is part of Russian territory, the use of the atmosphere, as distinct from airspace, is not regulated in the way that other natural resources are. However by Decree of 9 January 1991 the RSFSR Council of Ministers introduced payment for environmental pollution until the decree expired in 1993, and the 2002 Law on Protection of the Environment has continued the practice; the Procedure for Determining the Payment and the Maximum Amounts Thereof for Pollution of the Natural Environment, Siting of Wastes, and Other Types of Harmful Influence was confirmed by Decree of the Government of the Russian Federation on 28 August 1992, as amended.[25] Enterprises and organisations are required to receive an authorisation from competent agencies to discharge pollutants into the atmosphere, indicating when applying for the authorisation the nature, sources, and amounts of pollution being generated.

Fauna are defined in the Federal Law on Fauna of 24 April 1995[26] as the aggregate of living organisms, all types of wild fauna permanently or temporarily on the territory of Russia or the natural resources of the continental shelf and exclusive economic zone of the Russian Federation. All are in State ownership, and their possession, use, and disposition is a matter of joint jurisdiction between the Russian Federation and subjects of the Federation. Use is granted in the form of licences, and if use is authorised in the form of capture rather than killing, the

---

[22] The State for these purposes is the Russian Federation and that region on whose territory the subsoil plot is situated. Municipal and private ownership of the subsoil are precluded by this provision. See S A Bogoliubov (ed), Комментарий к Закону Российской Федерации 'О недрах' [*Commentary on the Law of the Russian Federation on the Subsoil*] (2001) 25.
[23] Ведомости РСФСР (1982), no 29, item 1027; (1985), no 4, item 117.
[24] СЗ РФ (1999), no 18, item 2222.
[25] САПП РФ (1992), no 10, item 726; СЗ РФ (1995), no 3, item 190; (2001), no 22, item 2236; no 26, item 2678.
[26] СЗ РФ (1995), no 17, item 1462.

fauna concerned become an object of private, municipal, or State ownership in accordance with civil legislation.[27]

E. Institutional Enforcement of Environmental and Natural Resource Legislation

A variety of institutions are involved in the enforcement of Russian legislation concerning the environment and natural resources. A distinction is made in doctrinal writings between general interdepartmental and departmental competence. Agencies of general competence would include, for example, the Government of the Russian Federation, which adopts decrees of general applicability on environmental matters but does not specialise only in environmental questions. Other agencies of general competence are the Ministry of Public Health, the Federal Service of Russia for Hydrometeorology and Monitoring of the Environment, the Committee for Standardisation, Metrology, and Certification of the Russian Federation, and the Ministry of Internal Affairs (motor vehicle pollutants).

Use of ecology and environmental protection generally are the responsibility of the Ministry of Natural Resources of the Russian Federation and the State Committee for Protection of the Environment. The use and protection of individual natural resources are the concern of the Committee for Fisheries, the State Forestry Service, the Ministry of Agriculture, and numerous others. These are routinely reorganised, merged, abolished, created, or renamed. Most maintain inspectorates to supervise compliance with pollution-control standards, use requirements, conservation measures, public health and sanitation rules, and the like. Their basic empowerment is to monitor the resource, notify serious instances of violation, suspend in some cases the operations of offending enterprises or users, apply administrative sanctions, and bring criminal violations to the attention of the relevant law enforcement agencies.

F. Sanctions for Violations of Environmental and Natural Resource Legislation

The 1996 Russian Criminal Code contains an entire chapter on ecological crimes (Chapter 26): violation of rules for environmental protection when performing work (Article 246); violation of rules for handling ecologically dangerous sub-

---

[27] See, eg, Decree No 156 of the Government of the Russian Federation of 19 February 1996 on the Procedure for Issuing Authorisations (or Regulations for Licences) for Turnover of Wild Fauna Belonging to Species Entered in the Red Book of the Russian Federation. СЗ РФ (1996), no 9, item 807.

stances and wastes (Article 247); violation of safety rules when handling micro-biological or other biological agents or toxins (Article 248); violation of veterinary rules and rules established for the struggle against diseases and pests of flora (Article 249); pollution of waters (Article 250); pollution of the atmosphere (Article 251); pollution of the marine environment (Article 252); violation of legislation of the Russian Federation on the continental shelf and on the exclusive economic zone of the Russian Federation (Article 253); spoilage of land (Article 254); violation of rules for the protection and use of the subsoil (Article 255); illegal extraction of aquatic fauna and flora (Article 256); violation of rules for the protection of fish stocks (Article 257); illegal hunting (Article 258); destruction of critical habitats for organisms entered in the Red Book of the Russian Federation (Article 259); illegal felling of trees and bushes (Article 260); destruction or damaging of forests (Article 261); violation of regime of specially protected nature territories and nature objects (Article 262).

Articles in other Chapters of the Criminal Code also concern what many would consider to be environmentally-related offences, eg, violation of sanitary-epidemiological rules (Article 236). Depending upon the nature and gravity of the crime committed, penalties range from fines, confiscation of property, deprivation of freedom, and others.

There are a vast number of administrative offences imposed by specially empowered agencies or officials in accordance with the 2001 CAdV or by administrative commissions attached to local agencies of self-government. In certain instances a disciplinary sanction may be substituted by an administrative penalty in accordance with the CAdV. If the harm is caused by a citizen, including during the course of his employment, there is a duty to compensate in full in accordance with legislation (see Article 77, 2002 Law on Protection of the Environment).

Both natural and juridical persons are civilly liable on general tort principles laid down in the Russian Civil Code for injury or harm caused to another or another's property through their fault (Article 1064). This general provision is replicated with respect to ecological violations in the 2002 Law on Protection of the Environment (Articles 77–79). Russian doctrine takes the view that there is a universal duty for the causer of harm to compensate the harm caused irrespective of whether other types of legal responsibility also are involved. Compensation must be in full and juridical persons and individual entrepreneurs must be liable for ecological harm caused by their workers, with the right of a regressive suit against the worker. Where so-called methods standards exist for calculating the harm caused to ecology, responsibility rests on the fact that harm was caused and not on the consequences of the harm. When such standards are not applicable or do not exist, the extent of the harm is based on the actual expenditures for restoration of the disturbed state of the environment taking into account losses sustained; losses for this purpose include lost advantage.

To these traditional types of sanctions Russian doctrine and legislation are adding the category of 'ecological legal responsibility', that is, special responsibility and sanctions imposed directly in ecological and natural resource legislation. These include limitation of the right to use a natural resource, or suspension of elements of the use of ecology pending rectification of a violation, or termination of the right to use a resource, such as revocation of a fishing licence, or deprivation of the right to use a natural resource, such as water, or non-compensation of expenditures invested by an offender in a nature object, for example, subsoil plots arbitrarily occupied would be returned to their original possessor without compensation or refund of investments made, or imposition upon an offender of the duty to restore a nature object at its own expense, for example, requiring that a building be demolished which was illegally built.

G. Restructuring Russian Environmental Policy

The transition to a market economy has required Russia fundamentally to transform its approach to environmental regulation. The process is perhaps nearly complete, the principal natural resource legislation and the 2002 Law on Protection of the Environment having been enacted. A major task of the 2002 Federal Law on environmental protection in the Russian Federation is to develop the constitutional principle that every citizen is entitled to a 'favourable environment'.

Russian legal doctrine suggests that a favourable environment can only be achieved by complying with certain principles. The legislator has set these out in Article 3 of the 2002 Law on Protection of the Environment:

- compliance with the human right to a favourable environment;
- ensuring favourable conditions for the vital activity of man;
- scientifically-substantiated combination of ecological, economic, and social interests of man, society, and the State for the purpose of ensuring stable development and a favourable environment;
- protection, regeneration, and rational use of natural resources as necessary conditions for ensuring a favourable environment and ecological security;
- responsibility of agencies of State power of the Russian Federation, agencies of State power of subjects of the Russian Federation, agencies of local self-government to ensure a favourable environment and ecological security on respective territories;
- payment for nature use and compensation for harm to the environment;
- independence of control in the domain of environmental protection;
- obligatoriness of conducting State ecological expert examination of projects and other documentation substantiating economic and other activity which may exert a negative influence on the environment and create a threat to life, health, and property of citizens;

- recording nature and socio-economic peculiarities of territories when planning and effectuating economic and other activity;
- priority of preserving natural ecological systems, nature landscapes, and nature complexes;
- admissibility of the influence of economic and other activity on the natural environment by proceeding from requirements in the domain of environmental protection;
- ensuring a reduction of the negative influence of economic and other activity on the environment in accordance with normative standards in the domain of environmental protection which may be achieved on the basis of using the best existing technologies, taking into account economic and social factors;
- obligatoriness of participation in activity with regard to environmental protection of agencies of State power of the Russian Federation, agencies of State power of subjects of the Russian Federation, agencies of local self-government, social and other non-commercial associations, and juridical and natural persons;
- preservation of biological diversity;
- ensuring integrated and individual approaches to establishing requirements in the domain of environmental protection for subjects of economic and other activity who effectuate such activity or are planning to do so;
- prohibition of economic and other activity, the consequences of whose influence are unpredictable for the environment, and also the realisation of projects which may lead to degradation of natural ecological systems, a change and/or destruction of the genetic fund of flora, fauna, and other organisms, depletion of natural resources, and other negative changes of the environment;
- compliance with the right of each to receive reliable information concerning the state of the environment, and also participation of citizens in adopting decisions affecting their rights to a favourable environment, in accordance with legislation;
- responsibility for a violation of legislation in the domain of environmental protection;
- organisation and development of a system of ecological education, nurturing, and the formation of ecological culture;
- participation of citizens, social organisations, and other non-commercial associations in resolving tasks of environmental protection;
- international cooperation of the Russian Federation in the domain of environmental protection.

These are the key components of the Russian legal concept of ecology use at the outset of the twenty-first century incorporated in the next generation of environmental legislation. The environment extends, under the 2002 Federal Law, to the ozone layer (Article 54). Ecological insurance is encouraged against ecological risks, and obligatory State ecological insurance to be introduced. For the most part, however, the 2002 Federal Law is a framework enactment contemplating subordinate normative legal acts to elaborate, define, and lay down normative standards for environmental behaviour.

Programmatic as the 2002 Federal Law may be, the purposes, orientations, tasks, and principles of State policies relating to the environment have been laid down in the Ecological Doctrine of the Russian Federation, approved by Regulation of the Government of the Russian Federation on 31 August 2002. State funding is likely to be based on this Doctrine.

16

LABOUR LAW

The demise of socialism in Russia has restored labour law to a normal stature within the legal system, although reforms in labour law have not been fully reflective of the requirements of a market economy.

A. Historical Background

Early Soviet legislation dealt piecemeal with labour conditions and social insurance. An eight-hour work-day was established and the following year an annual two-week holiday, pensions were increased, unemployment, disability, and sickness insurance introduced, and labour inspectorates reorganised. On or about 9 December 1918 the RSFSR Code of Laws on Labour was adopted.[1] The Code superseded all antecedent legislation and contracts contrary to its provisions and extended to all persons who worked for remuneration and to enteprises in both the socialised and private sectors. Every individual between the ages of 16 and 50, unless permanently disabled, had a 'labour duty', that is, a duty to work, under the Code.

---

[1] СУ РСФСР (1918), no 87–88, item 905.

553

Temporary exemptions were granted to the ill and to pregnant women, the latter up to eight weeks before and after birth. Persons obliged to work but not engaged in socially useful labour would be compulsorily recruited for employment by local soviets. The Code allowed individuals to work in their particular specialty at the established rates; equal pay for equal work was proclaimed. Transfer, dismissal, work hours, labour productivity, and labour safety also were regulated in the Code.

Soviet commentators attributed the strictness of the 1918 RSFSR Labour Code to the civil strife in which the country was then embroiled. The introduction of the NEP brought a new labour code approved on 30 October 1922[2] and in effect as from 15 November 1922 which differed markedly from its predecessor. The Chapter on 'Labour Duty' was supplanted by one 'On the Procedure for Hiring and Providing Labour'; labour relations were based on voluntary agreement. 'Labour duty' under the 1922 Code was restricted to exceptional situations, such as coping with natural disasters or an inadequate labour force to carry out certain State tasks. Both collective agreements and individual labour contracts were provided for in separate chapters. Management and labour were accorded broad discretion to modify Code provisions in labour contracts so long as minimum standards laid down by the Code were met. Trade unions were expected to negotiate on behalf of the labour force on these matters within the discretion of the parties, for example, wage rates, quality standards, work rules, and the like. Labour disputes were relegated under the Code either to people's courts or to price-conflict commissions, conciliation chambers, or mediation tribunals. The eight-hour work day was preserved and further limitations imposed on overtime.

In many respects the 1922 Labour Code resembled the labour legislation of Western industrialised countries. When, however, different regulations were necessary for State and private industry in the Soviet Union, State industry was favoured under the Code. The transition to national economic planning at the end of the 1920s altered or eliminated many premises upon which the 1922 Labour Code had been predicated. The State sector became the principal employer of labour. Trade unions were transformed from an adversary bargaining entity into a component of economic management. Their task was to assist in meeting planning targets, improving economic efficiency and labour productivity, and, if necessary, accepting short-term reductions in employee welfare to achieve these larger objectives. Most collective agreements in labour relations ceased after 1934; they were declared to be an institution which had outlived itself. Thereafter trade unions devoted themselves to administering social security and supervising the enforcement of safety regulations. Compulsory distribution of technical graduates was introduced in 1930 as part of manpower planning and

---

[2] СУ РСФСР (1922), no 70, item 903.

industrialisation. Shop work rules increasingly gave way to legislative regulation. Unjustified absence from work for even one day could result after 1932 in instant dismissal. Disciplinary penalties introduced in 1938 for being late to work or leaving early became serious criminal offences under wartime legislation. Decrees enacted in the early 1940s made it a crime to resign one's job without management consent and allowed the State to transfer employees at will without their consent.

Collective agreements were formally reintroduced again in 1947, apparently acknowledging that their actual continuance after 1935 at both plant and industry levels showed they had a purpose despite their nominal abolition in 1935.[3] Wage rates increasingly came to be centrally determined, although some local flexibility was allowed within minimum and maximum levels. Consequently, by the 1930–40s much of the 1922 Labour Code had become obsolete through subsequent legislation. Texts of the Code simply were no longer published. In the post-Stalin era some of the more draconian limitations on labour were removed. Workers were allowed to resign or to transfer jobs. Model rules adopted in 1957 relaxed the harsh requirements of wartime legislation. Although draft all-union labour legislation was published for discussion in 1959, it was not enacted until 1970 and formed the basis of the RSFSR Labour Code, adopted 9 December 1971, in force on 1 April 1972, and massively amended on 25 September 1992 to accommodate the transition to a market economy.[4] On 30 December 2001 the Labour Code of the Russian Federation was signed, in force as from 1 February 2002, as amended 24 July and 25 July 2002.[5]

B. Contemporary Regulation of Labour

In the Soviet era many premises of labour legislation were accorded constitutional status. The same is true, although the substance is quite different, of the 1993 Russian Constitution. The Constitution guarantees the right to create trade unions (Article 30), equal access to the State civil service (Article 32), the free use of one's abilities and property for entrepreneurial and other economic activity not prohibited by a law (Article 34), health protection and medical assistance (Article 41), education (Article 43), and guarantees of the right to free creativity (Article 41). Article 37 of the Constitution provides that labour shall be free. Each shall have the right to dispose freely of his capabilities to labour and to choose the nature of activity and profession. Forced labour is prohibited. Each has the right

---

[3] See H J Berman, *Justice in the USSR* (rev ed, 1963) 352.
[4] Ведомости Верховного Совета РСФСР (1971), no 50, item 1007. The Code was amended in hundreds of places in the years that followed.
[5] СЗ РФ (2002), no 1(I), item 3; no 30, items 3014 and 3033, transl in W E Butler, *Labour Code of the Russian Federation* (2002).

to labour in conditions which meet the requirements of safety and hygiene, to remuneration for labour without any discrimination whatever, and to the minimum amount of payment for labour established by a federal law, and also the right to defence against unemployment. Each has the right to engage in individual and collective labour disputes with the use of means established by a federal law for the settlement thereof, including the right to strike. Each has the right to leisure. The duration of work time, days off and holidays, and paid annual leave established by a federal law is guaranteed to a person working under a labour contract. But gone at the constitutional level are the right of guaranteed employment, the duty to labour, the reference to labour discipline, a constitutionally-determined work week, a commitment to reduce and ultimately abolish arduous physical labour, and a concern with the scientific organisation of labour.

In addition to the Constitution and the 2001 Labour Code, labour relations also are regulated by federal laws, edicts of the President of the Russian Federation, decrees of the Government, normative legal acts of federal agencies of executive power, the constitutions, charters, laws, and other normative legal acts of subjects of the Russian Federation, acts of agencies of local self-government, and local normative acts containing norms of labour law; guiding explanations of the Supreme Court of the Russian Federation, and legislation from the Soviet era which has not been repealed or replaced and is not deemed to be inconsistent with legislation of the Russian Federation.[6]

The architects of the 2001 Labour Code have followed the example of the Civil Code by trying to make, within its sphere of operation, the Labour Code supreme with respect to other sources of relevant rules. Norms of labour law 'contained in other laws must correspond to' the Labour Code, which is an attempt to frustrate the principle that the law latest in time governs; moreover, 'in the event of contradictions between' the Labour Code and 'other federal laws containing norms of labour law', the Labour Code shall apply (Article 5, 2001 Labour Code). Commencing from the bottom level of normative legal acts concerning labour, each must be in conformity with all sources and types of normative legal acts at the next superior level, following through to the 2001 Labour Code and the 1993 Russian Constitution at the apex. The bottom level consists of 'local' [локальный] normative acts originating at enterprise level (see Chapter 4).

---

[6] Articles 422 and 423 of the Labour Code repeal numerous normative legal acts linked with the 1971 RSFSR Labour Code but makes allowance for USSR and RSFSR enactments to remain in force: 'Other laws and other normative legal acts operating on the territory of the Russian Federation shall be subject to being brought into conformity with the present Code'.

C. Employment Relationship

Social partnership

The 2001 Labour Code incorporates the concept of 'social partnership', a system of mutual relations between workers or their representatives, employers or their representatives, and agencies of State power and local self-government intended to promote the coordination of interests of workers and employers.[7] Agencies of State power and local self-government find themselves in such a partnership either in their capacity as employers, or in other instances provided for by legislation. The concept directly involves the State, when necessary, in the resolution of divisive issues between management and workers and lays the groundwork for early State participation at plant level, if necessary, in labour disputes.

Labour contract

Russian law requires that a labour contract be concluded in writing between the employer and worker or employee, in two copies, each of which is signed by the parties; one copy is retained by the employer and the other handed over to the employee (Article 67, Labour Code). However, if the worker actually commences work with the knowledge of or on behalf of the employer or his representative and the labour contract is not duly formalised, he is deemed to be employed from that moment. In that event the employer is obliged to formalise a labour contract within three days in written form from the day that the employee actually was admitted to work. Hiring is formalised by an order or regulation issued by the employer on the basis of the concluded labour contract. The content of the order or regulation must correspond to the conditions in the labour contract and must be issued within three days under receipt from the day of signature of the labour contract; the employee has the right to require an attested copy of the order or regulation.

Labour relations also may arise on the basis of a labour contract as a result of election to an office or post, election by competition to fill a post, appointment to or confirmation in an office, a judicial decision concerning the conclusion of a labour contract, and other instances specified by the Labour Code.

Labour contracts are of two types under Article 58 of the 2001 Labour Code: for an indefinite period; or for a determined period not exceeding five years. A probationary period may be agreed by the parties for a period of up to three months

---

[7] See Россия и социальное партнерство [*Russia and Social Partnership*] (1993). The term 'social partnership' was used in the Edict of the President of the Russian Federation, adopted 15 November 1991, 'On Social Partnership and the Settlement of Labour Disputes (or Conflicts)'. Ведомости СНД и ВС РСФСР (1991), no 47, item 1611. The Edict lost force in 1996.

(and in specified instances, six months) and must be determined in the labour contract. Certain categories may not be subject to probation: youth under 18 years of age, pregnant women, and others. A worker dismissed during the probation period does not receive a severance benefit. The fixed-term contract is intended basically for situations when the job is temporary or the work is of a special nature requiring a fixed-term. The 2001 Labour Code contains a lengthy enumeration of instances when the fixed-term contract would be appropriate (Article 59). Moreover, once the fixed-term lapses, if the worker actually continues to work and neither party has requested termination of that contract, the fixed-term contract is transformed into a labour contract for an indefinite period.

By arrangement between management and the employee or worker, certain standard conditions of the labour contract are dispositive and may be drafted to suit the particular circumstances of the parties. For example, if a worker works on a holiday or on a day off, he may accept in lieu of overtime an additional day of leave or holiday or the overtime wage. Flexibility of this nature, the so-called non-standard work day introduced during *perestroika*, effectively alters the labour contract by removing constraints on the freedom of the parties to agree different conditions. The overall level of constraints in the form of imperative provisions, however, remains substantial.

Independent-work contract

The above relates to labour contracts. Individuals also may be retained under civil-law contracts, including independent-work contracts and service contracts. While the differences between the civil-law and the labour contracts can sometimes be difficult to ascertain, as a rule an individual who supplies services under an independent-work contract is not part of the personnel establishment of the employer, is not subject to the rules for internal labour order, has no superior in his employment, and is not subject to the orders or discipline of management or the administration. Remuneration is paid as provided in the civil-law contract, usually on the basis of work performed or services provided. Such contracts fall under the Civil Code of the Russian Federation, and the provisions of the Labour Code regulating work hours, holidays, disciplinary and material responsibility, settlement of labour disputes, and the like are not applicable.

Transfer

Many provisions of the Soviet labour codes treated problems of transfer or termination. In the economic reforms of the 1960s many enterprises found themselves overmanned, often because of new technology and automation or simply by reason of excessive hiring for social reasons. Wage costs and labour productivity became more prominent among the economic indicators of enterprise performance, but existing labour legislation, strongly enforced by the Soviet courts,[8] made it extremely difficult for planners and managers to redeploy the labour force. The 1970 FPLabL introduced greater flexibility to this end, and that flexibility was enlarged in 1988 and again in 1992. Under the 2001 Labour Code transfer to other permanent work within the same organisation at the employer's initiative or transfer to permanent work in another organisation or to another locality together with the organisation is permitted only with the employee's written consent. A worker who for medical reasons needs a different job must be transferred to other work with his consent by the employer, and if there is no such work, the labour contract is subject to termination. However, the worker's consent is not required if the worker is merely moved to another job site or structural subdivision within the same locality unless there is a material change of labour functions and conditions of the labour contract.

A change of material conditions of the labour contract is permitted for reasons connected with organisational or technological changes in the conditions of labour. The worker must be notified in written form at least two months in advance by the employer unless provided otherwise by the Labour Code or other federal law. If the worker does not consent, the employer must offer another job corresponding to his skills or health, and in the absence of such job, a vacant lower post or lower-paid work. In the absence of such possibilities or the refusal of the worker to accept the offer, he is subject to dismissal on the general grounds (Article 77(7), Labour Code). An employer may transfer a worker to other work in the same organisation for reasons of 'production necessity'; examples of the last include production accidents and catastrophes, natural disasters, down time for reasons of an economic, technological, technical, or an organisational character, destruction or spoilage of property, or to replace an absent worker.

Termination of contract

A labour contract may be dissolved under Russian legislation on the following grounds: agreement of the parties, expiry of the period of the labour contract concluded for a specified period but not exceeding five years or, provided that labour relations do not continue de facto, when the time designated for performing the work has elapsed; dissolution of the contract at the initiative of the worker or of the employer, transfer of the worker with his consent to another enterprise or taking up elective office, refusal of the worker to transfer to a job in another locality or a refusal to accept material changes in labour conditions, refusal of a worker to transfer to another job for reasons of health on the basis of a medical certificate,

---

[8] See M McAuley, *Labour Disputes in Soviet Russia 1957–1965* (1969); W E Butler, B A Hepple, and A C Neal (eds), *Comparative Labour Law: Anglo-Soviet Perspectives* (1987). A rather different picture is given for a later period by K Hendley, *Trying to Make Law Matter: Legal Reform and Labor Law in the Soviet Union* (1996).

refusal of a worker to continue work in connection with a change of owner of the property of an organisation, change of subordination of an organisation, or reorganisation thereof, a violation of the rules established by the Labour Code or other federal law for conclusion of a labour contract if such violation excludes the possibility of continuing work, and 'circumstances beyond the control of the parties'. The enumeration of occasions for termination is not exhaustive, nor confined to the Labour Code itself.

The worker has the right to dissolve a labour contract concluded for an indefinite period at any moment by giving two weeks notice in written form. By agreement between the worker and employer, the two-week period may be waived or shortened, or another period agreed. If the labour contract was concluded for a specified period or until specified work is performed, dissolution may occur if the worker becomes ill or disabled and cannot perform under the labour contract as agreed, or if the employer violates labour legislation or the conditions of the labour contract, or for other 'justifiable reasons'. If the employer does not object to termination of the labour contract, the contract is dissolved by agreement of the parties.

An employer may dissolve a labour contract if the enterprise is being liquidated or a natural person who is an employer terminates his activity, or if there is to be a reduction in the numbers or personnel establishment of the workforce. Management must give notice in person to workers being made redundant for reasons of production necessity at least two months beforehand and a severance benefit; further, the worker retains a right to average earnings for an additional period not exceeding two months (taking the severance benefit into account) in order to find a new job. If a worker objectively fails to meet the standards of his position for lack of skills or health reasons, this too is grounds for dissolution of the labour contract by the employer. The burden of proof lies with the employer, which as a rule will take the form of unsatisfactory work. If the reasons are medical, there must be a medical certificate. Age or lack of work experience per se are not reasons for dismissal under this criterion. Management may likewise dismiss a worker who systematically and without justifiable reasons fails to perform duties under the labour contract or rules for internal discipline on condition that a disciplinary sanction previously had been imposed, or if the worker is guilty of shirking (which is the failure to appear at work for an entire work day without justifiable reasons, or being absent from the workplace for four hours or more during the work day without justifiable reasons), or the worker appears at work in a state of intoxication or under the influence of narcotics, or if a worker commits a flagrant violation of labour duties, or if a worker divulges a State, commercial, employment, or other secret protected by a law which became known to the worker in connection with the performance of his labour duties, or if petty or other stealing of another's property, embezzlement, intentional destruction or damaging of property has been committed by a worker at his job as established by judgment of a court which has entered into legal force or by decree of an agency empowered to apply administrative sanctions, or if a worker violates requirements for the protection of labour provided that such violation entailed grave consequences or was known to create a real threat of such consequences ensuing, or if a worker directly servicing monetary or goods valuables commits guilty actions which cause the employer to lose trust in him, or if a worker fulfilling nurturing functions commits an amoral offence incompatible with his continuing such work, or if the director or deputy director of an organisation commits a flagrant violation of his labour duties, and so on. As a rule, a worker may not be dismissed while temporarily disabled or while on leave. The account above, while not exhaustive, materially increases the situations under which a worker or employee may be dismissed at the employer's initiative.

Termination of a labour contract for reasons beyond the control of the parties includes call-up to military service or being sent for alternative service, reinstatement in work of a worker who previously performed the job by decision of a State labour inspectorate or a court, failure to be elected to an office or post, sentencing of a worker to punishment which precludes continuing the former job in accordance with the judgment of a court which has entered into legal force, deeming of a worker to lack full labour capacity in accordance with a medical opinion, death of a worker or of a natural person who was an employer, or the deeming of the last to be missing, or the ensuing of extraordinary circumstances.

The procedure for dismissal is as follows: management issues an order which must cite the article and subpoint of the Labour Code on which the dismissal is based. For every worker who is employed more than five days the employer is required to keep a labour book. The labour book must be returned to the worker on the day of dismissal, and management must also give to the worker a document setting out the worker's speciality, qualifications, post, period of employment, and amount of earnings per month or per week. If a worker is dismissed without legal grounds or in violation of the established procedure for dismissal, or is illegally transferred to other work, the worker must be reinstated in his former job by the agency which considers labour disputes. When reinstating, the said agency will determine whether the worker should be paid average earnings for the period of enforced absence or the difference in earnings during the period that lower-paid work was performed, but not more than one year.

Personal data of employees

The 2001 Labour Code introduced protections for personal data concerning employees. Personal data is defined as information necessary for the employer to have in connection with labour relations and concerning a specific worker. Personal data may be processed solely for the purpose of ensuring compliance by the employer with laws and other normative legal acts, to assist in arranging employment for workers, promotion, advanced training, and the like, ensuring the protection of property, and evaluting the quantity and quality of work performed. All personal data is to be obtained from the employee himself. If the data is such that only third persons can provide it, the worker must be notified beforehand and his written consent obtained. Data concerning political, religious and other convictions and private life may not be obtained, although where relevant data on private life may be sought with the employee's consent. There also are protections for data concerning trade union membership and affiliation.

Employees have the right to full information concerning their personal data and free access to such data, including the right to receive copies of any entry containing personal data of the worker unless provided otherwise by a federal law. They may also require the deletion or rectification of untrue or incomplete personal data or data processed in violation of the Labour Code. If the employer refuses to delete or correct, the employee may record in written form his disagreement and substantiate his position. Where the personal data is of an evaluative nature, the worker may submit his own statement expressing his view. If an employer released untrue or incomplete data to other persons, an employee may require that all be notified about deletions, additions, and rectifications made. Any unlawful actions of the employer or failure to act in this connection may be appealed to a court. Persons guilty of violation of the norms concerning the obtaining, processing, and defence of personal data are subject to disciplinary, administrative, civil-law, or criminal responsibility.

Work time

Work hours are regulated by Russian legislation and vary according to the category of the worker. The normal duration of the work week is 40 hours, but for workers up to 16 years of age, 16 hours per week. A reduced work week operates for workers employed in jobs with what are classified as 'harmful labour conditions'. Whether an enterprise falls into this category is determined by the List of Production Entities, Shops, Professions, and Posts, confirmed by Decree of the State Committee of the Soviet Council of Ministers for Labour and Earnings and the All-Union Central Council of Trade Unions on 25 October 1974.

The normal work week is five days, followed by two days off. For production or other reasons, a six-day work week followed by one day off may be established. A work week with days off according to a sliding scale also is possible. The shift schedule must be brought to the information of workers, as a rule, one month beforehand. Shorter work days apply on the day before State holidays. A worker may not work two shifts in succession. Under work with a flexible work time regime the commencement, end, or total duration of the work day is determined by agreement of the parties. The employer is provided with a total quantity of work hours within respective recording periods (days, weeks, months, and so on)—this last regime is widely used in the natural resources industry.

Night work is deemed to be that performed between 22:00 hours and 06:00 hours. For night work the duration of work hours is reduced by one hour except for those workers who already have a reduced work day. Pregnant women, women with young children, and other designated categories of persons may not undertake night work, and disabled persons may do so only with a medical certificate.

Part-time work may be agreed in individual cases between the management and worker either when the worker is hired or later. It may take the form either of a shortened work day or a shorter work week. If a pregnant woman so requests, or a person having children at home of up to 14 years in age, or persons caring for a sick member of the family on the basis of a medical certificate, management must oblige with part-time work. Earnings are in proportion to the time worked or based on output (piece-work). Part-time work does not limit any entitlement to annual leave, calculation of labour experience, or other labour rights. In exceptional instances when enterprises operate 24 hours per day on all days of the week or in certain other situations when a normal work day is not practicable (for example, seasonal agricultural work), workers may work on a cumulative-time basis. Under this scheme there are no limits on the number of hours per week or per day, provided that the total number of hours worked in a particular time frame as provided by legislation is not exceeded.

There are limitations on overtime work. The basic approach is that overtime work is not permitted in excess of the established work hours per week or per shift, or the cumulative-time basis. Management may invoke overtime only with the written consent of the worker and in the instances enumerated in the Labour Code (Article 99). Other than the enumerated instances, overtime work is permitted with the written consent of the worker and the opinion of the elective trade union agency of the particular employer. Pregnant women, workers under 18 years of age, and certain other categories of workers in accordance with a federal law may not do overtime. Women having children under three years of age and disabled persons may undertake overtime work under specified conditions. The Labour Code provisions on overtime are strongly orientated to industrial production circumstances and not to service companies. Exceptional situations justifying overtime include work needed for the defence of Russia or to avert a production accident, or to eliminate the consequences of such an accident, or performing socially essential work relating to public utilities, communications, or transport, or when overtime is essential in order to complete work commenced which as a result of unforeseen or accidental delay cannot be completed within normal work hours, or when the next shift worker fails to appear and work cannot be interrupted, and others. Overtime must not exceed four hours for each worker within a two-day period, nor 120 hours per year.

Leisure time

Workers must be given a break for meals and nourishment for not more than two hours and not less than 30 minutes per day; the break is not included in the work hours and the time at which they may be taken is determined by the rules for internal labour order of the organisation or by agreement between employer and employee. There are 11 statutory holidays per year in Russia, which if they fall on a weekend are preceded or followed by a work day off. The holidays are: 1 to 2 January (New Year); 7 January (Christmas); 23 February (Day of Defender of the Fatherland); 8 March (International Women's Day); 1 to 2 May (Spring and Labour Days); 9 May (Victory Day); 12 July (Russia Day); 7 November (Anniversary of October Revolution. Day of Amity and Conciliation); 12 December (Constitution of the Russian Federation Day).

Annual leaves are provided with retention of job and average earnings. Basic paid leave is 28 calendar days per year; there is no maximum limit on the duration of leaves. Holidays which occur during a leave period are not calculated as part of the calendar days. Annual additional paid leaves are granted to workers engaged in jobs with harmful or dangerous labour conditions, workers with a non-standard work day, workers employed in the Far North or regions equated thereto, and others. For the first year of employment leave is granted to workers after six months of continuous work in the enterprise, with certain exceptions for younger workers and pregnant women. By agreement between employer and employee, the six-month period may be shorter. Leave may be carried over from one year to the next with the worker's consent but must be used within 12 months of the end of the work year for which it was granted. Leave exceeding 28 calendar days may at the written request of the worker be replaced by monetary compensation.

D. Labour Discipline

A worker in Russia is obliged under the Labour Code to perform in good faith, or conscientiously, his labour duties placed on him by the labour contract and to comply with the rules for internal labour order of the organisation (Article 21). Labour discipline under Russian law is a legal relationship expressing the subordination of a worker to rules of behaviour determined in accordance with legislation, the collective contract or agreements, the labour contract, and local normative acts of the organisation. Each enterprise, organisation, or institution has, or has the right to have, its own rules for internal labour order. Such rules are a local normative act of the employer regulating the procedure for hiring and dismissal of workers, the basic rights, duties, and responsibility of the parties to a labour contract, the work and leisure regime applicable to workers, measures of incentive and penalties, and the like. The labour contracts themselves may also contain such rules, and in certain branches of the national economy there are disciplinary charters or statutes which apply. As a rule, such rules are confirmed by the employer, having taken into consideration the opinion of the representative organ of workers in the organisation and are, also as a rule, appended to the text of the collective contract.

In addition to civil, criminal, and administrative responsibility, a worker also is subject to disciplinary responsibility for the commission of a disciplinary offence. There are two types of disciplinary responsibility: general and special. General disciplinary responsibility is applicable to all workers, whereas special disciplinary responsibility is applicable only to particular categories of workers specified in a special normative act.

The disciplinary sanctions engaged under general disciplinary responsibility are set out in Article 192 of the 2001 Labour Code. They would be applicable, for example, to workers who arrive at work late, who are idle during work time, who leave work early, and the like. The three principal disciplinary sanctions are: warning, reprimand, and ultimately dismissal on the respective grounds. When imposing a disciplinary sanction, the employer must have regard to the gravity of the offence committed, the circumstances under which it was committed, and the previous work performance and behaviour of the worker. The choice of disciplinary sanction lies with management, as does the option not to apply the measure and merely confine itself to an oral expression of opinion. A disciplinary sanction which has not been provided for by federal laws, charters, or statutes on discipline may not be imposed.

Before a sanction is imposed, explanations must be sought from the offender in writing and the sanction must be applied not later than one month after the day the offence was discovered and not later than six months from the day the offence was committed. If the offence relates to an internal audit, verification, or audit of financial-economic activity, a two-year period of limitations applies. Only one disciplinary sanction may be imposed for each offence, and the order, regulation, or decree concerning the sanction and specifying the reasons for applying it must be communicated under receipt to the worker who is being disciplined within three working days. A worker may appeal against a disciplinary sanction to the State labour inspectorate or agency for the consideration of individual labour disputes.

If within a year from the day of applying a disciplinary sanction a worker has not been subjected to a new disciplinary sanction, he is considered not to have a record of such a sanction being applied. The employer may at his own initiative or request of the worker concerned, or of the representative organ of workers, expunge the record of the disciplinary sanction, a practice which has analogies with the record of conviction in a criminal case.

E. Material Responsibility

Employee responsibility

This subject comes as something of a shock to foreigners in Russia. The basic principle of Russian law is that the employer and worker bear mutual responsibilities to one another. If a worker causes damage to his employer, he is obliged to compensate the damage; if the employer causes harm to the health or property of a worker, including by illegal dismissal, the worker has the right to compensation. The transition to a market economy has not materially changed these relationships. They are preserved in the 2001 Labour Code, where they are expressly linked with the labour contract, although any obligations of this nature survive dissolution of the labour contract. The formulation of the principle is: 'Material responsibility of a party to a labour contract ensues for damage caused to it by the other party to this contract as a result of its guilty unlawful behaviour (actions or failure to act) unless provided otherwise by the present Code or other federal laws' (Article 233, Labour Code).

Article 21 of the Labour Code requires workers to treat property of the employer with care and to take measures to avert damage. If a worker is at fault in causing direct actual damage to the employer, the worker is liable to pay compensation. Responsibility, however, is limited to average monthly earnings and does not extend to the full amount of damage caused except for certain instances. Lost revenues or lost advantage are not considered, but the worker is liable for damage to third persons for which the employer will be responsible. Nor is a worker liable for damage which falls into the category of normal production-economic risk, or is caused by insuperable force, extreme necessity, necessary defence, or the failure of the employer to perform his duties to ensure proper conditions for keeping the property entrusted to the worker. Management is required to create conditions for workers which are conducive to normal work and to ensuring the preservation of the property entrusted to him.

Two types of responsibility have been established for workers who caused damage to the employer: full and limited. As noted above, the limit of responsibility for actual direct damage caused by a worker is his average monthly earnings. That limit may be transcended when Russian law places full material responsibility on a worker for damage caused to the enterprise (for example, cashiers, who bear absolute responsibility for all valuables accepted by them and for any damage caused to the enterprise as a result of their intentional actions or a negligent or unconscientious attitude towards their duties), or when there is a contract in writing between the employer and the worker making provision for full material responsibility, or if the worker causes damage when not performing his labour duties, or when the worker received property or other valuables under a power of attorney or analogous documents, or when the worker who caused damage was intoxicated, or when damage was caused intentionally, or when damage was caused as a result of criminal actions established by judgment of a court or in consequence of an administrative offence established by a State agency. Of particular interest is the exposure of the worker to responsibility for the divulgence of information comprising an employment, commercial, or other secret protected by a law in instances provided for by federal laws.

If the damage caused did not exceed average monthly earnings, management may issue an order not later than within one month from the date of determining the amount of the damage caused and withholding the amount due from wages. Determining the amount of damage proceeds by calculating the market prices in the particular locality on the day the damage was caused, but not lower than the value of the property according to book-keeping data, taking into account wear and tear. Before taking a decision about the amount of damage to be compensated by a specific worker, the employer must verify the amount of damage caused and the reasons for it. An employer may create a commission to do this with the participation of specialists. The worker must provide an explanation in written form in order to establish the reasons why the damage was caused.

If the worker contests the deduction or the amount thereof, or the amount of damage exceeds his average monthly earnings, the recovery must be by way of a judicial proceeding. A worker may voluntarily compensate the damage caused in full or in part, and by agreement with the employer may pay compensation in instalments under a written obligation. With the consent of management a worker may repair damaged property or replace it with property of equal value.

In practice, the legal requirement that management sue if the employee or worker will not voluntarily pay compensation results in enterprises writing off small losses in the belief that bringing suit is too costly in time and trouble. The worker remains responsible to compensate the damage irrespective of whether he is brought to disciplinary, administrative, or criminal responsibility for the action or failure to act which caused damage to the employer. Having regard to the circumstances of the case, a court may reduce the amount of damage subject to compensation unless the damage was caused by a crime committed for a mercenary purpose.

Employer responsibility

The employer is obliged to compensate the worker for earnings not received by him in all instances when the worker is deprived of the possibility to work. This duty arises when earnings have not been received as a result of the illegal removal, dismissal, or transfer of a worker, refusal of an employer to perform or the untimely performance of a decision of an agency for the consideration of labour disputes or State legal inspector of labour to reinstate a worker in his former job, delays in issuing a labour book to a worker or making incorrect entries in the labour book concerning the reasons for dismissal, and others. If damage is caused to the property of a worker, the employer is liable in full at market prices in the particular locality when the damage was caused. Such damage may be compensated in kind if the worker consents.

If an employer violates the periods for payment of earnings, leave payment, severance, and other payments due to a worker, these must be compensated with interest at the rate determined in the 2001 Labour Code (Article 236) based on the refinancing interest of the Central Bank of the Russian Federation on the unpaid balance. Moreover, under the 2001 Labour Code a worker has the right to compensation for moral harm caused to a worker by unlawful actions or failure to act of the employer.

F. Social Insurance

The Russian Federation introduced its own pension system at the end of 1990, a year before the former Soviet Union dissolved, motivated in part by the desire to create a pension system separate from the Union with its own financial basis and separate from the State budget. As of 1998 about 38 million Russians receive State pensions. Pursuant to the Conception for Reform of the System of Pension Security in the Russian Federation, approved by the Government of the Russian Federation on 7 August 1995[9] and the Federal Law on the Fundamental Principles of Obligatory Social Insurance of 16 July 1999, as amended,[10] material changes have been introduced, including an increase in the minimum pensionable age and a reduction of the privileged age minimums for certain categories of citizens. Whatever reforms are made, however, Russian citizens have a constitutional right to social security for age, illness, disability, loss of breadwinner, nurturing children, and other instances established by law (Article 39, Russian Constitution).

So-called 'obligatory payments' for social security, pensions, and medical insurance have been transformed by Part II of the Tax Code (Chapter 24) into the uniform social tax, the proceeds of which are credited to State extra-budgetary funds: the Social Insurance Fund of the Russian Federation, the Pension Fund of the Russian Federation, and the obligatory medical insurance funds of the Russian Federation. Those who pay the uniform social tax include the following: (1) employers making payments to hired workers, including organisations, individual entrepreneurs, kinship and family communities of small peoples of the North engaging in traditional branches of economic management, peasant (or farmer)

---

[9] СЗ РФ (1995), no 33, item 3388.
[10] СЗ РФ (1999), no 29, item 3686; (2003), no. 1.

economies, and natural persons; (2) individual entrepreneurs, kinship and family communities of small peoples of the North engaging in traditional branches of economic management, heads of peasant (or farmer) economies, and advocates. If a taxpayer falls into two or more categories, he pays taxes for each category into which he falls. Taxpayers do not pay the tax with respect to the amounts credited to the Social Insurance Fund of the Russian Federation. The tax base is complicated, but includes both monetary and in kind payments. Payments are calculated for each worker or employee and based on graduated yearly remuneration scales.[11]

State social insurance

The Social Insurance Fund of the Russian Federation was formed as an autonomous credit-financial institution on 1 January 1991. Management of the Fund was placed on the Council of the Federation of Independent Trade Unions of the RSFSR and regulated by a Provisional Statute and Provisional Instruction of 29 May 1991. When the Soviet Union was dissolved, the social insurance fund was included in the group of property deemed to be exclusively in federal ownership. On 28 September 1993 management of the Fund was removed from the trade unions and transferred to the Government of Russia. At present the legal status of the social insurance fund is regulated by the Statute on the Social Insurance Fund of the Russian Federation confirmed by Decree of 12 February 1994, as amended.[12]

All workers in Russia are subject to obligatory State social insurance. The failure of an enterprise to pay social insurance contributions does not deprive the worker of the right to claim social insurance benefits. The social insurance fund pays for temporary lack of labour capacity, pregnancy and birth benefits, lump-sum benefits for the birth of a child, lump-sum benefits for women who in the early stages of pregnancy require medical supervision and consultations, child-care benefits until the child reaches 18 months of age, funeral and burial benefits, and payments for additional days off for parents who have disabled children.

Pensions

The uniform social tax and 2001 Labour Code were accompanied in December 2001 by three federal laws which have modernised and reformed the Russian pension system: the Federal Law on Obligatory Pension Insurance in the Russian Federation of 15 December 2001 as amended;[13] the Federal Law on State Pension Provision in the Russian Federation of 15 December 2001 as amended 25 July 2002;[14] and the

---

[11] See O V Staroverova, Налоговое право [*Tax Law*] (2001) 210–223.
[12] САПП РФ (1994), no 8, item 599; СЗ РФ (1995), no 31, item 3131; (1996), no 9, item 809; no 16, item 1908; (1997), no 1, item 174; no 48, item 5555; (1999), no 52, item 6417.
[13] СЗ РФ (2001), no 51, item 4832; (2002), no. 22, item 2026; (2003), no. 1.
[14] СЗ РФ (2001), no 51, item 4831; (2002), no 30, item 3033.

Federal Law on Labour Pensions in the Russian Federation of 17 December 2001, as amended 25 July 2002.[15] Subjects of the Russian Federation may have their own pension schemes in addition.

State pensions are paid to those who reach the age of retirement, for death of a breadwinner to members of his family who are unable to work, disability, or years of service in certain professions for the stipulated minimum period. The age of retirement for males is age 60 provided they have not less than 25 years general labour experience, and age 55 for females who have not less than 20 years general labour experience. Certain categories of workers qualify for a pension at a lower age limit or with fewer years of general labour experience. Pensioners who continue to work are paid the full amount of their pension, which comprises from 55–75 per cent of earnings depending upon the amount of labour experience. Women with many children and disabled persons qualify for pensions on a preferential basis. Under certain circumstances two pensions may be paid, and in any event these pensions are entirely separate from labour pensions.

Pension insurance is effectuated by the Pension Fund of the Russian Federation, whose budget is formed by insurance contributions, means of the federal budget, revenues from forfeits and other financial sanctions, revenues from investing temporarily free means, voluntary contributions, and other sources not prohibited by legislation. The Pension Fund provides the obligatory minimum for old-age labour pensions, labour disability pensions, labour pensions for loss of breadwinner, and the social benefit for burial of pensioners who are not employed on the day of death. The Pension Fund is financed by the uniform social tax and by individual accumulative portions credited to the personal pension account of each individual.

Labour pensions are paid for old-age, disability, and loss of breadwinner and consist of a base payment, insurance contributions, and accumulative portions.

Russian citizens who depart for permanent residence beyond the limits of the Russian Federation and who have on the day of departure the right to receive State pensions may upon request receive an advance payment equal to six months pension in Russian rubles. Pension amounts may be transferred abroad in foreign currency at the Central Bank rate. A citizen returning to Russia may claim back payment of pensions not paid during his absence abroad.[16]

Medical insurance

By Edict of the President of the Russian Federation of 28 June 1998, the Government of Russia was charged with confirming the Charter of the Federal Obligatory Medical Insurance Fund, which was duly accomplished on 29 July

---

[15] СЗ РФ (2001), no 52(I), item 4920; (2002), no 30, item 3033.
[16] СЗ РФ (2001), no 11, item 998.

1998. The Fund implements State policy in the domain of obligatory medical insurance for citizens as an integral part of State social insurance.

Voluntary medical insurance schemes are expanding in Russia, and many employers subscribe to these on behalf of their employees. Similarly, non-State pension funds are increasing in popularity, numbering in January 2000 more than 100 funds which served 2.4 million persons. These are regulated by the Federal Law on Non-State Pension Funds of 7 May 1998, as amended 12 February 2001 and 21 March 2002.[17]

G. Trade Unions

In the Soviet era virtually every employed person except military personnel and collective farmers was a trade union member. The 1993 Russian Constitution guarantees the right of citizens to combine into trade unions (Article 30), and the trade unions themselves are governed by the Federal Law on Trade Unions, Their Rights, and Guarantees of Activity, adopted 12 January 1996,[18] and relevant provisions of the 2001 Labour Code, together with a vast repository of subordinate legislation, including at the level of subjects of the Russian Federation.

A trade union is a voluntary social association of citizens linked by common production and professional interests with regard to the nature of their activity to be created for the purposes of representation and defence of their socio-labour rights and interests. Anyone aged 14 or above and engaging in labour or professional activity has the right to create a trade union, engage in trade union activity, or to withdraw from trade unions, such right to be exercised freely without preliminary authorisation. Foreign citizens and stateless persons who reside on the territory of the Russian Federation may join Russian trade unions unless prohibited from doing so by federal law or international treaties of the Russian Federation.

The reality is that in the early twenty-first century trade unions exist principally at State and quasi-State enterprises. Under the Labour Code, trade unions are viewed merely as one of the means by which workers are represented. It is uncommon for trade unions to be formed in other commercial firms or organisations for a variety of reasons, not least the fact that labour disputes which arise in commercial firms or organisations are usually of an individual rather than a collective nature. Management of an enterprise has a duty to create conditions that enable workers to be represented effectively *vis-à-vis* the management of the enterprise itself.

---

[17] СЗ РФ (1998), no 19, item 2071; (2001), no 7, item 623; (2002), no 12, item 1093.
[18] СЗ РФ (1996), no 3, item 148; with changes introduced by the Decree of the Constitutional Court of the RF, 24 January 2002. СЗ РФ (2002), no 7, item 745.

Where trade unions do exist, they continue to play a major role in labour protection and collective agreements. The trade union creates special inspectorates and committees to verify that sanitation and safety conditions comply with legislation. Such inspectorates have the right to inspect the premises at any time, including job sites, and to participate in the investigation of industrial accidents and otherwise defend the rights and interests of trade union members with regard to labour conditions and safety. If violations are discovered, the trade union may demand that management eliminate them and also apply to the Federal Labour Inspectorate for urgent measures to be taken.

H. Collective Contracts, Collective Agreements, and Strikes

Collective contract

In the late Soviet era the collective contract came to be linked with the role of the labour collective in deciding State and social matters, planning production and social development, and discussing and deciding management issues, and the like. The Russian Federation has linked the collective contract to the policy of social partnership in labour relations, an attempt of the Russian Government to encourage a transition from 'conflictual competition to conflictual cooperation'. On 1 December 1994 the Government of the Russian Federation confirmed the Statute on the Russian Tri-Partite Commission for the Settlement of Socio-Labour Relations (replacing an earlier version of 14 July 1993).[19] The principal tasks of the Commission include developing the system of social partnership and promoting the settlement of collective labour disputes by conducting collective negotiations and preparing and concluding a General Agreement between the All-Russian Associations of Trade Unions, the All-Russian Associations of Employers, and the Government of the Russian Federation. The current General Agreement was concluded for the years 2002–4 on 20 December 2001, the first for a three-year period instead of two years.[20]

The collective contract is regulated by the Law of the Russian Federation on Collective Contracts and Agreements adopted 11 March 1992, as amended 24 November 1995, 1 May 1999, and 30 December 2001,[21] and by Chapter 7 of the 2001 Labour Code. The legislation extends to all employers, workers, and representatives of employers and workers, and to agencies of executive power and local self-government. Indeed, the collective contract is characterised as a 'legal act

---

[19] СЗ РФ (1994), no 33, item 3443. The Decree lost force on 30 April 1997. See СЗ РФ (1997), no 20, item 2286.

[20] For the text see Российская газета [*Russian Newspaper*], 19 January 2002, 4–5.

[21] Ведомости СНД и ВС РФ (1992), no 17, item 890; СЗ РФ (1995), no 48, item 4558; (1999), no 18, item 2219 (2002), no 1(I), item 2.

regulating the socio-labour relations' between workers and their employer. Where such contracts are concluded, they are binding upon the employer; labour conditions in collective contracts which worsen the position of workers in comparison with that under legislation are invalid, and so too are conditions in individual labour contracts which contain conditions worse than those provided in the collective contracts.

A collective contract may be in force for up to three years, as the parties agree. The parties are the workers of the organisation in the person of their representatives, and the employer. The parties are at liberty to determine the content of the collective contract, but legislation suggests mutual obligations of the parties might include: the form, system, and amount of payment for labour, monetary remuneration, benefits, supplementary payments; a mechanism for regulating payment for labour, including adjustments for inflation, price increases, and the like; employment, retraining, and redundancy; duration of work hours and leisure or leaves; improvement of labour conditions; voluntary and obligatory medical and social insurance; housing; privatisation; ecological security and health protection; privileges for workers who undertake part-time study; control over fulfilment of the collective contract, renunciation of strikes, and others (Article 41, Labour Code).

Collective agreement

A collective agreement is a legal act regulating socio-labour relations between workers and employers but concluded at the level of the Russian Federation, subject of the Russian Federation, territory, branch, or profession. At each level the collective agreement fixed the general principles for regulation socio-labour relations, becoming more detailed at each lower level. In some cases such agreements are trilateral, involving State agencies and perhaps partial budget financing for certain measures.

A collective contract or agreement is subject within seven days from the day of signature to be sent for registration to an agency for labour. Such registration is for notification purposes, not constitutive, and entry into force of the contract or agreement does not depend upon the fact of registration.

Persons representing the employer who are guilty of violating or failing to fulfil the obligations under a collective contract or agreement are subject to a fine of up to 50 minimum amounts of payment for labour to be imposed by a court. At the request of representatives of the workers, the owner of the enterprise is obliged to take the measures provided for by legislation against an executive who violates or does not fulfil the conditions of the collective contract. Analogous sanctions are applicable to a representative of the employer who fails to provide information needed to conduct collective negotiations or to effectuate control over compliance with the collective contract or agreement.

Strikes

The 1993 Russian Constitution (Article 37) guarantees the right to strike, but that right must be exercised in accordance with the procedures laid down in the 2001 Labour Code and the Federal Law on the Procedure for the Settlement of Collective Labour Disputes, adopted 23 November 1995, as amended 6 November and 31 December 2001,[22] and subordinate legal acts issued by the Ministry of Labour and Social Development of the Russian Federation. A collective labour dispute is defined as 'unsettled disagreements between workers (or their representatives) and employers (or their representatives) with regard to the establishment or change of labour conditions (including earnings) or the conclusion, change, and fulfilment of collective contracts or agreements, and also in connection with a refusal of an employer to take into account the opinion of an elective representative organ of workers when adopting acts containing norms of labour law in organisations' (Article 398, Labour Code). Procedures are laid down for workers to put forward their demands in writing, a copy of which may be sent to the Service for the Settlement of Collective Labour Disputes, a department organised within the Ministry of Labour of the Russian Federation and operating on the basis of a Statute confirmed by Decree of the Government of the Russian Federation on 15 April 1996, as amended 21 March 1998.[23] The employer is obliged to accept the demands for consideration and to communicate his decision regarding them in written form within three days of receipt. If a dispute arises, it must first be referred to a conciliation commission and then to a mediator and/or labour arbitration.

A conciliation commission is formed ad hoc within a period of up to three work days from the moment the labour dispute commenced and is formalised by an order from the employer and a decision of the representative of the workers. Representatives of the parties serve on the commission on a parity basis; the employer may not evade creating the commission or refuse to serve on it and must create the necessary conditions for the commission to work. If the conciliation commission comes to a decision by agreement of the parties, the decision is formalised by a protocol and is binding upon the parties. If agreement is not reached, the conciliation process continues with the involvement of a mediator or a labour arbitration tribunal.

The mediator may be invited by the parties by recommendation of the Conciliation Service or independently of it. If within three work days of applying to the Service they do not reach agreement about the mediator, the Service will itself appoint one. The procedures to be followed by the mediator are agreed with

---

[22] СЗ РФ (1995), no 48, item 4557; (2001), no 46, item 4307; (2002), no 1(I), item 2.
[23] СЗ РФ (1996), no 17, item 1999; (1998), no 14, item 1579.

the parties to the dispute. The mediator has up to seven work days from the date of his appointment to complete his task, which takes the form either of an agreed decision in writing or a protocol of disagreements.

A labour arbitration tribunal is an ad hoc organ created by the parties to the collective labour dispute and the Service within a period of not more than three work days from the moment that the conciliation commission or mediator cease to consider the dispute. The tribunal comprises three persons recommended by the Conciliation Service or by the parties themselves; these persons may not be representatives of the parties. The tribunal considers the case within a period of up to five days from being formed and hears the representatives of the parties. The tribunal receives necessary documents and information relating to the dispute, informs agencies of State power and local self-government when necessary about the possible social consequences of the collective labour dispute, and works out recommendations regarding the essence of the dispute. These recommendations are passed to the parties in written form and, if the parties have so agreed in writing, are binding upon them.

If the conciliation procedures have been unsuccessful, or the employer does not fulfil the conciliation procedures, or does not fulfil an agreement reached during the settlement of the collective labour dispute, the workers have the right to use assemblies, meetings, demonstrations, and picketing, including the right to strike. Participation in strikes is voluntary; no one may be compelled to take part or not to take part in them. There must be a formal announcement of the strike by the meeting of workers who took the decision to strike, provided that such meeting had a proper quorum (two-thirds of the total number of workers). A majority of those present must vote in favour of the strike. A warning strike of one hour may be called after giving the employer notice in writing of at least three work days. Once a full strike is called, the employer must be given notice in writing ten calendar days in advance; the decision to strike must contain a list of disagreements of the parties which serve as the grounds for the strike, the date and time of commencement of the strike, its duration, and the proposed number of participants, the name of the agency heading the strike and the names of the representatives of the workers who are empowered to take part in conciliation procedures, and proposals relating to the minimum work or services required during the strike by the enterprise. During the period of the strike all workers have the right to receive their average earnings from the employer.

A strike declared without having regard to the periods, procedures, and requirements set out above is illegal, as is a strike which creates a real threat to the foundations of the constitutional system or the health of other persons. Certain groups are prohibited from striking: the Armed Forces, law enforcement agencies, and federal security agencies. The courts or a procurator have the right to adopt a decision to deem a strike to be illegal.

Strikes are uncommon in Russia at commercial organisations with foreign invest-ments or private enterprises. When such occur, they usually are at State enterprises which have large arrears in wages or where there is professional solidarity (eg, air controllers).

I. Work Permits

Foreign investment in the Russian Federation has been accompanied by a sub-stantial influx of foreign workers. By an Edict on the Recruitment and Use in the Russian Federation of Foreign Work Force issued by the President of the Russian Federation on 16 December 1993[24] and confirming a Statute bearing the same name, a priority right for Russian citizens to fill vacant positions has been created. Russian juridical persons (including those with foreign participation) who wish to employ foreign citizens in Russia must obtain a work permit from the Federal Migration Service of Russia; by an Edict of 29 April 1994 the same requirement has been extended to foreign juridical persons who employ foreign citizens in the Russian Federation, excluding those who send their workers to the Russian Federation to install equipment supplied by them.[25] Whether the Edicts extend to foreign citizens working at accredited representations of foreign firms is unclear. The personal accreditation of a foreign employee of a representative office may be regarded as the 'legalisation' of his presence on Russian territory; however, the Presidential edicts did not formally exclude foreigners employed by accredited representations from obtaining work permits. The definition of 'foreigner' for this purpose includes citizens of other CIS countries (except Belarus).

From 1 November 2002 the entire scheme for obtaining labour permits for foreigners has been changed by the Federal Law on the legal status of foreigners.

---

[24] САПП РФ (1993), no 51, item 4934.
[25] СЗ РФ (1994), no 2, item 77.

17

CRIMINAL LAW

The development of criminal law in the Russian Federation has been an expression of the democratisation of post-Soviet Russia and of difficult policy choices between a more humanistic attitude towards criminal behaviour and the need to cope with a rapidly accelerating crime rate and increase in organised crime.

A. Historical Background

The Soviet Government inherited in 1917 an Imperial Russian Criminal Code of 1903 that technically speaking was amongst the most advanced in Europe. That Imperial Code was not immediately repealed by the Soviet authorities. Rather, the local courts were directed to decide 'cases in the name of the Russian Republic and be guided in their decisions and judgments by laws of the overthrown governments only insofar as these have not been repealed by the revolution and are not contrary to the revolutionary conscience and revolutionary legal consciousness'. This provision extended only to courts, and not to revolutionary tribunals.[1]

---

[1] СУ РСФСР (1917), no 4, item 50. On this period in general with absorbing new details, see V A Bukov, От Российского суда присяжных к пролетарскому правосудию: у истоков тоталитаризма [*From the Russian Court of Jurors to Proletarian Justice: At the Sources of Totalitarianism*] (1997) 206–207.

Decree No 2 'On the Court' of 15 February 1918 established that 'the court shall be guided in civil and criminal cases by civil and criminal laws prevailing up to now only insofar as they have not been repealed by decrees of the Central Executive Committee and the Council of People's Commissars and are not contrary to socialist legal consciousness' (Article 36).[2] However, Decree No 3 'On the Court', adopted 20 July 1918, made no reference to the old laws and required that the courts be guided 'by decrees of the workers' and peasants' government and socialist conscience'.[3] And by November 1918 the RSFSR Statute on People's Courts prohibited 'references in judgments and decisions to laws of the overthrown governments' (although prohibiting a 'reference' is not the same as prohibiting application of those laws).[4]

In practice criminal offences and sanctions were established piecemeal in a number of early decrees. The first systematic attempt to codify criminal legislation was the so-called Guiding Principles of Criminal Legislation of the RSFSR, approved by the People's Commissariat of Justice on 12 December 1919.[5] Consisting of only 27 articles, the Guiding Principles addressed the concept of crime and punishment, attempt, preparation, types of punishment, and related matters.

During the period of New Economic Policy (NEP), codification was undertaken in the principal branches of law, including the criminal law, and in 1922 the RSFSR adopted a Criminal Code.[6] The formation of the Union of Soviet Socialist Republics on 30 December 1922 and adoption of the USSR Constitution in 1924 relegated the codification of criminal law to the union republics within the framework of 'Fundamental Principles' laid down by the all-union authority. Accordingly, the Fundamental Principles of Criminal Legislation were enacted in October 1924 at the USSR level.[7] Consisting of 39 articles, they required that the 1922 RSFSR Criminal Code be amended, which it was. On 22 November 1926 the RSFSR adopted a new Criminal Code which entered into force from 1 January 1927 and remained, as revised, the keystone of Soviet criminal policy for more than three decades.[8]

During the late 1930s, attention was given to drafting a Criminal Code of the USSR, as required by the 1936 USSR Constitution, but in fact a Soviet code was never adopted. In 1957 the USSR Constitution was amended to restore the scheme of all-union fundamental principles and union republic codes, and on 25 December 1958 the USSR enacted the All-Union Fundamental Principles of

---

[2] СУ РСФСР (1918), no 26, item 347.
[3] СУ РСФСР (1918), no 52, item 589.
[4] СУ РСФСР (1918), no 85, item 889.
[5] СУ РСФСР (1919), no 66, item 590.
[6] СУ РСФСР (1922), no 15, item 153.
[7] СЗ СССР (1924), no 24, item 205.
[8] СУ РСФСР (1926), no 80, item 600.

Criminal Law of the USSR and Union Republics, followed in 1959–61 by criminal codes in each of the 15 union republics.

The RSFSR Code enacted on 27 October 1960 and in force from 1 January 1961 served, as amended, for more than 35 years. The 1958 All-Union Fundamental Principles lost force when the former Soviet Union was dissolved in December 1991, but as their substance was entirely incorporated in the 1960 RSFSR Criminal Code, the disappearance of the Soviet Union created no crisis in the criminal law of the Russian Federation.

The 1996 Criminal Code of the Russian Federation replaced the 1960 RSFSR Criminal Code, having been adopted by the State Duma on 24 May 1996, approved by the Soviet of the Federation on 5 June 1996, signed by the President of the Russian Federation on 13 June 1996, and entered into force as from 1 January 1997, as amended to 25 July 2002.[9]

B. Criminal Law: General Part

The Russian Criminal Code is divided into two parts: a General Part containing general provisions applicable to the effect and operation of the Code as a whole, and a Special Part containing definitions and punishments for each specific offence. The Code is intended to be an exhaustive statement of the criminal law. Article 1 provides: 'Criminal legislation of the Russian Federation shall consist of the present Code'. Any new laws providing for criminal responsibility are to be incorporated into the Code, although the Code provides no consequences if such new laws are not so incorporated.

Purpose of criminal law

Fundamental to the reform of criminal law in post-Soviet Russia has been the elimination of the communist ideological foundations of criminal policy. In Soviet criminal law the statement of purpose was central to the course of criminal policy. The 1960 RSFSR Criminal Code had provided that the task of the Code was 'the protection of the social system of the USSR, of its political and economic system, of socialist ownership, of the person and the rights and freedoms of citizens, and of the entire socialist legal order, against criminal infringements' (Article 1). The 1995 Criminal Code in its definition of the tasks of the Code eliminates all references to protecting the social system or the socialist legal order and moves to first priority the protection of the individual: 'The tasks of the present Code

---

[9] СЗ РФ (1996), no 25, item 2954; (1998), no 22, item 2332; no 26, item 3012; (1999), no 7, items 871 and 873; no 11, item 1255; no 12, item 1407; no 28, items 3489, 3490, and 3491; (2001), no 11, item 1002; no 13, item 1140; no 26, items 2587 and 2588; no 33(I), item 3424; no 47, items 4404 and 4405; no 53(I), item 5028; (2002), no 10, item 966; no 11, item 1021; no 19, items 1793 and 1795; no 26, item 2518; no 30, items 3020 and 3029; no 44, item 4298.

shall be: protection of the rights and freedoms of man and citizen, ownership, public order and public security, the environment, and the constitutional system'.

The language of 'social danger' so characteristic of Soviet codes has been replaced by a general statement of tasks and the articulation of five principles. The general tasks of the Code are to establish the grounds and principles of criminal responsibility, determine which acts dangerous for the person, society, or the State are deemed to be crimes, and establish the types of punishments and other measures of a criminal-law character for the commission of crimes. The prevention of crime is also a task of the Code, but is listed secondarily.

The five principles which underlie criminal policy are: the principle of *legality*, which requires that the criminality and punishability of an act or any other criminal law consequences may be determined only by the Criminal Code and that the application of analogy is prohibited in the criminal law; the principle of *equality of citizens before the law*, which excludes such factors as sex, race, nationality, language, origin, property and official status, place of residence, attitude towards religion, convictions, affiliation to social associations, and similar circumstances from influencing criminal responsibility; the principle of *guilt*, which requires that a person is criminally responsible only for those socially dangerous actions or failures to act and the ensuing consequences for which guilt is established; the principle of *justness*, which demands that punishments meted out must correspond to the character and degree of social danger of the crime, the circumstances under which it was committed, and the personality of the guilty person; and the principle of *humanity*, which provides that punishment may not serve the aim of causing physical suffering or the demeaning of human dignity.

Operation of Criminal Code in time and space

All persons who commit crimes on the territory of the Russian Federation are subject to responsibility in accordance with the Russian Criminal Code unless they enjoy diplomatic privileges and immunities or are otherwise exempted from jurisdiction by international treaties of the Russian Federation. Territory for these purposes encompasses the land and subsoil thereof, internal and territorial waters or airspace of the Russian Federation, the continental shelf and exclusive economic zone, or on a vessel or aircraft registered in a port or aircraft register of the Russian Federation and which is situated on the open water or airspace beyond the limits of the Russian Federation.

Russian citizens and stateless persons permanently resident in the Russian Federation who have committed a crime beyond the limits of Russia are subject to criminal responsibility under the Russian Criminal Code if the act which they committed is deemed to be a crime in the State where it was committed and if those persons are not convicted in the foreign State. Russian military servicemen in

Russian military units stationed beyond the limits of Russia are responsible under the Russian Criminal Code for crimes committed on the territory of the foreign State unless an international treaty of the Russian Federation provides otherwise.

Foreign citizens and stateless persons who are not permanently resident in Russia and who have committed a crime beyond the limits of Russia which is directed against the interests of the Russian Federation may be prosecuted under the Russian Criminal Code. Where an international treaty so provides, such persons also may bear criminal responsibility in Russia if they were not convicted in the foreign State.

The criminality and punishability of an act are determined by the criminal law in force when the act was committed, except that a criminal law eliminating the criminality of an act, mitigating the punishment, or otherwise improving the position of the person who committed the crime has retroactive force whereas a law increasing punishment or establishing a new offence or otherwise worsening the position of the person being punished is not retroactive.

Both the 1993 Russian Constitution (Article 61) and the Criminal Code (Article 13) provide that Russian citizens who committed a crime on the territory of a foreign state are not subject to extradition to this state. Foreign citizens and stateless persons are subject to extradition for committing a crime beyond the limits of the Russian Federation either for prosecution or serving punishment in accordance with an international treaty of the Russian Federation.

Definition of crime

A crime is defined as a 'socially dangerous act committed guiltily which is prohibited' by the Criminal Code under threat of punishment. 'Act' is understood to encompass both an action or a failure to act. This definition represents a modification in comparison with the 1960 RSFSR Criminal Code. The 1996 Criminal Code imposes three requirements: first, the act must be expressly prohibited by the Criminal Code alone (and no other law); secondly, it must be socially dangerous; thirdly, it must be committed with guilt (intentionally or through negligence). Thus do the formal and material elements of crime continue to be combined. An action or failure to act even if dangerous to society cannot be treated as a crime unless the Criminal Code so provides. And even if an action or failure to act falls within the Criminal Code, it may be deemed not to be a crime by virtue of its insignificance since it does not represent a social danger by way of causing harm or threatening to cause harm to the person, society, or the State.

The standard of 'insignificance' was originally strengthened under the 1996 Criminal Code (Article 14(2)) by requiring that the 'person, society, and the State' must be taken into account. On 25 June 1998 the Criminal Code was amended to require merely that the act not represent a 'social danger'.

The measure of progress in Russian criminal law can be measured against the provisions of the 1926 RSFSR Criminal Code, which operated throughout the Stalin era until 1960. The 1926 Criminal Code had created quite a different equation between the elements of formality and materiality. That Code undertook to protect the socialist State against 'socially dangerous acts (crimes) by applying to persons committing the said acts the measures of social defence' provided for in the Code. There was no requirement that the law expressly prohibit such acts; social danger was the test. The flexibility (and therefore the uncertainty of precisely what behaviour was criminal) of this approach was extended by the principle of analogy in the 1926 Code: 'if any other socially dangerous act is not expressly provided for by the present Code the grounds and limits of responsibility therefore shall be determined according to those articles of the Code which provide for crimes most similar in nature' (Article 16). The analogy principle was controversial among Soviet jurists and deeply criticised abroad. Some dismissed it as a purely 'technical' matter having no 'political or socially nurturing significance'. They regarded it as a method of interpretation, and more dangerously, as a means of filling gaps in the law or a transformation of the Special Part of the Code into a 'model list' of crimes.[10] The omission of analogy in the 1958 FPCrimL was a major step forward in post-Stalin criminal law reform, and its express prohibition in the 1996 Criminal Code a no less welcome development (Article 3).

Intent and negligence

The 1996 Criminal Code continues to incorporate an element omitted in the 1926 RSFSR Criminal Code but introduced in the 1958 criminal law reforms: the moral guilt or fault of an accused. Guilt may be manifested in two ways: by intent and through negligence. Intent may be direct and indirect. The 1996 Criminal Code provides that a crime is deemed to be committed with direct intent 'if the person was aware of the social danger of his actions (or failure to act), foresaw the possibility of the ensuing of socially dangerous consequences, wishing the ensuing thereof' (Article 25). Indirect intent is present when a person is aware of the social danger of his actions or failure to act, foresaw the possibility of the ensuing of socially dangerous consequences, did not wish them, but consciously permitted those consequences or was indifferent to them. The majority of crimes require direct intent, some may be committed with either direct or indirect intent, and a few only with indirect intent.

Likewise there are two forms of negligence. The first, called thoughtlessness, arises when a person foresaw the possibility of the ensuing of the socially dangerous consequences of his actions or failure to act but without sufficient

---

[10] See V G Smirnov and M D Shargorodskii in O S Ioffe (ed), Сорок лет советского права 1917–1957 [*Forty Years of Soviet Law: 1917–1957*] (1957), I, 484–485, for an account of some of the early contending views.

grounds arrogantly counted on the prevention of these consequences. The second variety of negligence, carelessness, arises when a person did not foresee the possibility of the ensuing of the socially dangerous consequences of his actions or failure to act, although with necessary attentiveness and prudence these consequences should and could have been foreseen.

Just as in all legal systems these distinctions can be difficult to draw in practice. The state of mind in direct and indirect intent and in thoughtlessness is the foreseeing of socially dangerous consequences of the act or failure to act either as desired or as possible. An element of will is present in each of these instances, whereas in the case of dangerous consequences which should and could have been foreseen in the form of carelessness, a failure of will has occurred—to foresee socially dangerous consequences which should and could have been foreseen—although the guilty person intellectually should have been aware of his neglect of the requirements of the law or the interests of other persons.

If a socially dangerous consequence causally linked with the action or failure to act of a person causes harm but the person was not aware of and under the circumstances of the case could not be aware of the social danger, or such person foresaw the possibility that socially dangerous consequences would ensue but he could not prevent those consequences by virtue of the failure of his actions to conform to the psycho-physiological qualities of the requirements of extreme conditions or mental stress, such act or failure to act will be deemed to have been committed innocently. In this situation no crime has been committed.

Situations also arise in which two forms of guilt are present. An example is an intentional crime committed by a person who did not intend the grave consequences caused by his act or failure to act. Criminal responsibility for the consequences actually caused will arise only if the person foresaw the possibility of such consequences ensuing but without sufficient grounds arrogantly counted on their prevention or if the person did not foresee but should and could have foreseen the possibility that such consequences would occur.

Attenuation of criminal responsibility

Two factors may diminish or preclude criminal responsibility: age and mental disturbance or impairment. The 1996 Russian Criminal Code establishes the age of 16 as the minimum for criminal responsibility. There is no maximum age. For certain crimes minors aged 14 to 16 may be prosecuted for homicide, intentional causing of grave harm to health, intentional causing of average gravity of harm to health, stealing of a person, rape, forcible actions of a sexual character, theft, open stealing, assault with intent to rob, extortion, terrorism, vandalism, hooliganism, and a number of others. A minor who is mentally retarded or disturbed such that he could not while committing a socially dangerous act fully be aware of the actual character and social danger of his actions or failure to act or direct those actions is not subject to criminal responsibility.

Persons who are non-imputable, that is, at the time of committing a socially dangerous act could not be aware of the actual character and social danger of their actions or failure to act or direct such actions as a consequence of chronic mental disturbance, temporary mental disturbance, feeble-mindedness, or other state of mental illness are not subject to criminal responsibility. However, such persons may be subject to compulsory measures of a medical character under the Criminal Code. Mental disturbance not precluding putability must be taken into account by a court when assigning punishment or measures of a medical character.

A person who has committed a crime while in a state of intoxication caused by the use of alcohol, narcotic means, or other stupefying substances is not relieved of criminal responsibility.

Exculpatory circumstances

Even when an action falls within the constituent elements of a crime as defined by the Criminal Code, there are six types of exculpatory circumstances in addition to circumstances when an action or omission to act is not a crime if by reason of its insignificance it does not represent a social danger. Illegality is a legal expression of the social danger of an act or omission. Each case must be judged on the basis of the factual circumstances: the character of the act or omission, the situation and conditions under which it was committed, and the lack of material harmful consequences or insignifiance of harm caused. Factors relating to the character of the individual are not weighed in this connection, for they affect only the assignment of punishment.

In the 1996 Criminal Code the list of exculpatory circumstances has been enlarged and the ideological overtones of traditional ones eliminated or revised. Necessary defence was a principle closely linked in Soviet doctrine and practice to the concept of the ideal Soviet Man. In its initial post-Soviet version self-defence must have been resorted to first and foremost in order to protect the person and rights of the defender or other persons and secondarily to defend the interests of society protected by a law, or the State, against a socially dangerous infringement. This reversed the earlier equation, which placed State and social interests first.

On 14 March 2002 the 1996 Criminal Code was amended to strengthen substantially the right to resort to necessary defence.[11] 'Necessary' defence in its new definition is an 'infringement accompanied by force dangerous to the life of the defending or another person, or with the direct threat of using such force'. The qualification in the pre-2002 version that 'intentional actions which clearly do not correspond to the character and degree of social danger of the infringement shall be deemed to be exceeding the limits of necessary defence' under the

---

[11] СЗ РФ (2002), no 11, item 1021.

amended version applies only to an infringement not accompanied by force dangerous to the life of the defending or another person, or with the direct threat of using such force.

The Criminal Code incorporated judicial practice of the late Soviet era, expressly stipulating what in the past could only be found in decrees of the Soviet Supreme Court: a person may exercise his right of necessary defence irrespective of the possibility to escape a socially dangerous infringement or to apply for assistance to other persons or to agencies of power. All persons, moreover, have the right to necessary defence, including law enforcement officials, military servicemen, and the like. The Criminal Code grants this right irrespective of professional or other special training and official position (Article 37).

Closely related to necessary defence is harm caused to a person who has committed a crime and who is being turned over to law enforcement authorities. The aim is to keep the individual detained until the authorities arrive or until he is handed over to the authorities and to prevent new crimes being committed by the detained individual. Under these circumstances the Criminal Code does require other means of detention to be used if possible instead of committing harm and tolerates only those measures absolutely necessary to achieve this end. Exceeding these limits occurs when the harm caused was clearly excessive and not called for by the situation, but is criminally punished only if caused intentionally.

Extreme necessity arises when a person commits a criminal action in order to eliminate a danger directly threatening the person and rights of himself or other persons or the interests of society or the State protected by a law, provided that such danger could not be eliminated by other means and in so doing the limits of extreme necessity are not exceeded. The harm caused must correspond to the character and degree of the threatening danger and circumstances under which the danger was eliminated and must be less significant than the harm prevented. Examples of such danger are flooding, earthquakes, avalanche, illness, starvation, and others.

Harm caused as a result of physical coercion to interests protected by a criminal law is not a crime provided that the person being coerced could not direct his actions or failure to act.

Substantiated risk is exculpatory provided that the purpose of causing harm is to achieve a socially useful purpose. The risk is substantiated if the purpose could not be achieved by actions or failure to act unconnected with the risk and the person who permitted the risk undertook sufficient measures to prevent the harm to the interests protected by a criminal law. However, a risk is not substantiated if it knowingly was accompanied by a threat to the life of many people or of ecological catastrophe or social calamity.

Obeying an order or instruction which causes harm is not a crime by the person acting in performance of the order or instruction unless an intentional crime is committed in pursuance of an order or instruction known to be illegal; however, the person who gave the illegal order or instruction is criminally responsible.

Punishment

According to the 1996 Criminal Code, punishment serves three purposes: (1) restoring social justness; (2) reforming the convicted person; and (3) preventing the commission of new crimes. The Criminal Code enumerates exhaustively the 13 types of punishment which are subject to application (the 1960 RSFSR Criminal Code laid down 12 punishments).

The death penalty is treated by the Code as an 'exceptional measure of punishment' to be applied only for especially grave crimes infringing on life. Its existence and use have been as controversial in the late Soviet Union and Russian Federation as in most other countries. Proponents believe it serves as a deterrent to crime, an argument greatly strengthened in the public mind by the high incidence of organised crime and contract homicide in modern Russia. Opponents used to argue that it was contrary to the Marxian explanation of the causes of crime, and these days doubt its deterrent effects.

The existence of capital punishment has had its own history since 1917.[12] The 1924 Fundamental Principles of Criminal Legislation included capital punishment as a 'provisional measure' pending complete abolition. In May 1947 the death penalty was abolished, reintroduced in 1950 for treason, espionage, and sabotage, enlarged in April 1954 to embrace intentional homicide under aggravating circumstances, and expanded again in the law reforms of 1958, with yet further additions in 1962 to embrace economic offences such as speculation, counterfeiting, rape, stealing of State property, and others when committed on a large-scale or under aggravating circumstances.

Capital punishment under the 1996 Criminal Code may be assigned only for homicide, infringement on the life of a State or public figure, or for genocide. The death penalty may not be assigned to women, nor to persons who committed crimes at an age of less than 18 years, or to males who at the moment of rendering judgment by the court attained the age of 65 years. And when assigned, the death penalty may be replaced by deprivation of freedom for life or for a term of 25 years by way of a pardon. The death penalty is carried out by shooting. For many years the statistics of executions were a State secret, but are now known to have fluctuated from year to year and sometimes constituted several hundred, including in the post-Soviet era. In spring 1997 the Russian Federation suspended the application

---

[12] See A S Mikhlin, *The Death Penalty in Russia* (transl W E Butler, 1999).

of capital punishment in order to comply with treaty obligations undertaken as part of becoming a member of the Council of Europe. The Criminal Code has not been amended to incorporate those obligations. On 2 February 1999 the Constitutional Court of the Russian Federation decreed that the death penalty may not be assigned in any event until the Federal Assembly secured to all defendants throughout Russia being tried for a crime that may engage the death penalty the possibility of trial by jury.[13] This has created, as one Russian jurist noted, a 'paradoxical situation': on one hand, 'legally the death penalty as a measure of punishment is available in the arsenal of criminal-law measures, and, on the other hand, may not be assigned nor applied'.[14]

The Russian Criminal Code makes provision for 'deprivation of freedom' and does not use the terminology of imprisonment. In fact, confinement in a prison is but one form of deprivation of freedom. The Criminal Code defines deprivation of freedom as 'the isolation of the convicted person from society by means of sending him to a colony-settlement or premise in a correctional colony of general, strict, or special regime or to a prison' (Article 56). Deprivation of freedom may be assigned for a minimum of six months up to a maximum, when aggregating punishments, of 25 years or for life. A sentence to deprivation of freedom for life is possible only as an alternative to the death penalty. The same limitations on the death penalty with respect to women, minors, and males also apply to deprivation of freedom for life. The period of deprivation of freedom assigned and the type of crime committed influence the regime of colony in which the punishment will be served.

Exile and banishment, much despised during the Soviet period and Tsarist era, have been abolished as criminal punishments. The mildest form of criminal punishment is the fine, extensively used in the Special Part of the Code and expressed in a formula rather than a sum absolute: a multiple of the minimum amounts of payment for labour established by the State and revised from time to time in order to take account of inflation. Deprivation of special, military, or honorary title, class rank, or State awards and confiscation of property are exclusively supplementary types of punishment. Convicted persons may also be deprived of the right to occupy determined posts or to engage in a determined activity. The 1996 Criminal Code introduced 'obligatory tasks', which require the convicted person in time free from basic work or study to perform socially useful work free of charge by agreement with agencies of local self-government; these tasks are not to be confused with 'correctional tasks', which are a withholding from earnings of the convicted person at his place of work of from 5 to 20 per cent to the benefit of the

---

[13] Decree No 3-П, 2 February 1999. СЗ РФ (1999), no 6, item 867.

[14] See S V Zhil'tsov, Смертная казнь в истории России [*The Death Penalty in the History of Russia*] (2002) 441.

State. Correctional tasks may be assigned for a term of from two months up to two years, whereas obligatory tasks are assigned for a term of from 60 up to 240 hours and may not be served for more than four hours per day. Limitation in military service consists of deductions from military maintenance to the benefit of the State in an amount of up to 20 per cent and for a term not exceeding two years. Confiscation of property is applied for grave and especially grave crimes committed for mercenary motives and may be assigned only when the Special Part of the Code so stipulates.

Limitation of freedom is a form of supervised confinement in a special institution without isolation from society; it may be assigned to first offenders for an intentional crime or to persons who committed a crime through negligence. Arrest as a punishment consists of confinement of the convicted person under conditions of strict isolation for a term of from one up to six months. Minors under 16 years of age and pregnant women or women having children of up to eight years of age are exempted. Analogous in concept for military servicemen is confinement in a disciplinary military unit for a period of from three months up to two years.

In addition to exile and banishment being abolished, the 1996 Criminal Code also eliminated dismissal from office, making amends, and social censure as types of criminal punishment.

The 1996 Criminal Code preserves the distinction introduced in Soviet law between 'basic' and 'supplementary' measures of punishment. Obligatory tasks, correctional tasks, limitation in military service, limitation of freedom, arrest, confinement in a disciplinary military unit, deprivation of freedom for a determined period, deprivation of freedom for life, and the death penalty are basic measures of punishment. A fine and deprivation of a right to occupy determined posts or to engage in a determined activity may be either a basic or a supplementary punishment. Deprivation of a special, military, or honorary title, class rank, and State awards, and also confiscation of property, are exclusively supplementary punishments.

Assignment of punishment

When assigning punishment, the Russian courts are required to work within the requirements of the types and limits imposed for each crime in the Special Part and to have regard to the character and degree of social danger of the crime and the personality of the guilty person, including circumstances mitigating and aggravating punishment, and also the influence of the punishment assigned for reform of the convicted person and on the conditions of the life of his family. A punishment assigned must be 'just', that is, must be commensurate to achievement of the purposes of the punishment.

The Criminal Code contains an exemplary list of mitigating and aggravating circumstances. Mitigating circumstances include the crime being a first offence of minor gravity as a consequence of the accidental confluence of circumstances; the minority of the guilty person; pregnancy; the guilty person having young children; the confluence of arduous living circumstances or by reason of compassion; physical or mental compulsion or material, employment, or other dependence, violation of the conditions of the lawfulness of necessary defence, extreme necessity, detention of a person who committed a crime, substantiated risk, or obeying an order or instruction; unlawful or immoral behaviour of the victim which was the occasion for the crime; and rendering medical or other assistance to the victim immediately after committing the crime, voluntary compensation of property damage and moral harm caused by the crime, or other actions directed towards ameliorating the harm caused to the victim.

Among the aggravating circumstances are the repeatedness or recidivism of crimes, the ensuing of grave consequences as a result of commission of the crime; commission of a crime as part of a group of persons, a group of persons by prior collusion, an organised group, or a criminal society or organisation; playing an especially active role in the commission of a crime; involving minors or mentally incapacitated or intoxicated persons in the commission of a crime, committing a crime with respect to a woman known to be pregnant or a youth, other defenceless or helpless person, or person dependent on the guilty person; using specified weapons or other means; commission of a crime with special cruelty, sadism, mockery, or torment of the victim; and others.

In exceptional circumstances a court may assign a milder punishment than is prescribed as the lowest limit by the Criminal Code for the particular crime, or may assign a milder type of punishment than is provided for by the article, or may decline to apply a supplementary type of punishment which is ordinarily obligatory. The Criminal Code does not contain an exhaustive list of such exceptional circumstances. Amongst them is an inducement to assist the authorities in solving a crime; active assistance by the participant of a group crime in eliciting the crime. A milder punishment also may be assigned when the jurors recommend leniency; in this instance the punishment may not exceed two-thirds of the maximum term or extent of the most severe type of punishment provided for the crime committed. If the Special Part of the Code provides for the death penalty or deprivation of freedom for life, a recommendation of leniency precludes the application of these punishments.

If the court comes to the conclusion that, having assigned correctional tasks, limitation in military service, limitation of freedom, or confinement in a disciplinary military unit, or deprivation of freedom, that the reform of the convicted person is possible without actually serving the punishment, it may decree that the punishment assigned is a conditional punishment. In this event the court establishes a probation period during which the convicted person must prove his reform.

Relief from criminal responsibility

The 1996 Criminal Code establishes three circumstances under which a person who has committed a crime for the first time may nonetheless be relieved from criminal responsibility: (1) active repentance, which means voluntarily acknowledging his guilt, facilitating the eliciting of the crime, compensating damage caused, or otherwise making amends for the harm caused as a result of the crime; (2) reconciliation with the victim and making amends for harm caused; and (3) change of situation, by which is meant that either the person or the act committed by him ceased to be socially dangerous.

The Code further provides for periods of limitation, upon the expiry of which the person who committed the crime is relieved from criminal responsibility. These are fixed at two years after the commission of a crime of minor gravity; six years after a crime of average gravity; ten years after a grave crime; and 15 years after an especially grave crime. The periods run from the day of commission of the crime up to the moment of the entry of the judgment of a court into legal force. However, the running of the period of limitation is suspended if the person who committed the crime evaded the investigation or the court. If the offence committed is punishable by the death penalty or deprivation of freedom for life, it is in the discretion of the court as to whether the period of limitation should be applied or not. Crimes against the peace and security of mankind are not subject to a period of limitation.

Amnesty, pardon, and record of conviction

For the first time the Russian Criminal Code addresses amnesty and pardon in detail. An amnesty, under the 1993 Russian Constitution (Article 103), is a matter for the State Duma of the Federal Assembly and must be declared with respect to an individually indefinite group of persons.[15] An amnesty may relieve persons who committed a crime from criminal responsibility, or relieve convicted persons from punishment or may reduce the punishment assigned, or may substitute a milder type of punishment, or may relieve from a supplementary type of punishment, or may remove a record of conviction from persons who already have served a punishment. In practice amnesties are associated with major jubilees or holidays.

Pardons are granted, under the 1993 Russian Constitution, by the President of the Russian Federation to an individually determined person. They have been used with some frequency to commute capital punishment and less commonly to relieve from the further serving of punishment. A pardon may also remove a

---

[15] See, eg, the Decree of the State Duma on Declaring an Amnesty with Respect to Minors and Women, of 30 November 2001. СЗ РФ (2001), no 50, items 4694–4697.

record of conviction. The procedure for considering petitions to grant a pardon, previously centralised in a Commission attached to the President of the Russian Federation, has been partially decentralised by the creation of a network of pardon commissions set up in the subjects of the Federation. These commissions vet petitions and prepare opinions, which are then passed to the highest official of the subject of the Federation to prepare a recommendation for the President of the Russian Federation, with whom the ultimate right and power to pardon resides. Names of persons recommended for pardon are to be published in the media, together with the article of the Criminal Code under which they were convicted.[16]

A record of conviction has a technical meaning in Russian law which differs from that ordinarily used in Anglo-American law. It is deemed to exist from the day of entry of the judgment of guilt into legal force until the moment it is cancelled or removed. So long as the record of conviction is in place, it affects sentencing in the event recidivism of crimes occurs and when assigning punishment. A person relieved from punishment is not considered to have a record of conviction.

The cancellation or removal of a record of conviction annuls all the legal consequences connected with the record of conviction. This principle has caused difficulties for some foreign countries whose visa questionnaires ask whether an applicant has ever been convicted of a crime. A Russian applicant whose record of conviction has been cancelled or removed would respond with a negative answer to that question.

Compulsory medical and educational measures

Compulsory measures of a medical character arise when a person who has committed a crime is non-imputable under the Russian Criminal Code or with respect to whom after the commission of a crime a mental disturbance has ensued which makes the assignment or execution of punishment impossible, or who has committed a crime and suffers from mental disturbance not precluding putability, or who has committed a crime and needs treatment for alcoholism or drug addiction. The purpose of applying such measures is to cure or to improve their mental state and to prevent the commission of new acts by them provided for by the Special Part of the Criminal Code. Compulsory measures may be one of four kinds: out-patient compulsory observation and treatment by a psychiatrist; compulsory treatment in a psychiatric in-patent clinic of general-type; the same in an in-patient clinic of specialised-type; or in the last type of clinic with intensive observation.

---

[16] For the Statute on the Procedure for Consideration of Petitions Concerning a Pardon in the Russian Federation, confirmed by Edict of the President of the Russian Federation on 28 December 2001, No 1500, which sets out also the criteria for granting pardons, see СЗ РФ (2001), no 53(II), item 5149.

The application of compulsory medical measures is the right of a court, not the duty. They must be applied in judicial session on the basis of evaluating all the circumstances of the case linked with the crime and data relative to the personality of the person who committed the crime. Under Russian law such measures are not a punishment; their aim is to cure and socially rehabilitate the ill and protect society against dangerous behaviour resulting from a deranged mind. The medical measures are compulsory in the sense that the court may apply them irrespective of the wishes of the mentally-ill person, close relatives, or legal representatives, and only the court may change, extend, or terminate them.

The Criminal Code places no time limit on the duration of compulsory medical measures, nor does a court when applying such measures. Compulsory treatment continues until in the opinion of a commission of doctors-psychiatrists they are no longer necessary and an appropriate recommendation is made by the commission for submission to the court.

Compulsory measures of educational influence have reference to a minor who has committed a first offence and the court considers that his reform may be achieved by applying such measures. There are four compulsory measures of educational influence: warning; transfer to the supervision of parents or persons replacing them or to a specialised State agency; imposition of the duty to make amends for the harm caused; or limitation of leisure time and the establishment of special requirements for the behaviour of the minor. Several compulsory measures may be assigned in combination to a minor. In exceptional instances persons aged from 18 to 20 years may have compulsory educational measures applied to them.

C. Criminal Law: Special Part

As noted above, the Special Part of the Criminal Code defines individual crimes and the particular punishments applicable to each. The structure of the Special Part has changed significantly in the 1996 Russian Criminal Code in comparison with the codes of the Soviet era. The individual has become paramount in place of the State. The Special Part commences with crimes against the person, followed by crimes in the sphere of the economy, crimes against public security and public order, crimes against State power, crimes against military service, and crimes against peace and security of mankind. There is no longer in Russia a chapter concerning crimes constituting survivals of local customs.

To the extent that societies give expression to their philosophies or ideologies, objectives, prejudices, and problems in their criminal codes, the demise of communism and the transition of the Russian Federation to a market economy have produced a 1996 Criminal Code which is in the mainstream of Western-type criminal codes. Nonetheless, some crimes provided for in the Criminal Code are distinctive or unusual and offer particular insight into the social transformation in process.

Leaving in danger

Under Article 125 of the Russian Criminal Code, it is a crime to leave a person without assistance who is known to be in a state dangerous for life or health and who lacks the possibility to take measures for self-preservation by reason of youth, age, illness, or as a consequence of his own helplessness. The person guilty of committing such an action had to have had the possibility to render assistance to this person and was obliged to have concern for him, or himself to have placed the victim in a state dangerous for life or health. This Article is similar to an analogous offence in the 1960 RSFSR Criminal Code.

The object of the crime is the life and health of the person who lacks the possibility to take measures for self-preservation. The guilty person is one who fails to act, who fails to fulfil a duty to render assistance to this person. The helplessness may be the result of a disability or the consequence of an accident; a driver who knowingly left a victim as a result of a traffic accident would fall under this article, irrespective of whether the driver had violated traffic safety rules or not. However, a driver who could not assist by reason of his own injuries, or who entrusted medical assistance and the summoning of the police to other persons, or who failed to render assistance because of fear of reprisals from bystanders, or who counted upon eyewitnesses to render assistance, would not fall within Article 125.

The duty to have concern for other persons may be based on a law, or on blood relationship, trusteeship, or guardianship, employment (educator in a nursery, instructor in tourist group), the requirements of a contract (bodyguard, private detective), and the like. Placing the victim in a state dangerous for life or health presupposes behaviour of the guilty person who, without wishing this, nonetheless created a situation under which the ensuing of a state dangerous for life or health becomes real (placing a detained person in a premise with a low temperature or with carbon monoxide, jokingly persuading a person who does not know how to swim to jump into deep water).

The crime requires direct intent. The guilty person must be aware of having the possibility to render assistance to another who is knowingly in a state dangerous for life or health and being obliged to render assistance, must wish to avoid doing so and not render assistance. The motives may be various: revenge, fear of criminal responsibility, hostility, and others. The kidnapping of a newly-born child, if this knowingly created the possibility of the ensuing of the child's death, would fall under Article 125. Persons exercising necessary defence or law enforcement officers who gravely wound an attacker have a legal duty to give first aid and inform public health agencies at once; their failure to do so may also fall under this Article.

A person who in good faith was under a delusion as to his ability to take measures and the possibility of doing so to save the victim would not fall within Article 125.[17]

Pseudo-entrepreneurship

New to Russian criminal law is the crime of pseudo-entrepreneurship, defined as the creation of a commercial organisation without the intention to carry on entrepreneurial or banking activity but rather for the purpose of obtaining credits, tax relief, or deriving other property or financial advantage or concealing prohibited activity which has caused large-scale damage to citizens, organisations, or the State. The concept of a commercial organisation is defined in the Civil Code of the Russian Federation. It would extend to cooperatives, economic societies and partnerships, and others.

The aim of the Article is obscure, for read literally it would extend to activity which in a market economy is quite normal. Juridical persons are routinely organised solely to facilitate financial transactions, secure tax advantages, limit liability, and the like. The Commentaries mention money laundering or other legalising of means obtained by illegal means or deriving other property advantage. The Code contains no criteria for determining what is 'large-scale damage'. Entrepreneurial activity is defined as the 'production of goods, fulfilment of work, or rendering of services', which is a rather narrow definition.

The subjects of the crime are the founders of the pseudo-entrepreneurial organisation. The concept of a 'founder' differs from one juridical person to another; in the case of a joint-stock society, the founders are only those who acquire the initial emission of stocks. Shelf companies and many offshore companies would appear on the face of it to fall within Article 173. The Criminal Code does not require that the commercial organisation necessarily be registered in the Russian Federation.

Failure to return means in foreign currency from abroad

The origins of this offence lie in legislation introduced first by the USSR in 1990 and subsequently by the Russian Federation in the Law on Currency Regulation and Currency Control, adopted 9 October 1992, as amended.[18] The last requires that means in foreign currency received by enterprises or organisations who are

---

[17] See V V Eraksin, in V I Radchenko (ed), Комментарий к уголовному кодексу Российской Федерации [*Commentary on the Criminal Code of the Russian Federation*] (1996) 195–196; G N Borzenkov and V S Komissarov (eds), Уголовное право Российской Федерации. Особенная часть [*Criminal Law of the Russian Federation: Special Part*] (1997) 97–98.

[18] Ведомости СНД и ВС РФ (1992), no 45, item 2542; СЗ РФ (1999), no 1, item 1; no 28, item 3461; (2000), no 32, item 3341; (2001), no 23, item 2290; no 33(I), item 3432; (2002), no 1(I), item 2.

Russian residents are subject to obligatory deposit in an account in an empowered bank unless a licence issued by the Russian Central Bank provides otherwise. Residents are natural persons who have a permanent residence in Russia and enterprises and organisations created in accordance with Russian legislation and located in Russia, their branches and representations situated abroad, and diplomatic and other official representations of the Russian Federation situated outside Russia. 'Means in foreign currency' includes cash money and monies held in accounts in monetary units of foreign states or in international monetary or accounting units. Securities, including cheques, bonds, other payment documents and debt documents, are deemed to be means in foreign currency. Empowered banks are banks and other credit institutions who have been licensed by the Russian Central Bank to conduct currency operations. Transferring foreign currency to branches of empowered banks abroad does not meet the requirement of Russian legislation, nor do schemes to pledge or otherwise divert the foreign currency prior to deposit in a transit account in an empowered bank. The detailed rules are contained in the Basic Provisions on the Regulation of Currency Operations on the Territory of the USSR, confirmed by the USSR State Bank on 24 May 1991, which remains in force in Russia in relevant part as amended by letters and telegrams of the Central Bank of the Russian Federation. By Edict of the President of the Russian Federation, No 629, adopted 14 June 1992, as amended 27 December 1993 and 15 March 1999, a stipulated percentage of such foreign currency receipts must be sold for rubles.[19]

Article 193 of the Russian Criminal Code punishes not the failure to make the obligatory sale of rubles, but rather the failure to remit them from abroad. The subject of the crime is the director of the organisation or enterprise, who will be deemed to be the person who has the right of first signature on financial and banking documents for the enterprise. Criminal responsibility attaches when the failure to remit occurs on a large-scale, which is defined by the Criminal Code to mean an amount exceeding 10,000 times the minimum monthly amount of payment for labour.

The ostensible reason for the currency remittance and compulsory sale requirement is to promote the stability of the Russian ruble.

Hooliganism

In the Anglo-American world 'hooliganism' is a popular journalistic expression to describe public disorder at sporting events or other public gatherings. It is not a legal term. In Soviet law and now Russian law the term 'hooliganism' is a particular administrative and criminal offence defined in the respective codes of law.

---

[19] Ведомости СНД и ВС РФ (1992), no 25, item 1425; САПП РФ (1993), no 52, item 5084; СЗ РФ (1999), no 11, item 1279.

The term is believed to have entered the Russian language late in the nineteenth century. Various explanations of its origin have been tabled: some believe it first appeared in the works of Charles Dickens and found its way into the Russian language through translations of Dickens; others suggest the term is a corruption of the Irish surname Houlighan, as the Russian press reported on disturbances in Ireland associated with this family.

It is one of the offences most commonly committed in the Russian Federation. The Criminal Code defines hooliganism as the 'flagrant violation of public order expressed by a clear disrespect for society accompanied by the application of force to citizens or by the threat of the application thereof, and likewise by the destruction or damaging of another's property' (Article 213). It is to be distinguished from 'petty hooliganism', which is an administrative offence normally taking the form of swearing in public places or the pestering or bothering of individuals in an insulting manner or otherwise disturbing public order and quiet (Article 20.1, 2001 Code on Administrative Violations). The crime of hooliganism requires a 'flagrant' violation of public order and a 'clear disrespect' for society. The courts have stressed that in distinguishing between administrative and criminal hooliganism one must take into account the degree of violation of public order, and this is to be determined by having regard to the aggregate of circumstances, including the place where the disturbances occurred, the means by which they were caused, their intensity and duration, and the like.

There must also be the application of force or the threat thereof. Force may take the form of blows, light harm to health, and the like, but must not threaten the life or health of the victim. Hooliganism does not reach instances of family quarrels or fights within an apartment or house, as there must be a flagrant violation of 'public' order. However, a family quarrel which disturbs the neighbours would qualify as hooliganism.

Divulgence of State secret

The Criminal Code of the Russian Federation has moved crimes against the State from the first chapter of the Special Part well down in sequence, giving expression thereby to the enhanced importance of the individual in post-Soviet society. Article 283 punishes the divulgence of information constituting a State secret by a person to whom it was entrusted or became known through service or work, if this information became the weal of other persons and in the absence of the indicia of State treason. The protection of State secrets is regulated by the Law on State Secrets adopted 21 July 1993, as amended 6 October 1997,[20] and the State

---

[20] The Law on State Secrets was published on 21 September 1993 in Российская газета [*Russian Newspaper*], but because the official gazette of the Congress of People's Deputies and Supreme Soviet was suspended as a result of the attempted coup, the official newspaper version was never gazetted elsewhere. When changes and additions were made to the Law of 6 October 1997, the

Programme for Ensuring the Defence of State Secrets in the Russian Federation for 1996–7, and others. Article 283 is directed towards preventing the divulgence of a State secret to any outside persons which in turn would facilitate the leaking of secrets abroad to the detriment of Russian security.

Divulgence is making known, whether in conversation, public address, publication in the press, correspondence, drawings, sketches, documents, or manufactures, or otherwise, information constituting a State secret as a result of which it became known to outside persons or became the weal thereof as a result of the transfer of materials or articles to them for familiarisation. Divulgence also may take the form of lost unrecorded notebooks or sheets with extracts from documents containing a State secret, or leaving secret documents unsupervised. Any person who does not have access to the particular information, even if cleared generally for State secrets, is considered to be an outside person. The offence may be committed either intentionally or through negligence.

The crime does not require that the guilty person be aware that the transfer or making known of secret information is capable of harming the security of the Russian Federation nor that the information will become the weal of a foreign state or organisation. Criminal responsibility attaches only to the person to whom it was entrusted or became known through service or work; persons who have knowledge of a State secret by other means, for example, finding secret documents or private conversations with co-workers of the entrusted person, are not liable for divulgence under Article 283.

The Criminal Code of the Russian Federation has narrowed the definition of the crime in comparison with the 1960 RSFSR Criminal Code (Article 75). Under the 1996 Code, it is essential that the State secret has become the weal of other persons, whereas under the 1960 RSFSR Criminal Code the crime was committed from the moment of divulgence, that is, from the moment when the information could have become the weal of other persons.

Inclining to Consumption of Narcotic Means or Psychotropic Substances

'Inclining' to consumption is an ambiguous concept which includes a specific type of incitement to consume and a variety of dissemination of the narcotic means or psychotropic substances concerned. It follows that 'inclining' requires active, rather than passive, actions on the part of the guilty person. Article 230 of the Criminal Code punishes 'inclining' without offering a definition of either the concept itself or of the specific means and forms of committing it. The term was

---

original version was gazetted for the first time in the weekly official gazette but not assigned an item number; instead the correct citation is to pp. 8220–8235. The Law making changes in the original version was fully gazetted in the normal way. See СЗ РФ (1997), no 41, item 4673. The 1997 changes substantially enlarged the list of State secrets.

first introduced to Russian criminal law by amendments made in the 1960 Criminal Code of the RSFSR in 1974 through the addition of Article 224.

In Russian judicial practice 'inclining' is understood to comprise any intentional actions directed towards initiating or stimulating in another person the wish to consume narcotic means or psychotropic substances by means of persuasion, offer, advice, deceit, mental or physical coercion, limitation of freedom, or other actions with a view to compelling a person to receive, accept, or take them.[21] There need not be repeated or multiple actions to incline; one action is sufficient. Reference is made in the plural to 'actions' in the Supreme Court Decree in order to indicate the multiplicity of ways in which 'inclining' may be achieved rather than to a requirement that two or more actions be committed. Accordingly, a single offer for consumption is sufficient for criminal responsibility under Article 230.

Most 'inclining' takes oral form or coincident actions, although symbolic signs and written forms are known and would qualify under Article 230. Consumption consists of the reception of narcotic means or psychotropic substances by any means, including injection, tablets or powder, inhaling, smoking, and others. Russian doctrinal writings disagree as to when commission of the crime is completed. Some specialists believe that achievement of the purpose of inclining is not necessarily essential, that is, the desire to consume is manifested; others believe the desire to consume must be manifested; and yet a third group considers that consumption must actually commence. Construing Article 230 formally, however, the crime is completed from the moment when actions commence which are directed towards initiating in another person the desire to consume the respective means or substances irrespective of whether the initiating person succeeded or not in creating a desire to consume, or whether there was any consumption.

Express or direct intent and a special purpose is required on the subjective side, to create in the victim the desire to consume the narcotic means or substance.

The formulation and application of Article 230 has created difficulties for certain remedial programs, such as harmless needle schemes, intended to reduce the incidence of HIV-related diseases in Russia.

---

[21] See point 14, Decree of the Plenum of the Supreme Court of the Russian Federartion, 27 May 1998, no 9.

IV

THE LAW AND FOREIGN RELATIONS

18

THE LAW RELATING TO FOREIGNERS AND FOREIGN AFFAIRS

The legal regulation of Russian foreign relations in the broadest sense of the term is governed by several thousand normative acts, including international treaties of the Russian Federation. Some are directly concerned with inter-state relations, for example, claims to sovereign rights, territory, the procedure for concluding international treaties or a legal definition of aggression, whereas others touch upon foreign relations in passing; for example, statutes on ministries, family, civil, criminal, citizenship, or other branches of legislation.

Russian legal doctrine does not look upon foreign relations law as a separate branch of law, and there are no official efforts underway in Russia comparable to those in the United States to systematise the core principles in a *Restatement of Foreign Relations Law*. Pending systematic law reform in this domain, it probably would be premature to consider such a project. Although new rules regulating foreign relations have been set out in the 1993 Russian Constitution, major enactments survive from the former Soviet Union, the RSFSR, and the Russian Federation before the Constitution was adopted, complicating the legal regime of foreign relations considerably.

A. Legal Status of Foreign Citizens and Stateless Persons

Article 62(3) of the 1993 Russian Constitution provides: 'Foreign citizens and stateless persons shall enjoy in the Russian Federation the rights and bear the duties equally with citizens of the Russian Federation except for instances established by a federal law or by an international treaty of the Russian Federation'. This formulation extended the principle of national regime to stateless persons and permitted exceptions from that principle only on the basis of a 'federal law', rather than previously on the basis of any 'act of legislation'.

The USSR Law on the Legal Status of Foreigners in the USSR, adopted 24 June 1981 (in force as from 1 January 1982), with the changes introduced on 15 August 1996, remained in force until 25 September 2002.[1] The 1981 Law was the first of its kind in Soviet history, giving legislative sanction for the first time to a number of rules previously existing as administrative practices. The 2002 Federal Law on the Legal Status of Foreign Citizens in the Russian Federation is the most ambitious enactment on the subject in Russian history.[2]

General provisions

Foreign citizens are defined in Russian legislation as a natural person who is not a citizen of the Russian Federation and has evidence of citizenship of a Foreign State. Their legal status is governed by the Russian Constitution and the constitutive documents of subjects of the Federation, the 2002 Law mentioned above, all relevant legislative acts and judicial practice, and by generally accepted principles and norms of international law and international treaties of the Russian Federation. The basic principle is that foreign citizens enjoy the same rights and freedoms and bear the same duties as Russian citizens unless Russian federal laws or international treaties of the Russian Federation provide otherwise.

Foreign citizens are equal irrespective of origin, social and property status, racial and nationality affiliation, sex, education, language, attitude towards religion, nature and character of occupation, and other circumstances. Reciprocal limitations may be placed on the exercise of these rights and freedoms by the Russian Government if Russian citizens are limited in their rights in a particular foreign country. While the formulation in the 1993 Russian Constitution 'equally, . . . except for' has been justly criticised as being simply inaccurate with respect to areas of Russian public law, for example, the right to hold public office, where foreigners have no such right, the principle of national regime does operate for

---

[1] BBC CCCP (1981), no 26, item 836; СЗ РФ (1996), no 34, item 4029.
[2] СЗ РФ (2002), no 30, item 3032.

the most part with respect to private law.[3] Article 2(1) of the Civil Code provides that 'the rules established by civil legislation shall apply to relations with the participation of foreign citizens, stateless persons, and foreign juridical persons unless provided otherwise by a federal law'. The exceptions to the principle of national regime comprise numerically speaking a tiny percentage of overall Russian normative acts, but are nonetheless sufficiently numerous to speak about the 'rights of foreigners' as a special regime.

On 17 February 1998 for the first time in Russian legal history a stateless person filed suit in the Constitutional Court of the Russian Federation requesting the Court to declare unconstitutional the provision (Article 31, paragraph two) of the 1981 Law on the Status of Foreign Citizens which permitted a stateless person to be detained for the period necessary in order to organise his deportation from the country. No limit on the period of detention was provided for in the Law, which was inconsistent with the constitutional provision stipulating that a person may not be held under guard for more than 48 hours without the decision of a court. The Court found in favour of the petitioner and decreed that the respective provision of the 1981 Law was unconstitutional.[4]

The particular rights enjoyed by foreign citizens and stateless persons in Russia depend partly upon whether they are permanently or temporarily resident or own property, and partly upon whether work permits or visa quotas are available for their respective employers.

Citizenship and asylum

A single Federation citizenship operates in the Russian Federation; each citizen of a republic within the Federation is simultaneously a citizen of the Russian Federation. The 1993 Constitution requires that such citizenship shall be uniform and equal irrespective of the grounds of acquisition, that each citizen shall possess on Russian territory all the rights and freedoms and bear equal duties as provided for by the Constitution, and that a citizen may not be deprived of his citizenship or of the right to change it. The details were elaborated in the Federal Law on Citizenship of the Russian Federation of 31 May 2002, in accordance with Article 6 of the 1993 Russian Constitution. The 2002 Federal Law replaced that of 28 November 1991, as amended on 17 June 1993 and 6 February 1995, and changed by Decree of the Constitutional Court of the RF of 16 May 1996.[5]

---

[3] See A L Makovskii, in Правовое положение иностранных граждан в России: сборник нормативных актов [*Legal Status of Foreign Citizens in Russia: Collection of Normative Acts*] (1996) xxv–xxvi.

[4] СЗ РФ (1998), no 9, item 1142.

[5] Ведомости СНД и ВС РФ (1992), no 6, item 243; (1993), no 29, item 1112. СЗ РФ (1995); no 7, item 496; (1996), no 21, item 2579. For the 2002 law on Citizenship, see СЗ РФ (2002), no 22, item 2031.

Bilateral international treaties modify its provisions under certain circumstances, as does the 1996 Convention on Regulating the Procedure for the Acquisition of Citizenship by Citizens of States-Participants of the Commonwealth of Independent States. A remarkably extensive range of acts was applicable to determining affiliation to citizenship of the Russian Federation: acts of legislation of the Russian Federation and republics within the Federation, international treaties of the Russian Federation, of the former Soviet Union, or of the Russian State which existed before 7 November (25 October) 1917 and which operated at the moment of the ensuing of the circumstances with which the affiliation of a person to citizenship of the Russian Federation is linked. The reference to treaties of Imperial Russia in the 1991 Law on Citizenship was perhaps unique in legislation of the Russian Federation.

The 2002 Federal Law on Citizenship applies the criteria of both *jus soli* and *jus sanguinis* for the acquisition of Russian citizenship, together with others. Four individual grounds for the acquisition of citizenship are enumerated. Citizenship was 'deemed' to exist for all citizens of the former Soviet Union permanently residing on the territory of the Russian Federation on the date that the 1991 Federal Law entered into force unless within one year thereafter they declared their wish not to be citizens of the Russian Federation. Persons born on 30 December 1922 (the date the Treaty of the Union entered into legal force) or later and who lost citizenship of the Soviet Union were regarded as having citizenship of the Russian Federation by birth if they were born on the territory of the Russian Federation or one of their parents at the moment of the birth of a child was a citizen of the Soviet Union and permanently resided on the territory of the Russian Federation. In this connection the 'territory of the Russian Federation' meant that territory at the time of their birth.

A child whose parents at the moment of birth were citizens of the Russian Federation is itself such citizen irrespective of the place of birth. If the parents were of different citizenship when the child was born, the citizenship of the child was determined irrespective of the place of birth by written agreement of the parents. In the absence of such agreement the child acquired the citizenship of the Russian Federation if it was born on the territory of Russia or if it otherwise became a stateless person. If one parent was a Russian citizen at the moment of birth and the other was stateless, the child is a Russian citizen irrespective of the place of birth. A child situated on Russian territory, both of whose parents are unknown, was a citizen of the Russian Federation; if one of the child's parents, trustee, or guardian was discovered the citizenship of the child could be changed in accordance with the 1991 Law. A child born on Russian territory of parents who were citizens of another State(s) was a citizen of the Russian Federation unless one of the other States granted citizenship to it, but if the child was born on Russian territory of stateless persons, it was a Russian citizen.

Citizenship also could be acquired by way of registration by persons whose spouse or relative by direct line of ascent is a citizen of Russia, or who at the moment of birth had a parent that was a citizen of the Russian Federation but who acquired another citizenship by birth, provided they registered within five years after reaching 18 years of age, or who were the children of former citizens of the Russian Federation born after their parents terminated Russian citizenship, provided they registered within five years after reaching 18 years of age.

Registration also was applicable to those who were citizens of the former USSR residing on the territory of States within the former USSR or who arrived to reside on the territory of the Russian Federation after 6 February 1992 provided that they declared their wish to be citizens of Russia before 31 December 2000. However, this provision of the 1991 Law as amended was declared unconstitutional by Decree of the Constitutional Court of the Russian Federation on 16 May 1996[6] insofar as it extended to persons born on territory which at the moment of their birth was part of the territory of the Russian Federation, were citizens of the former Soviet Union, did not freely express their wish to terminate affiliation to citizenship of the Russian Federation, previously had left for permanent residence beyond the limits of the Russian Federation but within the limits of the former USSR, and subsequently returned for permanent residence within the limits of the Russian Federation. Under a literal interpretation of the 1991 Law on Citizenship such persons, although born on Russian territory but beyond its limits, albeit within the former Soviet Union, when the Law on Citizenship entered into force, were required to reacquire Russian citizenship by way of registration. Living outside Russia was therefore being used as a criterion to override the fact they had been born on Russian territory, and it was this construction of the 1991 Law on Citizenship that was held to be unconstitutional as well as a violation of Article 15 of the 1948 Universal Declaration of Human Rights.

The registration procedure extended to stateless persons who on the date of entry into force of the 1991 Law on Citizenship resided permanently on the territory of the Russian Federation or other republics within the former Soviet Union as of 1 September 1991 if within one year after the entry of the said Law into force they declared their wish to acquire citizenship of the Russian Federation, and also to foreign citizens and stateless persons irrespective of their place of residence if either they themselves or one of their relatives by direct ascent were subjects or citizens of Russia by birth and if these persons within one year after entry of the 1991 Law on Citizenship into force declared their wish to acquire Russian citizenship.

Under the 2002 Federal Law on Citizenship, any foreign citizen or stateless persons 18 years of age or older who has dispositive legal capacity may apply to be admitted to Russian citizenship in the general procedure irrespective of origin,

---

6 СЗ РФ (1996), no 21, item 2579.

social status, racial and nationality affiliation, sex, education, language, attitude towards religion, or political and other convictions. Foreign citizens and stateless persons who seek Russian citizenship ordinarily are required to have had permanent residence on the territory of the Russian Federation for five years without interruption from the day of receiving a residence permit until the day of application. 'Without interruption' means the applicant has not been outside the Russian Federation for more than three months within a year. Reduced periods may apply to refugees, to former citizens of the Soviet Union or the Russian Federation, to individuals of high achievement in science, technology, and culture or who have a profession or skills of interest to the Russian Federation, or who have rendered service to the Russian Federation, who have been granted political asylum on Russian territory, and others. Citizenship may be refused to applicants who favour the forcible change of the constitutional system of Russia or other actions creating a threat to the security of the Russian Federation, or who have been convicted and served punishment in the form of deprivation of freedom for actions prosecuted under the laws of the Russian Federation, or who were deported from the Russian Federation in accordance with federal laws, or who used forged documents or communicated false information in their application, among others.

The citizenship of children follows the citizenship of their parents or sole parent; if the parents or sole parent terminate Russian citizenship, the child thereof also loses Russian citizenship unless the child would thereby become a stateless person. A change of citizenship by parents deprived of parental rights who change their citizenship does not automatically change the citizenship of their children.

Dual citizenship is prohibited unless international treaties of the Russian Federation provide otherwise. Under the 2002 Federal Law on Citizenship, citizens of Russia having another citizenship are regarded by the Russian Federation only as a citizen of the Russian Federation unless a treaty provides to the contrary. Russian citizens who live beyond the limits of Russia retain their citizenship. Individuals who make application for Russian citizenship are, as a rule, expected to give evidence of having made application to renounce any foreign citizenship which they may hold.

Citizenship may be terminated by withdrawal, repeal of the decision to admit to citizenship, or by way of optation (if the state affiliation of territory changes, for example). The termination of Russian citizenship automatically means termination of the citizenship of republics within the Russian Federation. Withdrawal occurs upon the petition of an individual who wishes to lose Russian citizenship or by way of registration under specified circumstances. Petitions to withdraw from citizenship will not be granted if the individual concerned has been called up to active military or alternative service or before such service ends, or if the individual has been accused in a criminal proceeding or has been convicted by a court, or does not have another citizenship nor guarantees of acquiring such. Decisions to admit to citizenship may be repealed if they were adopted on the basis of information known to be false or forged documents and a Russian court determines the fact of such falseness or forgery; the decision may be repealed only within a five-year period after being adopted.

The principal agencies involved in matters of citizenship are the President of the Russian Federation, the federal agency of executive power concerning with internal affairs and its territorial agencies, and the Ministry of Foreign Affairs, diplomatic representations, and consular establishments of Russia.

Asylum was provided for in all Soviet constitutions from 1917. The 1993 Russian Constitution speaks of 'political asylum', which may be granted to foreign citizens and stateless persons 'in accordance with generally-recognised norms of international law' (Article 63(1)). The Statute on the Procedure for Granting Political Asylum in the Russian Federation was confirmed by Edict of the President of the Russian Federation on 21 July 1997,[7] replacing a Statute of 1995.

The grounds for granting asylum have changed dramatically in comparison with the Soviet era, when asylum was fundamentally ideological in character. Russia will grant political asylum to persons seeking protection against persecution or a real threat of becoming a victim of persecution in the country of which he is a citizen or of his usual residence by reason of his socio-political activity or convictions which are not contrary to democratic principles recognised by the international community nor to norms of international law. The persecution must be directed expressly against the person seeking asylum. Political asylum is granted by Edict of the President of the Russian Federation, who has the right to take into account the State interests of Russia when deciding to grant asylum or not.

Individuals granted asylum are assimilated to the legal regime for foreign citizens. Political asylum of the Russian Federation is not to be granted under certain circumstances: if the person is persecuted for actions (or failure to act) deemed in the Russian Federation to be a crime or is guilty of the performance of actions which are contrary to the purposes and principles of the United Nations; the person is being brought as an accused in a criminal case or with respect to him there is a judgment of conviction which has entered into legal force and is subject to execution on the territory of the Russian Federation; the person has arrived from a third country where he is not threatened with persecution; the person arrived from a country with developed and stable democratic institutions in the domain of the defence of human rights; the person arrived from a country with which the Russian Federation has an agreement on crossing the boundaries without visas, without prejudice to the right of the particular person to asylum in accordance

---

[7] СЗ РФ (1997), no 30, item 3601.

with the Law of the Russian Federation on Refugees; the person provided information known to be false; the person has the citizenship of a third country where he is not being persecuted. A person may be deprived of the political asylum granted to him by the Russian Federation for considerations of State security, and also if this person engages in activity which is contrary to the purposes and principles of the United Nations or if he has committed a crime and with respect to him there is a judgment of conviction of a court which has entered into legal force and is subject to execution. The 1997 Statute also enumerates situations under which political asylum may be forfeited.

Political asylum will not be granted to persons who arrive from countries which have designated treaties with Russia, which means principally other CIS members; and the duty is expressly placed on the Russian Ministry of Foreign Affairs to produce an annual list of countries having democratic and stable systems.

Quite distinct from asylum is the status of a refugee in Russia. Border conflicts have produced a substantial flow of refugees, as have air connections with African and Asian countries. The Law on Refugees adopted 19 February 1993, as amended 28 June 1997, 21 July 1998, 7 August 2000, and 7 November 2000[8] defines a 'refugee' as a person who is not a citizen of the Russian Federation and who by virtue of entirely substantiated apprehensions of becoming a victim of persecution by reason of race, confession of faith, citizenship, nationality, affiliation to a particular social group, or political convictions is situated outside the country of his citizenship and cannot take advantage of the defence of that country or does not wish to take advantage of such defence as a consequence of such apprehensions or, not having a specific citizenship and being outside the country of his previous usual residence as a result of similar events, cannot or does not wish to return to it as a consequence of such apprehensions (Article 1).

A refugee may petition for refugee status and enjoys limited rights until his or her status is determined.

Entry and exit

Foreign citizens entering the Russian Federation require valid foreign passports or other valid identity documents and a visa issued by a Russian diplomatic or consular representation abroad unless an international treaty of the Russian Federation provides otherwise. As a rule, visas are obtained by application to Russian embassies or consulates abroad; the Russian Federation is the legal successor to Soviet bilateral treaties with some countries allowing simplified procedures or multiple entry-exit visas and has negotiated several such treaties itself.

---

[8] Ведомости СНД и ВС РФ (1993), no 12, item 425; СЗ РФ (1997), no 26, item 2956; (1998), no 30, item 3613; (2000), no 33, item 3348; no 46, item 4537.

Entry or exit-entry visas may be issued when foreigners resident in Russia travel abroad for a determined period. Transit passage without a visa is permitted in the case of a forced landing, approved air route, or pursuant to an international treaty.

The Law on the Procedure for Exit from the Russian Federation and Entry to the Russian Federation, of 18 July 1996, as amended 18 July 1998 and 24 June 1999,[9] enumerates four grounds upon which a foreign citizen or stateless person shall not be allowed to enter Russia: (1) for the purpose of ensuring the security of the State; (2) he was convicted during a previous sojourn in Russia of committing a grave or especially grave crime or was deported from Russia; (3) documents needed to support a visa application have not been submitted; and (4) failure to submit an AIDS certificate when that is required (Article 27). These grounds are exhaustive and make no reference, unlike Soviet enactments on the subject, to subordinate legislation.

Under international treaties crew members of foreign merchant and fishing vessels are allowed visa-free entry to Soviet ports under special passes; analogous arrangements exist for foreign airline personnel. Tourists on cruise or excursion vessels may be allowed shore visits of short duration without a visa.

Foreign citizens also require a valid passport and visa or other authorisation in order to leave the Russian Federation. Exit may be refused if the person has been detained on suspicion of committing a crime or been formally accused of such until a decision is taken with regard to the case or a judgment of a court has entered into legal force, or has been sentenced for a crime committed on Russian territory, until the sentence has been served. Exit also will be refused if the person has evaded the performance of obligations imposed by a court, which may include financial obligations, and if a person has failed to fulfil obligations to pay taxes to the Russian Federation.

Freedom of movement

In the post-Soviet era the freedom of foreigners to move about the territory of the Russian Federation has been substantially increased. The Law on the Right of Citizens of the Russian Federation to Freedom of Movement and Choice of Place of Sojourn and Residence Within the Limits of the Russian Federation, adopted 25 June 1993,[10] provides that persons who are not citizens of Russia and who are legally situated on Russian territory have the right to freedom of movement and to choice of place of sojourn and residence in accordance with the 1993 Russian Constitution and laws and international treaties of the Russian Federation.

---

[9] СЗ РФ (1996), no 34, item 4029; (1998), no 30, item 3606; (1999), no 26, item 3175. See A A Sumin, Комментарий к Федеральному закону 'О порядке выезда из Российской Федерации и въезда в Российскую Федерацию' [*Commentary on the Federal Law 'On the Procedure for Exit from the Russian Federation and Entry into the Russian Federation*] (2001).

[10] Ведомости СНД и ВС РФ (1993), no 32, item 1227. Also see Article 11, 2002 Law on the Legal Status of Foreign Citizens.

However, by Decree of 4 July 1992, as amended on 17 November 1994, 27 November 1995, 27 December 1997, 2 February 2000, 30 October 2001, and 29 April 2002, the Government of the Russian Federation confirmed a List of Territories of the Russian Federation which may be visited by foreign citizens only with special authorisation.[11]

Although formal enforcement has been held in abeyance, foreign citizens and stateless persons who arrive in Russia for a period exceeding three months may be required to submit a medical certificate confirming the absence of AIDS as a condition of receiving a visa in accordance with the Federal Law on the Prevention of the Dissemination in the Russian Federation of Diseases Causing Immune Deficiency Virus in a Person, of 30 March 1995, as amended 9 January 1997 and 7 August 2000.[12] Foreign citizens or stateless persons in Russia who are found to have AIDS are subject to deportation.

Customs rules

Foreigners who cross the Russian frontier are subject to customs control. When entering the Russian Federation, foreign citizens importing goods or currency in excess of stipulated minimums are required to complete a customs declaration in which they must itemise currency, precious metals or stones, manufactures therefrom, weapons, works of art, pieces of luggage, and the like. An identical form is completed upon departure. Russian currency may be imported and exported within certain limits, but there is no limitation upon foreign currency in the possession of foreign citizens provided that it was declared upon entering or is duly justified upon departing. Certain countries (China, for example) have bilateral treaties with Russia governing customs procedures.

Administrative responsibility

Foreign citizens and stateless persons are bound under the 1993 Russian Constitution to respect and comply with Russian legislation, and likewise are subject to administrative responsibility just as is every Russian citizen (see Chapter 6). Certain administrative offences and sanctions are applicable only to foreigners. Under the 2001 CAdV, administrative deportation of foreign citizens and stateless persons is a sanction applicable only to them (Article 3.10). A fine with or without administrative deportation may be applied to foreigners who violate the rules for the sojourn of foreign citizens in Russia (Article 18.8). Fines are applicable to violations of customs regulations, violations of the border regime in frontier zones, violations of the Air Code or the Merchant Shipping Code, and others.

---

[11] САПП РФ (1992), no 2, item 37; СЗ РФ (1994), no 31, item 3286; (1995), no 49, item 4805, (1998), no 1, item 142; (2000), no 6, item 775; (2001), no 45, item 4267; (2002), no 18, item 1764.
[12] СЗ РФ (1995), no 14, item 1212; (1997), no 3, item 352; (2000), no 33, item 3348; (2001), no 53(I), item 5025.

Administrative arrest is wholly applicable to foreigners when provided for by law, in which case consular access may be allowed by treaty or at the discretion of the Russian authorities.

Foreigners may be detained by other duly authorised Russian officials for particular infringements, including hunting and fishing inspectors, frontier guards, masters of ships or river vessels, the captain of an aircraft, and others. The procedures for boarding and arresting foreign non-military vessels in waters under Russian jurisdiction are laid down in the 1983 United Nations Convention on the Law of the Sea, to which the Russian Federation is a party, and the Law on the State Boundary of the Russian Federation, adopted 1 April 1993, as amended.

Civil law rights

The Civil Code of the Russian Federation provides that the rules of civil legislation apply to relations with the participation of foreign citizens, stateless persons, and foreign juridical persons unless provided otherwise by a federal law (Article 2). In a market economy this provision has taken on a wholly different dimension for foreign citizens. Foreigners may engage in entrepreneurial activity without the formation of a juridical person (Article 23, Civil Code), registering in accordance with the Statute on the Procedure for the State Registration of Subjects of Entrepreneurial Activity, confirmed by Edict of the President of the Russian Federation on 8 July 1994, as amended;[13] engage in urban construction activity, pursuant to the Urban Construction Code of the Russian Federation of 7 May 1998, as amended 30 December 2001;[14] engage in auditing activity under the Federal Law on Auditor Activity, of 7 August 2001, as amended;[15] create or join social associations in accordance with the Law on Social Associations of 19 May 1995, as amended;[16] participate in philanthropic activity pursuant to the Law on Philanthropic Activity and Philanthropic Organisations, adopted 7 July 1995, as amended 21 March 2002 and 25 July 2002;[17] purchase insurance on the basis of the Law on Insurance, adopted 27 November 1992, as amended 31 December 1997, 20 November 1999, and 21 March 2002;[18] participate in exploiting the mineral resources of the seabed beyond the limits of the continental shelf, in accordance with the Decree of the Government of the Russian Federation of 25 April 1995;[19]

---

[13] СЗ РФ (1994), no 11, item 1194; (2001), no 36, item 3543.
[14] СЗ РФ (1998), no 19, item 2069; (2002), no 1(I), item 2.
[15] СЗ РФ (2001), no 33(I), item 3422; no 51, item 4829.
[16] СЗ РФ (1995), no 21, item 1930; (1997), no 20, item 2231; (1998), no 30, item 3608; (2002), no 11, item 1018; no 12, item 1093; no 30, item 3029.
[17] СЗ РФ (1995), no 33, item 3340; (2002), no 12, item 1093; no 30, item 3029; transl in W E Butler, *Russian Commercial and Company Legislation* (2002).
[18] Ведомости СНД РФ (1993), no 2, item 56; СЗ РФ (1998), no 1, item 4; (1999), no 47, item 5622; (2002), no 12, item 1093.
[19] See The Programme of the Government of the Russian Federation 'Reforms and Development of the Russian Economy 1995–1997', confirmed by Decree No 439. СЗ РФ (1995), no 21, item 1966.

extract water biological resources under the Federal Law on the exclusive economic zone, among others.

Among the exceptions or limitations are the following: persons who have received medical or pharmaceutical training in foreign states must undergo examinations in Russian educational institutions; only Russian citizens may engage in folk healing; foreign correspondents of foreign mass media must be accredited in order to enjoy the rights of a journalist; foreigners are limited in their right to act as insurers, or to be architects, or to be livestock breeders. Only citizens of Russia may be members of a Russian flag vessel or Russian civil aircraft unless special exceptions are obtained. The profession of private detective is limited to Russian citizens, as is the profession of patent attorney.

Although the practice may vary from one region to another, foreigners have experienced difficulties in becoming landowners outside the process of privatisation, now likely to be eased in view of the 2001 Land Code. There are also limitations with respect to the subsoil, activities on the continental shelf, fishing within the exclusive economic zone, and others.

Succession

Under Part Three of the Civil Code of the Russian Federation, foreign citizens may inherit and bequeath property in accordance with legislation of the Russian Federation. A normative document of the Central Bank of the Russian Federation provides that amounts of money passing by way of inheritance may be transferred abroad in foreign currency without restriction.

Unless provided otherwise by an international treaty of the Russian Federation, the Civil Code of the Russian Federation provides that relations relating to inheritance are determined according to the law of the country where the testator had his last place of residence, with certain exceptions for immoveable property. When Russian law is applicable, the group of heirs under intestate succession is governed by Part Three of the Civil Code of the Russian Federation. Foreigners who are heirs of any priority take equally with Russian citizens of the same priority. Last place of permanent residence is crucial. In the absence of treaty provisions, where the inheritance is to be opened under Russian law, the commentators suggest, the basis for deciding the applicable law is determined by residence. Some international treaties of the Russian Federation invoke the distinction between movable and immovable property as the basis for deciding the applicable law. The Civil Code of the Russian Federation provides that the inheriting of immovable property situated in the Russian Federation is determined according to Russian law, including immovable property entered in a State register in the Russian Federation. The same Law determines the capacity of the person to draw up or revoke a will and the form of the will.

As for wills, the Civil Code of the Russian Federation provides that the capacity of a person to draw up and revoke a will, the form of the will, and the document revoking it are determined according to the law of the country where the testator had his permanent place of residence at the moment of drawing up the act. However, if the requirements of the law of the place of drawing up the document or the requirements of Russian law are satisfied, the will or revocation thereof may not be deemed invalid as a consequence of the failure to comply with the form. Bilateral treaties of the Russian Federation in some instances follow a different principle, and most consular conventions concluded by the former Soviet Union and inherited by the Russian Federation allow consuls of the sending state to draw up, certify, and keep wills under the laws of the state, sometimes specifying precisely where the consul may perform these activities.

Foreign heirs by operation of law or by will must accept an inheritance at the notarial office where the inheritance was opened or at a consular representation of the Russian Federation within the usual six-month period. Foreigners may inherit equally with Russian citizens.

Authors' rights

Foreigners and stateless persons may have authors' rights in the Russian Federation and bequeath or inherit such rights. The Law on Author's Right and Neighbouring Rights of 9 July 1993, as amended 19 July 1995,[20] provides that the protection of the works of foreign authors depends upon a number of conditions. The authors' rights of foreigners are recognised and protected for those works which are published on the territory of Russia or are not published but are situated on Russian territory in any objective form. In this respect the legal status of foreign authors does not differ from that of Russian authors; the principle of national regime applies. When the work of a foreign author is published or is situated in objective form beyond the limits of the Russian Federation, its protection in Russia is based on international treaties of the Russian Federation. Accordingly, works issued after 27 July 1973, the date of Soviet accession to the Universal Convention on Copyright, by citizens of states parties to the said Convention are protected in the Russian Federation. The 1993 Law on Author's Right has introduced a rule previously unknown to Soviet legislation whereby a work is considered to be published in the Russian Federation if within 30 days after first publication beyond the limits of Russia it was published on the territory of the Russian Federation.

Authors' rights are protected in the Russian Federation for the lifetime of the author plus 50 years after this death. Once that period has elapsed, the work enters

---

[20] Ведомости СНД РФ (1993), no 32, item 1242; СЗ РФ (1995), no 30, item 2866; transl in W E Butler, *Intellectual Property Law in the Russian Federation* (2002) 42–73.

the public domain and may be freely used by any person without the payment of a royalty. However, the right of authorship, of name, and of defence of the reputation of the author remain in force without period of time. No longer are works in the public domain considered to be in the ownership of the State. The Government of Russia may, however, require special payments to be made for the use of works on the territory of Russia which are in the public domain; such payments may not exceed 1 per cent of the profit received from the use of these works.

Patents

Under the Patent Law of the Russian Federation, adopted 23 September 1992, as amended,[21] foreign citizens and juridical persons enjoy the same rights under the Patent Law as do natural and juridical persons of the Russian Federation either by virtue of international treaties of the Russian Federation or on the basis of reciprocity (Article 36). Applications for the issuance of a patent are submitted in the Russian language, although other documents accompanying the application may be in Russian or another language; in the last instance, a Russian translation must be provided.

Natural persons residing outside the Russian Federation or foreign juridical persons or their patent attorneys are to operate through Russian patent attorneys in order to receive a patent or to maintain one in force.

The Russian Federation is a party by legal succession to the 1883 Paris Convention on Industrial Property, the 1970 Treaty on Patent Co-operation, the 1971 Strasbourg Agreement of International Patent Classification, and others.

Labour activity

The 2002 Law on the Legal Status of Foreign Citizens in the Russian Federation distinguishes between the labour rights of foreigners permanently resident in Russia and those temporarily resident. Under a market economy, although the distinction continues to have meaning, the context has changed drastically. An Edict of the President of the Russian Federation adopted 16 December 1993 on the Recruitment and Use in the Russian Federation of Foreign Work Force[22] introduced a system of authorisations for hiring foreigners and confirmations for those foreigners already employed. Authorisations to hire foreigners may be issued to Russian juridical persons, enterprises with foreign investments operating on Russian territory, and individual Russian and foreign natural persons who use hired labour. The system is administered by the Federal Migration Service.

There are a number of exceptions to the authorisations system, including individuals working on Russian territory pursuant to inter-state agreements; workers

---

[21] Ведомости СНД и ВС РФ (1992), no 42, item 2319. СЗ РФ (2001), no 1(I), item 2; no 53(I), item 5030; transl in Butler (n 20 above) 104–24.
[22] САПП РФ (1993), no 51, item 4934.

of diplomatic and consular institutions or other organisations enjoying diplomatic status; religious figures performing activities in officially registered religious organisations, crew members of Russian sea-going and river vessels; students in Russian educational institutions; accredited correspondents and journalists, lecturers and instructors in Russian academies and educational institutions, and others. Foreign personnel of accredited representations of foreign juridical persons fall under a special quota regime established when the representation office is formed. Exceptions also exist for secondments and other forms of temporary assignments.

As noted above, foreigners may not hold offices or employment which by law are linked with being a Russian citizen. Foreigners consequently may not hold elective office, nor serve as a crew member on a Russian flag vessel or aircraft (unless a special exception is obtained), engage in commercial fishing, or serve in law enforcement agencies. Individuals trained in medicine or pharmacy outside Russia may be admitted to their profession in the Russian Federation by special examination; foreigners who receive such training in Russian institutions may practise in accordance with their degree and title.

Foreign citizens and stateless persons who reside on the territory of Russia may join Russian trade unions except for instances established by federal laws or by international treaties of the Russian Federation, pursuant to the Law on Trade Unions, Their Rights, and Guarantees of Their Activity, of 12 January 1996, as amended 24 January 2002 and 21 March 2002.[23]

Foreign citizens who have entered into labour relations with an employer enjoy the full protection of Russian labour legislation. Some foreigners choose to perform services on the basis of an independent work contract, governed by the Civil Code, instead of a labour contract. Foreigners are in principle eligible for State pension insurance, State benefits for citizens having children, and other social security unless provided otherwise by international treaties of the Russian Federation.

Criminal law and procedure

The scope of Russian criminal law extends fully to foreigners and stateless persons who are present on Russian territory (see Chapter 17). Certain articles of the Criminal Code extend only to foreigners; for example, espionage.

Foreign citizens enjoy procedural rights in court on the same basis as Russian citizens (see Chapter 7). The 1976 Consular Statute of the USSR and all bilateral consular conventions to which Russia is a party, including by right of legal succession, make provision for consular access to and defence of the rights of citizens who may be arrested or detained in other form. The consular conventions differ

---

[23] СЗ РФ (1996), no 3, item 148; (2002), no 3, item 148, no 12, item 1093.

in the specificity and time limits within which consular access must be granted, and whether a consul may visit persons serving sentence.

Other rights and freedoms

Marriage and family relations have been treated in Chapter 10. The Law of the Russian Federation on Education, adopted 10 July 1992, as amended 13 January 1996 and 16 November 1997, 20 July 2000, 7 August 2000, 29 December 2001, 13 February 2002 and 25 June 2002,[24] provides that foreign social and private foundations, and foreign citizens, may be founders of an educational institution in Russia. Foreigners and stateless persons have equal rights with Russian citizens in the sphere of cultural activity unless established otherwise by laws of the Russian Federation or of republics within the Federation, pursuant to the Fundamental Principles of Legislation of the Russian Federation on Culture, adopted 9 October 1992, as amended 23 March 1999, 27 December 2000, and 30 December 2001 (Article 19).[25] Foreign scholars may be appointed professor or docent if they are invited to teach in institutions of higher education.

Foreign citizens situated on Russian territory are guaranteed the right to health protection in accordance with international treaties of the Russian Federation. This provision of the Fundamental Principles of Legislation of the Russian Federation on Protection of the Health of Citizens, adopted 22 July 1993, as amended 2 March 1998, 20 December 1999, and 2 December 2000,[26] limits the rights of foreigners in comparison with the Soviet era. Stateless persons, on the other hand, who reside permanently in Russia, and refugees enjoy the right to health protection equally with Russian citizens unless international treaties provide otherwise.

Foreigners do not enjoy the right to vote in elections for State office or in all-people's referendums, and they are exempt from the duty to perform military service in the Russian Armed Forces.

B. Application of Foreign Law

The law applicable to civil-law relations with the participation of foreign citizens or foreign juridical persons, or civil-law relations complicated by 'another foreign

---

[24] Ведомости СНД РФ (1992), no 30, item 1797; СЗ РФ (1996), no 3, item 150; (1997), no 47, item 5341; (1999), no 28, item 3493; (2000), no 30, item 3120; no 33, item 3348; (2001), no 53(I), item 5025; (2002), no 7, item 631, no 26, item 2517.

[25] Ведомости СНД и ВС РФ (1992), no 46, item 2615; СЗ РФ (1999), no 26, item 3172; (2001), no 1(I), item 2; no 53(I), item 5030; (2002), no 1(I), item 2.

[26] Ведомости СНД и ВС РФ (1993), no 33, item 1318; СЗ РФ (1998), no 10, item 1143; (1999), no 51, item 6289; (2000), no 49, item 4740.

element' is regulated by Part Three of the Civil Code of the Russian Federation, and by Section VII of the Family Code of the Russian Federation (Articles 156–167), and international treaties of the Russian Federation. The basic approach is that foreign law is applicable to civil-law relations when legislative acts or international treaties of the Russian Federation so provide, or on the basis of agreement of the parties which is not contrary to Russian legislation or international treaties, or when international customs recognised in the Russian Federation so stipulate (Article 1186, Civil Code). Foreign law may not be applied in violation of Russian public policy (see below). The determination of the law subject to application by the international commercial arbitration tribunal is established by the Federal Law on International Commercial Arbitration.

The Civil Code requires that legal concepts be interpreted according to Russian law unless provided otherwise by a law; foreign law may be used when construing legal concepts which are unknown to Russian law, or are known in another meaning, or cannot be determined by means of an interpretation in accordance with Russian law. Individual provisions address reciprocity, renvoi, the procedures for determining the substance of foreign law, the application of imperative norms of law, and retorsion.

The personal lex of a natural person is the jus of the country of which he is a citizen; in the event of dual citizenship, one of which is Russian, Russian jus is considered to be the individual's personal lex, and the same applies if a foreign citizen has a place of residence in the Russian Federation. The civil-law capacity of a natural person is determined by his personal lex, although foreign citizens and stateless persons, while in Russia, enjoy civil-law capacity equally with Russian citizens except for instances established by a law.

The personal lex of a juridical person is the jus of the country where the juridical person was founded. The personal lex of a juridical person is used to determine the status of an organisation as a juridical person, the organisational-legal form of the juridical person, the requirements for the name of a juridical person, issues of the creation, reorganisation, liquidation, and legal succession of a juridical person, the content of the legal capacity of a juridical person, the procedure by which a juridical person acquires civil rights and assumes civil duties, internal relations of the juridical person, including those between the participants thereof and the juridical person, and the capacity of a juridical person to be liable for its obligations. A foreign organisation which is not a juridical person has as its personal lex the jus of the country where it was founded.

The content of the right of ownership to property is determined by the law of the country where such property is situated, as is whether property should be considered to be movable or immovable; however, the right of ownership to means of transport subject to State registration is determined according to the law of the country where such registration has been made. When the right of ownership arises or terminates is determined by the law of the country where the property was situated at the moment when the action or other circumstance occurred that served as the grounds for the right of ownership to arise or terminate unless Russian legislation provides otherwise. Individual rules provide for property which is the subject of a transaction, or is en route under a foreign economic transaction, or is the subject of demands. The form of a transaction is governed by the law of the place where it is concluded, but if concluded abroad may not be deemed invalid if the requirements of form of Russian law have been complied with. The form of foreign economic transactions concluded by Russian juridical and natural persons is determined by Russian legislation irrespective of where concluded. The rights and duties of the parties under a transaction are determined by the law of the place where it was concluded unless the parties provide otherwise; however, the place of concluding the transaction is determined by Russian law.

Russian law is principally dispositive with respect to the rights and duties of parties under foreign economic transactions, the parties being allowed to choose the applicable law. If the parties fail to so choose, the Civil Code makes this determination with respect to certain types of contract. In the case of obligations arising out of the causing of harm, the rights and duties of the parties are determined according to the law of the country where the action or other circumstance occurred which serves as the grounds for the demand for compensation. In the case of unjust enrichment, the law of the country where the enrichment occurred is the applicable law. Relations relating to inheritance are regulated by the law of the country where the testator had his last place of permanent residence.

The choice of law provisions must be read against Article 15(4) of the 1993 Russian Constitution. Russian judicial practice confirms that under a foreign economic transaction in which the parties have chosen Russian law as the applicable law, the parties have automatically included all international treaties of the Russian Federation since, according to Article 15(4) of the Russian Constitution and Article 7(1) of the Civil Code of the Russian Federation, these treaties are an integral part of the Russian legal system. Therefore, where the states of the parties concerned are both parties to an international treaty of relevance to the transaction, the treaty must be applied to the transaction. The choice of Russian law means 'the choice of the Russian legal system, and not individual laws regulating respective relations of the parties . . . when disputed questions are not regulated by an international treaty, the court shall apply the norms of municipal Russian Civil Law, including the norms of the Civil Code of the Russian Federation'.[27]

---

[27] See the Information Letter of the Supreme Arbitrazh Court of the Russian Federation, No 29, of 16 February 1998. Вестник Высшего Арбитражного Суда Российской Федерации [*Herald of the Supreme Arbitrazh Court of the Russian Federation*], no 4 (1998) 45–46.

C. Public Policy (*ordre publique*)

The Civil Code of the Russian Federation (Article 1193), the Family Code of the Russian Federation, and the MShC all contain public policy clauses. Of these the most recent is that contained in the Civil Code, which provides: 'Norms of foreign law subject to application in accordance with the rules of the present Section shall not be applied in exceptional instances when the consequences of the application thereof would clearly be contrary to the foundations of the legal order (public policy) of the Russian Federation. In this event the respective norm of Russian law shall be applied when necessary' (Article 1193). Russian commentators stress that the legislator has in view not a contradiction between a foreign law and the Russian system, but an application of that law. The classic textbook example is a foreign law permitting polygamous marriage. Even though polygamy is not permitted in the Russian Federation, Russian law would not deny alimony to the members of a polygamous marriage on the grounds of public policy. In practice, there have been few cases where public policy has been invoked under Russian law. On 15 November 1996 an arbitrazh court ruled that a violation of Russian currency legislation is a breach of public policy sufficient to make a contract with a foreign investor invalid.[28] The commentators stress that a differentiated approach must be taken to public policy matters. Thus, a polygamous marriage duly registered in a foreign state would be recognised in Russia, as would a child marriage, but citizens of a foreign State which permitted polygamous or child marriages would not, on public policy grounds, be permitted to register such a marriage in the Russian Federation.[29]

D. International Law and the Russian Legal System

Article 15(4) of the 1993 Russian Constitution provides: 'Generally-recognised principles and norms of international law and international treaties of the Russian Federation shall be an integral part of its legal system. If other rules have been established by an international treaty of the Russian Federation than provided for by a law, the rules of the international treaty shall apply'. This language has been carried over, with slight adjustments, to the 1995 Law on Treaties (Article 5). The formal recognition of generally recognised principles and norms of international law, that is, customary rules of international law, to be an integral part of the Russian legal system is one of the most momentous changes of the twentieth

---

[28] Translated in *Sudebnik*, II (1997), 435–441.
[29] See I V Panteleeva, in P V Krasheninnikov and P I Sedugin (eds), Комментарий к Семейному кодексу Российской Федерации [*Commentary on the Family Code of the Russian Federation*] (1997) 314–315.

619

century in the development of Russian law. While one may dispute as to which rules are generally recognised, Russian doctrinal writings have pointed expressly to the 1966 Covenant on Civil and Political Rights as containing rules which are deemed to be generally recognised, whereas its sister 1966 Covenant on Economic and Social Rights, given the objections to certain clauses by ratifying states, is regarded as containing treaty norms binding only upon the states-parties. There also is support for regarding the 1948 Universal Declaration of Human Rights, technically only a Resolution of the United Nations General Assembly and therefore having only recommendatory force, as containing norms of general international law because the State practice of the international community has so deemed them to be. Even those customary international legal norms of purely an inter-state character, it is suggested, by becoming part of the Russian legal system acquire a 'new legal quality', a constitutional guarantee of compliance by Russian State agencies with those norms.[30] Examples already exist of the Constitutional Court of the Russian Federation citing generally recognised principles of inter-national law and the 1970 Declaration of the Principles of International Law.

A judge of the Constitutional Court has written that:

> Generally-recognised principles and norms of international law, and also inter-national treaties of Russia, are applied by the Constitutional Court of Russia as being norms incorporated into national law. This incorporation is a variety of general incorporation. This means that any principles and norms of international law which are generally recognised in international relations are part of the Russian legal system. These are not only those generally-recognised principles and norms which are applied by States in the modern period, but also those which emerge in the future . . . The introduction of new generally-recognised international legal principles and norms into the system of Russian national law is effectuated, thus, automatically.[31]

Although generally recognised norms of international law are part of the Russian legal system, their precise place in that system is not determined by the 1993 Russian Constitution. Depending upon their subject matter, generally recognised norms of international law appear to enjoy two separate statuses in the Russian legal system. The 1993 Russian Constitution placed human rights at the very foundation of the legal system, stipulating that those basic rights and freedoms set out in the Constitution must not be interpreted as a denial of or impingement on other generally recognised rights and freedoms of man and citizen and that laws repealing or reducing the rights and freedoms of man and citizen may not be adopted (Article 55). Article 17 of the 1993 Russian Constitution further pro-

---

[30] See I I Lukashuk, in V P Zvekov and B I Osminin (eds), Комментарий к Федеральному закону 'О международных договорах Российской Федерации' [*Commentary on the Federal Law 'On International Treaties of the Russian Federation'*] (1996) 15–16.

[31] See O I Tiunov, 'Конституционный суд Российской Федерации и международное право' ['Constitutional Court of the Russian Federation and International Law'], Российский ежегодник международного права 1995 [*Russian Yearbook of International Law 1995*] (1996) 180.

vides that 'The rights and freedoms of man and citizen shall be recognised and guaranteed in the Russian Federation according to generally recognised principles and norms of international law and in accordance with the present Constitution'. This formulation places international law ahead of the Constitution and, in so doing, confers upon international law a special status in the Russian legal system. That same status is not accorded to other generally recognised norms of international law.

The proviso that international treaties of the Russian Federation take precedence over an inconsistent law was known to Soviet law but in Russia has been elevated for the first time to a rule of constitutional stature. The rule is repeated in dozens of other federal laws and codes, although by reason of the constitutional stature and generality of the rule, such repetition would appear to be superfluous. A literal interpretation of the provision requires that it extend to all treaties of the Russian Federation, including intergovernmental and interdepartmental. Some Russian jurists have taken the view that this point, read against Article 15(1) of the 1995 Law on Treaties, must be construed to mean that only ratified treaties take precedence over laws of the RF, with the result that treaties which are not subject to ratification fall outside the scope of Article 15(4) of the 1993 Russian Constitution and Article 5(1) of the 1995 Law on Treaties. This view was accepted in a Decree of the Plenum of the Supreme Court of the Russian Federation adopted on 31 October 1995, which provided that other rules of a treaty are subject to application only if the decision concerning consent to such rules being binding was adopted in the form of a federal law. Views among Russian jurists continue to be divided, although a literal interpretation of the Constitution would appear to provide unequivocally that all treaties of the Russian Federation take precedence over inconsistent laws of the Russian Federation and subjects of the Federation.

E. International Treaties

The Russian Federation has taken a fundamentally different approach to the sources of international law and to the role of treaties in domestic Russian law since the demise of the former Soviet Union.[32] The Soviet Union acceded to the 1969 Vienna Convention on the Law of Treaties with effect from 29 April 1986.[33] Although a 1978 USSR Law on the Procedure for the Conclusion, Execution, and Denunciation of International Treaties of the USSR[34] had reflected the 1969

---

[32] See W E Butler, *The Law of Treaties in Russia and Other Member Countries of the Commonwealth of Independent States* (2002).

[33] See A N Talalaev, Венская конвенция о праве международных договоров. Комментарий' [*The Vienna Convention on the Law of International Treaties: Commentary*] (1997).

[34] Ведомости Верховного Совета СССР (1978), no 28, item 439; transl in *International Legal Materials*, XVII (1978), 1115–1122; Butler (n 32 above).

Vienna Convention to a considerable extent, the 1995 Federal Law on International Treaties of the Russian Federation[35] is the first to reflect fully the 1969 Vienna Convention and the new status of international treaties in the Russian legal system pursuant to the 1993 Russian Constitution. Some account is taken in the 1995 Law on Treaties of the 1986 Vienna Convention on the Law of Treaties Between States and International Organisations or Between International Organisations. The Russian Federation is not a party to the 1978 Vienna Convention on the Legal Succession of States with Respect to Treaties.

The 1995 Law on Treaties incorporates and adapts to Russian circumstances the definition of a treaty contained in the 1969 Vienna Convention. The distinction is preserved in the 1995 Law on Treaties among inter-state, intergovernmental, and interdepartmental treaties of the Russian Federation. Inter-state treaties are those concluded in the name of the highest agencies of State power—the State in the person of the President in the name of the Russian Federation. Intergovernmental treaties are those concluded in the name of the Government of the Russian Federation, whereas those concluded in the name of federal agencies of executive power are treaties of an intergovernmental character. The expression 'international treaty' was introduced systematically in Soviet law on the basis of the 1978 Law on Treaties and has been carried over in the 1995 Law on Treaties. Whether a particular treaty falls into one or the other of the three categories is a matter partly for the 1993 Russian Constitution, the jurisdiction of the State agencies concerned, and policy decisions by the governments concerned.

F. Territory

The spatial limits of Russian frontiers are defined in the Law on the State Boundary of the Russian Federation of 1 April 1993, as amended 10 August 1994, 29 November 1996, 19 July 1997, 24 July 1998, 31 July 1998, 31 May 1999, 5 August 2000, 7 November 2000, 24 March 2001, 30 December 2001, and 24 December 2002.[36] The State boundary is defined in the 1993 Law as the line and the perpendicular surface passing along this line which determines the limits of State territory (land, waters, subsoil, and air space) of the Russian Federation, that is 'the spatial limit of the operation of State sovereignty of the Russian Federation' (Article 1). The State boundary of the Russian Federation is the boundary of the RSFSR consolidated by international treaties in force and by

---

[35] СЗ РФ (1995), no 29, item 2757; transl in Butler (n 32 above).

[36] Ведомости СНД и ВС РФ (1993), no 17, item 594; СЗ РФ (1994), no 16, item 1861; (1996), no 50, item 5610; (1997), no 29, item 3507; (1998), no 31, items 3805 and 3831; (1999), no 23, item 2808; (2000), no 32, item 3341; no 46, item 4537; (2001), no 51, item 4830; (2002), no 1(I), item 2; no. 52.

legislative acts of the former Soviet Union. Where the boundary with adjacent States has not been formalised under international law, it is subject to being consolidated by treaty.

Unless provided otherwise by international treaties of the Russian Federation, the land boundary is demarcated along characteristic points or relief lines or clearly visible orientation points; the boundary at sea is the outward limit of the territorial sea of the Russian Federation; on navigable rivers, along the middle of the principal channel or *thalweg*; and detailed provisions address the situation on non-navigable rivers, border lakes, hydro-installations, rail and road bridges, and the like.

The Russian Federation became a party to the 1982 United Nations Convention on the Law of the Sea with effect from 11 April 1997.[37] Pursuant to the Convention, the Russian Federation adopted the Federal Law on Internal Sea Waters, Territorial Sea, and Contiguous Zone of the Russian Federation, of 31 July 1998.[38] The Russian Federation has a territorial sea of 12 nautical miles calculated from the lowest ebb-tide line on the mainland and around islands which belong to the Russian Federation or from straight baselines joining appropriate points whose geographic coordinates have been confirmed by the Government of the Russian Federation. In individual instances, for example, with Finland, the breadth of the territorial sea may be established by international treaties or, in the absence thereof, in accordance with generally recognised principles and norms of international law.

Also part of Russian territory are internal waters, which under the 1998 Law encompass sea waters situated landward of straight baselines for calculating the breadth of the territorial waters of the Russian Federation; port waters; the waters of bays, inlets, coves, and estuaries whose entire coast belongs to the Russian Federation up to a straight line drawn from shore to shore in a place where, seaward, one or several passages are first formed, if the breadth of each of these does not exceed 24 nautical miles; the waters of bays, inlets, coves, and estuaries, seas, and straits historically belonging to the Russian Federation, a list of which is announced by the Government of the Russian Federation; and the waters of rivers, lakes, and other waters whose shores belong to the Russian Federation. Russian legislation has designated certain specific waters to be historic bays or straits, and Russian international lawyers sometimes have mentioned others.[39] The Northern Sea Route is an internal cabotage route extending from the port of St Petersburg to Vladivostok along the Arctic and Pacific coasts of the Russian

---

[37] The Federal Assembly ratified the Convention on 21 February 1997 with a Statement Concerning the Application of Certain Articles. СЗ РФ (1997), no 9, item 1013. The official Russian text of the Convention is published in СЗ РФ (1997), no 48, item 5493.

[38] СЗ РФ (1998), no 31, item 3833.

[39] See W E Butler, *The Soviet Union and the Law of the Sea* (1971); id, *Northeast Arctic Passage* (1978); id (ed), *The USSR, Eastern Europe, and the Development of the Law of the Sea* (1983).

Federation and within the joint jurisdiction, as a transport route, between the Russian Federation and contiguous subjects of the Russian Federation. The Republic Sakha (Iakutia) concluded on 28 June 1995 an Agreement with the Russian Federation demarcating powers over the administrative system of the Northern Sea Route.

Russian legislation lays down neither an upward boundary for air space nor a downwards boundary for the subsoil. Non-military vessels and warships enjoy the right of innocent passage through the territorial sea of the Russian Federation on condition of compliance with generally recognised principles and norms of international law, international treaties of the Russian Federation, and also legislation of the Russian Federation. Passage is peaceful if it does not disturb the peace, good order, or security of the Russian Federation. Violations of the State boundary regime can result in administrative or criminal sanctions which, in the case of illegal fishing, for example, may entail large fines or confiscation of the vessel.

The sovereign rights and jurisdiction of the Russian Federation over the continental shelf is regulated by the 1982 Convention on the Law of the Sea and by the Federal Law on the Continental Shelf of the Russian Federation, of 30 November 1995, as amended.[40] The Law contains (Article 6) an exhaustive enumeration of the competence of federal agencies of State power over the continental shelf, which allows for competence of subjects of the Federation whose coasts are adjacent to the sea. However, the competence of subjects of the Federation to conclude international treaties with respect to the shelf and activity thereon is excluded. The civil and commercial implications of continental shelf legislation have been addressed in an unpublished Letter issued by the Supreme Arbitrazh Court to lower arbitrazh courts on 15 February 1996, No C5–7/03–85. Information concerning the subsoil of the continental shelf may be exported only under license of the Ministry of Foreign Economic Activity issued on the basis of decisions adopted by the Committee of the Russian Federation for Geology and Use of the Subsoil (Roskomnedra).[41] Licenses for the right to use the subsoil of the continental shelf are formalised according to the established procedure for the State registration of licenses with certain modifications introduced by Roskomnedra.[42] On 16 June 1997 the Government of the Russian Federation adopted a Decree on the Procedure for Confirming the Geographic Coordinates of Points Determining the Line of the Outward Boundaries of the Continental Shelf of the Russian Federation.[43]

---

[40] СЗ РФ (1995), no 49, item 4694; (1999), no 7, item 879; (2001), no 33(I), items 3413 and 3429; (2002), no 1(I), item 4.

[41] See the Letter of the State Customs Committee of the Russian Federation, 16 June 1996, No 01–15/10319, unpublished.

[42] See the Letters of Roskomnedra No BO–61/2296, dated 10 September 1992 and No VD–47/584, dated 15 March 1993, both unpublished.

[43] СЗ РФ (1997), no 25, item 2939.

On the basis of the Law on the Continental Shelf, the Government of the Russian Federation has confirmed the Procedure for the Use of Weapons by Warships and Flying Apparatus of the Federal Border Service of the Russian Federation when Protecting the Continental Shelf of the Russian Federation in a Decree adopted 14 October 1996, No 1208, as amended 9 September 1999.[44] Weapons may be used against offending vessels in reply to the use of force by them, and in other exceptional instances when pursuing such vessels in accordance with international law by hot pursuit and all other measures under the circumstances have been exhausted which were necessary in order to terminate the violation and detain the offending vessel. Portions of this document are classified for official use only.

The Russian Federation has inherited an exclusive economic zone of 200 miles measured from the same baselines as the territorial sea, which was established by Edict of the Presidium of the Supreme Soviet of the USSR 'On the Economic Zone of the USSR', adopted 28 February 1984.[45] At present the status of and the sovereign rights and jurisdiction of the Russian Federation with respect to the exclusive economic zone are regulated by the 1982 Convention on the Law of the Sea and by the Federal Law on the Exclusive Economic Zone of the Russian Federation, of 17 December 1998, as amended.[46] The exclusive economic zone is defined as the maritime area beyond the limits of the territorial sea of the Russian Federation and adjacent thereto having a special legal regime established by the Federal Law of 17 December 1998, international treaties of the Russian Federation, and norms of international law.

Quotas for catches or the extraction of water biological resources within the exclusive economic zone, as well as internal sea waters and the territorial sea, are confirmed annually by the Government of the Russian Federation pursuant to a Decree of 27 December 2000.[47] The Rules for the Registration of Licences (or Authorisations) for Trade in Water Biological Resources in the Exclusive Economic Zone of the Russian Federation Issued to Russian and Foreign Juridical Persons and Citizens were confirmed on 12 February 2001 by the Russian Government.[48] Marine research in the Russian exclusive economic zone may be conducted on the basis of requests submitted pursuant to Rules confirmed by a Decree of 28 March 2001.[49]

The activity of Russian natural and juridical persons, irrespective of forms of ownership, including with the participation of foreign natural and juridical persons,

---

[44] СЗ РФ (1996), no 42, item 4806; (1999), no 38, item 4541.
[45] Свод законов СССР [Digest of Laws of the USSR], IV 548–1.
[46] СЗ РФ (1998), no 51, item 6273; (2001), no 33(I), item 3429; (2002), no 1(I), item 4; no 13, item 1093.
[47] СЗ РФ (2001), no 1(I), item 136.
[48] СЗ РФ (2001), no 8, item 753.
[49] СЗ РФ (2001), no 15, item 1490.

relating to the exploration and exploitation of mineral resources of the seabed beyond the limits of the continental shelf is, according to the Edict of the President of the Russian Federation on the Activity of Russian Natural and Juridical Persons Relating to the Prospecting and Exploitation of Mineral Resources of the Seabed Beyond the Limits of the Continental Shelf adopted 22 November 1994[50] and the Decree of the Government of the Russian Federation on the Procedure for Effectuating the Activity of Russian Natural and Juridical Persons Relating to Exploitation of Mineral Resources of the Seabed Beyond the Limits of the Continental Shelf, No 410,[51] to be effectuated in accordance with generally recognised principles and norms of international law, international treaties, and legislation of the Russian Federation. Such activity is regulated by the Committee of the Russian Federation for Geology and Use of the Subsoil by agreement with the Ministry of Foreign Affairs of the Russian Federation and other interested federal agencies of executive power.

G. Diplomatic and Consular Law

The central agencies of State power and administration of the Russian Federation concerned with conducting foreign relations are several. Under the 1993 Russian Constitution, the Russian Federation itself has jurisdiction over the foreign policy and international relations of the Russian Federation, international treaties of the Russian Federation; questions of war and peace; foreign economic relations of the Russian Federation; defence and security, determination of the status and defence of the State boundary, territorial sea, airspace, exclusive economic zone, and continental shelf of the Russian Federation (Article 71). However, the Russian Federation shares jurisdiction with the subjects of the Federation with regard to the coordination of international and foreign economic relations of subjects of the Russian Federation and the fulfilment of international treaties of the Russian Federation (Article 72, 1993 Russian Constitution).

The President of the Russian Federation, as the Head of State, determines the basic orientations of foreign policy of the State and represents the Russian Federation in international relations (Article 80, 1993 Russian Constitution). He appoints and recalls diplomatic representatives of the Russian Federation to foreign states and international organisations (Article 83, 1993 Russian Constitution), guides the foreign policy of the Russian Federation, conducts negotiations and signs international treaties, signs instruments of ratification, and accepts credentials and letters of recall of diplomatic representatives accredited to him (Article 86, 1993 Russian Constitution).

---

[50] СЗ РФ (1994), no 31, item 3252.
[51] СЗ РФ (1995), no 18, item 1675.

The chambers of the Federal Assembly adopt laws, inter alia, concerning the ratification and denunciation of international treaties of the Russian Federation, the status and defence of the State boundary of the Russian Federation, and war and peace (Article 106, 1993 Russian Constitution). The Government of the Russian Federation effectuates measures relating to the realisation of the foreign policy of the Russian Federation (Article 114, 1993 Russian Constitution). The jurisdiction of the Constitutional Court of the Russian Federation extends to international treaties of the Russian Federation which have not entered into legal force (Article 125, 1993 Russian Constitution). Ministries, State committees, and departments conduct foreign relations as determined by their respective statutes, and virtually all have some foreign relations function. The principal department concerned, however, is the Ministry of Foreign Affairs.

The Statute on the Ministry of Foreign Affairs (MID) was confirmed by Edict of the President of the Russian Federation on 14 March 1995, as amended 4 June 2001 and 16 September 2002.[52] The principal tasks of the Ministry include working out and submitting to the President the general strategy for foreign policy, realisation of the foreign policy course, coordination of international links of subjects of the Federation, ensuring the diplomatic protection of the interests of Russia, protecting the rights and interests of citizens and juridical persons of the Russian Federation abroad, coordinating the activity of and control over the work of federal agencies of executive power in the domain of foreign relations, and maintaining diplomatic and consular relations of Russia with foreign states and international organisations (point 4). In the legal sphere the MID works out draft international treaties, watches over compliance with treaties, participates in the preparation of proposals for bringing Russian legislation into conformity with international legal obligations, ensures the operation of a unified system for the registration and recording of treaties, keeps originals and official copies of treaties, and watches over the conformity of draft treaties to legislation of the Russian Federation and international law.

Given the large number of State agencies and subjects of the Federation which have a role in foreign affairs, the President of the Russian Federation, to whom MID is responsible, has accentuated the central role of MID in coordinating a unified foreign policy of the Russian Federation. The institutional channels and responsibilities of MID are elaborated in an Edict of the President adopted 12 March 1996 'On the Coordinating Role of the Ministry of Foreign Affairs of the Russian Federation in Conducting the Unified Foreign Policy Line of the Russian Federation'.[53] Procedural limits within which federal agencies of executive power

---

[52] СЗ РФ (1995), no 12, item 1033; (2001), no 23, item 2329.

[53] СЗ РФ (1996), no 12, item 1061. To this end MID may open representations on the territories of subjects of the Russian Federation to assist them in their foreign relations pursuant to a Statute confirmed on 11 March 2002. See Российская газета [*Russian Newspaper*], 8 May 2002, p 11.

and subjects of the Federation must react to queries and requests of MID are laid down in the Decree of the Government of the Russian Federation adopted 14 March 1997. Federal agencies of executive power and Russian State institutions were given the right, by decision of the President of the Russian Federation, to send their own personnel to be attached to Russian embassies abroad or to open their own representations pursuant to an Edict of the President of the Russian Federation adopted 14 June 1997 'On the Organisation and Procedure for the Effectuation by Federal Agencies of Executive Power and Russian State Institutions of Functions Connected with Activity Abroad'.[54]

Rather unusually in State practice, the status of a Russian embassy has been the subject of special legislation. By Edict of the President of the Russian Federation adopted 28 October 1996 the Statute on an Embassy of the Russian Federation was confirmed.[55] An embassy is defined as a State agency of foreign relations of the Russian Federation effectuating the representation of the Russian Federation in the receiving state. It is within the system of MID and is founded by decision of the Government of the Russian Federation in connection with the establishment, on the basis of an Edict of the President of the Russian Federation, of diplomatic relations with the respective foreign state at the level of an embassy. An embassy is a juridical person. Land plots, buildings, installations, and other property of an embassy which are the ownership of the Russian Federation are consolidated to it in the procedure established by Russian legislation. The embassy effectuates the rights of possession, use, and disposition of such property, taking into account the legislation of the receiving state.

The financial status of Ministry personnel is addressed in a Decree of the Government of the Russian Federation adopted 23 October 1995 on 'Questions of the Financial and Material Status of the Ministry of Foreign Affairs of the Russian Federation'.[56] The hard currency salaries of military, air, and naval attachés who are attached to embassies of the Russian Federation abroad and are fixed as percentages of the ambassadorial salary were confirmed by Decree of the Government of the Russian Federation adopted 13 August 1996.[57]

The Russian Consular Service is administered by the Consular Service Department, which is a functional structural subdivision of MID. The Department is governed by the Statute on the Department of the Consular Service of the Ministry of Foreign Affairs of the Russian Federation, confirmed by Order of MID on 14 August 1996. The 1976 Consular Statute of the USSR continues in force in the Russian Federation. The Soviet Union ratified the 1963 Vienna Convention on Consular

---

[54] СЗ РФ (1997), no 24, item 2743.
[55] СЗ РФ (1996), no 45, item 5090.
[56] СЗ РФ (1995), no 44, item 4183.
[57] СЗ РФ (1996), no 35, item 4181.

Relations in 1989. By way of legal succession the Russian Federation inherited 117 consular sections of embassies, 50 consulates general, eight consulates, and one consular agency. Consular establishments are being established in the other Independent States of the former Soviet Union. In addition to the bilateral consular treaties succeeded to from the Soviet era, the Russian Federation has concluded more than 30 bilateral consular conventions in its own name as of 2002.

Only a Russian citizen may be a consular officer, but with the consent of a receiving state a foreign citizen may be appointed an honorary consul. In early 1996 the Russian Federation had appointed 17 honorary consuls and accepted the appointment of three foreign honorary consuls in Russia.[58] With respect to Russian citizens a consul may protect their rights and interests when infringed, register them for military service, fulfil commissions of Russian investigative or judicial agencies, perform an adoption or take steps to establish a guardianship or trusteeship, protect and transmit property left by a deceased Russian citizen, assist citizens who may be detained or arrested by local authorities, issue or extend passports and visas, deal with citizenship matters, and register certain acts of civil status. Under the Fundamental Principles on the Notariat and the Consular Statute, a consul may certify an extensive number of transactions and documents and perform other notarial actions. The consul likewise has functions in regard to Russian vessels, aircraft, rail transport, and motor transport. In the absence of a trade representation or commercial counsellor, a consul sometimes may be concerned with commercial matters.

The status of foreign diplomatic and consular representations on the territory of the Russian Federation is governed principally by a Statute confirmed by Edict of the Presidium of the USSR Supreme Soviet on 23 May 1966. The 1966 Statute draws principally upon the 1961 Vienna Convention on Diplomatic Relations, which the USSR ratified in 1964. The Russian Federation also is a party to the 1973 Convention on the Prevention and Punishment of Crimes Against Persons Enjoying International Protection, Including Diplomatic Agents, but is not a party to the 1969 Convention on Special Missions. Premises occupied by a diplomatic representation are inviolable. Access requires the consent of the head of the representation or the person replacing him, and no enforcement actions, including search, seizure, and attachment, may be performed with respect to the premises, the property therein, or transport belonging to the representation. The right of communication is guaranteed, including by post or courier. On the basis of reciprocity a diplomatic representation and staff are exempt from all general State and local taxes and assessments. Customs exemptions are granted on items required for personal use. Diplomatic staff enjoy personal inviolability and may

---

[58] See I I Lukashuk, Международное право: особенная частв [*International Law: Special Part*] (1997) 57.

not be subject to detention or arrest, and immunity from criminal, civil, and administrative jurisdiction unless the immunity is expressly waived by the accrediting state. Civil immunity does not extend to instances when diplomatic staff enter into civil law transactions as private persons concerning structures belonging to them on Russian territory, inheritance, or activity beyond their official functions. Diplomatic staff may not be obliged to give testimony as witnesses nor be summoned by judicial or investigatory agencies. Family members of diplomatic staff who are not Russian citizens and reside together with the said staff enjoy the same privileges and immunities. Administrative and technical personnel enjoy more limited privileges and immunities unless special reciprocal arrangements are made.

Consular premises and the residence of the head of the consular representation enjoy inviolability on the basis of reciprocity. The personal immunity of consuls is limited. They may be detained or arrested in connection with a prosecution for a grave crime, for example, and are subject to civil suit for harm caused by road accidents. Their immunity against giving testimony appertains solely to matters connected with their official duties. Reciprocal exemptions are granted regarding payment of taxes and customs duties. The personal baggage of consular officials may be examined only if there are serious grounds to suppose that it contains articles prohibited for export or import. Such inspection must be conducted in the presence of the consular official. By special agreement other diplomatic privileges and immunities may be extended to consular personnel.

Representatives of foreign states and members of parliamentary and government delegations which arrive in the Russian Federation to participate in international talks, conferences, or meetings or are on other official missions are accorded full diplomatic privileges and immunities. The privileges and immunities granted to international intergovernmental institutions and their foreign representatives and officials are determined by international treaties governing these matters. The Russian Federation is a party to the 1946 Convention on the Privileges and Immunities of the United Nations (since 1953) and has ratified the 1975 Vienna Convention on the representation of states in their relations with universal international organisations.

19

FOREIGN INVESTMENT AND TRADE LAW

While a vast variety of normative legal acts regulate foreign investment in the Russian Federation, the foundation laws are the 1999 Federal Law on Investment Activity in the Russian Federation Effectuated in the Form of Capital Investments, as amended 2 January 2000,[1] and the 1999 Law on Foreign Investments in the Russian Federation, as amended 21 March 2002 and 25 July 2002.[2] They replaced the Law on Investment Activity in the RSFSR, adopted 26 June 1991, as amended

---

[1] СЗ РФ (1999), no 9, item 1096; (2000), no 2, item 143; transl in W E Butler, *Russian Company Law* (3rd edn, 2000) 575–592.

[2] СЗ РФ (1999), no 28, item 3493; (2002), no 12, item 1093; no 30, item 3034; transl in W E Butler, *Foreign Investment Law in the Commonwealth of Independent States* (2002) 681–696.

19 June 1995, 25 February 1999, 2 January 2000, and 10 January 2003[3], the Law on Foreign Investments in the Russian Federation, adopted 26 June 1991, as amended 24 December 1993, 19 June 1995, 16 November 1997, and 10 February 1999.[4] Foreign investors commonly overlooked the Law on Investment Activity, although it is this Law which defined in greatest detail what constitutes an investment and expressly applied to foreign investments (Article 4).

The 1991 laws on investment were enacted at the height of communist influence in the Russian parliament and consequently reflected strongly the values predominant at the time. The amendments to the Law were slight, caused in each case by the enactment of ancillary legislation. They must be read by each foreign investor who invested when they respectively were in force (and may therefore be 'grandfathered') against the network of foreign investment protection treaties that may be relevant, the Edict of the President of the Russian Federation of 27 September 1993 'On Improving Work with Foreign Investments',[5] and detailed regulation of individual aspects of foreign investment.

A. Concept of Foreign Investor and Investment

The 1999 Law on Foreign Investments contains an exhaustive enumeration of who may be a foreign investor in the Russian Federation. Of these the most common foreign investors are 'foreign juridical person, the civil law capacity of which is determined in accordance with legislation of the State in which it was founded and which has the right in accordance with legislation of the said State to effectuate investments on the territory of the Russian Federation' (Article 2).

Although Russian law does not use the terminology of a 'legal entity' which is not a juridical person, whereas in Anglo-American jurisdictions in particular there exist 'legal entities' without limited liability which are not juridical persons, account is taken in the definition of foreign investor: 'foreign organization which is not a juridical person, the civil law capacity of which is determined in accordance with legislation of the State in which it was founded and which has the right in accordance with legislation of the said State to effectuate investments on the territory of the Russian Federation'. The Anglo-American 'partnership' is a classic

---

[3] Ведомости СНД и ВС РСФСР (1991), no 29, item 1005; СЗ РФ (1995), no 26, item 2397; (1999), no 9, item 1096; no 28, item 3493; (2000), no 2, item 143; (2003), no. 2. This Law remains in force except insofar as its norms are contrary to the Federal Law of 25 February 1999.

[4] Ведомости СНД и ВС РФ (1991), no. 29, item 1008; (1993), no 52, item 5086; СЗ РФ (1995), no. 26, item 2397; (1997), no 47, item 5341; (1999), no 7, item 879; transl in Butler, (n 2 above), 613–631.

[5] САПП РФ (1993), no 40, item 3740. This Edict lost force on 29 August 2001, but the operation of the Edict may remain in force for some time. For repeal of the Edict, see СЗ РФ (2001), no 36, item 3543.

example. Foreign citizens, stateless persons, international organisations, and foreign States complete the category of possible foreign investors.

The concept of a foreign investment in Russian law is determined by the 1991 Law on investment activity, which offers essentially an economic definition of an investment: 'All types of property and intellectual valuables contributed to objects of entrepreneurial and other types of activity, as a result of which profit (or revenue) is formed or a social effect is achieved, shall be investments' (Article 1). The Law then proceeds to give examples of what in a market economy would be called 'capital turnover'. It is in substance an 'economic definition' which, if applied rigorously, causes difficulties and perplexities to lawyers as part of an endeavour to 'achieve doctrinal respectability'.[6] The 1999 Law on Foreign Investments is more legalistic and helpful: 'the investing of foreign capital in an object of entrepreneurial activity on the territory of the Russian Federation in the form of objects of civil rights which belong to the foreign investor if such objects of civil rights have not been withdrawn from turnover or have not been limited in turnover in the Russian Federation in accordance with federal legislation, including money, securities (in foreign currency and in currency of the Russian Federation), other property, property rights having the monetary value of exclusive rights to the results of intellectual activity (intellectual property), and also services and information'.[7] The expression 'objects' draws upon the terminology of the Civil Code of the Russian Federation.

The 1999 Law on Foreign Investments offers an exemplary definition of 'objects' of foreign investment. The formulation preserves the position under Russian law that one may not under Russian law contribute intellectual property as such to the charter fund of a Russian juridical person, merely the 'right' to such property. That is, one must draft the relevant documents so that the rights to such intellectual property are transferred by licence or other appropriate structure rather than a direct transfer of the rights, which will be invalid.

Definitions are offered of 'direct foreign investment', 'investment project', 'priority investment project', 'period of recoupment of investment project', 'reinvestment', and 'aggregate tax load'.

B. Foreign Investment Guarantees

The 1999 Law on Foreign Investments is addressed specifically to the basic guarantees of the rights of foreign investors to investments and to revenues and profit

---

[6] See M I Braginskii, W E Butler, and A A Rubanov, *Fundamental Principles of Legislation on Investment Activity in the USSR and Republics* (1991) 15–18.

[7] For a comparative analysis of all CIS foreign investment legislation, see Butler, (n 2 above).

received therefrom, as well as to the conditions of entrepreneurial activity of foreign investors on Russian territory. Every foreign investor in Russia has somewhere in its subconsciousness the apprehension that there may return to political power forces which would renationalise former State property and exclude the foreign investor from the country, or, less ambitiously, that in individual cases the Russian Federation or subjects of the Federation may seek to assert or reassert ownership over property in the ownership of a foreign investor.

The principal lines of defence against such a prospect are the investment protection treaties concluded by the former Soviet Union and by the Russian Federation with individual states, earlier foreign investment legislation for those investors who are 'grandfathered', and the 1999 Law on Foreign Investments. The 1999 Foreign Investments Law offers guarantees to the 'foreign investor'. It provides that 'the legal regime of the activity of foreign investors and the use of profit received from investments' enjoy 'full and unconditional legal defence'. The principle of national regime is invoked: the legal regime of the activity of foreign investors may not be 'less favourable than the legal regime of activity and the use of profit received from investments granted to Russian investors', with exceptions established by foreign laws.

The State guarantees are basically ten (as compared with three in the 1991 Law on Foreign Investments). They also extend to foreign investors and to commercial organisations with foreign investments on the territory of the Russian Federation in which the foreign investor(s) possess not less than 10 per cent of the participatory share(s) or contribution to the charter or contributed capital who reinvest. A Russian commercial organisation receives the status of a commercial organisation with foreign investments from the day that the foreign investor enters into participation of the organisation and loses it as and when all foreign investors withdraw from participation. We consider each briefly.

Guarantee of legal defence of activity

This guarantee refers to the full and unconditional defence of the rights and interests which are ensured by the 1999 Law on Foreign Investments, other federal laws and normative legal acts of the Russian Federation, and international treaties of Russia. The foreign investor has the right to compensation of losses caused to it as a result of the illegal actions or failure to act of State agencies, agencies of local self-government, or officials of those agencies in accordance with Russian civil legislation.

Guarantee of use of various forms to effectuate investments

The foreign investor has the right to effectuate investments on the territory of Russia in any forms not prohibited by Russian legislation. Capital invested is valued in accordance with Russian legislation and the valuation is made in Russian rubles.

Guarantee of transfer of rights and duties of foreign investor to another person

The right to assign rights and demands and to transfer debts in accordance with the Russian Civil Code is addressed in this guarantee. Specific protection is given to assignment or transfer by a foreign investor to a foreign state or State agency under a guarantee or insurance contract with regard to investments effectuated in the Russian Federation by the foreign investor.

Guarantee of contributory compensation in the event of nationalisation and requisition

Neither the 1999 Law on Foreign Investments nor the investment protection treaties address the wealth of terminology in the Russian language for the various forms of 'taking' of property. The 1999 Law on Foreign Investments speaks in this connection of foreign investments not being subject to 'compulsory seizure', including nationalisation or requisition, except for instances established by a federal law or international treaty of the Russian Federation. In the case of requisition only 'contributory compensation' is offered (which is not full compensation), whereas in the event of nationalisation, the terminology used implies full compensation.

The investment protection treaties add little to the issue, except to use the term 'expropriation', which is not a term of domestic Russian legislation, and to speak vaguely of a 'taking' of property 'in other form'. In addition to expropriation, seizure, nationalisation, and requisition, Russian law also recognises confiscation, sequestration, and 'removal' or 'taking' of property. These distinctions are important for several reasons, including the payment of compensation.

Certain compulsory seizures or other actions of State officials or agencies give rise to a right of compensation and reimbursement of losses. When State agencies or officials have acted on the basis of instructions which are contrary to Russian legislation, or they have improperly fulfilled their duties provided for by legislation with respect to a foreign investor or enterprise with foreign investments, the foreign investor has the right to receive compensation of losses, including lost advantage (Article 8). However, the standard of compensation having to correspond to the value of the investments is laid down in the 1999 Foreign Investments Law only with respect to instances of nationalisation or requisition, and even then the term 'real value' is not used. No other form of taking is mentioned in this connection, and a direct link between this requirement and losses caused to foreign investors by the actions of State agencies and officials is not established.

Guarantee against unfavourable changes in legislation

Investors commonly depend upon economic and legal projections based on the existing legal regime. When changes are introduced in legislation to increase taxes or introduce new taxes and charges or to otherwise disadvantage the foreign investor in comparison with the regime under which the investment was made, protections are commonly offered against such adverse changes. The 1993 Edict on improving work with foreign investments was mostly concerned with offering reassurances of this nature.

The 1999 Law on Foreign Investments offers a highly specific, detailed (Article 9) enumeration of the situations in which this guarantee is applicable. The guarantee is limited in scope and extends only to certain foreign investors or foreign investments. The greatest measure of stability is offered to large-scale investment projects formally registered as such.

Guarantee of proper settlement of dispute

This guarantee amounts to a restatement of the general position under Russian law to the effect that a foreign investor involved in a dispute which has arisen in connection with the effectuation of investments and entrepreneurial activity on Russian territory may seek settlement by way of international arbitration or in a court of ordinary jurisdiction or an arbitrazh court. The 1999 Law on Foreign Investments offers nothing that is not already provided by general Russian legislation.

Guarantee of use of revenues, profit, and other lawfully received monetary amounts

The essence of this guarantee is that after the payment of taxes and charges in Russia, the foreign investor has the right to free use of his revenues and profits for the purpose of reinvesting or other purposes not contrary to Russian legislation, or to transfer abroad revenues and other lawfully received monetary amounts received in connection with investments previously effectuated. Examples are offered of such revenues and monetary amounts, but the enumeration is not exhaustive. The question can arise for the foreign investor as to evidence that the amounts were lawfully received and that they were connected with or received by virtue of investments previously effectuated.

Guarantee of export of property and information initially imported as foreign investment

This guarantee refers to property and information in documentary or paperless form imported into Russia as an investment. Such intangibles under the 1999 Law on Foreign Investments may constitute an object of foreign investment.

Their unhindered export without quotas, licensing, or other non-tariff regulatory measures is guaranteed. The issue of evidence of import for the purpose stated would remain.

Guarantee of right to acquire securities

This guarantee merely refers to general Russian securities legislation and affirms the right of foreigners to acquire stocks and other securities of Russian commercial organisations and State securities in accordance with that general legislation.

Guarantee of foreign investor participation in privatisation

The guarantee can be read in two ways. Either the foreign investor may participate in privatisation generally, 'on the conditions and in the procedure which have been established by legislation', together with Russian investors; or whether foreign investors may or may not particiate in an individual privatisation turns on the conditions and procedure established by legislation. The true meaning of the clause will doubtless become important as land is made available for privatisation.

Guarantee of granting rights to foreign investor for use of land, natural resources, and other immovables

This guarantee offers nothing that general legislation in Russia does not offer. Foreign investors may acquire the right to land plots, other natural resources, buildings, installations, and other immovable property, including the right to lease a land plot, in accordance with Russian legislation.

From time to time the President of the Russian Federation introduced individual measures to improve the investment climate and reassure the foreign investment community. The most important of these was the aforementioned Presidential Edict of 27 September 1993, issued during the period of the so-called attempted coup against the President. The Edict provided that 'limitations on the activity of foreign investors on the territory of the Russian Federation may be established only by laws of the Russian Federation and by edicts of the President' (point 2). All normative acts adopted by the Government, ministries, and departments, and by subjects of the Federation which established limitations not provided for by laws and edicts were deemed to be invalid and not subject to application. The Edict also incorporated a 'grandfather clause' providing that newly adopted normative acts which worsened the conditions for the activity of foreign investors would not extend to them. The Edict reportedly enjoyed mixed success, and remained in force until 29 August 2001.

In an attempt to entice large-scale investment, the President of the Russian Federation by an Edict issued 23 May 1994, as amended 15 April 1995, offered a five-year tax holiday to enterprises with foreign participation registered after

1 January 1994 under conditions which few investors found attractive and was repealed on 5 December 2001 by reason of the enactment of Part II of the Tax Code.[8] An Edict of 25 January 1995 sought to encourage large-scale projects in the sphere of material production by introducing differentiated customs duties for the import of finished products on condition that the minimum size of the project was US $ 100 million and that the contribution of the foreign investor was not less than US $ 10 million. Only a handful of foreign investors pursued the offer; it was repealed on 9 September 2000 for budgetary reasons.[9]

C. Foreign Investment Vehicles

The 1991 Law on Foreign Investments already mostly had abandoned the 'joint enterprise' (see Chapter 11) as an organisational-legal form and referred instead to the 'enterprise with foreign investments'. The 1999 Law on Foreign Investments speaks of 'commercial organisations with foreign investments'. Such an organisation may be created and operate in the form of joint-stock societies and other economic societies and partnerships provided for by the Civil Code of the Russian Federation and other federal laws (Article 20). Among foreign investors by far the most popular Russian organisational-legal form is the closed joint-stock society.

Commercial organisations with foreign investments and their subsidiaries and branches may be either 100 per cent foreign-owned or may be owned partly by the foreign investor(s) and partly by Russian investors. Such enterprises may be created de novo or formed by the acquisition of stock or other equity in an existing enterprise. They are subject to State registration in accordance with Article 20, as amended 21 March 2002 and 25 July 2002. The 1999 Law on Foreign Investments further stipulates that a 'branch of a foreign juridical person' may be created and operate on the territory of Russia in order to effectuate activity which the head organisation effectuates beyond the limits of the Russian Federation. The reference to a 'branch' in this formulation differs from the Russian branch (филиал) and gave rise before 1999 in practice to the so-called 'unregistered branch', which for various reasons the Russian authorities have tolerated in practice so long as these branches paid their taxes (they qualified as a permanent establishment for tax purposes) but been reluctant to register formally. The 1999 Law on Foreign Investments requires that State control over the branch of a foreign juridical person is to be effectuated by means of accreditation in the procedure established by the Government of the Russian Federation. Documents for accreditation are submitted to the federal agency of executive power responsible for coordinating the attraction of direct foreign investments to the Russian Federation.

---

[8] СЗ РФ (1994), no 5, item 394; (1995), no 17, item 1510; (2001), no 50, item 4705.
[9] СЗ РФ (1995), no 5, item 400; (2000), no 38, item 3779.

Commercial organisations with foreign investments are at liberty to effectuate any types of activity for the purposes provided for in the charter of the enterprise unless such activity is expressly prohibited by Russian legislation. Certain types of commercial organisations with foreign investments require special licences (securities, insurance, banking, and others). Within the Russian Federation and beyond its limits commercial organisations with foreign investments may create subsidiaries, branches, and representations and may realise on a contractual basis goods, work, and services within the Russian Federation and abroad. If they so wish, commercial organisations with foreign investments may combine into unions, associations, concerns, and a variety of other combinations provided that these do not violate Russian legislation, principally anti-monopoly. Intellectual property may be in the ownership of commercial organisations with foreign investments in accordance with Russian legislation. Labour relations are regulated by Russian legislation except insofar as foreign workers may conclude contracts governed by another applicable law; even then, however, foreign workers enjoy the protections of the Labour Code of the Russian Federation.

Foreign investors have the right to acquire stocks, participatory shares, and shares or other securities of enterprises, subject to limitations that may be established by Russian legislation, which in some cases may prohibit direct investment by foreign investors or place a limitation on the percentage or amount of such investment.

D. Free Economic Zones

The 1991 Law on Foreign Investments in the RSFSR made provision for the creation on Russian territory of free economic zones for the purpose of attracting foreign capital, progressive foreign technology, and management experience and of developing the export potential of Russia; the 1999 Law on Foreign Investments excluded any references to free economic zones. Provision also is made in the 1995 Law on the State Regulation of Foreign Trade Activity (Article 23) and in individual treaties concluded between the Russian Federation and certain subjects of the Federation.[10]

Such zones offer a privileged regime for foreign investors and commercial organisations with foreign investments in comparison with the regime elsewhere in the Russian Federation. The types of privileges contemplated in such zones include simplified registration procedures for enterprises with foreign investments whose

---

[10] See, eg, Article 3 of the Russian Federation-Iakutia Agreement on the Delimitation of Powers in the Domain of International and Foreign Economic Links, concluded at Moscow on 28 June 1995.

charter capital exceeds stipulated threshholds, lower taxes, but not less than 50 per cent of the tax rates in Russia for foreign investors and commercial organisations with foreign investments, reduced payments for the use of land and other natural resources, a special customs regime featuring lower duties and simplified customs clearance procedures, and simplified procedures for the entry and exit of foreign citizens.

Although the concept of free economic zones was firmly established in many countries, in the former Soviet Union the early discussions about introducing so-called 'open sectors' were driven not by the usual considerations but rather by the desire to create on an experimental basis a territorial-administrative unit which could operate on market principles, more or less, without being stifled by the Planned Economy.[11] Working groups were formed within Gosplan to study the possibilities, and with support from the Soros Foundation, international working groups created to assist. As the Soviet Union began to introduce general market-oriented measures throughout the country, the discussion about open sectors shifted to the classic foreign economic zone as a vehicle to attract foreign investments. The Soviet Government took a decision in 1988 to form free economic zones in Nakhodka, Maritime Province, and Vyborg, Leningrad Region. More than 100 other regions or areas sought similar approval.

During 1990–1 both the USSR and Russian authorities became sympathetic to establishing free economic zones on a substantial scale. In 1991 the International Association for the Development of Free Economic Zones was founded in Russia for the purpose of supporting territorial initiatives and developing new management forms and methods for such zones. The President of the USSR, the Council of Ministers of the RSFSR, the Supreme Soviet of the RSFSR, and the Chairman of the Supreme Soviet of the RSFSR all created individual free economic zones on the basis of sundry normative acts: Nakhodka, Jewish Autonomous Region, Altai, Leningrad Region, Vyborg, Kuzbass, Kaliningrad, Novgorod, Chita Region, Sakhalin, Zelenograd, and others. The great majority of these have never truly functioned. Customs legislation was not in place satisfactorily, and the hierarchy of normative acts used to establish the zones created difficulties with the Russian tax agencies.

Attempts made to address the difficulties during 1992–6 were not very successful, although new free economic zones were formed at the Moscow Sheremetevo

---

[11] On the development of free economic zones in Russia, see Ia V Babitskii, 'Free Economic Zones in Belarus and Russia', *Sudebnik* VI (2001) 269–354; also see V Ignatov and V Butov, Своб-одные экономические зоны: Методические и организационные основы. Правовой и налоговый режим. Нормативная база [*Free Economic Zones: Methodological and Organisational Foundations. Legal and Tax Regime. Normative Base*] (1997); T P Dan'ko and Z M Okrut, Своб-одные экономические зоны: учебное пособие [*Free Economic Zones: Instructional Manual*] (1998).

Airports, Ingushetia, Sverdlovsk, Kabardino-Balkaria, Novosibirsk, and elsewhere. By 1996 18 free economic zones has been formally established in 15 territories which together constituted one-third of the land area of the Russian Federation. The zones ranged from free ports, to technoparks, export-production zones, and concessions. Originally a means of accelerating Russia's integration into the world economy, they have become in principle primarily a means for local economies to secure customs, tax, financial, and other economic and administrative preferences as against the federal authorities. Of the 18 free economic zones, only two are actually operating on a significant scale: Nakhodka and Kaliningrad. In addition to the 1999 Law on Foreign Investments and the individual normative acts in each free economic zone, the zones are regulated by the Edict of the President of the Russian Federation on Certain Measures Relating to the Development of Free Economic Zones (FEZ) on the Territory of the Russian Federation, adopted 4 June 1992, as amended 16 May 1997 and 29 August 2001;[12] the joint Letter of the State Tax Service of the Russian Federation (dated 29 June 1993) and Ministry of Finances of the Russian Federation (dated 25 June 1993), supplemented by a subsequent joint Letter from the same agencies dated 8 November 1994. A law on free economic zones, submitted to the Federal Assembly of the Russian Federation in 1995, has yet to be enacted.

E. Production Sharing Agreements

In principle one of the most promising spheres for foreign investment, Russia's oil, gas, mineral, and forestry resources have attracted foreign investments on a scale well below their potential. While policy reasons have played their part in this, there has been a vast gulf between the infrastructure offered by the Russian legal system and the expectations and practices of the foreign natural resources industries. After some years of experimentation with joint enterprises, contracts of joint activity (simple partnership), and other schemes, the President of the Russian Federation issued on 24 December 1993 an Edict on 'Questions of Production Sharing Agreements When Using Mineral Resources'.[13] The first Russian normative act to address this model of foreign investment, it opened, in the view of one Russian specialist, 'a new page in economic and legal relations when using mineral resources in Russia with potential investors'.[14]

The 1993 Edict, skeletal though it was, addressed several issues of Russian legislation causing difficulties to investors and Russian policy-makers. It established a

---

[12] Ведомости СНД и ВС РФ (1992), no 24, item 1325; СЗ РФ (1997), no 20, item 2243; (2001), no 36, item 3543.

[13] САПП РФ (1994), no 1, item 3.

[14] See N N Voznesenskaia, Соглашения о разделе продукции в сфере нефтедобычи [*Production Sharing Agreements in the Sphere of Oil Extraction*] (1997) 12.

scheme for foreign investment not mentioned in the 1991 Law on Foreign Investments, which had seemed to contemplate only concessions in this sphere.[15] Both Russian and foreign investors under the Edict were at liberty to conclude production sharing agreements, and the groundwork was laid for taxes to be paid in kind and/or in money. The Edict offered formal recognition to the 'consortium' under Russian law as an association of investors without the formation of a juridical person, although there remain certain questions about the relationship between the consortium and the simple partnership under Russian civil law. Perhaps the most important feature of the Edict was that it acknowledged the importance of production sharing agreements as an integrated 'investment package', all of whose features needed to be taken into account. Both the Law on the Subsoil in its 1995 version and the 1995 Law on the Continental Shelf made specific mention of production sharing agreements.

The Edict, however, was too skeletal to consummate production sharing agreements and was understood to be the harbinger of a fully-fledged law on the subject. The Law on Production Sharing Agreements of 30 December 1995 entered into force on 11 January 1996.[16] Although more substantial than the 1993 Edict, which it superseded, it is by common consent also less comprehensive than is required. Nonetheless, several production sharing agreements are underway on the basis of the Law.[17]

The legal conceptual foundations of the Law are unusual. To a considerable extent the Law depends upon the Law on the Subsoil to supply substance to such concepts as subsoil use, exploitation, and the like. Yet as a Law about a special type of agreement, or contract, of a civil-law nature, the Civil Code of the Russian Federation must also regulate production sharing relations. The observation in Russian doctrine that as lex specialis the 1995 Law on Production Sharing must 'prevail over all other national norms regulating the relations being considered' cannot be squared with the supremacy clause of the Civil Code relating to civil-law relations.

The parties to a production sharing agreement are the Government of the Russian Federation acting in the name of the State and the subject of the Russian Federation on those territory the subsoil plots are situated, whether onshore or offshore, on one side, and the natural and/or juridical persons or the associations of juridical persons created on the basis of a contract of joint activity, on the other,

---

[15] For the argument that the production sharing agreement is a species of concession and that the 1995 Law on Production Sharing Agreements owes its genesis to the 1991 Law on Foreign Investments, see S A Sosna, Комментарий к федеральному закону о соглашениях о разделе продукции [*Commentary on the Federal Law on Production Sharing Agreements*] (1997) 15.

[16] СЗ РФ (1996), no 1, item 18; (1999), no 2, item 246; (2001), no 26, item 2579.

[17] On the legislative history of the Law, see O V Radaeva, 'Production Sharing Agreements: The Investor and the State,' *Sudebnik* II (1997) 265–328.

that is, the investors. The Russian Federation and the respective subject of the Federation act as equal parties to the production sharing agreement on the side of the owners of the subsoil and resources concerned in furtherance of Article 72 of the 1993 Russian Constitution. On the side of the investors the unusual aspect is the association created which does not constitute a juridical person. As a matter of Russian civil law, that is not a novelty in itself; the novelty lies in the grouping formed not constituting the ultimate formation of the venture being undertaken, but rather a party to an additional venture, the production sharing agreement.

The Law on Producting Sharing Agreements makes provision in two articles for the right of ownership to the product produced (Article 9) and to property newly created or acquired by the investor and used by it to fulfil or relating to the agreement (Article 11). What the Law does not address is the nature of the right of ownership to the products or newly created property, that is, whether there is participatory share ownership [доля] or common undivided ownership [пай].

A number of provisions included in the Law on Production Sharing seek to address fundamental and perennial concerns of the foreign investor to a degree not present in general Russian foreign investment legislation. For example, investors and those under contract to the investor are exempted from the requirement of obligatory sale of hard currency for rubles with regard to hard currency receipts received when fulfilling work under the production sharing agreement (Article 15). State guarantees against future limitations on the investor are provided in much the same terms as they were in the Presidential Edict of 27 September 1993 (repealed 29 August 2001, see above), but include exceptions for safety and environmental regulations and for public and State security not found in the Presidential Edict (Article 17). The provisions on the responsibility of the parties do not extend to non-contractual obligations arising, for example, out of the causing of harm (tort, delict). The dispute settlement clause is unusually narrow, relating only to the performance, termination, and invalidity of production sharing agreements; nothing is said about the conclusion of those agreements (Article 22). Foreign parties enjoy a particular advantage in that production sharing agreements concluded with their participation may make provision for waiver by the State of judicial immunity, immunity against securing a suit, and immunity against the execution of a judicial decision and/or arbitral award.

F. Foreign Trade Law

On 22 April 1918 the RSFSR adopted a Decret on the Nationalisation of Foreign Trade which remained in force throughout virtually the entire Soviet period.[18]

---

[18] СУ РСФСР (1918), no 33, item 432; Вестник ЦИК, СНК и СТО СССР (1923), no 1, item 12.

The 1977 USSR Constitution relegated to all-union jurisdiction 'foreign trade and other types of foreign economic activity on the basis of the State monopoly' (Article 73(10)). During the era of *perestroika* the State monopoly was first dispersed and then dismantled. On 14 July 1990 the RSFSR Supreme Soviet adopted a Decree on the Basic Principles for Effectuating Foreign Economic Activities on the Territory of the RSFSR, which established that 'all juridical persons and individual citizens, irrespective of the form of ownership, . . . have the right of participation in foreign economic activities and direct access to the foreign market'.[19] In 1990–1 the Russian Federation asserted combinations of joint and exclusive competence to regulate questions of foreign trade and economic relations. The Decree of the Presidium of the RSFSR Supreme Soviet on Protecting the Economic Foundations of the Sovereignty of the RSFSR, adopted 9 August 1990, authorised the RSFSR Council of Ministers to prepare proposals concerning the procedure for the conclusion of foreign economic agreements and transactions with regard to the sale of diamonds, gold, platinum, precious stones, silver, oil, coal, gas, uranium, rare earth, ferrous, and non-ferrous metals, forestry materials, furs, grain, and others.[20] The Law of the RSFSR Supreme Soviet on Ensuring the Economic Foundations of the Sovereignty of the RSFSR, adopted 31 October 1990, provided that Union, union republic, and inter-republic foreign economic transactions with respect to resources situated on the territory of the RSFSR were void unless concluded with the consent of the RSFSR. Under the Law, the RSFSR Council of Ministers was given the exclusive right to determine the procedure for licensing and quotas for goods and services of participants of foreign economic activity under the jurisdiction of the RSFSR, determine customs duties relating to export-import operations, register participants of foreign economic activity, accredit foreign firms, banks, and other organisations having their offices on Russian territory, and carry on certain foreign economic licensing activities.[21] On 20 August 1991 an Edict of the President of the RSFSR on Ensuring the Economic Foundations of the Sovereignty of the RSFSR established Russian jurisdiction over the licensing of certain foreign economic activities, mandated the creation of Russian customs agencies, and proposed to agree rates of customs duties with the USSR. Decisions of Union agencies affecting the procedure for the import or export of goods were declared not to be valid in Russia unless agreed with empowered agencies of the RSFSR.[22] By late 1991 the RSFSR began to develop its own presence in foreign economic relations rather than simply react against the USSR policies. The Edict of the President of the RSFSR on the Liberalisation of Foreign Economic Activity on the Territory of the RSFSR of

---

[19] Transl in W E Butler, *Basic Legal Documents of the Russian Federation* (1992) 249.
[20] Transl in W E Butler (n 11 above) 39–40.
[21] Transl in Butler (n 10 above) 45–47.
[22] Ведомости СНД и ВС РСФСР (1991), no 34, item 1140; transl in Butler (n 19 above) 41–43.

15 November 1991 introduced currency licences, the concept of empowered banks, and the obligatory sale of part of currency receipts received by enterprises located or registered on the territory of the RSFSR to the Central Bank of the Russian Federation.[23]

The dismantling of the State monopoly of foreign trade left juridical and natural persons, including those juridical persons with foreign investments, at liberty to engage directly in foreign economic relations provided that they otherwise complied with Russian legislation. Most USSR foreign trade associations, part of the State monopoly of foreign trade, either were wound up or transformed themselves into economic societies and partnerships and undertook to trade in their own right. One, Mezhdunarodnaia kniga, celebrated its 75th anniversary in 1998, now a closed joint-stock society operating on a scale miniscule in comparison to the Soviet period. Through a combination of customs policies and tariffs, quotas, export and import prohibitions and incentives, licensing, and a multitude of special decrees the Russian Federation struggled to combine *laissez faire* and intrusive regulatory approaches to foreign commerce. Barter, a contract in the Civil Code of the Russian Federation (Articles 567–571), is subject, if a foreign trade transaction, to a host of subordinate normative acts regulating the procedure for concluding and performing barter agreements.

In the Federal Law on the State Regulation of Foreign Trade Activity of 13 October 1995, as amended 8 July 1997 and 10 February 1999, the Russian Federation undertook to determine the foundations for State regulation of foreign trade activity, the procedure for conducting foreign trade by Russian and foreign persons, and the rights, duties, and responsibility of Russian State agencies in the domain of foreign trade.[24] The aims of the Law are to defend the economic sovereignty and security of Russia, stimulate the development of the national economy, and effectively integrate Russia into the world economy. Foreign trade is understood for the purposes of the Law to be 'entrepreneurial activity in the domain of the international exchange of goods, work, services, information, and the results of intellectual activity, including exclusive rights to such activity'. It will be evident from this definition that there is overlap between 'foreign trade' and 'investment activity' as defined in the investment legislation above. The Law on foreign trade activity, for example, defines an 'import' as the import of a good, work, services, results

---

[23] Ведомости СНД и ВС РСФСР (1991), no 47, item 1612; (1992), no 25, item 1425; no 44, item 2517; transl. in Butler (n 19 above) 281. The Edict lost force on 23 December 2000. СЗ РФ (2001), no 1(II), item 63.

[24] СЗ РФ (1995), no 42, item 3923; (1997), no 28, item 3305; (1999), no 7, item 879; (2001), no 33(I), item 3413. The 1997 amendments consist of substituting the respective words 'вывоз' and 'ввоз' for 'экспорт' and 'импорт' in Articles 6(6) and 12(4) of the Law. The result is to introduce authentically Russian words for calques from a foreign tongue with no apparent change of meaning. If that be so, the change is a translator's nightmare, for both are translated respectively as 'export' and 'import'.

of intellectual activity, including exclusive rights thereto from abroad without the obligation to re-export—a definition which would reach the importation of such property for capital contributions to the creation of an economic society or partnership with foreign participation.

Participants in foreign trade

Russian participants of foreign trade are juridical persons created in accordance with Russian legislation and having a permanent location in Russia, as well as natural persons (which may include foreign citizens) who have a permanent or primary place of residence in Russia and are registered as individual entrepreneurs (see Chapter 11). Foreign participants are determined, in the case of juridical persons and other organisations which are not natural persons, according to the law of the foreign state in which they have been founded. This definition recognises legal entities from jurisdictions beyond the limits of Russia which are not juridical persons as participants in foreign trade activity, whereas, as noted above, foreign investment legislation does not recognise them. In this case the civil legal capacity of such legal entities is determined according to the law of the foreign state in which they were founded. Foreign citizens and stateless persons whose civil legal capacity and dispositive legal capacity is determined according to the law of the foreign state of which they are citizens or, for stateless persons, where they have a permanent place of residence, are foreign participants of foreign trade activity; as a rule, these will be not determined by Russian law since they are not permanently resident in Russia. However, the formulation does have potential and interesting implicit conflicts of laws considerations.

Principles of State regulation of foreign trade activity

Eight basic principles guide the State regulation of foreign trade in the Russian Federation. These are: (1) the unity of foreign trade policy as a constituent part of Russian foreign policy; (2) the unity of the system of and control over the State regulation of foreign trade; (3) the unity of export control policy; (4) the unity of the customs territory of Russia; (5) the priority of economic measures used as State regulation of foreign trade; (6) the equality of participants of foreign trade activity and non-discrimination between them; (7) State defence and protection of the rights and legal interests of participants of foreign trade activity; and (8) the exclusion of unjustified interference by the State and its agencies in foreign trade activity and the causing of damage to participants of foreign trade activity and the Russian economy as a whole.

Without invoking Article 15(4) of the 1993 Russian Constitution, the Law on foreign trade activity requires that relations of the Russian Federation with foreign states in the domain of foreign trade activity be structured on the basis of compliance with generally recognised principles and norms of international law and obligations arising from international treaties of the Russian Federation. The Law commits the Russian Federation to participate in international treaties concerning customs unions and free trade zones based on the establishment of a unified customs territory without the use of customs-tariff and non-tariff regulation of trade between member countries of those unions.

The 1993 Russian Constitution (Article 72(n)) relegates the 'coordination of international and foreign economic relations of subjects of the Russian Federation, and the fulfilment of international treaties of the Russian Federation' to the joint jurisdiction of the Russian Federation and subjects of the Federation. The 1995 Law on foreign trade activity sets out at considerable length those matters which are within the jurisdiction of the Russian Federation, disclosing at the same time an exceptionally broad understanding of the concept of foreign trade activity:

(1) the formation of the conception and strategy of the development of foreign trade links and basic principles for Russian foreign trade policy;

(2) ensuring the economic security and defence of the economic sovereignty and economic interests of the Russian Federation and the economic interests of the Russian Federation and Russian persons;

(3) State regulation of foreign trade activity, including financial, currency, credit, customs-tariff, and non-tariff regulation, export control, and certification of goods in connection with their export and import;

(4) establishment throughout Russian territory of standards and criteria for the safety and harmlessness for human beings of imported goods and the rules of control over such;

(5) determination of the procedure for the import and export of armaments, military technology, and property of military-technical designation, rendering technical assistance in the creation of military objects abroad, the transfer of technical documentation, military technology, and other services in the domain of military-technical cooperation, and cooperation with foreign States in the domain of missiles and space;

(6) determination for the export and import of fissionable materials, poisonous, explosive, toxic, psychotropic substances, virulent narcotic means, biologically and genetically active materials, flora and fauna nearing extinction, and others;

(7) determination of the procedure for the import, export, and use of dangerous wastes;

(8) determination of the procedure for the export of individual types of raw materials, equipment, technologies, scientific-technical information, and related services applicable when creating armaments and military technology, including those for peaceful purposes which may be used for creating weapons of mass destruction;

(9) determination of the procedure for the export of individual types of

strategically important raw materials connected with the fulfilment of international obligations of the Russian Federation and the import of raw material for processing on a customs territory of the Russian Federation and export of the products thereof;

(10) determination of the procedure for the import and export of precious metals, precious stones, manufactures therefrom, scrap of precious metals and stones, wastes from processing them and chemical compounds containing precious metals;

(11) establishment of the indicators for statistical reports of foreign trade activity obligatory throughout all of Russian territory;

(12) granting of State credits and other economic assistance to foreign states, juridical persons thereof, and international organisations, concluding international treaties on foreign borrowings of the Russian Federation and State credits granted by foreign states to the Russian Federation, and establishment of the maximum amount of State credits and external borrowings of the Russian Federation;

(13) the formation and use of the official gold and currency reserves of the Russian Federation;

(14) working out the balance of payments of the Russian Federation;

(15) attracting State, bank, and commercial credits under guarantee of the Government of the Russian Federation and control over their use;

(16) establishment of the ceiling of external State debt of the Russian Federation, management thereof, and organising the work to repay the debts of foreign states to the Russian Federation;

(17) conclusion of international treaties of the Russian Federation in the domain of foreign economic links;

(18) participation in the activity of international economic and scientific-technical organisations and the realisation of decisions adopted by them;

(19) creation and functioning of trade representations of the Russian Federation abroad, and also representations of the Russian Federation attached to international economic and scientific-technical organisations;

(20) possession, use, and disposition of federal State ownership of the Russian Federation abroad.

The enumeration of matters within the joint jurisdiction of the Russian Federation and subjects of the Federation in the domain of foreign trade activity is rather briefer:

(1) coordination of foreign trade activity of subjects of the Russian Federation, including export activity of those subjects in order that they might realise their full export potential;

(2) formation and realisation of regional and inter-regional foreign trade programmes;

(3) receipt of foreign trade credits under guarantee of budget revenues of subjects of the Federation, the use and repayment thereof in foreign trade activity;

(4) fulfilment of international treaties of the Russian Federation in the domain of foreign trade activity directly affecting the interests of respective subjects of the Federation;

(5) coordination of the activity of subjects of the Russian Federation relating to the creation and functioning of free economic zones and frontier trade regulation;

(6) informational provision for foreign trade activity.

Outside the matters enumerated above, the subjects of the Russian Federation enjoy the full plenitude of power with regard to foreign trade activity. The 1995 Law on foreign trade activity sets out by way of example some of the rights of the subjects of the Federation:

(1) effectuate foreign trade activity on their territory in accordance with Russian legislation;

(2) coordinate and control the foreign trade activity of Russian and foreign persons, as defined in the 1995 Law on foreign trade activity;

(3) form and realise regional foreign trade development programmes;

(4) offer additional financial guarantees to supplement federal guarantees to participants of foreign trade activity registered on their territories, on condition, however, that the Russian Federation is not liable under such additional guarantees;

(5) grant guarantees and privileges to participants of foreign trade activity registered on their territories, but only with respect to obligations of the budgets and extra-budgetary funds of the subjects of the Federation and without being contrary to international obligations of the Russian Federation;

(6) create insurance and pledge funds to attract foreign loans and credits;

(7) conclude agreements in the domain of foreign trade links with the subjects of foreign federated states and with administrative-territorial formations of foreign states. This would allow links with, for example, Scotland, individual states of the United States, and provinces of Canada;

(8) maintain their own representatives attached to trade representations of the Russian Federation in foreign states at their own expense.

On matters of joint jurisdiction between the Russian Federation and subjects of the Federation the 1995 Law on foreign trade activity lays down procedures to be followed in order to ensure that the subjects of the Federation are consulted, receive proper information, and, where their views are required, they are received or silence is construed as assent. In the case of each subject of the Federation, however, it must be determined whether the provisions in the 1995 Law on foreign trade activity have been elaborated or modified in a bilateral treaty between the Russian Federation and the subject of the Federation. Treaties of this nature are not gazetted and can be extremely difficult to locate. An example predating the 1995 Law on foreign trade activity is the Agreement between the Governments of Russia and Tatarstan delimiting powers in the domain of foreign economic relations. Concluded on 5 June 1993 for a five-year term subject to automatic prolongation in the absence of notice by one party to terminate, the treaty provides that Russia and Tatarstan shall coordinate the formation of the conception and programme for the development of foreign economic relations and agree them within the framework of questions relegated to their joint jurisdiction.

The detailed delimitation of powers in foreign economic relations between Russia and Tatarstan is very different from that set out above on the basis of the 1995 Law on foreign trade activity. Matters of joint jurisdiction, for example, include the establishment of quantitative limitations on the export of products under quota which are produced in Tatarstan, including oil and petrochemical products and the regulation of payment-settlement relations with foreign states. Neither of the latter figure in the 1995 Law on foreign trade activity. Moreover, the matters relegated in the treaty to the exclusive jurisdiction of Tatarstan go far beyond the 1995 Law on foreign trade activity: the conclusion of trade and economic agreements of the Republic Tatarstan with foreign states, or the formation and control over the use of the currency fund of the Republic Tatarstan.[25]

State regulation of foreign trade

Article 80(3) of the 1993 Russian Constitution provides that the President of the Russian Federation determines the basic orientations of internal and foreign policy of the State in accordance with the Constitution and 'federal laws'. The 1995 Law on foreign trade activity is one of those federal laws which elaborates and clarifies the jurisdiction of the President and of the Government of the Russian Federation. The President is responsible for directing the State foreign trade policy of Russia, setting out the state of foreign trade policy in his annual address to the Federal Assembly, regulating military-technical cooperation, determining the procedure for exporting precious metals and stones and fissionable materials, introducing economic sanctions recognised by international law, using conciliation procedures to settle disputes relating to State foreign trade policy between the Russian Federation and subjects of the Federation, and if those fail, referring the matter to a court, and, if necessary, suspending the operation of acts of agencies of executive power of subjects of the Federation in matters of State foreign trade policy until the question is decided by a court.

The Government of the Russian Federation ensures that the Russian Federation conducts a unified State foreign trade policy, prepares and submits to the Federal

---

[25] The text appears in W E Butler and J E Henderson (eds), *Russian Legal Texts* (1998) 84–85.

Assembly the federal programme for the development of foreign trade, adopts provisional measures to protect the internal markets of the Russian Federation, determines rates of customs tariffs within the limits established by a federal law and introduces quantitative export and import limitations, adopts decisions to negotiate and sign international treaties of the Russian Federation, manages federal ownership of the Russian Federation abroad, and effectuates other powers in the domain of foreign trade within its competence.

In the interests of a market economy the 1995 Law on foreign trade activity accentuates the use of customs-tariff and non-tariff regulation (in the form of quotas and licences) as the principal means of State regulation. Other methods are not prohibited so long as they do not constitute means of interference or the establishment of various limitations by agencies of State power of any level of the Russian Federation. The 1995 Law encourages reliance principally upon the use of customs duties. Export and import quotas are subject to introduction in compliance with specified criteria and require official publication at least three months before taking effect.

Export control is introduced in the interests of Russian national security and compliance with international treaty obligations. Individual types of goods whose export and/or import is a State monopoly and therefore subject to licensing are enumerated in individual federal laws; only State unitary enterprises may be licensed to do so, although the Law on foreign trade activity does not require that State unitary enterprises produce these products. If goods are imported in such large quantities or under such conditions that material damage or the threat thereof is caused to producers of similar or directly competitive products in Russia, the Russian Government may take 'defensive measures' with respect to the import of such goods. The principles of State export control policies, the legal bases for the activity of State agencies in the domain of export control, and the rights, duties, and responsibility of participants in foreign economic activity with regard to export control are determined by the Federal Law on Export Control of 18 July 1999, as amended 30 December 2001.[26]

'National interest' is another basis offered by the Law on foreign trade activity for prohibiting or limiting export and/or import. Compliance with public morality and legal order, protection of human health and life, or of flora and fauna, defence of cultural valuables, averting the exhaustion of irreplaceable natural resources, supporting the balance of payments of the Russian Federation, and fulfilling international obligations of Russia are among the national interests to be protected. Imported goods must comply with technical, pharmacological, sanitary, veterinary, phytosanitary, and ecological standards and requirements.

---

[26] СЗ РФ (1999), no 30, item 3774; (2002), no 1(I), item 2.

In a provision that could, if acted upon, provoke dumping or trade discrimination proceedings abroad, the Law on foreign trade activity authorised Russian juridical persons to combine into associations on branch, territorial, or other principles in order to defend the interests of their members, represent their common interests, avoid unfair competition, and develop and strengthen foreign trade links. The Government of the Russian Federation is expressly empowered to introduce retaliatory foreign trade measures when a foreign State introduces measures deemed to violate the economic or political interests of the Russian Federation provided that such measures are in accordance with generally recognised norms of international law.

With respect to defending the economic interests of Russia in foreign trade of goods, as distinct from services and intellectual property, the Federal Law on Measures Relating to the Defence of the Economic Interests of the Russian Federation when Effectuating Foreign Trade in Goods, of 14 April 1998,[27] introduced a variety of special defensive measures which may be taken: annual import quotas, anti-dumping policies, compensatory measures to offset foreign subsidies, limitations on import of goods to support the balance of payments, encourage the production of new types of goods, to protect structural adjustments to branches of the national economy, or to fulfil special-purpose federal programmes, special tariffs, and others. The actions of officials or their failure to act in the course of conducting investigations with a view to determining whether to introduce measures to defend the economic interests of Russia may be appealed to a court.

The Ministry of Foreign Economic Relations of the Russian Federation was abolished on 30 April 1998 and its functions distributed between the Ministry of Economy and the newly-formed Ministry of Industry and Trade of the Russian Federation.

G. Signing Foreign Trade Transactions

Under a USSR Decree of 14 February 1978 on the procedure for signing foreign trade transactions, certain imperative formalities must be complied with for such transactions to be valid: they must be in written form and they must be signed by two duly empowered persons. The names of the persons who ex officio have the right to sign foreign trade transactions, bills of exchange, and other monetary obligations are specified, as a rule, in the charter of the juridical person concerned. Russian doctrinal writings differ as to whether the 1978 Decree continues to be

---

[27] СЗ РФ (1998), no 16, item 1798. See R A Shepenko, Комментарий к федеральному закону О мерах по защите экономических интересов Российской Федерации при осуществлении внешней торговли товарами (постатейный) [*Commentary on the Federal Law on Measures Relating to the Defence of the Economic Interests of the Russian Federation when Effectuating Foreign Trade in Goods (Article-by-Article)*] (1999).

applicable. The Decree has never been formally repealed, and modern computer legislative databases in Russia include the text of the Decree. Irrespective of whether the Decree remains applicable or not, many Russian charters contain provisions concerning the right of officials to sign transactions. There is no doctrine of apparent authority in Russian law, and it therefore becomes a matter of due diligence to determine who precisely has the right of signature in the name of and on behalf of the Russian juridical person concerned in foreign trade or possibly even domestic transactions.

H. Foreign Representations in Russia

The expansion of Soviet commercial links in the 1970s led many Western corporations and banks to open their own offices in the Soviet Union. Until the early 1990s a rather selective procedure was in place to evaluate foreign companies who wished to create a permanent presence on the basis of the Statute on the Procedure for the Opening and Activity in the USSR of Representations of Foreign Firms, Banks, and Organisations, confirmed by Decree of the USSR Council of Ministers on 30 November 1989, as amended 10 August 1990, 19 January 1991, and 11 July 1991. It remains in force, although obsolete in many respects.[28] In particular, it no longer applies to foreign credit organisations, which are regulated in this respect by the Statute on the Procedure for the Opening and Activity in the Russian Federation of Representations of Foreign Credit Organisations, confirmed by Order of the Central Bank of the Russian Federation on 7 October 1997.[29]

Representations of foreign firms are not juridical persons under Russian law, although most by reason of their activities are treated as a permanent establishment for tax purposes and register with the Russian tax service. Accreditation is granted usually for two years and subject to renewal. Although the original conception was that such representations would perform purely liaison and marketing functions, in practice most became involved in revenue-producing operations. This was recognised by the 1995 Law on foreign trade activity, which provided: 'Foreign juridical persons shall have the right to open representations on the territory of the Russian Federation in order to conduct foreign trade activity in the name only of those foreign juridical persons' (Article 30). Bearing in mind the broad definition of foreign trade activity in the 1995 Law, the representation has considerable scope to operate. It should be noted that only foreign 'juridical' persons may open representations, which precludes Anglo-American partnerships, as a rule, from doing so.

---

[28] СП СССР (1990), no 1, item 8; no 21, item 104; the amendments of 19 January and 11 July 1991 appear not to have been gazetted.

[29] Вестник Банка России [*Herald of the Bank of Russia*], no 76 (20 November 1997).

20

COMMONWEALTH OF
INDEPENDENT STATES

The Soviet Union was dissolved in December 1991 when the original surviving founders formally denounced the Treaty of the Union of 30 December 1922 which had brought the Union of Soviet Socialist Republics into being.[1] The remaining members of the USSR associated themselves with this decision later in the same month. Simultaneously with the dissolution of the Union, the 12 Independent States (excluding the Baltic states) with varying degrees of enthusiasm and reluctance brought into being the Commonwealth of Independent States (CIS) as the principal vehicle to coordinate their future relations. In the eyes of some the CIS might become the means by which the former Soviet Union could be restored; others view the CIS as a means by which the Independent states may collaborate or consult when that is in their interests and pursue harmonised

---

[1] Belarus denounced the Treaty of the Union and ratified the Agreement on the Creation of the CIS on 10 December 1991 with one vote against and two abstentions. Ведомости Верховного Совета Республики Беларусь (1992), no 1. Ukraine acted on the same day without discussion, but entered reservations to the Agreement on the CIS. Ведомости Верховной Рады Украины (1992), no 12, item 180. In Russia the Supreme Soviet of the RSFSR voted 166 in favour, 3 opposed, with 9 abstentions to denounce the Treaty of the Union and ratified the CIS Agreement by a vote of 186 in favour, 6 opposed, with 7 abstentions.

policies when they prefer to do so.² The CIS has been described as a'Eurasian Union' with the potential of becoming, if its members so desire, a species of European Union with a common parliament and citizenship, perhaps a common currency, and the like. Only time will tell whether these elements of potential come to the forefront. Because in practice the CIS has adopted numerous enactments, many of which have the status of an international treaty and are therefore an integral part of the Russian legal system pursuant to Article 15(4) of the 1993 Russian Constitution, a work on Russian law cannot overlook this organisation and ancillary communities linked to the processes set in motion by the CIS.

A. Foundations of the CIS

The CIS combines a regional continental-geographic grouping of states who have formed a classical international organisation whose headquarters is situated in Minsk, Belarus. The organisation is treaty-based and not supranational; its decisions are based on the principle of sovereign equality of all of its members, each of whom has the right of withdrawal from the organisation. There are 12 members in all: Azerbaidzhan, Armenia, Belarus, Georgia, Kazakhstan, Kyrgyzstan, Moldova, Russia, Tadzhikistan, Turkmenistan, Ukraine, and Uzbekistan. Each has concluded or acceded to the Agreement on the Creation of the CIS of 8 December 1991, the Protocol to this Agreement of 21 December 1991, the Declaration of Almaty also dated 21 December 1991, and the Charter of the CIS of 22 January 1993.³ These constitutive documents are all regulated by public international law and have been ratified as international treaties by the states concerned. By a decision of the Council of Heads of State-Participants of the CIS, adopted 20 March 1992, all CIS members are legal successors of the former Soviet Union.⁴ The working language of the CIS is the Russian language.

The term 'commonwealth' was chosen for a variety of reasons. It stresses the international legal character of this league of sovereign independent states and its charter documents. Many writers contrast the commonwealth with the concept of a federation: the commonwealth has no single territory, no unified citizenship, no supranational constitutive document or constitution nor unified legal system, no

---

² For the major Russian study of the British legacy in the form of the Commonwealth of Nations, which appeared a few months before the CIS, see N S Krylova, Содружество наций: политико-правовые проблемы [*The Commonwealth of Nations: Politico-Legal Problems*] (1991).

³ These documents and other foundation CIS materials are collected in N A Mikhaleva, Практикум по конституционному праву стран Содружества Независимых Государств [*Practical Manual on the Constitutional Law of Countries of the Commonwealth of Independent States*] (1998).

⁴ The Decision overlooked the position of Russia as the 'legal continuer' of the former USSR, as distinct from 'legal successor'.

head of State or single parliament or government, no single or community currency, no unified armed forces, and no State symbolism.[5]

B. Purposes of the CIS

The essential aim of the CIS is to further cooperation amongst its member-states.
The fields of potential cooperation are immense: political, legal, socio-economic,
scientific, cultural, ecological, foreign policy, strategic-military, and others. The
principal orientations of member-states include expanding the treaty-law base of
their activities on the basis of the principles of equality, mutual advantage, non-
interference in internal affairs of one another, and developing a system of inter-
parliamentary cooperation, ensuring the rights and freedoms of compatriots
living in one another's states and the rights and freedoms of man and citizen
throughout the territories of member-countries, promoting the retention of a
common economic space and developing economic links, consistently averting
conflict situations in the CIS and settling disputes which arise by political means,
and complying with one another's political, economic, and strategic-military
interests.

In the economic, social, and legal spheres the CIS, for example, is dedicated to
forming a common economic space on the basis of market relations and free movement of goods, services, capital, and labour, coordinating social policy, developing
joint social programmes and measures to reduce social tension arising out of
economic reforms, developing transport and communications systems and electric
power, coordinating credit and finance policies, developing trade and economic
links among member-states, encouraging and protecting investment, standardising
and certifying industrial products and goods, protecting intellectual property,
developing a common information space, implementing nature-protection measures and extending mutual assistance to eliminate the consequences of ecological
catastrophes and other extraordinary situations, and implementing joint projects
and programmes in the domain of science and technology, education, public
health, culture, and sport.

The definitions of spheres of common interests thus are vast and programmatic
rather than normative. When specific measures are undertaken, it is not necessarily assumed that all member-states will, or should be, involved.

The interests of the Russian Federation in the CIS have been elaborated in the
Edict of the President of the Russian Federation which confirmed the Strategic
Course of the Russian Federation with States-Participants of the Commonwealth

---

[5] See, eg, N A Mikhaleva, Конституционное право зарубежных стран СНГ [*Constitutional
Law of Foreign Countries of the CIS*] (1998) 7–8.

of Independent States, adopted 14 September 1995.[6] The Strategic Course strikes a balance between Russian 'narrower' interests in the CIS and her 'larger' interests in the world community: relations with CIS countries are regarded as an important factor in integrating Russia into world political and economic structures. The priorities of Russian policies laid down in the Strategic Course are determined by the fact that the most vital interests of Russia in the domain of the economy, defence, security, and defence of the rights and freedoms of Russians are concentrated on the territory of the CIS and by the conviction that centrifugal trends in Russia itself are best counter-balanced by cooperation with other CIS member-countries.

The principal aim of Russian policy in the CIS is stated to be the creation of an economically and politically integrated association of states capable of claiming a worthy place in the world community. Russia is to pursue mutual compromises in her relations with these states without harming her own interests. Politically, these interests include: ensuring political, military, economic, humanitarian, and legal stability, promoting the formation of politically and economically stable structures in CIS member-countries which have a friendly attitude towards Russia, strengthening the position of Russia as the leading force in the creation of a new system of inter-state political and economic relations on post-Soviet territory, and encouraging integration processes within the CIS.

C. Membership of the CIS

There are two categories of membership in the CIS: full member and associate member/observer. The concept of full member encompasses both so-called founder-members who signed and ratified the Agreements of 8 and 21 December 1991 and the Charter of the CIS of 22 January 1993, and member-states who signed and/or ratified at a later stage.[7] No practical consequence flows from the distinction. The CIS is an open international organisation; any state which shares the purposes and principles and assumes the obligations contained in the Charter is in principle eligible for membership. Accession, however, requires the consent of all CIS members. Reservations and declarations may be, and in practice have been, made by states when ratifying the Charter and other constitutive documents of the CIS.

Associate membership is formalised by way of a decision of the Council of Heads of State, the highest organ of the CIS.

---

[6] СЗ РФ (1995), no 38, item 3667.
[7] The Russian Federation ratified the Charter of the CIS on 15 April 1993. See Ведомости СНД и Вероховного Совета РФ (1993), no 17, item 608.

There is an absolute right of withdrawal, exercised at least once by a member-country, which later rejoined. The formality of withdrawal consists of written notification to the depositary (the Government of Belarus) 12 months in advance of the withdrawal.

As in the case of any organisation, members are required to perform the obligations they have agreed to undertake and bear responsibility for the failure to do so. The Charter of the CIS attaches legal consequences and procedures to the failure to comply with Charter obligations. The systematic violation of the CIS Charter or of decisions of organs of the CIS by a member are to be considered by the Council of Heads of State, which may apply certain measures of pressure upon the offending state. In practice compliance with CIS obligations has been far from exemplary, but the Charter provisions intended to enforce compliance have never been invoked.

The budget of the CIS in 2001 was US $8.5 million, of which Turkmenistan was to contribute US $175,000; Kirgizia, Tadzhikistan, and Uzbekistan US $450,000 each, and Russia, US $3.5 million. Contributions are payable quarterly, a requirement widely ignored.

D. Organs of the CIS

The CIS is structured as a classical international organisation with a permanent secretariat and headquarters (in Minsk) and a network of organs having consultative and coordinating functions. Certain organs are sometimes called 'inter-branch organs' because they address all or several domains of cooperation. These include the most important CIS organs: the Council of Heads of State, the Inter-Parliamentary Assembly, the Council of Heads of Government, the Coordination-Consultative Committee, the Inter-State Economic Committee of the Economic Union, the Economic Court, and the Commission for Human Rights.

Other organs of the CIS are concerned with designated spheres of activity. They include the Council of Ministers of Foreign Affairs, the Council of Ministers of Defence, the Headquarters for the Coordination of Military Cooperation, the Council of Commanders of Border Guards, the Council of Ministers of Internal Affairs, the Statistical Committee, the Inter-State Bank, the Council of Directors of State Information Agencies, the Council for Cultural Cooperation, and a substantial number of others.

Inter-branch organs of the CIS

The Alma-Ata Agreement of 21 December 1991 actually provided that the Council of Heads of State and the Council of Heads of Government were to be the highest organs of the CIS. The Charter of the CIS adjusted the position to make the Council of Heads of State the highest organ (Article 1).

Council of Heads of State

The Council of Heads of State assembles as necessary (according to the Charter, twice a year) and is attended by the presidents or representatives of collective heads of states of CIS member-countries. The Council discusses questions of general concern to the CIS and establishes principles by which policies should be pursued. An extraordinary meeting of the Council may be convoked by any member of the CIS. Decisions are taken by consensus, and any state may declare its non-interest in a particular issue. Between 1991 and 2001 the Council held about 30 sessions.

The work procedure of the Council is regulated by the Rules of Procedure confirmed on 17 May 1996. Each member-country presides for a term of one year, unless the Council decides otherwise, in turn at meetings of the Council in the alphabetical sequence determined by the name of their country in the Russian language. The Council may create permanent or temporary working and auxiliary organs and may involve experts and advisors in their deliberations as required.

Following serious disagreements aired at Kishinev in October 1997 about the future of the CIS, a Special Inter-State Forum was arranged on 29 April 1998 and attended by Heads of Government to discuss ways of improving the activity of the CIS. The Forum endorsed the view unanimously that the decisions of the Heads of State and Heads of Government as organs of the CIS must be fulfilled by the member countries. The Forum proposed Conceptual Provisions of the Mechanism for the Realisation of Decisions, confirmed on 8 October 1999 by the Heads of Governments. On 1–2 April 1999 the Heads of State signed a Protocol on Making Changes in and Additions to the Agreement on the Creation of a Free Trade Zone of 15 January 1994, the basic provisions of which are consistent with the principles of the World Trade Organisation. The long-term strategy of the CIS was set out in a Declaration on the Basic Orientations of Development of the Commonwealth. The Economic Council of the CIS was formed and an Executive Committee established to combine the apparatuses of the majority of CIS organs. A decision was approved to demarcate the powers of the Council of Heads of State and the Council of Heads of Government which would relieve the former of less important issues. A Statute was confirmed on the Council of Ministers of Foreign Affairs, enhancing its role.

Council of Heads of Government

Consisting of the Prime Ministers of member-countries of the CIS, this organ coordinates cooperation among the agencies of executive power, principally in the economic and social spheres. The Charter of the CIS determines its legal status, and is governed by the same Rules of Procedure which govern the Council of Heads of State. The Council of Heads of Government is supposed to meet four times a year, but often postpones meetings; any member-Government may convoke an extraordinary meeting. Joint sessions are sometimes held with the Council of the Heads of State. In the decade from 1991 to 2001, the Council conducted about 40 sessions.

In other respects the Council operates similarly to that of the Heads of State. Meetings are chaired by countries in alphabetical sequence in the Russian language, and working bodies are formed as necessary on a permanent or temporary basis. Experts and advisors may be involved.

Inter-Parliamentary Assembly

The Assembly was founded on 27 March 1992 by seven states as a mechanism for encouraging inter-parliamentary cooperation among CIS member-countries. By 1999 all states except Turkmenistan had joined. The Assembly acquired the status of an inter-state organisation (but also is called an 'organ' of the CIS) under the Convention on the Inter-Parliamentary Assembly of States-Participants of the CIS, signed by the Council of Heads of State on 26 May 1995.[8] The Convention resulted in consequential changes to the Charter of the CIS.

The Inter-Parliamentary Assembly is not an independently elected parliament. Rather it consists of delegations sent by the parliaments of the CIS member-countries. The composition of each delegation changes from one session to the next, as each individual sending parliament may determine. The acts adopted by the Inter-Parliamentary Assembly are purely recommendatory. They take the form of statements, appeals, recommendations, model legislative acts, proposals, and memoranda. In addition to the Charter of the CIS and the 1995 Convention on the Inter-Parliamentary Assembly, inter-parliamentary cooperation is regulated by the Agreement on the Inter-Parliamentary Assembly of States-Participants of the CIS, concluded 27 March 1992,[9] and by the Reglament of the Inter-Parliamentary Assembly of the CIS, adopted 15 September 1992.[10]

All delegations to the Inter-Parliamentary Assembly have equal rights and one vote per delegation. Plenary sessions are held at least twice yearly, although in practice they have been postponed. Recommendations of the Assembly are sent, after adoption, for consideration to the parliaments of the CIS member-countries.

---

[8] Вестник Межпарламентской Ассамблеи государств-участников СНГ [*Herald of the Inter-Parliamentary Assembly of States-Participants of the CIS*], no 3 (1995) 224–234. The Agreement entered into force on 16 January 1996.

[9] Российская газета [*Russian Newspaper*], 31 March 1992.

[10] Информационный бюллетень Межпарламентской Ассамблеи государств-участников СНГ [*Information Bulletin of the Inter-Parliamentary Assembly of States-Participants of the CIS*], no 1 (1992) 26–34.

The heads of delegations to the Assembly serve on the Council of the Inter-Parliamentary Assembly, which acts as the internal executive organ of the Assembly. There also are permanent and temporary commissions. Observers from non-member countries of the CIS are sometimes invited to Assembly sessions.

The Inter-Parliamentary Assembly has nine permanent commissions, the work of which is guided by the Statute on the Permanent Commissions of the Inter-Parliamentary Assembly of States-Participants of the CIS, adopted 25 May 1993 as amended 18 March 1994. The permanent commissions include: legal questions, economics and finances, social policy and human rights, environmental problems, defence and security, culture, science, education, and information, foreign policy, control and budget, and State construction and local self-government. In order to be quorate official representatives of at least half of the parliaments must be present at a session of a commission.

The Assembly also has its own secretariat and support bodies. The secretariat is a permanently operating administrative organ of the Assembly responsible for preparing and circulating official materials and summarising information concerning the implementation of Assembly recommendations.

The recommendations of the Assembly may be directed, in addition to the constituent parliaments of member-countries, to other CIS organs, including the Council of Heads of State and/or of Government. The matters considered are various, reflecting the concerns of its permanent commissions. The approximation and harmonisation of legislation is a major domain of concern, and to this end the Assembly has encouraged the preparation of model codes of law, for example, a model civil code, criminal code, code of civil procedure, code of criminal procedure, to assist national parliaments in their own deliberations. The Assembly also attempts to synchronise procedures to ratify treaties concluded within the framework of the CIS.

Informational exchange among the national parliaments and CIS organs themselves is facilitated by the Coordination Centre for Inter-Parliamentary Information-Reference Service, an advisory body of the Assembly which coordinates the operations of similar services established by the national parliaments. The Service prepares and gives preliminary consideration to questions and draft decrees to be submitted to the plenary session of the Assembly or the Council of the Assembly. It also organises seminars, conferences, and similar measures and offers legal support to what are called 'integration processes' within the CIS.

The Inter-Parliamentary Assembly has its headquarters in St Petersburg, where it occupies the magnificent Tauride Palace. Proposals to transform the Assembly into a true legislative body with the right to enact binding laws have not as yet enjoyed significant support.

As a distinct international organisation, the Inter-Parliamentary Assembly has its own privileges and immunities as provided in the 1995 Convention on the Assembly. These are based on the 1946 Convention on the Privileges and Immunities of the United Nations. The Assembly also has the legal capacity under its constitutive documents to conclude international treaties. The Assembly also maintains links with the Parliamentary Assembly of the Union of Belarus and Russia and with the Inter-Parliamentary Committee of the Republic Belarus, Republic Kazakhstan, Kyrgyz Republic, and Russian Federation.

Executive Committee of CIS

Formed in 1999, its functions were previously performed by the Working Group for the Organisational-Technical Preparation and Conducting of Sessions of the Council of Heads of State and Council of Heads of Government of the CIS, the Statute thereon being confirmed in January 1992. It was succeeded by the Executive Secretariat of the CIS in May 1993.

The Executive Committee is the sole permanently operating executive, administrative, and coordinating organ of the CIS. It has responsibility under its Statute for organising the work of the Council of Heads of State, the Council of Heads of Government, the Council of Ministers of Foreign Affairs, the Economic Council, and other CIS organs. Its activities are financed from the unified budget of CIS organs. The personnel establishment for individuals working in CIS organs is 710 persons.

Economic Council of CIS

The predecessor of this entity was formed in October 1994 as the Inter-State Economic Committee of the Economic Union. All CIS countries except Turkmenistan signed the constitutive agreement. The Committee has been described as the first institute in the history of the CIS to be endowed with supranational control-administrative and executive functions insofar as it had the right with regard to certain questions to adopt decisions binding upon CIS members.

In 1999 the Committee was replaced by the Economic Council, the principal executive organ charged with ensuring the fulfilment of agreements adopted within the CIS framework, decisions adopted by the Council of Heads of State and the Council of Heads of Government on the formation and functioning of free trade zones, and other issues.

The Economic Council consists of deputy heads of governments of member countries of the CIS. The Chairman of the Executive Committee of the CIS is ex officio a deputy chairman of the Economic Council. Decisions with regard to the formation of free trade zones and other strategic issues are adopted by consensus; a qualified majority operates with regard to other questions according to a specially established procedure; and a simple majority adopts procedural questions.

Any State may declare its non-interest in a particular question, but later accede to the decision by written recourse to the Council.

Sessions of the Economic Council are held as required, but at least quarterly and held as a rule in Moscow.

Economic Union

Activities within the CIS directed towards the creation of a market economy by coordinating currency, banking, price-formation, taxation, customs, and analogous policies fall within the jurisdiction of the Economic Union, created by a Treaty concluded on 24 September 1993 between Azerbaidzhan, Armenia, Belarus, Kazakhstan, Kyrgyzstan, Moldova, Russia, Tadzhikistan, and Uzbekistan.[11] Turkmenistan and Ukraine are associate members. The Treaty lays down the principles of economic interaction and the stages for the formation and organisational and legal forms of cooperation. The aim of the Treaty is to encourage economic integration of states-parties on the basis of market principles, retaining existing economic links, on one hand, and encouraging mutual investments and other joint economic activity, on the other.

Under the Treaty, the states-parties express their intention to create a most-favoured-nation regime within the CIS and to coordinate price, budget, tax, and economic policies. These actions, it is anticipated, will lead to the formation of free trade zones, customs and payments unions, a common market and currency union, approximation of anti-monopoly policies, support for healthy competition, investment protection, unification in the social sphere, and greater interaction among enterprises, coordination of foreign economic activity, and the formation of a market infrastructure in the form of trade houses, stock exchanges, banks, and insurance companies. Regionalism in these matters, it is felt, will accelerate the integration of the CIS economies into the world economy.

Although the Economic Union pursues aims which if left unfettered could well lead to genuine economic integration, the Treaty stresses the inalienable right of each state-party to structure its own economic system and to pursue its own economic poicies. It is for each state-party to determine the level of integration it wishes to pursue within the Economic Union. The Economic Union coordinates its activities with the CIS generally through the Commission of the Economic Union, which is attached to the Coordination-Consultative Committee of the CIS (above).

In September 1994 the Inter-State Economic Committee of the Economic Union was created, the Statute thereon being confirmed by agreement of the parties on 21 October 1994.[12] This Committee was endowed with certain supranational

---

[11] Дипломатический вестник [*Diplomatic Herald*], no 19–20 (1993) 36–41.
[12] СЗ РФ (1997), no 13, item 1473. Azerbaidzhan and Turkmenistan did not participate.

functions, including the right to adopt binding decisions relating to unified oil pipeline, energy supply, railway, communications, and other matters. The Statute on the Committee contains three procedural variants for adopting decisions:

(1) consensus, with respect to strategic issues for the development of the Economic Union;

(2) qualified majority of not less than three-quarters, with respect to the advisability of implementing particular measures of economic development; and

(3) another qualified majority, with regard to deciding questions which require significant expenditures or may have for certain countries serious economic consequences. In this latter instance the majority basically consists of those willing to participate in large-scale economic projects with a limited number of participants.

An Agreement on a payments union has been signed within the framework of the CIS, but apparently is not yet in force. Within the Economic Union various councils have been formed: railway transport, electric power, machine-building, oil and gas, and supplementary agreements exist which elaborate the foundation documents of the Economic Union.

Economic Court

In accordance with the Charter of the CIS (Article 32), an economic court has been established at Minsk, Belarus, within the framework of the CIS to settle disputes arising out of the performance of economic obligations and other matters relegated to the jurisdiction of the Court. Reference to the Economic Court also is found in the Treaty on the Creation of an Economic Union of 24 September 1993; the Agreement on Measures Relating to Ensuring the Improvement of the Settlement of Accounts Between Economic Organisations of Participant Countries of the Commonwealth of Independent States (Article 5), of 15 May 1992;[13] the Agreement on the Status of the Economic Court of the CIS of 6 July 1992 and Statute thereon;[14] and the Reglament of the Economic Court, confirmed by Decree of the Court on 10 July 1997. The Court is empowered to interpret agreements and other acts of the CIS relating to economic questions, but only within the context of individual cases brought before the Court by interested parties. The Court only began to function in about March 1994 and had considered 24 cases during the first five years of operation.

The Agreement of 6 July 1992 was signed by eight members of the CIS: Armenia, Belarus, Kazakhstan, Kyrgyzia, Moldova, Russian Tadzhikistan, and Uzbekistan. Azerbaidzhan and Georgia, although parties to the Charter to the CIS, have not acceded to the Agreement of 6 July 1992 and therefore have no quota of judges on

---

[13] Translated in *Sudebnik* IV (1999) 679–681.
[14] Translated in *Sudebnik* IV (1999) 682–688.

the Court, do not finance the Court, and do not recognise decisions of the Court. Each member-state may have two judges on the Economic Court. In 2001 Kazakhstan, Moldova, and Tadzhikistan had two judges; Russia and Kyrgizia had one each; and Uzbekistan did not take part in the work of the Court. Judges are elected or appointed for a term of ten years.[15]

The Economic Court has jurisdiction over two types of economic disputes: those arising when performing economic obligations provided for by agreements or decisions of the Council of Heads of State, the Council of Heads of Government, and other CIS institutes; and the conformity of normative and other acts of member countries of the CIS on economic questions to the agreements and other acts of the CIS. In addition to considering disputes, the Court may issue two types of interpretation: the application of provision of agreements and other CIS acts, and acts of legislation of the former Soviet Union during the period of mutually-agreed application, including the admissability of applying acts as not contrary to agreements and other acts of the CIS adopted on the basis thereof.[16] The Court has no jurisdiction over the application of the CIS Charter or other constitutive documents of CIS organs.

Inter-State Bank of CIS

With a view to developing a unified banking, credit, monetary, and currency policy within the CIS, in 1993 the Inter-State Bank of the CIS was authorised to be created. Its fate is obscure.[17]

Commission for Human Rights

Formed in September 1993, the Commission is a consultative organ of the CIS charged with observing whether obligations assumed by member-countries of the CIS with respect to human rights are being fulfilled. The Commission consists of representatives of CIS countries and operates on the basis of a Statute confirmed by the Council of Heads of State.

The Commission is not concerned with human rights generally, but rather with those obligations arising out of the Declaration on International Obligations in the Domain of Human Rights and Basic Freedoms in Countries of the CIS, adopted 24 September 1993. On the same date were concluded the Agreement on Priority Measures Relating to the Defence of Victims of Armed Conflicts and the Agreement on Assistance to Refugees and Forced Migrants. Member-countries of

---

[15] See E G Moiseev, Десятилетие содружества [*Tenth Anniversary of the Commonwealth*] (2001) 130.

[16] The texts of an Advisory Opinion of 15 May 1996 and Decision of the Economic Court of 22 June 1998 are translated in *Sudebnik*, IV (1999), 937–972.

[17] See the Agreement on the Founding of the Inter-State Bank and the Charter thereof, respectively in the БМД, no 12 (1993) 3.

the CIS are obliged under the last Agreement, inter alia, to bring national legislation into conformity with international norms.

Branch organs of the CIS

These are usually denominated councils or committees. They perform the functions set out in the Charter of the CIS and in the individual Statutes confirmed for each of them. Generally speaking, they consider matters of multilateral interaction in the mutual interests of the member-countries. Any acts adopted are recommendatory, but organs of this nature may make proposals to the Council of Heads of Government.

Council of Ministers of Foreign Affairs

Created pursuant to Article 27 of the Charter of the CIS, this Council is guided in its work not only by CIS documents, but also by the purposes and principles of the United Nations, the Helsinki Final Act, agreements concluded within the framework of the CIS, and decisions adopted by the Council of Heads of State and the Council of Heads of Government. The Statute on the Council of Ministers of Foreign Affairs was confirmed on 24 September 1993, but not signed by Ukraine;[18] the Statute was adopted in a new version pursuant to the decision of 2 April 1999 to enhance the role of the Council. The new version was not signed by Turkmenistan.

The members of the Council are the Ministers of Foreign Affairs themselves. The Executive Secretary of the CIS may take part, as may invited observers. Attached to the Council is the Permanent Consultative Commission for Peaceloving Activity, whose aim is to realise international agreements and interaction in the field of security and disarmament. The principal tasks of the Council include: coordinating foreign policy activity, including in international organisations, consulting on issues of world politics of mutual interest, implementing decisions of the Council of Heads of State and the Council of Heads of Government on questions of international relations, ensuring the effectiveness of joint foreign policy actions, developing conceptual approaches to global problems, peaceful settlement of conficts and the creation of harmony and stability in the CIS, strengthening friendship and mutually advantageous cooperation, control over the non-proliferation of weapons of mass destruction and related technologies, counter-action against international terrorism, narcotics, and other inter-state crimes; and developing cooperation with the United Nations, OSCE, and other international institutions.

Sessions are to be held quarterly, as a rule on the eve of sessions of the Council of Heads of State or the Council of Heads of Government. Documents are circulated

---

[18] Дипломатический вестник [*Diplomatic Herald*], no 19–20 (1993) 42–43.

ten days in advance of the meeting. The agenda is based on proposals from individual ministers and commissions from the Councils of Heads of State or of Government. Decisions are taken by consensus, except on procedural questions, by majority vote. International treaties are commonly signed by ministers of foreign affairs within the Council on behalf of the member countries.

Council of Ministers of Defence

This Council acts as an organ of the Council of Heads of State. Its functions are determined in the Statute of 22 January 1993.[19] The Council considers conceptual approaches to military doctrine and may make proposals to the Council of Heads of State. It also coordinates military cooperation and may submit suggestions to prevent military conflicts on the territory of CIS member-countries or border areas thereof. It also encourages the approximation of legislation relating to military matters and social benefits for military servicemen. Ecological security at places where force groups are sited is within the jurisdiction of the Council.

Headquarters for Coordination of Military Cooperation

This organ is responsible for coordinating the Armed Forces of CIS member-countries and directing collective peace-keeping forces to maintain peace in the CIS. There are a variety of treaties concluded within the CIS addressing military matters: the Declaration on the Non-use or Threat of Force in Interactions Between States-Participants of the CIS, the Agreement on powers of the highest organs of the CIS related to defence questions, the Agreement on the legal foundations for activity of the United Armed Forces of the CIS, the Agreement on Unified Armed Forces in the transition period, the Agreement on the status of General Purpose Forces of the United Armed Forces of the CIS, and others. The CIS has been concerned to develop a general conception of military security and to protect the external boundaries of the CIS member-countries. It has dealt with the division of the Black Sea fleet between Russia and the Ukraine, the reduction or elimination of missiles in treaties with the United States, the prohibition of nuclear testing, and other similar issues. By mutual arrangement military objects of joint use may be placed on the territory of CIS member-countries, except for Ukraine, whose 1996 Constitution prohibits the siting of foreign military bases on Ukrainian territory.

Council of Commanders of Border Guards

The status of the Council is determined by the Statute thereon confirmed by the Council of Heads of State on 24 September 1993. Principal concerns of this Council include settling a range of border questions and laying the legal foundations for Russian border guard units to be stationed in the frontier areas of other CIS countries. Attention is given to schemes for unifying the command structure of CIS border guards.

---

[19] БМД, no 7 (1993) 3–7.

Council of Ministers of Internal Affairs

Created in 1995, the aim of this Council is to coordinate the interaction of law enforcement agencies in their efforts against organised crime, terrorism, narcotics trade, illegal weapons sales, smuggling, illegal immigration and emigration, counterfeit documents and money, as well as assistance in the enforcement of judicial decisions. The Council has proposed that recommendatory legislative acts be prepared on the subject of organised crime.

Council for Cultural Cooperation

Under its Statute confirmed on 26 May 1995,[20] the Council is to further cultural cooperation among CIS member-countries at the level of State agencies of cultural administration and of international, regional, and national cultural associations. One representative from each member-country serves on the Council, together with the Chairman of the Coordination Council of International Creative Social Associations of Figures of Culture and Art. Other may participate with an advisory vote.

E. Representations Attached to CIS Organs

Each member-country of the CIS has the right, under the Statute on Permanent Plenipotentiary Representatives of States-Participants of the CIS Attached to Charter and Other Organs of the CIS, of 24 December 1993,[21] to have a plenipotentiary representative attached to each CIS organ. The functions of the plenipotentiary include representation of his own country and defending its interests in relations with CIS organs, maintaining links between the CIS and the sending country, conducting negotiations and participating in sessions of charter and other CIS organs or in various forms of consultations, informing the sending state about the activity of CIS organs, ensuring that the sending country is represented in those CIS organs where special provisions regarding representation have not been established, and taking part in discussing and drawing up the agenda for the Councils of Heads of State and/or Government and the Coordination-Consultative Committee.

The Russian Federation has adopted special legislation to regulate its own plenipotentiaries: the Decree of the Government of the Russian Federation on the Permanent Representation of the Russian Federation attached to Charter and Other Organs of the CIS, adopted 11 June 1996.[22] The representation qualifies as

---

[20] БМД, no 3 (1996) 4–6.
[21] БМД, no 11 (1994).
[22] СЗ РФ (1996), no 40, item 4646.

a diplomatic representation of the Russian Federation and is within the system of the Ministry of Foreign Affairs of Russia. It is located in Minsk.

F. Union of Russian Federation and Belarus

On 2 April 1996 the Republic Belarus and the Russian Federation concluded a Treaty to create a Commonwealth of Russia and Belarus.[23] By a Treaty concluded on 2 April 1997[24] and a Charter confirmed on 23 May 1997,[25] the Commonwealth was transmuted into the Union of Belarus and Russia. On 25 December 1998 the Presidents of Russia and Belarus respectively signed a Declaration on the Further Unification of Russia and Belarus which set out the principle tasks to be resolved in creating a Union State. In pursuance of the Declaration the parties signed on the same day the Treaty of Equal Rights of Citizens[26] and the Agreement on the Creation of Equal Conditions for Subjects of Economic Management.[27] On 28 April 1999 the two Presidents signed 14 joint documents, including 'On Completion of the Forming of a Unified Customs Space of the Union of Belarus and Russia'; 'On the Conception of Security of the Union of Belarus and Russia', and 'On the Conception of Frontier Policy of the Union of Belarus and Russia'.

A draft treaty on the creation of a Union State was published on 8 October 1999 in Belarus and Russia for a discussion of the whole people, together with the draft Action Programme for Realisation of the said treaty. Some 1,159 comments were received, of which more than 400 were incorporated into the draft.[28] The final text was signed at Moscow on 8 December 1999 at a session of the High Council of the Union of Belarus and Russia.[29]

Under the Union in its 1997 version, each country retains its State sovereignty, independence, and territorial integrity, constitution, State flag, arms, and other attributes of statehood. Each acts in international relations as subjects of international law and maintains its independent relations with other countries. Referendums are to be held in both countries regarding the structure of the Union. However, the parties are obliged to coordinate their foreign policies and develop a common position on basic international issues, collaborate in ensuring security, protection of frontiers, and the struggle against criminality. With a view to creating a unified economic space, common market, and free movement of

---

[23] СЗ РФ (1996), no 47, item 5300.
[24] The Treaty was ratified by the Russian Federation on 10 June 1997. СЗ РФ (1997), no 24, item 2732. For the text of the Treaty, see БМД, no 9, (1997) 66–70.
[25] СЗ РФ (1997), no 30, item 3596; БМД, no 9 (1997) 68–72.
[26] БМД, no 2 (2000) 51–53.
[27] БМД, no 2 (1999) 57–61.
[28] Moiseev (n 15 above) 270.
[29] БМД, no 3 (2000), 54–85. Both documents entered into force on 26 January 2000.

goods, services, capital, and labour, the parties agree to synchronise the stages, periods, and tactics of economic reform and to form a unified normative-legal base for eliminating inter-state barriers and limitations and to ensure equal opportunities for free economic activity. The parties further have agreed to unify the system of anti-monopoly legislation, taxes, State support for production, investment regimes, rules for labour protection, and have a unified customs space.

In future the parties had in view a common transport system, unified electric power system, common scientific-technical space, and unified credit, monetary, and budgetary systems. Citizens of both countries are to have equal rights to receive education, employment, payment for labour, and social services. Natural persons are to have equal rights to acquire property in ownership and to possess, use, and dispose of it on their territories.

Neither the Treaty nor the Charter of the Union defined the legal nature or status of the Union. In substance the Union seems to be a species of confederation. The State Duma of the Russian Federation, on 4 April 1997, adopted the Statement on the Necessity of Step-by-Step State Reunification of the Russian Federation and the Republic Belarus, which suggests that in time a new federated state is intended.[30]

The organs of the Union are the High Council, the Parliamentary Assembly, and the Executive Committee, each formed on the principle of parity. Decisions in all three organs require consensus, that is, unanimity.

High Council

The High Council is composed of the Heads of State of Russia and Belarus and the Heads of Government, the chairmen of the chambers of the parliaments, and the Chairman of the Executive Committee of the Union with the right of an advisory vote. The functions of the High Council include deciding the major questions of development of the Union, considering questions affecting the rights and freedoms of citizens of the Union, forming the organs of the Union and determining their location and conditions of sojourn there, confirmation of the budget approved by the Parliamentary Assembly, the adoption of normative acts and confirmation of international treaties considered by the Parliamentary Assembly of the Union, ensuring the interaction with agencies of State power of the states-participants of the Union, adopting decisions relating to the security of the states-participants, collective defence against infringements from without, military construction, and the struggle against criminality, and hearing the report of the Executive Committee of the Union concerning the implementation of decisions adopted, including execution of the budget.

---

[30] Российская газета [*Russian Newspaper*], 16 April 1997.

The work of the High Council is conducted on the basis of a Statute and Rules of Procedure confirmed by it. The Presidents of each country vote in the High Council on the principle of 'one State—one vote'. The chairmanship of the High Council rotates every two years. Decisions adopted by the High Council are signed by both Presidents.

Parliamentary Assembly

The Parliamentary Assembly of the Union is formed by an equal number of parliamentarians from both parties. Its legal status is defined by the Agreement on the Parliamentary Assembly of the Commonwealth of Russia and Belarus of 29 April 1996 and by the Charter of the Union of Belarus and Russia of 23 May 1997 (Chapter 8). Each deputation sent by the national parliaments of both countries comprises 36 representatives. Each national parliament determines the term of office of each representative and the procedure for terminating such powers or recall of the representative. A quorum of the Parliamentary Assembly is two-thirds of each delegation, that is, 24 representatives. The Assembly meets twice yearly and creates permanent and temporary commissions which also interact with the two national parliaments and their commissions and committees. The Chairman of the Parliamentary Assembly and his first deputy are elected on a rotating basis for a term of one year by the Assembly. They may not both be citizens of the same State.

The Chairman and first deputy of the Assembly and the heads of the permanent commissions collectively form the Council of the Parliamentary Assembly, which has its own support apparatus. The right of legislative initiative is set out in the Charter of the Union of Belarus and Russia and belongs to: organs of the Union, the Heads of State, the parliaments, and the Governments of the states, each deputation, and groups of deputies numbering not less than one-fifth of the total number of deputies of the Parliamentary Assembly. Decisions are considered to be adopted by the Parliamentary Assembly if a majority within each deputation have voted in favour.

The Parliamentary Assembly has its own Reglament. In due course it is contemplated that the Parliamentary Assembly will be elected directly by citizens of the Union of Russia and Belarus.

The functions of the Parliamentary Assembly include: deciding questions of the development of the normative legal base for integration of the two states in the political, legal, economic, social, humanitarian and other domains, adopting normative legal acts having the status of model laws subject to priority consideration and adoption by the national parliaments of Russia and Belarus with a view to unifying their legislation, submitting proposals relating to the development of the normative legal base of the Union to the High Council and to agencies of Russia and Belarus who possess the right of legislative initiative, facilitating the unification of legislation of Russia and Belarus, ensuring the interaction of the national parliaments on questions of mutual interest, hearing information on the activity of the Executive Committee, considering the draft budget, exercising control functions under the Charter of the Union, faciliating the exchange of legal information and participating in the creation of a unified legal information system, concluding agreements on cooperation with the parliaments of foreign states and international organisations, and exercising other powers in accordance with the Charter of the Union.

Under the original Treaty between Russia and Belarus the Parliamentary Assembly met four times: 25 June 1996 (Smolensk), 24 October 1996 (Moscow), 11–12 March 1997 (Minsk), and 1 April 1997 (Moscow). When the relationship was transformed into the Union, the Assembly attached consecutive numbering to each session, taking into account the previous four (unnumbered) sessions: 12–13 June 1997 (Fifth, Brest), 3–4 November 1997 (Sixth, Kaliningrad), and 15 December 1997 (Seventh, Moscow), April 1997 (Eighth, Gomel). The Parliamentary Assembly has begun to refer to its enactments as a 'Law of the Union' [закон Союза]. On 15 December 1997 the Assembly adopted a Decree on the Procedure for the Publication and Entry into Force of Decisions of the Parliamentary Assembly of the Union of Belarus and Russia, authorising the appearance of its own official gazette.[31] The legal force of these enactments is controversial in Russian legal doctrine. Some argue that they are at best recommendatory unless and until introduced into the national law of Belarus and Russia by respective national laws confirming the draft law of the Union, although neither Russian legislation nor the Treaty of the Union recognise the concept of a 'Law of the Union'. Others favour a scheme whereby enactments of the Assembly would be referred to a committee by the State Duma and the prospects for unifying Russian and Belarus law assessed, or the State Duma would recommend the conclusion of an international treaty with Belarus on the basis of an acceptable recommendation from the Parliamentary Assembly, or a federal law adopted by the Russian Federal Assembly would transform the recommendation of the Parliamentary Assembly into Russian law.[32]

Executive Committee

The organ is concerned with organising the implementation of integration projects to be carried out in pursuance of the Union. The Chairman and his deputies are appointed to and relieved from office by the High Council of the Union.

---

[31] Информационный бюллетень Парламентского Собрания Союза Беларуси и России [*Information Bulletin of the Parliamentary Assembly of Belarus and Russia*], no 1 (February 1998). This issue collects all enactments adopted by the Assembly in 1996–7.

[32] See O G Rumiantsev, 'О Парламентском Собрании Союза Беларуси и России и его нормативных актах' ['On the Parliamentary Assembly of the Union of Belarus and Russia and Its Normative Acts'], Право [Law] no 2–3 (1998) 10–13.

The Committee consists of an equal number of representatives from Russia and Belarus, the personal membership being confirmed by the Presidents of Russia and Belarus. The Committee reports annually to the High Council and submits information to the Parliamentary Assembly on the fulfilment of projects and programmes. Decisions of the Executive Committee may be repealed or suspended by the High Council. The Committe has its own apparatus headed by an administrative manager who is appointed by the High Council.

The Executive Committee itself works out projects and programmes for realising the purposes and tasks of the Union, proposals for financing these measures, for creating organs and organisations of the Union, and the like, and submits these to the High Council. The Committee also develops measures to fulfil decisions of the High Council, coordinates the activity of other agencies and organisations involved by each party to implement projects and programmes, concludes civil-law contracts in its own name, and finances projects within the budget allocations of the Union. The draft Charter of the Union of Belarus and Russia made provision for the right of the Executive Committee within its competence to adopt acts having direct effect on the territory of Russia and Belarus, but these provisions disappeared from the final text of the Charter. One must therefore assume that acts of the Executive Committee require transformation into national legislation before they become effective under the domestic law of Russia and Belarus.

The Executive Committee may form on a parity basis organs and other bodies which are required to implement programmes or implement decisions of the High Council. Each organ operates on the basis of a Statute confirmed by the High Council or, on its behalf, by the Executive Committee. These organs, so-called 'branch organs', implement the common economic and social policy, form a unified normative-legal base, carry out measures directed towards unifying credit, monetary, tax, and budget systems, lay the groundwork for a common currency, form unified electric power, transport, and communications systems, site new and modernised production complexes, coordinate foreign economic links, jointly organise customs matters, and others.

The treaty creating the Union of Belarus and Russia is an open Treaty to which other states may accede.

G. Towards a Union State of Belarus and Russia

Under the Treaty on the Creation of a Union State of 8 December 1999, the parties affirm the aspiration to pursue the integration processes set in motion by the prior treaties between Belarus and Russia and to adhere to the purposes and principles of the United Nations Charter. The formation of a Union State is called a 'new stage in the process of unifying the peoples of the two countires into a democratic rule-of-law State' (Article 1). The purposes of the Union State are to ensure the peaceful and democratic development of the fraternal peoples of each state and strengthen their friendship, well-being, and standard of living; create a single economic space, comply with the basic rights and freedoms of man and citizen in accordance with generally recognised principles and norms of international law; conduct agreed foreign and defence policies; form a single legal system of a democratic state; conduct an agreed social policy; ensure the security of the Union State and struggle against criminality; and strengthen peace, security, and mutually-advantageous cooperation in Europe and the whole world and develop the CIS.

Integration is to be pursued in priority at the economic and social levels. The question of a Constitution for the Union State is to be considered later. In many respects the Union State as configured in the Treaty would be analogous to the former Soviet Union, an impression reinforced by use of the term 'Union' in this context. The Union State is to be based on the principles of sovereign equality of the states-participants, voluntariness, and good faith fulfilment of mutual obligations. There is to be a delimitation of subjects of jurisdiction and competence between the Union State, on one side, and Russia and Belarus on the other. The entire edifice is treaty-based (as was the former Soviet Union) and subject to the law of treaties.

The Union State, following the Belarus and Russian constitutions, is to be a 'secular, democratic, social, and rule-of-law State in which political and ideological diversity are recognised' under the Treaty (Article 5). The two member states of the Union State would retain their membership in the United Nations and other international organisations but by mutual arrangement might agree to single membership in some. The territory of the Union State will consist of the state territories of the two participants, who are charged with ensuring the integrity and inviolability of the territories of the Union State. However, it is foreseen that the Union State itself may one day assume responsibility for protection of its boundaries (Article 7).

All forms of ownership are to be recognised and defended on the territory of the Union State, and citizens have equal rights to acquire, possess, use, and dispose of property. These guarantees extend to juridical persons and citizen-entrepreneurs. The legal status and procedure for the activity of foreign juridical persons is, until legislation is unified on this question, to be effectuated in accordance with the legislation of Russia and Belarus and their treaties with third countries. However, the movable and immovable property of the Union State itself is to be in possession, use, and disposition on the basis of normative legal acts of the Union State.

The Union State will have all the symbolic attributes of statehood: arms, flag, anthem, and the like, to be established by the parliament of the Union State and subject to confirmation by the High State Council. The official languages of the Union State are the State languages of the participants. The Russian language is the working language in organs of the Union State. The High State Council will determine the location of agencies of the Union State.

A single currency will circulate from a single emission centre in the Union State. Citizens of Russia and Belarus will simultaneously be citizens of the Union State. No one may be a citizen of the Union State without acquiring the citizenship of either Belarus or Russia, the last being governed by the citizenship laws of each participant.

The Treaty lays down the subjects of exclusive jurisdiction of the Union State and joint jurisdiction between the Union State and participants. The exclusive jurisdiction of the Union State includes the creation of a single economic space and legal foundations for a common market ensuring the free movement of goods, services, capital, and workforce within the limits of the territories of states participant and equal conditions and guarantees for the activity of economic subjects. The Union State will have a single monetary-credit policy and currency, tax, and price policies; uniform rules for competition and consumer protection; unified transport and electric power systems; joint defence orders to ensure deliveries and realisation of arms and military technology and a unified system for technical provision to the armed forces of Belarus and Russia; unified trade and customs-tariff policies with respect to third countries and international organisations; and unified legislation on foreign investments. The Union State will have its own budget, manage its own property, conduct international activity and conclude international treaties with regard to questions within its exclusive jurisdiction; direct regional force groups; determine the frontier policy of the Union State, as well as the standards, hydrometeorological, metric, geodesy, cartographic, and other services or measures. Statistical and book-keeping records and unified databanks are within the jurisdiction of the Union State, as is the establishment of the system of agencies of the Union State, the forming thereof, and the procedure for their organisation and activity.

Within the joint jurisdiction of the Union State, on one hand, and Belarus and Russia on the other, are: admitting other states to membership in the Union State; coordination and interaction in the sphere of foreign policy connected with the Treaty of 8 December 1999; conducting an agreed course in strengthening the CIS; joint defence policy; interaction in international cooperation with regard to military and frontier questions, including the realisation of international treaties on reducing armed forces and limiting arms concluded by Belarus and Russia; interaction in effectuating democratic transformations and realising and defending the basic rights and freedoms of citizens of the Union State; harmonisation and unification of legislation of Belarus and Russia; effectuating investment policies in the interests of a rational division of labour; protection of the environment; joint actions in the domain of ecological security, prevention of natural and technogenic catastrophes and elimination of their consequences; among others.

The budget is based on annual agreed deductions from the states participant, but with the approval of agencies designated in the Treaty, other sources of finance may be used. The budget of the Union State may not have a deficit.

The organs of the Union State have been renamed in comparison with the Union of Belarus and Russia and given different powers. The *High State Council* is the highest agency of the Union State, comprising the Heads of State, Heads of Government, and leaders of the chambers of the parliaments of the member states. From the Union State itself, the Chairman of the Council of Ministers, Chairmen of the Chambers of the Parliament, and Chairman of the Court of the Union State are members of the High State Council. Acts of the High State Council must be adopted unanimously and are considered to be not adopted if one of the states participant opposes adoption (which would suggest that abstention does not defeat adoption of the act). The Head of State or person replacing him votes in the name of the state participant.

The *parliament* is the representative and legislative agency of the Union State. It consists of two chambers: the Chamber of the Union and the Chamber of Representatives. The Chamber of the Union consists of 36 members of the Soviet of the Federation and deputies of the State Duma delegated by the chambers of the Federal Assembly of the Russian Federation and 36 members of the Soviet of the Republic and deputies of the Chamber of Representatives delegated by chambers of the National Assembly of the Republic Belarus. The Chamber of Representatives of the Union consists of 75 deputies from the Russian Fedeation and 28 deputies from the Republic Belarus elected on the basis of universal suffrage by secret ballot. There is a four-year term of office in each chamber of the parliament.

The parliament, inter alia, adopts laws and Fundamental Principles of legislation of the Union State on questions relegated to the competence of the Union State; promotes the unification of legislation of states-participant; adopts the budget and hears yearly and semi-annual reports on the execution thereof; ratifies international treaties concluded in the name of the Union State; concludes agreements on cooperation with the parliaments of states which are not members of the Union State and with parliamentary organisations; appoints judges of the Court of the Union State; considers proposals of third states acceding to the Union State and adopting a respective recommendation. Laws are adopted by a majority vote in each chamber of the parliament and sent to the chairman of the High State Council for signature and promulgation. There is a 30-day period for signature, provided that both the Chairman of the High State Council and the Head of State of the participant which at the time is not Chairman of the High State Council do not object.

The *Council of Ministers* is the executive agency of the Union State and made up of the Chairman, Heads of Government, State Secretary (with the rights of deputy chairman of the Council of Ministers), ministers of foreign affairs, economy, and finances of the states participant, and leaders of the principal branch and functional agencies of administration of the Union State. The heads of the central banks and ministers of states-participant may be invited to sessions of the Council of Ministers. The High State Council appoints the Chairman of the Council of Ministers, who may be the Head of Government of Belarus or Russia by rotation. The functions of the Council of Ministers, composition thereof, and procedure for its activity is determined by a Statute confirmed by the High State Council.

The *Court of the Union State* is an agency called upon to ensure the uniform interpretation and application of the Treaty of 8 December 1999 and of normative legal acts of the Union State. There are to be nine judges appointed by the parliament of the Union State upon the recommendation of the High State Council. They act in a personal capacity, and must be citizens of the Union State who have high professional and moral qualities and meet the requirements for appointment to high judicial office in state participant. The judges are appointed for a term of six years and may be reappointed for one further term. One-third of the judges are renewed every two years. The chairman and deputy chairman of the Court may not be citizens of the same country. The Charter and Reglament of the Court is confirmed by the High State Council. Any questions connected with the interpretation and application of the Treaty of 8 December 1999 or normative legal acts of the Union State may be submitted to the Court by each state participant or by agencies of the Union State. Decisions of the Court are legally binding and subject to official publication; they are adopted by a two-thirds vote of the total number of judges in the respective judicial session.

The *Counting Chamber* is created to effectuate control over the finances of the Union State. It consists of 11 members appointed for a term of six years from among citizens of the states participants who have experience in internal audit, control, and auditing organisations. They are appointed by the Parliament of the Union State upon the recommendation of the Council of Ministers of the Union State. Parity is not a requirement here; but not more than seven members may be from one state.

The Union State is not perceived as a species of international organisation. Officials of agencies of the Union State are State employees of the Union State. They are required to act in the common interests without seeking or accepting instructions from any State agency of the states participant; cannot combine work in agencies of the Union State with other paid activity, except for teaching, scholarly, or other creative activity; and do not have the right to engage in activity incompatible with their status as officials of agencies of the Union State.

Acts of the Union State are sources of law in Belarus and Russia (see Chapter 4).

H. Integration of Belarus, Kazakhstan, Kyrgyzstan, and Russian Federation

On 29 March 1996 a Treaty was concluded between Belarus, Kazakhstan, Kyrgyzstan, and Russia on the deepening of integration in the economic and humanitarian domains with a view to creating in future a Commonwealth of integrated states.[33] The Treaty makes provision for the creation of a unified economic space, common market of goods, services, capital, and labour, and the development of unified transport, electric power, and information systems. Legislation is to be approximated, foreign policy to be coordinated, external frontiers jointly protected, and equal access to be ensured to education, among other aims of the incipient Commonwealth. The same countries had on 20 January 1995 (with Kirgizia acceding in 1996 and Tadzhikistan in 1998) concluded an Agreement on a Customs Union;[34] in the course of time there has been a certain level of merger between the structures organised under the 1995 Treaty on the Customs Union and the 1996 Treaty on deepening integration, although each retains its separate identity.

The 1996 Treaty provides for the creation of three organs: the Inter-State Council, the Integration Committee, and the Inter-Parliamentary Committee. The Inter-State Council is the highest management organ of integration. The Heads of State, Governments, and Ministers of Foreign Affairs are represented in it, and the Chairman of the Integration Committee has an advisory vote. The Chairman is elected for a one-year term on a rotating basis.

The Inter-State Council develops the strategy for cooperation, determines the basic stages, adopts decisions, and confirms Statutes on the management organs for integration and the procedure for financing them. Certain decisions adopted by the Inter-State Council are binding and have direct effect on the territory of the member-states, whereas others are subject to being transformed into national legislation.

The Integration Committee is the permanent executive organ responsible for implementing measures needed to achieve the principles and tasks of integration

---

[33] СЗ РФ (1997), no 17, item 1915. On 28 April 1998 the Republic Tadzhikistan acceded to the Union of Four, classifying it in the press as a customs union. See Народная газета [*People's Newspaper*], 8 May 1998 1, cols 4–6. The formalities of accession were completed in April 1999.

[34] БМД, no 6 (1995) 11–12.

fixed in the Treaty. Its members include the first deputy heads of government of each state-party to the Treaty and ministers responsible for cooperation with CIS member countries. The chairman of the Committee is appointed by the Inter-State Council on a rotating basis. Its duties are to supervise the fulfilment of decisions of the integration management organs, ensure that decisions of the Inter-State Council are implemented, and found inter-state commissions and committees and enlist independent experts as required.

The Inter-Parliamentary Committee operates on the basis of an Agreement[35] concluded by the four states on 28 May 1996 and a Provisional Reglament of 1 November 1996. It is conceived as a joint management organ of integration and of interparliamentary cooperation. It consists of parliamentary delegations from each of the four member-states, ten from each national parliament, elected in accordance with the internal regulations of each parliament. Each delegation has one vote in the Committee. If they wish, each national parliament may designate their parliamentary delegation to the Inter-Parliamentary Assembly of the CIS to represent their interests in the Inter-Parliamentary Committee.

The Inter-Parliamentary Committee adopts model legislative acts, prepares recommendations relating to the approximation and harmonisation of legislation and to synchronise the enactment of legislation in their national parliaments, submits proposals to develop the legal foundations for integration to the Inter-State Council and national parliaments, discusses questions of cooperation and sends its recommendations to the Inter-State Council, the Integration Committee, and/or to the national parliaments, and other analogous functions. Its recommendatory acts are sent to the national parliaments for consideration.

Sessions of the Inter-Parliamentary Committee are to be held once a month in St Petersburg or in the capital cities of the four member-states. The Chairman of the Committee and his deputies are elected for a term of one year on a rotating basis from the national parliamentary delegations. The Bureau of the Committee organises its activities. The Inter-Parliamentary Committee has formed four permanent commissions: for legal questions, for the economy and finances, for social and humanitarian questions, and for foreign links and security.

In April 1998 the parties to the Treaties on the customs union and on deepening integration began to meet under the aegis of both treaties, which in effect meant that the issues to be addressed under the treaties were so closely linked that joint decisions were required. Enormous difficulties had been experienced in proceeding with the customs union for a variety of political and economic considerations. It was decided to adopt a Statement on Ten Simple Steps for Ordinary People,

---

[35] Вестник Межпарламентской Ассамблеи государств-участников СНГ [*Herald of the Inter-Parliamentary Assembly of States-Participants of the CIS*], no 2 (1996) 253–256.

which included: introducing a simplified procedure for admitting to citizenship; ensuring citizens equal and free rights to cross the boundaries of other states at control points; creating identical conditions for citizens to receive urgent medical treatment; authorising the transfer of foreign currency in agreed amounts without obstructions; creating favourable conditions for television and radio broadcasting in one another's countries; and others. The Statement led to several treaties being concluded, including the Treaty on a Customs Union and Single Economic Space on 26 February 1999.

I. Eurasian Economic Community

On 10 October 2000 the presidents of the five States (Belarus, Kazakhstan, Kirgizia, Russia, and Tadzhikistan) who had created the customs union signed the Treaty on the Founding of the Eurasian Economic Community.[36] The Eurasian Economic Community (EurEC) was formed in order to advance effectively the process of establishing the Customs Union and Single Economic Space. All treaties concluded previously between the contracting parties and decisions of those agencies responsible for managing integration remain in force insofar as not contrary to the foundation treaty of the EurEC. The EurEC has four organs: the Inter-State Council, the Integration Committee, the Inter-Parliamentary Assembly, and the Court of the Community. It is the intention of the parties to have the Inter-State Council adopt a decision to terminate the activity of the management organs created by the Treaty of 29 March 1996 and the Treaty on the Customs Union of 26 February 1999.

The *Inter-State Council*, the highest organ of the EurEC, is composed of the Heads of State and Heads of Government of the contracting parties. The *Integration Committee* is the permanently operating organ of the EurEC and is located in Moscow and Almaty. The *Inter-Parliamentary Assembly*, located in St Petersburg, is an agency of parliamentary cooperation within the framework of the EurEC which considers questions of the harmonisation or approximation and unification of national legislation and bringing that legislation into conformity with the treaties concluded within the framework of the EurEC. It is made up of parliamentarians delegated by the parliaments of the contracting parties. The *Court of the Community*, based in Minsk, is to ensure the uniform application of the Treaty by the Contracting Parties and decisions adopted by organs of the EurEC. It also may consider disputes of an economic character arising between the contracting parties on questions of realising decisions of EurEC organs and treaty provisions, giving both explanations and opinions. The Court consists of not more than two representatives from each contracting party and are appointed

---

[36] СЗ РФ (2002), no 7, item 632. The Treaty entered into force for Russia on 30 May 2001.

by the Inter-Parliamentary Assembly upon the recommendation of the Inter-State Council for a term of six years.

Membership in the EurEC is open to all states who accept obligations arising from the Treaty and other treaties in force within the framework of the EurEC according to a list determined by decision of the Inter-State Council and who in the opinion of members of the EurEC can and intend to fulfil those obligations. There is a right to withdraw from the EurEC upon giving 12 months' advance notification, the actual date of departure depending upon the budget year of the EurEC.

The legal capacity of the EurEC is defined as that necessary to realise its purposes and tasks on the territory of each contracting party. The EurEC may establish relations with states and international organisations and conclude treaties with them. It enjoys the 'rights of a juridical person' and may, in particular, conclude contracts, acquire and dispose of property, appear in court, open accounts and perform operations with monetary means.

Decisions of the Integration Committee are taken by weighted voting. The distribution of votes is based on budget contributions as follows: Belarus (20 votes); Kazakhstan (20 votes); Kirgizia (10 votes); Russia (40 votes); and Tadzhikistan (10 votes).

The officials of EurEC are international civil servants and enjoy the privileges and immunities which are necessary for the fulfilment of their functions and achievement of the purposes provided for by the treaties operating within the framework of the EurEC.

J. Towards a Common Law of CIS Integration

The legal nature of the morass of treaties, declarations, decrees, resolutions, recommendations, model enactments, and the like has only begun to be the object of doctrinal analysis.[37] The body of available materials originates mostly in organisational structures firmly embedded in public international law, even when those structures make provision for acts adopted having direct effect in the national legal systems of their constituents. Indeed, in the Russian Federation, by virtue of Article 15(4) of the 1993 Russian Constitution, those documents of treaty-stature would have direct effect in any event.

---

[37] See Mikhaleva (n 2 above) 53–88; E G Moiseev, Правовой статус СНГ [*Legal Status of the CIS*] (1995); Moiseev, Международно-правовые основы сотрудничества стран СНГ [*International Legal Foundations of Cooperation of CIS Countries*] (1997), and V A Rzhevskii, 'О юридической природе форм нового Содружества Независимых Государств' ['On the Legal Nature of the Forms of the New Commonwealth of Independent States'], Государство и право [*State and Law*] no 6 (1992) 27–37.

Because, however, the professed aims of most of the structures include various levels of integration, there is an inclination in some doctrinal writings to classify the entire corpus of agreements creating the CIS and emanating from the CIS as an embryonic 'common law' of the CIS. The expression is not used in its Anglo-American meaning of unwritten law, for these materials all take written form in the CIS. Rather it refers to an emerging shared body of law which may in due course become a species of 'CIS community law' possibly supranational in character. As one Russian jurist views the matter:

> The common law of the CIS is in the process of formation. For the moment it is not a single internally consistent whole: the procedures for the creation of CIS acts and the mechanisms for the defence thereof are underdeveloped. The stimulus for the development of the common law of the Commonwealth is the reality, the requirement, of States-Participants of the CIS for economic, political, and strategic military integration. The norms of common law of the CIS possess all the necessary attributes of norms of law. They regulate the behaviour of participants of legal relations in countries of the CIS . . . the common law of the CIS is by its social nature supranational. It is a subsystem of international law. The norms of common acts of the CIS are orientators for the practical activity of national parliaments and other subjects of law-creation in the CIS.[38]

Whether the vision of a CIS common law comes to pass or not, the symbiotic role of the Russian legal system cannot fail to impress. It is Russian law and Russian legal concepts which serve as the principal model for legal development within the CIS, and it is the international legal system and, if it be such, the CIS subsystem of international law, which have become an integral part of the Russian legal system by virtue of the reception clause in the 1993 Russian Constitution.

---

[38] Mikhaleva (n 3 above) 61–62.

V

RESOURCE MATERIALS

21

RESOURCE MATERIALS ON RUSSIAN LAW

This chapter contains a bibliography of the principal official publications of the RF and subjects of the RF, together with references to secondary sources that develop observations or provide documentation relating to the main text in addition to items cited in the footnotes. The references to secondary sources are confined chiefly to those in the English language and to those relating to the RF since independence in 1991. Unless otherwise indicated, the place of publication is Moscow. For the Soviet period, see Chapter 21 in W E Butler, *Soviet Law* (2nd edn, London, Butterworths, 1988).[1]

A. Bibliography

On the late Soviet period, see I I Kavass, *Demise of the Soviet Union: A Bibliographic Survey of English Writings on the Soviet Legal System, 1900–1991* (Buffalo, W S Hein, 1992), updated for 1992 by Kavass in the *International Journal of Legal Information*, XXI (no 3, Winter 1993).

---

[1] The square brackets are used to distinguish website and email addresses from the text and do not comprise part of the address.

Recent Russian legal publications, together with review articles and personalia, are collected in Юридическая библиография [*Legal Bibliography*] (1997–), issued twice yearly. A quarterly bibliographic index of new legislation and books on financial and economic activity is Финансово-хозяйственная деятельность [*Financial-Economic Activity*], published quarterly.

Extensive bibliographies of CIS books on law, classified by subject, are to be found in each issue of *Sudebnik* (London, 1996–). These are integrated and substantially augmented in W E Butler and J Murjas (comps), *Russian Legal Bibliography* (London, Simmonds & Hill), published annually for 1996–99 and being cumulated for the first decade of legal publication.

B. Dictionaries

For Russian legal terminology, the best dictionary is W E Butler, *Russian-English Legal Dictionary* (Zertsalo, 2001), published together with an extensive bibliography of the author's translations in W E Butler, *Russian-English Legal Dictionary and Bibliographic Sources for Russian Law in English* (Ardsley, Transnational Publishers Inc., 2001). Also see A Kuznetsov, *Russian-English Legal Dictionary* (1995), which is based on a foreign terminological base. Russian equivalents of English legal terminology are to be found in S N Andrianov, A S Berson, and A S Nikiforov, Англо-российский юридический словарь [*Anglo-Russian Legal Dictionary*] (izd-vo Russkii iazyk, 1993); also see G A Komandin, Англо-российский юридический словарь [*Anglo-Russian Legal Dictionary*] (ТОО 'SKL Ltd.', 1993) and A S Mamulian and S Iu Kashkin, Англо-российский полный юридический словарь [*Anglo-Russian Comprehensive Legal Dictionary*] (Sovetnik, 1993).

C. Foreign Language Journals

Amongst Western journals, the *Review of Socialist Law* (1975–), published at the University of Leiden and renamed the *Review of Central and East European Law* as from 1994, appeared bi-monthly through 2001, and became again a quarterly. The *Parker School Journal of East European Law* (1994–) was issued six times yearly, but from 2001 returned to a quarterly. *Soviet Statutes and Decisions* (1964–), renamed *Statutes and Decisions* as from 1993, appears bi-monthly. Russian materials appear from time to time in the *Journal of Constitutional Law in Eastern and Central Europe* (1994–).

Sudebnik (1996–), the law review of the Moscow Higher School of Social and Economic Sciences and The Vinogradoff Institute, University College London, is published quarterly by Simmonds & Hill in London and from 2003 by The Vinogradoff Institute.

Several serials have been published in the RF in foreign languages. *Russland im Rundblick* was issued at St Petersburg in the German language and contained materials of legal interest. The *Russian Law Review* was published in Moscow, with texts both in Russian and English. *Law* was a Russian legal journal in the English language issued by the International Publishing Group Pravo at Moscow. Also in English, at least in part, are *Russian Commercial Law* and the *Russian Oil & Gas Journal,* which are both published in Moscow. *Diritto ed economia in Russia e nella CSI* appears at Moscow in the Italian language and in an English version, *Law and Economics in Russia and the CIS.* The extent to which these publications survived the August 1998 crisis has been difficult to determine.

D. Official Gazettes

Russian Federation

The RF has always regarded itself as the legal successor to the Russian Empire and as the legal continuer of the former Soviet Union. Accordingly, when the Soviet Union was dissolved in December 1991, the parliament of the RF continued to publish its weekly official gazette without interruption, the Ведомости съезда народных депутатов Российской Федерации и Верховного Совета Российской Федерации [*Gazette of the Congress of People's Deputies of the Russian Federation and Supreme Soviet of the Russian Federation*]. When the Congress of People's Deputies was suspended in September 1993 after the abortive attempt to capture the White House, publication ceased after issue No 34 and was resumed in spring 1994, back-dated to January 1994, as Ведомости Федерального собрания Российской Федерации [*Gazette of the Federal Assembly of the Russian Federation*] (11 issues appeared in 1994, 36 issues per year from 1996).

The verbatim transcripts, materials, and documents of the Constitutional Assembly convoked to draft the 1993 Constitution of the Russian Federation were published in 21 volumes (including index), Конституционное совещание. Стенограммы, Материалы, Документы. 29 апреля–10 ноября 1993 г. [*Constitutional Assembly. Transcripts, Materials, Documents. 29 April–10 November 1993*] (1995–96) by the Administration of the President of the RF.

Parliamentary, presidential, and governmental enactments have been published in the Собрание законодательства Российской Федерации [Collection of Legislation of the Russian Federation] weekly from May 1994, replacing the Собрание актов Президента и Правительства Российской Федерации [Collection of Acts of the President and Government of the Russian Federation], issued weekly from 1 July 1992.

The newspaper Российская газета [*Russian Newspaper*] enjoys the status of an official gazette, as did for some time Российские вести [*Russian News*]; the first is published five days per week and available at: [http://www.rg.ru/], whereas the second has had a difficult history, appearing episodically and then disappearing, deprived of its official stature. In October 1999 the newspaper Парламентская газета was given the stature of an official gazette.

The State Duma issues 18 times annually the Сборник федеральных конституционных законов и федеральных законов [Collection of Federal Constitutional Laws and Federal Laws] (1994–); and a monthly collection of its decrees and other documents: Государственная Дума. Постановления и другие документы [State Duma. Decrees and Other Documents] (1994–) and verbatim transcripts of its sessions in Государственная Дума. Стенограммы заседаний *(*Бюллетень*)* [State Duma. Transcripts of Sessions (Bulletin) (60 issues annually, 1994–), to which the Дневник заседании Государственной Думы [Diary of Session of State Duma] (1994–) is issued bi-monthly as a Supplement.

Subjects of the Russian Federation

The Republic Tatarstan publishes a monthly official gazette of the Supreme Soviet in the Russian and Tatar languages: Ведомости Верховного Совета Республики Татарстан [*Gazette of Supreme Soviet of the Republic Tatarstan*] (Kazan, 1992–).

The mayorate of Moscow published twice monthly the Вестник мэрии Москвы [*Herald of the Mayorate of Moscow*], as the successor to the monthly Известия совета депутатов города Москвы [*News of the Soviet of People's Deputies of the City of Moscow*] (1940–). The Ведомости Моссовета [*Gazette of the Moscow Soviet*] is retitled Ведомости Московской Думы [*Gazette of the Moscow Duma*] following the reforms of city government and appears bi-monthly.

The Moscow Regional Duma publishes a monthly gazette, Вестник Московской областной Думы [*Herald of the Moscow Regional Duma*] (1994–).

In St Petersburg the reorganised City Assembly commenced publication of the Вестник Санкт-Петербургского городского собрания [*Herald of the St Petersburg City Assembly*] (1995–), issued monthly. The Mayorate issued the monthly Вестник мэрии Санкт-Петербурга [*Herald of the Mayorate of St Petersburg*] (St Petersburg, 1993–).

The official gazettes of Sverdlovsk Region are a newspaper, Областная газета [*Regional Newspaper*], and the Собрание законодательства Свердловской области [Collection of Legislation of the Sverdlovsk Region] (1995–). The Sverdlovsk Regional Duma issues in booklet form the Ведомости Свердловской областной Думы [*Gazette of the Sverdlovsk Regional Duma*] (1994–).

The great majority (77) of the subjects of the Federation have their legislation available on Consultant Plus, the commercial computer database.

Departmental gazettes

The general gazette specialising in departmental legislation is that published by the Ministry of Justice of the RF, succeeding the bulletin commenced in 1972 by the Ministry of Justice of the USSR. Issued monthly, it is presently titled: Бюллетень нормативных актов министерств и ведомств Российской Федерации [Bulletin of Normative Acts of Ministries and Departments of the Russian Federation], also available on [http://www.systema.ru/]. The same Ministry also issues the Бюллетень Министерства юстиции РФ [Bulletin of the Ministry of Justice of the Russian Federation] (1995–), to appear six times yearly. With effect from 1 July 1996 and appearing twice monthly, the Бюллетень нормативных актов федеральных органов исполнительной власти [Bulletin of Normative Acts of Federal Agencies of Executive Power] (1996–) is an official publication containing the full texts of normative acts adopted by federal agencies of executive power which have been registered at the Ministry of Justice of the Russian Federation.

The newspaper Российская газета [*Russian Newspaper*] contains a weekly Departmental Supplement [Ведомственное приложение] which is subscribed to separately and contains departmental enactments registered by the Ministry of Justice. The draft Russian Civil Code was published there in instalments. For a separate subscription the same group publish the texts of codes, individual laws, or collections of laws, usually on a monthly basis.

From 1996 the Federal Commission for Securities and the Stock Market commenced publication of the Вестник Федеральной комиссии по ценным бумагам и фондовому рынку при правительстве Российской Федерации [*Herald of the Federal Commission for the Securities Market and Stock Exchange attached to the Government of the Russian Federation*] (1996–), the experimental issue being dated 30 January 1996.

The State Customs Committee of the RF publishes a monthly bulletin of official materials issued by it, Таможенные ведомости [*Customs Gazette*] (1994–) and the monthly Таможенный вестник [*Customs Herald*] (1993–).

Налоговый вестник [*Tax Herald*] (1995–), founded by the State Tax Service of the RF, is issued monthly.

The Ministry of Labour of the RF publishes the monthly Бюллетень Министерства труда Российской Федерации [Bulletin of the Ministry of Labour of the Russian Federation] which includes all material relating to labour, pension, social security, veterans. Constitutional Court decisions of relevance are published.

The Бюллетень государственного комитета Российской Федерации по высшему образованию [Bulletin of the State Committee of the Russian Federation for Higher Education] (1933–) is issued monthly by the State Committee of the RF for Higher Education.

Патенты и лицензии [*Patents and Licences*] (1966–) is the monthly gazette of the Committee of the RF for Patents and Trademarks. It contains informational materials, normative acts, and occasional international treaties in its subject area. Изобретение [*Invention*], the bulletin of the Committee of the RF for Patents and Trademarks, appears monthly at Moscow.

Панорама приватизации [*Panorama of Privatisation*] (November 1992–), issued twice monthly by the State Committee of the Russian Federation for the Administration of State Property, contains key GKI enactments, but ceased publication from a date indeterminate.

E. Principal Laws and Codes

Constitution

The Constitution of the Russian Federation, together with the Declaration of Independence and declarations on sovereignty, are translated in W E Butler and J E Henderson (eds), *Russian Legal Texts* (1998); and/or in W E Butler, *Constitutions of the Countries of the Commonwealth of Independent States* (The Hague, Kluwer, 2000). For the Russian-language version, see [http://www.nns/ru/sudy/konsti/konstirf.htm] (the English-language versions on websites are to be avoided).

The Treaties of the Federation, together with individual treaties concluded with Tatarstan, are translated in W E Butler and J E Henderson (eds), *Russian Legal Texts*. For Russian versions, see [http://www.misufa.ru/nb/shared/federationdogovorrf.htm].

The 1978 Constitution of the RSFSR, together with those of all autonomous republics within the RSFSR, are translated in W E Butler, *Collected Legislation of the USSR and Constituent Union Republics: Constitutions* (Dobbs Ferry, Oceana Publications, 1978–91), 2 vols.

President

The President of the Russian Federation website contains certain elementary information at [http://president/kremlin.ru].

Government

The Government of the Russian Federation website is more useful, containing materials (if updated) on the ministries and departments comprising the Government (frequently changed) and access to links with websites of subjects of the Federation. Beware the English versions. Governmental structure is elaborated at: [htto://www.gov.ru/main/ministry/isp-vlast47.html].

In a play on words dating from the Soviet era, Вся власть на www [All Power on www] has links with a vast variety of State and non-State websites. See [http://gosorgan.amursk.ru/]. Individual ministries sometimes place their departmental publications on websites; see below.

Among State agencies whose websites are of general concern should be included the State Committee for Statistics: [http://www.gks.ru]; and the Security Council: [http://www.scrf.gov.ru/]. Background histories on security agencies are given on individual websites: Ministry of Internal Affairs: [http://www.mvd.ru/]; Ministry of Defence: [http://www.mil.ru]; Federal Security Service: [http://www.fsb.ru]; Foreign Intelligence Service: [http://svr.gov.ru/]; Federal Agency for State Communications and Information (FAPSI): [http://www.government.ru/institutions/agencies/fapsi.html].

Federal Assembly

The Federal Assembly of the Russian Federation consists of two chambers, each of which has its own website. The State Duma, or lower chamber, information appears at [http://www.duma.gov.ru]. The Soviet of the Federation, or upper chamber, has the following website: [http://www.council.gov.ru].

The Library of the State Duma has an exceptionally rich website for the time period covered: [www.duma.ru/parlib/]. The data available includes from 1996 a bibliographic index to the СЗ РФ, Ведомости Федерального собрания РФ, and Российская газета, the index of publications, constitutions, and charters of subjects of the Federation (which index also appears in hard-copy form), and other materials.

Both governmental and commercial databases have begun to make recent legislation and normative legal acts routinely accessible in full text free of charge: among the relevant sites are: [http://rus-code.virtualave.net/] and [www.laws.ru]. Check Consultant Plus and Garant for current website addresses.

Judicial system

Each of the court systems has its own website, the English versions of which are defective. See for the Constitutional Court of the Russian Federation: [http://ks.rfnet.ru/]; for the Supreme Court of the Russian Federation: [http://www.supcourt.ru/]; and for the Supreme Arbitrazh Court of the Russian Federation: [http://www.arbitr.ru/].

Civil Code

The Civil Code of the Russian Federation was adopted in three separate parts, Part One having been enacted on 21 October 1994 (in force from 1 January

1995); Part Two, on 22 December 1995 (in force from 1 March 1996); and Part Three on 30 October 2001 (in force from 1 March 2002). In each case certain portions of the Code enter into force on different dates from the rest. Parts One and Two have since been amended. Countless texts of each or both parts have been issued in the Russian Federation, and translated in W E Butler, *Civil Code of the Russian Federation* (London, Simmonds & Hill, 1997; 2nd edn, 1998); W E Butler, *Civil Legislation of the Russian Federation* (The Hague, Kluwer Law International, 1999) (unique amongst English versions for having the totality of Russian Federation, RSFSR, and USSR civil laws in force as of 1999); W E Butler, *Civil Code of the Russian Federation* (Iurinfor, 2001) (in parallel Russian and English texts); in P B Maggs and A N Zhiltsov (transl), *The Civil Code of the Russian Federation. Parts 1 and 2* (International Centre for Financial and Economic Development, 1997); and C Osakwe, *Civil Code of the Russian Federation* (Moscow State University, 2000). Until Part Three was enacted, the 1964 RSFSR Civil Code and the 1991 Fundamental Principles of Civil Legislation of the USSR and Republics remained in force in relevant part.

For the Civil Code as of 1 September 2002, that is, Parts One to Three, see W E Butler, *Civil Code of the Russian Federation* (Oxford, OUP, 2002).

The modern generation of intellectual property legislation in Russia is collected in W E Butler (transl), *Intellectual Property Law in the Russian Federation: Basic Legislation* (London, Simmonds & Hill, 2002).

Family Code

The Russian Family Code was adopted on 8 December 1995 and entered into force on 1 January 1996. Translated in W E Butler and J E Henderson, *Russian Legal Texts* (1998), and in W E Butler, *Russian Family Law* (London, Simmonds & Hill, 1998).

Labour Code

The 2001 Labour Code of the Russian Federation entered into force on 1 February 2002, and is translated in W E Butler, *Labour Code of the Russian Federation* (Bicester, The Vinogradoff Institute, 2002).

The 1971 Labour Code of the RSFSR as amended to 1 December 1993 is available in a translation by W E Butler, *The Labour Code of the Russian Federation* (London and Moscow, Interlist, 1993).

Criminal Code

The Russian Criminal Code was adopted 24 May 1996 and entered into force as from 1 January 1997, replacing the 1960 Criminal Code of the RSFSR as amended. Translated in W E Butler, *Criminal Code of the Russian Federation*

(London, Simmonds & Hill, 1997; 3rd edn, The Hague, Kluwer Law International, 1999), and in W E Butler and J E Henderson, *Russian Legal Texts* (1998).

Code of Civil Procedure

The Code of Civil Procedure that remains partly in force is that of the RSFSR adopted in 1964 as amended. The most recent translation in English appears in W B Simons (ed), *Soviet Codes of Law* (Leiden, A W Sijthoff, 1980), and was replaced on 14 November 2002.

Code of Criminal Procedure

The Code of Criminal Procedure of the Russian Federation entered into force as of 1 July 2002. It replaced the Code of Criminal Procedure of the RSFSR adopted in 1960, as amended. The most recent translation in English appears in W B Simons (ed), *Soviet Codes of Law* (Leiden, A W Sijthoff, 1980).

Other Codes

The Air Code of the Russian Federation, Merchant Shipping Code of the Russian Federation, and the Code of the Russian Federation on Administrative Violations all replace their counterparts from the Soviet era. For the previous Merchant Shipping Code, see W E Butler (transl), *The Merchant Shipping Code of the USSR* (London and Moscow, Interlist, 1995).

Looseleaf services

Many of the earlier Soviet-era codes are in W E Butler (transl), *Collected Legislation of the USSR and Constituent Union Republics* (Dobbs Ferry, Oceana Publications, 1979–91), 7 vols. For more recent materials, see J N Hazard and V Pechota (eds), *Russia and the Republics: Legal Materials* (New York, Transnational Juris Publications, 1993–), a looseleaf service which uses translations supplied by many sources.

The publishing house Infra-M, based in Moscow, has instituted several loose-leaf services: Настольная книга бухгалтера [*Manual of a Bookkeeper*] (1996–); Собрание кодексов Российской Федерации [*Collection of Codes of the Russian Federation*] (1997–); Трудовое право Российской Федерации [*Labour Law of the Russian Federation*] (1997–); and Уголовное и уголовно-процессуальное законодательство Российской Федерации [*Criminal and Criminal Procedure Legislation of the Russian Federation*] (1997–). Российские законы [*Russian Laws*] is a looseleaf service issued by the publishing house BEK in Moscow (1995–); it was the first such commercial venture to appear in Russia, although in fact it was preceded by Российский рынок: сборник нормативных актов [*The Russian Market: Collection of Normative Acts*], a joint venture between the Russian law firm Kontrakt and the publishing house Rossiiskoe pravo (1992–).

F. Court Reports

The Supreme Court of the RF continues to publish the monthly Бюллетень Верховного Суда Российской Федерации [Bulletin of the Supreme Court of the Russian Federation], also available in full text on: [http://www.supcourt.ru/].

From December 1992 the Supreme Arbitrazh Court of the RF commenced publication of the monthly Вестник Высшего Арбитражного Суда Российской Федерации [Herald of the Supreme Arbitrazh Court of the Russian Federation], devoted principally to commentary, legislation, and decrees of the Plenum of the court, available from 1998 on: [http://www.vestnik-vas.ru].

The Вестник Конституционного Суда Российской Федерации [Herald of the Constitutional Court of the Russian Federation], issued bi-monthly, commenced publication in January 1993 with an experimental number '0', also available on: [http://ks.rfnet.ru/].

A special monthly journal for judges is Российский судья [Russian Judge] (1998–).

G. Unofficial Collected Legislation

Serials

Among journals publishing current legislation are Кадастр [Cadastre] (1991–), issued weekly by Informbank Agency; normative acts of other CIS States are sometimes published. Also see Нормативные акты по финансам, налогам и страхованию [Normative Acts on Finances, Taxes, and Insurance] (1991–), issued monthly as an Annex to Законодательство и экономика [Legislation and the Economy] (1992–) which contains economic legislation and commentary, issued twice monthly; and Экспресс-закон: Еженедельный сборник законодательных и нормативных актов Российской Федерации [Express-Law: Weekly Collection of Legislative and Normative Acts of the Russian Federation] (1992–), issued weekly. Кодекс [Kodeks] is published at St Petersburg weekly and contains legislation and commentary. Also see Правовое обозрение [Legal Survey], a monthly journal issued by the Ministry of Justice of the RF, Iniurkollegiia, and others.

Newspapers

Current legislative acts are published by Юридическая газета [*Legal Newspaper*], issued weekly by the Union of Jurists; and Юридический вестник [*Legal Herald*] (weekly, 1991–), issued by the Ministry of Justice of the RF. Экономика и жизнь

[*The Economy and Life*] (weekly, 1918–); Финансовая газета [*Financial Newspaper*] (weekly, July 1991–); Бизнес и банки [*Business and Banks*] (weekly, 1990–); and Бизнес, банки, биржа [*Business, Banks, and the Stock Exchange*] (weekly, 1991–4) are important for departmental tax, financial, economic, and banking (above Central Bank) materials.

Beyond doubt the best newspaper is the Russian legal weekly, Эж-Юрист (1998–), containing analytical articles, documents, and commentary.

Published twice monthly, Налоги [*Taxes*] (1993–) contains tax legislation and instructions.

H. International Treaties

The publication of international treaties of the RF commenced in the monthly Бюллетень международных договоров [Bulletin of International Treaties] (March 1993–), which is issued by the Administration of the President of the RF.

The Ministry of Foreign Affairs of the RF continues to publish the annual collection of treaties in force, renamed in 1994 (vol. 47–) Сборник международных договоров СССР и Российской Федерации [Collection of International Treaties of the USSR and Russian Federation], containing treaties which entered into force during the calendar year 1991 and which are treaties of the Russian Federation as the state-continuer of the USSR. The journal Дипломатический Вестник [*Diplomatic Herald*] (monthly, 1992–), issued by the Ministry of Foreign Affairs, contains the texts of diplomatic documents, also available on: http://www.mid.ru].

International treaties also are published in the Российский ежегодник международного права 1992– [*Russian Yearbook of International Law*], published since 1994 at St Petersburg by the Russian Association of International Law (continuing the Советский ежегодник международного права [*Soviet Yearbook of International Law*] (1958–91), and in the journals Московский журнал международного права [Moscow Journal of International Law] (quarterly, 1991–); Журнал международного частного права [Journal of Private International Law] (twice yearly, St Petersburg, 1993–); and the bilingual quarterly (supplemented by special issues), Международное право [International Law] (1998–), which from 2002 becomes the organ of the Russian Association of International Law. The Association of Maritime Law (formerly the Soviet Association of Maritime Law) issues the Ежегодник морского права [*Yearbook of Maritime Law*].

Devoted to public and private international law and including some documents is the quarterly Международное публичное и частное право [International Public and Private Law](2000–).

Внешняя торговля continues to be issued monthly in separate Russian and English [*Foreign Trade*] language versions by the Ministry of Foreign Economic Relations and contains the texts of commercial treaties. The monthly Международная жизнь, now a quarterly published by the Ministry of Foreign Affairs, occasionally contains international documents; there is an English-language version, *International Affairs*, published in Minneapolis, Minnesota.

I. Law Reviews

The pre-eminent law review in the RF is the venerable monthly journal of the Institute of State and Law of the Russian Academy of Sciences, Государство и право [State and Law] (1930–). The Law Faculty of Moscow State University publishes Вестник Московского университета, серия 11—право [Herald of Moscow University, series 11—Law], bi-monthly. St Petersburg University continues to combine law with philosophy, politology, sociology, and psychology in Вестник Санкт-Петербургского университета, серия 6—право [Herald of St Petersburg University, series 6—Law], issued quarterly. The Известия высших учебных заведений, серия право [News of Higher Educational Institutions, series Law], is issued bi-monthly. The Centre for Private Law issues the Журнал российского права [Journal of Russian Law] (1997–) monthly with an accent on law reform. In Ekaterinburg the Российский юридический журнал [Russian Legal Journal] (1995–), founded by the Ural State Legal Academy and the Ministry of Justice of the RF, is published quarterly, and in Saratov, the Вестник Саратовской государственной академии права [Herald of the Saratov State Academy of Law]. Право и жизнь [Law and Life], described as an independent scientific-popular journal, appears as an irregular quarterly in Moscow. Правовед [Jurist] (1995–) appears bi-monthly in Moscow.

While all the above journals include materials on legal history, the specialist bi-monthly История государства и права (1998–) is devoted entirely to the subject area.

Российская юстиция [Russian Justice] (1923–), published monthly by the Ministry of Justice of the RF, contains articles for the practitioner and the notary (available on CD-ROM from 1995 onwards). The Procuracy reads the monthly journal Законность [Legality], issued at Moscow since 1922 and, since 1997, a quarterly journal issued for the procuracies of all CIS countries, Прокурорская и следственная практика [Procuracy and Investigative Practice]. Notaries have a special publication in St Petersburg, the Информационный бюллетень нотариальной палаты Санкт-Петербурга [Information Bulletin of the Notarial Chamber of St Petersburg], monthly, and in Moscow, Нотариус [Notarius] (1996–) issued by the Youth Union of Jurists, and thereafter issued under the same name (1997–) together with the Federal Notarial Chamber, Moscow City Notarial Chamber, Regional notarial chambers, and the Notarial Chamber of the Republic Belarus, as well as the Бюллетень нотариальной практики [Bulletin of Notarial Practice] (1998–). The Federal Counter-Intelligence Service of the RF publishes bi-monthly the Журнал Федеральной службы контрразведки Российскоий Федерации [*Journal of the Federal Counter-Intelligence Service of the Russian Federation*] (1995–). Forensic medicine is the subject of Судебно-медицинская экспертиза [*Forensic Medical Expert Examination*], published quarterly by the Ministry of Public Health. For the policeman, the monthly journal Милиция [*Police*] is supplemented by a quarterly almanack Профессионал [*Professional*]. The professional investigator consults Следователь [*Investigator*] (1996–), published by the Youth Union of Jurists, now appearing monthly as Российский следователь. The amateur or professional private detective reads Частный сыск и охрана [*Private Detective and Protection*], issued by Interpol-Moscow each month. Criminalistics are addressed in a serial publication which includes a substantial amount of bibliographic material: Вестник криминалистики (2000–). Developments in foreign criminology are followed in the monthly journal Борьба с преступностью за рубежом [*Struggle Against Criminality Abroad*]. Penology is treated in Преступление и наказание [*Crime and Punishment*], a monthly journal of the Ministry of Internal Affairs of the RF.

In the field of civil and arbitrazh procedure there is the monthly Арбитражный и гражданский процесс [Arbitrazh and Civil Procedure] (1998–).

For those interested in military law, Закон и Армия [Law and the Army] (1996–) appeared monthly and from 1996, independently, as an annex to the journal Юрист [Jurist] (1994–), published by the Youth Union of Jurists.

There are a number of law societies which issue journals and newspapers. The Moscow City Advokatura, together with the International Union of Advocates, publishes a monthly newspaper, Адвокат [Advocate] (1993–). Юрист [Jurist] is issued monthly with the participation of the Youth Union of Jurists. Российский адвокат [Russian Advocate], founded by the Guild of Russian Advocates, is published in Moscow. Молодой юрист [Young Jurist], a monthly newspaper, is published by the Youth Union of Jurists, which also issues Московский юрист [Moscow Jurist] (1996–). The Kazan City Society of Young Jurists, a regional division of the Youth Union of Jurists, issues Право и практика [Law and Practice]. The Association of Jurists in the Sverdlovsk Region publishes Юридический Вестник [Legal Herald] twice monthly. The Youth Union of Jurists also issues two annual reference volumes: Вся юридическая Россия [All Legal Russia] (1994–) and Вся юридическая Москва [All Legal Moscow] (1994–). Адвокатская практика (1998–) appears bi-monthly, being issued by the Youth Union of Jurists.

An excellent monthly journal, each issue devoted to a particular theme, combining commentary with selected legislation is Закон [Law] (1992–), published by Izvestia. The Ministry of Justice has commenced Право: Всероссийский юридический жунрал [Law: All-Russian Legal Journal] (1997–), published monthly, to monitor current legislation and judicial practice.

The Association of Legal Institutions of Higher Education has founded its own journal published six times yearly, Вестник юридических вузов [*Herald of Legal Institutions of Higher Education*] (February 1996–), by the Publishing House of the Legal College of Moscow State University. It contains legislation on higher legal education, the texts of State Standards, local acts, bibliography, and commentaries. Of interest to the law teaching profession generally is the quarterly Юридическое образование и наука [Legal Education and Science] (1998–).

Commentary on issues of economic law, including court decisions, is to be found in Хозяйство и право [The Economy and Law] (1977–), presently the organ of the Supreme Arbitrazh Court and the Ministry of Justice of the RF. Право и экономика [Law and the Economy], an annex to the newspaper Деловой мир [*Business World*], is issued in Moscow. Legislation on book-keeping and accounting is discussed and sometimes reproduced in Бухгалтерский учет [*Accounting*] (1937–), issued monthly by the Ministry of Finances of the Russian Federation, and in Новое в бухгалтерском учете и отчетности Российской Федерации [*New in Accounting and Reports of the Russian Federation*] (1996–). Also see Бухгалтерский бюллетень [*Book-keeping Bulletin*] (1996–), which is published with an annex, 'Архив бухгалтера' ['Archive of a Book-keeper']; and 'Бухгалтерский Вестник' [*Book-keeping Herald*] (1995–), with a monthly annex 'Законодательство для бухгалтера' ['Legislation for the Book-keeper']. For subscribers to its book-keeping database, but generally available separately, is a monthly journal, Главная книга (2001–) issued by Consultant Plus. The commentary is sufficiently general to be of interest to business lawyers.

For the entrepreneur Закон и бизнес [Law and Business] appears in Moscow, and Нефть, газ и право [Oil, Gas and Law] is published monthly at Tiumen. Дело и право [Business and Law] (1992–), a monthly, is linked to a computer database service. Право и экономика [Law and the Economy] appears twice monthly under the auspices of the Russian Union of Industrialists and Entrepreneurs in Moscow. Норма [Norm] is issued by the Conference of Unions of Entrepreneurs of Russia. Юридический консультант [Legal Consultant] offers material of commercial interest, issued monthly. Законодательное обеспечение бизнеса в России [Legislative Provision for Business in Russia] (1991–) is issued bi-monthly in English and Russian.

Shipping, carriage by air, river, rail, and motor vehicle are dealt with in their legal aspects quarterly by Транспортное право [Transport Law] (1998–).

Environmental issues are discussed in Экология и закон [Ecology and Law], issued monthly in Moscow, and in Экологическое право [Ecological Law], issued quarterly. In the field of energy studies the journal of legal and commerical information, Нефть, Газ и Право [Oil, Gas and Law] (1995–), is issued six times annually and once yearly Нефтегаз, Энергетика и Законодательство [Oil and Gas, Electric Power and Legislation] (2001–).

Intellectual property is treated in the monthly journals Изобретатель и Рационализатор [Inventor and Rationalizer] and Интеллектуальная собственность [Intellectual Property]. Computer technology is treated in 'Компьютер и право' ['Computer and the Law'], published monthly as an annex to Человек и компьютер [*Man and Computer*].

Banking law is addressed in a quarterly journal bearing the same name, Банковское право [Banking Law] (1998–). The monthly journal Деньги и кредит [*Money and Credit*] (1927–) contains much of legal interest. Securities are treated in Рынок ценных бумаг [*Securities Market*] (1995–), issued bi-monthly. Insurance is the subject of Страховое дело [*Insurance*], issued monthly; in Российский страховой бюллетень [*Russian Insurance Bulletin*] (1993–); and Страховое право: вопросы теории и практики [Insurance Law: Questions of Theory and Practice] (1998–). Financial materials are reproduced monthly in Финансы в документах [*Finances in Documents*] (1997–). Legal aspects of financial securities have their own journal, Ценные бумаги: вопросы права [Securities: Questions of Law] (1998–), and there is much of interest in Вестник НАУФОР (October 1996–), the monthly *Herald of the National Association of Stock Market Participants*, and in Финансовое право [Financial Law] (1999–), issued quarterly.

The President and the Government each have popular informational journals intended for the layman but containing much of legal interest. Российская Федерация [*Russian Federation*] (1994–) is issued twice monthly by the Government of the RF. Президентский контроль [*Presidential Control*] (1994–) is issued bi-monthly by the Administration of the President of the RF. Public law issues are treated in the quarterly Конституционное и муниципальное право [Constitutional and Municipal Law] (1998–) and in the quarterly Государственная власть и местное самоуправление [State Power and Local Self-Government] (1998–).

The commercial press contains much of legal interest. Коммерсант [*Commersant*] (1992–), published weekly as a journal and five times weekly as a newspaper with a less frequent English-language version, is a good example, the best of its kind being Ведомости (2000–), co-sponsored by the *Financial Times* and the *Wall Street Journal*.

The layman continues to be catered for by the monthly Человек и закон [Man and Law] (1968–) issued by the Ministry of Justice of the RF. Also for the layman are Человек и право [Man and Law], described as an international newspaper and published in Moscow; Щит и меч [Shield and Sword], a legal socio-political newspaper; and Домашний адвокат [Home Advocate], issued free of charge in Moscow. Ваше право [Your Law] is issued by the Ministries of Labour and of Social Defence of the RF for the layman.

Правозащитник [Legal Defender] is a journal specialising in the legal problems of non-govermental organisations and issued at Moscow, as is the Бюллетень некоммерческих организаций [Bulletin of Non-commercial Organisations] (1998–).

International legal matters are treated with frequency in Морской сборник [*Maritime Collection*], issued monthly since the nineteenth century by the Russian Navy. On merchant shipping, see Морской флот [*Maritime Fleet*], published bi-monthly.

J. Legal Databases

The information below has been gathered from a variety of sources, including advertising material of the firms themselves. Direct inquiries should be made in each case regarding upgrading policies, software details, CD-ROM and on-line availability, compatibility, networking, and delivery. Most sources are adding daily to their databases and changing their technologies to take into account recent developments.

Since 2000 there has been considerable consolidation and fall-out in the domain of legislative computer databases. Consultant Plus has about 65 per cent of the market, Garant about 30 per cent, Kodeks about 3 per cent, and the remainder is divided amongst the rest. Consultant Plus adds about 10,000 documents monthly, in total as of March 2002 has over 800,000 documents available. Kodeks is moving increasingly into CD-ROM based materials in hard copy with accompanying discs. State offices are increasingly accepting commercial databases supplied without cost as the official databases fall behind in technology and coverage.

Official databases

Система [*Sistema*]: The official database of the Russian Federation, it contains about 65,000 documents as of February 2002, the texts of which have official status. Free of charge to users within Russia, but fees are imposed upon users beyond the Russian Federation. In coverage and quality of search apparatus, it is inferior to the commercial databases. See [http://www.systema.ru/].

Эталон [*Etalon*]: Created by the Scientific Centre for Legal Information of the Ministry of Justice of the Russian Federation for courts and justice agencies, but widely installed in central government offices and available commercially. Contains about 50,000 documents as of February 2002. The system is obsolete in comparison with its commercial competitors and *Sistema*. Publisher: Ministry of Justice, at: [http://www.scli.ru/dbs/ras1etal.asp].

Commercial databases

The three largest commercial databases in order of size are:

Консультант плюс [*Konsultantplus*]: The Regional Information Centre GARANT offers reference systems of the Konsultant Plus (Consultantplus) Family, including Russian legislation divided into thematic topics, both current and repealed versions, documents of the Supreme Court and Supreme Arbitrazh Court of the RF, and all federal district arbitrazh courts, Moscow legislation, Central Bank, Ministry of Finances, State Tax Service, and other departmental acts, most regions, sample notarial, legal, and financial documents, and commentary. Publisher: Konsultant Plus [http://www.consultant.ru].

Гарант [*Garant*]: One of the earliest legislative database systems to appear on the market, Garant is widely used in Russian government offices. Available on-line or in CD-ROM form. Recent legal materials can be consulted free of charge in a generally accessible section on 'hot documents'. A separate English-language version is to be avoided. Publisher: Garant [http://www.garant.ru/].

Кодес [*Kodeks*]: St Petersburg-based, this legal database is moving increasingly towards CD-ROM publications, with a variety of subject categories: economic legislation, book-keeping and finances for enterprises, banking and finance, customs law, international law, securities and privatisation, arbitrazh law and practice, construction and architecture, insurance, legal commentaries and advice, samples of legal and business documents, customs legislation of the CIS and the Baltic, banking legislation of the CIS and Baltic, judicial practice of all federal arbitrazh district courts. The English versions are to be avoided. Updated weekly. Available on-line or CD-ROM or supplied in disk form. Publisher: Kodeks [http://www2. kodeks.net/n-zak].

Other databases include:

Аргумент [*Argument*]: Issued by Agenstvo 'Biznes-Press' in Moscow, the databases include material on central and local governmental structures and officials, as well as the press centres of State agencies of the RF. Thematic offerings include the Regions of Russia, the Structures of Power of Russia, the CIS, and Baltic Countries, Official Moscow. Publisher: Agenstvo 'Biznes-Press', Volgogradskii pr-t 26, Office 608, Moscow, Russia. Tel: 095–277–0660, 215–5610; fax: 095–270–9090.

Дело и право [*Delo i pravo*]: Moscow-based, this complex of databases claims to have all legislation 'from the commencement of the formation of market relations in Russia'. Three basic services are offered: Russia, Moscow and Moscow Region, and Taxes. Publisher: Delo i pravo, ul. Iablochkova dom 5, 127254 Moscow, Russia. Tel/fax: 095–210–2221.

ИНЕК [*INEK (INEC)*]: Situated in Moscow, this firm offers more than 15,000 documents in subject categories: economic law and the market (tax, land, labour, housing, investment, and other legislation), insurance, banking law (includes basic legislation, instructions, letters, telegrams), foreign economic activity, legislative acts of the city of Moscow. Commentaries on individual enactments and branches of law are a speciality. Fully cross-referenced, including after upgrades. Tel: 095–150–8608, 150–9213, 150–8604.

Юр-Профи [*Iur-Profi*]: An agency of the Youth Union of Jurists, this group maintains and offers databases containing the principal normative legal acts regulating higher education and a separate database of law schools and faculties in Russia. Publisher: Iur-Profi, PO Box 15, 125057 Moscow, Russia. Tel/fax: 095–238–8885; fax: 095–246–2020.

ЮСИС [*IUSIS (JUSIS)*]: Issued by the Legal Information Agency Interlex, legislative databases exist for Russian legislation (State Duma, President, Government, Central Bank, Ministry of Finances, Ministry of Labour), Moscow, Moscow Region, St Petersburg, Leningrad Region, court decisions, notarial practice, arbitrazh practice, commentaries, and model documents [http://www.intralex.ru/].

Право [*Pravo*]: Offers database containing information regarding Russian legislation in force, full texts with issuance data, renewable weekly or monthly. Also offers electronic versions of journals which it publishes. Publisher: Iuridicheskii dom Iustitsinform, Kotel'nicheskaia nab. 17, 109240 Moscow, Russia. Tel/fax: 095–298–3841.

Референт [*Referent RT*]: Database containing 35,000 documents and several informational modules: Russia, Regions, Финансовая газета [*Financial Newspaper*] (1994–), Auditor. Publisher: ZAO 'Referent-Servis' [http://www. referent.ru/].

Russian search engines

There are several, including: Апорт/Aport [http://www.aport.ru/]; Рэмблер/ Rembler [http://www.rambler.ru/]; Яндекс/Yandex: [http://www.yandex.ru].

APPENDIX

CONSTITUTION
of the
RUSSIAN FEDERATION

[Adopted by Referendum, 12 December 1993, as amended
by Edicts of the President of the Russian Federation, 9 January
1996, No 20, 10 February 1996, No 173, and 9 June 2001, No 209.
Российская газета, 25 December 1993; СЗ РФ(1996),
no 3, item 152; no 7, item 676; (2001), no 24, item 2421]

We, the multinational people of the Russian Federation,
united by a common fate on our land,
affirming the rights and freedoms of man and civil peace and harmony,
retaining the historically-formed State unity,
proceeding from generally-recognised principles of equality and self-determination of peoples,
honouring the memory of ancestors who transmitted to us love and respect for the Fatherland and faith in good and justness,
renewing the sovereign Statehood of Russia and affirming the inviolability of its democratic foundations,
endeavouring to ensure the well-being and prosperity of Russia,
proceeding from a responsibility for the Motherland to the present and future generations,
aware of being part of the world community,
adopt the Constitution of the Russian Federation.

Section One

CHAPTER 1. FOUNDATIONS OF THE CONSTITUTIONAL SYSTEM

Article 1

1. The Russian Federation—Russia is a democratic federated rule-of-law State with a republic form of government.

2. The names Russian Federation and Russia are of equal significance.

Article 2

Man, his rights and freedoms are the highest value. Recognition of, compliance with, and defence of the rights and freedoms of man and citizen shall be the duty of the State.

Article 3

1. The bearer of sovereignty and the sole source of power in the Russian Federation shall be its multinational people.

705

2. The people shall effectuate their power directly and also through agencies of State power and agencies of local self-government.

3. The highest direct expression of the power of the people shall be the referendum and free elections.

4. No one may appropriate power in the Russian Federation. The seizure of power or the appropriation of the powers of rule shall be prosecuted according to a federal law.

Article 4

1. The sovereignty of the Russian Federation shall extend to all of its territory.

2. The Constitution of the Russian Federation and federal laws shall have supremacy throughout the entire territory of the Russian Federation.

3. The Russian Federation shall ensure the integrity and inviolability of its territory.

Article 5

1. The Russian Federation shall consist of republics, territories, regions, cities of federal significance, autonomous region, autonomous national areas — which shall be equal subjects of the Russian Federation.

2. A republic (State) shall have its own constitution and legislation. A territory, region, city of federal significance, autonomous region, or autonomous national area shall have its own charter and legislation.

3. The federated structure of the Russian Federation shall be based on its State integrity, unity of the system of State power, delimitation of the subjects of jurisdiction and powers among the agencies of State power of the Russian Federation and agencies of State power of the subjects of the Russian Federation and the equality and self-determination of peoples in the Russian Federation.

4. All subjects of the Russian Federation shall be equal between themselves in mutual relations with federal agencies of State power.

Article 6

1. Citizenship of the Russian Federation shall be acquired and shall terminate in accordance with a federal law and shall be uniform and equal irrespective of the grounds of acquisition.

2. Each citizen of the Russian Federation shall possess on its territory all the rights and freedoms and bear equal duties provided for by the Constitution of the Russian Federation.

3. A citizen of the Russian Federation may not be deprived of his citizenship or the right to change it.

Article 7

1. The Russian Federation shall be a social State whose policy is directed towards the creation of conditions ensuring a life of dignity and the free development of man.

2. Labour and human health shall be protected in the Russian Federation, a guaranteed minimum amount of payment for labour shall be established, State support of the family, motherhood, fatherhood, childhood, disabled persons, and aged citizens shall be ensured, the system of social services shall be developed, and State pensions, benefits, and other guarantees of social defence shall be established.

Article 8

1. The unity of economic space, free movement of goods, services, and financial assets, support of competition, and freedom of economic activity shall be guaranteed in the Russian Federation.

2. Private, State, municipal, and other forms of ownership shall be equally recognised and defended in the Russian Federation.

Article 9

1. Land and other natural resources shall be used and protected in the Russian Federation as the basis of the life and activity of peoples residing on the respective territory.

2. Land and other natural resources may be in private, State, municipal, and other forms of ownership.

Article 10

State power in the Russian Federation shall be effectuated on the basis of separation into legislative, executive, and judicial. Agencies of legislative, executive, and judicial power shall be autonomous.

Article 11

1. State power in the Russian Federation shall be effectuated by the President of the Russian Federation, the Federal Assembly (Soviet of the Federation and the State Duma), the Government of the Russian Federation, and the courts of the Russian Federation.

2. State power in the subjects of the Russian Federation shall be effectuated by agencies of State power formed by them.

3. Delimitation of the subjects of jurisdiction and powers among the agencies of State power of the Russian Federation and agencies of State power of the subjects of the Russian Federation shall be effectuated by the present Constitution, by the Treaty of the Federation, and by other treaties on the delimitation of the subjects of jurisdiction and powers.

Article 12

Local self-government shall be recognised and guaranteed in the Russian Federation. Local self-government within the limits of its powers shall be autonomous. Agencies of local self-government shall not be within the system of agencies of State power.

Article 13

1. Ideological diversity shall be recognised in the Russian Federation.

2. No ideology may be established as State or obligatory.

3. Political diversity and a multi-party system shall be recognised in the Russian Federation.

4. Social associations shall be equal before the law.

5. The creation and activity of social associations whose purposes or actions are directed towards the forcible change of the foundations of the constitutional system and a violation of the integrity of the Russian Federation, subverting the security of the State, the creation of armed formations, incitement of social, racial, nationality, and religious enmity shall be prohibited.

Article 14

1. The Russian Federation is a secular State. No religion may be established as State or obligatory.

2. Religious associations shall be separate from the State and equal before the law.

Article 15

1. The Constitution of the Russian Federation shall have the highest legal force, direct effect, and be applied throughout the entire territory of the Russian Federation. Laws and other legal acts applicable in the Russian Federation must not be contrary to the Constitution of the Russian Federation.

2. Agencies of State power, agencies of local self-government, officials, citizens, and their associations shall be obliged to comply with the Constitution of the Russian Federation and laws.

3. Laws shall be subject to official publication. Unpublished laws shall not be applied. Any normative legal acts affecting the rights, freedoms, and duties of man and citizen may not be applied if they have not been published officially for general information.

4. Generally-recognised principles and norms of international law and international treaties of the Russian Federation shall be an integral part of its legal system. If other rules have been established by an international treaty of the Russian Federation than provided for by a law, the rules of the international treaty shall apply.

Article 16

1. The provisions of the present Chapter of the Constitution shall comprise the foundations of the constitutional system of the Russian Federation and may not be changed other than in the procedure established by the present Constitution.

2. No other provisions of the present Constitution may be contrary to the foundations of the constitutional system of the Russian Federation.

CHAPTER 2. RIGHTS AND FREEDOMS OF MAN AND CITIZEN

Article 17

1. The rights and freedoms of man and citizen according to generally-recognised principles and norms of international law and in accordance with the present Constitution shall be recognised and guaranteed in the Russian Federation.

2. The basic rights and freedoms of man shall be inalienable and shall belong to each from birth.

3. The effectuation of the rights and freedoms of man and citizen must not violate the rights and freedoms of other persons.

Article 18

The rights and freedoms of man and citizen shall be of direct effect. They shall determine the sense, content, and application of laws and the activity of legislative and executive power and local self-government and shall be ensured by justice.

Article 19

1. All shall be equal before law and court.

2. The State shall guarantee the equality of rights and freedoms of man and citizen irrespective of sex, race, nationality, language, origin, property and official position, place of residence, attitude towards religion, convictions, affiliation to social associations, and also other circumstances. Any forms of the limitation of the rights of citizens according to indicia of social, racial, nationality, language, or religious affiliation shall be prohibited.

3. Man and woman shall have equal rights and freedoms and equal opportunities for the realisation thereof.

Article 20

1. Each shall have the right to life.

2. The death penalty may until the abolition thereof be established by a federal law as an exceptional measure of punishment for especially grave crimes against lie while granting to the accused the right to consideration of his case by a court with the participation of jurors.

Article 21

1. The dignity of the person shall be protected by the State. Nothing may be grounds for demeaning it.

2. No one may be subjected to tortures, force, or other cruel treatment or punishment humiliating human dignity. No one may be subjected without voluntary consent to medical, scientific, or other experiments.

Article 22

1. Each shall have the right to freedom and personal inviolability.

2. Arrest, confinement under guard, and maintenance under guard shall be permitted only according to a judicial decision. Before a judicial decision a person may not be subjected to detention for a period of more than 48 hours.

Article 23

1. Each shall have the right to inviolability of private life, personal and family secrecy, and defence of his honour and good name.

2. Each shall have the right to secrecy of correspondence, telephone conversations, postal, telegraph, and other communications. Limitation of this right shall be permitted only on the basis of a judicial decision.

Article 24

1. The collection, keeping, use, and dissemination of information concerning the private life of a person without his consent shall not be permitted.

2. Agencies of State power and agencies of local self-government and their officials shall be obliged to ensure to each the opportunity to familiarise himself with documents and material directly affecting his rights and freedoms unless provided otherwise by a law.

Article 25

A dwelling shall be inviolable. No one shall have the right to penetrate into a dwelling against the will of the persons residing therein other than in the instances established by a federal law or on the basis of a judicial decision.

Article 26

1. Each shall have the right to determine and specify his nationality affiliation. No one may be forced to determine and specify his nationality affiliation.

2. Each shall have the right to use his native language and to the free choice of language for communion, nurturing, study, and creativity.

Article 27

1. Each who is legally on the territory of the Russian Federation shall have the right to freely move about and choose a place of sojourn and residence.

2. Each may freely depart from the limits of the Russian Federation. A citizen of the Russian Federation shall have the right without hindrance to return to the Russian Federation.

Article 28

Each shall be guaranteed the freedom of conscience, freedom of religious belief, including the right to propagate any religion individually or jointly with others, or not to propagate, freely choose, have, and disseminate religious and other convictions and to act in accordance with them.

Article 29

1. Freedom of thought and speech shall be guaranteed to each.

2. Propaganda or agitation inciting social, racial, nationality, or religious enmity and hatred shall not be permitted. Propaganda of social, racial, nationality, religious, or linguistic supremacy shall be prohibited.

3. No one may be forced to express his opinions and convictions or to renounce them.

4. Each shall have the right to freely seek, receive, transmit, produce, and disseminate information by any legal means. A list of information constituting a State secret shall be determined by a federal law.

5. The freedom of mass information shall be guaranteed. Censorship shall be prohibited.

Article 30

1. Each shall have the right to association, including the right to create trade unions in order to defend their interests. The freedom of activity of social associations shall be guaranteed.

2. No one may be forced to join any association or to be therein.

Article 31

Citizens of the Russian Federation shall have the right to assemble peacefully without weapons, hold assemblies, meetings, and demonstrations, processions, and picketing.

Article 32

1. Citizens of Russian Federation shall have the right to participate in the administration of affairs of the State both directly and through their representatives.

2. Citizens of the Russian Federation shall have the right to elect and to be elected to agencies of State power and agencies of local self-government, and also to participate in a referendum.

3. Citizens deemed by a court to lack dispositive legal capacity, and also maintained in places of deprivation of freedom by judgment of a court, shall not have the right to elect and to be elected.

4. Citizens of the Russian Federation shall have equal access to State service.

5. Citizens of the Russian Federation shall have the right to participate in the dispensing of justice.

Article 33

Citizens of the Russian Federation shall have the right to have recourse personally, and also to send individual and collective appeals to State agencies and to agencies of local self-government.

Article 34

1. Each shall have the right to free use of his abilities and property for entrepreneurial and other economic activity not prohibited by a law.

2. Economic activity directed towards monopolisation and unfair competition shall not be permitted.

Article 35

1. The right of private ownership shall be protected by a law.

2. Each shall have the right to have property in ownership, possess, use, and dispose of it both as one person and jointly with other persons.

3. No one may be deprived of his property other than by decision of a court. The compulsory alienation of property for State needs may be done only on condition of advance and fair compensation.

4. The right of inheritance shall be guaranteed.

Article 36

1. Citizens and their associations shall have the right to have land in private ownership.

2. The possession, use, and disposition of land and other natural resources shall be effectuated by their owners freely unless this brings damage to the environment and does not violate the rights and legal interests of other persons.

3. The conditions and procedure for the use of land shall be determined on the basis of a federal law.

Article 37

1. Labour shall be free. Each shall have the right to freely dispose of his capabilities to labour and to choose the nature of activity and profession.

2. Forced labour shall be prohibited.

3. Each shall have the right to labour in conditions which meet the requirements of safety and hygiene, to remuneration for labour without any discrimination whatever, and to the minimum amount of payment for labour established by a federal law, and also the right to defence against unemployment.

4. The right to individual and collective labour disputes with the use of means established by a federal law for the settlement thereof, including the right to strike.

5. Each shall have the right to leisure. The duration of work time, days off and holidays, and paid annual leave established by a federal law shall be guaranteed to a person working under a labour contract.

Article 38

1. Motherhood and childhood and the family shall be under the defence of the State.

2. Concern for children and their nurturing shall be the equal right and duty of the parents.

3. Children capable of labour who have attained 18 years of age must be concerned for parents who are not capable of labour.

Article 39

1. To each shall be guaranteed social security for age, illness, disability, loss of breadwinner, nurturing children, and in other instances established by a law.

2. State pensions and social benefits shall be established by a law.

3. Voluntary social insurance and the creation of additional forms of social security and philanthropy shall be encouraged.

Article 40

1. Each shall have the right to housing. No one may be arbitrarily deprived of housing.

2. Agencies of State power and agencies of local self-government shall encourage housing construction and create conditions for the effectuation of the right to housing.

3. Indigent and other citizens specified in a law who need housing shall be granted such free of charge or for affordable payment from State, municipal, and other housing funds in accordance with norms established by a law.

Article 41

1. Each shall have the right to health protection and medical assistance. Medical assistance in State and municipal public health institutions shall be rendered to citizens free of charge at the expense of assets of the respective budget, insurance contributions, and other proceeds.

2. Federal programmes for the protection and strengthening of health of the populace shall be financed in the Russian Federation, measures shall be taken for the development of State, municipal, and private public health systems, activity shall be encouraged which promotes the strengthening of the health of man, the development of physical culture and sport, and ecological and sanitary-epidemiological well-being.

3. The concealment by officials of facts and circumstances threatening human life and health shall entail responsibility in accordance with a federal law.

Article 42

Each shall have the right to a favourable environment, reliable information concerning the state thereof, and compensation for damage caused to his health or property by an ecological violation.

Article 43

1. Each shall have the right to education.

2. The general accessibility of and free preschool, basic general and secondary vocational education in State or municipal educational institutions and at enterprises shall be guaranteed.

3. Each shall have the right on a competitive basis to receive higher education free of charge in a State or municipal educational institution or at an enterprise.

4. Basic general education shall be obligatory. Parents or persons replacing them shall ensure by receipt of basic general education by children.

5. The Russian Federation shall establish federal State educational standards and shall support various forms of education and self-education.

Article 44

1. To each shall be guaranteed the freedom of literary, artistic, scientific, technical, and other types of creativity and teaching. Intellectual property shall be protected by a law.

2. Each shall have the right to participation in cultural life and the use of institutions of culture and of access to cultural valuables.

3. Each shall be obliged to be concerned for the preservation of the historical and cultural heritage and to care for monuments of history and culture.

Article 45

1. The State defence of the rights and freedoms of man and citizen shall be guaranteed in the Russian Federation.

2. Each shall have the right to defend his rights and freedoms by all means not prohibited by a law.

Article 46

1. To each shall be guaranteed the judicial defence of his rights and freedoms.

2. Decisions and actions (or omissions to act) of agencies of State power, agencies of local self-government, social associations, and officials may be appealed to a court.

3. Each shall have the right in accordance with international treaties of the Russian Federation to apply to inter-State agencies for the defence of the rights and freedoms of man if all available intra-State means of legal defence have been exhausted.

Article 47

1. No one may be deprived of the right to consideration of a case in that court and by those judges to whose jurisdiction it has been relegated by a law.

2. A person accused of committing a crime shall have the right to consideration of his case with the participation of jurors in the instances provided for by a federal law.

Article 48

1. To each shall be guaranteed the right to receive qualified legal assistance. In the instances provided for by a law, legal assistance shall be rendered free of charge.

2. Each person detained, confined under guard, or accused of committing a crime shall have the right to take advantage of the assistance of an advocate (or defender) from the moment respectively of the detention, confinement under guard, or presentation of the accusation.

Article 49

1. Each person accused of committing a crime shall be considered to be innocent until his guilt is proved in the procedure provided for by a federal law and established by the judgment of a court which has entered into legal force.

2. An accused person shall not be obliged to prove his innocence.

3. Ineradicable doubts of the guilt of a person shall be interpreted to the benefit of the accused person.

Article 50

1. No one may be convicted a second time for one and the same crime.

2. When effectuating justice the use of evidence obtained in violation of a federal law shall not be permitted.

3. Each person convicted for a crime shall have the right to a review of the judgment by a superior court in the procedure established by a federal law, and also the right to request a pardon or mitigation of punishment.

Article 51

1. No one may be obliged to testify against himself, his spouse, or near relatives, the group of which shall be determined by a federal law.

2. Other instances of being relieved from the duty to give witness testimony may be established by a federal law.

Article 52

The rights of victims of crimes and abuses of power shall be protected by a law. The State shall ensure the victim access to justice and contributory compensation for damage caused.

Article 53

Each shall have the right to compensation by the State for harm caused by the illegal actions (or omissions to act) of agencies of State power or their officials.

Article 54

1. A law establishing or aggravating responsibility shall not have retroactive force.

2. No one may bear responsibility for an act which at the moment of its commission was not deemed to be a violation of law. If after the commission of a violation of law responsibility therefor has been eliminated or mitigated, the new law shall be applied.

Article 55

1. The enumeration in the Constitution of the Russian Federation of the basic rights and freedoms must not be interpreted as a denial or diminution of other generally-recognised rights and freedoms of man and citizen.

2. Laws abolishing or diminishing the rights and freedoms of man and citizen must not be issued in the Russian Federation.

3. The rights and freedoms of man and citizen may be limited by a federal law only in the extent to which this is necessary for the purposes of defence of the foundations of the constitutional system, morality, health, rights, and legal interests of other persons and ensuring the defence of the country and security of the State.

Article 56

1. Under conditions of an extraordinary situation in order to ensure the safety of citizens and defence of the constitutional system individual limitations of the rights and freedoms may be established by a federal constitutional law, specifying the limits and the period of their operation.

2. An extraordinary situation throughout the entire territory of the Russian Federation and individual localities thereof may be introduced when the circumstances are present and in the procedure established by a federal constitutional law.

3. The rights and freedoms provided for by Articles 20, 21, 23 (paragraph 1), 24, 28, 34 (paragraph 1), 40 (paragraph 1), 46–54 of the Constitution of the Russian Federation shall not be subject to limitation.

Article 57

Each shall be obliged to pay legally established taxes and charges. Laws establishing new taxes or worsening the position of taxpayers shall not have retroactive force.

Article 58

Each shall be obliged to preserve nature and the environment and to care for that relegated to natural wealth.

Article 59

1. Defence of the Fatherland shall be the obligation and duty of a citizen of the Russian Federation.

2. A citizen of the Russian Federation shall bear military service in accordance with a federal law.

3. A citizen of the Russian Federation shall, in the event his convictions or religious belief is contrary to bearing military service, and also in other instances established by a federal law, have the right to replace it with alternative civilian service.

Article 60

A citizen of the Russian Federation may autonomously effectuate his rights and duties in full from 18 years of age.

Article 61

1. A citizen of the Russian Federation may not be deported beyond the limits of the Russian Federation or extradited to another State.

2. The Russian Federation shall guarantee to its citizens defence and protection beyond its limits.

Article 62

1. A citizen of the Russian Federation may have the citizenship of a foreign State (dual citizenship) in accordance with a federal law or international treaty of the Russian Federation.

2. That a citizen of the Russian Federation has the citizenship of a foreign State shall not diminish his rights and freedoms nor relieve him from duties arising from Russian citizenship unless provided otherwise by a federal law or by an international treaty of the Russian Federation.

3. Foreign citizens and stateless persons shall enjoy in the Russian Federation the rights and bear the duties equally with citizens of the Russian Federation except for instances established by a federal law or by an international treaty of the Russian Federation.

Article 63

1. The Russian Federation shall grant political asylum to foreign citizens and stateless persons in accordance with generally-recognised norms of international law.

2. The extradition to other States of persons being persecuted for political convictions, and also for actions (or omission to act) which are not deemed to be a crime in the Russian Federation, shall not be permitted in the Russian Federation. The extradition of persons accused of committing a crime, and also the transfer of convicted persons to serve punishment in other States, shall be effectuated on the basis of a federal law or international treaty of the Russian Federation.

Article 64

The provisions of the present Chapter shall constitute the foundations of the legal status of the person in the Russian Federation and may not be changed other than in the procedure established by the present Constitution.

CHAPTER 3. FEDERATED STRUCTURE

Article 65

1. There shall be subjects within the Russian Federation:
Republic Adygeia (Adygeia), Republic Altai, Republic Bashkortostan, Republic Buriatiia, Republic Dagestan, Republic Ingushetia, Kabardino-Balkarian Republic, Republic Kalmykiia, Karachaevo-Cherkessy Republic, Republic Karelia, Republic Komi, Republic Marii El, Republic Mordoviia, Republic Sakha (Iakutiia), Republic Northern Osetia-Alaniia, Republic Tatarstan (Tatarstan),

Republic Tyva, Udmurt Republic, Republic Khakasiia, Chechen Republic, Chuvash Republic-Chuvashia [as amended by Edicts of the President of the Russian Federation, 9 January 1996, 10 February 1996, and 9 June 2001];

Altai Territory, Krasnodar Territory, Krasnoiarsk Territory, Maritime Territory, Stavropol Territory, Khabarovsk Territory;

Amur Region, Arkhangel Region, Astrakhan Region, Belgorod Region, Briansk Region, Vladimir Region, Volgograd Region, Vologda Region, Voronezh Region, Ivanovo Region, Irkutsk Region, Kaliningrad Region, Kaluga Region, Kamchatka Region, Kemerovo Region, Kirov Region, Kostroma Region, Kurgan Region, Kursk Region, Leningrad Region, Lipetsk Region, Magadan Region, Moscow Region, Murmansk Region, Nizhegorod Region, Novgorod Region, Novosibirsk Region, Omsk Region, Orenburg Region, Orlovsk Region, Penza Region, Perm Region, Pskov Region, Rostov Region, Riazan Region, Samara Region, Saratov Region, Sakhalin Region, Sverdlovsk Region, Smolensk Region, Tambov Region, Tver Region, Tomsk Region, Tula Region, Tiumen Region, Ul'ianovsk Region, Cheliabinsk Region, Chita Region, Iaroslavl Region;

Moscow, St. Petersburg—cities of federal significance;

Jewish Autonomous Region;

Agin Buriat Autonomous National Area, Komi-Permiats Autonomous National Area, Koriak Autonomous National Area, Nentsy Autonomous National Area, Taimyr (Dolgano-Nentsy) Autonomous National Area, Ust-Ordyn Buriat Autonomous National Area, Khanty-Mansiisk Autonomous National Area, Chukotsk Autonomous National Area, Evenkiisk Autonomous National Area, Iamalo-Nentsy Autonomous National Area.

2. The admission to the Russian Federation and the formation within it of a new subject shall be effectuated in the procedure established by a federal constitutional law.

Article 66

1. The status of a republic shall be determined by the Constitution of the Russian Federation and the constitution of the republic.

2. The status of a territory, region, city of federal significance, autonomous region, or autonomous national area shall be determined by the Constitution of the Russian Federation and by the charter of the territory, region, city of federal significance, autonomous region, or autonomous national area adopted by the legislative (or representative) agency of the respective subject of the Russian Federation.

3. Upon the recommendation of legislative and executive agencies of an autonomous region or autonomous national area, a federal law on the autonomous region or autonomous national area may be adopted.

4. The relations of autonomous national areas within a territory or region may be regulated by a federal law and by a treaty between the agencies of State power of the autonomous region and, respectively, the agencies of State power of the territory or region.

5. The status of a subject of the Russian Federation may be changed by mutual consent of the Russian Federation and the subject of the Russian Federation in accordance with a federal constitutional law.

Article 67

1. The territory of the Russian Federation shall incorporate the territories of its subjects, internal waters, and the territorial sea, and airspace above them.

2. The Russian Federation shall possess sovereign rights and effectuate jurisdiction on the continental shelf and in the exclusive economic zone of the Russian Federation in the procedure determined by a federal law and norms of international law.

3. The boundaries between subjects of the Russian Federation may be changed with their mutual consent.

Article 68

1. The Russian language shall be the State language of the Russian Federation throughout all of its territory.

2. Republics shall have the right to establish their own State languages. They shall be used, together with the State language of the Russian Federation, in agencies of State power, agencies of local self-government, and State institutions of the Republic.

3. The Russian Federation shall guarantee to all of its peoples the right to preserve the native language and the creation of conditions for its study and development.

Article 69

The Russian Federation shall guarantee the rights of native small peoples in accordance with generally-recognised principles and norms of international law and international treaties of the Russian Federation.

Article 70

1. The State flag, arms, and anthem of the Russian Federation, the description thereof, and the procedure for the official use shall be established by a federal constitutional law.

2. The capital of the Russian Federation shall be the city of Moscow. The status of the capital shall be established by a federal law.

Article 71

There shall be within the jurisdiction of the Russian Federation:
- (a) the adoption and change of the Constitution of the Russian Federation and federal laws, and control over compliance therewith;
- (b) the federated structure and territory of the Russian Federation;
- (c) the regulation and defence of the rights and freedoms of man and citizen; citizenship in the Russian Federation; regulation and defence of the rights of national minorities;
- (d) the establishment of the system of federal agencies of legislative, executive, and judicial power, and the procedure for their organisation and activity; the formation of federal agencies of State power;
- (e) federal State ownership and the administration thereof;
- (f) the establishment of the fundamental principles of federal policy and federal programmes in the domain of State, economic, ecological, social, cultural, and nationality development of the Russian Federation;
- (g) the establishment of the legal foundations of a single market; financial, currency, credit, and customs regulations, monetary emission, foundations of price policy; federal economic services, including federal banks;
- (h) federal budget; federal taxes and charges; federal regional development funds;
- (i) federal electric power system, nuclear power, fissionable materials; federal transport, railways, information, and communications; activity in outer space;
- (j) foreign policy and international relations of the Russian Federation, international treaties of the Russian Federation; questions of war and peace;
- (k) foreign economic relations of the Russian Federation;
- (l) defence and security; defence production; determination of the procedure for the sale and purchase of weapons, ammunition, combat technology, and other military

property; production of poisonous substances, narcotic means, and the procedure for the use thereof;

(m) determination of the status and defence of the State boundary, territorial sea, airspace, exclusive economic zone, and continental shelf of the Russian Federation;

(n) court organisation; procuracy; criminal, criminal procedure, and criminal-executory legislation; amnesty and pardon; civil, civil procedure, and arbitrazh procedure legislation; legal regulation of intellectual property;

(o) federal conflicts of law;

(p) meterological service, standards, metric system, and calculation of time; geodesy and cartography; names of geographic objects; official statistical and bookkeeping records;

(q) State awards and titles of honour of the Russian Federation;

(r) federal State service.

Article 72

1. There shall be within the joint jurisdiction of the Russian Federation and the subjects of the Russian Federation:

(a) ensuring the conformity of the constitutions and laws of the republics and the charters, laws, and other normative legal acts of territories, regions, cities of federal significance, autonomous region, and autonomous national areas to the Constitution of the Russian Federation and to federal laws;

(b) defence of the rights and freedoms of man and citizen; defence of the rights of national minorities; ensuring legality, legal order, and public security; the regime of border zones;

(c) questions of the possession, use, and disposition of land, subsoil, water, and other natural resources;

(d) delimitation of State ownership;

(e) nature use; protection of the environment and ensuring ecological security; specially protected nature territories; protection of monuments of history and culture;

(f) general questions of nurturing, education, science, culture, physical culture and sport;

(g) coordination of questions of public health; defence of the family, motherhood, fatherhood, and childhood; social defence, including social security;

(h) effectuation of measures relating to the struggle against catastrophes, natural disasters, epidemics, and liquidation of their consequences;

(i) establishment of general principles of taxation and charges in the Russian Federation;

(j) administrative, administrative procedure, labour, family, housing, land, water, and forest legislation, legislation on the subsoil and on environmental protection;

(k) personnel of judicial and law enforcement agencies; advokatura, notariat;

(l) defence of the natural habitat and traditional way of life of small ethnic communities;

(m) establishment of general principles for the organisation of the system of agencies of State power and local self-government;

(n) coordination of international and foreign economic relations of subjects of the Russian Federation, and the fulfilment of international treaties of the Russian Federation.

2. The provisions of the present Article shall in equal measure extend to the republics, territories, regions, cities of federal significance, autonomous region, and autonomous national areas.

Article 73

Beyond the limits of jurisdiction of the Russian Federation and powers of the Russian Federation relating to subjects of joint jurisdiction of the Russian Federation and subjects of the Russian Federation, the subjects of the Russian Federation shall possess the entire plenitude of State power.

Article 74

1. The establishment of customs boundaries, duties, charges, and any other hindrances to the free movement of goods, services, and financial means shall not be permitted on the territory of the Russian Federation.

2. Limitations on the movement of goods and services may be introduced in accordance with a federal law if this is necessary in order to ensure security, defence of human life and health, protection of nature, and cultural valuables.

Article 75

1. The monetary unit in the Russian Federation shall be the ruble. Monetary emission shall be effectuated exclusively by the Central Bank of the Russian Federation. The introduction and emission of other monies in the Russian Federation shall not be permitted.

2. The defence of and ensuring the stability of the ruble shall be the principal function of the Central Bank of the Russian Federation, which it shall effectuate independently from other agencies of State power.

3. The system of taxes recovered to the federal budget and the general principles of taxation and charges in the Russian Federation shall be established by a federal law.

4. State loans shall be issued in the procedure determined by a federal law and shall be placed on a voluntary basis.

Article 76

1. Federal constitutional laws and federal laws having direct effect throughout the entire territory of the Russian Federation shall be adopted with regard to the subjects of jurisdiction of the Russian Federation.

2. Federal laws and laws and other normative legal acts of subjects of the Russian Federation adopted in accordance therewith shall be issued with regard to the subjects of joint jurisdiction of the Russian Federation and subjects of the Russian Federation.

3. Federal laws may not be contrary to federal constitutional laws.

4. Beyond the limits of the jurisdiction of the Russian Federation and the joint jurisdiction of the Russian Federation and subjects of the Russian Federation, the republics, territories, regions, cities of federal significance, autonomous region, and autonomous national areas shall effectuate own legal regulation, including the adoption of laws and other normative legal acts.

5. Laws and other normative legal acts of subjects of the Russian Federation may not be contrary to federal laws adopted in accordance with paragraphs one and two of the present Article. In the event of a contradiction between a federal law and another act issued in the Russian Federation, the federal law shall operate.

6. In the event of a contradiction between a federal law and a normative legal act of a subject of the Russian Federation issued in accordance with paragraph four of the present Article, the normative legal act of the subject of the Russian Federation shall operate.

Article 77

1. The system of agencies of State power of republics, territories, regions, cities of federal significance, autonomous region, and autonomous national areas shall be established by the subjects of the Russian Federation autonomously in accordance with the foundations of the constitutional system of the Russian Federation and the general principles for organising representative and executive agencies of State power established by a federal law.

2. Within the limits of the jurisdiction of the Russian Federation and powers of the Russian Federation with regard to the subjects of joint jurisdiction of the Russian Federation and the subjects of the Russian Federation, federal agencies of executive power and agencies of executive power of the subjects of the Russian Federation shall form a unified system of executive power in the Russian Federation.

Article 78

1. Federal agencies of executive power may, in order to effectuate their powers, create their territorial agencies and appoint the respective officials.

2. Federal agencies of executive power by agreement with agencies of executive power of subjects of the Russian Federation may transfer to them the effectuation of part of their powers if this is not contrary to the Constitution of the Russian Federation and federal laws.

3. Agencies of executive power of subjects of the Russian Federation by agreement with federal agencies of executive power may transfer to them the effectuation of part of their powers.

4. The President of the Russian Federation and the Government of the Russian Federation shall ensure in accordance with the Constitution of the Russian Federation the effectuation of the powers of federal State power throughout the entire territory of the Russian Federation.

Article 79

The Russian Federation may participate in inter-State associations and transfer to them part of its powers in accordance with international treaties if this does not entail a limitation of the rights and freedoms of man and citizen and is not contrary to the foundations of the constitutional system of the Russian Federation.

CHAPTER 4. PRESIDENT OF THE RUSSIAN FEDERATION

Article 80

1. The President of the Russian Federation shall be the head of State.

2. The President of the Russian Federation shall be the guarantor of the Constitution of the Russian Federation and the rights and freedoms of man and citizen. In the procedure established by the Constitution of the Russian Federation he shall take measures to protect the sovereignty of the Russian Federation, its independence and State integrity and ensure the coordinated functioning and interaction of agencies of State power.

3. The President of the Russian Federation shall in accordance with the Constitution of the Russian Federation and federal laws determine the basic orientations of internal and foreign policy of the State.

4. The President of the Russian Federation as the head of State shall represent the Russian Federation within the country and in international relations.

Article 81

1. The President of the Russian Federation shall be elected for four years by citizens of the Russian Federation on the basis of universal, equal, and direct suffrage by secret ballot.

2. A citizen of the Russian Federation not younger than 35 years and permanently residing in the Russian Federation for not less than 10 years may be elected President of the Russian Federation.

3. One and the same person may not occupy the office of President of the Russian Federation for more than two terms in succession.

4. The procedure for elections of the President of the Russian Federation shall be determined by a federal law.

Article 82

1. When taking up the office, the President of the Russian Federation shall take the following oath to the people:

"I swear when effectuating the powers of President of the Russian Federation to respect and protect the rights and freedoms of man and citizen, to comply with and defend the Constitution of the Russian Federation, to defend the sovereignty and independence, security, and integrity of the State, and to loyally serve the people."

2. The oath shall be taken in a solemn ceremony in the presence of members of the Soviet of the Federation, deputies of the State Duma, and judges of the Constitutional Court of the Russian Federation.

Article 83

The President of the Russian Federation shall:

(a) appoint with the consent of the State Duma the Chairman of the Government of the Russian Federation;
(b) have the right to preside at sessions of the Government of the Russian Federation;
(c) take the decision concerning the resignation of the Government of the Russian Federation;
(d) submit to the State Duma a candidacy for appointment to the office of Chairman of the Central Bank of the Russian Federation; place before the State Duma the question of relieving from office the Chairman of the Central Bank of the Russian Federation;
(e) upon the proposal of the Chairman of the Government of the Russian Federation, appoint to and relieve from office the deputy chairmen of the Government of the Russian Federation and federal ministers;
(f) submit to the Soviet of the Federation candidacies for appoint to the office of judges of the Constitutional Court of the Russian Federation, Supreme Court of the Russian Federation, Supreme Arbitrazh Court of the Russian Federation, and also the candidacy of the Procurator General of the Russian Federation; submit to the Soviet of the Federation a proposal concerning the relieving from office of the Procurator General of the Russian Federation; appoint judges of other federal courts;
(g) form and head the Security Council of the Russian Federation, the status of which shall be determined by a federal law;
(h) confirm the military doctrine of the Russian Federation;
(i) form the Administration of the President of the Russian Federation;
(j) appoint and relieve plenipotentiary representatives of the President of the Russian Federation;
(k) appoint and relieve the high command of the Armed Forces of the Russian Federation;
(l) appoint and recall after consultations with the respective committees or commissions of the chambers of the Federal Assembly diplomatic representatives of the Russian Federation to foreign States and international organisations.

Article 84

The President of the Russian Federation shall:

(a) designate elections of the State Duma in accordance with the Constitution of the Russian Federation and a federal law;
(b) dissolve the State Duma in the instances and procedure provided for by the Constitution of the Russian Federation;

(c) designate a referendum in the procedure established by a federal constitutional law;

(d) submit draft laws to the State Duma;

(e) sign and promulgate federal laws;

(f) address the Federal Assembly with annual messages on the situation in the country and the basic orientations of internal and foreign policy of the State.

Article 85

1. The President of the Russian Federation may use conciliation procedures in order to settle disagreements between agencies of State power of the Russian Federation and agencies of State power of subjects of the Russian Federation, and also between agencies of State power of subjects of the Russian Federation. In the event of the failure to reach an agreed decision, he may transfer settlement of the dispute for consideration of the respective court.

2. The President of the Russian Federation shall have the right to suspend the operation of acts of agencies of executive power of subjects of the Russian Federation in the event these acts are contrary to the Constitution of the Russian Federation and federal laws or international obligations of the Russian Federation or violate the rights and freedoms of man and citizen until this question is decided by the respective court.

Article 86

The President of the Russian Federation shall:

(a) effectuate guidance over the foreign policy of the Russian Federation;

(b) conduct negotiations and sign international treaties of the Russian Federation;

(c) sign instruments of ratification;

(d) accept credentials and letters of recall of diplomatic representatives accredited to him.

Article 87

1. The President of the Russian Federation shall be the Supreme Commander-in-Chief of the Armed Forces of the Russian Federation.

2. In the event of aggression against the Russian Federation or a direct threat of aggression the President of the Russian Federation shall introduce a military situation on the territory of the Russian Federation or in individual localities thereof, immediately notifying the Soviet of the Federation and the State Duma thereof.

3. The regime of a military situation shall be determined by a federal constitutional law.

Article 88

The President of the Russian Federation shall, under the circumstances and in the procedure provided for by a federal constitutional law, introduce on the territory of the Russian Federation or in individual localities thereof an extraordinary situation, immediately notifying the Soviet Federation and the State Duma thereof.

Article 89

The President of the Russian Federation shall:

(a) decide questions of citizenship of the Russian Federation and grant political asylum;

(b) award State awards of the Russian Federation, confer titles of honour of the Russian Federation and the highest military and highest special ranks;

(c) effectuate a pardon.

Article 90

1. The President of the Russian Federation shall issue edicts and regulations.

2. Edicts and regulations of the President of the Russian Federation shall be binding for execution throughout the entire territory of the Russian Federation.

3. Edicts and regulations of the President of the Russian Federation must not be contrary to the Constitution of the Russian Federation and federal laws.

Article 91

The President of the Russian Federation shall possess inviolability.

Article 92

1. The President of the Russian Federation shall embark upon the performance of powers from the moment of taking the oath and shall terminate the performance thereof with the expiry of the period of his sojourn in office from the moment of the newly elected President of the Russian Federation taking the oath.

2. The President of the Russian Federation shall terminate the performance of powers before time in the event of his resignation, becoming unable by reason of state of health to effectuate the powers belonging to him, or impeachment. In so doing elections of the President of the Russian Federation must take place not later than three months from the moment of the termination of the performance of powers before time.

3. In all instances when the President of the Russian Federation is not in a state to fulfil his duties, the Chairman of the Government of the Russian Federation shall perform them. The person performing the duties of the President of the Russian Federation shall not have the right to dissolve the State Duma, designate a referendum, nor make proposals concerning amendments to and the revision of provisions of the Constitution of the Russian Federation.

Article 93

1. The President of the Russian Federation may be impeached by the Soviet of the Federation only on the basis of an accusation put forward by the State Duma of treason to the State or commission of another grave crime confirmed by an opinion of the Supreme Court of the Russian Federation concerning the existence in the actions of the President of the Russian Federation of the indicia of a crime and opinion of the Constitutional Court of the Russian Federation concerning compliance with the established procedure for putting forward the accusation.

2. The decision of the State Duma to put forward an accusation and the decision of the Soviet of the Federation to impeach the President must be adopted by two-thirds of the votes of the total number in each of the chambers at the initiative of not less than one-third of the deputies of the State Duma and in the presence of an opinion of a special commission formed by the State Duma.

3. The decision of the Soviet of the Federation to impeach the President of the Russian Federation must be adopted not later than within a three-month period after the State Duma put forward the accusation against the President. If within this period the decision of the Soviet of the Federation is not adopted, the accusation against the President shall be considered to be rejected.

Chapter 5. The Federal Assembly

Article 94

The Federal Assembly—the parliament of the Russian Federation—shall be the representative and legislative agency of the Russian Federation.

Article 95

1. The Federal Assembly shall consist of two chambers — the Soviet of the Federation and the State Duma.

2. In the Soviet of the Federation shall be two representatives from each subject of the Russian Federation: one each from the representative and executive agencies of State power.

3. The State Duma shall consist of 450 deputies.

Article 96

1. The State Duma shall be elected for a term of four years.

2. The procedure for the formation of the Soviet of the Federation and the procedure for elections of the State Duma shall be established by federal laws.

Article 97

1. A citizen of the Russian Federation who has reached 21 years of age and has the right to participate in elections may be elected a deputy of the State Duma.

2. One and the same person may not be simultaneously a member of the Soviet of the Federation and a deputy of the State Duma. A deputy of the State Duma may not be a deputy of other representative agencies of State power and agencies of local self-government.

3. Deputies of the State Duma shall work on a professional permanent basis. Deputies of the State Duma may not be in State service and engage in other paid activity, except for teaching, scientific, and other creative activity.

Article 98

1. Members of the Soviet of the Federation and deputies of the State Duma shall possess inviolability throughout the entire term of their powers. They may not be detained, arrested, subjected to search, except for instances of detention at the site of a crime, and also subjected to personal inspection, except for instances when this has been provided for by a federal law in order to ensure the safety of other people.

2. The question of deprivation of inviolability shall be decided upon the recommendation of the Procurator General of the Russian Federation by the respective chamber of the Federal Assembly.

Article 99

1. The Federal Assembly shall be a permanently operating agency.

2. The State Duma shall assemble for the first session on the thirtieth day after election. The President of the Russian Federation may convoke a session of the State Duma earlier than this period.

3. The first session of the State Duma shall be opened by the deputy most senior in age.

4. From the moment of the commencement of work of the State Duma, new convocation, the powers of the State Duma of the previous convocation shall terminate.

Article 100

1. The Soviet of the Federation and the State Duma shall sit separately.

2. Sessions of the Soviet of the Federation and the State Duma shall be open. In the instances provided for by the Reglament of the chamber, it shall have the right to hold closed sessions.

3. The chambers may assemble jointly in order to hear messages of the President of the Russian Federation, messages of the Constitutional Court of the Russian Federation, and addresses of leaders of foreign States.

Article 101

1. The Soviet of the Federation shall elect from its membership the Chairman of the Soviet of the Federation and his deputies. The State Duma shall elect from its membership the Chairman of the State Duma and his deputies.

2. The Chairman of the Soviet of the Federation and his deputies and the Chairman of the State Duma and his deputies shall conduct sessions and the internal order of the chamber.

3. The Soviet of the Federation and the State Duma shall form committees and commissions and hold parliamentary hearings regarding questions within their jurisdiction.

4. Each chamber shall adopt its own Reglament and decide questions of internal order of its activity.

5. In order to effectuate control over the execution of the federal budget the Soviet of the Federation and the State Duma shall form the Chamber of Accounts, the membership and procedure for the activity of which shall be determined by a federal law.

Article 102

1. There shall be relegated to the jurisdiction of the Soviet of the Federation:
    (a) confirmation of changes of boundaries between subjects of the Russian Federation;
    (b) confirmation of an edict of the President of the Russian Federation concerning the introduction of a military situation;
    (c) confirmation of an edict of the President of the Russian Federation concerning the introduction of an extraordinary situation;
    (d) deciding of the question of the possibility of the use of the Armed Forces of the Russian Federation beyond the limits of the territory of the Russian Federation;
    (e) designation of elections of the President of the Russian Federation;
    (f) impeachment of the President of the Russian Federation;
    (g) appointment to office of judges of the Constitutional Court of the Russian Federation, Supreme Court of the Russian Federation, and Supreme Arbitrazh Court of the Russian Federation;
    (h) appoint to and relieving from office of the Procurator General of the Russian Federation;
    (i) appoint to and relieving from office of the deputy chairman of the Chamber of Accounts and half of the auditors thereof.

2. The Soviet of the Federation shall adopt decrees regarding questions relegated to its jurisdiction by the Constitution of the Russian Federation.

3. Decrees of the Soviet of the Federation shall be adopted by a majority of votes of the total number of members of the Soviet of the Federation unless another procedure for the adoption of decisions has been provided for by the Constitution of the Russian Federation.

Article 103

1. There shall be relegated to the jurisdiction of the State Duma:
    (a) giving the consent of the President of the Russian Federation to the appointment of the Chairman of the Government of the Russian Federation;
    (b) deciding the question of confidence in the Government of the Russian Federation;
    (c) appointing to and relieving from office the Chairman of the Central Bank of the Russian Federation;

(d) appointing to and relieving from office the Chairman of the Chamber of Accounts and half of its auditors;

(e) appointing to and relieving from office the Plenipotentiary for Human Rights acting in accordance with a federal constitutional law;

(f) declaration of an amnesty;

(g) putting forward an accusation against the President of the Russian Federation to impeach him.

2. The State Duma shall adopt decrees regarding questions relegated to its jurisdiction by the Constitution of the Russian Federation.

3. Decrees of the State Duma shall be adopted by a majority of the votes of the total number of deputies of the State Duma unless another procedure has been provided to adopt decisions by the Constitution of the Russian Federation.

Article 104

1. The right of legislative initiative shall belong to the President of the Russian Federation, the Soviet of the Federation, members of the Soviet of the Federation, deputies of the State Duma, the Government of the Russian Federation, and legislative (or representative) agencies of subjects of the Russian Federation. The right of legislative initiative shall also belong to the Constitutional Court of the Russian Federation, the Supreme Court of the Russian Federation, and the Supreme Arbitrazh Court of the Russian Federation with regard to questions of their jurisdiction.

2. Draft laws shall be submitted to the State Duma.

3. Draft laws concerning the introduction or abolition of taxes, exemption from the payment thereof, the issuance of State loans, change of financial obligations of the State, and other draft laws providing for expenses to be covered at the expense of the federal budget may be submitted only when there is an opinion of the Government of the Russian Federation.

Article 105

1. Federal laws shall be adopted by the State Duma.

2. Federal laws shall be adopted by a majority vote of the total number of deputies of the State Duma unless provided otherwise by the Constitution of the Russian Federation.

3. Federal laws adopted by the State Duma shall be transferred within five days for consideration by the Soviet of the Federation.

4. A federal law shall be considered to be approved by the Soviet of the Federation if more than half of the total number of members of this chamber have voted for it or if within fourteen days it was not considered by the Soviet of the Federation. In the event of the rejection of a federal law by the Soviet of the Federation, the chambers may create a conciliation commission in order to overcome disagreements which have arisen, after which the federal law shall be subject to consideration a second time by the State Duma.

5. In the event that the State Duma fails to agree with the decision of the Soviet of the Federation, a federal law shall be considered to be adopted if during the second vote not less than two thirds of the total number of deputies of the State Duma have voted for it.

Article 106

Federal laws adopted by the State Duma shall be subject to obligatory consideration in the Soviet of the Federation with regard to questions of:

(a) the federal budget;

(b) federal taxes and charges;

(c) financial, currency, credit, customs regulation, monetary emission;

(d) ratification and denunciation of international treaties of the Russian Federation;

(e) status and defence of the State boundary of the Russian Federation;

(f) war and peace.

Article 107

1. A federal law adopted shall be sent within five days to the President of the Russian Federation for signature and promulgation.

2. The President of the Russian Federation shall sign the federal law within fourteen days and promulgate it.

3. If the President of the Russian Federation within fourteen days from the moment of receipt of a federal law rejects it, the State Duma and the Soviet of the Federation shall in the procedure established by the Constitution of the Russian Federation consider the said law anew. If during a second consideration a federal law is approved in the version previously adopted by a majority of not less than two-thirds of the votes of the total number of members of the Soviet of the Federation and deputies of the State Duma, it shall be subject to signature by the President of the Russian Federation within seven days and to promulgation.

Article 108

1. Federal constitutional laws shall be adopted with regard to questions provided for by the Constitution of the Russian Federation.

2. A federal constitutional law shall be considered to be adopted if it was approved by a majority of not less than three-quarters of the votes of the total number of members of the Soviet of the Federation and not less than two-thirds of the votes of the total number of deputies of the State Duma. A federal constitutional law adopted shall be subject to signature within fourteen days by the President of the Russian Federation and to promulgation.

Article 109

1. The State Duma may be dissolved by the President of the Russian Federation in the instances provided for by Articles 111 and 117 of the Constitution of the Russian Federation.

2. In the event of the dissolution of the State Duma the President of the Russian Federation shall designate the date of elections so that the newly elected State Duma shall assemble not later than within four months from the moment of dissolution.

3. The State Duma may not be dissolved on the grounds provided for by Article 117 of the Constitution of the Russian Federation within a year after its election.

4. The State Duma may not be dissolved from the moment of putting forward an accusation against the President of the Russian Federation until the adoption of a respective decision by the Soviet of the Federation.

5. The State Duma may not be dissolved during the period of the operation throughout the territory of the Russian Federation of a military or extraordinary situation, and also within six months before the ending of the term of powers of the President of the Russian Federation.

CHAPTER 6. GOVERNMENT OF THE RUSSIAN FEDERATION

Article 110

1. The Government of the Russian Federation shall effectuate executive power of the Russian Federation.

2. The Government of the Russian Federation shall consist of the Chairman of the Government of the Russian Federation, the deputy chairmen of the Government of the Russian Federation, and federal ministers.

Article 111

1. The Chairman of the Government of the Russian Federation shall be appointed by the President of the Russian Federation with the consent of the State Duma.

2. A proposal concerning a candidacy for Chairman of the Government of the Russian Federation shall be submitted not later than within two weeks after the newly elected President of the Russian Federation takes office or after the resignation of the Government of the Russian Federation or within a week from the date of the State Duma rejecting the candidacy.

3. The State Duma shall consider the candidacy submitted by the President of the Russian Federation for Chairman of the Government of the Russian Federation within a week from the date of submitting the proposal concerning the candidacy.

4. After the State Duma rejecting three times the candidacies submitted for Chairman of the Government of the Russian Federation, the President of the Russian Federation shall appoint the Chairman of the Government of the Russian Federation, dissolve the State Duma, and designate new elections.

Article 112

1. The Chairman of the Government of the Russian Federation shall not later than a week after appointment submit to the President of the Russian Federation proposals concerning the structure of the federal agencies of State power.

2. The Chairman of the Government of the Russian Federation shall propose to the President of the Russian Federation candidacies for the offices of deputy chairmen of the Government of the Russian Federation and federal ministers.

Article 113

The Chairman of the Government of the Russian Federation shall in accordance with the Constitution of the Russian Federation and federal laws and edicts of the President of the Russian Federation determine the basic orientations of activity of the Government of the Russian Federation and organise its work.

Article 114

1. The Government of the Russian Federation shall:
    (a) work out and submit to the State Duma the federal budget and ensure its execution; submit to the State Duma the report concerning execution of the federal budget;
    (b) ensure the implementation in the Russian Federation of a unified financial, credit, and monetary policy;
    (c) ensure the implementation in the Russian Federation of a unified State policy in the domain of culture, science, education, public health, social security, and ecology;
    (d) effectuate the administration of federal ownership;
    (e) effectuate measures relating to ensuring the defence of the country, State security, and the realisation of the foreign policy of the Russian Federation;
    (f) effectuate measures relating to ensuring legality, the rights and freedoms of citizens, protection of ownership and public order, and the struggle against criminality;
    (g) effectuate other powers placed on it by the Constitution of the Russian Federation, federal laws, and edicts of the President of the Russian Federation.

2. The procedure for the activity of the Government of the Russian Federation shall be determined by a federal constitutional law.

Article 115

1. On the basis of and in execution of the Constitution of the Russian Federation, federal laws, and normative edicts of the President of the Russian Federation, the Government of the Russian Federation shall issue decrees and regulations and ensure their execution.

2. Decrees and regulations of the Government of the Russian Federation shall be binding for execution in the Russian Federation.

3. Decrees and regulations of the Government of the Russian Federation may in the event of their failure to conform to the Constitution of the Russian Federation, federal laws, and edicts of the President of the Russian Federation be repealed by the President of the Russian Federation.

Article 116

The Government of the Russian Federation shall lay down its powers to a newly elected President of the Russian Federation.

Article 117

1. The Government of the Russian Federation may offer to resign, which may be accepted or rejected by the President of the Russian Federation.

2. The President of the Russian Federation may adopt a decision concerning the resignation of the Government of the Russian Federation.

3. The State Duma may express lack of confidence in the Government of the Russian Federation. The decree concerning lack of confidence in the Government of the Russian Federation shall be adopted by a majority vote of the total number of deputies of the State Duma. After the expression by the State Duma of lack of confidence in the Government of the Russian Federation, the President of the Russian Federation shall have the right to declare the resignation of the Government of the Russian Federation or not to agree with the decision of the State Duma. If the State Duma within three months expresses its lack of confidence a second time in the Government of the Russian Federation the President of the Russian Federation shall declare the resignation of the Government or dissolve the State Duma.

4. The Chairman of the Government of the Russian Federation may place before the State Duma the question of confidence in the Government of the Russian Federation. If the State Duma refuses confidence, the President shall within seven days adopt a decision concerning the resignation of the Government of the Russian Federation or dissolution of the State Duma and the designation of new elections.

5. In the event of resignation or laying down powers, the Government of the Russian Federation shall on behalf of the President of the Russian Federation continue to operate until the formation of a new Government of the Russian Federation.

CHAPTER 7. JUDICIAL POWER

Article 118

1. Justice in the Russian Federation shall be effectuated only by a court.

2. Judicial power shall be effectuated by means of constitutional, civil, administrative, and criminal procedure.

3. The judicial system of the Russian Federation shall be established by the Constitution of the Russian Federation and by a federal constitutional law. The creation of extraordinary courts shall not be permitted.

Article 119

Citizens of the Russian Federation who have attained 25 years of age and have a higher legal education and work experience in the legal profession of not less than five years may be judges. Additional requirements for judges of courts of the Russian Federation may be established by a federal law.

Article 120

1. Judges shall be independent and subordinate only to the Constitution of the Russian Federation and to a federal law.

2. A court, having established when considering a case the failure of an act of a State or other agency to conform to a law shall adopt a decision in accordance with the law.

Article 121

1. Judges shall not be removable.

2. The powers of a judge may be terminated or suspended not other than in the procedure and on the grounds established by a federal law.

Article 122

1. Judges shall be inviolable.

2. A judge may not be brought to criminal responsibility other than in the procedure determined by a federal law.

Article 123

1. The examination of cases in all courts shall be open. The hearing of cases in closed session shall be permitted in the instances provided for by a federal law.

2. The examination of criminal cases in courts in absentia shall not be permitted except for instances provided for by a federal law.

3. Court procedure shall be effectuated on the basis of contentiousness and equality of the parties.

4. In the instances provided for by a federal law court procedure shall be effectuated with the participation of jurors.

Article 124

The financing of the courts shall be only from the federal budget and must ensure the full and independent effectuation of justice in accordance with a federal law.

Article 125

1. The Constitutional Court of the Russian Federation shall consist of 19 judges.

2. The Constitutional Court of the Russian Federation shall, at the requests of the President of the Russian Federation, Soviet of the Federation, State Duma, one-fifth of the members of the Soviet of the Federation or deputies of the State Duma, Government of the Russian Federation, Supreme Court of the Russian Federation and Supreme Arbitrazh Court of the Russian Federation, agencies of legislative and executive power of subjects of the Russian Federation, settle cases concerning the conformity to the Russian Constitution of:

   (a) federal laws, normative acts of the President of the Russian Federation, Soviet of the Federation, State Duma, and Government of the Russian Federation;

   (b) constitutions of the republics, charters, and also laws and other normative acts of subjects of the Russian Federation issued with regard to questions relegated to the jurisdiction of agencies of State power of the Russian Federation and the joint jurisdiction of agencies of State power of the Russian Federation and agencies of State power of subjects of the Russian Federation;

   (c) treaties between agencies of State power of the Russian Federation and agencies of State power of subjects of the Russian Federation, and treaties between agencies of State power of subjects of the Russian Federation;

   (d) international treaties of the Russian Federation which have not entered into legal force;

3. The Constitutional Court of the Russian Federation shall settle disputes concerning the competence:

   (a) between federal agencies of State power;

   (b) between agencies of State power of the Russian Federation and agencies of State power of subjects of the Russian Federation;

   (c) between the highest State agencies of subjects of the Russian Federation.

4. The Constitutional Court of the Russian Federation shall verify the constitutionality of a law being applied or subject to application in a specific case in the procedure established by a federal law with regard to appeals against a violation of constitutional rights and freedoms of citizens and at the requests of courts.

5. The Constitutional Court of the Russian Federation shall at the requests of the President of the Russian Federation, Soviet of the Federation, State Duma, Government of the Russian Federation, and agencies of legislative power of subjects of the Russian Federation give an interpretation of the Constitution of the Russian Federation.

6. Acts or individual provisions thereof deemed to be unconstitutional shall lose force; international treaties of the Russian Federation which do not conform to the Constitution of the Russian Federation shall not be subject to introduction into operation and application.

7. The Constitutional Court of the Russian Federation at the request of the Soviet of the Federation shall give an opinion concerning the compliance with the established procedure of the putting forward of an accusation against the President of the Russian Federation of treason against the State or commission of another grave crime.

Article 126

The Supreme Court of the Russian Federation shall be the highest judicial agency with regard to civil, criminal, administrative and other cases within the jurisdiction of the courts of general jurisdiction, effectuate judicial supervision over their activity in the procedural forms provided for by a federal law, and give explanations regarding questions of judicial practice.

Article 127

The Supreme Arbitrazh Court of the Russian Federation shall be the highest judicial agency for the settlement of economic disputes and other cases to be considered by arbitrazh courts, effectuate judicial supervision over their activity in the procedural forms provided for by a federal law, and give explanations regarding questions of judicial practice.

Article 128

1. Judges of the Constitutional Court of the Russian Federation, Supreme Court of the Russian Federation, and Supreme Arbitrazh Court of the Russian Federation shall be appointed by the Soviet of the Federation upon the recommendation of the President of the Russian Federation.

731

2. Judges of the other federal courts shall be appointed by the President of the Russian Federation in the procedure established by a federal law.

3. The powers, procedure for the formation, and activity of the Constitutional Court of the Russian Federation, Supreme Court of the Russian Federation, Supreme Arbitrazh Court of the Russian Federation, and other federal courts shall be established by a federal constitutional law.

Article 129

1. The Procuracy of the Russian Federation shall comprise a unified centralised system with the subordination of inferior procurators to superior and to the Procurator General of the Russian Federation.

2. The Procurator General of the Russian Federation shall be appointed to and relieved from office by the Soviet of the Federation upon the recommendation of the President of the Russian Federation.

3. The procurators of subjects of the Russian Federation shall be appointed by the Procurator General of the Russian Federation by agreement with the subjects thereof.

4. Other procurators shall be appointed by the Procurator General of the Russian Federation.

5. The powers, organisation, and procedure for activity of the procuracy of the Russian Federation shall be determined by a federal law.

CHAPTER 8. LOCAL SELF-GOVERNMENT

Article 130

1. Local self-government in the Russian Federation shall ensure the autonomous deciding by the populace of questions of local significance and the possession, use, and disposition of municipal ownership.

2. Local self-government shall be effectuated by citizens through referendums, elections, and other forms of the direct expression of will and through elective and other agencies of local self-government.

Article 131

1. Local self-government shall be effectuated in city and rural settlements and on other territories by taking into account historical and other local traditions. The structure of agencies of local self-government shall be determined by the populace autonomously.

2. A change of the boundaries of the territories in which local self-government is effectuated shall be permitted by taking into account the opinion of the populace of the respective territories.

Article 132

1. Agencies of local self-government autonomously shall administer municipal ownership, form, confirm, and execute the local budget, establish local taxes and charges, effectuate the protection of public order, and also decide other questions of local significance.

2. Agencies of local self-government may be endowed by a law with individual State powers with the transfer of necessary material and financial assets for the effectuation thereof. The realisation of the powers transferred shall be under the control of the State.

Article 133

Local self-government in the Russian Federation shall be guaranteed by the right to judicial defence, contributory compensation of additional expenses which arose as a result of decisions adopted by agencies of State power, and the prohibition against the limitation of the rights of local self-government established by the Constitution of the Russian Federation and by federal laws.

Chapter 9. Constitutional Amendments and Revision of the Constitution

Article 134

Proposals concerning amendments to and revision of provisions of the Constitution of the Russian Federation may be submitted by the President of the Russian Federation, Soviet of the Federation, State Duma, Government of the Russian Federation, legislative (or representative) agencies of subjects of the Russian Federation, and also groups numbering not less than one-fifth of the members of the Soviet of the Federation or deputies of the State Duma.

Article 135

1. The provisions of Chapters 1, 2, and 9 of the Constitution of the Russian Federation may not be revised by the Federal Assembly.

2. If a proposal concerning a revision of the provisions of Chapters 1, 2, and 9 of the Constitution of the Russian Federation is supported by three-fifths of the votes of the total number of members of the Soviet of the Federation and deputies of the State Duma, then in accordance with a federal constitutional law a Constitutional Assembly shall be convoked.

3. A Constitutional Assembly either shall confirm the immutability of the Constitution of the Russian Federation, or work out a draft new Constitution of the Russian Federation, which shall be adopted by the Constitutional Assembly by two-thirds of the votes of the total number of its members or shall be submitted to an all-people's referendum. When an all-people's referendum is held the Constitution of the Russian Federation shall be considered to be adopted if more than half of the electors who took part in the voting voted for it on condition that more than half of the electors have taken part in it.

Article 136

Amendments to Chapters 3–8 of the Constitution of the Russian Federation shall be adopted in the procedure provided for the adoption of a federal constitutional law and shall enter into force after their approval by agencies of legislative power of not less than two-thirds of the subjects of the Russian Federation.

Article 137

1. Changes in Article 65 of the Constitution of the Russian Federation determining the composition of the Russian Federation shall be made on the basis of a federal constitutional law concerning the admission to the Russian Federation and formation within it of a new subject of the Russian Federation and on changing the constitutional law status of a subject of the Russian Federation.

2. In the event of a change of name of a republic, territory, region, city of federal significance, autonomous region, or autonomous national area, the new name of a subject of the Russian Federation shall be subject to inclusion in Article 65 of the Constitution of the Russian Federation.

Section Two

Concluding and Transitional Provisions

1. The Constitution of the Russian Federation shall enter into force from the day of its official publication according to the results of the all-people's vote.

The day of the all-people's vote on 12 December 1993 shall be considered to be the date of adoption of the Constitution of the Russian Federation.

The operation of the Constitution (Basic Law) of the Russian Federation-Russia adopted 12 April 1978, with subsequent changes and additions, shall terminate simultaneously.

In the event of the failure of the provisions of the Constitution of the Russian Federation to conform to the provisions of the Treaty of the Federation—the Treaty of the Delimitation of the Subjects of Jurisdiction and Powers Between Federal Agencies of State Power of the Russian Federation and Agencies of State Power of the Sovereign Republics within the Russian Federation, the Treaty on the Delimitation of the Subject of Jurisdiction and Powers Between Federal Agencies of State Power of the Russian Federation and Agencies of State Power of Territories, Regions, and the Cities of Moscow and St. Petersburg of the Russian Federation, the Treaty on the Delimitation of Subjects of Jurisdiction and Powers Between the Federal Agencies of State Power of the Russian Federation and the Agencies of State Power of the Autonomous Region and Autonomous National Areas within the Russian Federation, and also other treaties between federal agencies of State power of the Russian Federation and agencies of State power of subjects of the Russian Federation and treaties between agencies of State power of subjects of the Russian Federation—the provisions of the Constitution of the Russian Federation shall operate.

2. Laws and other legal acts which have operated on the territory of the Russian Federation before the entry into force of the present Constitution shall be applied in that part which is not contrary to the Constitution of the Russian Federation.

3. The President of the Russian Federation elected in accordance with the Constitution (Basic Law) of the Russian Federation-Russia shall from the date of entry into force of the present Constitution effectuate the powers established by it until the expiry of the term for which he was elected.

4. The Council of Ministers-Government of the Russian Federation shall from the date of entry into force of the present Constitution acquire the rights, duties, and responsibility of the Government of the Russian Federation established by the Constitution of the Russian Federation and thenceforth shall be named—the Government of the Russian Federation.

5. The courts in the Russian Federation shall effectuate justice in accordance with their powers established by the present Constitution.

After the entry into force of the Constitution the judges of all courts of the Russian Federation shall retain their powers until the expiry of the term for which they were elected. Vacant posts shall be filled in the procedure established by the present Constitution.

6. Until the introduction into operation of a federal law established the procedure for the consideration of cases by a court with the participation of jurors, the previous procedure for the judicial consideration of the respective cases shall be retained.

Until criminal procedure legislation of the Russian Federation is brought into conformity with the provisions of the present Constitution the previous procedure for arrest, confinement under guard, and detention of persons suspected of committing a crime shall be retained.

7. The Soviet of the Federation, first convocation, and the State Duma, first convocation, shall be elected for a term of two years.

8. The Soviet of the Federation shall assemble for its first session on the thirtieth day after the election. The first session of the Soviet of the Federation shall be opened by the President of the Russian Federation.

9. A deputy of the State Duma, first convocation, may simultaneously be a member of the Government of the Russian Federation. The provisions of the present Constitution concerning the inviolability of deputies with respect to responsibility for actions (or omissions to act) connected with the fulfilment of employment duties shall not extend to deputies of the State Duma who are members of the Government of the Russian Federation.

Deputies of the Soviet of the Federation, first convocation, shall effectuate their powers on a non-permanent basis.

INDEX OF NAMES

SUBJECT INDEX